ASSESSING THE ABILITIES AND INSTRUCTIONAL NEEDS OF STUDENTS

ASSESSING THE ABILITIES
AND INSTRUCTIONAL NEEDS
OF STUDENTS

A Practical Guide for Educators, Psychologists, Speech Pathologists, and Diagnosticians

EDITED BY
Donald D. Hammill

CONTRIBUTIONS BY
Linda Brown
Brian R. Bryant
Herbert P. Ginsburg
Stephen C. Larsen
Patricia I. Myers
J. Lee Wiederholt

5341 Industrial Oaks Boulevard
Austin, Texas 78735

Library of Congress Cataloging-in-Publication Data

Assessing the abilities and instructional
   needs of students.

   Bibliography: p.
   Includes index.
   1. Ability—Testing. 2. Handicapped
children—Identification. 3. English
language—Ability testing. 4. Children—
Language—Testing. 5. Mathematical ability—
Testing. 6. Behavioral assessment of
children. I. Hammill, Donald, D., 1934–
II. Brown, Linda L.
LB1131.A759 1986   371.2′6   86-15133
ISBN 0-89079-137-6

5341 Industrial Oaks Boulevard
Austin, Texas 78735

10 9 8 7 6 5 4 3 2   88 89 90 91 92

CONTENTS

PART I

AN OVERVIEW OF ASSESSMENT PRACTICES

Donald D. Hammill

The discussion of how the specific needs of students can be assessed productively begins with an introductory chapter dealing with general assessment principles and practices. This single chapter provides a basic understanding of the assessment process and how that process can be related to the appraisal of spoken language, reading, writing, arithmetic, and socioemotional behavior—the five constructs examined in this book.

1 / ASSESSING STUDENTS IN THE SCHOOLS

Assessment is the act of acquiring and analyzing information about students for some stated purpose, usually for diagnosing specific problems and for planning instructional programs. This information includes knowledge about an individual's personal attributes, cognitive abilities, environmental status, academic achievement, health, or social competence and is acquired by a variety of techniques of which testing, observation, interviews, record reviews, and analytic teaching are the most frequently used.

The contents of this chapter provide readers with a basic background about assessment concepts and procedures that are currently employed in schools and clinics. Specifically discussed are (a) the purposes for assessing students, (b) the domains of human behavior that are usually measured, (c) the techniques that are most often used to obtain useful information, (d) the frames of reference used to interpret assessment findings, and (e) the role of standardization in assessment.

PURPOSES FOR ASSESSING STUDENTS

There are important reasons for assessing students. Chief among these are (a) to screen students to find those who need special assistance, (b) to diagnose their problems, (c) to identify their instructional needs, (d) to document their progress in special programs, and (e) to provide information for use in research projects.

Screening

The first step in a comprehensive assessment program is to locate youngsters who may need special attention. This entails surveying all students enrolled in a school to screen out those who are at risk. Since large numbers of students have to be surveyed, the screening procedures must be time efficient and cost effective.

Generally, two procedures are employed. First, some schools routinely refer for special attention all students who score below a particular level on the group administered readiness or achievement tests that are regularly given. Second, students selected by their teachers as experiencing significant problems may be referred for further study. Children who are identified as somehow deficient through these screening procedures are usually targeted for more in-depth assessment.

Diagnosing

Diagnosis, originally a medical term, is the recognition of diseases from their symptoms. The physician knows that a fever may be a symptom of many different diseases and that it is necessary to diagnose the disease that is the culprit so appropriate treatment can be prescribed.

In psychoeducational parlance, diagnosis is the use of observed behaviors and events (symptoms) to infer underlying causes and conditions (diagnosis). For example, a child whose speech is characterized by severe word finding problems and unusual syntax, who was late in developing oral language, who has a history of breech birth, and who had a near normal IQ when measured by nonverbal tests (the symptoms) might be labeled as suffering from *specific language disorder* or, as it is sometimes called, *developmental dysphasia* (the diagnosis).

Ideally, a diagnosis should involve not only a label, but also a theory that explains the symptoms. In other words, a diagnosis is the examiner's best estimate of *why* a child acts as he or she does, not a listing or inventory of *what* the child does. For example, to note that Bill is reading four years behind where he should be, given his IQ, is an observation of a symptom, not a diagnosis. To analyze Bill's strengths and weaknesses in reading (e.g., to note that he makes frequent miscues in oral reading, tends to miss inferential comprehension questions, reads slowly, and fails *bl* blends) is nothing more than an elaborate listing of symptoms and should not be considered a diagnosis. Such compendiums of symptoms are useful and contribute to making a diagnosis, but they are not in themselves the diagnosis, because they do not explain why the problems are being evidenced.

Diagnoses may involve organic as well as functional causes. An assessment of Bill, a poor reader, may reveal (a) that reading is not highly prized in his home, (b) that he has many unexcused absences from school, and (c) that he has little interest in learning to read. This particular cluster of symptoms rules out dyslexia (a severe reading problem due to brain dysfunction) as a diagnosis and points to functional causes of Bill's reading problem.

The diagnosis occurs only after the student's academic and behavioral patterns have been determined, the medical, school, and developmental histories have been reviewed, and the parents and teachers have been interviewed. Because of the scope and depth of information that must be interpreted, diagnoses are usually made by multidisciplinary teams. Depending on the nature and severity of the student's symptoms, the team could be composed of any combination of the following: teachers (regular, special, or remedial), physicians, parents, psychologists, speech pathologists, audiologists, optometrists, and physical/occupational therapists, among others.

A diagnosis may or may not be greatly relevant to classroom instruction and planning. To diagnose the problem based on school absences would be highly useful instructionally; however, to classify Sally as autistic tells us little about how to treat her and even less about specific skills she needs to learn. It does, however, influence what might be said to her parents regarding prognosis and expectations and which program she might be referred to for services.

The diagnosis also qualifies Sally for protection under federal and state laws. According to these laws, children diagnosed as having particular handicaps (as in the preceding example, autism) must be served. Undiagnosed children exhibiting similar problems don't have to be served in the schools, even though they may be antisocial, noncompliant, disruptive, abusive, and nonproductive. Under these laws, a clear distinction is drawn between students who are *diagnosed* as having physical, intellectual, emotional, or learning handicaps and those who are not, regardless of their behavior.

Identifying Instructional Needs

As important as screening and diagnosis are, from the teacher/therapist's point of view, the most useful assessments are those that yield educationally relevant information about a problem. This type of assessment will answer such questions as: Which areas are problematic and which are relatively intact? Which specific skills or behaviors within a problem area are defective or missing? In what order should the defective or missing skills be taught?

Determining Strengths and Weaknesses. A comprehensive assessment will determine a student's relative competence in a variety of important areas, especially in the achievement, aptitude, and affective areas. Comparisons of abilities within an area may also be of interest (e.g., within the achievement area, one might assess a student's reading, writing, math, and science proficiency). Even within a single achievement area, such as reading, skill and knowledge comparisons may be made. For example, an examiner occasionally will need to know a student's relative competence among reading comprehension, word recognition skill, phonic and alphabet knowledge, and oral reading rate.

Selecting Instructional Targets. While information about a student's general strengths and weaknesses is important, even more detailed information is required before a final comprehensive instructional plan can be generated. For example, the examiner can easily determine the broad content areas in which a student is experiencing problems (e.g., that a child has a problem in math but not in reading). Also, it is a simple matter to recognize that the weakness is centered in subtraction and not in multiplication, addition, or division.

Assuming that a student has difficulty with subtraction, the examiner would need to determine the specific subtraction errors being made. For example, errors might involve problems with borrowing, mistakes due to zero in the minuend, reversals, adding instead of subtracting, ignoring a digit, and so forth. In this case, an analysis of subtraction errors would likely yield content targets that were appropriate for instructional intervention. The correction of these targeted errors becomes an important goal of remediation.

Inherent in selecting instructional targets is attempting to understand the cognitive strategies that the student uses to do school work. Such knowledge has considerable educational and diagnostic importance, because it helps explain why the student makes an error, thereby suggesting how the error can be remediated. For example, Ms. Burton, a third grade teacher, knows from scores on a math test that Jenny ranks in the 10th percentile of mathematical performance, a value indicating a pronounced problem. She knows from direct teaching experience that Jenny fails subtraction problems that require borrowing but passes other kinds of subtraction problems. Now Ms. Burton wants to determine why Jenny has trouble when doing subtraction with borrowing with a problem like $52 - 14 = 42$. Through the use of techniques described in Part V of this book, Ms. Burton learns that Jenny's mistake results from her overzealous use of the rule, "Always subtract the smaller from the larger." Thus, Jenny solves the problem by using the following unproductive strategy: She subtracts 2 from 4, since "you always have to take away the small number from the big one." Similar approaches can be undertaken in reading, writing, spelling, speech, and behavior to discover the strategies employed by students to answer questions and solve problems.

Determining the Sequence of Instructional Tasks. Having isolated general areas of difficulty and identified specific errors of concern, the examiner must now decide the order in which the errors are to be corrected. In this endeavor, the examiner will find the use of a scope and sequence chart most helpful. On a scope and sequence chart, the broad theoretical categories (the scope) are depicted on one axis, and the skills that comprise the categories (the sequence) are listed in order of development or difficulty on the other axis. A scope and sequence chart displaying the rules governing capitalization and the order (in terms of grade levels) in which they are usually taught is presented in Table 1.1.

TABLE 1.1. Scope and Sequence of Capitalization

Words to Capitalize	K	1	2	3	4	5	6	7	8
First word of a sentence	•	•	+	'	'	'	'	'	'
First and last names of a person	•	+	'	'	'	'	'	'	'
Name of street or road	•	•	+	'	'	'	'	'	'
The word *I*	•	+	'	'	'	'	'	'	'
Name of city or town		•	+	'	'	'	'	'	'
Name of a school or special place	•	•	+	'	'	'	'	'	'
Names of months and days	•	•	+	'	'	'	'	'	'
First and important words in titles	•	•	•	+	'	'	'	'	'
Abbreviations: Mr., Mrs., St., Ave.	•	•	+	'	'	'	'	'	'
Each line of a poem		•	+	'	'	'	'	'	'
First word of salutation of a letter		•	+	'	'	'	'	'	'
First word of complimentary close		•	+	'	'	'	'	'	'
Initials		•	•	+	'	'	'	'	'
Titles used with names of persons			•	•	+	'	'	'	'
First word in an outline topic				•	•	+	'	'	'
Names of organizations			•	•	+	'	'	'	'
Sacred names			•	•	•	+	'	'	'
Proper names generally: countries, oceans			•	•	•	+	'	'	'
Proper adjectives					•	•	+	'	'
Titles of respect and rank and their abbreviations			•	•	+	'	'	'	'

• Introduction; + Suggested teaching; ' Maintenance

From *Experiences in Language: Tools and Techniques* (p. 195) by W. T. Petty, D. C. Petty, and M. F. Becking, 1973, Boston: Allyn & Bacon. Reprinted by permission of the publisher.

If a systematically designed, commercially available program is to be used for instruction (e.g., Silver Burdett's Spelling or SRA's Distar), the examiner should consult the charts that usually accompany such packages. These scope and sequence charts will show both the gross subject matter content areas that are addressed by the program and the specific skills under each for which lessons are provided. Also, entry tests often accompany these programs. Their use will show where the student is performing in terms of the levels and content of the program and, therefore, where to enter the program for the purpose of beginning instruction.

Scope and sequence charts are also available for depicting developmental abilities and skills as well as for subject matter content. These charts are particularly common in the areas of language and motor abilities. Lee (1974) provides an example for spoken grammar. An abbreviated version of her chart is presented in Table 1.2. This particular scope is composed of broad categories of word types, including Personal Pronouns, Main Verbs, Secondary Verbs, Negatives, and so forth. The sequence of skills is grouped into seven developmental levels. The sequence for the Personal Pronouns category begins with first and second personal pronouns (I, you), progresses to third person pronouns (he, she), and continues systematically to plurals (we, us), reflexives (myself, themselves), and *wh-* pronouns (who, which), among others. In scope and sequence charts of this type, the sequence is based on observation of the actual development of children rather than on a purely logical organization of subject matter content.

Often these scope and sequence charts serve as guides in determining the sequence in which needed skills will be taught. For example, from reading a series of essays written by a student, the teacher may identify a set of consistent errors in capitalization. The material in Table 1.1 provides a rationale for listing these errors in preferred order of instruction.

Monitoring Student Progress

Another important purpose of assessment is to monitor the success or failure of students receiving special attention. It is through such assessments that examiners, teachers, and parents learn whether or not the prescribed intervention has been beneficial. If the student has shown little or no growth or improvement in targeted areas, a change of instructional activities and/or a reevaluation might be appropriate.

Often the documentation of student improvement (or lack of it) is required by law or by school policy. Also, many nonschool agencies make their funding of programs and research contingent upon the testing of students who receive service or who serve as subjects. Even when periodic reassessment is not required, it is a desirable practice to do so, because reassessment provides evidence about whether the instructional program is appropriately meeting the student's needs.

TABLE 1.2. An Abbreviated Scope and Sequence of Language Training

Score "Developmental Level"	Indefinite Pronouns or Noun Modifiers	Personal Pronouns	Main Verbs	Secondary Verbs
1	it, this, that	1st and 2nd person: I, me, my, mine, you, your(s)	A. Uninflected verb: I *see* you. B. Copula: is or 's: *It's red.* C. is + verb + ing: He *is coming.*	
2		3rd person: he, him, his, she, her, hers	A. -s and -ed: *plays, played* B. Irregular past: *ate, saw* C. Copula: *am, are, was, were* D. Auxiliary: *am, are, was, were*	Five early-developing infinitives I wanna *see* (want to *see*) I'm gonna *see* (going to *see*) I gotta *see* (got to *see*) Lemme [to] *see* (let me [to] *see*) Let's [to] play (let us [us to] *play*)
3	A. no, some, more, all, lot(s), one(s), two (etc.), other(s), another B. something, somebody, someone	A. Plurals: we, us, our(s), they, them, their B. these, those		Non-complementing infinitives I stopped to *play.* I'm afraid to *look.* It's hard to *do* that.
4	nothing, nobody, none, no one		A. can, will, may + verb: *may go* B. Obligatory do + verb: *don't go* C. Emphatic do + verb: I *do see*	Participle, present or past: I see a boy *running.* I found the toy *broken.*
5		Reflectives: myself, yourself, himself, herself, itself, themselves		A. Early infinitival complements with differing subjects in kernels: I want you to *come.* Let him [to] *see.* B. Later infinitival complements: I had *to go.* I told him *to go.* I tried *to go.* He ought *to go.* C. Obligatory deletions: Make it [to] *go.* I'd better [to] *go.* D. Infinitive with wh word: I know what *to get.* I know how *to do* it.
6		A. Wh- pronouns: who, which, whose, whom, what, that, how many, how much I know *who* came. That's *what* I said. B. Wh- word + infinitive: I know *what* to do. I know *who(m)* to take.	A. could, would, should, might + verb *might come, could be* B. Obligatory does, did + verb C. Emphasis does, did + verb	
7	A. any, anything, anybody, anyone B. every, everything, everybody, everyone C. both, few, many, each, several, most, least, much, next, first, last, second (etc.)	(his) own, one, onself, whichever, whoever, whatever Take *whatever* you like	A. Passive with *get*, any tense. Passive with *be*, any tense B. must, shall + verb *must come* C. have + verb + en *I've eaten.* D. have got *I've got* it.	Passive infinitival complement: With *get:* I have *to get dressed.* I don't want to *get hurt.* With *be:* I want *to be pulled.* It's going *to be locked.*

From *Interactive Language Development* (pp. 4–5) by Laura Lee, R. A. Koenigsknecht, and S. T. Mulhern, 1975, Evanston, IL: Northwestern University Press. Reprinted by permission.

Conducting Research

Another purpose of collecting data on students is to participate in research projects. Each year the school district will initiate or cooperate in a number of research projects which will require the testing of students. The results of this research are important to education, especially when they lead to definitive conclusions about the effectiveness of intervention programs, the validity of theoretical positions, the relationship among instructionally relevant abilities, the statistical adequacy of assessment devices and procedures, and the availability of local norms for tests used in the district.

FREQUENTLY ASSESSED DOMAINS

After an extensive survey of the assessment literature, Hammill, Brown, and Bryant (in press) concluded that almost all of the variables evaluated in schools could easily be grouped under three headings or domains: aptitude, achievement, and affect.

Aptitude Domain

The term *aptitude* refers to natural capacity, potential, or ability. Most aspects of what is considered general intelligence and the specific mental abilities that are used to measure the concept can fairly be considered aptitudes. Aptitudes are considered to be developmental abilities that are acquired through common, everyday experience. As such, they are present to some degree in all people, unless the individual has physical limitations (e.g., blindness, deafness, cerebral palsy). For example, all people possess some proficiency in language, thinking, or manual dexterity, though they vary widely in their relative competence in these abilities.

In schools, aptitude is generally assessed to obtain an estimate of a student's potential for successful school work. The underlying assumption in aptitude evaluation is that a youngster who has not profited from incidental experience will likely have problems in school mastering formally taught subject matter. Of course, a competent aptitude evaluation will go well beyond merely documenting that a student has not profited from everyday experience by seeking to explain why the student has not profited from such experience.

Achievement Domain

The term *achievement* refers to those skills that a person has mastered as a result of direct instruction. The skills may be teacher-taught, parent-taught, or self-taught; but they exist only in those individuals who have had specific training. As such, achievement skills (e.g., reading, writing, computer use, alphabet knowledge, or typewriting) are not present in all persons. In the school, achievement assessments are conducted mostly to discover how much a student knows about a particular content, which subskills need to be taught, and what success was attained as a result of instruction.

Affect Domain

The term *affect* refers to the feelings that people have toward themselves or toward other people, institutions, or ideas. Assessments of this domain in school aged students is done most frequently to secure information about attitudes, interests, and feelings involving school, community, home, peers, work, and self.

Obviously, a comprehensive assessment of a student who evidences a serious problem should include all three domains (aptitude, achievement, and affect). Information pertinent to these domains must be integrated if a student's difficulty is to be diagnosed accurately and if an individual plan of instruction is to be prepared.

ASSESSMENT TECHNIQUES

In this section, the techniques most frequently used to assess students are described. Any of these techniques can be used to assess any of the domains described above and to achieve any of the purposes previously stated. In the discussions that follow, the emphasis is placed on the use of the techniques for instructional purposes, that is, for obtaining educationally useful information. Six techniques are described: testing, product analysis, direct observation, interviews, analytic teaching, and record review.

Testing

A test "may be thought of as a set of tasks or questions intended to elicit particular types of behaviors when presented under standardized conditions and to yield scores that have psychometric properties" (American Psychological Association, 1974, p. 2). According to this definition, a wide variety of school assessment techniques would have to be considered tests.

The tasks or questions on a test (usually called *items*) can measure different aspects of a student's academic knowledge, skill mastery, behavior, athletic performance, values, interests, or some other physical, mental, or behavioral attributes. The particular format of these items may vary considerably. On some occasions, a student's knowledge may be tested directly, as on an IQ test or a teacher's daily math test. In these cases, actual competence is measured by having the student answer objective questions, solve problems, and so on.

At other times, checklists and rating scales are used. Items on these tests are statements that are actually inferred questions. These statements or questions are prepared to solicit specific information about a person's opinion or observation of something. Sometimes the user of these tests is a person who is describing the behavior of another person; sometimes a person is describing his or her own behavior. The main difference between rating scales and checklists is that on the rating scale the informant can indicate the degree to which a characteristic is present (e.g., Johnny is absent: rarely, seldom, occasionally, often), while on the checklist the informant is limited to a simple yes or no (e.g., Johnny can count from 1 to 10: yes, no).

The instructions for taking tests may be written or oral; and the responses may require writing, speaking, or performing some action. In responding to items, students may be expected to choose between dichotomous answers (yes-no; true-false), to select an answer from among multiple choices, to give a correct answer to a factual question (Who discovered America?), to compose an essay, to relate a story, to point to answers, or to employ any of countless other possibilities.

Regardless of the test's content or format, its results can be interpreted from a norm, criterion, or nonreferenced point of view. Also, depending on the intention of its author, a test can vary markedly in its degree of standardization. The roles of referencing and standardization are important measurement concepts that determine greatly how assessment results are interpreted. Since these topics are germane to all assessment techniques, they will be discussed in detail later in this chapter.

Readers interested in the procedures, statistical and otherwise, used to construct tests are referred to the comprehensive texts of Anastasi (1982), Gronlund (1985), and Nunnally (1978). For narrative overviews of an exhaustive number of tests, Mitchell's (1985) *The Ninth Mental Measurements Yearbook* is the prime source. When objective critiques of tests' standardization and norming properties are required, Hammill, Brown, and Bryant's (in press) *A Consumer's Guide to Tests in Print* is recommended.

Product Analysis

A particularly useful assessment technique involves the analysis of samples of students' products. These products may be samples of speech, written material, or math assignments. The strength of this approach is that it allows the examiner to see firsthand the products of a student's performance in spontaneous, everyday situations.

Speech and Language Samples. When collecting a speech and language sample, it is often helpful to tape-record the child's vocalizations so they can be analyzed at leisure at another time. It is also wise to collect several samples over a period of a week or so. The samples should deal with different topics and different speech situations. For example, samples of the child describing the contents of a picture, engaged in free social conversation, or responding to direct questions might be obtained.

These samples can be subject to loose or highly structured analyses. For example, examiners may listen to the speech of the child and note the presence or absence of various parts of speech, sentence types, vocabulary items, and grammatical forms using a gross checklist as a guide; or they may use an elaborate, systematic analysis such as the *Developmental Sentence Analysis* offered by Lee (1971, 1974).

Reading Samples. A popular method for assessing reading involves the assessment of errors (or "miscues") made by students during oral reading. Students are asked to read aloud printed passages that vary in difficulty. Their oral production is assessed in terms of their approximation of the printed message. All deviations from the printed version are noted and analyzed for significance.

Wiederholt (1985) provides an example in his report on Dori (Figure 1.1). In reading Story 11 from the *Formal Reading Inventory*, Dori mispronounced *indolence* and *procrastination*, substituted /inherited/ for *inherent*, and omitted *tenacious*. She missed three comprehension questions (noted by the check marks immediately below the story). Each departure from print is listed and classified. Other sophisticated systems for analyzing oral reading miscues are provided in Goodman and Burke's *Reading Miscue Inventory* (1972) and Wiederholt and Bryant's *Gray Oral Reading Tests–Revised* (1986).

Writing Samples. The analysis of students' spontaneously written material, including stories, letters, and essays, is highly productive from an assessment point of view. These compositions can be assessed from many different perspectives. A glance is all that is necessary to make judgments about legibility and length; more care is needed in conducting a thorough assessment of such factors as proficiency in vocabulary, grammar, syntax, spelling, punctuation, capitalization, and idea expression.

A teacher-diagnostician could have a class or two write a story on some given topic of interest. After reading 30 or so essays on the same topic, the teacher should be quite sensitive to the themes, vocabulary, grammar, and so on, used by most of the students. Departures from modal responses are likely to be of clinical interest. Compositions that make use of dialogue, humor, philosophic or moral themes, complex story sequences, paragraphs, and imagination tend to be more mature than those that do not. The quality of the vocabulary used can be estimated by consulting graded word lists

---

FIGURE 1.1. Example of an Analysis of Oral Reading

Student's Name __Dori__

Form _____ Oral Reading Level __11__

TEACHER'S COPY OF STORY

Story 11

        indōlence   prostication   inherited/

1.   Although indolence and procrastination were inherent in Jane's constitution,

        vīgor

2.   she prospered in learning through the sheer vigor of her intellect. From an early

3.   age she was uncommonly inquisitive, and her memory was so(tenacious)that

    meators   incrucials as   reaction/

4.   her mentors were forever incredulous at her powers of retention. Endowed with

flauntless   porsosly   desulong

5.   boundless and restless mental(faculties.)Jane read prodigiously but in a desul-

                        a

6.   tory manner, and seemed to acquire knowledge by an intuition unbuttressed by

              dilīgence   genus/

7.   the steady application of diligence. In(that)particular parish, genius had an aura

          tomatic

8.   of the divine, and(it)was axiomatic that anyone with a love of letters was naturally

    pamady   stranded

9.   disposed to pedagogy.(So)when Jane's father found himself in straitened cir-

10.   cumstances and Jane was compelled to earn her keep, she was soon engaged

                        in patience

11.   as a governess. The truth is, however, that she lacked the patient and

methoginal   graderate

12.   methodical nature that would fit her to conduct her charges in learning by grada-

                resend the   in appropriations

13.   tions. This made it difficult to descend to particulars and mince her precepts for

14.   her pupils to swallow.

    1. ✓   2. _____   3. ✓   4. ✓   5. _____

FIGURE 1.1. continued

DEPARTURE FROM PRINT ANALYSIS

Student's Name __Dori__

Form _____ Oral Reading Level __11__

NO.	LINE	TEXT WORD	MISCUE	Meaning Similarity	Function Similarity	Graphic/Phonemic Similarity	Multiple Sources	Self-Correction
1	1	indolence	indolence	0	0	1	0	0
2	1	procrastination	prostication	0	0	1	0	0
3	1	inherent	inherited/ι	1	1	1	1	1
4	2	vigor	vigor	0	0	1	0	0
5	4	mentors	meators	0	0	1	0	0
6	4	incredulous	incrucials	0	0	1	0	0
7	4	at	as	0	1	1	1	0
8	4	retention	reaction/ι	0	1	1	1	1
9	5	boundless	flauntless	0	0	1	0	0
10	5	prodigiously	porsosly	0	0	1	0	0
11	5	desultory	desulong	0	0	1	0	0
12	7	diligence	diligence	0	0	1	0	0
13	7	genius	genus/ι	0	0	1	0	1
14	8	axiomatic	tomatic	0	0	1	0	0
15	9	pedagogy	pamady	0	0	1	0	0
16	9	straitened	stranded	0	1	1	1	0
17	11	patient	patience	0	1	1	1	0
18	12	methodical	methoginal	0	0	1	0	0
19	12	gradations	graderate	0	0	1	0	0
20	13	descend	resend	0	1	1	1	0
21	13	to	the	0	1	1	1	0
22	13	precepts	appropriations	0	1	1	1	0
23								
24								
25								
			TOTAL YES	1	8	22	8	3
			TOTAL NO	21	14	0	14	19

OTHER MISCUES

Type

Omissions O	
Additions ∧	
Dialect ∨	
Reversals ~	

OTHER OBSERVATIONS

Type

Slow reading rate	
Word-by-word reading	
Poor phrasing	
Lack of expression	
Pitch too high or low; voice too soft or strained	
Poor enunciation	

Type

Disregard of punctuation	
Head movement	
Finger pointing	
Loss of place	
Nervousness	
Poor attitude	
Other _____	

Adapted from *Formal Reading Inventory* (pp. 54–55) by J. L. Wiederholt, 1985, Austin, TX: PRO-ED. Reprinted by permission of the author and the publisher.

or by simply noting the number of large words (those with seven or more letters) used in relation to the total number of words in the composition. Analyzing the grammatic character of individual "thought units" or sentences is often used as an estimate of syntactic complexity. Errors in spelling, grammar, punctuation, and capitalization are easy to identify and can be noted for later instruction.

Math Samples. The most popular way to assess computation skills involves error analysis using samples of math problems as the basis. It has been noted that students do not tend to make random mistakes. Instead, their errors seem to follow fairly consistent patterns. To this point, Howell and Kaplan (1980) state:

> . . . little information is obtained by simply reporting the number of errors a student makes. The knowledge that "Jenny got five wrong" is not particularly valuable. However, hearing that "Jenny made five multiplication errors and they all involve ×8" could lead you to think that you should teach Jenny her 8's. (p. 245)

In addition to studying the pattern of errors, the teacher may be interested in learning how the student came to make the error. To determine how a student reaches a wrong answer is often a simple task—just ask the student to verbalize the process he or she uses while working out a problem. For example:

Problem A	*Problem B*
17	17
+ 5	+ 5
112	85

While working Problem A, Sally verbalizes, "Seven and five are twelve. Put twelve below the line and bring down the one up there next to the seven. That makes 112." In this problem, she is using a process to solve the problem that she thinks is correct, a process that she likely applies to all similar problems.

While working Problem B, Bill verbalizes, "Seven times five is 35. Put the five below the line and hold the three. Five times one is five. Add three to it and put the eight below the line in front of the five. The answer is 85." He has obviously misread the sign and has multiplied instead of adding.

The error analysis and verbalizing technique is applicable to assessing arithmetic reasoning and geometry skills as well. For readers who wish to know more about error analysis, there are several fine sources, including Ashlock (1976), and Howell and Kaplan (1980). Readers who are interested in a particularly thorough and systematic technique for analyzing math errors are referred to the *Diagnostic Test of Arithmetic Strategies* (Ginsburg & Mathews, 1984).

Direct Observation

Valuable assessment information about a student can also result from direct observation. In using this technique, targeted students are watched carefully, and their behaviors are noted and analyzed. The data collector (i.e., the observer) can be the classroom teacher or a specially trained person.

Direct observation provides some unique data about a student and is particularly useful when assessing behavior problems, breaches of discipline, acting out behavior, or social maladjustment. Direct observation of the youngster in the classroom can confirm or raise questions about the validity of the referral. Of all the assessment techniques available, this one permits the evaluation of individuals while they are in a natural environment (i.e., when they are functioning in an everyday setting). The technique is also useful in assessing the nature of teacher-student interactions and the classroom climate.

In discussing the reasons for and advantages of direct observation, Wiederholt, Hammill, and Brown (1983) list several:

> First, observation can confirm or disconfirm statements or hypotheses made about the student. Second, patterns of student participation and interaction with people, with tasks, and with objects (such as trading cards, marbles, or furniture) can be noted and documented. A third purpose for observation is to note consistencies and inconsistencies in patterns of behavior, both over time and from setting to setting. Fourth, factors that appear to influence the student's behavior can be identified. And fifth, any student behaviors of concern may be described more accurately as the observer sees what the student actually does. (p. 24)

The manner in which observations are noted varies widely along a nonstructured to highly structured continuum. At one end, the observer might merely watch the student engaged in everyday play or classroom activity and thereby secure an overall picture of the situation. At the other end of the continuum, each of the student's behaviors might be classified and frequencies of occurrence tallied over a specified period of time. On those occasions where student-teacher interactions are being observed, there exist several elaborate systems for recording and interpreting the nature of the interactions noted (Brophy and Good, 1969; Flanders, 1970; Medley, Schluck, & Ames, 1968).

Regardless of how much care is taken in faithfully recording observed behaviors, examiners often become overly subjective in specifying the cause for or the meaning of the behaviors observed. The degree to which an observer can analyze behaviors accurately depends heavily on the training and experience of the observer.

Bloom and Lahey (1978) illustrate this point by giving the example of how a professional jockey and a casual appreciator of horses might view a particular horse. Without doubt, the jockey is in a position to see more, understand more, suspect more, and speculate with more assurance than someone with less experience.

Interviews

An interview is "a conversation directed to a definite purpose other than satisfaction in the conversation itself" (Bingham, Moore, & Gustad, 1957, p. 3). Because interviews always have a predetermined purpose (i.e., are undertaken to obtain specific information about something), they play an important role in many comprehensive assessment efforts.

Much useful information about students' needs and problems can be assembled by interviewing parents, teachers, and the students themselves. The results of these interviews can be used to study attitudes, perceptions, and feelings about the causes, nature, and consequences of a particular problem area; settings and situations in which problems occur; and countless other nuances associated with a suspected difficulty.

Most teachers value the information derived from interviews and spend considerable time each year talking with and seeking data from parents, students, and other teachers about specific students. The interview approach provides a convenient way of obtaining perceptions that a person has about a situation or event that is current or historic. For example, interviewing the parents of a student with behavioral problems will yield insights into how the student is perceived and treated at home and what the parents believe is causing or contributing to the problems. These perceptions are usually highly idiosyncratic and subjective and, therefore, should not be taken at face value. Yet they do provide the teacher-diagnostician with clues concerning factors that might be influencing a specific situation.

A good interview is not a haphazard undertaking. On the contrary, the interviewer must decide in advance the particular purposes for the conversation, the questions that are to be asked, the most expedient method for initiating the interview, and other pertinent procedural matters. There is a definite art and science to interviewing. Fortunately, there are several useful how-to books available. Among these are books by Stewart and Cash (1985), Gordon (1970), and McCallon and McCray (1975). Also of interest is Part V of this book, in which Ginsburg shows how the interview technique can be applied to instructional assessment, especially math assessment.

Analytic Teaching

Many assessment oriented practitioners have devised methods of analyzing a student's behavior while the student is engaged in dynamic, ongoing instructional situations. Information from these analyses is used to form hypotheses about the nature of the problem and to determine the next steps in assessment or instruction. The procedure is also used to observe student progress and to discover the elements that need to be changed where expected progress is not evident.

Analytic teaching is known by many names, including "diagnostic teaching," "prescriptive teaching," "directive teaching," "adaptive teaching," and "clinical teaching." All of the systems represented by these terms involve the breaking down of observed behaviors into their component parts so they can be more fully examined for instructional or diagnostic purposes. This is the very essence of the word *analysis* and the reason we prefer to call these systems "analytic teaching."

Wiederholt, Hammill, and Brown (1983) note that analytic teaching methods share at least four characteristics:

> (1) The practitioner has to observe the student engaged in the behavior of interest; (2) the student's responses must be noted and analyzed within some constant frame of reference; (3) the selection of future steps to be taken depends on the interpretation of the results of the successive response analyses; and (4) the methodologies are flexible enough to be applied to almost all aspects of a student's school performance, including academic, linguistic, emotional, and social areas. Methodologies that share these characteristics are grouped under the heading analytic teaching. (p. 32)

Analytic teaching methodologies are exemplified by the clinical teaching techniques of Johnson and Myklebust (1967) and the directive teaching approach of Stephens (1970). The adaptive testing assessment method of Hausserman (1958) is also a technique that combines behavioral analysis of responses with ongoing instruction.

A simple example of an analytic teaching session is provided by Hammill and Bartel (1986) and involves the attempt of a teacher to learn about a student's knowledge of colors. In this instance, the teacher wishes to discover the extent of John's understanding of concepts related to colors. To accomplish this, the teacher probes for answers to the following questions:

1. Can John match the basic colors (place red chips together, blue chips together, and so forth)? If not, what colors does he have difficulty in matching?
2. If asked to point to the red chip, then to the blue chip, and so forth, can John select the correct chip from among others of different colors?

3. If the teacher points to the red chip, then to the blue chip, and so forth and says "What color is this?" does John answer correctly?

These three questions all relate to the general question of whether or not the child can recognize colors, but they also provide different kinds of information about the level of his knowledge, the particular colors he does not know, and how to begin to teach him. First he learns to discriminate among the colors, then he learns the labels (receptive language), and finally he uses the labels in speech (expressive language). (p. 9)

Analytic teaching is particularly useful (a) in detecting areas of weakness and strength; (b) in verifying, probing, or discarding the conclusions and recommendations derived from other sources; (c) in deducing specific instructional or behavioral needs; and (d) in formulating remedial programs. This is accomplished through an ongoing process of teaching the child and analyzing his or her responses to various instructional tasks.

Reviewing School and Anecdotal Records

The usefulness of reviewing school records, especially as the practice relates to assessment, is described quite adequately in Chapter 2 of *The Resource Teacher* by Wiederholt, Hammill, and Brown (1983). Rather than attempt to "gild the lily," their comments are simply quoted at this time.

The analysis and review of records made about the student is one of the most important of assessment activities, and it is also one of the most overlooked sources of information. Review of records is relatively unobtrusive, is inexpensive, and is one of the major sources of information for generating assessment questions.

Records are often in disarray and may be poorly organized because no one may have taken or been given the responsibility of records collection and organization. When they are not organized, it is impossible to evaluate the relevance of information gathered. People may continue to collect information superstitiously, believing that it is of value when it is not, or they may understandably complain about collecting information that is never used. People rarely mind collecting information that can be shown to be helpful to a student. Especially where the resources for data or information collection are limited, the resource teacher, usually in conjunction with others in the school, will want to make a careful study of the records system.

The kind of information we can expect from a review and analysis of records is reflected in the following questions:

1. What is the nature of the information provided? The information should be relevant to any presenting problems. It should also be comprehensive enough to describe the problem or the student adequately. Both positive and negative information are important. We will also want to know if information that should

be there is missing. This is especially true of information that is needed to rule out possible causes of problems or certain instructional methods. Instructional records often lack enough detail to permit a real analysis of the instructional history of the student.

2. How current is the information? There is no need to duplicate information that is already available. On the other hand, if people are making decisions on old information, there should be an updating to be sure that the information used is currently valid.

3. How reliable and valid is the information? The data base for any statements made about the student must be known. The data base is then evaluated literally as to its goodness. Some statements, such as "John has a central auditory processing disorder, because he mispronounces words such as *chimney* as *chimley* and *came* as *come*," are clearly in need of further interpretation. In addition, statements based upon a one-time observation, or upon only a single setting may be suspect. Observable fact must be separated from professional fiction.

4. What discrepancies about the student or his or her behavior are apparent from the records? These discrepancies may be between one time and another, between one setting and another, or between an expectation and an actual performance. The sudden onset of social, emotional, or academic problems, as well as gradual declines (as in IQ scores) are signals either of invalid information or a serious adverse change in the student or in his or her environment.

5. What consistent patterns of behaviors, comments about the student, or test scores are noted? Consistencies provide some evidence of reliability in information and evidence for the chronic nature of a problem. On the other hand, we would be concerned about the effectiveness of the instructional program if records showed a consistent pattern of no change during any time of remedial effort.

6. How is the information in the records organized? Although this question is not about the student, it has implications both for the wise use of the resource teacher's time and energy and for public relations with those who will be asked to gather information on behalf of the student. When records are not organized, it becomes impossible to evaluate the relevance of the information recorded, and people continue to collect information that is irrelevant or unused.

In addition to the need for organizing records, the form of the organization is important. While there is an apparent advantage in having a purely chronological account of a student, eventually the information should also be reorganized around presenting problems as well. The problem-oriented record described by Weed (1971) is often used in settings where more than one person works with a student or is to observe the student or where the problem is persistent across time and settings.[1]

---

[1]From *The Resource Teacher* (pp. 23–24) by J. L. Wiederholt, D. D. Hammill, and V. Brown, 1983, Austin, TX: PRO-ED. Reprinted by permission.

INTERPRETING ASSESSMENT RESULTS

The results of assessment activity, whether test scores, records of anecdotal events, answers to interview questions, or descriptions of performance, are at best merely observations of behavior. To be of maximal use, these findings must be interpreted (i.e., some system must be applied that gives these sterile observations meaning). In general, interpretative systems are of two types: referenced and nonreferenced.

The two most prevalent forms of referenced interpretation are norm referenced and criterion referenced. Both of these referenced systems interpret behavior in terms of some absolute standard existing outside the student. Norm referenced interpretation assumes some idea of normalcy for rating scores. Criterion referenced interpretation involves precisely stated objectives to indicate skill mastery. In addition to these two approaches, this section covers what we have designated nonreferenced interpretation.

Norm Referenced Interpretation

According to Gronlund (1985), norm referenced interpretations can be applied to all kinds of assessment data and need not be restricted to test derived scores. When norm referenced interpretations are made, a test score or an observed behavior is compared to some real or hypothetical average representation of persons who share common characteristics with the individual being evaluated (the normative referent group). A test score or a particular behavior might be described as being more or less equal to, above, or below the average of the normative sample. Thus, norm referenced interpretations are made to describe interindividual differences among people (i.e., to see how far a person's behavior is from some perceived or statistically determined average).

Interpretation of Raw Scores. When norm referenced interpretations are based on test performance, the total number of correct responses (the raw score) made by students in the normative sample are converted to values that truly reflect their distance from the average score of the group. There is a simple procedure for doing this. At each age interval, the raw scores made by students are plotted on a cumulative frequency distribution chart from which percentiles and standard scores are calculated. Percentiles are particularly useful when describing test results to parents, teachers, and the child tested. For example, to say that Phil reads at the 85th percentile means that he performs better than 85 out of a 100 students his age.

The test data derived from the normative sample can also be used to calculate other normative scores, such as age and grade equivalents. Their use results in such statements as Phyllis does math at the 8.5 grade level or Richard is at the second year level in gross motor development. These values are not as accurate as percentiles and standard scores, and their use sometimes can lead to a distorted picture of a child's true abilities. Most authorities recommend strongly that such scores be avoided in school practice.

Demographic Characteristics of Norm Sample. The group whose scores are used to compute test norms may represent the national population, students attending school in a particular district, a single classroom of students, or even a class of handicapped people. In any case, test developers are required to show that their normative sample is representative of the desired population. To illustrate, where the reference group is the country's general population, test developers will show that the demographic characteristics of the normative sample are essentially the same as those for the national population. The characteristics might be sex, age, social class, urban-rural residence, geographic area, educational level of parents, and so forth.

The normative referent does not have to be statistically determined or based on some formally identified normative sample. Rather, norms may be based simply on the experience of a teacher, therapist, or examiner. In such a case, a student's performance is compared with the professional's knowledge of how most people the student's age have in the past performed a given task in a particular situation. For example, most competent third grade teachers with ten years classroom experience need no normative tables to tell them what typical behavior is for third graders. It is against this experiential background that the teacher judges an individual student's performance as good, average, or poor.

The Norm Referencing Process. Consider four-year-old Sally, who is suspected of being mentally retarded. Mr. Jones, the examiner, could use information obtained from both tests with formally derived norms and other unnormed assessment procedures to reach a norm referenced decision. For example, he could administer the *Detroit Tests of Learning Aptitude–Primary* (Hammill & Bryant, 1986) and use its tables to secure norm referenced data about Sally's intellectual competence.

Next, Mr. Jones could devote an hour or so to observing Sally at free play, asking her questions about the everyday world, watching her interact with other kids, and interviewing her parents. After all of this, Mr. Jones would compare his observations with his knowledge about how children Sally's age usually perform under the conditions that were observed. Here, he is using his "internal norms," norms that are derived from his training and experience, as the basis for interpreting Sally's performance.

Examples of norm referenced statements are listed below.

1. Bob scored at the 23rd percentile on the Graduate Record Exam.

2. Cynthia was third in her class in reading and received an A.

3. Professor Wylie curved the grades on his last test.

4. Six-year-old Willie's behavior was considered poor by his teacher, because he was acting like a four-year-old.

5. The new student did math at the sixth grade level, even though his grade equivalent for his math score on the *Metropolitan Achievement Test* was 4.4.

6. Sam has a two-year discrepancy between his IQ and achievement test score.

7. For her age, she is a very good girl.

8. William scored 23 points in the game, which was four points above the school average.

Criterion Referenced Interpretation

As is the case with norm reference, criterion reference refers to a method of interpreting assessment findings, a method applicable to all types of assessment techniques, including standardized tests, interviews, and informal teacher made tests. Unlike norm referencing, however, criterion referencing is undertaken to learn what an individual can do unrelated to the performance of others. In other words, student performance is interpreted in an absolute rather than in a relative sense. Sometimes this method is called content, domain, universe, or mastery referencing.

Generally, the domain to be evaluated is clearly defined in terms of skills, tasks, or test items; and the criterion for successful mastery is specified (e.g., the student either passes or fails an activity; he or she can pass an activity 75% of the time). To use an example from Salvia and Ysseldyke (1985), criterion referenced assessments "provide answers to specific questions such as 'Does Maureen spell the word *dog* correctly?'" (p. 30). For such a question, Maureen's spelling proficiency compared to her peers is irrelevant; spelling the word correctly is evidence of her mastery of the task. While the performance criterion in norm referenced interpretation is the average performance of some specified population, in criterion referenced interpretation, the criterion is a predetermined level of performance on some task or series of tasks.

Obviously, criterion referenced assessment has considerable relevance for instruction and is widely practiced in the classroom. It can be used to inventory a student's instructional needs, to monitor success in a program of study, or to place a youngster into a curriculum. Classroom teachers frequently apply this frame of reference to the results of their own classroom tests. For example, on Monday a teacher may give his or her students 20 new words to learn to spell by Friday. On Friday the students are tested. Instances where students spell 17 words correctly are taken as evidence that they have mastered those words on the test. Misspelled words are singled out for special instruction, and the student is retested later on these words.

Examples of criterion referenced statements are listed below.

1. Mary could spell only 5 of the 20 words.

2. Though otherwise proficient, Billy missed 5 of 10 words containing *bl* blends.

3. James has mispronounced words having r's in them in 7 out of 10 trials.

4. Of all the spelling rules, Nell has the most trouble with "i before e except after c."

5. William scored 23 points in the game and was added to the school's athletic Hall of Fame.

6. Having passed 85% of the questions on Form A of the test, the student undertook to answer the questions on Form B.

7. Since Morris made 8 baskets in 10 trials, he qualified for the team.

8. Tom made a B in algebra class.

Nonreferenced Interpretation

Like norm and criterion referenced interpretations, nonreferenced interpretations also are concerned with what students do. But in this case, the concern is focused on learning what strategies or systems students use to solve problems and reach answers.

Naturally, answers that students give to problems and to teachers' questions, even when incorrect, are not always reached by guessing. Usually, students use what for them seems to be a logical procedure for reaching their answers. Knowledge of these procedures is useful for the examiner, because if the teacher understands how a student has reached an erroneous conclusion or how a student has reached an acceptable conclusion in an inefficient way, it is often an easy matter to provide the student with a new strategy that works better.

How Nonreferencing Works. While the other types of referencing have clear-cut criteria for correctness (right-wrong) or mastery (pass-fail), nonreferenced interpretations have no hard and fast rules governing correctness. Consider the example provided in Figure 1.2. By watching students attack the problem or by asking them how they did it, the examiner can easily learn the strategies that were employed to achieve the task. There are many approaches to solving the problem, some more efficient than others, none entirely worthless. For example, one student may count the number of right angles, another student may begin by counting the smaller triangles and work up systematically to the larger ones, another student may take a pencil and shade each triangle after counting it (as a reminder not to count it twice), another student may start counting in the lower left corner and expand to the rest of the figure, and so forth. All of these strategies work to some extent; perhaps some work better for some students than for others. The example provided is a simple one, purposely chosen to show clearly what is meant by nonreferencing and why there can be no rigid criteria for correctness.

FIGURE 1.2. Triangle Problem

Task: How many triangles are
embedded in this picture?

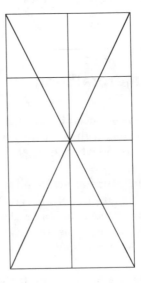

Nonreferencing as a Designation. Some authorities might consider nonreferenced interpretation a subtype of criterion referencing. Millman (1974), for example, uses criterion referencing in a very general sense and assigns to that category all absolute interpretations, including even those where no explicit criterion for success is stated and where scores are used for purely descriptive purposes. Most writers, however, do not consider this type of interpretation an example of criterion referencing.

As no name could be found in the literature for this kind of interpretation, I called it *nonreferencing*, recognizing that this term is not completely satisfactory. Perhaps in time a better term will be coined, but for now this one will suffice. Alternative terms were considered (e.g., intrinsic, self, individual, idiosyncratic, strategy, and solution referencing), but all were discarded for one reason or another.

Examples of nonreferenced statements are listed below.

1. David failed to carry in problem 12, and in problem 16 he transposed digits in the remainder.

2. When Lois does something she shouldn't, she always tries to lie her way out of it.

3. William misses many baskets on days when he is criticized by his coach.

4. Mary spells words the way she says them, misspelling the ones she mispronounces.

5. James used the mnemonic device H-O-M-E-S to help recall the names of the Great Lakes.

6. In oral reading, Billy substitutes semantically similar words for words he does not know (e.g., reading aloud "He drove down the road" for "He drove down the thoroughfare").

7. Jan can tell the story better if she has time to rehearse and make notes.

STANDARDIZED AND NONSTANDARDIZED ASSESSMENT

One frequently reads about the importance of using standardized methods in assessment, but much confusion exists as to what constitutes a standardized method. To help clarify this situation, this section discusses (a) the elements that comprise the concept of standardization, (b) the evidence required to prove that a technique is in fact standardized, and (c) the value of using nonstandardized techniques.

The Three Elements of Standardized Assessment

Paraphrasing Nunnally (1978) and Anastasi (1982), a well-standardized technique will have clear rules governing its use and will require uniform skills in administering the test and interpreting its results. These are the elements that form the concept of *standardized assessment*. To a considerable degree, it is the presence of these elements that help make reliability and validity of a technique possible. Each element is discussed below.

Set Administration Procedures. All standardized assessments include precise instructions governing how the technique is to be administered. These instructions specify a variety of things, including what may be said to the student, what materials are needed, how picture books, blocks, or other physical components are to be managed, when to discontinue the procedure, and many other important aspects required in using a particular technique. Set administration procedures are important to all types of assessments, including tests, interviewing, direct observation, and analytic teaching.

Objective Scoring Criteria. Another factor in standardized assessment is the provision of some system for scoring or reporting behavior objectively. If the technique is a test, the system will include specific criteria for what constitutes a correct or incorrect answer. For nontest assessments, other systems are available for noting behaviors, for example, classifying different types of teacher-student interactions in classroom observation situations and recording student comments during or immediately after interviews. In all cases, care is taken to prepare the examiner to see the behavior clearly, to classify it according to some system, and to record it properly.

A Specified Preferred Frame of Reference. The authors or proponents of a well-standardized technique will indicate clearly the frame of reference that is best applied to its results. If the technique calls for a norm referenced interpretation, information will be provided for using normative tables or developmental levels. If a criterion referenced interpretation is to be applied, specifications for item mastery will be offered. If a nonreferenced interpretation is the goal, a particular system for classifying errors or identifying strategies will be provided.

In standardized assessment, these guidelines governing administration, scoring, and interpretation are not mere recommendations; they are to be followed to the letter. Adherence to the stated procedures is so important that any divergence is assumed to invalidate the results to some extent. As a consequence of using these guidelines, there is a higher degree of consistency in results among examiners. This is a basic assumption underlying standardized assessment—namely, that different examiners will obtain more or less the same results when using the same procedure. Following the designated procedures minimizes error and increases the probability that what an examiner sees or hears will truly reflect the student's abilities, knowledge, or behavior.

The Two "Proofs" of Adequate Standardization

Standard administration procedures, standard scoring criteria, and standard means of interpretation represent the very essence of standardization, and it is difficult to see how any assessment technique that did not handle these three elements well could be considered standardized. Yet their presence alone does not ensure that a technique is in fact standardized. To be certain that a technique is properly standardized, the examiner must consider evidence concerning the two proofs of adequate standardization: reliability and validity. Without the availability of convincing evidence regarding these proofs, no technique can be considered adequately standardized.

Evidence of Reliability. The experimental demonstration of a procedure's reliability is an important proof of a proper standardization. Unreliable procedures yield untrustworthy results; untrustworthy results lead directly to errors in their interpretation; and errors in the interpretation of results invariably end up producing negative consequences for the individuals who were assessed. There are several sources of error that influence reliability; errors associated with content sampling, time sampling, and interobserver sampling are the most frequently studied.

Content sampling is associated exclusively with the reliability of tests. The amount of error that exists as a function of the items selected to create a test is called content sampling error and is estimated by any of several statistical procedures, including split-halving and application of the Küder-Richardson or coefficient Alpha formulas.

Time sampling is associated with all types of assessment techniques. Error due to the random fluctuations from one assessment session to another is called time sampling error and is usually estimated by the test-retest method.

Interobserver reliability can also be computed on test data but more frequently is used to estimate reliability of other types of techniques (e.g., the analysis of students' written products or speech and language samples). Error due to different observers is called interobserver sampling error and is estimated by intercorrelating the observations or by computing the percentage of agreement among observers.

Most of these methods yield a summative statistic, the reliability coefficient. The magnitude of this coefficient tells how much confidence one should place in the results of a procedure. In the case of interobserver reliability, the percentage of agreement serves this purpose.

Evidence of Validity. Simply put, validity refers to the evidence that an assessment procedure measures what it is said or believed to measure. In the case of standardized measurement, the evidence must be thoroughly demonstrated, usually through logical or experimental means. Three kinds of validity are generally considered appropriate for standardized techniques: content, criterion related, and construct.

Content validity. Gronlund (1985) writes that "content validation is the process of determining the extent to which a set of test tasks provides a relevant and representative sample of the domain of tasks under consideration" (p. 59). Although Gronlund is writing specifically about tests, his definition can be generalized to all forms of assessment.

Obviously, content validity has to be built into the assessment technique from the beginning. In doing this, great care must be taken to construct test items, interview questions, error analysis systems, and so forth, that adequately represent significant aspects of the domain being assessed.

The content validity of a spelling test could be demonstrated by showing that its items were consistent with the material that is actually being taught in the school. This would be sufficient for a teacher's purposes, but authors of a test built for commercial distribution should go further and demonstrate through item analytic procedures the suitability of their items.

The content validity of a list of questions being prepared for use in an interview to learn a person's interests in a particular occupation could be validated by submitting the list to a panel of practitioners in that field. These practitioners could judge the extent to which the questions reflect significant aspects of their occupation.

The content validity of an error analysis system could be demonstrated by showing that the errors are classified in a way that is consistent with current theory. For example, a system for classifying articulation errors could reflect current ideas about feature analysis, especially relative to place, manner, and voicing. A classification system for oral reading errors might reflect the newer ideas about miscues, especially relative to semantically, phonically, and graphically similar substitutions.

Criterion related validity. Criterion related validity is defined as the extent to which performance measured or observed by some procedure is related to some other valued measure of the same performance. This form of validity can be established by using the results to predict future performance or by correlating the results with those from some already accepted procedure. For example, the results of teachers' overall ratings of reading readiness could be used to predict first grade reading success, or the scores from a new test of reading could be correlated with those of an older well-established reading test. Both of these examples provide evidence of criterion related validity.

Construct validity. This type of validity refers to the degree to which the underlying constructs of a procedure can be identified and the extent to which these traits reflect the theoretical model on which the procedure is based. Gronlund (1985) offers a three-step procedure for demonstrating construct validity. First, several constructs presumed to account for performance are identified. Second, hypotheses are generated that are based on the identified constructs. Third, the hypotheses are verified by logical or empirical methods. For example, the developers of a new test of reading might as a result of their knowledge of the reading process hypothesize that reading should be related to age (because reading is developmental in nature), to IQ (because reading is a cognitive ability), and to grades (because reading is a key skill helpful in all academic subjects). If the new test did correlate highly with age, IQ, and grades, it would be evidence that the new test possessed construct validity. Though this example pertains to the construct validity of a test, the concept is equally applicable to the results of all kinds of assessment techniques.

Conclusion. In concluding this discussion about standardization, three important points should be made. First, even though the majority of the evaluation literature discusses standardization almost exclusively in terms of its relation to tests, the reader should recognize that the elements and proofs represent important generic concepts in measurement. As such, they are applicable to all assessment techniques and should not be restricted to tests. To be sure, knowledge of reliability and validity is as critical to interpreting data acquired from interviewing, observing, and analytic teaching as it is to interpreting data acquired from testing.

Second, the reader will note that the presence of norms is not included among either the elements or the proofs of standardization. While norms are often associated with highly standardized devices, especially those built for the expressed purpose of making norm referenced interpretations, their presence is by no means an essential criterion for standardization. Many assessment techniques are perfected specifically for research uses or for making criterion or nonreferenced interpretations. In such instances, norms are superfluous. Yet these procedures need precise administration instructions, reliable results, and consistent interpretations as much as those intended for norm referenced use.

Third, assessment techniques can easily be classified into three groups—highly standardized, standardized, and nonstandardized—according to their degree of standardization in terms of the previously described proofs. Techniques for which exhaustive evidence (e.g., multiple studies) is available that shows acceptable reliability and validity can fairly be called *highly standardized*. Techniques that have only minimal evidence (e.g., one or two studies showing acceptable reliability and validity) qualify for a *standardized* rating. Techniques for which no proof of reliability or validity is available, only nonsupportive evidence exists, or evidence is provided for only one of the two proofs must be considered *nonstandardized*. In general usage, *formal* is used as a synonym for "standardized" or "highly standardized"; *informal* is used as a synonym for "nonstandardized."

The Value of Nonstandardized Techniques

The advantages of using well-built, highly standardized techniques are obvious: Their use yields reliable and valid results, the kind of results that are most needed for justifying placement decisions about students and for documenting growth. But a high price often is paid for this standardization; for example, the examiner's freedom to improvise and to probe is sacrificed, the breadth and depth of the content assessed has to be restricted or arbitrarily fixed, and the setting in which the assessment takes place has to be contrived to satisfy the demands expected of standardized techniques.

To prepare instructional plans for students and to diagnose their problems properly, examiners frequently need information that lies outside the purview of standardized assessment. Sometimes examiners want to assess areas for which standardized techniques are simply not available. Sometimes they want to probe the extent of a student's knowledge of a subject in ways that are impossible under standardized conditions. The three examples that follow show how the use of nonstandardized procedures can produce relevant, useful assessment information.

Example #1. If the student doesn't understand what is asked of him or her, the examiner can reformulate the instructions to a simpler level and try again. If the student still doesn't understand, the examiner can demonstrate over and over again until the student finally gets the idea.

Example #2. Knowledge of whether or not students misspelled this or that word or failed a particular task is not as important for many purposes as trying to learn why they did not achieve as expected and determining the conditions under which they might have performed well. For example, when students give the wrong answer to a problem, the examiner could (a) tell them to be more careful and to do the problem again, (b) call their attention to particularly relevant elements in the problem before asking them to attempt it a second time, or (c) ask them how they came to the answer that was given. Knowing how a student's performance is altered on an assessment task under each of the conditions listed may have significant educational implications.

Example #3. On a given day, Ms. Foster, a fifth grade teacher, may decide to test her students' mastery of multiplication, because it has been the subject of instruction for the past week. She prepares a test in which the problems require knowledge of those aspects of multiplication that had been taught. Usually she makes up the problems to be included on the test; occasionally the problems are drawn from workbooks, teacher's manuals, or other classroom sources. It is Ms. Foster's personal judgment about the need for and relevance of the information to be assessed that determines the nature of the items placed on the test. Without doubt, the teacher has used some rationale in constructing her test, but she will rarely see the need or have the desire for expressing it formally.

The flexibility in administering, scoring, and interpreting procedures evidenced by these examples is simply not permitted when using standardized procedures. Yet the examples illustrate how instructionally important assessment information can result from the use of nonstandardized procedures. Surely the findings obtained through nonstandardized techniques are not substitutes for those derived from standardized methods, but they can augment such findings and from the teacher's point of view are often infinitely more valuable.

CONCLUSION

Finally, there are four questions that examiners should consider carefully when thinking about assessment. These are the Whys?, Whats?, Whiches?, and Hows? that underlie the understanding of all assessment efforts.

1. Why is the assessment being undertaken? Is it done to diagnose students, to document progress, or to acquire instructionally relevant information?

2. What is going to be measured—that is, which attributes in the achievement, aptitude, or affective domains are the targets for assessment?

3. Which of the available assessment techniques are to be employed: tests, interviews, analytic teaching, direct observation, review of records, or analysis of student production?

4. How are the resulting data to be interpreted? Are they going to be subjected to a norm, criterion or nonreferenced interpretation?

REFERENCES

American Psychological Association. (1974). *Standards for educational and psychological tests.* Washington, DC: Author.

Anastasi, A. (1982). *Psychological testing* (5th ed.). New York: Macmillan.

Ashlock, R. B. (1976). *Error patterns in computation.* New York: McGraw-Hill.

Bingham, W., Moore, B. V., & Gustad, J. W. (1957). *How to interview.* New York: Harper & Row.

Bloom, L., & Lahey, M. (1978). *Language development and language disorders.* New York: John Wiley.

Brophy, J. E., & Good, T. L. (1969). *Teacher-child dyadic interaction: A manual for coding classroom behavior.* Austin, TX: Research and Development Center for Teacher Education. The University of Texas.

Flanders, N. (1970). *Analyzing teaching behavior.* Menlo Park, CA: Addison-Wesley.

Ginsburg, H. P., & Mathews, S. C. (1984). *Diagnostic Test of Arithmetic Strategies.* Austin, TX: PRO-ED.

Goodman, Y., & Burke, C. L. (1972). *Reading Miscue Inventory.* New York: Macmillan.

Gordon, T. (1970). *Parent effectiveness training.* New York: Wyden.

Gronlund, N. E. (1985). *Measurement and evaluation in teaching* (5th ed.). New York: Macmillan.

Hammill, D. D., & Bartel, N. (1986). Meeting the special needs of children. In D. D. Hammill & N. Bartel (Eds.), *Teaching students with learning and behavior problems* (pp. 1–21). Austin, TX: PRO-ED.

Hammill, D. D., Brown, L., & Bryant, B. (in press). *A consumer's guide to tests in print.* Austin, TX: PRO-ED.

Hammill, D. D., & Bryant, B. (1986). *Detroit Tests of Learning Aptitude–Primary.* Austin, TX: PRO-ED.

Hausserman, E. (1958). *Developmental potential of preschool children.* New York: Grune & Stratton.

Howell, K. W., & Kaplan, J. S. (1980). *Diagnosing basic skills.* Columbus, OH: Charles E. Merrill.

Johnson, D., & Myklebust, H. (1967). *Learning disabilities: Educational principles and practices.* New York: Grune & Stratton.

Lee, L. (1971). Developmental sentence scoring. A clinical procedure for estimating syntactic development in children's spontaneous speech. *Journal of Speech and Hearing Disorders, 36,* 315–331.

Lee, L. (1974). *Developmental sentence analysis.* Evanston, IL: Northwestern University Press.

Lee, L., Koenigsknecht, R. A., & Mulhern, S. T. (1975). *Interactive language development.* Evanston, IL: Northwestern University Press.

McCallon, E., & McCray, E. (1975). *Planning and conducting interviews.* Austin, TX: Learning Concepts.

Medley, D., Schluck, C., & Ames, N. (1968). *Assessing the learning environment in the classroom: A manual for users of OSCAR 5.* Princeton, NJ: Educational Testing Services.

Millman, J. (1974). Criterion-referenced measurement. In W. J. Popham (Ed.), *Evaluation in education. Current applications* (pp. 309–397). Berkeley, CA: McCutchan.

Mitchell, J. V. (Ed). (1985). *The ninth mental measurements yearbook.* Lincoln, NE: The University of Nebraska Press.

Nunnally, J. S. (1978). *Psychometric theory* (4th ed.). New York: McGraw-Hill.

Salvia, J., & Ysseldyke, J. E. (1985). *Assessment in special and remedial education* (3rd ed.). Boston: Houghton Mifflin.

Stephens, T. M. (1970). *Directive teaching of children with learning and behavior handi-caps.* Columbus, OH: Charles E. Merrill.

Stewart, D. J., & Cash, W. B. (1985). *Interviewing: Principles and practices* (4th ed.). Dubuque, IA: Brown.

Wiederholt, J. L. (1985). *Formal Reading Inventory.* Austin, TX: PRO-ED.

Wiederholt, J. L., & Bryant, B. (1986). *Gray Oral Reading Tests–Revised.* Austin, TX: PRO-ED.

Wiederholt, J. L., Hammill, D. D., & Brown, V. (1983). *The resource teacher.* Austin, TX: PRO-ED.

PART II

ASSESSING
ORAL LANGUAGE

Patricia I. Myers

The reader can discover many resources dealing with the assessment of oral language, but many of these rely on the observation of children in natural settings and on lengthy language or speech samples. In the following chapters are a number of structured techniques for eliciting specific linguistic features. The value of language samples is not denigrated; procuring samples may be the most accurate method of language assessment. However, one must remember that recording and analyzing a language sample is a tedious process for which the public school speech pathologist seldom has the time.

The rationale presented rests upon the speech pathologist having a working knowledge of language development and language structure. The author's belief is that nothing can substitute for such knowledge. Without it, tests or assessment procedures can be of little value beyond their screening capabilities.

Chapter 2 covers an introduction to the topic of language assessment. Because of the importance assigned to speech and language structure and development, the next two chapters are devoted to these topics. Chapter 5 is devoted to techniques of informal speech and language assessment. Here a number of comprehensive assessment devices are described.

2 / AN OVERVIEW OF LANGUAGE ASSESSMENT

The assessment of children's language abilities and disabilities has been a preoccupation of speech pathologists, psychologists, and other appraisal personnel for well over twenty years. Psycholinguistic models of assessment enjoyed great popularity with such professionals during the 1970s and gave rise to a number of standardized tests—some more related to language than others—such as the *Illinois Test of Psycholinguistic Abilities* (ITPA) (Kirk, McCarthy, & Kirk, 1968), the *Utah Test of Language Development* (Mecham, Jex, & Jones, 1978), and others. During this time, content validity was asserted by simply using face validity as evidence that psycholinguistic abilities were measured by a test. The extensive use of these tests means that the assessment process has become vested in a model that yields little in-depth information regarding a child's language abilities (Muma, 1983).

Already enchanted with psychometric models, professionals in language assessment became equally entranced with Chomsky's theories of generative grammar. If these professionals considered themselves too progressive to continue using the ITPA, they simply exchanged it for some other instrument, such as the *Developmental Sentence Analysis* (Lee, 1974) or one of the developmental profiles. However, the 1970s began with the "semantic revolution" heralded by Bloom (1970), Bowerman (1973a), Schlesinger (1971), and Slobin (1973) and ended with the "pragmatics revolution" led by Bates (1976a), Bates et al. (1979), and Dore (1975). As Leonard (1983) notes, the gains made in the 1970s were solidified by the substantive data that became available at that time and by expanded knowledge about the learning of language.

This knowledge will continue to bring about profound changes in all aspects of language and its assessment. For example, assessment and treatment procedures focusing on psycholinguistic abilities or on grammar must be altered radically to reflect the discovery that the linguistic structure of children's speech is determined by the dual needs to be meaningful and to have some social effect.

Chapter 5 discusses assessment procedures, including the value of traditional measures of articulation, grammar, and other language abilities. There are children with only articulation problems, children who need improved vocabularies, and children in need of syntactic refinements. For those children, the conventional assessment procedures will serve. However, more and more children with severe language disorders are being seen in our schools and clinics—children who are retarded, autistic, or in some other way severely deficient in language—for whom the traditional approaches to assessment and remediation are seriously inadequate.

Any discussion of language assessment must deal with at least four major areas: the assessment framework, the nature and structure of language, the development of language, and the specific assessment procedures. Because this book is devoted to assessment for instructional purposes, the assessment framework is discussed first. The work of Chapman (1976), Miller (1978, 1981), and Muma (1983) has provided a basis for many of the concepts in this book.

The approach to oral language assessment set forth in the following chapters is fundamentally developmental. It focuses on defining and describing the developmental status of the child for each of the basic language processes: comprehension, production, and communication. These processes are discussed in Chapter 3 under the more traditional categories of phonology, syntax, semantics, and pragmatics. Regardless of the taxonomical problems in describing language, the following problems in assessment must be considered.

- It is difficult to quantify many of the elusive aspects of deviant language.

- Developmental data are often incomplete, fragmented, and sometimes inconsistent.

- Theories and models of language behavior are often too narrow, too broad, vary greatly from one another, or simply ignore deviant language.

- Many excellent approaches to assessment are too time-consuming to be employed outside of an experimental situation.

These difficulties must be accepted. One must assume a positive approach to assessment, accept the challenge, and attempt to apply what is known, what is best, and what is feasible.

The most efficient approach to assessment is attempting to answer the three questions posed by Miller (1978):

1. Why are we assessing the child?

2. What are we going to assess?

3. How are we going to assess the child? (p. 273)

The answer to any of the questions will affect the others, because they are interactive, relating to each other in a reciprocal fashion. For example, if assessment is being done because the child has a functional articulation disorder, the "what" and "how" are to some extent predetermined.

WHY ASSESS LANGUAGE?

Obviously, children's language is assessed to discover whether their language behaviors are deviant and, if so, to what degree. However, assessment involves much more than the designation of "problem/no problem" that arises when someone questions the child's language behavior with regard to its quantity or quality. The basic aim of assessment is deceptively simple; it implies that one will be able to establish the normalcy or deviance of the child's language and that one knows what constitutes normal language behavior in a 3 year old or an 8 year old. In the past, clinicians have relied upon standardized norm referenced tests to provide the answers to these questions. However, severely language delayed or disordered children presently being referred for assessment are unable to respond to the requirements of a standardized testing situation. Moreover, research is indicating more and more that language development can be highly idiosyncratic and that what is normal for most children may not be normal for the individual child.

A second reason for assessing the child's language is to provide baseline information regarding the different components of language. The establishment of baseline functioning enables the evaluator to estimate the developmental level at which children are performing by comparing their performances to test norms or to developmental data. The existence of a developmental delay or disorder can be established only after the child's developmental level is determined. It should be noted here that there is little agreement on the terms *language delay* and *language disorder*. Some authors equate the two terms (Coggins, 1976; Miller & Yoder, 1973; Morehead & Ingram, 1973), but others differentiate them, using the rationale that some children are delayed in language acquisition but are progressing in normal sequence, while other children's development is violating the sequence at least insofar as that sequence is known (Bax & Stephenson, 1977; Cousins, 1979; Menyuk, 1968).

A third reason for assessment, and the most important from the viewpoint of the clinician, is to provide information for the design and development of a therapeutic program. The data gathered in the assessment can determine the developmental level at which therapy should begin and aids the clinician in determining which processes and components of language should be included in the therapy program. Although the treatment of language disorders is not within the purview of this text, it should be noted that the baseline information obtained in assessment is important in determining whether progress is being made by the child and at what rate the progress, if any, is occurring.

WHAT IS TO BE ASSESSED?

The elements, the components, the processes of language are to be assessed, and determining what those elements are forms the basis of the answer to the question, "What?" The reader will find that language is discussed throughout the text in terms of four components: phonology, syntax, semantics, and pragmatics. As mentioned earlier, it would be possible to categorize the content of assessment into the same elements as those of language or to use other divisions, such as the processes of language: comprehension, production, and pragmatics. It is also possible to use the first categorization system and, with the exception of pragmatics, break down the components into their receptive and productive aspects.

Another aspect of language that must be preserved in assessment is the complexity of language. The field of language assessment is notorious for the use of quick and easy tests of "simple" processes. One of the reasons given for the use of such tests is that large numbers of children must be assessed, and, therefore, easily-administered instruments are necessary. The difficulty arises when these tests are used for diagnostic purposes and when therapeutic programs are designed based on the results. Unfortunately, some professionals who know better use and advocate such tests which violate a fundamental principle of language therapy by reducing language to simple, and sometimes irrelevant, dimensions.

HOW TO CONDUCT AN ASSESSMENT

The third question to be asked before assessing a child is, "How am I going to go about the assessment?" This may be the most difficult question of the three, because there are more obstacles and pitfalls in selecting instruments and in eliciting appropriate responses than there are in the other two areas of problem identification and language taxonomy. Assessment procedures can be divided into at least four basic categories: standardized tests, developmental scales, nonstandardized tests, and behavioral observations.

Standardized Tests

Miller (1978) gives a particularly lucid and succinct definition of a standardized test when he says that it

> . . . is one that has been given to large numbers of children from various populations, has demonstrated reliability (internal and/or test retest), is valid as determined by external or face-validity criteria, and has normative data that provide either scale-score, age-equivalent, or numerical-score comparisons for individual children tested. (p. 291)

Some of the commonly used standardized tests of language are: the *Illinois Test of Psycholinguistic Abilities* (Kirk, McCarthy, & Kirk, 1968), the *Test for Auditory Comprehension of Language* (Carrow, 1973), the *Test of Language Development–Primary* (Newcomer & Hammill, 1982) and *Intermediate* (Hammill & Newcomer, 1982), the *Clinical Evaluation of Language Functions* (Semel & Wiig, 1980), the *Test of Adolescent Language* (Hammill, Brown, Larsen, & Wiederholt, 1987), and the *Carrow Elicited Language Inventory* (Carrow, 1974). Standardized tests of oral language are discussed further in Chapter 5.

Standardized tests of language have numerous drawbacks with regard to comprehensive assessment for purposes of program planning. They are seldom, if ever, appropriate for children under 3 years of age, and they are not always appropriate to all populations. In selecting a standardized test, one should search for agreement among the procedures of the test, the child's behavior, and the goals of assessment. Availability of a test is never an adequate substitute for suitability; there are many alternatives to standardized tests.

Developmental Scales

Developmental scales sample the child's major performance areas across a developmental period and are administered to determine the specific developmental level the child has attained. The scales are only as good as the milestones in development they sample, and a prospective user should examine these milestones very carefully. Sometimes the behaviors sampled are not sequenced discretely enough to allow the examiner to determine at what level the child is really functioning. One behavior at age 2.0 years followed by another at age 3.0 gives the examiner a very cloudy picture of what is going on between ages 2 and 3. Examiners using developmental scales should be grounded in knowledge of language development as thoroughly as possible.

Some of the developmental scales used in schools and clinics are: the *Developmental Activities Screening Inventory* (Fewell & Langley, 1984), the *Minnesota Child Development Inventory* (Ireton & Thwing, 1972), the *Birth to Three Developmental Scale* (Bangs & Dodson, 1979), and the *Utah Test of Language Development* (Mecham, Jex, & Jones, 1978). Developmental scales may require the examiner to check off specific tasks the child is asked to perform or may involve indirect reporting by parents.

Other Assessment Procedures

The last two types of assessment procedures include the use of partially standardized tests and simple behavioral observations. Tests of language having less than complete standardization include language sample analysis, elicited production, comprehension, and elicited imitation (Miller, 1981). The procedures have a comfortable degree of face validity, suggested administrative procedures, and systems for interpretation, but, more important, they allow for flexibility and modification. As Miller (1978) remarks, these partially standardized tests conform to the child rather than requiring the child to conform to them. A number of these procedures will be discussed in greater detail in the section on assessment procedures (Chapter 5).

Behavioral observation is critical to all types of assessments from standardized to the most nonstandardized of testing to the assessment of specific behaviors in controlled or unstructured, naturalistic situations. Observing a child's behavior requires only meticulous listening, observing, and recording of that behavior, and the results are sometimes considered nonevidential and pedestrian. However, if the literature on the language acquisition process is surveyed, one can conclude without doubt that most of the data on language production have been obtained through observation. As Miller (1978) states, we must know the goals of observation more specifically than with any other type of assessment, as there is no goal inherent in the procedure. "We must know what we are looking for in order to observe the occurrence, frequency, antecedent, and consequent events, and contingencies of specific behaviors of interest" (p. 304).

In summary, assessment must be conducted with a developmental approach, the goal being to assess language behavior directly through the components of phonology, syntax, semantics, and pragmatics and through the language processes of acquisition and use. We should be most interested in what the child is able to do rather than what his or her disabilities are, and we should be even less interested in the labels that test results can provide.

REFERENCES

Bangs, T., & Dodson, D. (1979). *Birth to Three Developmental Scale.* Dallas: Developmental Learning Materials.

Bates, E. (1976a). *Language and context.* New York: Academic Press.

Bates, E. (1976b). Pragmatics and sociolinguistics in child language. In D. Morehead & A. Morehead (Eds.), *Normal and deficient child language* (pp. 411–463). Austin, TX: PRO-ED.

Bates, E., Benigni, L., Bretherton, I., Camaioni, L., & Volterra, V. (1979). *The emergence of symbols: Cognition and communication in infancy.* New York: Academic Press.

Bax, M., & Stephenson, P. (1977). Analysis of a developmental language delay. *Proceedings of the Royal Society of Medicine, 70,* 727–728.

Bloom, L. (1970). *Language development: Form and function in emerging grammars.* Cambridge, MA: MIT Press.

Bowerman, M. (1973a). *Early syntactic development: A cross-linguistic study with special reference to English.* Cambridge, MA: Cambridge University Press.

Bowerman, M. (1973b). Structural relationships in children's utterances: Syntactic or semantic? In I. E. Moore (Ed.), *Cognitive development and the acquisition of language* (pp. 346–378). New York: Academic Press.

Carrow, E. (1973). *Test for Auditory Comprehension of Language.* New York: Teaching Resources.

Carrow, E. (1974). *Carrow Elicited Language Inventory.* New York: Teaching Resources.

Chapman, R. (1976). Eliciting answers to questions: The development of question comprehension in pre-school children. In J. Miller (Ed.), *Procedures for assessing children's language: A developmental process approach* (p. 450). Madison, WI: Waisman Center on Mental Retardation and Human Development, University of Wisconsin.

Coggins, T. (1976). Early semantic development in retarded children. Unpublished doctoral dissertation, University of Wisconsin, Madison, WI.

Cousins, A. (1979). Grammatical morpheme development in an aphasic child: Some problems with the normative model. Paper presented at the 4th Annual Boston University Conference on Language Development, Boston, MA.

Dore, J. (1975). Holophrases, speech acts, and language universals. *Journal of Child Language, 2,* 21–40.

Fewell, R., & Langley, M. (1984). *Developmental Activities Screening Inventory.* Austin, TX: PRO-ED.

Hammill, D. D., Brown, V., Larsen, S., & Wiederholt, J. L. (1987). *Test of Adolescent Language.* Austin, TX: PRO-ED.

Hammill, D. D., & Newcomer, P. (1982). *Test of Language Development–Intermediate.* Austin, TX: PRO-ED.

Ireton, H., & Thwing, E. (1972). *Minnesota Child Development Inventory.* Minneapolis, MN: Behavior Science Systems.

Kirk, S., McCarthy, J., & Kirk, W. (1968). *The Illinois Test of Psycholinguistic Abilities.* Urbana, IL: University of Illinois Press.

Lee, L. (1974). *Developmental Sentence Analysis.* Evanstan, IL: Northwestern University Press.

Leonard, L. (1983). Discussion: Part II: Defining the boundaries of language disorders in children. In J. Miller, D. Yoder, & R. Schiefelbusch (Eds.), *Contemporary issues in language intervention* (ASHA Reports 12, pp. 107–115). Rockville, MD: American Speech-Language-Hearing Association.

Mecham, M., Jex, J., & Jones, J. (1978). *Utah Test of Language Development.* Austin, TX: PRO-ED.

Menyuk, P. (1968). The role of distinctive features in children's acquisition of phonology. *Journal of Speech and Hearing Research, 11,* 138–146.

Miller, J. (1978). Assessing children's language behavior: A developmental process approach. In R. Schiefelbusch (Ed.), *Bases of language intervention* (pp. 269–319). Austin, TX: PRO-ED.

Miller, J. (1981). *Assessing language production in children: Experimental procedures.* Austin, TX: PRO-ED.

Miller, J., & Yoder, D. (1973). Assessing the comprehension of grammatical form in mentally retarded children. Paper presented at the International Association for the Scientific Study of Mental Deficiency, The Hague.

Morehead, D., & Ingram, D. (1973). The development of base syntax in normal and linguistically deficient children. *Journal of Speech and Hearing Research, 16,* 330–352.

Muma, J. (1983). Speech-language pathology: Emerging clinical expertise in language. In T. Gallagher & C. Prutting. (Eds.), *Pragmatic assessment and intervention issues in language* (pp. 195–215). San Diego, CA: College-Hill Press.

Newcomer, P., & Hammill, D. D. (1982). *Test of Language Development–Intermediate.* Austin, TX: PRO-ED.

Schlesinger, I. (1971). Production of utterances and language acquisition. In D. Slobin (Ed.), *The ontogenesis of grammar* (pp. 63–101). New York: Academic Press.

Semel, E., & Wiig, E. (1980). *Clinical evaluation of language functions: Diagnostic battery examiner's manual.* San Antonio, TX: Psychological Corporation.

Slobin, D. (1973). Cognitive prerequisites for the development of grammar. In C. Ferguson & D. Slobin (Eds.), *Studies of child language development.* New York: Rinehart, Holt, and Winston.

3 / THE NATURE AND STRUCTURE OF LANGUAGE

The arguments and professional debates are endless regarding which characteristic, capacity, or ability sets humans apart from the other animals. There are proponents of the opposable thumb, advocates for the ability to problem solve, those who would argue for the capacity to think in abstract terms, and many of us who believe that the one uniquely human capacity is the ability to acquire, develop, use, and continuously expand a verbal symbol system. To those who view a linguistic system as the only characteristic possessed by humans alone, the attempts at teaching language to other primates are feeble experiments in what is little more than sign behavior and rank fairly close to the highly trained animal's ability to follow very complicated signals provided by a trainer.

Human infants do not have to be taught to comprehend and use a linguistic system; they have only to be exposed to an environment in which spoken language is used. Unless children are seriously impaired, probably having a severe to profound hearing loss or a severe dysfunction of critical neurological functions, they will speak the language of their families and communities. Children with mild problems may experience some delay or dysfunction in their linguistic abilities—delays that may be cumulative as they become older. However, humans acquire and use a verbal symbol system that is governed by sets of rules that are phonological, syntactic, and semantic. They use the system in a practical fashion, dependent upon the context, and are never formally taught the system rules until they enter school. By that time the child's basic language, at least in its spoken form, has already been learned, and the only ensuing development is in the direction of enhancing and enriching the child's linguistic system.

Mention was made above of phonological, syntactic, and semantic rules of language. As these are not yet household terms, some explanation of the components of the linguistic system and of its development is in order. The following section provides only a summary of the nature, structure, and development of language; however, ample references are given so that the reader who wishes to pursue a particular topic in depth may do so.

Most authorities in linguistics arbitrarily divide language into three major components: phonology, syntax, and semantics. Others elaborate somewhat on this division and speak of morphology as an element of both syntax and semantics. In recent years, a number of authors discuss pragmatics as a linguistic component separate and apart from syntax and semantics. For our purposes, we will deal with the three major components of phonology, syntax, and semantics and will subsume pragmatics under semantics.

PHONOLOGY

Phonology refers to the three components of the speech-sound system of a language: segmental features, the rules for combining the segmental features, and supra-segmental features. The segmental features of the sound-system are the phonemes—the discrete speech sounds—of the language; the rules for combining phonemes are known as phonological rules; and the supra-segmental features are the intonational or prosodic elements of speech. Menyuk (1972) provides a lucid example of the three components of phonology by comparing two sentences:

S_1 She's a white housekeeper.
S_2 He's a lighthouse keeper?

On the segmental—or phonemic—level, a native English speaker distinguishes the difference between *sh/e's* and *h/e's* and between *wh/ite* and *l/ight* because of the differences in the phonemes that form the first segments of the words. Jakobson, Fant, and Halle (1963) hypothesize that these differences are perceived because each phoneme is made up of a particular bundle of distinctive features based on articulatory and acoustic characteristics. Theoretically there is a pool of universal features from which all of the speech sounds of all languages are drawn. One feature that is demonstrated in the two example sentences is the consonantal feature that divides consonants from vowels and from the glides (h, y, w). In the example sentences, *white house* can be distinguished from *lighthouse*, because the latter possesses the consonantal feature, whereas the former does not. Some other distinctive features include the quality of voicing, sibilancy, nasality, and so on. It is possible to plot each phoneme on a table of features, thereby distinguishing each from the other.

Menyuk's two sentences probably would be distinguished from each other first on the supra-segmental level; the speaker would immediately recognize that one is a statement, while the other is a question, because they differ in their fundamental frequency contours. The statement sentence has a falling fundamental frequency contour, and the question has a rising contour. The voice drops at the end of a statement; it rises at the end of a question. There is also a difference in stress in the two sentences. In the first sentence, the stress falls on the syllable *house* in *white housekeeper*, whereas the stress in the second sentence is the syllable *light* in *lighthouse*. The difference in the stress patterns indicates that in S_1 the speaker is referring to a housekeeper who is white, while in S_2 the reference is to a keeper of a lighthouse.

The phonological rules operating in the two sentences are similar with regard to certain sequential rules. For example, in both sentences the vowel in *she's* and *he's* is lengthened, because the final strident consonant is voiced (pronounced with laryngeal tone). The stop consonants /k/ and /p/ are aspirated in both sentences; if they were not, the segment *keeper* would sound like *geeper*. Many phonological rules govern the articulatory and acoustic characteristics of vowel-consonant, consonant-vowel, and consonant-consonant production in the English language. Of course, other languages use different rules, which is why it is difficult for speakers of one language to produce accurately the phonemic strings of another language. Some of the very common rules that most of us recognize once they are called to our attention are:

- Initial cluster consonants can take only the form of consonant + /w/, /r/, or /l/ unless the consonant is /s/.

- Tense, number, and possession indicated by the addition of *s* or *es* take the following phonomic forms:

  - /z/ after voiced phonemes—play + /z/, tree + /z/, bum + /z/

  - /s/ after unvoiced phonemes—muff + /s/, rat + /s/, dip + /s/

  - /Iz/ after stridents—rose + /Iz/, pass + /Iz/, crash + /Iz/

- Tense indicated by the addition of *ed* takes the following forms:

  - /d/ after voiced phonemes—pay + /d/, sign + /d/, glove + /d/

  - /t/ after unvoiced phonemes—kick + /t/, muff + /t/, rough + /t/

  - /Id/ after /t/ and /d/ phonemes—pat + /Id/, side + /Id/

In evaluating articulatory disorders, the following information about the phonological system is critical and must be known by the individual who undertakes such an assessment:

- Phonetic transcription of the 43 or so phonemes
- Phonological features that distinguish phonemes in words
- Rules for combining matrices of features
- Prosodic features of sentences

The information is critical, because articulation disorders generally result from a failure in one or more of the last three areas, and appraisal must be related to those areas if the results are to be of any value in a therapy program. It goes without saying that the therapist must be able to transcribe in written form exactly what the child is producing, and, therefore, a knowledge of phonetic transcription is vital to preserving a record of articulation proficiency.

SYNTAX

Syntax is the branch of grammar that is concerned with the arrangement of words in sentences and with the means by which such relations are shown (e.g., word order or inflection). An important element of syntax is morphology, which is the study and analysis of the structure of words, particularly the forms and classes of words (e.g., declensional endings like walks, walked, or walking and derivational endings like the ness in goodness. Morphological analysis is used to describe the grammatical elements in a language by observing their form and function, their phonological variants, and their distribution and mutual relationships within larger stretches of speech.

This section covers three main topics: innate capacity for language, competence versus performance, and the linguistic rules of grammar. Much of the information comes from Noam Chomsky, who revolutionized the study of linguistics, the study of child acquisition and development, and the approaches to remediation of childhood language disorders. The linguistic theory based on Chomsky's work is known as transformational-generative grammar and has been expanded by such authors as Lyons (1968), Postal (1968), Burt (1971), Fowler (1971), Fillmore and Langendoen (1971), and King (1969). Chomsky criticized the traditional schools of linguistics as being merely taxonomic; that is, as simply labeling and listing phonetic, grammatical, and other units of language, thereby neglecting the underlying processes of human speech. According to Chomsky, the object of linguistic analysis must be to discover those elements in language that are universal and regular in the human's innate ability to understand and produce new "grammatical" sentences, even though the individual may never have heard those specific sentences before.

Innate Capacity

The debate regarding the innate quality of human characteristics has been carried on for years, and the "nature-nurture" arguments are too extensive to recapitulate. Let us say that linguistics and psychologists study the process of language learning by comparing input with output, that is, by comparing the language an infant or young child is exposed to with the language he or she in turn produces. Exactly how the brain is structured to acquire language competence is not known, but the term *language acquisition device* (LAD) was applied by Chomsky (1957) to the unknown function shown in the model below.

Language is learned and is not instinctive; however, Chomsky and others regard it as an innate capability that requires only the triggering of a speaking environment for its development. More recently, some researchers working in the area of pragmatics have questioned the existence of the LAD and have placed much greater emphasis on the "nurture" aspects of language acquisition.

Competence Versus Performance

Also implicit in transformational-generative grammar is the concept of competence as opposed to performance. The distinction was drawn originally by Chomsky but has been studied by numerous other linguists and psychologists. Competence refers to the ability that all native speakers have of being able to understand and produce sentences they have never heard before; in this sense, competence refers to the code that underlies all utterances in a given language. On the other hand, performance refers to the utilization of this code in situations where language is used. In transformational-generative grammar, competence features are represented in the deep structure, whereas features of performance are represented in the surface structure. Deep structure is produced by the syntactic component of the grammar, and surface structure is produced by the phonological component. Competence and performance have been likened to a symphony in which competence is the underlying musical rules of tonality, harmony, and so on, and performance is the production that the listener hears.

Grammar in the above sense must account for all the sentences that may be formed in a language and judged correct according to the linguistic intuition of native speakers. At a somewhat deceptively simple level, this intuition can be demonstrated in very young children, who will accept as an English word *splik* but will reject *jrik*. Their linguistic intuition tells them that one is "correct" but that the other is not, even though they have never heard either word nor have they been taught any of the acceptable phonetic combinations of English.

Linguistic Rules

According to Chomsky, the sentence is the basic unit of language, and he describes relationships between items in the structure of a sentence in terms of abstract statements called *phrase structure rules* and *transformation rules*. A phrase structure rule is a series of syntactic rewrites (can be rewritten as instructions). The rules generate strings and assign a structure to the string. Each rule is in the form of an expansion rule with only one symbol to the left of the arrow; for example, S → NP + VP, which means that a sentence has the structure of a noun phrase (NP) plus a verb phrase (VP). The particle NP → Det + Nom means that a noun phrase consists of a determiner (such as an article) plus a nominal.

$$VP \longrightarrow \begin{Bmatrix} Vt + NP \\ Vi \end{Bmatrix}$$

means that the verb phrase consists of transitive verb plus a noun phrase or an intransitive verb standing alone. If these rules are applied, one by one, in the following order:

1. S $\longrightarrow$ NP + VP (A sentence is a noun phrase plus a verb phrase.)

2. NP $\longrightarrow$ Det + Nom (A noun phrase is a determiner plus a nominal.)

3. VP $\longrightarrow$ $\begin{Bmatrix} Vt + NP \\ Vi \end{Bmatrix}$ (A verb phrase is a transitive verb plus a noun phrase or an intransitive verb alone.)

a series of strings such as the following could be produced:

1. NP + VP (The boy + kicks the ball.)

2. NP + Vt + VP   (The boy + kicks + the ball.)

3. Det + Nom + Vt +   (The + boy + kicks + the + ball.)

From the examples given above, the reader can see the words form a lexicon (dictionary), and the application of appropriate morphophonological rules produce the sentence, "The boy kicks the ball." The generation of such a sentence can be represented diagrammatically as

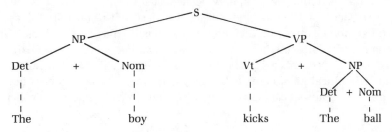

When all of the phrase structure rules have been applied, the result is a terminal string.

In addition to phrase structure rules, Chomsky postulated transformational rules which lay down procedures for converting one grammatical pattern into another. Such a rule may change one sentence type into another, delete or add elements, change the order of elements, or substitute one element for another. Transformational rules operate on the output, that is, the terminal string of the phrase structure rules. As one example, observe the transformation of a declarative sentence into an interrogative sentence. The rule applied is: NP + Pas + be + X $\rightleftharpoons$ Pas + be + NP + X, in which Pas = past tense, NP = noun phrase, and X = any construction. Application of the rule results in the following:

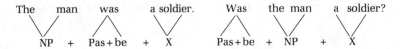

The reader can see that the phrase structure rules describe the basic structures of the language concerned, whereas more complicated structures lend themselves to description as transformations of basic structures by means of transformation rules. In the earliest type of transformational-generative grammar, the rules themselves are usually referred to in terms of three components: first, the *phrase structure component*, consisting of phrase structure rules; second, the *transformation component*, producing strings of formatives (bound morphemes such as prefixes, suffixes, etc.); and third, the *morphophonemic component*, which is a series of rules converting the string of formatives into a phonetic representation.

Before discussing the semantic component of language, a few additional words should be said about morphemes, because a great deal of research has dealt with the acquisition and development of morphological elements. A *morpheme* is a minimum distinctive unit of grammar and, in fact, has been called the smallest unit of meaningful language. A word is composed of one or more morphemes. Like phonemes, a morpheme is a formal element, and a particular morpheme may be represented by different variants (or *allomorphs*) in different environments. For example, the English plural morpheme often symbolized as s_2 may occur as /-s/ in cats, /-z/ in dogs, or /iz/ in horses. Because the morpheme is the smallest unit of meaningfulness, a word like *home* cannot be divided into its constituent parts such as *h, ho, ome, me,* and so forth, without the original meaning being lost or changed. Thus, *home* represents a single free morpheme—free, because it can stand alone. The plural morpheme /-s/, along with others, is said to be a bound morpheme, because it can occur only in conjunction with another morpheme.

SEMANTICS

In Chomsky's later publications (1968), he added a semantic component to the transformational-generative grammar, because he had come to the conclusion that meaning should have the same formal treatment as grammar. Semantics was then included as an integral part of the grammatical analysis of language. The emphasis in transformational-generative grammar is on the elaboration of a logically consistent theory that can explain adequately and formulate explicitly the deep structures of sentences.

In the discussion of semantics, four major areas are discussed: the relationship between the semantic and grammatic components, the referential features of semantics, the semantic features, and the relational features. The first section deals primarily with the work of Chomsky and other transformational grammarians, while the latter sections draw from the work of other theorists.

Semantics and Grammar

The grammatical relationships inherent in the elements of a phrase or sentence but not immediately apparent from their linear sequences are referred to as the deep structure or, infrequently, the deep grammar. Consider the following English sentences:

1. John expected mother to bring a present.

2. John persuaded mother to bring a present.

The surface structure of the two sentences is identical, as they both consist of Nominal + verb + nominal + marked infinitive + determiner + nominal, but the deep structure of the two sentences is quite different, as can be seen by the fact that the first can be transformed as follows:

3. John expected that mother would bring a present.

However, the second cannot be similarly transformed:

4. John persuaded that mother would bring a present.

Diagrammatically, the difference between the two sentences can be shown as follows:

1. John expected mother to bring a present.

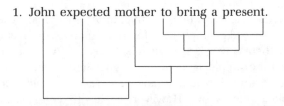

2. John persuaded mother to bring a present.

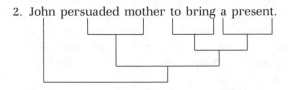

From the above diagrams it can be seen that the difference lies in the nature of the relationship of the verbs *expected* and *persuaded* with the words that follow them. In sentence 1, *expected* is directly related to all of what follows; in sentence 2, *persuaded* is related only to *mother*. In summary, we may say that transformational grammarians view semantics as a study in logical relationships.

Many authors have found the transformational-generative semantics difficult to apply when dealing with acquisition, development, and disorders of language, and the theories have never enjoyed the popularity and discipleship that the theories related to phonology and syntax have had. Leaving the work of Chomsky and other strict transformational linguists, one may define the semantic system of a language as the knowledge that a native speaker must have to understand sentences and to relate them to his or her knowledge of the world. Such a definition obviously implies a strong cognitive element, and many writers in the area of semantics acknowledge their debt to Piaget, Bruner, and other cognitive psychologists.

Semantics includes the knowledge of lexical items individually as well as the meaning of a sentence as determined by the meanings of both the individual lexical items and the structure of the sentence. Lexical items are simply units of the vocabulary of a language—such as words, phrases, or terms—as listed in the dictionary. They usually have a pronounceable or graphic form, fulfill a grammatical rule in a sentence, and carry semantic meaning. It is increasingly apparent that semantics deals with meaningfulness and that a fourth component of language—namely, pragmatics—is more or less embedded in it. For purposes of clarity, pragmatics is discussed in the following section as a component apart from semantics, but, as with all of the language components, that is a highly artificial division.

Referential Features

One of the earliest theories of semantic meaning is the referential theory in which the meaning of a word is simply its referent or that object to which the word points. In this theory, words are symbols that stand for something other than themselves; for example, *table* refers to a particular piece of furniture, *cat* to a particular animal, *blue* to a particular range of colors, and so on. This is all simple and attractive. However, we also have to account for the meanings of words like *at*, *but*, *is*, and other words that have no immediate referents, as well as words that have more than one referent (e.g., *you*) and those that have referents that are difficult to identify (e.g., *unicorn*). Proponents of the referential theory have attempted to deal with words like those above, but as Alston (1964) notes, the explanations raise even more problems.

If every object in the world had exactly one name and every name had only a single referent, it would be much simpler to explain the meaning of meaning. The problem, as pointed out by Brown (1973), is that almost all names actually refer to categories, and every object can be named by a variety of terms. For example, the word *cat* refers to all four-legged animals of a certain type, and the terms *furry creature*, *tabby*, and so on, all refer to cats. Learning about the referents of words is actually a matter of learning about how human beings organize the world about them.

Semantic Features

Katz and Postal (1963) and Katz (1966) propose the best known theory for understanding semantic development. (See Chapter 4 for a detailed discussion of language development.) Katz and Postal hypothesize that the meaning of a word consists of two parts: its semantic features and its selection restrictions. Semantic features, of which each word may have several, express parts of the meaning of the word. For example, *cat* has the following features, in addition to many others: *living, animal, four-legged, furry, purring,* and so on. The word *dog* has the same set of features as those given for *cat,* with the exception of *purring,* for which *barking* could be substituted. Dale (1976) lists some of the semantic features of the words *bachelor* and *wife* and illustrates how the term *bachelor's wife* violates the selection restrictions, because *bachelor* includes the feature *unmarried,* while *wife* includes the feature *married.*

Relational Features

Norman, Rumelhart, and their research group (1975) take issue with the notion that the meaning of a term is the sum of its semantic features. They believe that relational information is also necessary. In considering the word *pay,* one must take into account not only the semantic features of the word but also the relations among the *payer,* the *payee, money, giving,* and *obligation.*

There are numerous other theories and subtheories regarding the nature of semantics, but the majority of the work that has been done in the area focuses on the semantic functions of words within the context of an utterance. For example, Slobin (1970) classifies early two-word utterances in terms of whether they express need, possession, location, and so on, and he finds striking similarities in the types of utterances used by English, Finnish, Russian, German, Luo, and Samoan children. Brown (1973) concentrates on the acquisition of morphology, while performing detailed semantic analyses, and comes to the conclusion that new morphological markers are acquired only after the child knows their underlying semantic distinctions.

PRAGMATICS

Until the 1970s, much of the research in linguistics, language acquisition, assessment, and therapy focused on grammar and syntax. In the 1970s and early 1980s, authors tended to highlight two facts about language performance—that language always occurs in a context and that contexts are not all the same. Regrettably, these two facts frequently have been seen as obvious and possibly trivial. As Cook-Gumperz and Gumperz (1978) point out, the issue is not that contexts exist or that they vary, but whether contexts are static backgrounds within which language occurs, "a 'label' for a cluster of extralinguistic or extra-grammatical factors" (p. 5), or whether they are dynamic aspects for both the speaker and the listener. Pragmatic theories of language address language as it is used and characterize both linguistic and contextual elements as parts of one interactive communicative whole (Austin, 1962, Bates, 1976a; Searle, 1969). Hymes (1971) speaks of competence for use or communicative competence and points out that equating competence with the speaker/hearer's knowledge of the grammatical rules of language is a narrow view that neglects a body of observable data that depends on rules for the appropriate use of utterances in relevant contexts. Hymes further states that to give a full account of the facts we need an explanation of what the speaker/hearer knows about who can say what, in what way, where and when, by what means, and to whom.

Theories of Language Pragmatics

The pragmatics of language is vitally concerned with who can say what, as indicated by Hymes. However, earlier researchers such as Morris (1938) discuss the relationship between signs and their interpreters. More recently, Lakoff (1972) states that it is essential to take extralinguistic contextual factors in account, and Bates (1976b) defines pragmatics of language as rules governing the use of language in context. Halliday (1975) relates the structure of language to its individual and social functioning. Searle (1969) discusses the four basic components of how understanding between communicative beings is accomplished:

- the utterance act—uttering words

- the propositional act—referring and predicating

- the illocutionary act—stating, questioning, asserting, etc.

- the perlocutionary act—the effects such acts have on the beliefs, thoughts, actions of the hearer

Searle's classification has been used by Prutting and Kirchner (1983) in developing a pool of pragmatic behaviors for assessment purposes.

Duchan (1983) states that pragmatic knowledge leads to the choice of linguistic structures but does not affect their packaging. According to Bates and MacWhinney (1983), who call their approach *functionalism*, pragmatics is the deepest level of activity in language performance. Because they feel pragmatics provides a foundation for choosing linguistic forms, it seems that pragmatics would be the first aspect or component of language for them to consider. It would precede phonology, syntax, and semantics and, probably, underlie all other components. Duchan (1983) agrees that the change of focus from viewing language form as more significant than the intent behind the form contains the impetus for moving away from a structuralistic, multilevel view of language to a more dynamic, functionalistic model. According to Duchan's theory, the barriers between the components of language (phonology and syntax, syntax and semantics, etc.) would be disregarded in favor of emphasizing the structures within each component. These structures could be classed together in terms of the functions they serve.

Decoding Speech

Let us return for a moment to Searle's (1969, 1975a, 1975b) description of the *speech act*, a term closely associated with his work. He states that the same sentences may be used as different speech acts. For example, the sentence, "It's almost lunchtime," can serve as a statement of fact; however, if it is said in hope that the listener will provide lunch, it functions as a request. Rees (1978) uses the example of Grandmother's sentence made while sitting with her family at the dining table, "Has everyone had enough?" How do her listeners know that she is saying that she would like someone to pass the food so she can have a second helping? It is certainly not a message that is conveyed by a syntactic/semantic analysis of the utterance. How, in fact, does any listener manage to comprehend any speaker's intentions when the message is conveyed indirectly? Searle (1975a) suggests:

> In indirect speech acts the speaker communicates to the hearer more than he actually says by way of relying on their mutually shared background information, both linguistic and nonlinguistic, together with the general powers of rationality and inference on the part of the hearer. (pp. 60–61)

If a listener is to decode the intended meaning of a sentence, a listener must be able to decide on a particular set of circumstances or prior information to which the information in the heard sentence is related (Rees, 1978). Sometimes the related information is in a previous sentence. Transcriptions of dyadic conversations reveal quite readily that sentences often make no sense unless the reader relates them to the context and to previous sentences in the sample. Freedle and Carroll (1972) give a cogent and lucid example of the interpretation of relations:

> Suppose Frank and Joe are walking down the street and are about to pass a hamburger stand. Frank says, "Would you like to eat here?" Such a question contains assumptions of at least time and space: The time is not "right now" but "pretty soon, after we get served," and the place is not "right here on the street" but "at the counter of the hamburger stand." Yet if Frank and Joe are walking in the park and carrying a picnic basket, the question "Would you like to eat here?" we would assume that the time is "right now, as soon as we unload the basket" and the place could be "right here." In either case, the total situation supplies the context which evokes the semantic assumptions that are most consistent with the utterance. (p. 361)

In addition to context and previous sentences providing interpretive clues to the meaning of a sentence, so do cultural expectations and pragmatic presuppositions (Bates, 1976b). For example, the sentence, "Can you zip me up, honey?" carries with it some very definite cultural expectations for most of us. We would expect that the speaker is a woman and that the listener is a man, a close woman friend, or possibly a child. Rarely would we expect that the listener and speaker are both men. If we hear the sentence, "Could you turn the TV down?" we would be likely to come to one of two conclusions: (a) The speaker and listener are social equals or (b) the speaker is socially superior to the listener but was reared to be polite to social inferiors. However, decide for yourself what the pragmatic presuppositions are for the form of the same sentence, "Turn the TV down!"

The Cooperative Principle

Another facet of pragmatics, which Grice (1975) calls the cooperative principle, deals with the principles or rules of conversation. He identifies four maxims, or rules, and subrules that listeners and speakers expect each other to observe. These are extracted and simplified by Rees (1978):

    A. Quantity (the quantity of information to be provided)
      1. Make your contribution as informative as is required (for the current purposes of the exchange).
      2. Do not make your contribution more informative than is required, or your listener will be misled or think you talk too much.
    B. Quality (try to make your contribution one that is true)
      1. Do not say what you believe to be false.
      2. Do not say that for which you lack adequate evidence.
    C. Relation (be relevant, whatever that may turn out to mean, specifically)
    D. Manner (be perspicuous)
      1. Avoid obscurity of expression.
      2. Avoid ambiguity.
      3. Be brief (avoid unnecessary prolixity).
      4. Be orderly. (p. 207)

SUMMARY

Language is a highly complex, species-specific, continually developing characteristic of the human being. In this chapter language has been discussed in its phonological, syntactic, semantic, and pragmatic aspects. However, the reader should remember that these divisions of language are artificial and that each aspect of language has a significant and dramatic impact on the others. Although the development of language is discussed in the next chapter using the same divisions as those given above, no pretense is made that the different components are separate or that each can be assessed or treated apart from the others.

REFERENCES

Alston, W. (1964). *Philosophy of language.* Englewood Cliffs, NJ: Prentice-Hall.

Austin, J. (1962). *How to do things with words.* Cambridge, MA: Harvard University Press.

Bates, E. (1976a). *Language and context.* New York: Academic Press.

Bates, E. (1976b). Pragmatics and sociolinguistics in child language. In D. Morehead & A. Morehead (Eds.), *Normal and deficient child language* (pp. 411–463). Austin, TX: PRO-ED.

Bates, E., & MacWhinney, B. (1983). Functionalist approaches to grammar. In L. Gleitman & E. Wanner (Eds.), *Language acquisition: The state of the art* (pp. 126–154). New York: Cambridge University Press.

Brown R. (1973). *A first language: The early stages.* Cambridge, MA: Harvard University Press.

Burt, M. (1971). *From deep to surface structure: An introduction to transformational syntax.* New York: Harper and Row.

Chomsky, C. (1968). *The acquisition of syntax in children from 5 to 10.* Cambridge, MA: MIT Press.

Chomsky, N. (1957). *Syntactic structures.* The Hague: Mouton.

Cook-Gumperz, J., & Gumperz, J. (1978). Context in children's speech. In N. Waterson & C. Snow (Eds.), *The development of communication* (pp. 214–238). New York: John Wiley.

Dale, P. (1976). *Language development: Structure and function* (2nd ed.). New York: Holt, Rinehart and Winston.

Duchan, J. (1983). Language processing and geodesic domes. In T. Gallagher & C. Prutting (Eds.), *Pragmatic assessment and intervention issues* (pp. 83–101). San Diego: College-Hill Press.

Fillmore, C., & Langendoen, D. (Eds.). (1971). *Studies in linguistic semantics.* New York: Irvington.

Fowler, R. (1971). *An introduction to transformational syntax.* London: Routledge.

Freedle, R., & Carroll, J. (1972). Language comprehension and the acquisition of knowledge: Reflections. In R. Freedle & J. Carroll (Eds.), *Language acquisition and the acquisition of knowledge* (pp. 361–368). New York: John Wiley.

Grice, H. (1975). Logic and conversation. In P. Cole & J. Morgan (Eds.), *Syntax and semantics, Vol. 3: Speech acts* (pp. 43–59). New York: Academic Press.

Halliday, M. (1975). *Learning how to mean: Explorations in the development of language.* London: Edward Arnold.

Hymes, D. (1971). Competence and performance in linguistic theory. In R. Huxley & E. Ingram (Eds.), *Language acquisition: Models and methods* (pp. 3–24). New York: Academic Press.

Jakobson, R., Fant, G., & Halle, M. (1963). *Preliminaries to speech analysis.* Cambridge, MA: MIT Press.

Katz, J. (1966). *The philosophy of language.* New York: Harper and Row.

Katz, J., & Postal, P. (1963). *An integrated theory of linguistic descriptions.* Cambridge, MA: MIT Press.

King, R. (1969). *Historical linguistics and generative grammar.* Englewood Cliffs, NJ: Prentice-Hall.

Lakoff, R. (1972). Language in context. *Language, 48,* 907–927.

Lyons, J. (1968). *Introduction to theoretical linguistics.* London: Cambridge University Press.

Menyuk, P. (1968). The role of distinctive features in children's acquisition of phonology. *Journal of Speech and Hearing Research, 11,* 138–146.

Menyuk, P. (1972). *The development of speech.* New York: Bobbs-Merrill.

Miller, J. (1981). *Assessing language production in children: Experimental procedures.* Austin, TX: PRO-ED.

Morris, C. (1938). *Foundations of the theory of signs.* Chicago: University of Chicago Press.

Norman, D., Rumelhart, D., & the LNR Research Group. (1975). *Explorations in cognition.* San Francisco: Freeman.

Postal, P. (1968). *Aspects of phonological theory.* New York: Harper and Row.

Prutting, C., & Kirchner, D. (1983). Applied pragmatics. In T. Gallagher & C. Prutting (Eds.), *Pragmatic assessment and intervention issues in language* (pp. 29–65). San Diego: College-Hill Press.

Rees, N. (1978). Pragmatics of language: Applications to normal and disordered language development. In R. Schiefelbusch (Ed.), *Bases of language intervention* (pp. 191–269). Austin, TX: PRO-ED.

Searle, J. (1969). *Speech acts.* London: Cambridge University Press.

Searle, J. (1975a). Indirect speech acts. In J. Morgan & P. Cole (Eds.), *Studies in syntax and semantics. Vol. 3: Speech acts* (pp. 133–169). New York: Academic Press.

Searle, J. (1975b). Speech acts and recent linguistics. In D. Aaronson & R. Rieber (Eds.), *Developmental linguistics and communication disorders* (pp. 45–61). New York: Academy of Sciences.

Slobin, D. (1970). Universals of grammatical development in children. In G. Flores d'Arcais & W. Levelt (Eds.), *Advances in psycholinguistics* (pp. 48–61). Amsterdam: North Holland Publishing.

4 / THE DEVELOPMENT OF LANGUAGE

In assessing spoken language proficiency, it is desirable that the examiner understand both the structure and the acquisition of language. When nonstandardized testing is done, it is especially important that examiners have a working knowledge of the development of language. They cannot rely on normative data as is provided by standardized tests but must depend on information about the sequential development of spoken language and the approximate ages at which various structures emerge. Many of the strategies discussed in Chapter 5 are only vaguely age-referenced, but they are presented in sequence.

When do children acquire and develop adult oral language? In the early and mid 1960s, researchers concentrated on the development of the formal structures of language. In the 1970s, they moved on to investigate the semantic structures underlying the morphophonemic and syntactic structures. By the late 1970s to the present, the greatest interest has been in how language is acquired. In addition, the study of pragmatic aspects of language acquisition has greatly increased in recent years. In this chapter, acquisition and development in their phonological, syntactic, semantic, and pragmatic aspects are discussed, although it should be emphasized again that it is actually impossible to divide language into separate, discrete components. All components are interrelated, and the reader will see later in this chapter when Brown's research on development is discussed that there is definite overlap between syntactic and semantic development.

PHONOLOGICAL DEVELOPMENT

The first reviews of speech sound acquisition and development dealt with the ages at which various phonemes were acquired by young children. Tables of development were generated by numerous authors, and general agreement was found among those authors (Davis, 1938; Irwin, 1947, 1948; Templin, 1957). The results of two early definitive studies are reproduced in tables 4.1 and 4.2. Table 4.1 shows the earliest age levels at which mastery of common consonants was achieved by 100% of the children studied by Davis (1938). In Table 4.2 Templin (1947) gives the age levels at which 75% of the children tested achieved mastery. Since the publication of the work of Davis and Templin, there has been little need to study the age levels at which phoneme mastery is attained. In recent years, research in phonological development has centered upon the ages at which phonemes emerge, not when they are mastered.

Production of Phonemes

For many years, speech pathologists used tables such as those discussed above to determine whether articulation development was proceeding according to schedule. However, more recently they have focused on the child's production of phonemes and their relation to the words he or she is trying to produce. Even in the area of phonemics—the study of speech sounds—interest has shifted from the mere production of isolated phonemes to the acquisition of the distinctive features that make up the phonemes and to the acquisition of morphophonemic rules of syntax.

The child at the one-word stage of speech development creates sentences that have differing syntactic and semantic structures but that also preserve certain aspects of the phonemic segmental features within the words. For example, the child who says *ba-tuh* for *bottle* is preserving part of the consonant-vowel-consonant-vowel (C-V-C-V) segments of the word, and beyond that he or she is preserving the sequence of stop C + back V + stop C + back V (a statement in which C = consonant and V = vowel).

To account for what is preserved phonemically and what is not, Jakobson (1968) proposed the principle of maximum contrast and used it to explain the fact that infants' earliest utterances are usually *mama* and *papa*. These two utterances represent maximum contracts between +consonantal with −vocalic features (a consonant) and −consonantal with +vocalic (a vowel) and the lip sounds (/p/ and /m/). These consonants and vowels represent the largest degree of contrast, going from the anterior closure of the vocal mechanism to the opening of the posterior part. As further differentiations are made, additional phonemic features are acquired. For example, children

TABLE 4.1. Earliest Age Level at Which Mastery was Attained by 100% of Children Tested

Age Levels in Years	Phonemes						
3.5	m	p	b	w	h		
4.5	n	t	d	ɥ	k	g	j
5.5	f	v	s*	z*			
6.5	ʃ	ʒ	l	θ	ð		
8.0	r	hw	s	z			

*/s/ and /z/ appear consistently at age 4.5 years but disappear when the anterior deciduous teeth are lost; they reappear after anterior dentition is complete.

Adapted from "The Speech Aspects of Reading Readiness" by I. Davis, 1938, *17th Yearbook of the Department of Elementary School Principals, 17*, pp. 282–289. Reprinted by permission.

TABLE 4.2. Earliest Age Level of 75% Consonant Mastery

Age Levels in Years	Phonemes						
3.0	m	n	n	p	f	h	w
3.5	j						
4.0	b	d	k	g	r		
4.5	s	ʃ	tʃ				
6.0	t	l	v	θ			
7.0	ð	z	ʒ	dʒ			

Adapted from *Certain Language Skills in Children* by M. Templin, Institute of Child Welfare Monograph Series No. 26, 1957, Minneapolis: University of Minnesota Press. Reprinted by permission.

can learn to distinguish between the oral feature of /p/ and the nasal feature of /m/, and they can begin to differentiate back vowels into their wide /a/ and narrow /i/ features.

Sequence of Development

Based on the extensive work of researchers like Davis (1938) and Templin (1957) discussed earlier, there is a strong indication of a sequence in the development of differentiation of segmental features. This conclusion can be drawn simply because the data in tables 4.1 and 4.2 demonstrate that some phonemes are mastered before others. Menyuk (1968) analyzed these data and concluded that sounds that are +nasal, +grave, and +voice are mastered before those that are +diffuse, +continuant, and +strident.

With regard to the perceptual differentiation of segmental features, Edwards (1974), Lyamina and Gagua (1966), and Shvachkin (1966) all report that there is a sequence of development and that perceptual distinctions are made before productive distinctions. Whether the order of development is the same in perceptual and productive segments was investigated by Menyuk (1972) when she compared the results of her research on production substitutions with the research of Koenigsknecht and Lee on perceptual substitutions. The results indicate that the rank order for features preserved in perception and in production are not the same, although, as the reader may see in Table 4.3, there are similarities.

The earliest productive distinctions, that is, those made by children at age three, seem to be the following:

• oral versus nasal (*p, b, w* versus *m*)

• labial versus non-labial (*m, p, b* versus *n, t, d*)

• voiced versus non-voiced (*b, d* versus *p, t*)

• fricative versus stop (*f, v* versus *p, b*)

• lingual versus velar (*t, d, n* versus *k, g*)

TABLE 4.3. Rank Order of Features Preserved in Perception and Production

Perception	Production
Nasality	Nasality
Voicing	Voicing
Continuancy	Stridency
Place	Continuancy
	Place

From *The Development of Speech* (p. 26) by P. Menyuk, 1972, New York: Bobbs-Merrill. Reprinted by permission.

Children may distinguish these sounds earlier than others because these are the easiest ones to hear and because these are the perceptual distinctions that are easiest to translate into articulatory movements. The last sounds to be acquired (tables 4.1 and 4.2) are those in which the tongue must be moved to some position other than the normal rest position. Consider the differences in tongue movements for the production of /p/ or /b/ and for the production of /r/, /s/, or /ʃ/.

The Morphophonemic Rules

In addition to acquiring the segmental features of phonology, the child at the same time is acquiring and developing certain sequential rules that relate to the syntax of his or her language—the morphophonemic rules. Newfield and Schlanger (1968) provide evidence that such rules are not fully mastered even by age 7. It appears, however, that it is the very specific rather than the general rules that are late in being learned. Some of the rules that are mastered late include:

- the past tense forms of strong verbs, such as *ring, rang*
- the /Iz/ versus the /s/ or /z/ ending for forming plurals or the third person singular
- The /Id/ versus the /t/ or /d/ ending for past tense

However, there is some evidence indicating that these rules are understood long before they are mastered in production (Menyuk & Klatt, 1968). As stated earlier, very young children are also able to differentiate between English and non-English clusters of consonants in reproducing non-English consonant clusters; they attempt to preserve the integrity of English rules, but they try to maintain the distinctive feature composition of the non-English clusters. Therefore, it may be concluded that these children are observing rules while also composing in segments. The reader probably knows from experience with young children that it is quite common to find them substituting /w/ for /r/ and /l/, as in *wabbit* for *rabbit* or *wady* for *lady*. These are perfectly acceptable English sound sequences and are not rejected by children making such substitutions.

In summary, children acquire and develop, in more or less identified sequence, the distinctive features that distinguish the phonemes of their language and the morphophonemic rules that govern the sequencing of the segments. In spite of the large body of research accrued in the past forty to fifty years, the study of the acquisition and development of the phonological system is still in its infancy. There has been a marked diminution of investigation in phonology; it is hoped that interest and activity will again increase in the not too distant future.

SYNTACTICAL DEVELOPMENT

There is evidence that children in the early stages of speech development use single words as sentences, but the analysis of syntactic structures in development usually begins when the child has begun using two- and three-word sentences. Braine (1963) classifies the lexical items used by children in two categories: the open class and the pivot class. Generally, a small group of morphemes in the pivot class can occur in conjunction with many morphemes in the open class. McNeill (1970) assumes that the child generates sentences by selecting from the open class (O) in the case of one-word sentences or from either the open class twice (O,O) or the pivot and open class (P,O) in the case of longer utterances. A pivot grammar may describe a number of children's utterances, but, in general, it is too restrictive; children's language is hardly ever as simple as the pivot grammar concept would indicate (Bowerman, 1973). Many recent authors reject Chomsky's notion that there is a structure dependency of rules, that there are universal grammatical relations and categories (McNeill, 1966), or that grammatical rules are both analytic and productive. Instead, current theory and research indicate that the syntactic rules are semantic and that their source may be the child's cognitive structures.

This section on syntactical development encompasses structural development, Brown's stages of language development, and imitation. As the reader will note, there is considerable overlap among the various components of language, but the thread of syntax runs throughout the discussion.

Structural Development

After children acquire base structure rules that define the subject-object relationship in sentences, they seem to acquire understanding of the concept that various sentence types can be generated by joining various elements such as negation + sentence, question + sentence, and so on. Under the heading of structural development, the emergence of complex and compound sentences is discussed. Menyuk (1971) provides a graphic explanation of the development of sentence types as shown in Table 4.4.

Complex Sentences. After the child has acquired true sentences, another equally important event in linguistic development occurs—the joining together of two simple sentences to form a complex sentence. If auxiliaries are excluded, one may say that any sentence containing two verbs represents two sentences in deep structure. The first complex sentences are often object noun-phrase complements and appear when the child has a mean length of utterance (MLU) of approximately 3.5 to 4.0 morphemes. In a

TABLE 4.4. Stages in the Development of Declarative, Negative, Question, and Imperative Sentences

	A Early	B In Between	C Later
Declarative	That box Big boat Rick go	That's box That big boat Rick going	That's a box That's a big boat Rick is going
Negative	No play No a book No fall down	I no play That not book (a) I not falling down (b) I'm not fall down	I won't play That's not a book I'm not falling down
Question	See shoe? Truck here? Where baby?	Mommy see shoe? Truck's here? (a) Where baby is? (b) Where's baby is?	Do you see the shoe? Is the truck here? Where's the baby?
Imperative	Want baby! No touch! Have it!		I want the baby or Give me the baby! Don't touch it! Give it to me!

From *The Acquisition and Development of Language* (p. 106) by P. Menyuk, 1971, Englewood Cliffs, NJ: Prentice-Hall. Reprinted by permission.

sentence with an object noun phrase complement, another full sentence can take the place of the object of the verb. For example:

• Watch me draw squares.

• I don't want you to watch TV.

• I saw you come in.

In these examples of children's language, the embedded sentence that is the object of the verb is present in the surface structure in its unembedded form. However, in adult English, complements appear to be quite different from simple sentences. "It annoys the neighbors for John to play basketball in the backyard" has as its object complement "John plays basketball." This is a type of complement that does not appear in child language until much later.

Sentences containing *wh-* clauses are a second type of complex sentence. The *wh-* clause allows one sentence to serve virtually any role in another sentence. The following are some examples of sentences with *wh-* clauses with embedded sentences shown in parentheses:

- (Whoever did this) will pay for it   Subject
- He did (what he could)   Object
- I know (where he is)   Locative

Relative clauses appear slightly later than the constructions noted above. They are related to *wh-* clauses, even though they are different from them. As indicated above, *wh-* clauses are embedded sentences used in a particular slot as a noun phrase. The relative clause, instead of being a noun phrase, modifies a noun phrase, as in "The man who came to dinner stayed a month," in which "The man who came to dinner" modifies and further specifies the subject of "the man stayed a month." Children first produce relative clauses to modify objects and predicate nominals and then later use them to modify subjects, as in the example given above. As a general rule, objects are modified before subjects whether the case is one of simple or complex modification.

Compound Sentences. Compound or conjoined sentences also begin to appear at this stage of development, but their mastery takes much longer. The first conjoined sentences produced by children seem to be simple groupings of two sentences without a conjuction, but shortly afterward the conjunction *and* makes its appearance. First sentences may be those like, "I see the book; you see the book." Later sentences would be like, "I was mad and I thought it was funny," in which the two sentences require the conjunction to establish the relationship between them.

Brown's Stages of Language Development

Another way of looking at both syntactic and semantic language development in young children is provided by Brown (1973), who outlines five stages of development and discusses the first two stages in great detail. The following section deals with the results of Brown's extensive research into language development and the hypotheses he has derived from analyzing the results of that investigation.

Brown proposes five stages in language development, beginning with the first emergence of multiword utterances at Stage I and continuing through the development of complex sentences at Stage V. The stages are defined by increments of .5 to the mean length of utterance (MLU), but it should be remembered that there is a great deal of variation in length of utterance at any stage. Saying that a child has an MLU of 2.0 means that he or she may produce utterances that vary from one to six morphemes in length. However, children of comparable MLUs are as close to the same in language development as it is possible to find. Each stage is discussed below.

Stage I. Brown characterizes children's Stage I speech in several ways. The first aspect of construction he calls relations or roles within the simple sentence. More descriptively, he discusses Stage I as a time of telegraphic speech and the pivot grammar. Telegraphic speech is exactly what the term seems to mean: an absence of the small functional words, such as prepositions, articles, conjunctions, auxiliary verbs, and so on. Those words that we leave out of telegrams are omitted from the speech of Stage I children.

The pivot grammar was discussed briefly in the previous section of this chapter. However, more explanation of the Stage I construction is warranted. In the production by a child of a single sentence, "Mommy sock," Bloom (1970) concludes that the context in which the utterance is made determines the meaning of the sentence. Viewed contextually, the sentence is actually at least two different sentences. In one sentence, *Mommy* is a possessive modifier of sock in *Mommy's sock*, and in the second, *Mommy* is the agent of the sentence and *sock* is the object. A pivot grammar could not distinguish between the two sentences, but it is clear that the relationship between *Mommy* and *sock* differs in the two. There are other common semantic relationships in Stage I sentences, as shown in Table 4.5. As with Bloom's *Mommy sock* sentence, it is necessary to know the context to determine the semantic relationship.

Brown has extended further the explanation of semantic relations in the Stage I sentence by defining and exemplifying some of the semantic roles played by noun phrases in simple sentences. Table 4.6, which demonstrates some of the roles, is taken from *A First Language* (Brown, 1973).

The essential points to be remembered in the analysis of a language sample with regard to Stage I language behavior are that (a) it is marked by a reliance on telegraphic speech, (b) the semantic relationships between words in sentences are as shown in Table 4.5, and (c) the noun phrases in simple sentences may play a number of roles as described in Table 4.6. All of this behavior is typical of the Stage I child whose MLU is 1.01 to 1.99 morphemes.

Stage II. The child with an MLU of 2.00 to 2.49 is said to be in Stage II of language development—a stage referred to by Brown (1973) as a stage of modulating meaning within the simple sentence. In English, modulations are defined as structures such as the inflection of the noun for plurality; inflection of the verb for tense; provision of the copula *be*; provision of definite and indefinite articles that are used to mark a referent; and some prepositions like *in* and *on* that are used to further specify locations suggested by word order alone. Brown selected 14 grammatical morphemes

TABLE 4.5. Semantic Relations in Stage I Sentences

Semantic Relation	Form	Example
1. Nomination	that + N	that book
2. Notice	hi + N	hi belt
3. Recurrence	more + N, 'nother + N	more milk
4. Nonexistence	allgone + N, no more + N	allgone rattle
5. Attributive	Adj + N	big train
6. Possessive	N + N	mommy lunch
7. Locative	N + N	sweater chair
8. Locative	V + N	walk street
9. Agent-Action	N + V	Eve read
10. Agent-Object	N + N	Mommy sock
11. Action-Object	V + N	put book

Adapted from *Psycholinguistics* (p. 220) by R. Brown, 1970, New York: Free Press, a Division of Macmillan. Reprinted by permission.

for study, as shown in Table 4.7. These morphemes are almost totally missing from Stage I; in Stage II they begin to appear, but even by Stage V some children have not yet reached the 90% mastery level on some morphemes. The inflections of meaning occur in a lengthy development—a property that English may share with other languages. The modulations shown in Table 4.7 do not constitute an exhaustive list for English; Brown selected only forms for which it is possible to identify contexts in which the form is obligatory.

Stage III. In stages I and II, Brown describes the major semantic relations and development of inflections (modulations) in what are essentially declarative and affirmative simple sentences. In Stage III other sentence modalities are considered: *yes-no* interrogatives, constituent interrogatives, imperatives, and negatives. Brown uses the sentence, "Mr. Smith cut the rope with a knife," to demonstrate that it can be transformed into an interrogative that requires a *yes* response if assenting or a *no* if dissenting. The interrogative transformation becomes, "Did Mr. Smith cut the rope with a knife?" None of the semantic relations nor modulations discussed under Stage II are altered in this transformation, although the reader should note that the

TABLE 4.6. Some Semantic Roles Played by Noun Phrases in Simple Sentences

Role	Definition	Examples
Agent	Someone or something that causes or instigates an action or process. Usually animate but not always, an agent must be perceived to have its own motivating force.	*Harriet* sang. *The men* laughed. *The wind* ripped the curtains.
Patient	Someone or something either in a given state or suffering a change	*The wood* is dry. He cut *the wood*.
Experiencer	Someone having a given experience or mental disposition	*Tom* saw the snake. *Tom* wanted a drink.
Beneficiary	Someone who profits from a state or process, including possession	*Mary* has a convertible. This is *Mary's* car. Tom bought *Mary* a car.
Instrument	Something that plays a role in bringing about a process or action but which is not the instigator; it is used by an agent	Tom opened the door with *a key*. Tom used *his knife* to open the box.
Location	The place or locus of a state, action, or process	The spoon is in *the drawer*. Tom sat in *the chair*.
Complement	The verb names an action that brings something into existence. The complement, on a more or less specific level, completes the verb. This use of the word "complement" is not, incidentally, its most common use in linguistics.	Mary sang *a song*. John played *checkers*.

TABLE 4.7. The Acquisition of 14 English Grammatical Morphemes

Morpheme	Order of Acquisition	Semantic Description	Example
present progressive	1	temporary duration	The dog *is barking.*
on	2.5	support	The book is *on* the table.
in	2.5	containment	The candy is *in* the box.
plural	4	more than one	The boy*s* are here.
past irregular	5	earlierness	He *came.*
possessive	6	ownership	The man*'s* hat is black.
uncontractible copula	7	identity	*These are* white.
		membership	*These are* cocker spaniels.
		attribute possession	The dogs *are* white.
		location	Here it *is.*
Articles	8	specific	*The* horse is brown.
		nonspecific	I have *a* box.
past regular	9	earlierness	They *walked* to town.
third person singular regular	10	tense, number (often is redundant)	The boy *walks.*
third person singular irregular	11	tense, number	The boy *has* a hat.
uncontractible auxiliary	12	temporary duration	*These are* going on the shelf.
		earlierness	*They were* going to town.
contractible copula	13	identity	*He's* John.
		membership	*Daddy's* a man.
		attribute possession	The *book's* blue.
		location	*Mary's* at home.
contractible auxiliary	14	temporary duration	*He's* talked too long.
		earlierness	*He'd* talked too long.

From *A First Language: The Early Stages* (p. 31) by R. Brown, 1973, Cambridge, MA: Harvard University Press. Reprinted by permission.

auxiliary *do* had to be supplied and marked for past tense—*did.* In addition, there are tag questions such as, "You're going, aren't you?" that are also requests for confirmation through a *yes-no* response. However, tag questions are very late in the course of development, and some Stage V children still have not acquired them.

Another form of interrogative sentence that makes its appearance in Stage III is the question requesting that a constituent be named—or more commonly, the *wh-* question. These are termed *wh-* questions, because in almost all instances the question is initiated by *who, whose, what, where, when, why,* or *how* (e.g., "Who will take out the trash?"). The constituent required in the response to the question is a subject noun: "X will take out the trash."

In Stage III the negative sentence, as opposed to the syntactic expression of negation (No!), begins to appear. Bloom (1970) distinguishes three types of negation: nonexistence, rejection, and denial. Nonexistence of a referent can be expressed as, "There isn't any milk," ordinarily meaning that there was some milk but now there is not. Rejection is exemplified in a sentence such as, "I don't want any milk," or "No more milk." Finally, there is the negative sentence that denies the truth of some proposition, such as, "Texas is not part of the U.S."

Imperative sentences are those in which the speaker asks, demands, insists, and so on, that something occur. In English, we have no difficulty identifying the imperative, because it is usually expressed without a subject and begins only with the uninflected verb, as in, "Pass the butter," "Give me a hand," and so on. The imperative is considered a characteristic of Stage III but is present even in Stage I children. On purely linguistic grounds, imperatives are almost impossible to identify, because the Stage I child so often produces subjectless sentences. Therefore, it is only from context that we know the child is expressing an imperative. By Stage III the child will use subjects in sentences, and we can easily recognize the imperative when it appears.

Many of the transformations of Stage III make their initial, unstructured appearance as far back as Stage I, but they become truly identifiable only in Stage III. Furthermore, the elaboration of the transformations occurs after Stage III and even past Stage IV. The most acceptable method of categorizing a child as being in Stage III is to apply the MLU method: If the child's MLU is 2.50 to 2.99 morphemes, we may say that he or she is in Stage III.

Stage IV. Three varieties of embedded sentences begin to appear in Stage IV: object noun phrase complements, indirect or embedded *wh-* questions, and relative clauses. Remember that we are discussing a child with a predicted chronological age of only 3.0 to perhaps 3.5 years and that the discussion of embedded sentences does not apply in its fullest sophistication to such a young child. Rather, one sees the early beginnings of embedding in Stage IV, and the full elaboration of embedding may not be observed in many adults.

The easiest embeddings to recognize are the object noun phrase complements which take the form of, "I hope I don't hurt it," "I think it's the wrong way," and other sentences recorded by Brown (1973). These were early productions of the children he observed. In these sentences, one can see that with certain transitive verbs, (e.g., *think, know, guess, tell, hope,* and *mean*), a simple intact sentence may take the place of a simple noun object and play the role of a noun. It is much more difficult to recognize the simple sentence, "Mary plays the piano," in the more complex sentence, "It bothers the neighbors for Mary to play the piano," and yet the same kind of complement is used in the two sentences.

The second type of embedding involves the use of *wh-* questions. Brown (1973) recorded a number of these sentences, a few of which are:

> Whoever broke this must fix it.
> When I get big I can lift you up.
> Mary sang what I like to hear. (p. 22)

These sentences are indirect (or embedded) *wh-* questions in which the *wh-* word plays the role of the object or some other role.

A classically constructed sentence with a relative clause is, "The man who came to dinner stayed a month," in which there are two propositions made about the same noun phrase. Because a relative pronoun (e.g., *who*, *whom, which*) may replace a noun phrase, it is not always apparent that there are two propositions.

Stage V. Stage V is marked by an MLU of 4.00 to 4.49 morphemes with a predicted chronological age of 43.4 to 46.6 months, as may be seen in Table 4.8. It is a stage titled by Brown as "coordination of simple sentences and propositional relations." Early examples of coordinated simple sentences are, "I have one and you have one," "John plays and Mary plays," and so on. Each of the simple sentences is complete and can stand alone, but it usually demonstrates a continuity of thought. The sentence, "I am an educator and Mary has a cat," is not patently ungrammatic, but it violates the underlying semantic relationships that we expect in coordinated sentences. As language develops, children eliminate the redundancy in the sentences given above and instead replace them with, "You and I have one," or, "John and Mary play."

Brown (1973) summarizes the five stages as follows:

> In summary five major processes of sentence construction have been described in both semantic and syntactic terms . . . They are:
>
> 1. Semantic roles such as agent, patient, instrument, locative, etc., in simple sentences expressed by linear order, syntactic relations, prepositions or postpositions.
>
> 2. Semantic modulations such as number, specificity, tense, aspect, mood, etc., expressed by inflections or free forms belonging to small closed classes.
>
> 3. Modalities of the simple sentence: *yes-no* interrogation, request for specification of a constituent, negation, imperative.
>
> 4. Embedding of one simple sentence as a grammatical constituent or in a semantic role in another including all the roles of 1, all the constituents which one may ask to be specified in 3.

5. Coordination of full sentences or of partially identical and partially distinct (but structurally matched) sentences with deletion of one representation of the identical stretches. The coordinated sentences appear with connector words that approximate in meaning to relations of propositional logic. (p. 32)

Imitation

So far we have discussed only the spontaneous production of language, but a great deal of research effort has been spent on investigating the imitation performance of children. Two types of imitation have been studied: spontaneous imitation (in which the child imitates an adult's production without being cued) and elicited imitation (in which an adult asks the child to imitate him). In general, three conclusions can be drawn from the studies done by Ervin (1964), Kemp and Dale (1973), and Bloom, Hood, and Lightbown (1974). These studies are prototypical of many others that have been done.

First, imitations have essentially the same structure as the child's free speech no matter how complicated the stimulus is. Second, the imitations may even be simpler in structure than the child's free speech. Third, children may imitate new words that have not occurred in their free speech yet may *not* imitate words that are in their everyday productive vocabulary. This last point, that children may not imitate words or structures that are in their spontaneous speech, is a particularly interesting one. Bloom (1974) hypothesizes that in spontaneous speech, the child is talking about the present—the here and now—and that this temporal contextual support plays an important role in the formulation of sentences. Without this support, children do not seem to be able to produce utterances in imitation that they have produced spontaneously the day before.

In regard to syntactic development, another aspect should be discussed, that of comprehension. If a child does not spontaneously produce a particular structure, such as plurals, and does not imitate plural words, can one be sure that the concept of plurality is not a part of the child's competence? It does seem that children comprehend language long before they produce it, but sometimes their apparent ability to comprehend is deceiving. Consider that when a child hears a word, he or she has several clues to its meaning: his or her own general knowledge of the world, the nonlinguistic context in which the word occurs, the linguistic context, and the child's knowledge of words and syntactic structures. When any of us hears a word, we call upon these clues. A child may respond appropriately to the command, "Come here," only because of minimal gestural cues. He or she may respond to, "Give it to daddy," because of the linguistic context and because it is the child's mother speaking.

The first systematic attempt to investigate and compare imitation, comprehension, and production was made by Fraser, Bellugi, and Brown (1963).

TABLE 4.8. Predicted Chronological Ages and Age Ranges Within One Standard Deviation of the Predicted Value for Each MLU

Brown's stage	MLU	Predicted chronological age[a]	Predicted age ±1 SD[b] (middle 68%)
Early Stage I	1.01	19.1	16.4–21.8
MLU = 1.01–1.49	1.10	19.8	17.1–22.5
	1.20	20.6	17.9–23.3
	1.30	21.4	18.7–24.1
	1.40	22.2	19.5–24.9
	1.50	23.0	18.5–27.5
Late Stage I	1.60	23.8	19.3–28.3
MLU = 1.50–1.99	1.70	24.6	20.1–29.1
	1.80	25.3	20.8–29.8
	1.90	26.1	21.6–30.6
	2.00	26.9	21.5–32.3
Stage II	2.10	27.7	22.3–33.1
MLU = 2.00–2.49	2.20	28.5	23.1–33.9
	2.30	29.3	23.9–34.7
	2.40	30.1	24.7–35.5
	2.50	30.8	23.9–37.7
Stage III	2.60	31.6	24.7–38.5
MLU = 2.50–2.99	2.70	32.4	25.5–39.3
	2.80	33.2	26.3–40.1
	2.90	34.0	27.1–40.9
	3.00	34.8	28.0–41.6
Early Stage IV	3.10	35.6	28.8–42.4
MLU = 3.00–3.49	3.20	36.3	29.5–43.1
	3.30	37.1	30.3–43.9
	3.40	37.9	31.1–44.7
	3.50	38.7	30.8–46.6
Late Stage IV–	3.60	39.5	31.6–47.4
Early Stage V	3.70	40.3	32.4–48.2
MLU = 3.50–3.99	3.80	41.1	33.2–49.0
	3.90	41.8	33.9–49.7
	4.00	42.6	36.7–48.5

TABLE 4.8. continued

Brown's stage	MLU	Predicted chronological age[a]	Predicted age ±1 SD[b] (middle 68%)
Late Stage V	4.10	43.4	37.5–49.3
MLU = 4.00–4.49	4.20	44.2	38.3–50.1
	4.30	45.0	39.1–50.9
	4.40	45.8	39.9–51.7
	4.50	46.6	40.3–52.9
Post Stage V	4.60	47.3	41.0–53.6
MLU = 4.50+	4.70	48.2	41.9–54.5
	4.80	48.9	42.6–55.2
	4.90	49.7	43.4–56.0
	5.00	50.5	42.1–58.9
	5.10	51.3	42.9–59.7
	5.20	52.1	43.7–60.5
	5.30	52.8	44.4–61.2
	5.40	53.6	45.2–62.0
	5.50	54.4	46.0–62.8
	5.60	55.2	46.8–63.6
	5.70	56.0	47.6–64.4
	5.80	56.8	48.4–65.2
	5.90	57.5	49.1–65.9
	6.00	58.3	49.9–66.7

[a]Age is predicted from the equation Age (in months) = 11.199 + 7.857 (MLU)
[b]Computed from obtained standard deviations

From *Assessing Language Production in Children: Experimental Procedures* (p. 26) by J. Miller, 1981, Austin, TX: PRO-ED. Reprinted by permission.

Using the Imitation–Comprehension–Production Test (ICP), they combined pairs of sentences that differed in only one aspect, such as plurality, and asked children to imitate the sentences, to point to the picture that correctly depicted the sentences, and to produce a correct sentence when shown a picture. For the ten pairs of sentences, the results were remarkably clear-cut and consistent. The children scored highest on the imitation task, second highest on the comprehension section, and lowest on production. In fact, this pattern occurred in almost all of the children tested. The children ranged in age from 37 to 43 months. The study was so intriguing that it was replicated by Lovell and Dixon (1967) with children aged 2 to 6 years and with retarded 6 and 7 year olds. Their results were the same as those of the earlier study, with the addition of the finding that scores increased with age and with intellectual level.

The results of studies mentioned above do not necessarily refute the findings of Bloom and others; the children were tested on elicited and not spontaneous imitations. However, other problems with the ICP type of studies have been noted by Baird (1972) and Fernald (1972).

After the age of 5 or 6 years, syntactic development—at least in production—appears to approximate adult language quite closely, with a few common difficulties that can be noted. These problems include subject-verb agreement, case endings on personal pronouns, acquisition of the irregular past tense, and acquisition of perfect forms. As the reader can see, these are relatively minor matters of development. For all purposes one may say that the basic syntactic structure of the majority of the older child's sentences is the same as that of adult grammar, with the one notable exception of complex sentences. For information on later syntactic development with regard to specific structures, the reader may refer to Chomsky (1968), Cromer (1970), Kessel (1970), and Cambon and Sinclair (1974).

SEMANTIC AND PRAGMATIC DEVELOPMENT

During the past ten years or so, many studies have addressed themselves to the relationship between cognitive and linguistic development (Bates, Camaioni, & Volterra, 1975; Blank, 1974, 1975; Bowerman, 1976, 1977; Cromer, 1981; Duchan, 1983; Morehead & Morehead, 1974; Schlesinger, 1974, 1977; Sinclair-de-Zwart, 1969; Wells, 1975). No attempt will be made to summarize the work and/or positions of all these authors; suffice it to say there seem to be three major propositions: (a) Cognitive development precedes language development; (b) cognition and language develop in a parallel but noncausally related fashion; and (c) some unidentified "deeper" structures account for both cognitive and language development. At present, the state of the field is one in which one author supposes and another disposes; however, all seem to be very polite to one another at this juncture, probably because it is anyone's guess as to who is correct. Simply, the results are not yet in.

Setting aside the above issues, we will concentrate on a somewhat demographic view of semantic and pragmatic development. Again, emphasis will be on *what* rather than *how* or *why*. It is convenient to follow Katz and Langendown (1976) in relating pragmatics to the study of meaning and making a distinction between grammatical meaning and utterance meaning. They equate pragmatics with semantic performance and indicate that pragmatics may be viewed as the performance aspect of the semantic component of grammar.

Lexical Growth

Semantic development has been reviewed by most authors in terms of lexical growth—the acquisition of words that have meaning to the child. Bloom (1973) originally contended that single words might be used by the child to express an entire sentence and that the child omitted the rest of the words because of limited performance factors such as memory span or breath control. Bloom also wrote that the single words used by the child were gross approximations of the adult word and that by adding semantic features, the child could come closer and closer to the dictionary meaning of the word. Within this notion are two well-known facts related to the development of word meaning: overextension and underextension (or overlap). Overextension refers to word meanings that are overgeneralized (e.g., the use of *dog* to refer to all animals). On the other hand, underextensions are word meanings that are too specific (e.g., *dog* used to refer only to the family pet).

From the literature, it appears that overextension is the more common failing of children developing language, but there are notable exceptions. Seldom are proper names overgeneralized, and diaries of children's language development are replete with underextensions. Therefore, it is probably impossible to say which failure is the more common. One serious problem with H. Clark's (1970) theory is her failure to account for the occurrence of underextensions.

Variable Word Meanings

Briefly, some of the research dealing with the development of the meaning of specific terms will be discussed. The terms *more* and *less* were studied in 3 year olds by Donaldson and Balfour (1968) and Palermo (1973), all of whom found that the terms were treated generally as synonyms. The children reacted as if they knew that the terms referred to quantity, but they did not distinguish between them.

Dimensional terms (e.g., *big, little, long, short, thick, thin*) have been extensively explored by Donaldson and Wales (1970), H. Clark (1970), E. Clark (1972), Maratsos (1973), and Eilers, Oller, and Ellington (1974). Some of the findings are: (a) Fewer errors were recorded for the *big/little* contrast than for any of the others and (b) there were fewer on *long/short* than on *wide/narrow*, indicating a developmental trend from general to specific terms. However, for all three contrasts, correct responses occurred most frequently on the negative item in the pair—that is, *little, short*, and *narrow*. Maratsos' findings suggest a three-stage development in the meanings of *big* and *long*, as follows:

• About age 3: *big* refers to global (overall size, and *long* refers to only one dimension

- About age 4–5: *long* is still interpreted correctly, but now *big* is treated as synonymous with *long*, particularly with reference to height

- About age 5+: the two terms are again distinguished correctly

Apparently, learning the meanings of words is not merely a matter of the child attending to the adult language features of the word; in fact, quite different features may be used during language development.

In addition to the above research, various authors have investigated causality and verbs, verbs of possession and transfer, color names, and many other structures. Some good reviews can be found in Bloom (1973), Hayes (1970), John and Moskovitch (1970), Moore (1973), and Slobin (1973).

SUMMARY

Language development was discussed in this chapter with reference to the young child's development of phonological, syntactic, and semantic structures and rules. In addition, a fairly lengthy review of the stages of language development according to Brown (1973) was presented because of its marked relevance to the analysis of language samples. As stated in the beginning of the chapter, the discussion of development was felt to be necessary, because the orientation to assessment presented throughout the text is developmental. Without a thorough grounding in language development, the clinician will have great difficulty in adopting such an approach. Although the discussion is brief in relation to the body of knowledge regarding language development, the clinician should be able to extend his or her knowledge by pursuing some of the references given.

REFERENCES

Baird, R. (1972). On the role of chance in Imitation–Comprehension–Production Test results. *Journal of Verbal Learning and Verbal Behavior, 11*, 474–477.

Bates, E., Camaioni, L., & Volterra, V. (1975). The acquisition of performatives prior to speech. *Merrill-Palmer Quarterly, 21*, 205–226.

Blank, M. (1974). Cognitive functions of language in the preschool years. *Developmental Psychology, 10*, 229–245.

Blank, M. (1975). Mastering the intangible through language. In D. Aaronson & R. Rieber (Eds.), *Developmental psycholinguistics and communication disorders* (pp. 234–249). New York: New York Academy of Sciences.

Bloom, L. (1970). *Language development: Form and function in emerging grammars.* Cambridge, MA: MIT Press.

Bloom, L. (1973). *One word at a time.* The Hague: Mouton.

Bloom, L. (1974). Talking, understanding, and thinking. In R. Schiefelbusch & L. Lloyd (Eds.), *Language perspectives: Acquisition, retardation, and intervention* (pp. 285–311). Austin, TX: PRO-ED.

Bloom, L., Hood, L., & Lightbown, P. (1974). Imitation in language development. *Cognitive Psychology, 6,* 380–420.

Bowerman, M. (1973). Structural relationships in children's utterances: Syntactic or semantic? In I. E. Moore (Ed.), *Cognitive development and the acquisition of language* (pp. 346–378). New York: Academic Press.

Bowerman, M. (1976). Semantic factors in the acquisition of rules for word use and sentence construction. In D. Morehead & A. Morehead (Eds.), *Directions in normal and deficient child language* (pp. 99–179). Austin, TX: PRO-ED.

Bowerman, M. (1977). The acquisition of rules governing "possible lexical items": Evidence from spontaneous speech errors. Stanford University Department of Linguistics, *Papers/Reports on Child Language Development, 13,* 148–156.

Braine, M. (1963). The ontogeny of English phrase structure: The first phrase. *Language, 39,* 1–14.

Brown, R. (1973). *A first language: The early stages.* Cambridge, MA: Harvard University Press.

Cambon, J., & Sinclair, H. (1974). Relations between syntax and semantics: Are they "easy to see?" *British Journal of Psychology, 65,* 133–140.

Chomsky, C. (1968). *The acquisition of syntax in children from 5 to 10.* Cambridge, MA: MIT Press.

Chomsky, N. (1957). *Syntactic structures.* The Hague: Mouton.

Chomsky, N. (1968). *Language and mind.* New York: Harcourt, Brace & World.

Clark, E. (1972). On the child's acquisition of antonyms in two semantic fields. *Journal of Verbal Learning and Verbal Behavior, 11,* 750–758.

Clark, E. (1973). What's in a word? On the child's acquisition of semantics in his first language. In T. E. Moore (Ed.), *Cognitive development and the acquisition of language* (pp. 65–110). New York: Academic Press.

Clark, H. (1970). The primitive nature of children's relational concepts. In J. Hayes (Ed.), *Cognition and the development of language* (pp. 324–333). New York: John Wiley.

Cromer, R. (1970). Children are nice to understand: Surface structure clues for the recovery of a deep structure. *British Journal of Psychology, 61,* 397–408.

Cromer, R. (1981). Reconceptualizing language acquisition and cognitive development. In R. Schiefelbusch & D. Bricker (Eds.), *Early language: Acquisition and intervention* (pp. 51–138). Austin, TX: PRO-ED.

Davis, I. (1938). The speech aspects of reading readiness. *17th Yearbook of the Department of Elementary School Principals, 17,* 282–289.

Donaldson, M., & Balfour, G. (1968). Less is more: A study of language comprehension in children. *British Journal of Psychology, 59,* 461–472.

Donaldson, M., & Wales, R. (1970). On the acquisition of some relational terms. In J. Hayes (Ed.), *Cognition and the development of language* (pp. 112–123). New York: John Wiley.

Duchan, J. (1983). Language processing and geodesic domes. In T. Gallagher & C. Prutting (Eds.), *Pragmatic assessment and intervention issues* (pp. 83–101). College-Hill Press.

Edwards, M. (1974). Perception and production in child phonology: The testing of four hypotheses. *Journal of Child Language, 1,* 205–219.

Eilers, R., Oller, D., & Ellington, J. (1974). The acquisition of word meaning for dimensional adjectives: The long and short of it. *Journal of Child Language, 1,* 195–204.

Ervin, S. (1964). Imitation and structural change in children's language. In E. Lenneberg (Ed.), *New directions in the study of language* (pp. 163–189). Cambridge, MA: MIT Press.

Fernald, C. (1972). Control of grammar in imitation, comprehension, and production: Problems of replication. *Journal of Verbal Learning and Verbal Behavior, 11,* 606–613.

Fraser, C., Bellugi, U., & Brown, R. (1963). Control of grammar in imitation, comprehension, and production. *Journal of Verbal Learning and Verbal Behavior, 2,* 121–135.

Hayes, J. (Ed.). (1970). *Cognition and the development of language.* New York: John Wiley.

Irwin, O. (1947). Infant speech: Consonantal sounds according to place of articulation. *Journal of Speech Disorders, 12,* 187–201.

Irwin, O. (1948). Infant speech: Development of vowel sounds. *Journal of Speech and Hearing Disorders, 13,* 31–34.

John, V., & Moskovitch, S. (1970). Language acquisition and development in early childhood. In A. Marckwardt (Ed.), *Linguistics in school programs* (pp. 167–214). Chicago: National Society for the Study of Education.

Katz, J., & Langendoen, D. (1976). Pragmatics and presuppositions. *Language, 52,* 1917.

Kemp, J., & Dale, P. (1973, March). Spontaneous imitation and free speech: A grammatical comparison. Paper presented to the Society for Research in Child Development, Philadelphia.

Kessel, F. (1970). The role of syntax in children's comprehension from ages six to ten. *Monographs of the Society for Research in Child Development, 35,* No. 6 (Serial No. 139).

Lovell, K., & Dixon, E. (1967). The growth of the control of grammar in imitation, comprehension, and production. *Journal of Child Psychology and Psychiatry, 8,* 31–39.

Lyamina, G. M., & Gagua, N. I. (1966). On the formation of the correct pronunciation of words in children from 1½ to 3 years of life. In F. Smith & G. A. Miller (Eds.), *The genesis of language* (pp. 374–375). Cambridge, MA: MIT Press.

McNeill, D. (1966). Developmental psycholinguistics. In F. Smith & G. Miller (Eds.), *The genesis of language* (pp. 15–84). Cambridge, MA: MIT Press.

McNeill, D. (1970). *The acquisition of language: The study of developmental psycholinguistics.* New York: Harper and Row.

Maratsos, M. (1973). Decrease in the understanding of the word "big" in preschool children. *Child Development, 44,* 747–752.

Menyuk, P. (1968). The role of distinctive features in children's acquisition of phonology. *Journal of Speech and Hearing Research, 11,* 138–146.

Menyuk, P. (1971). *The acquisition and development of language.* Englewood Cliffs, NJ: Prentice-Hall.

Menyuk, P. (1972). *The development of speech.* New York: Bobbs-Merrill.

Menyuk, P., & Klatt, D. (1968). A child's production of initial consonant clusters. *Quarterly Progress Reports of the Research Laboratory of Electonics, MIT, 91,* 205–213.

Moore, T. (1973). *Cognitive development and the acquisition of language.* New York: Academic Press.

Morehead, D., & Morehead, A. (1974). From signal to sign: A Piagetian view of thought and language during the first two years. In R. Schiefelbusch & L. Lloyd (Eds.), *Language perspectives: Acquisition, retardation, and intervention* (pp. 153–190). Austin, TX: PRO-ED.

Newfield, M., & Schlanger, B. (1968). The acquisition of English morphology by normal and educable mentally retarded children. *Journal of Speech and Hearing Research, 11,* 693–706.

Palermo, D. S. (1973). More about less: A study of language comprehension. *Journal of Verbal Learning and Verbal Behavior, 13,* 211–221.

Schlesinger, I. (1974). Relational concepts underlying language. In R. Schiefelbusch & L. Lloyd (Eds.), *Language perspectives: Acquisition, retardation, and intervention* (pp. 129–151). Austin, TX: PRO-ED.

Schlesinger, I. (1977). The role of cognitive development and linguistic input in language acquisition. *Journal of Child Language, 4,* 153–169.

Shvachkin, N. (1966). Development of phonemic speech perception in early childhood. Abstracted by D. Slobin. In F. Smith & G. Miller (Eds.), *The genesis of language* (pp. 381–382). Cambridge, MA: MIT Press.

Sinclair-de-Zwart, H. (1969). Developmental psycholinguistics. In D. Elkind & J. Flavell (Eds.), *Studies in cognitive development* (pp. 315–366). New York: Oxford University Press.

Slobin, D. (1973). Cognitive prerequisites for the development of grammar. In C. Ferguson & D. Slobin (Eds.), *Studies of child language development* (pp. 183–186). New York: Rinehart, Holt, and Winston.

Templin, M. (1957). *Certain language skills in children.* Institute of Child Welfare Monograph Series, No. 26. Minneapolis: University of Minnesota Press.

Wells, G. (1975). Interpersonal communication and the development of language. Paper presented at the Third International Child Language Symposium, London, September.

5 / THE ASSESSMENT PROCEDURES

The present chapter deals with the assessment and description of oral language delay or disorder in children who may have a variety of other handicapping conditions. The philosophy of assessment reflected in this text centers around the need to describe the child's comprehension and production of language through a developmental investigation of the processes of language. The chapter is presented in three main sections: standardized measures of oral language, the language sample, and other assessment procedures. The section on standardized measures of oral language deals briefly with a few of the more commonly used instruments, because they are considered the best vehicle for identifying children with significant linguistic discrepancies. The second section describes one of the oldest techniques for assessing oral language production—the collecting and analyzing of a language sample. In the third section, which is by far the longest of the three, a number of informal assessment strategies are discussed.

STANDARDIZED MEASURES OF ORAL LANGUAGE

A variety of frequently used standardized and often normed measures of oral language are on the commercial market. Some of these measures assess only one dimension of language, such as articulation or syntax; others purport to assess almost all parameters of spoken language. In the following section, two general types of tests are discussed: (a) measures of only phonology and (b) measures that assess syntax, semantics, and, sometimes, articulation.

Tests of Phonology

In this section phonological tests of both reception and production are discussed. Phonological reception may be considered synonymous with speech sound discrimination, while phonological production is discussed in terms of articulatory performance. The tests reviewed in this section are at least partially standardized in that specific instructions are provided for administration and scoring. There is a great deal of latitude permitted in the interpretation of the scores, and the reader will find that there are no exact norms.

Tests of Speech Sound Discrimination. Most investigators have found a relationship between speech sound discrimination and articulatory proficiency that they feel indicates the following: (a) Children's speech sound discrimination ability improves as they grow older, at least during the period between the ages of 3 and 8 years: and (b) children who have articulation deficits also tend to have poor speech sound discrimination. Clinicians usually assess articulation defective children in speech sound discrimination as a precursor to teaching them to hear the differences among sounds in the auditory training phase of therapy. Only two tests of speech sound discrimination are discussed, because there is a marked similarity among all such tests.

Auditory Discrimination Test. The *Auditory Discrimination Test* (Wepman, 1958) is the prototype for many discrimination tests, both standardized and nonstandardized. It was constructed for children between the ages of 5 to 8 years and consists of 40 word pairs, such as *sake/shake*. The test is administered by having the child turn his or her back to the examiner and indicating whether the two words produced by the examiner are the same or different. The test incorporates a validity check to determine whether the child understands the task and is able to cooperate in taking it. As would be expected, it is necessary to determine whether the child understands the concepts of *same* and *different* before administering a test like this. Broadly stated age norms are provided.

Language Related Tests of Speech-Sound Discrimination (LTSD). The LTSD (Bryen, 1974) was developed as a means of determining whether a child has adequate speech sound discrimination in standard English, black English, and Spanish. The test consists of three different forms, one in each language area, and has 35 items per form. It is appropriate for children 6 to 12 years old. The LTSD uses the Wepman paradigm in which the first word is presented, followed by a second word, which is the same as the first or which differs in only one phoneme. The child responds by indicating whether the two words are the same or different.

The test can serve several purposes. First, information can be obtained as to how children are developing phonologically in their own spoken language, and second, one can determine how well children are developing in standard English regardless of the language they use. Statistical data provided indicate that the age-related construct validity of the LTSD is partially supported and that the test-retest reliability coefficients for all three forms are significant. Mean scores and tables of content analysis are provided as well.

Tests of Articulation. Articulation tests, such as those described below, measure only a fairly limited number of dimensions no matter how complex they may seem. These dimensions are place and manner of articulation, presence of voicing, elicited production or imitation, and phonemic context.

Which articulators, or speech organs, are involved in the production of the phoneme? The answer to such a question reveals the place of articulation. The articulators are usually assumed to be the lips, teeth, alveolar ridge (the area behind the upper teeth), palate, and tongue. When two of the articulators are brought together in the production of a phoneme, the place of contact between them is called the place of articulation. For example, /p/ is a bilabial phoneme, because it is produced by bringing the two lips together; /k/ is a lingua-palatal phoneme, because its production requires the tongue and palate to come into contact.

The manner of articulation refers to how the phoneme is produced. It may be with a puff of air, such as /p/ and /b/; with friction, as in /f/; or with hissing, as in /s/. As the reader can deduce, all of these sounds are produced with varying degrees of closure between articulators. The classes of closure are often categorized as stops (or plosives), fricatives, nasals, affricates, glides, and laterals.

Voicing is a very simple dimension of articulation denoting merely whether the phoneme is produced with or without vocal tone. All vowels are produced with voice, but the voicing feature is used as a description of consonants, because many of them are distinguished from one another only by the voicing feature, such as /p/ and /b/, /t/ and /d/, and /s/ and /z/.

A number of articulation tests allow for the assessment of sounds that are produced either spontaneously or only in imitation of the test administrator's production of the sound. Even if the test does not allow for imitation, most clinicians will use it.

Only a few commercial tests of articulation include techniques for distinctive feature analysis of phonemic errors. Such an analysis is a procedure for contrasting the features (manner and place of articulation and voicing) that may be represented in a child's articulation errors. For example, a feature analysis of a given child's articulation test profile could indicate that the child's errors are the result of the lack of a particular feature, such as the absence of the labio-dental feature in place of articulation.

At least two, and perhaps more, of the commercially available tests of articulation feature the assessment of phonemes within a variety of phonemic contexts. For example, in English the phoneme /r/ is never followed by the phoneme /s/ in single words; however, in contextual speech the combination may occur quite frequently as in the production of such word combinations as *barstool*. Testing phonemes in context often reveals contexts in which a defective phoneme is produced correctly, and that context can form a point of origin for therapy.

Templin-Darley Test of Articulation.   The oldest test of articulation that is still used widely is probably the *Templin-Darley Diagnostic Test of Articulation* (Templin & Darley, 1969), which is based on the Templin (1957) normative data. It is a 141 item, single word test that is designed to elicit all phonemes in all positions (initial, medial, and final) and in common blends. As with almost all articulation tests, it is a picture presentation test, although for some older persons there are sentences that can be used. The score obtained by the child is the number of items produced correctly, and the score can be evaluated by comparing it with means and standard deviations that are given for each one-half year level from ages 3 to 5 years and at one year intervals from 5 to 8 years. The variables of sex and socioeconomic status are also considered in the norms. There is probably little value to the reliability and validity coefficients that are presented in the manual, because, in the last analysis, articulation tests are used diagnostically rather than formally by speech pathologists who have determined the presence of an articulation disorder prior to administering a lengthy diagnostic instrument. The data obtained from the test are used for therapeutic rather than identification purposes.

A Deep Test of Articulation.   Another older and less frequently used test of articulation is McDonald's (1964) *A Deep Test of Articulation*, in which pairs of pictures or written sentences are presented to elicit the production of a phoneme in many different phonetic contexts. Using a screening test of any kind, the speech pathologist first determines the error sounds and then employs the appropriate combination of pictures or sentences to elicit the phoneme in about 30 different contexts in which the test phonemes comes after the context sound. For example, if the child manifests a defective /s/, the picture card *house* from the first pack of cards in the test is presented in combination with all of the picture cards from the second pack, each depicting a word that begins with a different sound. The child is instructed to say the unusual two-syllable words that are formed from pairing the two pictures, such as *housetie* or *housecow*. McDonald indicates that if the sound is produced correctly in 75% of the contexts, therapy is probably not necessary. Moreover, if therapy is necessary, it would probably be best to begin with those combinations in which the child produces the phoneme correctly.

Goldman-Fristoe Test of Articulation. The *Goldman-Fristoe Test of Articulation* (Goldman & Fristoe, 1969) samples both spontaneous and imitative phonemic production and includes both single word and conversational speech production. In addition, phonemes are assessed in the initial, medial, and final positions as appropriate. The test manual provides test-retest and interrater reliability percentages ranging from 71 to 100%. Percentile rank norms are given for males and females aged 6–0 to 16+ years on spontaneous production of words and on elicited production of syllables.

Fisher-Logemann Test of Articulation Competence. A test designed to assist in the assessment of distinctive features is the *Fisher-Logemann Test of Articulation Competence* (Fisher & Logemann, 1971). Three parameters were chosen for the analysis of the distinctive features of consonants and four parameters for the analysis of vowels. Voicing, place of articulation, and manner of articulation are analyzed in consonants; height of tongue, place of articulation, degree of tension, and lip rounding are evaluated in vowel production. The system of distinctive feature analysis presented by Jakobson, Fant, and Halle (1963) is not used by the authors, because they felt that it was much too complex for the routine articulation testing that is done by most school speech pathologists. Instead, the authors adapted the Jakobson approach and designed a much more simplified analysis.

The test consists of 109 pictures on 39 cards plus 15 sentences for children or adults who read. Consonants are tested in prevocalic position (before a vowel in a syllable), postvocalic position (after a vowel), and intervocalic position (between two vowels). The twelve vowels are tested in either single syllable words or in words with the test vowel receiving primary stress. In addition, 23 blends and four diphthongs are tested. As with most articulation tests, the test procedures and test data are similar to the Templin-Darley. One advantage to the test is that the test record blank is arranged to facilitate the analysis of distinctive features, thereby assisting the examiner in the interpretation of test results. One disadvantage of the test is that it may require a much higher degree of proficiency in phonetic transcription than many school speech pathologists possess.

Test of Articulation Performance. One of the most recently published articulation tests is the *Test of Articulation Performance* (Bryant & Bryant, 1983), which has both a standardized screening form (TAP–S) and an inventory for feature analysis (TAP–D). The diagnostic inventory is the most comprehensive of articulation tests in that it measures six different parameters of speech production: phonemes in isolated words, distinctive features, articulation of adjacent phonemes, phonemes in continuous speech, phonemic modeling, and the speaker's attitude toward his or her speech. The TAP–D incorporates elements of all of the tests previously discussed as well as adding the factor of attitude. Reliability coefficients for the TAP–S, ranging from .88 to .96, are given for internal consistency and test-retest reliability; interrater reliability is estimated at 95%. All components of the TAP–S were examined with regard to content, criterion related, and construct validity, as appropriate, and were determined to have significantly high validity coefficients. A readily apparent advantage of the TAP–D and the TAP–S is their comprehensiveness. The examiner is able to assess a variety of articulatory dimensions using a single instrument.

Tests of Syntax and Semantics

In this section six standardized tests of language performance are discussed briefly. As opposed to the instruments discussed above, which were limited to the measurement of only a single language ability, these tests are generally much more comprehensive. For the most part they assess syntax and semantics in both comprehension and production modes; some measure other attributes as well. The selection of the tests for review was arbitrary, the major selection criterion was that they deal with language in a linguistic paradigm rather than in a psychological or even psycholinguistic model. For this reason one of the best known tests, the *Illinois Test of Psycholinguistic Abilities* (Kirk, McCarthy, & Kirk, 1968) was not chosen for inclusion, because it contains many visual and memory elements that are difficult to reference in a linguistic model.

All of the tests reviewed here have advantages and disadvantages. The primary advantage to all of them is that they are, for the most part, well-standardized. This gives the examiner a reliable reference point for identifying children who have language delays or disorders severe enough to warrant therapeutic intervention. The disadvantage of these tests and of all others like them is that they contain too few items to represent the domains measured and, therefore, cannot be used to inventory children's special needs. These tests may provide baseline information about the child's linguistic performance, but they do not thoroughly explore the deficits that the child may be manifesting. Such an investigation requires the use of other assessment techniques. However, the information obtained from the tests reviewed here is valuable when applied appropriately and should not be underrated.

Six tests are discussed in this section, but the reader is not to assume that these six are recommended over and above any other well-standardized measures. As stated before, they were selected because they are prototypes of standardized language tests and because they are commonly used by practitioners in the field. Table 5.1 presents a more comprehensive listing of various types of oral language measures for the reader who would like to make some comparisons among instruments.

Test for Auditory Comprehension of Language. The TACL (Carrow, 1973) is a very popular test that purports to measure a number of lexical and structural elements in both English and Spanish. The language categories measured by the TACL are (a) form classes and function words, (b) morphological constructions, (c) grammatical categories, and (d) syntactic structure. Each of these categories may contain four to seven subcategories, and each subcategory may be assessed with only 1 to 18 items, the average being 4.21 items per subcategory. For subcategories like nouns that have 12 items, adjectives with 18 items, and verbs with 8 items, there may be enough test items to warrant making conclusions regarding the child's performance in these areas. However, when a subcategory like interrogatives is tested with only 3 items, conclusions cannot be made regarding the child's knowledge in that area. The test has value because it is one of the few standardized linguistic measures that can be used with Spanish-speaking children. Means and standard deviations are given for four test components: lexical, morphological, grammatical, and syntactical subtests and for the total for children at the kindergarten and first grade levels. Reliability coefficients indicate that the total score and all subtest scores except the syntactic are adequate.

Test of Adolescent Language. The TOAL (Hammill, Brown, Larsen, & Wiederholt, 1987) is the only standardized, nationally normed test of language for students aged 11–1 to 18–11 years. It is a comprehensive test composed of eight subtests that measure the expressive and receptive components of reading and writing and the lexical and grammatic aspects of listening and speaking. In addition to providing subtest scores, the instrument allows the examiner to calculate a number of composite scores, such as those for spoken language, written language, receptive language, expressive language, vocabulary, grammar, and a number of others. Coefficients for internal, test-retest, and interrater reliability are all high, and the test is a valuable addition to the examiner's repertoire of language tests.

Clinical Evaluation of Language Functions. The CELF (Semel & Wiig, 1980) is composed of eleven subtests that measure certain aspects of language in the areas of semantics (word meanings), syntax (sentence structure), and memory (recall and retrieval). In addition, two subtests are devoted to the assessment of phonology (articulation and discrimination of speech sounds). The CELF Screening Test was standardized on a stratified sample of 1,405

TABLE 5.1. Tests of Oral Language

Test	Purpose		Elements		
	Identification	Instruction	Phonology	Syntax	Semantics
Auditory Discrimination Test (Wepman, 1958)	X		X		
Assessment of Children's Language Comprehension (Foster, Giddan, & Stark, 1972)	X	X		X	X
Basic Concept Inventory (Englemann, 1967)	X				X
Birth to Three Developmental Scale (Bangs & Dodson, 1979)	X	X		X	X
Carrow Elicited Language Inventory (Carrow, 1974)	X	X		X	X
Clinical Evaluation of Language Functions (Semel & Wiig, 1980)	X			X	X
Denver Developmental Screening Test (Frankenburg, Dodds, Fandal, Kazuk, & Cohrs, 1975)	X			X	X
Developmental Activities Screening Inventory (Fewell & Langley, 1984)	X			X	X
Developmental Sentence Analysis (Lee, 1974)	X	X		X	
Fisher-Logemann Test of Articulation Competence (Fisher & Logemann, 1971)	X	X	X		

TABLE 5.1. continued

Test					
Goldman-Fristoe Test of Articulation (Goldman & Fristoe, 1969)	X	X	X		
Illinois Test of Psycholinguistic Abilities (Kirk, McCarthy, & Kirk, 1968)	X	X		X	X
Language-Related Tests of Speech-Sound Discrimination (Bryen, 1974)	X		X		
Linguistic Analysis of Speech Samples (Angler, Hannah, & Longhurst, 1973)	X	X		X	X
Miller-Yoder Test of Grammatical Comprehension (Miller & Yoder, 1972)	X	X		X	
Minnesota Child Development Inventory (Ireton & Thwing, 1972)	X			X	X
Northwestern Syntax Screening Test (Lee, 1969)	X			X	
Peabody Picture Vocabulary Test (Dunn, 1981)	X				
Screening Test of Spanish Grammar (Toronto, 1973)	X			X	
Templin-Darley Tests of Articulation (Templin & Darley, 1969)	X	X	X		
Test for Auditory Comprehension of Language (Carrow, 1973)	X			X	X
Test of Adolescent Language (Hammill, Brown, Larsen, & Wiederholt, 1987)	X			X	X

TABLE 5.1. continued

Test			
Test of Articulation Performance (Bryant & Bryant, 1983)	X		X
Test of Early Language Development (Hresko, Reid, & Hammill, 1981)	X	X	X
Test of Language Development–Intermediate (Hammill & Newcomer, 1982)	X	X	X
Test of Language Development–Primary (Newcomer & Hammill, 1982)	X	X	X
Utah Test of Language Development (Mecham, Jex, & Jones, 1973)	X		X
Verbal Language Development Scale (Mecham, 1958)	X		X
Vocabulary Comprehension Scale (Bangs, 1977)	X		X

Adapted from *Learning Disabilities: Basic Concepts, Assessment Practices, and Instructional Strategies* (pp. 56–57) by P. Myers and D. Hammill, 1982, Austin, TX: PRO-ED. Reprinted by permission.

children in grades K–12; however, the Diagnostic Battery was standardized on only 159 of the students who took the Screening Test. It would appear that the reliability coefficients, which are all within acceptable limits, should be viewed with some reservations due to the small size of the sample used. The validity coefficients are also open to the same criticism.

The CELF has some interesting variations, particularly those that allow for evaluation of grammaticality and complexity and the subtests that allow for probes of incorrect responses. The test manual also contains a number of appendixes, some of which are particularly useful, such as the description of dialectical variations in morphology and syntax and the overview of informal extension testing formats at the syntactic level.

Test of Early Language Development. The TELD (Hresko, Reid, & Hammill, 1981) measures spoken language in the expressive and receptive modes for the dimensions of content and form. Content is defined as a semantic dimension and is related to the expression or reception of word meaning, conceptual categories, and interpretation of meaning within varying contexts. The dimension of form refers to syntax, morphology, and phonology. The TELD was standardized on 1,184 children between the ages of 3–0 and 7–11 years. Reliability coefficients for internal and test-retest reliability are within acceptable limits. Content, criterion related, and construct validity were examined, and the authors state that the validity of the test is well supported.

Clark-Madison Test of Oral Language. The Clark-Madison (Clark & Madison, 1981) is designed for young children ages 4–0 and 8–11 years and is one of the most widely used tests of spoken language in early childhood education programs. It was developed to assess young children's expressive abilities in various grammatical and syntactic components of language as well as target modifiers, determiners, prepositions, verbs, pronouns, and inflections. It uses a unique nominative elicitation technique in its administration. The authors have reviewed much of the research related to the relationship between spontaneous language sampling and structured elicitation. They found that the nominative elicitation technique as used in the Clark-Madison test results in children producing 52% of the target structures that were not produced when spontaneous speech samples were taken.

To understand the item administration technique better, a couple of examples are given. The child is shown a picture of a boy carrying a large box and two boys carrying some small boxes between them. The examiner points to the first picture and says, "Listen. His box is big." The examiner then points to the second picture and says, "Tell me about them." The correct response is, "Their boxes are small," in which the target item is *their* or *theirs.* As one might expect, demonstration items are scattered throughout the test because, as the authors concede, the administration technique places large demands on the child's memory capacity. The authors give some examples of how poor memory may affect the child's responses and suggest that if a memory deficit is thought to be interfering with the administration of the test, some other measurement device should be used.

The authors recognize that the standardization sample of 144 children is of minimal size, and they report that extensive standardization and normative data analysis is underway. The reliability and validity coefficients as reported in the 1981 test manual are within acceptable limits but should be viewed with reservation because of the small sample size.

Test of Language Development–Primary and *Test of Language Development–Intermediate.* The TOLD–P (Newcomer & Hammill, 1982) and the TOLD–I (Hammill & Newcomer, 1982) are very widely used measures of oral language that have been carefully standardized and normed. The tests employ a two-dimensional model of language function to measure the receptive and expressive modes of phonology, syntax, and semantics. The TOLD tests have been used as the criteria in many studies examining the criterion related validity of other tests because of their excellent construction and statistical characteristics.

Reliability coefficients for internal and test-retest reliability are quite high, as are the validity coefficients. The TOLD was meticulously standardized, and a great deal of statistical information is available in the test manuals.

A Statement on the Results of Standardized Testing

Therapists, diagnosticians, and other appraisal personnel know that it is often difficult to determine whether a child has a language disorder. The great advantage to standardized tests, for the experienced professional as well as for the novice, is that they are often excellent tools for identifying broad areas of language disability. When a test is well standardized and well normed, it can be used to answer the primary diagnostic question: Does the child have a problem? At the same time, the examiner must remember that in the moderately or severely delayed youngster, the characteristics of mental retardation, cultural deprivation, emotional disturbance, and language disorder can be misinterpreted. The examiner cannot always be sure what is the origin of the language deficiency. The child has a problem to be sure, but what is the nature of that problem? What is the most appropriate intervention? What are the skills to be taught? What are the reasonable expectations for progress? These are not questions answered by the kinds of standardized tests discussed above. To be fair, the test authors do not usually indicate that their tests supply such answers. More generally, authors caution the examiner against making such diagnostic or instructional inferences. Answers to many of the diagnostic questions surrounding an oral language disorder can be discovered only through informal criterion referenced assessment, involving observation and elicitation of speech samples in a variety of contexts, and diagnostic teaching. The remaining sections of this chapter deal with the analysis of language or speech samples and other testing techniques.

ANALYSIS OF LANGUAGE SAMPLES

The analysis of spontaneous speech samples was first advocated as an assessment tool by McCarthy (1930), who used the child's output as a basis for calculating the mean length of response and for analyzing structural complexity and vocabulary. Since that time many authors have used language samples in both structured and unstructured analyses of children's linguistic behavior. The analysis of language samples taken over a period of time in varying situations exemplifies the holistic or molar approach to assessment, although obviously, even the analysis of a language sample can be done in a highly specific, molecular fashion. It is important to remember that any language assessment should provide the examiner with the maximum amount of information about the total language functioning of the child and with data related to all aspects of the child's behavior as he or she interacts verbally and nonverbally with the environment.

The discussion of language samples is divided into four sections: (a) collecting and recording the language sample; (b) information on the appropriate size of the sample; (c) analysis of linguistic elements; and (d) interpretation of the mean length of utterance (MLU).

Collecting and Recording the Language Sample

Much of the information in this section is adapted from Miller (1981), who gives a detailed explanation of the use of language samples in assessment. Miller acknowledges that the most difficult part of collecting a free-speech sample, particularly with very young or developmentally delayed children, is initiating the therapist-child interaction and convincing the child that he or she wants to talk to the therapist. Some of the strategies advocated are as follows:

1. Do not say anything to the child after the first friendly greeting for the first five minutes of the interaction.

2. Engage in parallel play with the child for the first few minutes but do very little talking. It is suggested that this is a very effective technique with children who are functioning at a cognitive level below 30 months.

3. Engage in interactive play with the child but still do little talking. This works best with children at the 3 to 5 year cognitive level.

4. Finally, engage in interactive play without an introduction. Simply begin playing with the child and then invite discussion after the activity is finished.

Usually, one of these strategies will be effective in initiating the child's speech production; if not, the clinician may need to enlist the participation of the child's mother, a sibling, or another child. Children must feel comfortable, and it is important not to pressure them. With many recalcitrant children, the pressure applied on them to make them talk will result in even greater resistance, and the entire session may have to be abandoned.

Language samples can be collected in almost any setting in which the child is comfortable and, for very young children, should probably be collected in more than one setting to obtain a representative sample. It appears that older children (at least 3 to 4 years old) produce quite representative samples in the clinical setting. The clinician should keep in mind that the sample should be representative of the child's linguistic development and that certain settings tend to evoke only limited types of language production. For example, a sample taken in a classroom will often reflect classroom language behavior: questions during working time, declaratives during "show and tell."

The materials used during the collection of a language sample should be varied, and, if possible, some toys new to the child should be provided. Certain types of games are not productive because they tend to evoke rote types of utterances. For example, playing with Old Maid cards will usually result in very limited, routine productions; playing games will often evoke nothing more than, "It's your turn," or counting; and picture books can lead to routines such as "Once upon a time, there were three little pigs."

The language sample can be recorded in several manners: shorthand or speedwriting, audiotape recordings, or videotape recordings. The first, manual transcription, is not recommended unless recording equipment is unavailable or impractical to use. It is very difficult to write down everything that children say unless their verbal output is quite small. Probably the most effective method is using the audiotape recorder. The microphone may inhibit children initially, although not nearly as much as will a videotape recorder. Some time should be spent showing the equipment to the children and letting them get used to it. It is best to use multidirectional microphones placed about one to two feet from the child instead of lavalier or tie-tack microphones, which are restrictive to movement and are distracting.

Size of Language Sample

The examiner may take two approaches to the question of language sample size: either specify the number of utterances at 50, 100, or 200 or specify the amount of time that will be devoted to taking a sample. Miller (1981) recommends the latter approach because he feels it has greater flexibility. Using 30 minutes as the time for interaction, about 100 to 200 utterances can be produced by children functioning at 24 months of age and up. Children functioning below that level will produce fewer than 100 utterances, with children between 18 and 24 months producing about 30 to 60 utterances. Children who are functioning between 12 and 18 months will produce very few utterances, and samples should be supplemented either by the parents at home or by the clinician in ongoing sessions.

Even though a very good microphone may be used for recording every utterance the child produces and though transcription may be highly accurate, it is still important for the clinician to make contextual notes during the session. Bloom (1970) underlines the necessity for keeping a record of the child's activities while he or she is producing the utterances. Bloom's classic example of the utterance, "Mommy sock," could not have been interpreted without knowing that the child produced the utterance while holding the mother's sock, thus indicating a possessive relationship. If the child were holding his or her own sock, speaking with proper stress, and indicating *mother*, one could infer an agent-object request ("Mommy, put on my sock"). To further ensure that the context of the child's utterances is preserved, the transcription of the sample must include the examiner's utterances as well as the child's. Figure 5.1 shows the type of transcription format used by Miller (1981).

Analysis of Linguistic Elements

A number of authors have suggested various methods of analyzing linguistic elements in a language sample. Table 5.2, taken from Miller (1981), details some of those procedures, the linguistic elements that have been quantified, the size of the language sample that is advised, and the age range for which the procedure may be used. Table 5.3 is a listing of measures that rely on a language sample as the primary source of data for assessment.

Of the measures detailed in Table 5.2, probably the most useful is the mean length of utterance (MLU), a time-honored method of analyzing children's free speech. Mean length of utterance, as a quantifiable indicator of children's linguistic capacity, is better understood if Brown's (1973) description of the stages of language development is considered.

Counting Rules for the Mean Length of Utterance. In calculating and interpreting the MLU, one uses the guidelines provided by Chapman

FIGURE 5.1. Format for Transcription of Language Sample

Name of child: _____ Mark _____

Clinic number: _____

Chronological age: _____ 6–8 _____

Date of evaluation: _____

Examiners: _____

_____

Key:

C = Child   [ ] Gloss or Contextual notes

E = Examiner   ( ) Questionable Transcription

XXX = unintelligible   / / Phonetic Transcription

. . . = pause

Situation variables:

Time of day: _____ 1:30 p.m. _____

Setting: _____ Waisman Center (Rm. 145) _____

Materials used: Blocks, puzzle, PAT pictures, DLM pictures, puppet

Length of interaction: _____ 18 minutes _____

Participants/Type of interactions: 1. _____ Clinician-child _____

2. _____

3. _____

4. _____

Child MLU: _____ 2.50 _____

Number of utterances: _____ 53 _____

Number of intelligible utterances: _____ 52 _____

Sources of transcription: _____ Audiotape _____

Adult MLU:

1. Mother _____

2. Clinician _____

3. _____

FIGURE 5.1. continued

Pragmatics		Speaker	Utterance Number / Dialogue	Morpheme Count		Syntax	Semantics
Child	Adult			Child	Adult		
		C	1. Hey, that Cookie Monster stands.				
		E	1. That stands?				
			2. It sure does.				
			3. Mark, do you know who this is?				
		C	2. Oscar.				
		E	4. Is that Oscar?				
			5. Or is that the Cookie Monster?				
		C	3. Oscar.				
		E	6. Oscar!				
		C	4. Cookie Monster in there. [box]				
		E	7. The Cookie Monster's in there?				
			8. I thought this was the Cookie Monster?				
		C	[shakes head]				

From *Assessing Language Production in Children: Experimental Procedures* (p. 15) by J. Miller, 1981, Austin, TX: PRO-ED.

TABLE 5.2. General Analysis Procedures for Quantifying Transcripts of Free-Speech Samples

Content	Measure	Sample size advised	Range of use	Reference
Syntax	Mean Length of Utterance in Morphemes (MLU)	50 utterances or more	1.5–5 years	Brown, 1973; this volume
	Mean Length of Utterance in Words (MLR)	50 utterances	1.5–8 years	Templin, 1957
	Mean Length of T-unit or Communication Unit (MLTR)	30 T-units	5–18 years	Loban, 1976
	Frequency distribution—Number of utterances by length	50 utterances[a]	1.5–18 years	This volume
	Frequency distribution—Number of utterances by structural type	50 utterances[a]	1.5–18 years	This volume
	Developmental Sentence Score (DSS)	50 utterances or more	3–7 years	Lee, 1974
	Length-Complexity Index (LCI)	15–50 utterances	4–8 years	Shriner, 1967, 1969; Miner, 1969; Barlow and Miner, 1969; Griffith and Miner, 1969
Semantics	Type-Token Ratio–Vocabularity Diversity	50 utterances or more	3–8 years	Templin, 1957

TABLE 5.2. continued

Phonology	Percent intelligible, partially intelligible, and unintelligible utterances	1–18 years	50 utterances[a]	
Communicative interaction	Frequency distribution of number of utterances per speaking turn for each speaker, Mom's MLU–Child's MLU ratio, number of Mom's utterances to number of Child's utterances	1–18 years 1.5–5 years 2–18 years	50 utterances[a] 50 utterances[a] 50 utterances[a] 50 utterances[a]	Retherford, Schwartz, and Chapman, in press Retherford, Schwartz, and Chapman, in press

[a]Number of utterances may vary for these analysis procedures. Fifty utterances is considered a minimum target providing enough data for interpretation. Note that as sample size increases, representativeness is likely to increase.

From *Assessing Language Production in Children: Experimental Procedures* (p. 23) by J. Miller, 1981, Austin, TX: PRO-ED. Reprinted by permission.

TABLE 5.3. Measures of Spontaneous Language Analysis Procedures

Measure	Author
Mean length of utterance (MLU)	McCarthy (1970)
Length-complexity index	Miner (1969)
Developmental sentence types (DST)	Lee (1966)
Linguistic analysis of speech samples (LASS)	Engler, Hannah, & Lonehurst (1973)
Co-occurring and restricted structure procedure (CORS)	Muma (1973)
Developmental sentence scoring (DSS)	Lee (1974)
Tyack and Gottsleben's language analysis system	Tyack & Gottsleben (1974)
Grammatical analysis of language disability	Crystal, Fletcher, & Garman (1976)
Trantham and Pederson's modified DSS	Trantham & Pederson (1976)
Case relation analysis	Scroggs (1977)
Language sample analysis	Bloom & Lahey (1978)
Assigning structural stage (ASS)	Miller (1981)

From "Assessment of Language Disorders: Linguistic and Cognitive Functions" by D. Geffner, 1981, *Topics in Language Disorders, I*, pp. 1–10. Reprinted by permission of Aspen Publishers.

(in Miller, 1981), who says that the first consecutive 50 intelligible morphemes in the sample are counted. The reader should recall that a morpheme is a minimal meaningful unit of language; for example, *dogs* consists of two morphemes, *dog* and the plural -*s*. The counting rules given below are adapted from Brown (1973) and Chapman.

1. *Repetitions.* If stuttering occurs it should be noted, but the word is counted only once. If a word is repeated for emphasis, it should be counted each time.

2. *Fillers.* Utterances such as *mm* or *uh* are not counted; actual words, even though used as fillers, such as *yeah* or *no*, are counted.

3. *Compound words, proper names, and reduplications.* Each is counted as a single word, even though it may consist of two utterances, such as *tick-tock*, *John Brown*, or *seesaw*.

4. *Irregular past tense.* Verbs in the irregular past tense, such as *did, went, saw,* and so on, are counted as single morphemes because there is no evidence that children view them as anything separate from the present tense.

5. *Diminutives.* All count as one word because diminutives are standard forms for children.

6. *Auxiliaries and concatenations.* All are counted as separate, single words. Concatenations, such as *gonna, hafta,* and so on, are standard forms for children and are only representations for *going to, have to,* and so on. All inflections, such as regular past *-ed,* progressive *-ing,* possessive *-e,* plural *-s,* and third person singular *-s,* are counted as separate morphemes.

Checking the Validity of the Mean Length of Utterance.

Transcripts of samples should be checked to investigate their representativeness of the MLU. Several characteristics can affect the MLU by either inflating or deflating it. If more than 20% of the child's utterances are imitations of the previous speaker, the MLU may be spuriously high. To check this, one may calculate separate MLUs for the imitations and for the spontaneous utterances.

If self-repetitions occur frequently in the sample, the MLU may be higher than warranted. Brown (1973) included these utterances, but Bloom (1973) excluded them. One way to check the validity of the MLU is to calculate it with and without the self-repetitions similar to the method suggested for checking on imitations. A high proportion of questions-answers in the sample will tend to reduce spontaneous speech and may deflate the child's MLU. In collecting the sample, try to keep the questioning technique at a minimum, or the sample may consist of a great many *Yes, No,* and *Here* responses.

Some children's language samples may be marked by a high proportion of what are termed *routines* (i.e., nursery rhymes, commercial jingles, alphabets, counting, etc.). The MLU may be upwardly biased by the inclusion of these utterances. Again, the procedure recommended by Brown is to calculate the MLU with and without the routines. It is not uncommon for language samples reflecting MLUs of 4.0 to 5.0 or higher to contain frequent instances of sentence conjunction. Older children commonly use run-on sentences, continually beginning a new sentence with "And then." Chapman (in Miller, 1981) recommends that the MLU not be computed for such children but that other utterance measures be used that are better designed to assess the increasing grammatical sophistication of the child. One of the measures that might be used is the T-unit or communication unit count described by

Loban (1976), which treats each clause headed by *and* as a single unit of communication.

To compute the MLU, first count the total number of morphemes produced and then divide by the total number of utterances counted, as shown in the formula below:

$$\text{MLU} = \frac{\text{Number of Morphemes}}{\text{Number of Utterances}} \quad \text{or} \quad \text{MLU} = \frac{M}{U}$$

Recall that an utterance is similar to a sentence but is not the same as what we consider an adult sentence. Utterances will have to be marked off by using the criterion of terminal intonation contour—falling intonation for declarative utterance, rising for interrogative.

Interpretation of the Mean Length of Utterance

The MLU is a valuable index only if it represents the child's normal discourse. Some suggestions were given above as to ways that representativeness can be investigated. Some other factors that can affect the MLU are the child's familiarity with the examiner, the setting itself, the topic of discourse, the child's present health and mood, and so on. The MLU is a general indicator of structural language development and can be reliably interpreted only when it falls between 1.01 and 4.49 morphemes. Two methods of interpretation of the MLU are structural stages and distributional analysis.

Stages of Structural Development. The MLU is interpreted in terms of Brown's stages I through V. Each stage, as discussed in Chapter 4, is associated with distinct developmental achievements and defines the predictable structures in the child's expressive language. An MLU of 2.80 places the child at Stage III, while an MLU of 4.30 reflects Stage V development. As may be seen in Table 4.8, the former MLU gives a child a predicted chronological age of 33.2 months and the latter an age of 45.0 months. By the same token, the examiner is able to predict the MLU and MLU ranges within one standard deviation for children 18 to 60 months of age by using Miller's (1981) data shown in Table 5.4. Miller notes that the data shown in tables 4.8 and 5.4 should not be considered exhaustively normative, because the sample upon which they are based was a relatively small sample of middle-class children from Madison, Wisconsin. Although the data may not be generalized to all populations of young children, they do give the examiner a starting point for estimating MLU or predicting chronological age.

Distributional Analysis. Another way of analyzing the MLU and the language sample as a whole is to reorganize the transcript of the sample

TABLE 5.4. Predicted MLUs and MLU Ranges Within One Standard Deviation of Predicted Mean for Each Age Group

Age ±1 Month	Predicted MLU[a]	Predicted SD[b]	Predicted MLU ±1 SD (middle 68%)
18	1.31	0.325	0.99–1.64
21	1.62	0.386	1.23–2.01
24	1.92	0.448	1.47–2.37
30	2.54	0.571	1.97–3.11
33	2.85	0.633	2.22–3.48
36	3.16	0.694	2.47–3.85
39	3.47	0.756	2.71–4.23
42	3.78	0.817	2.96–4.60
45	4.09	0.879	3.21–4.97
48	4.40	0.940	3.46–5.34
51	4.71	1.002	3.71–5.71
54	5.02	1.064	3.96–6.08
57	5.32	1.125	4.20–6.45
60	5.63	1.187	4.44–6.82

[a]MLU is predicted from the equation MLU $= -0.548 + 0.103$ (age).
[a]SD is predicted from the equation $SD_{MLU} = -0.0446 + 0.0205$ (age).

From *Assessing Language Production in Children: Experimental Procedures* (p. 27) by J. Miller, 1981, Austin, TX: PRO-ED.

by specific utterance characteristics. Some of the segments that Chapman (in Miller, 1981) recommends are (a) sentence length, (b) syntactic structures, and (c) number of utterances per speaking turn. If one reorganizes the transcript by sentence length, the MLU will be clarified by quantifying the number of utterances of each length that were produced. There are variations around the mean to be expected, but a number of spuriously long sentences may seriously inflate the MLU, and the examiner should consider such MLUs invalid.

A distributional analysis by syntactic structures provides the examiner with data regarding the structural variety in the child's language production. One favored technique is known as Assigning Structural State (ASS), but any type of sample segmentation that reveals the variety and number of syntactic structures used by the child would be acceptable. Some children may generate enough words and utterances to obtain a fairly high MLU, but an analysis of their syntactic structures may reveal a significant degree of poverty in the variety of structures produced.

The third distributional analysis that the examiner could use requires segmenting the language sample into the number of utterances produced by the child in each of his or her turns to speak. This involves analysis on a more pragmatic level of language. The number of the utterances produced by both the child and the examiner is segmented; the relationship between the two reflects the distribution of talking for each and the child's turn-taking ability in discourse. It may also indicate how much the examiner (or other adult) allowed the child to talk.

Although the language sample can be analyzed in a number of ways not described here (see Miller, 1981), the procedures given above are the usual techniques discussed by most authors for analyzing free-speech samples of children.

USING INFORMAL ASSESSMENT PROCEDURES

Standardized or nonstandardized (informal) approaches to language assessment are chosen according to the reason for assessment. The first question to be asked is why a child is being evaluated. Is information needed to decide whether the child's language is deviant? If so, quantitative, normed, standardized approaches are valuable in supplying the answer. If, however, the question is related to the direction that intervention should take, the informal approaches are beneficial in generating courses of therapy. The standardized measures, such as those discussed in the previous section, can resolve the question of deviance through comparison with norms but can provide little information about the parameters of the problem or the type of therapy needed. Similarly, because of the lack of normative data, informal tasks give little information regarding the question of deviance.

Some of the informal assessment procedures discussed in this section yield a type of age-related information, but the strength of the procedures lies in their flexibility and in their usefulness for designing an intervention program. The clinician must decide what the assessment questions are and then use the best measures to resolve those questions.

In this section, informal assessment procedures are described for the following areas of the oral language evaluation: assessment of language comprehension, assessment of language production, and assessment of pragmatics. All of the procedures found in this section are informal because they lack both standardization of administration and normative data. The examiner should feel free to adapt, extend, or in any other way modify the assessment procedures, suggested materials, and/or number of items.

Assessment of Language Comprehension

Language comprehension is often assessed before language production because of the almost universally accepted dictum that reception precedes expression. Therefore, most clinicians feel that the investigation of the child's receptive or comprehension abilities gives significant clues as to what areas of production can and should be explored.

If the child is not "hard to assess," it is common practice to administer standardized tests, such as those described in a previous section. In this section, we will discuss other procedures that can be followed to assess in depth the child's speech sound discrimination, understanding of vocabulary, and comprehension of syntactic/semantic elements.

Speech Sound Discrimination. According to Aungst and Frick (1964), at least four types of auditory discrimination tasks are important for speech production: (a) matching two externally produced sounds, (b) matching an external sound to one produced by the child, (c) matching an external speech sound to an internal criterion, and (d) matching an internally produced sound with an internal criterion. The tasks are arranged in order of increasing difficulty. The first type of discrimination is probably the easiest, and often children with severe articulatory deficiencies can perform well on such a task. Matching two externally produced sounds is the paradigm followed by Wepman (1958) in the *Auditory Discrimination Test* and by most other authors of speech sound discrimination tests.

The second task that the clinician may ask the child to perform is matching an external speech sound to a sound produced by the child. The clinician produces the speech sound, and the child imitates it. Then the child is asked to determine whether the two sounds are the same or different. The sounds used should be those that the child is misarticulating. If the child is unable to tell whether his or her imitation matches the sound produced by the clinician, it will be difficult for correction to take place through imitation.

The next task is for the child to determine whether two sounds produced in syllables and words are correct or incorrect. To monitor and evaluate the clinician's speech sound production, the child must have an internal auditory image of the correct production to compare with what is heard. For some children, this task may be fairly easy, because it does not require that they monitor their own speech.

In the last type of discrimination task, the child produces the targeted sound and then judges whether the production was accurate. Successful performance on this task indicates that the child is able to monitor his or her own speech; failure would suggest that the child is unable to listen to and evaluate his or her speech production.

Vocabulary. Formal tests of vocabulary comprehension, such as those mentioned previously, reveal whether the child's understanding of single words is adequate for his or her age. If the test results indicate that the child's understanding of words is significantly impaired, the clinician should endeavor to discover whether this is a generalized deficit or whether the child's lack of comprehension is restricted to certain classes or categories of words. The classes of words should be both linguistic and cognitive. The following abbreviated chart (Table 5.5) contains a number of such classes of words for which the clinician can devise a picture test. For older children, the number of classes could be extended, and the accompanying words could be more difficult.

The pictures depicting the various words should be presented in the same fashion as the picture plates for the *Peabody Picture Vocabulary Test* (Dunn, 1981). At least four pictures should be presented to the child in random order. The child is asked to point to the picture named, and the clinician determines whether the child is responding incorrectly to certain classes of words or to a large number of unspecified words.

If possible, the clinician should also compare the child's vocabulary comprehension with his or her vocabulary production as expressed in ongoing language samples. In the usual course of language development, children's comprehension vocabularies far outstrip their expressive vocabularies in both numbers of words and complexity. If this is not the case, the clinician must examine or arrange for the evaluation of the child's intellectual and emotional status. That is not to say that the child may not have a language disorder, but it is an indicator that the child might be mentally retarded or emotionally disturbed rather than, or in addition to, being language disordered. The clinician must also consider the possibility of a hearing loss, but it should go without saying that any child being referred for oral language assessment should first be given a thorough audiological examination.

Syntax/Semantics. No attempt will be made to separate the components of syntax and semantics in the assessment of oral language comprehension; the two are inextricably interwoven. As only one example of this correlation between the two, consider the plural noun and its phonological, syntactic, and semantic properties. An analysis of the plurality of the words *cat* and *dog* follows:

1. *Phonological elements:* The plural of *cat* is formed by adding the phoneme /s/, while the plural of *dog* requires the addition of the phoneme /z/.

2. *Syntactic elements:* The plurals of both *cat* and *dog* are characterized by the addition of only the appropriate morpheme, not specifying which phoneme, and are shown schematically by *cat* + /-s/ or *dog* + /-s/.

3. *Semantic elements:* No distinction is made between the plural of *cat* and *dog*. The criterion is that the child have the concept of plurality or "more than one." As the reader can easily see, asking the child to identify a plural requires at least syntactic and semantic knowledge from the child; asking him or her to produce a plural also requires phonological knowledge.

Bellugi-Klima (1971) suggests a variety of ways in which the clinician can assess syntactic structures that are known to children. The procedures

---

TABLE 5.5. A List of Example Classes and Words to be Used in Assessing Vocabulary Comprehension

CLASSES			
Cognitive[1]	**Words[2]**	**Linguistic[3]**	**Words[2]**
Animals	Cat	Nouns	Box
	Dog		Car
	Rabbit		Train
Furniture	Bed	Action Verbs	Running
	Chair		Catch
	Sofa		Shove
Toys	Doll	Pronouns	She
	Teddy Bear		It
	Choo-choo		Our
People	Man	Prepositions	On
	Woman		Beneath
	Lady		Over
Family	Mother	Adjectives	Pretty
	Father		Bad
	Sister		Big
Occupations	Teacher	Adverbs	Quietly
	Policeman		Quickly
	Farmer		Very
Geographical Features	Hill		
	Mountain		
	Valley		

[1]Can be extended upwards developmentally through adding more abstract classes
[2]Can be extended by using more difficult vocabulary
[3]Can be extended by adding more complex linguistic classes

require that situational clues be eliminated from the presentation of the tasks, that the child know the vocabulary being presented, that the objects used in assessment be familiar to the child, and that the construction of the task require an understanding of the syntax of the sentences presented rather than some other feature. Bellugi-Klima's general approach entails providing the child with a number of familiar objects, producing a sentence, and asking the child to act out the meaning of the sentence. As an example, the passive construction can be tested by giving the child a boy and a girl doll, presenting two sentences that differ only in the syntax, and having the child demonstrate the meaning of the sentences (e.g., "The boy is pushed by the girl" and "The girl is pushed by the boy") by manipulating the dolls. It is possible to assess a number of syntactic structures in this fashion. The following tasks are some of those recommended by Bellugi-Klima.

Active sentences. In the majority of English sentences, the first noun is the subject (or actor), and the noun following the verb is the object or recipient of the action. The first question to be asked in the assessment of syntax is, "Given a verb, does the child know that the first noun is the actor and the second noun is the object?" Test as follows:

• Place a number of small objects before the child.

• Determine that the child knows what the objects are and knows the names of each.

• Determine that the child knows the meaning of the verbs that will be presented.

• Present two sentences that differ only in the subject-object relationship.

• Ask the child to demonstrate the meaning of the sentence by manipulating the objects.

Examples:

Show me: The boy feeds the girl.
Show me: The girl feeds the boy.

The general testing instructions will not be repeated for each of the syntactic structures that are discussed in this section, but the clinician should be sure to follow the procedures for all tasks.

Singular/plural noun. The inflection on the plural noun is one of the earliest inflections to appear in children's language development. In some cases the plural inflection on the noun is redundant, as there are other clues in the sentences. For example, the use of a plural copula *are*, plural demonstratives *these* and *those*, a plural such as *some*, and plural adjectives like *two* all signal plurality. Such words should be avoided in presenting assessment tasks; the sentences used should contain no other cues to plurality beyond the plural inflection on the noun.

Examples:

Give me the ball.
Give me the balls.

Give me the flower.
Give me the flowers.

Give me the cat.
Give me the cats.

Possessive. The possessive inflection of nouns occurs after the plural inflection, even though noun plus noun constructions (e.g., "Mommy dress") do appear fairly early in development. In assessing possessives, test the child's understanding of the fact that two nouns occur, the first being a modification of the second. In such cases, it is the second noun that is the head noun of the noun phrase. Instead of saying, "the girl's dress," one could paraphrase the sentence to say, "The dress that belongs to the girl." To assess the possessive, the clinician can set up minimal pairs as follows:

Examples:

Show me the girl's mommy.
Show me the mommy's girl.

Show me the car's driver.
Show me the driver's car.

Show me the captain's ship.
Show me the ship's captain.

Negative/affirmative statements. In the early stages of language development, it is not clear whether children are able to process negation when it is embedded in a sentence and attached to the auxiliary verb. Very often, in fact, the aspect of negation is contracted with the auxiliary, is unstressed, and is not very noticeable. It is very easy, and often likely, for the young child simply to overlook the addition of the phonemic element in a contraction such as *can't*.

Examples:

Show me: The doll can close her eyes.
Show me: The doll can't close her eyes.

Show me: The doll is standing.
Show me: The doll is not standing.
Show me: The doll isn't standing.

Show me: The dog has a bone.
Show me: The dog doesn't have a bone.

Negative affirmative questions: In this task, which is similar to the previous one, the child is presented with *wh-* questions rather than statements.

Examples:

What can you eat?
What can't you eat?

What can the girl wear?
What can't the girl wear?

What do you play with?
What don't you play with?

Singular/plural with noun and verb inflections: Even though the noun inflection for plurality appears early in language development, the verb inflection for third person singular appears much later. In singular and plural sentences in the third person such as, "The dog barks," and, "The dogs bark," the inflection occurs on the verb for the singular and on the noun for the plural.

Examples:

(Two boy dolls lying down. Demonstrate *walking*.)

Show me: The boy walks.
Show me: The boys walk.

(Two toy dogs. Demonstrate *jumping*.)

Show me: The dog jumps.
Show me: The dogs jump.

Adjectival modification. In a noun phrase, an adjective can be used to modify or alter the meaning of the head noun in the noun phrase. This applies to only the head noun of the phrase in which the adjective appears. So, in the sentence, "The little girl hit the boy," the adjective *little* applies only to the girl and provides no information about the object or *boy*. This seems quite simple, but often children in the middle stage of language development confuse the modification issue if the subject and the object of a sentence both are modified by adjectives.

Examples:

Show me: The little girl has a big doll.
Show me: The big girl has a little doll.

Put the round peg in the square hole.
Put the square peg in the round hole.

Show me the red dress with buttons.
Show me the dress with red buttons.

Negative affix. In the previous tasks, negation was dealt with on the level of sentence negation. Another type of negation is communicated through the use of affixes and is an inflection of only the word to which the affix is attached. Some such affixes that are negative are *un-*, *mis-* and *dis-*. The most familiar and earliest negative affix to appear is *un-* as in *untied.* In assessing negative affix, the clinician must determine whether the child learned words such as *tied* and *untied* as separate vocabulary items instead of learning the use of the affix to denote negation.

Examples:

Show me: The blocks are piled.
Show me: The blocks are unpiled.
Show me: The blocks are not piled.

Show me: The boxes are opened.
Show me: The boxes are not opened.
Show me: The boxes are unopened.

Reflexivization. Reflexives such as, "I looked at myself in the mirror," appear relatively late in language development. An earlier form that often appears is the object case pronoun instead of the reflexive pronoun in sentences like, "I saw me."

Examples:

Show me: Mommy washed her.
Show me: Mommy washed herself.

Show me: Billy hit him.
Show me: Billy hit himself.

Show me: The cat licked her.
Show me: The cat licked herself.

Comparatives. Another late appearing construction is the comparative, no doubt making its appearance only after the child has internalized the concept of comparison. As with the negative affix, the clinician must take care that some comparative words such as *more* and *less* have not been learned as separate vocabularly items that are synonymous with *big* and *little*. It would probably be advisable to avoid testing such words and to concentrate on comparative adjectives with -*er* suffixes.

Examples:

Give me a red stick shorter than a blue stick.
Give me a red stick longer than a blue stick.

Give me a short stick wider than a long stick.
Give me a short stick narrower than a long stick.

Show me the big box.
Show me the bigger box.

Passives. Passive sentences are those in which the normal word order of subject-verb-object is reversed. Thus, "The boy hit the girl," becomes, "The girl is hit by the boy." The two sentences are equivalent in meaning even with the reversal. The passive is another late appearing construction in language development and is often not fully comprehended until the child is about 4 years old. Younger children will often react to passive sentences as if they were active sentences, ignoring everything but the supposed subject-verb-object. In the sentence above, a child might focus upon, "The girl (is) hit (by) the boy," and interpret the sentence as if the words in parentheses were not present.

Examples:

Show me: The cat is chased by the dog.
Show me: The dog is chased by the cat.

Show me: The girl is washed by the boy.
Show me: The boy is washed by the girl.

Self-embedded sentences. One of the most interesting things about languages is that sentences can be of almost infinite length. One way that this is achieved is by "opening" the sentence and adding additional sentences of constituents to it. Consider the sentence, "The woman drove the car." One can insert another sentence, "The woman has a large dog," and produce the finished sentence, "The woman who has a large dog drove the car." In addition, one can insert the sentence, "The dog chased the cat," and produce, "The woman who has a large dog that chased the cat drove the car." There is no need to belabor the point, but this type of embedding can go on forever, as in the familiar nursery rhyme, "This is the House That Jack Built."

Examples:

(Use dolls and demonstrate *hitting* and *falling.*)

Show me: The boy that the girl hit fell down.
Show me: The girl that the boy hit fell down.

Show me: The cat that the dog chased jumped.
Show me: The dog that the cat chased jumped.

Show me: The cat that chased the dog jumped.
Show me: The dog that chased the cat jumped.

Assessment of Language Production

In this section assessment techniques and procedures are discussed for the evaluation of (a) the oral speech mechanism, (b) articulatory proficiency, (c) syntax, and (d) semantics. Although the interrelatedness of comprehension and production and of syntax and semantics should be reemphasized, for purposes of discussing assessment, it is necessary to separate and dichotomize what are highly integrated aspects of language.

Assessment of the Oral Speech Mechanism. Assessment of the speech mechanism should encompass the examination of structure and function. All too often speech pathologists perform a speech mechanism examination in a ritualistic, perfunctory manner simply because they were taught in their training programs that such an examination is always done. However, if the clinician does not know the range of normalcy in oral anatomy and physiology, he or she can gain nothing from looking in children's mouths or asking them to say "puh-tuh-kuh" as fast as they can.

The examination should be systematic and rapid, which requires a considerable amount of practice. The clinician should use a process such as that outlined in this section to provide systematization and should take every opportunity to perfect his or her technique and observational skills. The proposed process, offered ·in a checklist format (Figure 5.2), is adapted from Sanders (1972) and provides for examination of both the structure of the speech mechanism and the function of the speech organs.

The results of the oral speech mechanism examination should provide the clinician with information related to the adequacy of the child's speech mechanism for the production of speech. In such an examination we do not usually find dramatic deviations of the oral structures that can be conclusively related to specific speech deviations, because most people are able to compensate for a number of structural irregularities. As a result we find that if the speaker can produce a sound correctly in some context, particularly in connected speech, the observed structural irregularities that he or she may have cannot be highly significant. However, we cannot overlook the

FIGURE 5.2. A Checklist for the Peripheral Speech Mechanism Examination

I. *The Speech Mechanism at Rest and in Passive Motion*

  A. General Body Position

    1. Sitting Balance

      _____ Good, with head erect

      _____ Poor (see below)

         _____ Chest "collapsed"

         _____ Head and shoulders forward

         _____ Flattened upper rib cage

         _____ Must be held in position by assistive devices

    2. Head Balance

      _____ Good

      _____ Poor (see below)

         _____ Involuntary movements; tremors

         _____ Turning to one side

         _____ Unable to lift in supine or prone position

         _____ Total body extensor tonus in supine position

         _____ Total body flexor tonus in prone position

    3. Tonic Neck Reflex

      _____ Absent

      _____ Present

  B. General Configuration and Muscular Control

    1. Facial Symmetry

      _____ Normal

      _____ Abnormal (see below)

         _____ Facial muscles droop on one side (specify) _____

         _____ One eye droops (specify) _____

         _____ Facial musculature pulled to one side (specify) _____

         _____ Absence of naso-labial line on one side (specify) _____

         _____ Greater retraction of one side of mouth (specify) _____

         _____ Mandible pulls to one side (specify) _____

FIGURE 5.2. continued

2. Feature Configuration

_____ Normal

_____ Abnormal (see below)

_____ Unusual slant of palpebral fissures of the eye

_____ Round flabby facies

_____ Protruding lips

_____ Rigid smile

_____ Protruded, retruded, or underdeveloped mandible (check)

_____ Scarred upper lip

3. Mouth

_____ Normal

_____ Abnormal (see below)

_____ Open with tongue protruding

_____ Drooling

_____ Mouth breathing

4. Facial Musculature

_____ Normal

_____ Abnormal (see below)

_____ Involuntary movement (specify)_____

_____ Primitive or infantile lip or tongue reflexes

_____ Lip and tongue movement toward the side of the mouth, if stroked

_____ Reflexive sucking

_____ Reflexive pursing of the mouth when lips are tapped

_____ Reflexive biting

5. Thoracic and Abdominal Musculature

_____ Normal

_____ Abnormal (see below)

_____ Movement of the upper thoracic area during breathing

_____ Evidence of opposition breathing

_____ Resting breathing rate (specify) _____

_____ Irregular breathing pattern

_____ Stridorous noises during breathing

FIGURE 5.2. continued

II. *Voluntary Muscle Control During Speech*

    A. Coordination of the Articulators During Speech

        1. Range and Motion of Articulation Muscles

            _____ Adequate

            _____ Poor (see below)

            _____ Cannot move and shape articulators for phonemes that are

                _____ labial

                _____ labial-dental

                _____ lingua-dental

                _____ lingua-alveolar

                _____ lingua-palatal

                _____ nasal

                _____ glottal

        2. Muscles of Respiration, Phonation, and Velopharyngeal Closure

            _____ Good

            _____ Poor (see below)

                _____ Difficulty initiating phonation during exhalation

                _____ Jaw thrust when initiating phonation

                _____ Nasal emission of air during speech

                _____ Inadequate velopharyngeal closure for plosive and fricative consonants

                _____ General incoordination of all muscles during speech

    B. Phonation and Resonance

        1. Pitch

            _____ Good

            _____ Poor (see below)

                _____ Too high

                _____ Too low

                _____ Pitch breaks

        2. Intensity

            _____ Good

            _____ Poor (specify) _____

        3. Quality

            _____ Good

FIGURE 5.2. continued

_____ Poor (see below)

     _____ Hoarse

     _____ Breathy

     _____ Nasal

     _____ Denasal

     _____ Glottal "fry"

     _____ Diplophonia

     _____ Other (specify) _____

III. _Voluntary Muscle Control During Nonspeech Activities_

  A. Mandible

     _____ Good

     _____ Poor (see below)

        _____ Cannot open and close easily on cue

        _____ Temporamandibular facet slip

        _____ Cannot click teeth together at the rate of two times per second

  B. Lips

     _____ Good

     _____ Poor (see below)

        _____ Cannot purse and retract lips easily on cue

        _____ Cannot purse and retract at the rate of two times per second

        _____ Diminished mobility of upper lip due to scarring or tightness

        _____ Cannot show teeth by raising upper lip and depressing lower lip

  C. Tongue

     _____ Good

     _____ Poor (see below)

        _____ Cannot protrude and retract easily on cue

        _____ Cannot elevate and depress to reach just beyond vermilion border of lips

        _____ Cannot lateralize smoothly

        _____ Cannot lateralize at the rate of two cycles per second

        _____ Involuntary movements when protruded for 3 to 4 seconds

FIGURE 5.2. continued

_____ "Wave-like" movements

_____ Deviation to one side during protrusion (specify) _____

_____ Cannot point the tip

_____ Cannot alternately narrow and flatten the blade

_____ Cannot touch specific locations on the lips when stimulated

_____ Thrust between the teeth during swallowing

_____ Does not fit well in oral cavity (specify) _____

D. Dental Occlusion

_____ Good

_____ Poor (see below)

    _____ Obvious malocclusion

    _____ Space between incisors when molars are occluded

    _____ Maxillary arch lies within mandibular arch

    _____ Missing, extra, misplaced, or tilted teeth (specify) _____

E. Palate

_____ Good

_____ Poor (see below)

    _____ High and vaulted or low and flattened (check)

    _____ Evidence of a repaired or unrepaired cleft

    _____ Inadequate movement of palate and posterior pillars during production of /a/

    _____ Inadequate oral air pressure using an oral manometer

    _____ Inadequate fit of a speech appliance

F. Larynx and Muscles of Respiration

_____ Good

_____ Poor (see below)

    _____ Cannot sustain phonation for 10–15 seconds

    _____ Undue tension in neck muscles during phonation

    _____ Undue elevation of thyroid cartilage during phonation

    _____ Phonation during inhalation

In most cases the oral speech mechanism examination may be conducted as shown above. However, with some very young, severely mentally retarded, or severely neuromuscularly involved children, the examination may have to be conducted on a vegetative or emotional level. The following points should be checked:

FIGURE 5.2. continued

I. Vegetative Level

  A. Biting, Chewing, and Swallowing

    _____ Adequate

    _____ Poor (see below)

        _____ Cannot open mouth to receive food

        _____ Does not use teeth to bite and chew

        _____ Accomplishes mastication by forward protrusion and elevation of tongue against palate

        _____ Cannot lateralize tongue to move food to chewing edge of teeth

        _____ Cannot use tongue to retrieve food from lip corners

        _____ Tongue thrust in swallowing

        _____ Tips head back to swallow

        _____ Chokes easily on soft foods

  B. Drinking

    _____ Adequate

    _____ Poor (see below)

        _____ Tips head back to swallow when drinking from cup

        _____ Liquid escapes from nose

        _____ Cannot hold lips around a straw

        _____ Cannot develop negative pressure to drink from straw

  C. Range of Motion in Eating

    _____ Adequate

    _____ Poor (see below)

        _____ Cannot feel bits of cracker or peanut butter placed on the lip or between the teeth and lips and retrieve them with the tongue

        _____ Cannot elevate tongue to retrieve bits of food placed behind the upper teeth or on the palate

        _____ Cannot protrude, point, or narrow tongue to lick lollipop held in front of mouth

II. Emotional Level

    _____ Adequate (in crying, laughing, smiling, showing fear or anger, etc.)

    _____ Poor (see below)

        _____ Does not retract lips in smiling

        _____ Does not open mouth to laugh

FIGURE 5.2. continued

_____ Does not cup or thin the tongue

_____ Does not elevate the soft palate

_____ Does not sustain phonation

_____ Other (from previous checklist items) _____

_____

_____

Adapted, with permission, from _Procedure Guides for Evaluation of Speech and Language Disorders in Children_, 4th ed., by Lois Joan Sanders, 1979, Danville, IL: Interstate.

possibility that some inadequacy of the oral mechanism may account for, or contribute to, the speaker's inability to articulate proficiently. The clinician can teach some children with high, arched palates who have /r/ distortions to produce the /r/ correctly by artificially lowering the palate height (using chewing gum) and then, through a series of approximations, teaching the child to make the /r/ when the palate is allowed to return to its usual height by using less gum to occlude the space between the tongue and the palate.

Assessment of Speech Sound Production. To plan an articulation therapy program, as in other areas of language therapy, it is not enough simply to know that the child has an articulation error. The clinician must be concerned with four basic areas:

- What sounds are produced incorrectly? What are the characteristics of the misarticulations? These points are discussed in the following section (Phonemic Analysis) and are the points covered by most articulation tests.

- How does the child misarticulate? This question is related to the oral speech mechanism examination, because it centers around the specific muscle patterns that produce the misarticulations.

- What is the variability of the misarticulation? Under what acoustic or contextual conditions does the misarticulation vary?

- Why does the child misarticulate? Can any related deficiencies be identified, such as poor speech sound discrimination, structural anomalies, inadequate neuromuscular abilities, or inappropriate linguistic models? Answers to all of these questions may not be possible, but because children with so-called "functional" articulation problems often have syntactic and semantic disorders as well, it is worthwhile to investigate the full parameters of what may look like a simple speech problem.

Phonemic analysis. Almost any standard articulation test will suffice to answer the first diagnostic question, "What sounds are misarticulated and what are the characteristics of the misarticulation?" The results of such a test will reveal (a) which sounds are in error, (b) what type of misarticulations are present (omissions, substitutions, or distortions), (c) where the errors occur (in initial, medial, or final position), and (d) in some tests, where the place of articulation is (e.g., labial, dental, alveolar). Some clinicians have been taught to make their own articulation tests, but with the number of good instruments on the market, there seems little benefit to be gained from such a time-consuming and tedious task. No doubt it is a useful exercise to make beginning students more aware of phonemes and to enhance their own listening skills, but because phonemic analysis is so well-covered by commercial tests, examiner-constructed tests will not be further discussed.

Kinetic analysis. Van Riper (1963) describes a way to assess articulation disorders that he terms *kinetic analysis.* This procedure investigates what specifically a child is doing to produce the phonemes in a defective manner. To conduct such an analysis, the clinician must draw on Powers' (1957) description of the necessary motor requirements for accurate sound production. She suggests that there must be precision of movement in terms of placement of structures, direction of movements, amount of contact surface, and the shape of the contact between structures. Articulatory movements must also be made at the appropriate speed, they must be made with enough energy or pressure, and there must be synergy of the sequential movements necessary for connected speech.

To conduct the kinetic analysis, three methods may be employed. First, the clinician can ask the child to tell what he or she is doing. This is probably the least fruitful approach, because even adult clients can seldom describe how they are producing a given sound. As children and adults progress in therapy, they are better able to describe phonemic production, but they still have difficulty describing anything more complex than whether the tip of the tongue is elevated. The second method is to watch what the child is doing. For example, does the tongue protrude between the incisors when the /s/ or /z/ is produced? Does the mandible shift to one side when sibilants are uttered? If either of these two phenomena are observed, it is likely that a major reason for a central or lateral lisp has been discovered, and a central focus for therapy has been established. If the reader has any doubt on this score, he or she should try producing the word *some* with the tongue protruding between the central incisors during the production of the initial /s/. The result will be a classic central lisp—*thum* instead of *some.* The third method of kinetic analysis is probably the best. Taking advantage of their trained ears and knowledge of motor phonetics, clinicians can attempt to duplicate in their own production what the child is doing. By listening carefully and experimenting with the placement of the articulators, the clinician can learn to make the child's error, providing a basis for altering the child's production in an objective, systematic fashion.

The kinetic analysis may reveal obvious motor disorders; indeed, such an analysis could be incorporated into the initial stages of the oral speech mechanism examination. Regardless, the clinician must learn as much as possible about motor phonetics to understand the motor elements of phonemic production. Only through such knowledge will the clinician become an accurate observer or imitator of the movements of speech production.

Sources of variability. Identifying misarticulated phonemes and determining how the phonemes are being produced is only half of the diagnostic task. The clinician must also investigate the circumstances that may improve the child's articulatory production. Because inconsistency of production is an important clinical sign, we must discover whether children ever produce their error sounds correctly. If the error sounds are produced correctly, even only occasionally, we can assume children have the normal capability of improving their articulation. It is a good prognostic sign and provides a starting point of therapy. Four types of variability are discussed in the following section: connected speech, stimulability, key words, and deep testing.

1. *Connected speech.* The major problem with articulation tests is that they are designed to evoke single words, and that is not how we speak—not even the most taciturn of us. Speech is a dynamic, overlapping, incredibly swift, flowing activity. If one has good ears and listens carefully, one can distinguish individual phonemes in the flow, but each of these phonemes is influenced by the phonemes which precede and follow it. This phenomenon is known as *coarticulation* and may extend across four or five phonemes. Because of this, a complete assessment of a child's articulation cannot be limited to the examination of single words but must include an evaluation of spontaneous, connected speech that will more accurately reflect habitual articulation behavior.

Connected speech samples can be elicited in a number of ways, such as conversing, retelling a story, narrating a recent event, reading a paragraph, and so on. The speech sample can be tape recorded and an articulation inventory done at the clinician's leisure. The results of the analysis of the speech sample should be compared with the results of an articulation test to determine whether there is inconsistency in phonemic production under the two differing conditions and, if so, what the characteristics of the variability are.

2. *Stimulability.* In many cases, children are able to imitate the correct production of their error sounds by imitating their clinician's productions. Even if the production is not truly accurate, there may be movement away from the error toward the correct production. Testing for stimulability is a feature of several articulation tests, but further testing by the clinician should be done to determine whether children can imitate correct production of their error sounds on single words, in isolation, in nonsense syllables,

and in limited connected speech. If the child is stimulable, there are usually no significant obstacles that would prevent eventual acquisition of the sound. Results of stimulability assessment also give the clinician a starting point for therapy when a child produces a number of defective sounds. The sounds that are most stimulable are the ones that should be corrected first.

3. *Key words.* It is not unusual to find that children will produce correctly their error sounds in certain words, often words that are discovered only in conversation with them. It is valuable to discover such key words because, as Van Riper (1963) says,

> . . . they provide for the person a model in his own mouth for the sound we seek to teach him. We can use these key words to help us perceive the characteristics of the standard sound, both acoustic cues and the postures and movements required for their production. They can be used in discriminating error words from normally spoken words. (p. 231)

Van Riper's statement is important not only with reference to key words but to any condition under which a child is able to produce a sound correctly.

4. *Deep testing.* The phenomenon of coarticulation (i.e., the fact that each phoneme produced by a speaker is influenced by the phonemic context in which it occurs) is discussed above. Most articulation tests provide for only a superficial evaluation of the many possible phonemic contexts in which a child's misarticulated sound may occur. McDonald (1964) developed the *Deep Test of Articulation* to assess a child's misarticulation in all possible phonemic contexts. The *Test of Articulation Performance–Diagnostic* (Bryant & Bryant, 1983) also provides for deep testing, although in a more limited fashion than the McDonald test. Deep testing need not be administered routinely during a diagnostic evaluation, but the clinician should use either the test or the procedure during the initial stages of therapy to determine the phonemic contexts in which a misarticulated sound is produced correctly, thereby providing a starting point for therapy.

Linguistic analysis. For some time, clinicians have observed that children with functional articulation disorders are also deficient in other language skills. Authors such as Compton (1970), Fisher and Logemann (1971), and McReynolds and Huston (1971) pointed out some time ago that individuals with articulation disorders do not simply have an incomplete, random system of phonemic production. Rather, a careful phonological analysis of the speech of such individuals reveals that in many cases logical and coherent principles underlie their idiosyncratic use of speech sounds. According to McReymolds and Huston (1971),

> when articulation errors occur, they may consist of a phoneme system organized differently from the adult phoneme system. The more the systems differ,

the more severe the child's articulation problem. The child's system may be complete for the child and as lawful as the adult's but it is his own system, and his rules are at variance with the adult or the standard system. (pp. 155–156)

In terms of assessment, attention is shifted from the child's actual error sound to the underlying patterns that the errors follow. Clinicians may use one of the commercially available tests that include the dimension of distinctive feature analysis, such as the Fisher-Logeman or the TAP–D. Or clinicians may do their own analysis using the results of articulation assessment as described above and recording the data on a chart such as the one shown in Figure 5.3. The data to be recorded would be only correct productions, and the clinician would be able to determine quite easily which distinctive features the child is missing. The only features selected for analysis are the common ones of place of articulation, manner of articulation, and voicing. The results of such an analysis are shown in Figure 5.4. One might draw several conclusions with regard to a therapy program from these results.

The child whose correct productions are recorded in Figure 5.4 has only six correct phonemes—/m/, /p/, /b/, /t/, /d/, and /h/. For /k/, /t/ or /h/ was substituted; for /g/, /d/ and /h/ were substituted; for / θ /, /t/ was substituted; and for /ð / and /n/, /d/ was substituted. All other phonemes were replaced by the voiceless, glottal /h/. Based on this information, the following suggestions for therapy could be made.

- Teach some of the features that classify sounds—for example, teach the feature of friction as it relates to changes at the place of articulation.

- Use words like *hip* and *ship* to show how meaning is changed when the place of articulation changes from the common /h/ to the lingua-palatal contrast. Enlarge the categories for the auditory discrimination of speech sounds.

- Do all types of auditory training exercises using the correct sounds and contrasts.

- Use tongue exercises to help explore the structures of the mouth and the variety of movements possible among articulators.

Other excellent presentations of phonological analysis procedures are available in addition to those already mentioned. Some of these approaches are the description of distinctive feature analysis by Pollack and Rees (1972), generative phonology by Schane (1973), and natural generative phonology by Ingram (1976). Shriberg and Kwiatkowski's (1980) natural process approach is particularly helpful in linking developmental phonology with syntax and semantics.

Assessment of Syntactic Production. Two general procedures are presented for the assessment of both syntactic and semantic production: the

FIGURE 5.3. A Chart for the Analysis of Phonemic Errors Using a Distinctive Features Approach

	Labial		Labiodental		Dental		Alveolar		Palatal		Velar		Glottal	
	V	N-V	V	N-V	V	N-V	V	N-V	V	N-V	V	N-V	V	N-V
Glide														
Semivowel														
Nasal														
Stop														
Fricative														

V = voiced
N-V = non-voiced

FIGURE 5.4. A Child's Articulation Performance.

	Labial		Labiodental		Dental		Alveolar		Palatal		Velar		Glottal	
	V	N-V	V	N-V	V	N-V	V	N-V	V	N-V	V	N-V	V	N-V
Glide														
Semivowel														
Nasal	m													
Stop	b	p					d	t						
Fricative														h

V = voiced
N-V = non-voiced

language sample analysis and elicited production tasks. Readers should refer to the beginning of this chapter to refresh their memory regarding the procedures for securing a language sample and estimating the mean length of utterance (MLU). The first assessment is computing the MLU; the second is a distributional analysis. These are followed by de Villiers and de Villiers' (1973) stage assignments for Brown's 14 grammatical morphemes, an example of Miller's (1981) assessment profile, and finally, a series of elicitation techniques. For a variety of other techniques and procedures that can be used to assess syntactic production in depth, see Table 5.6 as suggested by Miller (1981).

Distributional analysis. A distributional analysis is a reorganization of the transcript of a language sample by specific utterance characteristics. Three types of segmentation of transcripts can be effected: by sentence length, by syntactic structure, and by number of utterances per speaking turn. The MLU will be clarified by a distributional analysis of sentence length. Ideally, variations in sentence length around the mean should exist but should not be extreme in their variance. A number of spuriously long sentences will significantly inflate the MLU and render it nonrepresentative. If the language sample consists of utterances that are all only one or two words in length, there may be a limitation in production due to functional problems in the oral speech mechanism. To analyze the distribution of sentence length, simply make a list of the utterances with one morpheme, two morphemes, three morphemes, and so on. By reviewing such a list the clinician can quickly determine whether the MLU seems to be representative.

Analyzing the distribution of syntactic structures in the language sample provides the clinician with a view of the structural variety within the sample. At the same time that the clinician is examining the specific structures produced, he or she may record the length of utterance associated with the structures. A very simple way to go about this type of analysis is to list the structures, the number of utterances in which each structure occurred, and the length of the utterances as shown below :

Structural Analysis	Total Number of Utterances	MLU per Type of Structure
Noun phrase elaboration		
Verb phrase elaboration		
Noun inflections		
Verb inflections		
Yes/no questions		
Wh- questions		
Negation		

TABLE 5.6. Procedures for In-Depth Analysis of Children's Syntactic Production

Content	Procedure	Sample size	Range of use	Reference
Syntax	Developmental Sentence Types (DST)	100 utterances	22 months–6 years	Lee (1966)
	Developmental Sentence Analysis (DSS)	50 complete sentences	3–7 years	Lee (1974)
	Language Sampling, Analysis and Training (LSAT)	100 utterances	2–10 years	Tyack and Gottsleben (1974)
	Language Assessment, Remediation and Screening Procedure (LARSP)	30 minutes 100–200 utterances	22 months–5 years	Crystal, Fletcher & Garman (1976)
	Scale of Children's Clausal Development (SCCD)	Transcript of unspecified length	18–40 months	Dever and Bauman (1974)
	TALK-Assessing Current Functioning	6–8 pages (200+ utterances)	1.5–5 years	Dever (1978)
	Co-occurring and Restricted Structure Procedure (CORS)	Representative sample (usually requiring several samples in varying situations)	1.5–5 years	Muma (1973)
	Linguistic Analysis of Speech Samples (LASS)	75–100 utterances	5–11 years	Engler, Hannah and Longhurst (1973)
	Assigning Structural Stage (ASS)	At least 50 utterances in at least two contexts	18 months–7 years	Miller (1981)

From *Assessing Language Production in Children: Experimental Procedures* (p. 30) by J. Miller, 1981, Austin, TX: PRO-ED. Reprinted by permission.

Structures that are produced within longer utterances or low frequency utterances may be found in the initial stages of acquisition.

The analysis of the distribution of utterances per speaking turn is not really related to syntactic production but is, instead, one way of assessing the more pragmatic level of language. Categorically, this analysis would be done at the same time that the other distributional analyses are done. See the Assessment of Pragmatics section later in this chapter for a discussion of this segmentation.

de Villiers and de Villiers' 14 morpheme analysis. Table 5.7 shows de Villiers and de Villiers' (1973) stage assignments for the 14 grammatical morphemes used by Brown (1973) in researching the stages of normal language

TABLE 5.7. Stage Assignments for 14 Grammatical Morphemes

Stage	Morpheme	Example
II	*-ing*	Me playing.
	plural	That books.
	in	Cookie Monster in there.
III	*on*	Doggie on car.
	possessive	Mommy's shoe.
V	regular past	He walked.
	irregular past	She came.
		We went.
	regular third person singular	It jumps. She plays.
	articles *a, the*	That's a puppy. Here is the paper.
	contractible copula *be*	Here's my coat. Those are my crayons.
V+	contractible auxiliary *be*	They're playing. I am coming.
	uncontractible copula *be*	Who's here? I am.
	uncontractible auxiliary *be*	Who's playing? I *am*.
	irregular third person singular	She has. He does.

Adapted from "A Cross-Sectional Study of the Acquisition of Grammatical Morphemes in Child Speech" by J. de Villiers and P. de Villiers, 1973, *Journal of Psycholinguistic Research, 2,* 267–268. Reprinted by permission.

development. The clinician will need some type of worksheet for recording the 14 morpheme analysis, and the one developed by Miller (1981) can serve as a prototype (see Figure 5.5). Whatever kind of worksheet the clinician designs, it will need to have space for recording several types of information, as follows:

• a space for each morpheme

• a space to indicate the number of the utterance in which the morpheme is present

• a way of indicating that the morpheme is obligatory in the specific utterance (Miller uses a check to indicate the presence of a morpheme and a minus to indicate the absence of it in the obligatory context.)

• space for recording the percentage of occurrence, which is obtained by dividing the number of morphemes present in one realm, such as plurals, by the number of obligatory contexts

The reader should note that the terms *contractible* and *uncontractible* refer to whether the verb can be contracted in Standard English, not to whether the child has or has not contracted the verb in his or her language sample. It makes no difference to the stage assignment for the child if he or she has said "I am going" or "I'm going." Uncontractible verbs are usually found in the sentence-final position and can never be correctly contracted. One may say "I am" in response to the question "Who's here?" but may not respond "I'm."

Elicited production. Elicited production is not to be confused with elicited imitation, which is an outright imitation by the child of the clinician's production. However, in elicited production the situation is structured so that the child is led into producing the desired oral response without the need for imitation. Elicitation techniques may be used for a variety of reasons: (a) when the clinician wishes to assess specific aspects of language, (b) when certain structures appear only infrequently in naturalistic settings, and (c) when time for assessment is limited. The following procedures for eliciting specific structures are taken from Bellugi (in Slobin, 1967) and are considered appropriate for children aged 3 through 12 years.

1. *Interrogation.* Using dolls or puppets, tell the child to "Ask the doll _____," using the indirect form of the question (e.g., "Ask the doll what she wants"). Try to focus on eliciting questions that are structurally difficult or rare. The verb phrase can be anything that the clinician feels is appropriate to the situation.

FIGURE 5.5. Worksheet for 14 Morpheme Analysis.

II

-ing

plural | 49) blocks ✓ | 100%

in | 4) in ✓ | 38) in ✓ | 100%

on

possessive

III

irregular past

article | 18) the ✓ | 40) a ✓ | 100%

regular past

regular third person singular | 1) stands ✓ | 52) comes come | 50%

V

contractible auxiliary be

irregular third person singular | 38) does ✓ | 100%

uncontractible auxiliary be

uncontractible copula be

contractible copula be
4) 's	–
19) 's	✓
21) is	✓
22) is	✓
28) 's	–
36) 's	✓
49) 're	–
50) is	✓
	63%

V+

From *Assessing Language Production in Children: Experimental Procedures* (p. 30) by J. Miller, 1981, Austin, TX: PRO-ED. Reprinted by permission.

Examples:

Vary the interrogative word

What she wants
Where she put it
When she'll do it
How she got it

Vary the noun phrase and the auxiliary verb

What she can do
What I might have
What they will have been doing
What the boy is supposed to see

Vary with negative

Why she doesn't help
Why I can't do it
Why they aren't here yet

Vary the subject and object

Who pushed John
Who did John push

Instead of using dolls or puppets with older children, it would probably be more appropriate to bring into the room a third person and phrase the command, "Ask Mr. Smith _____" (e.g., "Ask him what his name is," "Ask Mr. Smith why he is here," etc.).

2. *Tag questions.* The production of tag questions ("He did it, didn't he?") appears relatively late in children's language development. It follows a declarative sentence and generally asks for confirmation of the statement. Other common forms are: "He's here, right?" "Give me the book, okay?" and "Huh?" after a statement. These less elegant productions usually occur in children's speech well before the true tag questions.

Tag questions are of particular interest, because the form of the tag is explicitly determined by the syntax of the sentence it follows. According to Bellugi (in Slobin, 1967), the following processes are involved in the formation of tags:

1. The speaker must pronominalize the noun phrase subject of the sentence.

2. The speaker must locate (and perhaps supply *do* or the full form of) the first auxiliary verb of the main clause of the sentence.

3. The speaker negates the auxiliary of the sentence if it is affirmative but not if it is negative.

4. Finally, the speaker must invert the auxiliary verb and the pronominalized noun phrase.

As the reader can see, the speaker must follow a very complex procedure in producing tag questions. The procedure for assessing children's ability to produce such structures can provide information about their ability to locate the subject of a sentence, pronominalize nouns and noun phrases, handle conjoined noun phrases, define sentence negation, handle auxiliaries that they may not produce, locate the first element of an auxiliary verb, handle subject-verb agreement and tense agreement, define the subject and auxiliary of an imperative sentence, and so on.

The examiner can begin to elicit tag questions using a set of instructions such as those suggested by Miller (1981):

> Suppose I want to say something, and I'm not really sure about it. I might say: "The sun is shining today," and then, I might add: "Isn't it?" We're going to play a game like that. I'll say something, and you can add the last part, like this. I say, "That alligator can bite very hard," and you say, "_____."
> (p. 146)

The range of information available to the examiner through this elicitation procedure is shown in Table 5.8 adapted from Bellugi (in Miller, 1981).

3. *Negativization.* In Slobin (1967), Bellugi discusses elicitation procedures that can be used to assess children's ability to produce a variety of negatives, which are generally more easily elicited than some of the other structures discussed. Basically, the child is asked to provide the negative of a sentence that is supplied by the examiner, who may use a variety of techniques to initiate the process. It probably would be easiest to begin by asking the child to imitate sentences, thus giving him or her a clue as to what patterns are expected and what patterns are beyond the child's capacity.

The examiner gives the following instructions: "I'll say something and then you say the opposite. I'll say, 'The boy can run,' and you say, 'The boy can't run.'" The various types of negatives that can be assessed are given below with sample sentences:

Vary Auxiliary

The boy can run.	The boy _____.
The dish will break.	The dish _____.
The girl is crying.	The girl _____.
The cat went outside.	The cat _____.

TABLE 5.8. Examples of the Range of Information Available in Tag Questions (Bellugi, in Slobin, 1967)

Affirmative/negative interaction

I will do it.
I won't do it.

He could come.
He couldn't come.

Be and have

It's been done now.
It's coming now.

John's tired.
John's finished his lunch.

They're doing it.
I was going.

They were annoyed.
I'm coming.

First element of auxiliary

He could have done it.
I will have been swimming since this morning.
They would have been coming anyway.

Tense agreement

I go there often.
I went there yesterday.

He walked farther.
He walks frequently.

Location of grammatical subject

The girl pushed the boy.
The boy was pushed by the girl.

John and you played together.
Three boys and a girl are playing together.

Definition of sentence negation

He came here.
He never came.

He is unhappy.
He is happy.

I saw the boy who didn't go to school.
The boy who didn't go to school was fishing.

Nobody likes me.
Everybody likes me.

They have no sense.
They have little sense.

Modal auxiliaries

I could have found it.
They should arrive soon.
He will ask us.
She can do it.

Subject and auxiliary of imperatives

Help me find this book.
Sit down.
Come here.

Do as auxiliary verb

I need some cookies.
You see the truck.

Subject-verb agreement

I hit the ball.
He hits the ball.

You throw the stone.
John throws the stone.

Pronominalization

John came home early.
Sue is running.
The boys are playing.
The chair tipped over.

Both of them did it.
The two of us want some.

John and Bill played together.
John and I played together.

Yesterday after we came home from a long walk, the little girl came out to greet us.
I know where the boy is hiding.
The boys who jumped over the fence in my neighbors' yard ran away.

Limit on applicability of tag

Who finished this?

From *Assessing Language Production in Children: Experimental Procedures* (p. 147) by J. Miller, 1981, Austin, TX: PRO-ED. Reprinted by permission.

Negative with Indefinite

The girl ate some soup.   The girl _____.

He wants some cookies.   _____.

Someone saw her.   _____.

Someone is coming in.   _____.

Imperatives

Come in here.   _____.

Sit down over there.   _____.

Multi-Propositional Sentences

I saw the cat who came.   _____.

She asked him to do it.   _____.

Someone wants him to take some.   _____.

Why does she do that?   _____.

4. *Reflexivization.* Reflexivization is a grammatical structure that can be elicited in only a limited way. In English, whenever the subject and the object of certain verbs are the same, the object is reflexivized. In children's speech, and indeed in the speech of adults in some geographic regions of the country, the intermediate stage of reflexivization is often encountered. "I made me a glass of tea" is heard in place of "I made myself a glass of tea."

To begin eliciting reflexives, the examiner should have several sets of pictures illustrating the same action being performed on the individual represented and on another individual. For example, in one picture a girl may be washing her face, and in another picture she may be washing her doll's face. The pictures are presented to the child with the accompanying sentences: "The girl washed the doll." "The girl washes herself." Because reflexives may be difficult to elicit, the examiner should be prepared with several sets of pictures to assist the child in setting the appropriate pattern. Some of the sentences that the examiner might use to elicit reflexives are

Pronominalization

The girl washed _____ (herself) _____.

The boy cut _____ (himself) _____.

The girl looked at _____ (herself) _____.

I see _____ (myself) _____.

Imperatives

Behave _____ (yourself) _____.

Protect _____ (yourself) _____.

It should be noted that according to English rules of grammar, reflexivization does not occur outside of sentence boundaries. Prepositions are reflexivized; therefore, one cannot reflexivize the subject of the main clause, as in "I want her to take care of (herself, not myself)" or "Mary wanted John to help her (himself, not herself)."

Assessment of Semantic Production. In assessing semantics it is important to distinguish between semantics and other developmental functions, such as cognition, and to distinguish between semantics and syntax and pragmatics. One may consider the underlying concepts that children acquire as cognition and the means for expressing these concepts in words as semantics. For the purposes of this discussion, we will limit the subject to children's expressions of meanings through language. The distinction between semantics and syntax or semantics and pragmatics is very elusive because of the generous overlaps among them. For example, many of the early semantic roles that researchers have investigated (e.g., agent, action, object) are both semantic and syntactic, because they characterize the meaning of the words that fill the slots in the sentence and they represent something about their grammatic function as well. Agents, a semantic characterization, are almost always sentence subjects, a grammatic representation. Consistent word order in a child's speech reflects that the child knows these roles fulfill more than meaningful categorization. And children seem to know that these categories must be combined in a certain structure or sequence to express the desired meaning—a grammatic sequence. Bloom and Lahey (1978) refer to these early semantic role combinations as *semantic-syntactic relations*. In assessing semantics, the specifically semantic component of the grammar will be extracted as much as possible.

As mentioned above, semantics and pragmatics overlap to such a degree that it is often impossible to separate the meaning of a sentence from its use. If I say, "Can you hand me that book?" the literal meaning of my sentence ("Are you able to hand me the book?") is not what I probably intended you to understand.

For several reasons, this section presents a very limited introduction to the area of investigating a child's use of semantic knowledge. First, many semantic taxonomies have been developed and presented in the developmental literature, but very little work has been done in applying these taxonomies to clinical populations as assessment tools. Second, and more important, there is not a clear developmental sequence for the acquisition of semantic production beyond the period of Brown's stages I or II. What is presented here is a framework for thinking about semantic development.

In 1973, de Villiers and de Villiers proposed a distinction between referential meaning and relational meaning in their discussion of semantic development. Referential meaning concerns the one-to-one link between words and the objects for which they stand. Relational meaning has to do with the connections between and among concepts, words, and sentences.

Referential meaning. In assessment, referential meaning is investigated primarily through an analysis of the child's use of individual words. Two types of analyses are suggested by Miller (1981): (a) the type-token ration and (b) semantic field analysis. The type-token ration, developed by Templin (1957), provides the examiner with an index of lexical diversity. The procedure used by Templin calculates vocabulary usage based on the number of different words produced by the child in a 50-utterance sample and the total number of words in the sample. The relationship between these two measures is derived by dividing the total number of words used into the total number of different words used, as shown below:

$$\text{Type-Token Ration} = \frac{\text{Total Number Different Words}}{\text{Total Number Words}}$$

Templin, who studied the type-token ratios (TTR) of 480 children, reported ratios of approximately .50 occurring consistently across all age groups, sex groups, and socioeconomic status groups. Because of this consistency, the TTR is a remarkably useful measure.

Type-token ratios are easy to compute from transcripts. The following procedures for the computation (Templin, 1957) should be followed as closely as possible.

I. *Utterance sample*

Templin employed McCarthy's (1930) procedures in collecting speech samples. She used pictures and toys as stimulus materials and recorded 50 consecutive utterances. Utterance boundaries were determined by what were called "a natural break in the verbalization of the child."[1]

II. *Rules for counting numbers of words*

A. Contractions of subject and predicate like *it's* or *I'll* are counted as two words.

---

[1]From *Certain Language Skills in Children* (Institute of Child Welfare Monograph Series No. 26) (p. 15) by M. Templin, 1957, Minneapolis, MN: University of Minnesota Press. Reprinted by permission.

    B. Contractions of the verb and the negative such as *isn't* are counted as one word.

    C. Each part of a verbal combination is counted as a separate word; thus, *have been playing* is counted as three words.

    D. Hyphenated and compound words are counted as one word.

    E. Expressions that function as one word, such as *oh boy, all right,* etc. are counted as one word.

    F. Articles—*a, an, the*—are counted as one word.

    G. Bound morphemes (such as *-ness, -ly,* etc.) and noun and verb inflections are not counted as separate words.[2]

III. *Computing the Type-Token Ratio*

    A. Identify 50 consecutive utterances from the sample, preferably the middle 50.

    B. Count the total number of words expressed using the rules given above under II.

    C. Count the total number of different words produced.

    D. Divide the total number of different words by the total number of words produced. The result is the TTR.[3]

The second type of referential semantic assessment is the semantic field analysis, which provides the examiner with another way of investigating the range of a child's vocabulary. For this particular analysis, there is no standardized procedure. Instead, the examiner must create a set of meaning categories for the words that appear in the transcript of the speech sample. Noun categories might be animals, people, vehicles, toys, and so on; verb categories could be movement, existence, desire, and so on; and adverb or adjective categories could be duration (*long, short*), temporal sequence (*first, last*), manner (*hard, loud*), and distance (*near, far*).

The words in the transcript are classified according to the various categories created, and the examiner then has some idea regarding the diversity and complexity of the child's vocabulary in terms of both the number of meaningful categories and the number of different words in each category. For example, if the categorical concepts are encoded by children who have low levels of structural development, the examiner could predict a discrepancy between their cognitive and linguistic performance.

Relational meaning. At least three levels of analysis of the semantics of relational meaning can be posited: intrasentence relations, intersentence relations, and contextual (or nonlinguistic) relations. The most extensively studied aspect of the semantics of relational meaning is intrasentence relations

---

[2]Ibid., p. 160.

[3]Ibid., p. 160.

(Bloom, 1973; Brown, 1970, 1973; Greenfield & Smith, 1976; and Schlesinger, 1971). It appears that children produce a rather restricted number of intra-sentence relations in 2- to 3-word sentences even though they could produce a great many. Brown (1973) describes a set of common relations to look for in Stage I to II children, and Retherford, Schwartz, and Chapman (in Miller, 1981) present a scheme for coding the relations in a speech sample transcript, as shown in Figure 5.6.

Note that there are no developmental data for semantic role analysis for children above Stage II, and, therefore, analysis of children above that stage of development would be unreliable. The examiner who is well versed in the literature on semantic development could devise assessment procedures to evaluate some of the more complex semantic relations at the intrasentence level (e.g., conjunctions joining two propositions within one utterance, the content of requests, and the content of questions).

A number of intersentence and contextual relations, such as pronominal reference, deixis, discourse cohesion, and communicative intent, could be investigated by the examiner. However, there are very little developmental data in these areas, and they overlap so closely with pragmatics that it would be better not to consider them semantic functions. To summarize, semantic analyses can include the assessment of referential and relational meanings. While referential meaning is examined with regard to single words, relational meaning can be explored within a single sentence or between sentences.

Assessment of Pragmatics

To reemphasize a major point regarding pragmatics and not, it is hoped, to belabor the point, language always occurs in a context, and all contexts are not the same. Implicit in this statement is the assumption that language production varies with the context in which it is produced. Although the research is not reviewed here, there is evidence that language varies with the communicative partner and within different physical contexts. For the interested reader, Gallagher (1983) presents a brief and lucid review of the literature.

An entirely new vocabulary must be learned to read the literature on pragmatics in childhood language. It is not within the parameters of the present book to present, define, and discuss this vocabulary or the many taxonomies of pragmatic function that have been developed. The decision was made to review briefly the work of Prutting and Kirchner (1983), Halliday (1975), and Dore (1975), because it seems that their work provides a framework for the examiner to develop assessment strategies.

FIGURE 5.6. Definitions of the 21 Semantic Categories

Action[a] A perceivable movement or activity engaged in by an agent (animate or inanimate).

Entity (One-term utterances only) any labeling of the present person or object regardless of the occurrence or nature or action being performed on or by it.

Entity (Multi-term utterances only) The use of an appropriate label for a person or object in the absence of any action on it (with the exception of showing, pointing, touching, or grasping); or someone or something that caused or was the stimulus to the internal state specified by a state verb or any object or person that was modified by a possessive form. (**Entity** was used to code a possession if it met either of the preceding criteria).

Locative The place where an object or action was located or toward which it moved.

Negation[b] The impression of any of the following meanings with regard to someone or something, or an action or state: non-existence, rejection, cessation, denial, disappearance.

Agent The performer (animate or inanimate) of an action. Body parts and vehicles, when used in conjunction with action verbs, were coded **Agent**.

Object A person or thing (marked by the use of a noun or pronoun) that received the force of an action.

Demonstrative The use of demonstrative pronouns or adjectives, *this, that, these, those,* and the words *there, right there, here, see,* when stated for the purpose of pointing out a particular referent.

Recurrence A request for or comment on an additional instance or amount; the resumption of an event; or the reappearance of a person or object.

Attribute An adjectival description of the size, shape, or quality of an object or person; also, noun adjuncts which modified nouns for a similar purpose (e.g., *gingerbread* man).

Possessor A person or thing (marked by the use of a proper noun or pronoun) that an object was associated with or to which it belonged, at least temporarily.

Adverbial[c] Included in this category were the two subcategories of action/attribute and state/attribute.
  Action/Attribute A modifier of an action indicating time, manner, duration, distance, or frequency. (Direction or place of action was separately coded as **Locative, Repetition** and **Recurrence**).
  State/Attribute A modifier indicating time, manner, quality, or intensity of a state.

Quantifier A modifier that indicated amount or number or a person or object. Prearticles and indefinite pronouns such as *a piece of, lots of, any, every,* and *each* were included.

State A passive condition experienced by a person or object. This category implies involuntary behavior on the part of the **Experiencer**, in contrast to voluntary action performed by an **Agent**.

Experiencer Someone or something that underwent a given experience or mental state. Body parts, when used in conjunction with state verbs, were coded **Experiencer**.

Recipient One who received or was named as the recipient of an *object* (person or thing) from another.

Beneficiary One who benefited from or was named as the beneficiary of a specified action.

Name The labeling or request for naming of a person or thing using the utterance forms: *my (his, your, etc.) name is _____* or *what's _____ name?*

Created Object Something created by a specific activity, for example, a *song* by singing, a *house* by building, a *picture* by drawing.

Comitative One who accompanied or participated with an agent in carrying out a specified activity.

Instrument Something that an **Agent** used to carry out or complete a specified action.

From Retherford, Schwartz, and Chapman in *Assessing Language Production in Children: Experimental Procedures* (p. 44) by J. Miller, 1981, Austin, TX: PRO-ED. Reprinted by permission.

Halliday's Functions of Language. Halliday categorized children's early uses of language in two phases: Phase I (9 to 15 months of age) and Phase II (16 to 35 months). Within the total age range, he lists seven functions of language as given below:

1. The *instrumental*, in which the *I want* function of seeking satisfaction of material needs is served by language

2. The *regulatory*, in which language serves the *Do as I tell you* function and regulates the behavior of communicative partners

3. The *interactional*, in which language serves to link *you and me* in an interaction between self and others

4. The *personal*, in which language is used for the expression of feelings and attitudes and for the personal element in interaction between communicative partners

5. The *heuristic*, in which language is used to investigate reality and to learn about things—*Tell me why*.

6. The *imaginative*, the *Let's pretend* function, in which language serves to create the child's own environment

7. The *informative*, in which language serves the function of communicating new information about something

The first six functions are exemplified in Table 5.9, which categorizes a number of Halliday's son's vocalizations at 16 to 18 months of age. Using this table, the examiner can begin to develop evaluation strategies for determining which functions a child may be using in a variety of contexts. For example, within the relatively high structure of the appraisal situation does the child produce more or fewer functions than in the mother-child context or in the peer context? Which functions are used in which context? Can unused functions within one context be elicited in that context?

Although the seven functions of language are used throughout an individual's life, Halliday identifies two principal functions during Phase II: the pragmatic and the mathetic. Apparently, older children combine the instrumental, regulatory, and interactional functions into what Halliday refers to as the general pragmatic function of speech when the symbolic system is used by the child to act on reality and becomes the language of requests. The interactional, personal, and heuristic functions combine into what Halliday terms the mathetic function, and the symbolic system is used as a means of learning about reality or reflecting it.

The reader should keep in mind that the examples shown in Table 5.9 are reflective of only one child's development and do not constitute anything approaching normative data. Other children may use Halliday's functions

TABLE 5.9. Halliday's Functions of Language (exemplified in one child)

Function and example	Vocalization Gloss
Instrumental	
Generalized request for object	/m/ = Give me that.
Request for food	*more* = I want some more.
	cake = I want some cake.
Request for specific objects or	*ball* = I want my ball.
entertainment	*Dvořak* = I want the Dvořak record on.
	fish = I want to be lifted up to where the fish picture is.
Regulatory	
General request for action	/ɛ/ = Do that (again).
Specific requests for action	*book* = Let's look at a book.
	lunch = Come for lunch.
Request for permission	*stick-hole* = Can I put my stick in that hole?
Request for assistance	/ɛ/ = Pick me up (gestures).
Interactional	
Greeting person	/a/ouha/ = hello
	Anna
Seeking person	*Anna?* = Where are you?
Finding person	*Anna* = There you are.
Initiating routines	*devil* = You say, "ooh you are the devil."
Expressions of shared regret	/ʔ a:/ = Let's be sad; it's broke.
Response to "look"	/m/ = Yes, I see.
Response to *where* question	/de/ = There is it.
Personal	
Comment on appearance of object	*star* = There's a star.
Comment on disappearance	*no more* = The star has gone.
Express feelings of:	
interest	/ɸ/ = That's interesting.
pleasure	/ayi:/ = That's nice.
surprise	/o/ = That's funny.
excitement	/ʘ/ = Look at that.
ritual joy	/ɛ/ = That's my _____!
warning	/ɥ:/ = Careful, it's sharp.
complaint	/ɛ:he/ = I'm fed up.
Heuristic	
Request for information	/ɜ$^{ad^v da}$/ = What's that called?
Acknowledgment	/m/ = I see.
Imitating	(imitates name) = It's a _____.
Imaginative	
Pretend play	(g^{w}ɣ|···/ = Let's pretend to go to sleep.
	/ɹa::o/ = Roar; let's pretend to be a lion.
Jingles	*cockadoodledo*
Rhymes	(supplies final word)

From *Learning How to Mean: Explorations in the Development of Language* (pp. 156–157) by M. Halliday, 1975, London: Edward Arnold. Reprinted by permission.

earlier or later than his son did and may not use them in the same sequence as that given.

Dore's Primitive Speech Acts. Dore (1975) defined a set of early "primitive" speech acts that he identified in the one-word speech of children who were just beginning to talk. These acts include labeling, repeating, answering, requesting action, requesting answers, calling, greeting, and protesting. Examples are given in Table 5.10.

The examiner may seldom or never assess children who are just beginning to speak, but it would not be unusual to assess older, nonverbal children who may produce only a few words. In such cases, Dore's framework provides a useful reference to the types of pragmatic speech acts that are common to children at very low levels of language development. In addition, the eight pragmatic categories identified in nonverbal children by Coggins and Carpenter (1978) provide clues as to pragmatic function in preverbal or nonverbal children. The categories and definitions developed by Coggins and Carpenter are shown in Table 5.11.

Prutting-Kirchner Assessment of Pragmatic Behavior. Prutting and Kirchner (1983) begin their description of assessment with a detailed review of school-age and adult pragmatic behaviors, organizing them within a speech act framework. According to this study, all of the behaviors should be present and used appropriately by school-age children. For the assessment of younger or developmentally delayed children, the authors refer the reader to the work of such authors as Dore (1975).

As described by Prutting and Kirchner, the utterance act is extended to include paralinguistic and nonverbal as well as verbal behaviors. The second broad behavior they describe is termed *propositional acts*. These behaviors consist of linguistic dimensions of sentence meaning and serve to orient both of the communicative partners. The third area includes the *illocutionary* and *perlocutionary* acts, which are shared behaviors regulated by the communicative partners. The illocutionary act is the speaker's intention, while the perlocutionary act is the effects of the act on the listener. Table 5.12 is an abbreviated listing of the pool of pragmatic behaviors as given in Prutting and Kirchner (1983).

Based on the pool of pragmatic behaviors, Prutting and Kirchner developed an assessment strategy, the results of which can be analyzed at two different levels: the molar and the molecular. As the authors state, assessment should be conducted for the purpose of designing therapy programs and should be no more detailed than is necessary for designing the program.

The protocol is organized around four areas: the utterance act, the propositional act, the illocutionary act, and the perlocutionary act. Observation of the child's pragmatic behaviors can indicate where the problem

TABLE 5.10. Dore's Primitive Speech Acts

Speech act	Definition	Example
Labeling	Uses word while attending to object or event. Does not address adult or wait for a response.	C touches a doll's eyes and says *eyes*.
Repeating	Repeats part or all of prior adult utterance. Does not wait for a response.	C overhears Mother's utterance of *doctor* and says *doctor*.
Answering	Answers adult's question. Addresses adult.	Mother points to a picture of a dog and asks *What's that?* C answers *bow-wow*.
Requesting action	Word or vocalization often accompanied by gesture signaling demand. Addresses adult and awaits response.	C, unable to push a peg through hole, utters *uh uh uh* while looking at Mother.
Requesting	Asks question with a word, sometimes accompanying gesture. Addresses adult and awaits response.	C picks up book, looks at Mother, and says *book?* with rising terminal contour. Mother answers *Right, it's a book.*
Calling	Calls adult's name loudly and awaits response.	C shouts *mama* to his mother across the room.
Greeting	Greets adult or object upon its appearance.	C says *hi* when teacher enters room.
Protesting	Resists adult's action with word or cry. Addresses adult.	C, when his mother attempts to put on his shoe, utters an extended scream of varying contours while resisting her.
Practicing	Use of word or prosodic pattern in absence of any specific object or event. Does not address adult. Does not await response.	C utters *Daddy* when he is not present.

From "Holophrases, Speech Acts, and Language Universals" by J. Dore, 1975, *Journal of Child Language*, 2, pp. 21–40. Reprinted by permission.

TABLE 5.11. Pragmatic Behaviors in Nonverbal Children

Category	Definition
Requesting	Solicitation of a service from a listener:
Object requests	Gestures or utterances that direct the listener to provide some object for the child
Action requests	Gestures or utterances that direct the listener to act upon some object in order to make it move. The action, rather than the object, is the focus of the child's interest.
Information requests	Gestures or utterances that direct the listener to provide information about an object, action, or location
Greeting	Gestures or utterances subsequent to a person's entrance that express recognition
Transferring	Gestures intended to place an object in another person's possession
Showing off	Gestures or utterances that appear to be used to attract attention
Acknowledging	Gestures or utterances that provide notice that the listener's previous utterances were received
Answering	Gestures or utterances from the child in response to a request for information from the listener

lies. It may be at any one level or across levels, and difficulties at one level may lead to difficulties at another. For example, if the child has a problem with propositional acts (linguistic dimensions of sentence meaning), it is more likely that problems will be noted in conversational interaction than if he or she has a problem at the utterance level.

The examiner should always be aware that a pragmatic deficit can occur in combination with linguistic or cognitive deficits or may occur in isolation from other deficits. There is no evidence as to the incidence of pragmatic deficits either in isolation or in combination with other problems, and according to Prutting and Kirchner, there is no good evidence whether a pragmatic deficit would or should qualify as a legitimate problem needing therapeutic attention. At this time individual clinicians must decide for themselves whether the time needed to assess pragmatic behaviors is worth the results.

TABLE 5.12. Pool of Pragmatic Behaviors

Taxonomy	Modality	Description and Coding
UTTERANCE ACT		
1. Intelligibility	Verbal/paralinguistic	the trappings by which the act is accomplished
1. Intelligibility		the extent to which the message is understood
4. Prosody		the intonation and stress patterns of the message
6. Physical contacts	Nonverbal	the distance which speaker and listener sit or stand from one another
PROPOSITIONAL ACT	Verbal	linguistic dimension of the meaning of the sentence
1. Lexical selection/use		
A. specificity/accuracy		lexical items of best fit considering the context
2. Specifying relationships between words		
A. Word order	Verbal	grammatical word order for conveying message
ILLOCUTIONARY AND PERLOCUTIONARY ACTS		intentions of the speaker and effects on the listener
1. Speech act pair analysis		the ability to take both speaker and listener role appropriate to the context
B. Turntaking		smooth interchanges between speaker and listener

From "Applied Pragmatics" by C. Prutting and D. Kirchner, 1983, *Pragmatic Assessment and Intervention Issues in Language*, edited by T. Gallagher and C. Prutting, San Diego: College-Hill Press. Reprinted by permission.

SUMMARY

This chapter has dealt with the informal assessment of oral language production—namely, the examination of the oral speech mechanism; assessment or articulatory proficiency; and the assessment of syntax, semantics, and pragmatics in oral production. As indicated previously, the assessment strategies reviewed are generally not normative and, in some instances, are based on only minimal developmental data. In no way does informal assessment take the place of standardized evaluation, except with children too young or too severely handicapped to be assessed with standardized instruments. For this reason, some of the well-standardized measures have been reviewed.

The procedure that we continue to suggest is: (a) Administer well-standardized, appropriate measures of language ability to determine whether a problem actually exists, (b) assess children in areas of deficit using strategies such as those discussed above to determine and design a therapeutic program, and (c) design the therapeutic program using the assessment information gained to determine a starting place for therapy and to measure progress. There should be no real quarrel between the advocates of standardized testing and advocates of informal assessment. There is a place for both, and both are equally valuable.

REFERENCES

Angler, L., Hannah, E. P., & Longhurst, T. M. (1973). Linguistic analysis of speech samples: A practical guide for clinicians. *Journal of Speech and Hearing Disorders, 38*, 192–204.

Aungst, L., & Frick, J. (1964). Auditory discrimination ability and consistency of articulation of /r/. *Journal of Speech and Hearing Disorders, 29*, 76–85.

Bangs, T. E. (1977). *Vocabulary Comprehension Scale.* Dallas: Developmental Learning Materials.

Bangs, T., & Dodson, D. (1979). *Birth to Three Developmental Scale.* Dallas: Developmental Learning Materials.

Bellugi-Klima, U. (1971). Some language comprehension tests. In C. Lavatelli (Ed.), *Language training in early childhood education* (pp. 157–170). Urbana, IL: University of Illinois Press.

Bloom, L. (1970). *Language development: Form and function in emerging grammars.* Cambridge, MA: MIT Press.

Bloom, L. (1973). *One word at a time.* The Hague: Mouton.

Bloom, L., & Lahey, M. (1978). *Language development and language disorders.* New York: John Wiley.

Brown, R. (1970). The first sentences of child and chimpanzee. In R. Brown (Ed.), *Psycholinguistics.* New York: Free Press.

Brown, R. (1973). *A first language: The early stages.* Cambridge, MA: Harvard University Press.

Bryant, B., & Bryant, D. (1983). *Test of Articulation Performance–Diagnostic.* Austin, TX: PRO-ED.

Bryen, D. N. (1974). Special education and the linguistically different child. *Exceptional Children, 40,* 589–599.

Carrow, E. (1973). *Test for Auditory Comprehension of Language.* New York: Teaching Resources.

Carrow, E. (1974). *Carrow Elicited Language Inventory.* New York: Teaching Resources.

Clark, J. B., & Madison, C. L. (1981). *Clark-Madison Test of Oral Language.* Tigard, OR: C.C. Publications.

Coggins, T., & Carpenter, R. (1978). Categories for coding pre-speech intentional communication. Unpublished manuscript, University of Washington, Seattle.

Compton, A. (1970). Generative studies of children's phonological disorders. *Journal of Speech and Hearing Disorders, 35,* 315–339.

de Villiers, J., & de Villiers, P. (1973). A cross-sectional study of the acquisition of grammatical morphemes in child speech. *Journal of Psycholinguistic Research, 2,* 267–268.

Dore, J. (1975). Holophrases, speech acts, and language universals. *Journal of Child Language, 2,* 21–40.

Dunn, L. (1981). *Peabody Picture Vocabulary Test.* Circle Pines, MN: American Guidance Service.

Englemann, S. (1967). *Basic Concept Inventory.* Chicago: Follett.

Fewell, R., & Langley, M. (1984). *Developmental Activities Screening Inventory.* Austin, TX: PRO-ED.

Fisher, H., & Logemann, J. (1971). *Fisher-Logemann Test of Articulation Competence.* Boston: Houghton Mifflin.

Foster, C. R., Giddan, J. J., & Stark, J. (1972). *Assessment of Children's Language Comprehension.* Palo Alto, CA: Consulting Psychologists Press.

Frankenburg, W., Dodds, J., Fandal, A., Kazuk, E., & Cohrs, M. (1975). *Denver Developmental Screening Test.* Denver: LADOCA.

Gallagher, T. (1983). Pre-assessment: A procedure for accommodating language use variability. In T. Gallagher & C. Prutting (Eds.), *Pragmatic assessment and intervention issues in language* (pp. 1–29). San Diego: College-Hill Press.

Goldman, R., & Fristoe, M. (1969). *Goldman-Fristoe Test of Articulation.* Circle Pines, MN: American Guidance Service.

Greenfield, P., & Smith, J. (1976). *The structure of communication in early language development.* New York: Academic Press.

Halliday, M. (1975). *Learning how to mean: Explorations in the development of language.* London: Edward Arnold.

Hammill, D. D., Brown, V. L., Larsen, S. C., & Wiederholt, J. L. (1987). *Test of Adolescent Language.* Austin, TX: PRO-ED.

Hammill, D. D., & Newcomer, P. L. (1982). *Test of Language Development–Primary.* Austin, TX: PRO-ED.

Hresko, W. P., Reid, D. K., & Hammill, D. D. (1981). *The Test of Early Language Development.* Austin, TX: PRO-ED.

Ingram, D. (1976). *Phonological disability in children.* London: Edward Arnold.

Ireton, H., & Thwing, E. (1972). *Minnesota Child Development Inventory.* Minneapolis, MN: Behavior Science Systems.

Jakobson, R., Fant, G., & Halle, M. (1963). *Preliminaries to speech analysis.* Cambridge, MA: MIT Press.

Kirk, S., McCarthy, M., & Kirk, W. (1968). *Illinois Test of Psycholinguistic Abilities.* Urbana, IL: University of Illinois Press.

Lee, L. (1969). *Northwestern Syntax Screening Test.* Evanston, IL: Northwestern University Press.

Lee, L. (1974). *Developmental Sentence Analysis.* Evanston, IL: Northwestern University Press.

Loban, W. (1976). *Language development.* Urbana, IL: National Council of Teachers of English.

McCarthy, D. (1930). *The language development of the preschool child* (Institute of Child Welfare Monographs Series No. 4). Minneapolis, MN: University of Minnesota.

McDonald, E. (1964). *A Deep Test of Articulation.* Tucson, AZ: Communication Skill Builders.

McReynolds, L., & Huston, K. (1971). A distinctive feature analysis of children's misarticulations. *Journal of Speech and Hearing Disorders, 36,* 155–166.

Mecham, M. (1958). *Verbal Language Development Scale.* Circle Pines, MN: American Guidance Service.

Mecham, M., Jex, J., & Jones, J. (1973). *Utah Test of Language Development.* Austin, TX: PRO-ED.

Miller, J. (1981). *Assessing language production in children: Experimental procedures.* Austin, TX: PRO-ED.

Miller, J., & Yoder, D. (1984). *Miller-Yoder Test of Grammatical Comprehension.* Austin, TX: PRO-ED.

Newcomer, P. L., & Hammill, D. D. (1982). *Test of Language Development*#*Intermediate.* Austin, TX: PRO-ED.

Pollack, E., & Rees, N. (1972). Disorders of articulation: Some clinical applications of distinctive feature theory. *Journal of Speech and Hearing Disorders, 37,* 451–461.

Powers, M. (1957). Functional disorders of articulation: Symptomatology and etiology. In L. Travis (Ed.), *Handbook of speech pathology* (pp. 98–131). New York: Appleton-Century-Crofts.

Prutting, C., & Kirchner, D. (1983). Applied pragmatics. In T. Gallagher & C. Prutting (Eds.), *Pragmatic assessment and intervention issues in language* (pp. 29–65). San Diego: College-Hill Press.

Sanders, L. (1972). *Procedural guides for evaluation of speech and language disorders in children.* Danville, IL: Interstate.

Schane, S. (1973). *Generative phonology.* Englewood Cliffs, NJ: Prentice-Hall.

Schlesinger, I. (1971). Production of utterances and language acquisition. In D. Slobin (Ed.), *The onotogenesis of grammar* (pp. 63–101). New York: Academic Press.

Semel, E., & Wiig, E. (1980). *Clinical Evaluation of Language Functions–Diagnostic Battery.* San Antonio, TX: Psychological Corporation.

Shriberg, L., & Kwiatkowski, J. (1980). *Natural process analysis: A procedure for phonological analysis of continuous speech samples.* New York: John Wiley.

Slobin, D. (1967). *A field manual for cross-cultural study of the acquisition of communicative competence.* Berkeley, CA: University of California Press.

Templin, M. (1957). *Certain language skills in children* (Institute of Child Welfare Monograph Series No. 26). Minneapolis, MN: University of Minnesota Press.

Templin, M., &. Darley, F. (1969). *The Templin-Darley Tests of Articulation* (2nd ed.). Iowa City, IA: Bureau of Educational Research and Service, University of Iowa.

Toronto, A. S. (1973). *Screening Test of Spanish Grammar*. Evanston, IL: Northwestern University Press.

Van Riper, C. (1963). *Speech correction: Principles and methods*. Englewood Cliffs, NJ: Prentice-Hall.

Wepman, J. (1958). *Auditory Discrimination Test*. Los Angeles: Western Psychological Service.

PART III

ASSESSING
READING

**J. Lee Wiederholt
Brian R. Bryant**

The assessment of students' reading abilities and instructional needs is a major, if not *the* major, component of school appraisal programs. With few exceptions, all students in a school district are assessed annually on reading achievement. The resulting scores for each grade level are often used to evaluate the success of the school's reading program. In addition, the performance of each student is examined. Where a test score is sufficiently low, the student is tested further and, if necessary, a remedial program is implemented.

Sometimes a particular student will be referred for assessment by parents or a teacher because the student is experiencing extreme difficulty in learning to read. The assessment that follows these referrals is usually more in-depth than the annual school district assessment efforts.

The purpose of this section is to describe the assessment of students' reading problems. The chapters serve as a guide to understanding the nature of reading, the assessment of the various aspects of reading, and the different types of reading disabilities.

The first chapter addresses the nature of the reading process. Definitions of reading are provided, theories on the acquisition of reading competence are overviewed, and the numerous factors that could affect learning to read are detailed.

Chapter 7 describes the techniques used to determine the presence and degree of reading problems. Classroom observation techniques, group administered standardized tests, and individually administered reading tests are discussed.

Chapter 8 delves into specific assessment methods used to determine a student's instructional needs. First, the assessment of environmental factors that may affect reading achievement is discussed. Second, the student's attitudes and feelings about reading are considered. Next, methods for analyzing oral reading miscues made by students are described. Techniques for matching a student to a textbook level are then noted, and strategies for analyzing specific vocabulary and skill abilities of students are presented.

Chapter 9 describes the classification of students with reading problems into various diagnostic categories. These include dyslexic and corrective readers, as well as students with mental, learning, vision, or hearing impairments. Issues concerning placement of individuals into diagnostic categories are also discussed, and a brief history of categorization efforts in reading is presented.

6 / THE NATURE OF READING

The nature of reading is indeed complex and not completely understood. What Huey said in 1908 still holds true today:

> . . . to completely understand what we do when we read would almost be the acme of . . . achievement, for it would be to describe very many of the most intricate workings of the human mind, as well as to unravel the tangled story of the most remarkable specific performance that civilization has learned in all its history. (p. 6)

Despite this lack of a complete understanding, a great deal of progress regarding the nature of reading has been made over the last several decades. This chapter contains a discussion of some of this progress. Specifically, three areas are overviewed: (a) definitions of reading, (b) acquisition of reading, and (c) factors that affect reading proficiency.

DEFINITIONS OF READING

Dechant (1964) states that "there are as many definitions or descriptions of reading as there are reading experts" (p. 15). Yet an analysis of definitions indicates that almost all of them share a common property. That is, they stress that reading is *gaining meaning* from printed or written symbols. For example, as early as 1908, Huey defined reading as "thought getting"; Thorndike in 1917 defined it as "reasoning."

More recent definitions also adhere to the idea of reading as gaining meaning from printed or written symbols. For example, Smith, Goodman, and Meredith (1976) define reading as "the active process of constructing meaning from language represented by graphic symbols (letters) systematically arranged" (p. 265). In a similar vein, Harris and Sipay (1980) state that "Reading is the meaningful interpretation of printed or written symbols" (p. 8).

Dictionary definitions also note the importance of meaning in reading. For example, *Webster's II New Riverside University Dictionary* (1984) gives the following definitions:

> 1. To examine or grasp the meaning of (written or printed characters, words, or sentences). 2. To utter or express aloud (written or printed materials). 3. To interpret the meaning or nature of through close examination or observation. 4. To determine the intent, moods, or thoughts of. 5. To attribute (a particular meaning) to something read.

Most individuals would agree with the intent of all the preceding definitions. That is, they would concur that when a person is reading, he or she is actively involved in gaining meaning or comprehending a word, sentence, or text. If any confusion exists, it is not about the definition of reading but rather the manner in which the word *reading* is sometimes used in daily conversation. Oftentimes one is said to be "reading" when no comprehension is involved. Consider instances where adults read material from which they derive no meaning (e.g., an Internal Revenue Tax Form, directions for assembling a child's toy, a highly technical manual). They may even be able to say the individual words correctly. E. B. Smith et al. (1976) note that in cases like these, "Adult readers can use generalizations they have acquired about letters and sounds to say the words . . . , but that is not reading, because no meaning is involved" (pp. 268–269).

Reasons that adults might be able to correctly word call a passage but not comprehend it usually relate to the grammar (syntax) or vocabulary (semantics) used in the text. Consider the following two passages:

> The latter of the two queens, whose name was Victocris, a wiser princess than her predecessor, not only left behind her, as memorials of her occupancy of the throne, the works which I shall presently describe, but also observing the great power and restless enterprise of the Medes, who had taken so large a number of cities, and among them Vinevih, and expecting to be attached in her turn, made all possible exertions to increase the defenses of her empire. (from "The History of Herodotus," *Great Books of the Western World*, 1952, p. 41)

> In the anurice of acute nephritis (q.v.) no treatment will be effective until the swelling of the glomerulor capillary endothebuim diminishes. Hot applications to the loins, and high, hot colonic irrigations may be of some value. Diuretics, hypertonic solutions of sodium chloride or of dextrose are ineffective. (from the *Merck Manual of Diagnosis and Therapy*, 1956, p. 726)

Most adults would have difficulty comprehending either of the passages, even though they may pronounce most of the words correctly. This is because in the first passage the grammar is extremely complex; in the second case, the vocabulary is technical and specific to the medical field.

Another very common instance where the word *reading* is used in an imprecise manner is in the early grades of school. Consider instances where children have a reading lesson on sound blending and naming the letters of the alphabet; or where children word call from a list of words. These same children may correctly sound blend and name letters of the alphabet. In addition, some words may be said properly. Yet blends and the alphabet have no meaning in and of themselves. The words said properly may also have no meaning, such as *the, is, a,* and so forth. Since no meaning is derived from the sounds, alphabet, or these words, we would have to say that the criteria of "reading" are not met. Children usually do these tasks because some teachers believe that students need to do them to enable them to read. This issue has to do with the acquisition of reading, not the definition of reading, and is the topic of the next section.

In sum, the precise use of the word *reading* means comprehending words, sentences, paragraphs, and/or entire texts. What this means is that children who can call some words but cannot attach meaning to them are not reading. Also, while most adults have acquired generalizations about letters and sounds and can effectively word call, few, if any, can read everything.

This discussion of the appropriate and inappropriate use of the word *reading* is more than an exercise in polemics. It is necessary in scientific endeavors to use words in a precise manner. Imprecise word use causes confusion and misinterpretation of what writers and speakers are attempting to convey. Reading means comprehending, and it is used in this manner in the remainder of this text.

THE ACQUISITION OF READING

Since reading means comprehending words, sentences, paragraphs, and/or entire texts, how do people, primarily young children, acquire this ability? Venezky (1978) notes that the acquisition of reading ability is viewed by most educators as "an obscure process" (p. 2). However, several attempts have been made to describe this process (e.g., Laberge & Samuels, 1976; Rumelhart, 1977; Smith, 1982; Stanovich, 1980). Harris and Sipay (1980), after reviewing these often conflicting theories about the acquisition of reading, have classified them into one of three categories: (a) bottom-up, (b) top-down, and (c) interactive models. Each of these is described in this section, along with the application of stage theory to the three models.

Bottom-Up Models

Bottom-up models are based on oral language competency and the decoding of written language. Professionals who adhere to this orientation believe that written language is subservient to oral language and that decoding printed symbols is the only activity unique to reading. It is believed that once individuals have learned to break the written language code, all they need to do to comprehend the material is to apply it to their oral language knowledge. As Harris and Sipay (1980) note:

> In bottom-up models of the reading process, reading is basically a translating, decoding, or encoding process. The reader starts with letters (or larger units), and as he attends to them, begins to anticipate the words they spell. As words are identified, they are decoded to inner speech, from which the reader derives meaning in the same way as in listening. Reading comprehension is believed to be an automatic outcome of word recognition. (p. 6)

Laberge and Samuels (1974) present a model of reading acquisition that is basically a bottom-up orientation. They place a great deal of importance on automatic processing as critical to the acquisition of reading and give the following example. In the skill of basketball, ball handling is regarded as automatic by an experienced player. However, ball handling consists of several subskills, such as dribbling, passing, and catching. Each of these subskills and the transitions between them must be automatic as well. So it is with reading—it consists of several subskills that must be automatic as well as the interaction among these subskills.

Figure 6.1 depicts portions of this particular bottom-up model. In this model, the first reading system on the left is vision memory (VM). Graphemic information (letters or larger units) enters into the reader's visual memory bank. This information is then analyzed by feature detectors, which in turn are translated into word codes. One feature might be a spelling pattern code. The authors stress that only well-learned information can attract the attention of the reader and be automatically activated.

The second system, phonological memory (PM), is activated by visual memory. The PM system contains units closely related to acoustic and articulatory inputs. The acoustic unit might include memory of such features as phonemes, then syllables, and finally words. The articulatory system is also hypothesized as being hierarchical. For example, to respond with a word, a reader would give attention to the phonology, then to the syllabic unit, and perhaps from these to the word.

The third system in this model is the Semantic Memory Component (SM). Once the visual memory makes contact with the phonological word code, these word codes are translated into the reader's experiences with spoken language. Laberge and Samuels (1974) note:

FIGURE 6.1. A Bottom-Up Model

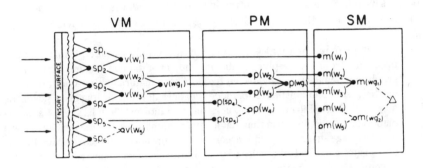

From "Toward a Theory of Automatic Information Processing in Reading" (p. 312) by D. Laberge and S. J. Samuels, 1974, *Cognitive Psychology, 6*. Reprinted by permission.

> Most of the connections between phonological word codes and semantic meaning codes have already been learned to automaticity through extensive experience with spoken communications. In fact, authors of children's books purposely select vocabularies in which words meet this condition. This takes the attention off the processing of meaning and frees it for decoding. (p. 307)

This overview of the Laberge-Samuels model is not as comprehensive or detailed as the authors' original work. However, it does present an example of a bottom-up model. As Rumelhart (1977) notes, the Laberge-Samuels model is strictly bottom-up, because it follows a basic sequence. That is, the reader moves from features to letters, from letters to spelling patterns, from spelling patterns to visual word representations, from visual word representations to phonological word representations, and finally from phonological word representations to word or word group meanings. Also, critical to a bottom-up model, no higher level can modify a lower level sequence. For example, knowledge of word group meanings would not act upon the lower level phonological word representations. The sequence to meaning must be followed in hierarchical fashion. These points are in direct contrast to top-down models.

Top-Down Models

Top-down models are based on the premise that the reader's cognitive and language competencies are the major factors in constructing meaning from printed materials. The major difference between models of this sort and the bottom-up models is that in top-down models graphic information is believed to be used only to support or reject hypotheses the reader has previously made regarding the meaning of the text. Specifically, individual words are not likely to be pulled from the reader's visual and graphic memory unless they fit with the semantic and syntactic clues the reader is using while actively processing a text. Harris and Sipay (1980) note about top-down models:

> Meaning (comprehension) is obtained by using only as much information as necessary from the graphic, syntactic, and semantic cue systems. Graphic or graphophonemic cues are derived from printed material; other cues are based on the reader's linguistic competence. Readers develop strategies to select the most useful graphic cues. As readers become more skilled, less graphic information is needed, because they have better sampling techniques, more control over language structures, and a larger store of concepts on which to draw. Prediction strategies, based on the use of semantic and syntactic cues, allow the reader to comprehend the material (obtain the deep structure) and anticipate what will probably occur next in print. The validity of these predictions is checked through the use of confirmation strategies; when predictions are inaccurate, correction strategies are employed in which additional cues are processed in a search for meaning. (p. 7)

F. Smith (1979), in *Reading Without Nonsense*, presents a top-down model of reading. His position is that we (readers) first need to "comprehend meaning in order to identify words and that we normally try to identify words in order to identify letters" (p. 107). Specifically, he asserts that in reading, meaning precedes and sometimes does not even include the identification of individual letters or words and that normal reading demands comprehension prior to or even without the identification of letters and words.

Smith's position is based in part upon the fact that two unrelated words would be read in a single second. However, twice that many words would be read in the same amount of time if the words make sense. Because of this, something about the meaningfulness of words in context must facilitate the identification of individual words. Specifically, something about the meaning of phrases or sentences must have been comprehended before any of the words were identified.

Smith also asserts that meaning cuts down on the possible alternatives of what a word can be. When words are in a meaningful sequence, the number of alternatives is small (i.e., about one in two hundred). Conversely, isolated random words could be one in many thousands of words. As a result, the fewer the number of meaningful alternatives, the less likely it is that we need to look at the distinctive graphic features of a word.

In addition, Smith notes that when fluent readers orally read and make an error, the error usually makes sense. On the other hand, poor readers tend to make errors that may be graphically similar (e.g., *sand* for *said*) but that make no sense at all.

Finally, it is noted that comprehension precedes the identification of individual words for the simple reason that words in isolation are essentially meaningless. For example, readers cannot tell the part of speech or the meaning of such common words as *chair, table, house, narrow, empty, waste,* and so forth, unless they have some idea of what they are reading.

For these reasons, Smith believes that comprehension precedes the actual word. Harris and Sipay (1980) note that Smith's model is top-down, because readers are believed to go directly to meaning before processing the word by letter or groups of letters. In addition, readers can obtain meaning without accurate word identification, as well as make transformations in vocabulary or syntax that do not change the meaning of the text.

Interactive Models

Other theoreticians have postulated that top-down and bottom-up processing seem to occur simultaneously. In other words, comprehension is dependent on both graphic information and information in the reader's mind. Comprehension is believed to be obstructed when the reader is lacking an actual skill or a piece of knowledge relative to the text. According to Harris and Sipay (1980), in interactive models "when comprehension is hampered, the skilled reader compensates by decoding a word, relying on context, or both" (p. 8).

Rumelhart (1977), a well-known theorist within the interactive school of reading, suggests:

> Reading is a process of understanding written language. It begins with a flutter of patterns on the retina and ends (when successful) with a definite idea about the author's intended message. This reading is at once a "perceptual" and a "cognitive" process. It is a process which bridges and blurs these two traditional distinctions. Moreover, a skilled reader must be able to make use of sensory, syntactic, semantic, and pragmatic information to accomplish his task. These various sources of information appear to interact in many complex ways during the process of reading. A theorist faced with the task of accounting for reading must devise a formalism rich enough to represent all of these different kinds of information and their interactions. (pp. 573–574)

Rumelhart developed much of his theory of reading from models on language processing for computers. Two primary systems were used: the General Syntactic Processor (Kaplan, 1973) and the HEARSAY II (see Lesser, Fennell, Erman, & Reddy, 1974). These systems consist of totally independent processes that communicate by means of a global, highly structured data storage system. Rumelhart calls this data system the "message center." Figure 6.2 illustrates this two dimensional message center.

FIGURE 6.2. A Two Dimensional Slice of the Message Center

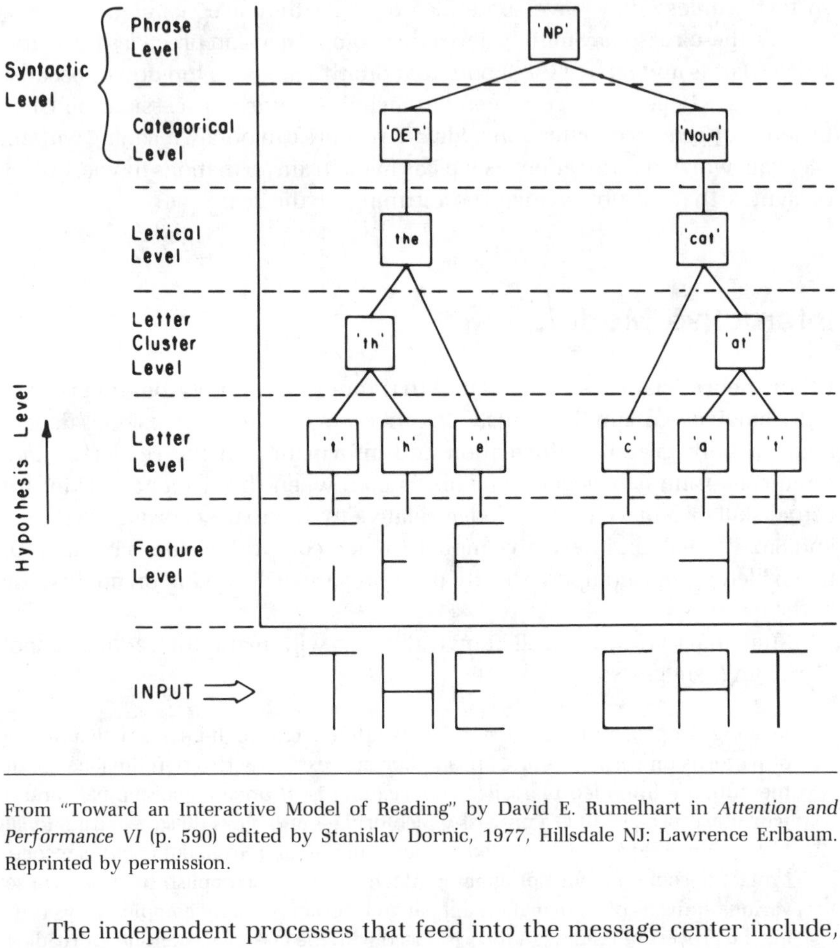

From "Toward an Interactive Model of Reading" by David E. Rumelhart in *Attention and Performance VI* (p. 590) edited by Stanislav Dornic, 1977, Hillsdale NJ: Lawrence Erlbaum. Reprinted by permission.

The independent processes that feed into the message center include, but are not limited to, graphic, syntactic, lexical, letter cluster, letter level, and feature level knowledge sources. Each of these sources has specialized knowledge about some aspect of the reading process. The message center contains the hypothesis about the nature of the input from each process. In the reading act, each knowledge source scans the message center for the hypothesis relative to its own knowledge. The message center in turn confirms, disconfirms, or removes the hypothesis, and a new hypothesis is added to the center. The process continues until a decision is made about the text.

As noted earlier, the message center is a two dimensional space with one space representing the hypothesis level (feature, letter, letter cluster, etc.) and another dimension representing different levels of decision making regarding alternative hypotheses. Each level interacts with the other levels. In other words, information flows back and forth instead of only up or down, as in the top-down and bottom-up models. For example, in Figure 6.2 the input is THE CAT. The hypothesis that the first word in the string is THE is supported by the hypothesis that the first letter in the string is T. In addition, the word THE supports the hypothesis that the string begins with a noun phrase.

Interactive reading models are neither purely bottom-up nor top-down. Instead, they view reading as all levels of processing interacting together. In addition, information is believed to be generated by any level (i.e., the meaning of the text, the structure of the language, or the features of words or letters).

Stages and the Models

Other authors argue for the idea of reading stages within the models. For example, Shuy (1977) suggests that early readers rely more heavily upon word and letter identification, while more efficient readers rely more upon syntactic and semantic features. Chall (1983) proposes the following stages of reading development as they interact with the models.

Stage 0. Prereading: Birth to Age 6. During this stage, children grow in control over syntax and words. The meaning of words and sentences is emphasized. Therefore, this stage is top-down in regard to reading acquisition.

Stage 1. Initial Reading, or Decoding, Stage: Grades 1–2, Ages 6–7. During this stage, children learn the arbitrary sets of letters and associates these with the corresponding parts of spoken words. Insight is gained about the nature of the spelling system and the particular alphabetic language used. Since decoding is emphasized, this stage is bottom-up in regard to reading acquisition.

Stage 2. Confirmation, Fluency, Ungluing from Print: Grades 2–3, Ages 7–8. With the decoding skills, the syntax, and the vocabulary developed at earlier stages, students can take advantage of these skills and concentrate on what is said—the meaning of a story or book. In addition, more complex phonic elements are learned. Since both decoding and meaning are part of acquisition, this is viewed as both a bottom-up and top-down model. (Although Chall does not use the term *interactive model*, it can be applied to this model).

Stage 3. Reading for Learning the New: A First Step: Middle School, Ages 9–13. Reading at this stage is for factual information, concepts, and how to do things. There is a growing importance of word meaning and prior knowledge of the student, but students still use decoding skills learned earlier to derive meaning. Chall characterizes the stage again as both top-down and bottom-up in regard to reading acquisition.

Stage 4. Multiple Viewpoints: High School, Ages 14–18. The difference between this stage and Stage 3 is that in Stage 4 students learn to deal with more than one point of view in reading. Chall also characterizes this stage as top-down and bottom-up.

Stage 5. Construction and Reconstruction—A World View: College, Age 18 and above. At this stage students are able to use selectively the printed materials that are of interest to them. Readers learn to construct knowledge for themselves in what they read, that is, to balance their comprehension of the ideas read, their analysis of them, and their own ideas of them. This is also characterized as top-down and bottom-up.

Chall notes that these age stages are hypothetical in that some readers may reach higher stages earlier than others. Conversely, some readers may never achieve the highest stages. However, what Chall has done has related models of reading acquisition to different ages or stages of readers. This indicates that certain models may be more relevant than others during the development of reading competence.

In this section we have described several models of reading acquisition. The bottom-up models with their emphasis on decoding and oral languages; the top-down models with their emphasis on meaning and prior knowledge; and the interactive models with their emphasis on simultaneous use of several aspects of reading, including decoding and meaning. Finally, we have noted the use of these models within stages of reading acquisition. These models provide some guidance in the assessment process, but none account for all aspects of the reading process. As Harris and Sipay (1980) note, "No model can be called the most acceptable; the search continues" (p. 6). We concur with this statement in that continued theory development and research on reading acquisition is necessary. However, we believe that interactive models are the most accurate representation of the reading process. It is to these models that our efforts to better understand reading should most likely be directed.

FACTORS THAT AFFECT READING PROFICIENCY

A number of problems can occur in reading. It is, of course, necessary in the assessment of reading to be aware of the numerous areas that could affect comprehension. For this reason, three efforts to delineate problems in reading are overviewed in this section: (a) cue systems, (b) author and reader components, and (c) classes of variables.

Cue Systems

Smith, Goodman, and Meredith (1976) state that three kinds of cue systems operate in reading to cue meaning. These are cue systems (a) within words, (b) in the flow of language, and (c) within the reader.

Cue Systems Within Words. Smith et al. (1976) believe that reading is learned from whole to part. That is, like in F. Smith's (1979) top-down model, readers can get the meaning of a sentence long before they can recognize each word in isolation. However, they also believe that all proficient readers have acquired the ability to use cue systems within words. These cue systems include:

> Letter-sound relationships
> Shape, or word configuration
> Known little words in new words
> Affixes
> Recurrent spelling patterns
> Whole known words (Smith et al., 1976, p. 269)

Smith et al. (1976) give an example of how this cue system works for a first grader encountering "monkey" for the first time in his reading. He might try to recall sounds he has learned to associate with letters in the word. He may notice and remember the shape of this new word; he may try to pick out little words in the new word (in this case, *key*); he may try to pick out a word that has the same affix and use it to attempt the word; or he may try a word that is spelled in a somewhat similar manner. He will usually rely on remembering the entire word.

According to Smith et al. (1976), readers who rely heavily on the cues within words are often led away from the true purpose of reading—that is, gaining meaning from print. This is because they focus on minute details and must then build back toward meaningful language units. Interestingly, "few children who become remedial readers lack the ability to attack words. Many just can't get the meaning" (p. 270).

Cue Systems in the Flow of Language. Cue systems in the flow of language are those that exist outside the word itself but within language. These cue systems include:

> Patterns of words or function order
> Inflection and inflectional agreement
> Function words
> Intonation (stress, pitch, and juncture)
> Contextual meaning
> Redundancy in language cues (Smith et al., 1976, p. 271)

They use an example of the child who encounters the new word "monkey" in the following sentence:

> "Tom saw a *monkey*. A man played some music. The little *monkey* clapped his hands. Tom gave the *monkey* a penny." (Smith et al., 1976, p. 271)

The first cue consists of the common patterns in which the sentence or phrase is arranged. In this case, "Tom saw a monkey" is subject-verb-object or noun-verb-noun, one of the most common sentence structures in the English language. Smith et al. (1976) note that when children come to school, they have mastered all of the basic patterns of the language. Therefore, the boy would use the cue that *monkey* is something Tom saw.

The second cue used might be inflectional endings. There is a pattern of consistency in the use of these inflectional endings, and they are used as cues. For example, if the boy read, "The boys sees the monkey," it would simply not sound right to him in most dialects of English.

The third cue would be that of those small number of words in the English language that have little or no meaning but perform key roles as structure cues. In the sentence, "Tom saw a *monkey*," *a* is a noun marker—indicating that monkey is a noun. If the student read, "Tom saw a money," he would likely recognize an error, as *a* does not precede a noun such as money. Smith et al. (1976) note that this is usually not a reasoned or conscious decision but simply a reliance on the child knowledge of language.

The fourth cue is the stress, pitch, or juncture of written language that the reader imposes on the passage. These three all work together in oral language. If the boy read *Tom, saw, a,* and *monkey* in isolation, the words would probably have a different stress, pitch, and juncture than in a meaningful sentence. In reading connected discourse, understanding the flow of the language facilitates meaning.

The fifth cue lies in the prior words or subsequent words and the whole utterance. This meaning is cued by nearby function words, inflectional ending, the position of the word in the pattern, interactions, and the meaning of nearby words.

The final cue employed is the tendency of written language to provide several cues to the same bit of information. These successive redundancies narrow the number of possible words that could fit into the text. In rereading the example sentence, it can be seen that *monkey* is used in three situations where all the previous cues systems in the flow of language and redundancy can be used to derive the meaning. If a student makes one mistake, there are almost always redundant additional cues to help him or her select the proper word.

The authors note that even if a reader does not know all the words in the text, the meaning of the words can still be determined through the flow of the language. As evidence, the authors cite research by K. Goodman in which first grade students were able to read two-thirds of the words they had missed on a list when these same words occurred in a story. Second graders read three-fourths of words missed on a list correctly when they occurred in a story; third graders got more than four of five right in the story. The authors state, "they were able to do this because of the cue systems that exist in the flow of language, but not in words" (Smith et al., 1976, p. 277).

Cues Within the Reader. What readers bring to the reading act depends a great deal upon how effective their abilities to interpret texts are. Smith et al. (1976) note that what the reader brings to the reading act is as important as the cues in the language of the text itself. These cues include:

Language facility (the internationalization of a dialect)
Physiology (as it affects perception and expression)
Learned responses and strategies
Experiential background of the reader
Reader's conceptual background and ability (pp. 277–278)

The first cue is the agreement of language between the writer and the reader. Some readers will be confused if the language of the basal readers is different from their own speech patterns (i.e., their dialect). Similarly, older students may be confused when reading classics that employ archaic dialects. The closer readers are able to interpret the writer's language, the greater their comprehension.

Physical factors, such as visual and hearing problems or physical or mental health of the reader, also affect ability to learn to read. While these cues have a history of acceptance in the field of reading, Smith et al. (1976) note that "research has failed to find any substantial cause for reading failure in physical, mental, or perceptual difficulties" (p. 279).

The third set of cues affecting the reader is their learned responses to letters, single or in groups. Readers may learn to use these letters in a natural manner, just as they have learned to talk and understand oral language. Or they may have learned systems of reading, such as word attack skills or phonics.

The fourth set of cues are those related to the experiential background of the reader. If the content of the text does not relate to the experiences the reader has had with the events, places, people, and objects portrayed, it will be more difficult to derive meaning from the written discourse.

The final set of cues relates to the conceptual ability of the reader. Obviously, readers cannot read written language that is beyond their ability to understand. In other words, readers must have the intellectual ability to be able to understand the concepts being presented in the text.

In summary, the cue systems include those within words, those within the flow of language, and those within the reader. Smith et al. (1976) state:

Research on the reading process among readers from low-proficiency second-graders to highly proficient adults has demonstrated that the major difference between weak and strong readers is in how well they have the process together. Regardless of level of proficiency, all readers are users of language. They attempt to use graphic, syntactic, and semantic cues to get meaning from within language, and all readers use all types of cues. Proficient readers are both efficient and effective. As *effective* readers, they get the most meaning out of the task. As *efficient* readers, they do it with the least amount of effort and energy. They are highly selective, using only enough cues to get to the meaning. (p. 282)

Author and Reader Components

V. Brown, Hammill, and Wiederholt (1986), like the authors of cue systems, have developed a somewhat different but similar model of what factors play a part in reading. These include (a) author component and (b) reader component.

Author Component.   V. Brown et al. (1986) note that reading comprehension is closely tied to the understanding and skill of the author. Within this they include (a) intended meaning, (b) expectations about the reader, and (c) the expression of intended meaning. Each of these is discussed in this section.

An author's intentions are probably never reconstructed exactly in the minds of their readers. There are good reasons for misfit between an author's intention and a reader's comprehension. First, the meaning may be fuzzy in the mind of the author. Also, the writer may not have the skills needed to bring the ideas to the mind of the reader. They note that it is important to remember that written language (i.e., the surface representation of meaning) can never perfectly characterize the author's actual intentions. Life experiences and specific language competence are so unique to each reader that they can never perfectly characterize the author's actual intentions.

The implications of the problem an author has in representing intended meaning are related to the reader's complementary task: The reader must recover as much as possible of the author's underlying meaning. The better the author is at expressing his or her ideas in written language, the more likely it is that the reader will comprehend the meaning. V. Brown et al. (1986) note that in the hands of a poor author, poor readers can be created.

The second factor in the author's component is his or her expectations about the reader. Usually authors have certain expectations about the reader that influence the choice of elements used in written language. Vocabulary selection, complexity of syntax, and the organization of material are all choices of the writer. V. Brown et al. (1986) suggest considering the case of an author who is writing about "Behavior Modification." If the audience is assumed to be knowledgeable about the topic, it is likely that words and phrases such as *contingency management, reinforcer,* and *baseline* will appear in the text. However, unless the author assumes extensive reader experience with the topics, such words and phrases will be explained at length. When authors have grossly misjudged their audience, a comprehensive problem is created. Where the reader does not have the background assumed by the author, attempts to recover the author meaning are unlikely to be successful.

The third author component factor that affects meaning contains several parts, including (a) readability, (b) study skills, (c) written language, and (d) the author as an answerer of questions. In the past when writers spoke of readability or text difficulty, they were primarily referring to such matters as the number of different words among the total number of words, the syllabic length of words, the number of words per sentence, and the complexity of sentence structure (i.e., simple versus complex and compound sentences). In determining readability, formulas such as the Fry, Flesch, or Dale-Chall were used to determine the difficulty level of a text.

Durkin (1981) has noted that "almost as old as the readability formulas are doubts about their ability to yield accurate information" (p. 32). For example, short sentences (a criterion for a low readability level) were at one time believed to be easier to read than long sentences. However, Irwin (1980) found that some short sentences may be more difficult to read, as they often require the reader to make inferences about previously stated or unstated information. The research in this area resulted in a joint communique from the presidents of the International Reading Association and The National Council of Teachers of English on November 7, 1984, suggesting that everyone involved with text selection stop rating reading level of difficulty primarily by word or sentence length (Cullinan & Fitzgerald, 1984). Klare (1984) has summarized the research on readability formulas and offered some suggestions for their use. Specifically, he notes that these formulas can be used with caution as surface readability indicators but should not be used alone as indicators of the readability of text.

Several important factors other than those measured by traditional readability formulas are related to readability. Some of these factors include the structure of the sentence, the logical connections between sentence and clauses, and the coherence of topics. Meyer and Rice (1984) refer to text structure as

> how the ideas in a text are interrelated to convey a message to a reader. Some of the ideas in the text are of central importance to the author's message, while others are of less importance. Thus, text structure specifies the logical connections among ideas, as well as subordination of some ideas to others. (p. 319)

Study skills are also a part of the author's expression of intended meaning. Specifically, this is the manner in which authors aid the reader in organizing the text information prior to reading. Ausubel (1968) recommends that authors write "advanced organizers" (an outline of major and subordinate ideas) to help readers better understand the author's intention.

Written language is the third part of the author's expression of intended meaning. Written language is basically thought to employ the full range of syntactic transformations, most of which are not produced in spoken language. The fact that written language employs transformations that are not usually employed in spoken language (e.g., "Bowing awkwardly, he left the room") may present special problems for comprehension. Authors who use complex syntactical structures may be interfering with the reader's ability to comprehend.

The fourth and final part of the author's expressing of intended meaning is concerned with the author as an answerer of questions. F. Smith (1978) believes that comprehension occurs as an author answers the reader's continuous, often implicit, questions. The reader as a question asker is illustrated in Robinson's (1961) SQ3R study technique (Survey, Question, Read, Recite, Review). Students are taught to ask consciously the questions they believe the author will answer. In F. Smith's (1978) view, the skilled writer is the one who can get the reader to ask the right questions (i.e., the questions that the author intends to answer).

The author's component, therefore, includes the intended meaning, the expectations about the reader, and the expression of intended meaning. The second part of the V. Brown et al. (1986) reading equation is the reader component.

Reader Component. V. Brown et al. (1986) note three major factors associated with the reader's role in comprehension: (a) the reader's expectations about the text or the author, (b) the reader's experience with language in its written form, and (c) implicit text processing.

Reader expectations are believed to be predictions about ideas or about specific language elements that are either confirmed or disconfirmed as one reads. Predictions of the reader are not always at the conscious level. Implicit knowledge of what is permissible, either in language or in life, influences expectations. For example, careful attention to, "The boy up ran the hill," would make most readers reread the sentence, because the word order does not fit our expectations about language. Also, reading that, "The sun went down in a bright green blaze," should trigger some curiosity about the meaning or perhaps the truth of such a reported event.

Reader language is also a part of the reader component. General competence of the reader with language provides access to comprehension. The role of language in reading is usually assumed but often rather vaguely.

Implicit text processing is the final component. Fisher and Smith (1977) "speak of a text as being implicitly and actively processed when the reader generates the fabric which relates sentences to each other and to the larger fabric of which they are a part" (p. 24). They believe that four concepts are involved in this view of comprehending: (a) prior knowledge, (b) skills in determining logical relationships, (c) systematic integration of the total text, and (d) active processing.

Prior knowledge is concerned with the student's understanding of the ideas being expressed in the text. Comprehension is believed to be built on what is known already. The person who has no prior knowledge of urbanization is likely to experience problems with a social studies chapter dealing with that topic. Forming relationships from one unknown to another unknown is sure to affect the ability to comprehend a text.

Skill in determining logical relationships is consistent with the ideas of relational meaning. Relational meaning considers the characteristics and various cognitive categories to which events in a text belong. The more interrelationships among cognitive categories, the more meaning the reader can assign to the text. F. Smith (1975) states:

> It is thought that the manifold ways in which our cognitive categories are related to each other make our environment meaningful. These interrelations are the core of the entire cognitive system of our theory of the world. They enable us to summarize our past experiences, make sense of present and predict the future. (p. 17)

Obviously, the more cognitive experience readers have with the areas expressed in the text, the better their ability to comprehend the information presented.

Systematic integration of the total text refers to the assumption that the reader who accounts for all of the information in a text "may 'understand more' than the reader who processes only the relations between continuous sentences" (Fisher & Smith, 1977, p. 24). As readers read, they should develop some ideas of the whole text to which the sentences or sections are related.

The last concept within implicit text processing is simply that of active processing. It is singled out to note that the reader's role is one of active involvement as contrasted to the view that the reader's role is one of a passive word caller or information recipient.

V. Brown et al. (1986) note:

> There is solid agreement that (a) if meaning is to be "gained" by the reader, the reader must "construct" it, and (b) if the reader constructs his/her own meaning, it would undoubtedly be different from that which the writer intended. Further, different readers will construct different types and degrees of meaning because readers vary in their knowledge background, grasp of language, and other abilities. (p. 4)

Classes of Variables

Idol (in press), like the other authors, notes the problems that can occur in learning to read and in reading. She believes that reading is an interactive process, with good readers using more top-down processing and beginning and poor readers often relying more on bottom-up processing. She has specified three classes of problems: (a) those that are text-related, (b) those that are teacher-related, and (c) those that are student-related.

Figure 6.3 depicts Idol's (in press) model of the reading process. In the center of the figure, the circle with arrows represents the interactive reading process where readers integrate decoding and conceptual processes (indicated by the large arrow at the top). The two-way arrows with broken lines leading to the box labeled *Context* depict how the reader derives two different kinds of understanding from a text (i.e., those that are explicitly stated and those that are implicit throughout the text). The box at the left of the interactive circle, labeled *Memory*, represents how readers apply meaning or semantics to what is being read. *Attention* variables, listed in the box at the bottom of the chart, indicate reader-related influences. A discussion of some of the variables relating to text, teacher, and student are as follows.

Text Variables. Many of Idol's (in press) text-related variables are similar to those presented by Smith et al. (1976) in their cue systems and Brown et al. (1986) in their reader and author components. For example, variables within text language are similar to cue systems in the flow of language; text organization is similar to factors noted in the author component. However, some variables are unique to Idol's list, and these will be discussed in this section.

Idol (in press) notes under Text Organization the importance for opportunities for reader practice, teacher presentation, and comprehension checking that could influence reading. Under reader practice, she particularly stresses that slower achieving students may not have had sufficient opportunity to practice reading. Under teacher presentation, the importance of teachers having opportunities to present instructional information prior to reading as well as at various points within the total reading assignment is emphasized. She cites research indicating that teachers are more likely to give assignments and check comprehension only after reading a text and that teachers' manuals rarely provide sufficient directions on prior and continued instructional opportunities.

A unique aspect of Idol's (in press) model is opportunities for comprehension checking within the text. She states:

> A third type of text organization is the opportunities for readers to check on their own comprehension as they are reading. Are the materials organized in such a way that readers are prompted to engage in ongoing self-checking? And, are the materials structured so that readers are provided with alternative strategies and solutions for finding answers if the results of comprehension checking are negative? (p. 8)

Comprehension checking is easily explained as an example of metacognition in reading. In reading, metacognition is used to account for the self-knowledge or self-awareness readers have about their own abilities to think, organize, understand, and conceptualize in relation to the required learning task. In

FIGURE 6.3. Classes of Variables

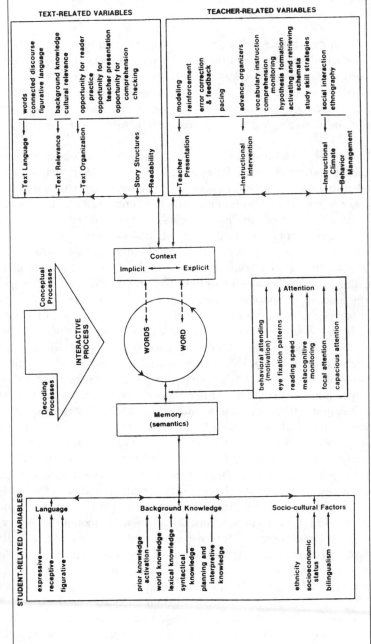

From *Johnny Can't Read: Does the Fault Lie with the Book, the Teacher, or Johnny?* by L. Idol, in press, Urbana, IL: Center for the Study of Reading, University of Illinois. Reprinted by permission.

addition, it includes planning a next step and checking the outcome of a strategy that has been used as well as revising strategies. Comprehension checking in relation to text organization refers to how the text facilitates these metacognitive strategies.

Teacher Variables. Idol's (in press) specification of the importance of teacher variables is also a unique addition in comparison to the cue systems and author-reader components discussed earlier. She specifies four types of teacher variables, including teacher presentation, instructional intervention, instructional climate, and behavior management. Teachers who do not use the variables may not be instructing students in an appropriate manner.

Teacher presentation refers to the techniques teachers employ in learning activities. Some of these techniques include modeling whereby teachers may demonstrate how to search for important clues prior to textual reading, how to fill in a story map while reading, how to summarize and ask reciprocal questions about reading, or how sounds are pronounced.

The components of reinforcement include punishment, negative reinforcement, and positive reinforcement. Idol (in press) notes how each of these when used by teachers may affect reading achievement. Error correction and feedback refer to how teachers correct student responses and the amount of specific feedback given to the learner. Finally, pacing under teacher presentation refers to the teacher's exactness of the match between the student's ability and a task, how long teachers can sustain responses, and how fast teachers move students through the lesson.

The second major class of teacher-related variables are those related to instructional intervention. These include the teacher's use of advanced organizers, vocabulary instruction, comprehension monitoring, hypothesis formation, activating and retrieving schemata, and study skill strategies. Advanced organizers and study skills have been discussed earlier by V. Brown et al. (1986), and the reader is referred to that section for definitions, if necessary. To Idol (in press) vocabulary instruction includes *meaning* vocabulary and *word recognition* vocabulary. The former type of teacher instruction focuses upon the meaning or meanings of words in context and is viewed as being the most recommended practice in instruction. The latter, word recognition, refers to teaching words in isolation. Comprehension monitoring is teaching students to check if comprehension is occurring and to use self-remediation strategies to correct errors. Hypothesis formation is teaching readers to make interpretations of the text and to make predictions about what will happen in the text. Finally, activating and retrieving schemata is teaching students to store and apply information within their own knowledge base.

The last two classes of teacher-related variables include instructional climate and behavior management. Instructional climate is concerned with factors that deal with the social interactions that take place within a classroom as well as the effects of various ethnic groups as they relate to student-student and student-teacher interactions. Behavior management refers to the teacher's ability to organize the classroom in such a way that students can apply their talent to learning to read in an efficient manner. If these teacher behaviors are lacking in instruction, comprehension could be affected.

Student Variables. Idol's (in press) student-related variables are in many instances similar to Smith et al. (1976) cue systems within the reader, and Brown et al. (1986) reader component. However, Idol's special attention to sociocultural factors, such as ethnicity, socioeconomic status, and bilingualism, deserves comment. She notes that

> the question of background knowledge and its influence on comprehension is particularly relevant to the understanding of problems of poor readers from diverse cultural groups. This is especially relevant if the reader is from a minority group yet receiving reading from the majority point of view. Differences in prior knowledge due to cultural variables can account for many of the reading problems of the minority student. (p. 33)

Idol (in press) stresses the need for careful attention to the match or lack of a match among ethnic or social class values of students, their teachers, and the materials used for teaching them. She also recommends that variables that may need to be addressed are the manner in which question-answer or discussion groups are organized and how these relate to the social conventions of the student's culture.

In this section, three efforts to delineate problems in reading were overviewed (i.e., cue systems, author and reader components, and classes of variables). While these systems overlap in many ways, each also has a unique focus upon problems that can occur in reading and learning to read. As can be seen, the number of problems that can occur are numerous and present quite a challenge to those charged with assessing the cause of a reading problem in an individual student.

CONCLUSION

In this chapter reading was defined as comprehending words, sentences, paragraphs, and/or entire texts. While the acquisition of reading ability is not completely understood, the interactive models appear to be very appropriate in describing learning to read. Finally, a great number of factors which affect reading proficiency were delineated.

While Huey's statement in 1908 about our incomplete understanding of the nature of reading still holds true today, we have obviously made a great deal of progress in unraveling this mystery. Certainly, our progress has been great enough to focus the attention of those responsible for reading assessment on critical variables that either help or hinder reading competency. How this is accomplished is the discussion of the following chapters.

REFERENCES

Ausubel, D. P. (1968). *Educational psychology. A cognitive view.* New York: Holt, Rinehart and Winston.

Brown, V. L., Hammill, D. D., & Wiederholt, J. L. (1986). *Test of Reading Comprehension.* Austin, TX: PRO-ED.

Chall, J. S. (1983). *Stages of reading development.* New York: McGraw-Hill.

Cullinan, B., & Fitzgerald, S. (1984) *Background information bulletin on the use of readability formulae.* Urbana, IL: National Council of Teachers of English.

Dechant, E. V. (1964). *Improving the teaching of reading.* Englewood Cliffs, NJ: Prentice-Hall.

Durkin, D. (1981). What is the value of the new interest in reading comprehension? *Language Arts, 58,* 23–43.

Fisher, D. L., & Smith, M. S. (1977). An information processing approach. In S. F. Wanat (Ed.), *Linguistics and reading series: 2. Language and reading comprehension.* Arlington, VA: Center for Applied Linguistics.

Harris, A. J., & Sipay, E. R. (1980). *How to increase reading ability: A guide to developmental and remedial methods* (7th ed.). New York: Longman.

Huey, E. B. (1908). *The psychology of pedagogy of reading.* New York: Macmillan.

Idol, L. (in press). *Johnny can't read: Does the fault lie with the book, the teacher or Johnny?* Urbana, IL: Center for the Study of Reading, University of Illinois.

Irwin, J. (1980). The effects of explicitness and clause order on the comprehension of reversible causal relationships. *Reading Research Quarterly, 15,* 477–488.

Kaplan, R. M. (1973). A general syntactic processor. In R. Rustin (Ed.), *Natural language processing* (pp. 193–242). New York: Algorithmics Press.

Klare, G. R. (1984). Readability. In P. D. Pearson (Ed.), *Handbook of reading research* (pp. 681–744). New York: Longman.

Laberge, D., & Samuels, S. J. (1974). Toward a theory of automatic information processing in reading. *Cognitive Psychology, 6,* 293–323.

Laberge, D., & Samuels, S. J. (1976). Toward a theory of automatic information processing in reading. In H. Singer & R. B. Ruddell (Eds.), *Theoretical models and processes of reading* (2nd ed., pp. 548–579). Newark, DE: International Reading Association.

Lesser, V. R., Fennell, R. D., Erman, L. D., & Reddy, D. R. (1974). Organization of the HEARSAY II speech understanding system (Working papers in Speech Recognition III). Pittsburgh: Carnegie-Mellon.

Meyer, B. J. F., & Rice, G. E. (1984). The structure of text. In P. D. Pearson (Ed.), *Handbook of reading research* (pp. 319–351). New York: Longman.

Robinson, F. P. (1961). *Effective study.* New York: Harper and Row.

Rumelhart, D. E. (1977). Understanding and summarizing brief stories. In D. Laberge & S. J. Samuels (Eds.), *Basic processes in reading: Perception and comprehension* (pp. 265–304). Hillsdale, NJ: Lawrence Erlbaum Associates.

Rumelhart, D. E. (1980). Schemata: The building blocks of cognition. In R. J. Spiro, B. C. Bruce, & W. F. Brewer (Eds.), *Theoretical issues in reading comprehension* (pp. 33–58). Hillsdale, NJ: Lawrence Erlbaum Associates.

Shuy, R. W. (Ed.). (1977). *Linguistic theory: What can it say about reading?* Newark, DE: International Reading Association.

Smith, E. B., Goodman, K. S., & Meredith, R. (1976). *Language and thinking in school* (2nd ed.). New York: Holt, Rinehart and Winston.

Smith, F. (1975). *Comprehension and learning: A conceptual framework for teachers.* New York: Holt, Rinehart and Winston.

Smith, F. (1978). *Understanding reading: A psycholinguistic analysis of reading and learning to read* (2nd ed.). New York: Holt, Rinehart and Winston.

Smith, F. (1979). *Reading without nonsense.* New York: Teachers College Press, Columbia University.

Smith, F. (1982). *Understanding reading* (3rd ed.). New York: Holt, Rinehart and Winston.

Stanovich, K. E. (1980). Toward an interactive-compensatory model of individual differences in the development of reading fluency. *Reading Research Quarterly, 16,* 32–71.

Thorndike, E. L. (1917). Reading as reasoning: A study of mistakes in paragraph reading. *Journal of Educational Psychology, 8,* 323–332.

Venezky, R. L. (1978). Reading acquisition: The occult and the obscure. In F. Murray & J. Pikulski (Eds.), *The acquisition of reading* (pp. 1–22). Baltimore, MD: University Park Press.

Webster's II New Riverside University Dictionary. (1984). Boston: Riverside.

7 / DETERMINING THE PRESENCE AND DEGREE OF A READING PROBLEM

Most students learn to read regardless of the instructional approach used. For some, however, learning to read is a difficult task that challenges both the learners and those responsible for their education. Often these students need individualized instruction designed to meet their specific needs. In order to receive special service or help, these students must usually be identified as having a significant problem in learning to read. Identifying problem readers and determining the degree to which the problem exists have been a vital part of education for years.

While the procedures used in this process may vary, they generally follow a consistent pattern. First, classroom teachers observe that a student is experiencing problems with the skills in reading or the abilities that may be factors in learning to read (i.e., the teacher may note that the child is experiencing reading problems concurrently with difficulties in general learning abilities, seeing, hearing, etc.). Second, group administered standardized test results may be examined to determine how the student performed on the portions of the test that measure reading. If a deficiency is noted, the teacher may refer the child for further evaluation. Third, diagnosticians administer a series of norm referenced standardized tests to determine whether a deficiency indeed exists and, if so, to what degree. This chapter describes how non-standardized procedures and norm referenced standardized tests are used to identify reading problems and to document the degree of severity.

IDENTIFYING A PROBLEM USING
NONSTANDARDIZED PROCEDURES

The first step in the identification process is to screen for children who are deficient in reading. This can easily be accomplished using nonstandardized procedures (i.e., through informal means). Procedures of this nature are described by Hammill in the first chapter of this volume as "techniques for which no proof for the reliability or validity is available, only nonsupportive evidence exists, or evidence is provided only for one of the two proofs [i.e., proof of validity or reliability]."

Experienced teachers have little difficulty identifying problem readers using nonstandardized procedures. Their knowledge of reading allows them to observe students in the classroom and to determine both the presence of a reading difficulty in a student and the degree to which it is a problem. Familiarity with the elements of reading (e.g., word recognition, word identification, comprehension) allows the teacher to develop performance expectations for students at particular reading levels; that is, experienced professionals know what reading skills are used by most first graders, second graders, and so on. Such knowledge may be accrued during teacher training, but usually occurs as a result of years of internalizing the skills sequences found in basal reading series.

With most basal approaches, the skills of reading programs are sequenced to some degree in what is believed to be easy to difficult order. For example, basal series introduce skills in preprimers that are presumed to be easier than those covered in primers. In addition, the base skills of the preprimer are designed to be learned prior to the skills presented in the primer; thus, the skills sequence is hierarchical in nature. While not all approaches to reading instruction teach the skills at the same level, most basal series are more similar than different. Of the differences that do exist, D. Brown (1982) notes that "these variations are not usually of major proportions, and a teacher can learn much about the development of reading skills by reviewing the scope and sequence charts from two or three basal series" (p. 38). This section describes scope and sequence charts and explains how they may be used to create informal evaluation instruments (i.e., checklists and rating scales) for assessing the students' observed reading behaviors.

Scope and Sequence

Scope and sequence charts are outlines depicting the skills within a particular content area—in this case, reading. They are used by publishers to diagram for teachers the sequence of skills that are to be taught in a particular series. Similarly, they are used to identify skills that will be assessed on teacher made or commercially prepared tests. They are also used by educators as foundations for planning the content of remedial education programs.

While providing a useful breakdown of skills within a content area, scope and sequence charts cannot be used without question. Bartel (1986) cautions that the skills sequences "are based on the judgment of 'experts' and on tradition. Such sequences or hierarchies of skills have not yet been validated" (p. 41). Bartel notes that teachers cannot be sure that all children's learnings conform to these skills sequences. That is, not all children need to master skill A at step 1 before they progress to skill B at step 2; likewise, proficiency in skill B may not enhance the opportunity to learn skill C, and so on. Still, teachers must understand skills sequences if they are to realistically evaluate a student's ability.

An Example. Bartel (1986) provides a scope and sequence chart that is an adaptation of one presented by Kaluger and Kolson (1978). This chart (see Table 7.1) presents skills from the first through sixth grades that are classified according to category (i.e., Word-Study Skills, Comprehension Skills, Study Skills). Note the comprehension skills that appear at the Preprimer Stage. These include associating text and pictures, following oral directions, determining the main idea, noting details, recognizing sequence, drawing conclusions, and seeing relationships. At the Primer Stage, the skills include all those previously described plus three new ones: forming judgments, making inferences, and classifying. Presumably, these new skills build upon what has been learned previously and prepare the way for later skills. As a result of their training and experience, reading teachers internalize a skills sequence such as the one provided here. Thus, when they observe children in the classroom, signs of achievement difficulties are easily recognized.

Advantages and Disadvantages. As might be expected, scope and sequence charts have their advantages and disadvantages. Groups that are commissioned to select a series for district adoption can examine the skills sequence of several series and select the one most compatible with the philosophy of the staff and/or administration. Teachers can examine the scope and sequence charts to get a listing of the skills covered by the texts at each level. Test authors can use the charts to establish the content validity of their achievement tests. If authors can demonstrate that the skills appearing on their tests are those consistently taught in schools, then the device is presumed to have been built on a solid foundation. Further, as will be seen, such tests may be used by teachers as bases for checklists and rating scales.

The primary disadvantage of scope and sequence charts is that their use may lead to the creation of atomistic remedial reading programs. At the heart of atomistic teaching is the concept that each major element within a construct has several subelements. These subelements can be taught, and presumably acquisition of knowledge in these parts leads to the attainment

TABLE 7.1. Typical Scope and Sequence of Reading Skills Usually Taught at the Elementary Level

		Word-Study Skills	Comprehension Skills

First Grade	**Preprimer Stage**	A. Word meaning and concept building
		B. Picture clues
		C. Visual discrimination
		D. Auditory skills
		   1. Initial consonants—e.g., *b, c, d, f*
		   2. Rhyming elements
		E. Structural analysis
			A. Associating text and pictures
			B. Following oral directions
			C. Understanding main idea
			D. Understanding details
			E. Understanding sequence
			F. Drawing conclusions
			G. Seeing relationships

	Primer Stage	A. Review, reteach, or teach all skills not mastered and expand vocabulary
		B. Context clues
		C. Phonetic analysis
		   1. Initial consonants
		   2. Rhymes
		   3. Learning letter names—*n, l, p, d, g, r, c*
		D. Structural analysis
			A. Understanding all those skills listed at preprimer level
			B. Forming judgments
			C. Making inferences
			D. Classifying

	First Reader	A. Review all previous skills
		B. Phonetic analysis
		   1. Final consonants
		   2. Initial blends—*st, pl, bl, br, tr, dr, gr, fr*
		C. Structural analysis
		   1. Verb forms—*ed, ing*
		   2. Compound words
			A. Reviewing all previously taught skills
			B. Recalling story facts
			C. Predicting outcome
			D. Following printed directions

Second Grade	**Book One**	A. Review and practice all first-grade skills
		B. Phonetic analysis
		   1. Rhyming words visually
		   2. Consonants
		     a. Initial—*j*
		     b. Final—*x, r, l*
		     c. Blends—*cr, sn, sl, pr, cl*
		     d. Digraphs—*ai, oa*
		C. Structural analysis
		   1. Plural of nouns—adding *s* and *es*
		   2. Variant forms of verbs
		     a. Adding *es, ing*
		     b. Doubling consonants before adding *ing* or *ed*
			A. Reviewing all previously taught skills
			B. Making generalizations
			C. Seeing relationships
			D. Interpreting pictures

TABLE 7.1. continued

	Word-Study Skills	Comprehension Skills

Second Grade — Book Two

Word-Study Skills:

A. Review all previously taught skills
B. Recognize words in alphabetical order
C. Phonetic analysis
  1. Consonant blends—*thr, gl, squ, apr, str*
  2. Phonograms—auditory and visual concepts of *ar, er, ir, ow, ick, ew, own, uck, ed, ex, ouse, ark, oat, ound*
  3. Vowel differences
    a. Vowels lengthened by final *e*
    b. Long and short sounds of *y*
    c. Digraphs—*ee, ea*
    d. Diphthongs—different sounds of *ow*
D. Structural analysis
  1. Contractions—*it's, I'm, I'll, that's, let's, don't, didn't, isn't*
  2. Variant forms of verbs—dropping *e* before adding *ing*
  3. Plural forms of nouns—changing *y* to *ies*

Comprehension Skills:

A. Practicing and using all previously taught skills
B. Making inferences
C. Seeing cause and effect relationships

Third Grade — Book One

Word-Study Skills:

A. Review all previously learned skills
B. Word meaning
  1. Opposites
  2. Adding *er, est* to change meaning of words
  3. Words with multiple meanings
C. Phonetic analysis
  1. Consonants
    a. Hard and soft sounds—*c, g*
    b. Recognizing consonants
    c. Digraphs—*ck*
  2. Vowels
    a. Silent vowels
    b. Digraphs—*ai, ea, ou,* etc.
D. Structural analysis
  1. Contractions
  2. Possessive words
  3. Suffixes—*en, est, ly*
  4. Variant forms of verbs
E. Alphabetizing—first letter
F. Syllabication—up to three-syllable words

Comprehension Skills:

A. Practicing all skills previously learned
B. Detecting mood of situation
C. Relating story facts to own experiences
D. Reading pictorial maps
E. Skimming

TABLE 7.1. continued

	Word-Study Skills	Comprehension Skills

Third Grade / Book Two	A. Review all previously learned skills
	B. Word meaning
	  1. Homonyms—*dew, do; sea, see;* etc.
	  2. Synonyms—*throw, pitch; quiet, still; speak, say;* etc.
	C. Phonetic analysis
	  1. Consonants—hard/soft sounds of *g, c*
	  2. Vowels
	    a. Diphthongs—*ou, ow, or,* etc.
	    b. Sounds of vowels followed by *r*
	D. Structural analysis
	  1. Plurals—change *f* to *v* when adding *es*
	  2. Contractions—*doesn't, you'll, they're*
	  3. Suffixes
	  4. Prefixes—*un* changes meaning of words to the opposite
	E. Alphabetizing—using second letter
	F. Syllabication
	  1. Between double consonants
	  2. Prefixes and suffixes as syllables
	G. Accent—finding emphasized syllables
		A. Practicing all previously learned skills
		B. Solving problems

Fourth Grade	A. Word meaning
	  1. Antonyms
	  2. Synonyms
	  3. Homonyms
	  4. Figures of speech
	  5. Sensory appeals in words
	B. Word analysis
	  1. Phonetic analysis
	    a. Consonants
	      (1) Silent
	      (2) Two sounds of *s*
	      (3) Hard and soft sounds of *c* and *g*
	      (4) Diacritical marks
	        (a) Long sounds of vowels
	        (b) Short sounds of vowels
		A. Practicing all previously learned skills
		B. Reading for comprehension
		C. Finding the main ideas
		D. Finding details
		E. Organizing and summarizing
		F. Recalling story facts
		G. Recognizing sequence
		H. Reading for information
		I. Reading creatively
		  1. Classifying
		  2. Detecting the mood of a situation
		  3. Drawing conclusions
		  4. Forming judgments
		  5. Making inferences
		  6. Predicting outcomes

TABLE 7.1. continued

	Word-Study Skills	Comprehension Skills
Fourth Grade	(5) Applying vowel principles (a) Vowel in the middle of a word or syllable is usualy *short* (b) Vowel coming at the end of a one-syllable word is usually *long* (c) When a one-syllable word ends in *e*, the medial vowel in that word is usually *long* (d) When two vowels come together, the first vowel is usually *long* and the second vowel is *silent* 2. Structural analysis a. Hyphenated words b. Finding root words in word variants c. Prefixes—*dis, re, un, im* d. Suffixes—*ly, ness, ment, ful, ish, less* e. Syllabication (1) When a vowel is followed by one consonant, that consonant usually begins the next syllable (2) When a vowel sound in a word is followed by two consonants, this word is usually divided between the two consonants f. Accent	7. Seeing cause and effect relationships 8. Solving problems J. Following printed directions K. Skimming
Fifth Grade	A. Antonyms—review and practice B. Expand vocabulary C. Review figures of speech and introduce new ones to enrich vocabulary D. Homonyms—review and introduce new ones E. Synonyms—review and introduce new ones to expand vocabulary F. Use of dictionary and glossary G. Phonetic analysis 1. Review consonant sounds	A. Continuing development in the following areas: 1. Understanding main idea 2. Understanding sequence 3. Reading for details 4. Appreciating literary style 5. Drawing conclusions 6. Enriching information 7. Evaluating information 8. Forming opinions and generalizing 9. Interpreting ideas

TABLE 7.1. continued

	Word-Study Skills	Comprehension Skills

Fifth Grade

Word-Study Skills:
2. Review pronunciation of diacritical marks
3. Review phonograms
H. Structural analysis
  1. Compound words
  2. Words of similar configuration
  3. Prefixes, review and introduce *in-, anti-, inter-, mis-*
  4. Suffixes, review and introduce *-sp, -or, -ours, -ness, -ward, -hood, -action, -al*
  5. Syllabication
  6. Application of word analysis in attacking words outside the basic vocabulary

Comprehension Skills:
10. Using alphabetical arrangement
11. Using dictionary or glossary skills
12. Interpreting maps and pictures
13. Skimming for purpose
14. Classifying ideas
15. Following directions
16. Outlining
17. Summarizing
18. Reading for accurate detail
19. Skimming
B. Introducing
  1. Discriminating between fact and fiction
  2. Perceiving related ideas
  3. Strengthening power of recall
  4. Using encyclopedias, atlas, almanac, and other references
  5. Using charts and graphs
  6. Using index and pronunciation keys
  7. Reading to answer questions and for enjoyment of literary style

Sixth Grade

Word-Study Skills:
A. Word meaning
  1. Antonyms—review and practice
  2. Homonyms—develop ability to use correctly
  3. Classify words of related meaning
  4. Enrich word meaning
  5. Review use of synonyms
  6. Use of context clues in attacking new words
  7. Expand vocabulary
  8. Become aware of expressions that refer to place and time and develop skill in

Comprehension Skills:
A. Continuing development in the following areas
  1. Understanding main ideas
  2. Understanding sequence
  3. Reading for details
  4. Appreciating literary style
  5. Drawing conclusions
    a. Predicting outcomes
    b. Forming judgments
    c. Seeing relationships
  6. Extending and enriching information

A. Reviewing skills in the following
  1. Arranging alphabetically
  2. Using dictionary and glossary
  3. Using encyclopedia, almanac, and other references
  4. Interpreting maps and pictures
  5. Skimming for a purpose
  6. Classifying ideas
  7. Following directions
  8. Summarizing
  9. Outlining
  10. Reading for accurate detail

TABLE 7.1. continued

	Word-Study Skills		Comprehension Skills	

Sixth Grade

Word-Study Skills

interpreting such
expressions
9. Use dictionary
and glossary
B. Word analysis
1. Phonetic
analysis—review
consonant sounds,
diacritical marks,
and vowel sound
principles
2. Structural analysis
a. Review
compound and
hyphenated
words
b. Review
prefixes and
introduce
trans-, pre-,
fore-, ir-, non-
c. Review suffixes
and introduce
-able, -ance,
-ence, -ate, -est,
-ent, -ity, -ic,
-ist, -like
d. Review
principles of
syllabication
e. Review
accented
syllables
f. Apply word
analysis to
words outside
the basic
vocabulary

7. Interpreting
pictures
8. Evaluating
information
9. Interpreting
ideas
10. Using facts to
form opinions,
generalizing
B. Introducing the skills
of
1. Enriching
imagery
2. Discriminating
between fact and
fiction
3. Strengthening
power of recall

Comprehension Skills

11. Using index and
pronunciation
keys
12. Using charts and
graphs
B. Introducing the
following skills
1. Using facts and
figures
2. Using headings
and type style—
especially italics
3. Using an index
4. Using the library
5. Using a table of
contents
6. Taking notes
7. Reading
informational
material
8. Reading poetry

From "Teaching Students Who Have Reading Problems" by N. R. Bartel, 1986, in *Teaching Students with Learning and Behavior Problems* (pp. 70–75) by D. D. Hammill and N. R. Bartel, Boston: Allyn & Bacon. Reprinted by permission.

of the whole—in this case, in the ability to read. Obviously, scope and sequence charts fit this scheme nicely. As was noted earlier, however, the validity of the charts themselves has been questioned, and we have serious reservations about teaching reading using an atomistic approach.

Observations

In Chapter 1 of this volume, Hammill notes that valuable information can be obtained through direct observation of a student. Observing reading behaviors is fundamental to the continuous diagnosis of reading that goes on in the classroom. Informal observations provide the most naturalistic technique for gathering diagnostic information. It is a technique that teachers can use effectively to observe a child's general performance, learn about his or her interests and attitudes, examine problem solving strategies, and detect physical anomalies. While observations may be general (e.g., "The child is reading fluently"), they usually target a particular skills area (e.g., word-study, comprehension).

Philosophy of the Observer. Observations tend to reflect the general reading philosophy of the observer. For example, earlier we noted that approaches to reading instruction generally fall within one of three categories: bottom-up, top-down, and interactive. Observers with a bottom-up philosophy will be primarily concerned with a student's ability to apply phonics generalizations when identifying individual words. Thus, their observations might be inclined to report on a student's ability to use *sl* blends, respond to inflectional ending clues, or identify multisyllabic words. Scope and sequence charts will often be used to list the skills to be observed.

Conversely, the observer with a top-down philosophy will likely focus on the manner in which readers use previous knowledge to gain meaning from the text. Or the top-down observer might be interested in the reader's ability to make meaningful substitutions when reading orally. For example, the top-down observer would find clinically useful the reading of "Tom ran to the store as fast as he could" as "Tom raced to the store as fast as he could," since the substitution *raced* for *ran* demonstrates the ability to make meaningfully similar miscues; that is, substituting *raced* for *ran* does not dramatically change the meaning of the sentence.

Finally, the observer with an interactive orientation might target behaviors that would be of concern to either the bottom-up or the top-down observer. That is, such factors as using inflectional endings in words to contribute to the meaning of a passage might be deemed important during an observation.

Applications. Cooper and Petrosky (1976) provide a number of observations characteristic of good and poor readers that reflect the interactive approach to reading instruction. These behaviors have been adapted by Bartel (1986) and are presented in Table 7.2. Clay (1979) provides an example of the types of observations that are relevant to beginning readers (see Table 7.3). These observation systems reflect an interactive or top-down approach and are provided here because they reflect current theories of reading instruction.

Lists of observable reading behaviors are helpful in that they (a) allow scope and sequence charts to be put to practical use and/or (b) allow observers to focus on behaviors that reflect their particular reading orientation. That is, they provide the means to observe behaviors that are either listed in scope and sequence charts or are determined by experts in the field to be important in reading.

Checklists and Rating Scales

Nonstandardized checklists and rating scales are used to measure behaviors that are of interest to the observer. Gronlund (1985) notes that checklists and rating scales are similar in both appearance and use. He describes the basic difference in the two devices in terms of the types of judgments that are made during observations. With a rating scale, "one can indicate the *degree* to which a characteristic is present or the *frequency* with which a behavior occurs. The checklist, on the other hand, calls for a simple *yes-no* judgment. It is basically a method of recording whether a characteristic is present or absent" (p. 400).

An example of a reading comprehension checklist is provided in Table 7.4. This checklist is based on Kaluger and Kolson's (1978) scope and sequence chart previously shown in Table 7.1. The inability to accomplish the tasks outlined in the checklist might lead to developing intervention strategies designed to teach the deficient skills or, at the very least, to referring the child for in-depth assessment.

Table 7.5 provides an example of a rating scale that is not based specifically on any scope and sequence chart but rather on skills considered important by Goodman (1976) and by us. Note that these skills represent an interactive approach to reading.

To describe how checklists and rating scales may be used effectively, consider the case of Jonathan, a third grade student who has been placed in the Chickadee reading group. After two weeks of working with his fellow Chickadees, Jon's lack of progress was noted by his teacher, Mrs. Wright. Over a period of the next several days, Mrs. Wright observed Jon's reading behaviors and completed the rating scale and checklist found in tables 7.3 and 7.4. Based on the results of the observations, Jon was referred for additional testing.

TABLE 7.2. Comparison Between Good and Poor Readers

What the Good Reader Does	What the Poor Reader May Do
Notes the distinctive features in letters and words	Fails to notice distinctions between b and d, or was and saw, or m and n, or the configuration of other letters and words; focuses only on certain characteristics, e.g., beginnings of words
Predicts the endings of words (e.g., "right?"), phrases (e.g., "once upon a _____"), or sentences (e.g., "the fire _____ed") with feasible hypothesis	Cannot predict reasonable or possible endings of words, phrases, or sentences
Expects what he or she reads to make sense in terms of his or her own background	Fails to relate reading content to his or her own background
Reads to identify meaning rather than to identify letters or words	Reads to identify individual letters or individual words, or reads because he or she has to
Shifts speed and approach to the type and purpose of reading	Approaches all reading tasks the same way
Formulates hypotheses or expectations about the way the passage will develop an idea	Cannot/does not develop expectations or predictions concerning the direction or main idea of a passage
Takes advantage of the graphic, syntactic, and semantic cues in a passage to speed reading and improve comprehension	Becomes bogged down in attempting to decipher the passage on a letter-by-letter or word-by-word basis

From "Teaching Students Who Have Reading Problems" by N. R. Bartel, 1986, in *Teaching Students with Learning and Behavior Problems* (p. 33) by D. D. Hammill and N. R. Bartel, Boston: Allyn & Bacon. Reprinted by permission.

TABLE 7.3. Observations of Students During the Early Stages of Reading

Location and movement

Does he control directional movement?
  left to right?
  top to bottom?
  return sweep?
Does he locate particular cues in print? Which cues?
Does he read word by word?

Language

Does he control language well?
Does he read for meaning?
Does he control book language?
Does he have a good memory for text?
Does he read for the precise message?

Behavior at difficulties

Does he seek help?
Does he try again?
Does he search for further cues? How?
Note unusual behaviors.

Substitutions

Do the substitutions the child uses make sense? (Meaning)
Do they make an acceptable sentence in English? (Structure)
Could they occur in grammar?
Are some of the letters the same? (Visual or graphic cues)

Self-correction

Does he return to the beginning of the line?
Does he return back a few words?
Does he repeat the word only?
Does he read on to the end of the line?
Does he repeat only the initial sound of a word?
Note unusual behavior.

Cross-checking strategies

At an early stage of text reading
does he ignore discrepancies?
does he check language with movement?
does he check language with visual cues?
does he try to make language, movement and visual cues match?

From *The Early Detection of Reading Difficulties: A Diagnostic Survey with Recovery Procedures* (p. 30) by M. M. Clay, 1979, Portsmouth, NH: Heinemann. Reprinted by permission.

TABLE 7.4. A Sample Checklist Based on Kaluger and Kolson's Scope and Sequence Chart

---

Reading Comprehension

Instructions: At each stage of reading, behaviors have been identified that demonstrate the ability to comprehend what has been read. Place a check on the line next to each behavior if it has been observed of the student.

Preprimer Stage

_____ Associates text and pictures

_____ Follows oral directions

_____ Determines the main idea

_____ Notes details

_____ Recognizes sequences

_____ Draws conclusions

_____ Sees relationships

Primer Stage

_____ Forms judgments

_____ Makes inferences

_____ Classifies

First Reader

_____ Recalls story facts

_____ Predicts outcomes

_____ Follows printed directions

Adapted from *Reading and Learning Disabilities* by G. Kaluger and C. J. Kolson, 1978, Columbus, OH: Charles E. Merrill. Adapted by permission.

TABLE 7.5. A Sample Rating Scale Based on Goodman's Important Reading Skills

Instructions: Below are listed several behaviors that relate to reading. Based on observations of the student, rate the degree to which the child demonstrates proficiency in each ability by circling the number that corresponds to the degree of mastery.

The reader has the ability to . . .

	Not at all				At all Times
scan.	1	2	3	4	5
fix or focus the eye on a line of print.	1	2	3	4	5
select the most important graphic cues, such as initial consonants.	1	2	3	4	5
predict the graphic presentation from syntactic and growing semantic constraints.	1	2	3	4	5
form an image to check what is actually seen with what one is expected to see.	1	2	3	4	5
search memory so that language knowledge as well as experience and conceptual level can be brought to bear.	1	2	3	4	5
formulate a tentative hypothesis or make guesses on the basis of the minimal number of cues and relevant knowledge related to syntax and semantics.	1	2	3	4	5
incorporate semantic and syntactic testing (i.e., asking whether what has been read makes sense and whether it sounds like language).	1	2	3	4	5
determine if the working hypothesis has failed either the semantic or syntactic tests, to recall the graphic image for a match, and to gather more graphic information if needed.	1	2	3	4	5
regress when an hypothesis has failed so that the point of error may be located and the text can be processed.	1	2	3	4	5
decode (i.e., integrate new stimulus with those learned previously to form meaning).	1	2	3	4	5

Adapted from "Reading: A Psycholinguistic Guessing Game" by K. Goodman in *Theoretical Models and Processes of Reading,* edited by M. Singer and R. Ruddell, 1976, Newark, DE: International Reading Association. Adapted by permission.

In sum, experienced teachers internalize the skills progression associated with reading. They observe students' reading habits informally and use checklists and rating scales to determine to what extent children exhibit proficiency in targeted areas. Failure to demonstrate proficiency is crucial to the determination of a reading problem. Further, the degree to which a deficiency exists often determines whether a student is referred for further evaluation. For example, observations may indicate that a student can identify words adequately but exhibits mild to moderate weaknesses in comprehension; perhaps this student would remain in the regular classroom and receive supplemental instruction. In contrast, the student who is observed to have a severe deficiency in word identification and comprehension might require additional testing to see if he or she qualifies for special intervention in remedial reading or special education. While further assessment will continue to examine the student's performance relative to specific reading skills, it will also likely examine areas that are presumed to affect reading performance. These areas are the focus of the next section.

IDENTIFYING OTHER PROBLEMS ASSOCIATED WITH READING

Several nonreading factors are of concern to teachers, diagnosticians, and others associated with reading assessment. These factors are often considered correlates of reading, since specific deficits in them may impact the development of reading proficiency. Many factors are purported to relate to reading proficiency, including intelligence, affect, spoken language, sight, and hearing. Each is examined here, and an example case, Jonathan, will show how nonstandardized procedures may be used to evaluate the constructs listed.

Intelligence

Intelligence, or aptitude, refers to the basic mental ability that is needed to perform a task—in this case, reading. The importance of the relationship between intelligence and reading ability is illustrated by the fact that many reading test authors attempt to demonstrate the construct validity of their devices by showing a significant correlation between the scores achieved on their reading tests and those achieved on an intelligence measure. This is because research has indicated that intelligence can be a reasonable predictor of reading achievement. As early as 1940, Kirk noted that intelligence factors can have a limiting effect on a child's potential level of reading success. Harris (1970) also notes that intelligence test scores have been an important factor in determining a child's readiness for reading. Hammill and McNutt

(1981) reviewed 100 different studies that yielded 486 correlation coefficients examining the relationship between intelligence and reading performance. The median coefficient of .61 suggests that a high correlation exists between the two constructs. Harris (1970) notes that intelligence test scores have been an important factor in determining a child's readiness for reading.

Bond, Tinker, Wasson, and Wasson (1984) caution, however, that "intellectual development alone does not determine how well a given child will or should read" (p. 69). In fact, Vernon (1957) states that a low intelligence quotient is not a direct cause of reading disability. In summarizing the evidence against a direct comparison of mental age and reading level, Spache (1981) notes:

1. Intelligence tests do not show a very close relationship to reading tests, even when they are group tests of intelligence that actually involve reading. Individual tests show even less of a relationship.

2. At primary grades, particularly, the similarity between mental and reading test results exists in very moderate form. The relationship increases somewhat as the age of the pupil increases and reading tests become stronger measures of the reasoning factor. But the parallelism is never great enough to permit individual predictions. Mental tests vary in their content: some measure elements important in the reading act as vocabulary and reasoning; others stress quantitative and spatial thinking that is irrelevant. Hence different tests vary greatly in their relationship to reading performance.

3. Reading success is more dependent upon instructional method and degree of personalized attention than upon mental age. Pupils with similar mental ages will not necessarily make the same progress under the same method or organizational pattern.

4. Since human beings normally vary in their development of cognitive processes or reading skills, mental age cannot be expected to predict performances in a variety of areas, as vocabulary, word analysis, comprehension, and rate.

5. The only level at which mental ages and reading levels tend to be similar is in the IQ range from 90 to 110. Above this range, reading tends to be significantly lower; while below this range, reading tends to excel mental age.

Both mental and reading test scores have sizeable errors of estimate that are often ignored in these comparisons. Differences in some cases should be greater than a year or even two or three before they can be considered real. Since intelligence and environment interact to determine the individual's functioning, no simple comparison or predictive formula can work for any sizeable number of pupils, for it ignores all the environmental, linguistic, socioeconomic, and personality factors present in each case.[1]

---

[1]From *Diagnosing and Correcting Reading Disabilities* (p. 85) by G. Spache, 1981, Boston: Allyn & Bacon. Reprinted by permission.

Given the differing views of Spache (1981) and Kirk (1940), among others, reading specialists are left in a quandary as to the emphasis that should be placed on intelligence as it relates to reading. Given the data, one can safely assume that intelligence and reading are related to some degree, thus justifying consideration of intelligence in the evaluation of reading difficulties. However, since the relationship between the two constructs is far from perfect, reading specialists must be cautious when examining the data that they have.

Intelligence is examined quantitatively using a norm referenced standardized test such as the *Wechsler Intelligence Scale for Children–Revised* (Wechsler, 1974), the *Kaufman Assessment Battery for Children* (Kaufman, 1983), or the *Detroit Tests of Learning Aptitude* (Hammill, 1985; Hammill & Bryant, 1986). In addition to tests, however, valuable evidence of intellectual maturity can be gathered through observations. Such qualitative assessment practices require knowing the characteristics of slow learners that have been provided over the years (Baker, 1929; Haring & Schiefelbusch, 1967; Ingram, 1950; Kephart, 1971). Kennedy (1977) has surveyed the literature and provides several behaviors that are of interest. While cautioning that many of the behaviors can be recognized among children of average or superior intelligence, "they do furnish a point of departure for classifying slow learners" (p. 439). Several of the behaviors noted by Kennedy have been used to form a rating scale (Table 7.6), which can provide the observer with the means to rate students informally.

Earlier, we introduced Jonathan, a third grader who is experiencing reading difficulties. As part of the screening process, Mrs. Wright, Jonathan's teacher, completed the rating scale shown in Table 7.6 and determined that Jonathan's behaviors were indicative of normal intelligence. She consulted the school records and found that his performance on the *Short Form Test of Academic Aptitude* (Sullivan, Clark, & Tiegs, 1978), a group administered intelligence test, fell in the average range. Thus, she concluded that Jon's reading problem was probably not related to low level intellectual functioning.

Affect

Affect refers to emotional adjustment, including self-image, ego involvement, and so forth. The status of personal affect influences the way people perceive themselves in relation to society, which includes the schools. One of the major concerns of researchers who examine the relationship between affect and reading performance is whether emotional maladjustment contributes to a reading problem or whether the reading problem contributes to emotional difficulties. As Fernald (1943) notes, "Some children fail to learn because they are emotionally unstable; others become emotionally unstable because they

TABLE 7.6. Slow Learner Rating Scale

Directions: Rate each behavior 1 to 4 as it applies to the student. Use the following descriptors:

> 1 = Not at all like the student
> 2 = Not much like the student
> 3 = Somewhat like the student
> 4 = Very much like the student

The student . . .

1 2 3 4   is slow to perceive and react to objects or happenings in the environment.

1 2 3 4   asks few questions and has little desire to follow up the answers to a question.

1 2 3 4   uses rote memory rather than reasoning in learning.

1 2 3 4   lacks fluency, clarity, and precision in using language.

1 2 3 4   has a poor sense of time and of time relationships.

1 2 3 4   shows little interest in trying new ways of performing a task.

1 2 3 4   is unable to give logical reasons for a belief or opinion.

1 2 3 4   can learn few words or new ideas at one sitting or in any given length of time.

1 2 3 4   needs much repetition in order to learn skills or understand new ideas.

1 2 3 4   requires much personal recognition, individual attention, and sincere praise.

1 2 3 4   is retarded in physical growth.

1 2 3 4   has poor motor coordination.

1 2 3 4   seems unsure and hesitant when responding to questions.

1 2 3 4   uses short, choppy sentences in conversation.

1 2 3 4   misses school frequently because of illness.

Adapted from *Classroom Approaches to Remedial Reading* (p. 439) by E. C. Kennedy, 1977, Itasca, IL: Peacock. Adapted by permission.

fail to learn" (p. 7). Either way, we agree with Rabinovitch (1968), who notes that "no discussion of reading problems in children should avoid mention of the inordinate suffering experienced by otherwise normal youngsters, cut off from communication channels that are increasingly vital for survival today" (p. 10).

Spache and Spache (1977) note that such personality traits as excessive timidity or fearfulness, hyperactivity, or overaggressiveness handicap young learners in the classroom. Richek, List, and Lerner (1983) describe five psychodynamic symptoms that have been cited in the literature as associated with poor readers: learning block, hostile-aggressive behavior, passive-withdrawn behavior, low self-esteem and depression, and anxiety. While discrete symptoms, all can result from the frustration that is associated with reading failure. For example, the student who is conditioned to failure may develop a low self-esteem, which may cause him or her to withdraw and balk at instruction (i.e., develop a learning block that is difficult to break through). It is particularly important to note, however, that many students with emotional problems have little difficulty in learning to read. Similarly, many students with reading problems experience little apparent difficulty in emotional adjustment. This is illustrated by Hammill and McNutt's (1981) survey of thirty studies involving affect and reading achievement. The researchers found that the range of the 603 coefficients was from nonsignificant to .77, with the median coefficient being nonsignificant.

Spache and Spache (1977) note that teacher appraisal is an effective tool for assessing emotional problems in students. Bader (1980) provides a series of behaviors that fit nicely into a rating scale that can be useful to professionals interested in gaining information of an emotional nature for their nonreaders (Table 7.7).

Continuing with our example of Jonathan, during the screening process Mrs. Wright made note of Jonathan's affective behaviors by completing the rating scale depicted in Table 7.7. She also met with Jonathan's father, who described his son as a generally happy child who gets along well with other family members and his friends. In fact, the boy's father noted that Jonathan seemed happy with school and with how he was doing. This information, coupled with her observations of Jonathan's affective behaviors in the classroom and on the playground, led Mrs. Wright to suspect that the reading difficulty was not related to behavior problems.

Spoken Language

Spoken language skills involve the ability to meaningfully interpret spoken symbols. Clay (1979) notes that "children bring to the reading situation, fluent oral language. This consists of an unconscious control of most of the sounds of the language, a large vocabulary of word labels for meanings that are

TABLE 7.7. Affect Rating Scale

Instructions: Using the numeric descriptors 1 to 4, rate the student's affective behaviors listed below.

1 = Very much like the student
2 = Somewhat like the student
3 = Not much like the student
4 = Not at all like the student

The student is . . .

1 2 3 4 impulsive; responds quickly without thinking.

1 2 3 4 resistant; reluctant to change.

1 2 3 4 dependent; relies on others instead of figuring out the next step.

1 2 3 4 inflexible; finds difficulty in shifting to alternative strategies.

1 2 3 4 unable to concentrate; cannot focus on the task at hand.

1 2 3 4 lacking confidence; unable to risk making a mistake.

1 2 3 4 lacking in ability to generalize; has difficulty deducing the principle or seeing the point.

1 2 3 4 unable to transfer learning; has difficulty in applying knowledge in different settings.

1 2 3 4 unable to identify critical differences; has difficulty focusing on critical elements.

1 2 3 4 lacking persistence; unable to stay on task for reasonable length of time.

1 2 3 4 unwilling to practice; impatient with reviews and repetition.

1 2 3 4 unable to accept failure; failure results in strong emotional interference with further efforts.

understood, and strategies for constructing sentences" (p. 2). Thus, one would expect oral language competence to be highly related to reading performance. Research, however, provides conflicting evidence as to the relationship between spoken language and reading. Some researchers point to a low to nonsignificant relationship between oral language abilities and reading performance in primary students. Others, (e.g., Dechant, 1964; Harris, 1970; Heilman, 1972; Loban, 1963; Strickland, 1969; Zintz, 1970) have described the importance of language skills to reading. Vogel (1974, 1975) and Wiig and Semel (1976) suggest that language delay may be an indication of later difficulty in learning to read for many students.

Hammill and McNutt (1981) surveyed eight studies involving 33 coefficients and found the median to be .51, a moderate relationship. This led the researchers to conclude, "To find that oral language relates to reading is not surprising; however, to discover that it is only 'marginally' predictive of reading is most surprising. Apparently, good spoken language is no guarantee that a person will also be a good reader" (p. 36).

Bryant, Bryant, Bunney, and Schuele (1984) provide a rating scale that can be used to examine children's spoken language skills (Table 7.8). The device can be used to gauge children's functional use of speech, as it was used with Jonathan, our example. Upon completion of the rating scale, Mrs. Wright noted with concern Jonathan's apparent spoken language weaknesses. Specifically, Jon seemed to have deficiencies in the area of syntax. This, she hypothesized, might be related to Jonathan's inability to provide functionally similar substitutions when reading orally. She decided to note this observation and discuss it with the diagnostician upon referral.

Visual Impairment

The research concerning the relationship between sight deficiencies and reading has also provided conflicting results. Bond, Tinker, Wasson, and Wasson (1984), however, after reviewing the literature involving visual deficiencies, cite fairly consistent trends.

1. There is a slightly greater percentage of visual deficits among children with reading disability than among children without reading disability.

2. Children with visual defects, as a group, tend to read more poorly than children without visual defects.

3. On the other hand, many children with visual defects learn to read as well as or better than children without visual defects.

4. No matter what kind of visual deficiency is studied, some children can be found who have that specific kind or type of visual deficiency who are making good progress in reading. (p. 53)

TABLE 7.8. Spoken Language Rating Scale

1 = Not at all like the student
2 = Not much like the student
3 = Somewhat like the student
4 = Very much like the student

The ability to . . .

. . . attend to the speaker.	1 2 3 4
. . . verbalize complete thoughts.	1 2 3 4
. . . name common objects when given a verbal description.	1 2 3 4
. . . describe more than one dimension/trait of an object.	1 2 3 4
. . . provide concise descriptions of common objects.	1 2 3 4
. . . use conventional grammatical word order.	1 2 3 4
. . . use prosody (stress, intonation, pitch) to aid in meaning.	1 2 3 4
. . . use inflectional endings to provide meaning.	1 2 3 4
. . . give verbal directions in logical order.	1 2 3 4
. . . relate simple personal experiences in proper order.	1 2 3 4
. . . adapt language appropriately to different situations.	1 2 3 4
. . . pronounce words appropriately for age.	1 2 3 4
. . . speak clearly and distinctly.	1 2 3 4
. . . participate in conversations appropriately (does not monopolize).	1 2 3 4
. . . identify rhyming words.	1 2 3 4
. . . produce rhyming words.	1 2 3 4
. . . answer what, where, and who questions (literal comprehension).	1 2 3 4
. . . answer why, how, and what if questions (inferential comprehension).	1 2 3 4
. . . identify multiple meanings in words.	1 2 3 4
. . . use compound sentences (uses conjunctions to combine complete thoughts).	1 2 3 4
. . . understand simple prepositions.	1 2 3 4
. . . follow simple directions.	1 2 3 4
. . . give opposites when requested.	1 2 3 4
. . . identify synonyms on request.	1 2 3 4
. . . use contractions appropriately.	1 2 3 4
. . . talk in sentences of six or more words.	1 2 3 4
. . . mark tense appropriately.	1 2 3 4
. . . formulate questions to elicit desired response.	1 2 3 4

The last observation is of particular significance. The presence of sight deficiency may contribute to a reading problem or may not. Clearly, however, children with sight problems should be identified, since the presence of a significant deficit may result in a disturbance of the reading process. The following useful behavioral symptoms for sight are provided by Knox (1953). These behaviors are readily observable to the teacher during class time.

1. Facial distortions

2. Book held close to face

3. Tenseness during visual work

4. Head tilting

5. Head thrust forward

6. Body tenseness while looking at distant objects

7. Poor sitting position

8. Head moving excessively while reading

9. Eyes rubbed frequently

10. Tendency to avoid close visual work

11. Tendency to lose place in reading (pp. 54–55)

Such observations can be incorporated into a helpful checklist like the one provided in Table 7.9 (Kennedy, 1977). If behaviors such as those noted in the checklist are present, the child should be given a complete visual examination by an eye care professional. In our example, Jonathan's teacher completed the checklist and observed that there were few instances where sight problems appeared to be in evidence. Thus, she concluded that a referral to an eye care specialist was not warranted.

Hearing Impairment

Most hearing deficits result in a loss in acuity. Early investigators (e.g., Betts, 1957; Henry, 1948; Johnson, 1957) found that hearing impairments were related to low reading performance, particularly when the losses were within the high frequency ranges. In addition, Dechant (1971) noted that, in general, marked hearing loss is associated with reading retardation.

Conversely, Robinson (1953) found that a loss in hearing acuity was an infrequent cause of reading disability. Perhaps the most meaningful observation has been made by Kirk, Kliebhan, and Lerner (1978), who stated, "Although it is well established that hard-of-hearing children are retarded in reading, the research does not indicate that the hearing acuity of the

TABLE 7.9. Checklist of Visual Difficulties

Name_____ Date_____

Date of last professional eye examination_____

Checklist completed by_____ Referred_____

Symptom	Check if Symptom Exists	
	Yes	No
1. Acuity low on test instruments.	____	____
2. Specific difficulties detected with instruments.	____	____
3. Has had professional examination within one year.	____	____
4. Eyes or eyelids are red, bloodshot, or swollen.	____	____
5. Eyes water after close work.	____	____
6. Squints or shields eyes when facing light.	____	____
7. Complains of frequent headaches.	____	____
8. Closes or covers one eye when reading.	____	____
9. Holds book at an odd angle when reading.	____	____
10. Turns head to one side when reading.	____	____
11. Complains that words look fuzzy or blurred.	____	____
12. Complains of seeing double images or lines.	____	____
13. Complains of painful, stinging, itching eyes.	____	____
14. Has difficulty in reading from chalkboard or charts.	____	____
15. Reads significantly better when print is large.	____	____
16. Loses place more often when print is small.	____	____
17. Has trouble with the return sweep when reading orally.	____	____
18. Keeps moving book to different distances from eyes.	____	____
19. Holds book too close or too far away from eyes.	____	____
20. Frowns or seems to be in a strain when reading.	____	____
21. Tires easily when doing close work.	____	____
22. Is irritable after close reading.	____	____
23. Selects books with large print and pictures.	____	____
24. Rubs eyes frequently when reading.	____	____
25. Blinks or closes eyes often when reading.	____	____

From *Classroom Approaches to Remedial Reading* (p. 385) by E. C. Kennedy, 1977, Itasca, IL: Peacock. Reprinted by permission.

general population of school children is highly correlated with reading achievement" (p. 19).

Bond et al. (1984) provide a list of observations concerning hearing abilities. Hearing deficits may be suspected if some of the following behaviors are observed:

1. Inattention during listening activities

2. Frequent misunderstanding of oral directions or numerous requests for repetition of statements

3. Turning one ear toward the speaker or thrusting head forward when listening

4. Intent gazing at the speaker's face or strained posture while listening

5. Monotone speech, poor pronunciation, or indistinct articulation

6. Complaints of earache or hearing difficulty

7. Insistence on closeness to sound sources

8. Frequent colds, discharging ears, or difficult breathing (p. 57)

Behaviors such as those presented here may be incorporated into a checklist that is helpful for targeting hearing weaknesses. Devices such as that offered in Table 7.10 (Kennedy, 1977) may provide justification for referral to a hearing specialist. For our example child, Jonathan, Mrs. Wright completed the checklist and noted that Jonathan's hearing did not appear to be a problem. She also recalled that, in her conversation with the child's father, he had noted that Jon had had tubes in his ears as a young child, and that recent pure tone tests by an audiologist had determined that hearing problems no longer existed.

Summary

This section has described a variety of reading correlates (i.e., factors that may impact the development of reading abilities). Clearly, the presence of correlational deficiencies need not be interpreted as a cause for a reading disability, though on occasion they may be. Likewise, the student with con-current reading and correlational deficits should not be expected to be "cured" of the reading problem once the correlate deficiency is remedied. However, professionals involved with reading assessment should account for intelligence, affect, spoken language, sight, and hearing when determining the presence of a reading problem. We have provided examples of how checklists and rating scales can be used during the screening process to identify deficiencies not only in correlational abilities but in the skills directly related to reading. After identifying a reading problem and determining that

---

TABLE 7.10. Checklist of Hearing Difficulties

Name_____ Date_____

Date of last professional auditory examination_____

Checklist completed by_____ Referred_____

| Symptom | Check if Symptom Exists |
	Yes	No
1. Inclines one ear toward speaker when listening.	___	___
2. Holds mouth open while listening.	___	___
3. Holds head at an angle when taking part in discussions.	___	___
4. Reads in an unnatural tone of voice.	___	___
5. Uses faulty pronunciation on common words.	___	___
6. Enunciation is indistinct.	___	___
7. Invariably asks to have instructions and directions repeated.	___	___
8. Breathes through the mouth.	___	___
9. Has discharging ears.	___	___
10. Frequently complains of earache or sinusitis.	___	___
11. Has frequent attacks of head colds.	___	___
12. Complains of buzzing noises in the ears.	___	___
13. Seems to be lazy, inattentive, or indifferent.	___	___
14. Does not excel in games requiring observance of oral directions.	___	___
15. Cannot follow the "trend of thought" during oral discussions.	___	___

From *Classroom Approaches to Remedial Reading* (p. 391) by E. C. Kennedy, 1977, Itasca, IL: Peacock. Reprinted by permission.

it is severe enough to warrant further testing, the teacher usually refers a student for a more complete evaluation. As already noted, the diagnostic testing will include the use of nonstandardized procedures and standardized tests. The manner with which standardized tests are used to identify the degree of a reading deficit is the subject of the remainder of this chapter.

IDENTIFYING A PROBLEM USING STANDARDIZED PROCEDURES

In Chapter 1, Hammill describes a standardized test as one having "clear rules governing its use and [one which] will require uniform skills in administering the test and interpreting its results." Several considerations affect a user's selection of a particular test. These include (a) the technical adequacy of a test, including its reliability, validity, and the characteristics of the device's normative sample; (b) the format of the test (e.g., whether it is designed to be administered to groups or individuals; the types of stimulus/response required by the test, i.e., whether speaking, listening, or marking is involved); (c) the time it takes for the test to be administered; and (d) the ages or grades for which the test is intended. This information is described in detail by Hammill in this volume and by Brown and Bryant (1984).

A cursory inspection of texts that list standardized tests (e.g., *Tests*, Sweetland & Keyser, 1983; *Tests in Print*, Buros, 1974; *A Consumer's Guide to Tests in Print*, Hammill, Brown, & Bryant, in press) indicates that hundreds of instruments are available to measure reading performance. This section examines how standardized tests are used to assess three essential elements in reading: (a) recognizing letters and words in print, (b) understanding words and ideas in print, and (c) reading passages with speed.

Recognizing Letters and Words in Print

Many tests of reading attempt to assess an individual's ability to recognize letters and words in print. This skill is measured in two basic areas: (a) word recognition and (b) word identification. Each is discussed in this section, including a description of the content and how it is measured by a number of available tests.

Word Recognition. The ability to recognize words in print is assessed by having a person read aloud isolated words presented in flash, graded word lists, sentences, or passages or to recognize words in print that are stated by the examiner. As might be expected, the ability to recognize individual words in print may be assessed using different formats. The user must decide upon the format that best meets the needs of the testing situation. For example, tests that require oral responses obviously prohibit the administration of the test to more than one student at a time. In addition, some examiners might wish to distinguish between the ability to recognize words presented in flash (i.e., when words are shown for a brief period of time) and the ability to simply read words without any time limits. Thus, the nature of the formats used by the tests must be considered when selecting a reading test.

The Word Identification subtest of the *Woodcock Reading Mastery Test* (WRMT) (Woodcock, 1973), the Word Identification subtest of the *Diagnostic Achievement Test For Adolescents* (DATA) (Newcomer & Bryant, 1986), items from the Reading Recognition subtest of the *Peabody Individual Achievement Test* (PIAT) (Dunn & Markwardt, 1970), the Reading subtest of the *Wide Range*

Achievement Test–Revised (WRAT–R) (Jastak & Wilkinson, 1984), The Words: Untimed subtest of the *Gates-McKillop-Horowitz* (GMH) (Gates, McKillop, & Horowitz, 1981), and the *Slosson Oral Reading Test* (SORT) (Slosson, 1983) all use a similar format to assess word recognition abilities. An example of the word in isolation format is provided in Figure 7.1, which shows a copy of the DATA Word Identification subtest. The list of words is presented to the examinee, who reads them one at a time; no time limits are imposed, although the examiner is told not to spend too much time with individual

FIGURE 7.1. Word Identification Subtest of DATA

man
house
stop

Practice

1–9	10–19	20–29
transfusion	artery	configuration
undertone	unfounded	align
recede	impartial	affirmative
monogram	villain	miscellaneous
nymph	feminine	aviation
victorious	garrison	antagonize
immeasurable	discipline	betroth
utensil	orientation	ultimate
cancellation	rehabilitate	hospitable
	denomination	indignity

30–37	38–45
obituary	fuselage
domicile	trepidation
excruciating	extemporaneous
dubious	variegated
sanctify	reconnaissance
lithe	magnanimous
equilibrium	cynosure
benighted	bucolic

From *Diagnostic Achievement Test for Adolescents* by P. L. Newcomer and B. R. Bryant, 1986, Austin, TX: PRO-ED. Reprinted by permission.

items. Usually the words included in the tests are selected from graded word lists. For example, on DATA the words selected for the Word Identification subtest are from the Reading Vocabulary list of the *EDL Core Vocabularies in Reading, Mathematics, Science, and Social Studies* (Taylor, Frackenpohl, & White, 1979). Such lists generally reflect the words commonly found in school textbooks.

The Words: Flash subtest of the GMH provides an example of word recognition assessment where words are presented in flash. Here, the tachistoscope, a piece of heavy stock paper with a peephole that exposes a single word, is used to present each word (e.g., *interest*) for about one-half second. Such a technique presumes to distinguish between words recognized on sight and those that need to be decoded using word analysis strategies.

A third format used to assess word recognition is demonstrated with the R level of the *Gates-MacGinitie Reading Tests* (GM) (MacGinitie, 1978). Here, the student selects from a series of response choices the word that is stated by the examiner. For example, when the teacher says the word *plate* aloud, the child marks the oval below his or her choice from one of four response choices provided.

A final example is provided in Figure 7.2 by the *Gray Oral Reading Test–Revised* (GORT–R) (Wiederholt & Bryant, 1986). With this subtest, the student reads a paragraph orally, and each deviation from print (i.e., error) is marked with a slash by the examiner. This index contributes to the GORT–R's Passage Score. A similar technique for assessing word recognition is available on the Oral Reading section of the GMH.

With regard to the different ways of assessing word recognition, Spache (1981) cautions examiners not to regard errors made on words presented in isolation in the same way as errors made on words in context. The reader is forced to rely almost exclusively on graphic and phonemic clues when words are isolated, whereas words in sentences may allow the context to play an important role in word recognition. The work of K. Goodman, cited by Smith, Goodman, and Meredith (1976), reinforces this view. In several studies, first, second, and third graders were able to read over two-thirds of the words they had missed on a list when the words appeared in the context of a story. Thus, we suggest that word recognition be examined in the context of running words, if students are able to respond to such a format. Younger readers, and those with serious deficits, may more appropriately be tested using graded word lists. When possible, however, reading assessment should be undertaken in a natural reading environment. This would involve contextual reading.

FIGURE 7.2. Sample GORT–R Paragraph

A-5 Prompt: Say, "THIS STORY IS ABOUT ANIMALS HAVING A PROBLEM. READ THE STORY TO FIND OUT WHAT THE PROBLEM IS AND HOW IT WAS SOLVED."

1. A blue jay was perched on a limb looking for water. Having just
2. flown a great distance, she was very thirsty. At that moment she
3. happened to spot a water jar on the ground, so she flew down and
4. tried to get a drink from the jar. But there was so little water in the
5. jar that she was unable to drink. Just as she felt that she would
6. surely die of thirst, an idea struck her. The jay gathered a pile of
7. stones and began dropping them in the jar. Little by little the water
8. rose and at last the jay could drink her fill.

Comp. 1. (a) ____ 2. (a) ____ 3. (c) ____ 4. (c) ____ 5. (b) ____ Comp. Score ____ Rate ____ Dev. from Print ____

From *Gray Oral Reading Tests–Revised* (p. 12) by J. L. Wiederholt and B. R. Bryant, 1986, Austin, TX: PRO-ED. Reprinted by permission.

Word Identification. Word identification is used synonymously here with *word analysis* and *word attack* and describes the reading strategies that are employed to decode unknown words. This ability includes all aspects of alphabet knowledge, including the ability to discriminate among letters, associate sounds with letters, and analyze the phonetic and structural aspects of words. Once again, numerous tests reflecting a variety of formats are available to consumers to examine the ability to apply word attack strategies. In this section, the areas within word identification are divided into three categories: (a) letter identification, (b) phonetic analysis, and (c) structural analysis.

Letter identification. Almost every test that measures word identification devotes items or subtests to assessing students' knowledge of letter names or the ability to match lower and upper case letter forms. The Letter Identification subtest of the WRMT, items from the Alpha/Word Knowledge subtest of the *Diagnostic Achievement Battery* (DAB) (Newcomer & Curtis, 1983), and items from the PIAT provide examples of one method that is available to assess alphabet knowledge. With these devices, the student is shown a series of letters, and he or she states what the letters are. An example of such a format as it is used on the Letter Identification subtest of the WRMT is provided below. As can be seen in the example, both upper and lower case letters are provided as stimuli, and the student calls out loud the name of each letter.

X   B   S   i   C

Level 10 of the *California Achievement Tests* (CAT) (CTB/McGraw-Hill, 1978) provides an example of a different means to assess letter identification. In the first item, students identify letters that are named by an examiner by filling in the bubble below the letter. The pictures to the left of the item are used to help the students keep their place. In the next item, the student matches the upper and lower case forms of a letter once again by marking the response choice.

TEST 3   LETTER NAMES

^		L l	S s	T t	R r
		○	●	○	○

As with all instances involving assessment, the examiner must ask why something is being tested. In the vast majority of cases, letter identification testing is of little clinical use, unless readiness is being tested. Even then, we would recommend that little time be spent determining whether a child knows the letters of the alphabet.

Phonetic analysis. The measurement of a reader's ability to make associations between letters and sounds, usually referred to as grapheme-phoneme correspondences, is often a vital component of a reading test. The Phonetic Analysis subtest of the *Stanford Diagnostic Reading Test* (SDRT) (Karlsen, Madden, & Gardner, 1974) requires the student to identify the letter or letter combinations that match(es) the initial or final sound(s) of words. As is seen below, a picture of the earth is on the student's booklet. The child is given the verbal instructions, "In box number 9, you see a picture of the earth. Mark the space next to the letters that tell the ending sound of 'earth.' "

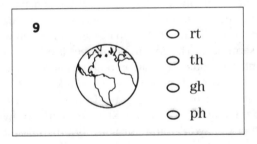

The same format is used on the Letter Sounds subtest of the CAT, Level 10. The Word Analysis subtest from the Early Primary Battery of the *Iowa Tests of Basic Skills* (ITBS) (Hieronymus, Lindquist, & Hoover, 1982) is similar but uses pictures instead of letters. Here, the examiner asks the child to mark the picture that begins (or ends) with the sound(s) presented in a stimulus word. For example, item 13 (shown below) requires the child to fill in the oval under the picture whose name begins with the same sound as *prune*.

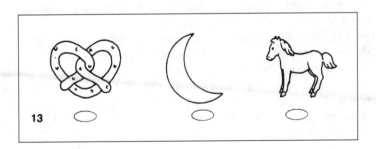

A popular method for assessing phonetic analysis skills is used on the Word Attack subtest of the WRMT. The student is shown a series of nonsense words (e.g., *tat*) and is asked, "How do these words sound?" Credit is awarded if the child's response matches the pronunciation provided in the test manual.

---

tat

Unfortunately, in many cases much more time may be spent in reading assessment examining phonetic analysis skills than is probably needed. The most important question to be asked is whether readers can use phonetic clues in conjunction with context clues to identify unknown words. For example, when the sentence, "The Indian chief held a pow-wow with his warriors," is encountered, could the reader combine context clues with phonetic clues to identify the word *chief*, if that word is unknown? That is, given the ability to read, "The Indian _____ held a pow-wow with his warriors," could the student combine the context clues with knowledge that the unknown word begins with *ch* to figure out that the missing word is *chief*? Sadly, we know of no standardized reading test that provides such a means to assess phonetic analysis. Thus, we would question the value of assessing phonetic skills independent of context, particularly if the intent is to teach those phonetic skills that are deficient.

Structural analysis. This form of word analysis deals with the use of structural attributes of words (e.g., affixes, roots, compounds, contractions, and syllables) in decoding. The Word Analysis subtest of the WRMT provides an example of one format for measuring structural analysis abilities. The nonsense words include selected items that can be decoded with the assistance of structural clues (e.g., *wip's*).

Level 12 of the CAT examines compounds, syllables, contractions, roots, and affixes using a different format (Figure 7.3). The first two items require a child to select the response choice that forms a compound when combined with the stimulus word (e.g., foot + ball = football). Items 3 and 4 require the child to identify the number of syllables contained in the stimulus word (e.g., 1 for *raise*, 2 for *cabin*). Items 5 and 6 are used to elicit the two words that form the stimulus contraction (e.g., in item 5, *that is* for *that's*). Items

FIGURE 7.3. Structural Analysis Subtest of CAT

1 foot	ball ○	head ○	game ○	shoe ○
2 birth	hill ○	day ○	toy ○	coal ○
3 raise	1 ○	2 ○	3 ○	4 ○
4 cabin	1 ○	2 ○	3 ○	4 ○

5 that's
  ○ that is
  ○ that was
  ○ that says
  ○ that does

6 hadn't
  ○ had to
  ○ had not
  ○ had never
  ○ had taken

7 ○ refill
  ○ dishes
  ○ splashed
  ○ following

8 ○ fields
  ○ roaring
  ○ shouted
  ○ handful

9 ○ boats
  ○ helping
  ○ jumped
  ○ friendly

10 ○ asleep
  ○ unable
  ○ wrong
  ○ brother

11 ○ across
  ○ belong
  ○ farmer
  ○ happen

7 through 9 assess a student's ability to identify an underlined root word (e.g., *refill* for item 7). Items 10 and 11 examine the student's ability to identify affixes, with item 10 providing an underlined prefix (i.e., *un*able) and item 11 providing an underlined suffix (i.e., farm*er*). The SDRT Structural Analysis subtest for the Green level uses a similar format, focusing on what its authors call Word Division and Blending.

Our comments concerning the assessment of structural analysis skills are similar to those regarding phonetic analysis. The use of structural clues to identify unknown words is helpful when combined with contextual clues. Proficiency in isolated skills tells little about a student's ability to read.

Understanding Words and Ideas in Print

As noted in Chapter 6, the essence of reading is meaning; that is, reading is defined as gaining meaning from printed or written symbols. The ability to understand print is known as comprehension and is usually divided into two components: the understanding of individual words (i.e., vocabulary comprehension) and the understanding of running text (i.e., sentence and passage comprehension). The methods used to assess these two, using norm referenced standardized tests, are described here.

Understanding Words. Vocabulary comprehension is the ability to know what individual words in print mean. If readers do not know the meanings of most of the words used by the writer, they will not be able to understand the message being conveyed in print. Further, if readers are unable to associate multiple meanings with words, the message from the writer may be garbled. Consider, for example, the sentence, "The winner of the fencing competition won the gold medal." Some readers might think that the medal was won, not by a swordsman, but by a fence builder. Clearly, vocabulary knowledge is a fundamental aspect of reading comprehension.

In reading assessment, a distinction is made between a sight vocabulary and a meaning vocabulary. For example, a word may be identified properly by a student at sight, but the student may not have an understanding of what the word means. This occurs frequently, particularly with a word that may have been heard and perhaps even used, but incorrectly. To illustrate, one might be able to "call" the word *psycholinguistics*, particularly if one is familiar with the educational literature. Perhaps the word has been seen and heard several times and even an association made, in this case, with spoken language. But the word is not in a person's meaning vocabulary unless he or she is able to define what *psycholinguistics* means. This is but one example of a situation that occurs often in reading situations. Thus, for purposes of this section, the terms *vocabulary comprehension* and *meaning vocabulary* are used synonymously.

Several tests of reading provide measures of vocabulary. While the formats may vary, they all attempt to assess knowledge of what individual words mean. For example, the WRMT uses a system of analogies. With this technique, the student looks at three words that provide some type of relationship and responds with a word that completes the analogy. For example, *dog* is to *walks* as *bird* is to what word? To do this exercise, students must identify the three stimulus words and also know what the three words mean. Only if they can do both tasks can students have a chance to respond correctly to the item. The CAT assesses vocabulary differently, as shown below.

TEST 3   READING VOCABULARY

SAMPLE ITEM A

  <u>put</u> outside

  O use

  O set

  O find

  O work

Here, the reader is given a descriptive phrase (e.g., *put* outside) and must select from four alternatives the one word that goes with the underlined stimulus word (*put*). The bubble is filled in next to the student's response, in this case *set*. Again, identification is necessary to accomplish this task, but clearly the primary content being measured is vocabulary. A third technique is demonstrated below by the *Test of Reading Comprehension* (TORC) (Brown, Hammill, & Wiederholt, 1986). With this device, the stimulus consists of three words that are related in some way. Four response choices are provided, and the student must select two words from the response choices that go with the stimulus words. In the example, *yellow, red,* and *blue* are colors. The student studies the four response choices and selects the two that are common to the stimulus words, in this case *black* and *green,* since they are also colors. A useful feature of the TORC is that, along with the General Vocabulary subtest pictured below, three similar specialized vocabulary subtests are available to measure specific subject matter vocabulary (i.e., Mathematics Vocabulary, Science Vocabulary, and Social Studies Vocabulary).

TORC SUBTEST #1: GENERAL VOCABULARY

DIRECTIONS for each item:

1. Read the 3 words in the box. Think about why they might go together, or how they are alike.
2. Read all the words under the box. Choose the 2 you believe are most like the words in the box.
3. Put X's over the letters that stand for the 2 words you chose.

EXAMPLES

▲ yellow red blue

A. black
B. grass
C. green
D. yes

● teeth nose arm

A. hair
B. air
C. legs
D. too

Vocabulary measures provide an important contribution to reading assessment, as they give the examiner information pertinent to the reading process. Specifically, information concerning the size and nature of a student's meaning vocabulary directly relates to what he or she can be realistically expected to read. For example, most people would have no chance of comprehending the passage on acute nephritis presented in Chapter 6, because the meaning of the words in this passage are generally known only to physicians. The breakdown lies in limited vocabulary, not in an inability to recognize main ideas or make inferences. Thus, vocabulary assessment can yield important clinical data to the examiner about a student's ability to comprehend.

Understanding Ideas in Print. The second element of reading comprehension that is commonly assessed is the understanding of ideas when presented in print. This is the most important assessment, since comprehending passages is the primary goal of reading instruction. In fact, any standardized test purporting to be a comprehensive measure of reading that does not assess sentence or passage comprehension should be considered inadequate. This is true even in early reading assessment. Some form of comprehension should be included, such as that provided on the *Test of Early Reading Ability* (TERA) (Reid, Hresko, & Hammill, 1981). With this test, a story is read to the child, who responds to questions posed by the examiner about the story.

As with all other types of assessment offered thus far, understanding ideas in print is measured using different formats. Knowledge of these formats provides the discerning examiner with a means to select the test that best fits a student or situation. The SDRT demonstrates the use of one format (see below).

TEST 5: Reading Comprehension   Part A

SAMPLES

A The ball is big.

With this measure, the student reads a sentence and selects the picture that goes best with the idea expressed in the sentence. In the example provided, the reader fills in the bubble under the big ball, since that choice goes along with the sentence. A similar technique is available with the Reading Comprehension subtest of the PIAT, wherein a sentence is read by students (e.g., See the boy with the hat), and they select from a set of four pictures the one that is best described by the sentence (Figure 7.4). The primary

---

FIGURE 7.4. Sample Item from the Reading Comprehension Subtest of the PIAT

From *Peabody Individual Achievement Test* (p. 26) by L. Dunn and F. Markwardt, 1970, Circle Pines, MN: American Guidance Service. Reprinted by permission.

difference between the formats of the SDRT and the PIAT is that, with the latter test, the sentence is removed from view as the picture plate is shown. This requires the student not only to comprehend the sentence but to remember briefly what was read.

Figure 7.5 shows another format used to assess passage comprehension. This example is from the *Formal Reading Inventory* (FRI) (Wiederholt, 1985). The FRI requires the student to silently read passages and respond to multiple choice questions that follow each story. Some tests of passage comprehension, such as those provided on the DATA and DAB, also require the student to read paragraphs. However, instead of using multiple choice questions and leaving the passage in front of the student, these devices use open ended questions, such as, "Name two things Tony got at the grocery store," after the passage is removed from view. While tests such as these may involve different types of comprehension questions (e.g., literal, inferential, critical, and affective), most tests provide only one score; that is, a separate score for each comprehension form (e.g., literal, inferential) is not provided.

A third popular method of assessing comprehension is exhibited by the Passage Comprehension subtest of the WRMT. This measure uses the cloze procedure, in which a word is omitted from a sentence or paragraph, and the student is required to generate a word based on the context of the passage. The reader silently peruses the passage and orally provides one word that best fits the context of the passage (see below).

The duck is swimming in the ____.

As noted earlier, knowledge of the formats used by different tests provides a means to select the test that best fits the need of a student and situation. For example, the formats of the WRMT and PIAT do not allow the tests to be administered to groups of students. In addition, the examiner who prefers to examine a variety of comprehension forms (e.g., literal, inferential) might select tests like the FRI, since its questions tap these forms consistently.

Reading with Speed

To read quickly is generally considered a sign of reading proficiency. While reading rate is influenced by numerous factors (e.g., purpose for reading,

---

FIGURE 7.5. Sample Item from the FRI

Story 12

As a poet Mr. Treadwell seems to occupy an indeterminate position between the transcendentalists and the great body of versifiers who address the intellect and sympathies of the multitude. His poems, to accord them their due, are not altogether devoid of meaning. Indeed, they might have won their creator greater notoriety but for an inveterate propensity for allegory, which is apt to invest his doggerel with ethereal conceptions and shadowy imagery. A wearisome perusal of the bibliography of his works reveals that his muse is voluminous; he continues to write and publish with indefatigable verve as if the products of his genius were showered with the accolades that attend a poet laureate. Too ephemeral to suit the popular taste and too stultifying to satisfy even somnambulists, Mr. Treadwell seems destined to appeal only to the mausoleum coterie.

1. What kind of poetry does Mr. Treadwell write?

   a. epics
   b. ballads
   c. lyrics
   d. none of the above

2. According to this passage, the poet Treadwell _____.

   a. enjoys widespread acclaim
   b. is a prolific writer
   c. has captured the quintessence of pragmatism
   d. makes precocious observations

3. This passage is probably written as a(n) _____.
   a. epithet
   b. eulogy
   c. montage
   d. critique

4. What is the tone of this passage?

   a. caustic
   b. blasphemous
   c. magnanimous
   d. noncommittal

5. What do you think the writer feels about Mr. Treadwell's works?

   a. They deserve recognition.
   b. They are paragons for other writers.
   c. They will appeal to connoisseurs of the arts.
   d. They are vapid and nebulous.

From *Formal Reading Inventory* by J. L. Wiederholt, 1975, Austin, TX: PRO-ED. Reprinted by permission.

content), it is considered to be an important skill for mature readers who are often faced with the task of having to read large quantities of material for school assignments. Spache and Spache (1977) note differences in oral and silent reading rates, stating that early studies involving rapid eye movement demonstrated that the average reader could read from one and one-half times to twice as fast silently as orally. Guszak (1985) reports the reading rates identified by McCracken and shown below. As can be easily noted, the rates are similar at the early reading levels, with silent reading rate becoming much higher starting at the third grade.

Standard Reading Inventory Minimum Speeds

Grade	Oral (wpm)	Silent (wpm)
1	60	60
2	70	70
3	90	120
4	120	150
5	120	170
6	150	245
7 and above	150	300

Both measures of silent and oral reading rate are available. The SDRT provides two indices of silent reading rate. The Brown level has the subtest Reading Rate and the Blue level has the subtest Fast Reading. These subtests measure the ability to read relatively simple material quickly.

The GORT–R provides an index of rate for oral reading. Students read aloud a passage, and the time in seconds it takes for the passage to be read is noted. This index contributes to the test's Passage Score. A valuable feature of the GORT–R is that the test, in addition to providing an index of reading speed, provides a measure of oral reading comprehension. As Spache (1981) notes, "Rate of reading scores are relatively meaningless without a related comprehension measure. . . ." (p. 291). We agree; if a measure of rate is to be used, it should always be accompanied by a comprehension score. Speed without understanding is of no practical value to the reader.

IDENTIFYING THE DEGREE OF THE PROBLEM

As previously discussed, experienced professionals have little difficulty in making qualitative judgments about the degree of a reading problem. The further behind the child is, the greater the degree of the deficit. Norm referenced standardized tests provide a means of quantifying the deficiency. These data may be analyzed in two ways. First, the scores may be examined with regard to the degree of the deficit (e.g., mild, moderate, or severe). Second, standard scores may be profiled for graphic presentation. Each method of data analysis is described here.

For purposes of this discussion, the terms *mild, moderate,* and *severe* are used to denote the degree of the deficit. In reality, however, the terms are inadequate to describe the degree of a reading problem. That is, a mild reading problem may not be mild to the student with the deficit. The terms actually describe the degree to which the reading problem is severe, since the problems that reading difficulties can present (e.g., difficulty in academic areas, embarrassment) are severely restricting to the problem reader. Thus, when a child has a "mild" deficit, understand that the deficit is indeed mildly severe.

To judge the degree of a reading deficit quantitatively, the results of the norm referenced standardized tests are examined. Most tests report their results in terms of percentile ranks and standard scores. Percentile ranks designate a person's score in relation to those scores obtained by the normative group. For example, if a child scores at the 60th percentile, then 40% of the normative sample at that age did better than he or she did. Standard scores are deviations of percentile ranks that are based on the distribution of raw score points that have a set mean and standard deviation. As seen in Table 7.11, several standard scores are available for use, the most common being quotients (M = 100, SD = 15), normal curve equivalents (NCEs) (M = 50, SD = 21), T-scores (M = 50, SD = 10), z-scores (M = 0, SD = 1), and stanines (M = 5, SD = 1.96).

To interpret test scores with degree of deficit in mind, a variation of Wiederholt and Bryant's (1986) classification of scores is used (Table 7.12). Using Wechsler (1974) as a guide, Wiederholt and Bryant provide descriptors for the quotient scores achieved on their reading test (GORT–R). As can be seen, approximately 50% of students score from 90 to 110 (i.e., the 26th through the 74th percentiles). This is considered Average performance. The next classification, Below Average, occurs from 80 to 89 (i.e., the 9th through the 25th percentiles). For determining the degree of a reading problem, this would be considered a Mild deficit. Poor performance occurs from 70 to 79 (i.e., between the 2nd and 8th percentiles), which is considered a Moderate deficit. Finally, performance falling below 70, or the 2nd percentile, would be considered Very Poor, or in this case, a Severe deficit. These data allow for a clear degree classification that falls across a variety of standard scores (see Table 3.11).

The second means by which scores may be used to determine the degree of a deficit is through profiling. That is, standard scores can be depicted in graphic form to give a visual presentation of performance. One test that allows for this type of inference is the TORC. Figure 7.6 shows a profile of scores made by Jonathan, the child used in several previous examples. Note that each standard score is provided on the profile sheet to the left of the

TABLE 7.11. Relation of Various Standard Scores to Percentile Rank and to Each Other

Percentile rank	Standard Scores					Deficit
	Quotients	NCE scores	T-scores	z-scores	stanines	
99	150	99	83	+3.33	9	
99	145	99	80	+3.00	9	
99	140	99	77	+2.67	9	
99	135	99	73	+2.33	9	
98	130	92	70	+2.00	9	
95	125	85	67	+1.67	8	
91	120	78	63	+1.34	8	none
84	115	71	60	+1.00	7	
75	110	64	57	+0.67	6	
63	105	57	53	+0.33	6	
50	100	50	50	+0.00	5	
37	95	43	47	−0.33	4	
25	90	36	43	−0.67	4	
16	85	29	40	−1.00	3	mild
9	80	22	37	−1.34	2	
5	75	15	33	−1.67	2	moderate
2	70	8	30	−2.00	1	
1	65	1	27	−2.33	1	
1	60	1	23	−2.67	1	severe
1	55	1	20	−3.00	1	

TABLE 7.12. Classification of Scores

Quotient	Rating	% Included
>130	Very Superior	2.34
121–130	Superior	6.87
111–120	Above Average	16.12
90–110	Average	49.51
80–89	Below Average	16.12
70–79	Poor	6.87
<70	Very Poor	2.34

FIGURE 7.6. Profile of Jonathan's Scores on TORC

SECTION III. TORC PROFILE

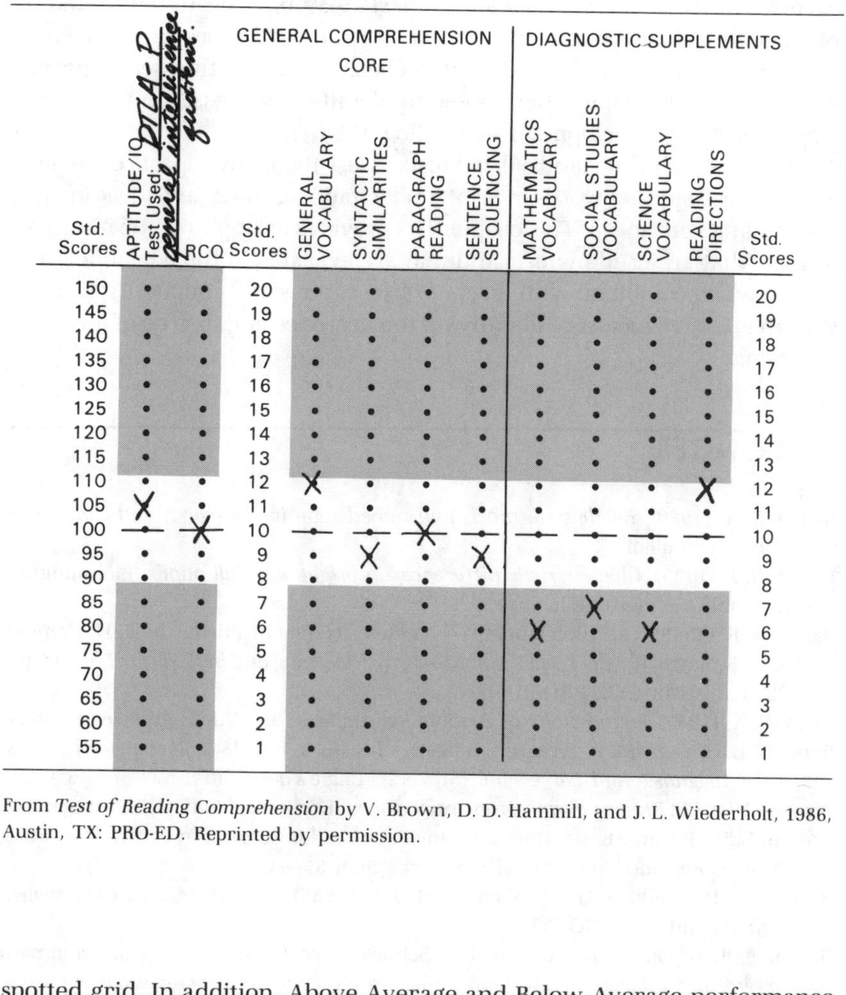

Aptitude/IQ Test Used: *PTLA-P general intelligence quotient* (handwritten)

Std. Scores	RCQ Std. Scores	GENERAL COMPREHENSION CORE				DIAGNOSTIC SUPPLEMENTS				Std. Scores
		GENERAL VOCABULARY	SYNTACTIC SIMILARITIES	PARAGRAPH READING	SENTENCE SEQUENCING	MATHEMATICS VOCABULARY	SOCIAL STUDIES VOCABULARY	SCIENCE VOCABULARY	READING DIRECTIONS	
150	20									20
145	19									19
140	18									18
135	17									17
130	16									16
125	15									15
120	14									14
115	13									13
110	12	X							X	12
105	11									11
100	10			X						10
95	9		X		X					9
90	8									8
85	7						X			7
80	6					X		X		6
75	5									5
70	4									4
65	3									3
60	2									2
55	1									1

From *Test of Reading Comprehension* by V. Brown, D. D. Hammill, and J. L. Wiederholt, 1986, Austin, TX: PRO-ED. Reprinted by permission.

spotted grid. In addition, Above Average and Below Average performance areas are shaded for easy reference.

The examiner marks the appropriate spot on the profile to depict the child's level of performance on each subtest and the total score. Such a depiction allows for a quick and helpful overview of the student's performance. Since space is also available on the profile sheet for recording data from other tests that have been administered, TORC scores can be compared not only to one another, but to related tests as well.

SUMMARY

Identifying the presence and degree of a reading problem is a task that involves the use of nonstandardized procedures and norm referenced standardized tests. Scope and sequence charts may be used to determine the reading behaviors that children should master as they progress through a curriculum. Observations and related checklists and rating scales provide a means to check pupil progress and to identify weaknesses in factors that may impact the development of reading abilities.

Norm referenced standardized tests assess the many aspects of reading, including recognizing words in print, understanding words and ideas in print, and reading with speed. This chapter has provided examples of the numerous formats that are used by tests and that are available to the consumer. Test scores, when combined with teacher observations and comments, can provide an effective means of identifying the presence and degree of a reading problem.

REFERENCES

Bader, L. A. (1980). *Reading diagnosis and remediation in classroom and clinic.* New York: Macmillan.

Baker, H. J. (1929). *Characteristic differences in bright and dull pupils.* Bloomington, IL: Public School Publishing.

Bartel, N. R. (1986). Teaching students who have reading problems. In D. D. Hammill & N. R. Bartel (Eds.), *Teaching students with learning and behavior problems* (pp. 23–89). Austin, TX: PRO-ED.

Betts, E. A. (1957) *Foundations of reading instruction.* New York: American Books.

Bond, G. L., Tinker, M. A., Wasson, B. B., & Wasson, J. B. (1984). *Reading difficulties: Their diagnosis and correction.* (5th ed.). Englewood Cliffs, NJ: Prentice-Hall.

Brown, D. (1982). *Reading diagnosis and remediation.* Englewood Cliffs, NJ: Prentice-Hall.

Brown, L., & Bryant, B. R. (1984). A consumer's guide to tests in print: The rating system. *Remedial and Special Education, 5*(1), 55–61.

Brown, V., Hammill, D. D., & Wiederholt, J. L. (1986). *Test of Reading Comprehension.* Austin, TX: PRO-ED.

Bryant, B. R., Bryant, D. L., Bunney, S., & Schuele, C. M. (1984). *A cooperative approach to remediating language disorders.* Paper presented at annual convention of Texas Council for Exceptional Children.

Buros, O. K. (1974). *Tests in print.* Lincoln, NE: University of Nebraska Press.

CTB/McGraw-Hill. (1978). *California Achievement Tests.* Monterey, CA: CTB/McGraw-Hill.

Clay, M. M. (1979). *The early detection of reading difficulties: A diagnostic survey with recovery procedures.* Auckland, New Zealand: Heinemann.

Cooper, C. R., & Petrosky, A. R. (1976). A psycholinguistic view of the fluent reading process. *Journal of Reading, 20,* 184–207.

Dechant, E. V. (1964). *Improving the teaching of reading*. Englewood Cliffs, NJ: Prentice-Hall.

Dechant, E. V. (1971). *Detection and correction of reading difficulties*. New York: Meredith.

Dunn, L., & Markwardt, F. (1970). *Peabody Individual Achievement Test*. Circle Pines, MN: American Guidance Service.

Fernald, G. M. (1943). *Remedial techniques in basic school subjects*. New York: McGraw-Hill.

Gates, A. I., McKillop, A. S., & Horowitz, E. C. (1981). *Gates-McKillop-Horowitz Reading Diagnostic Tests*. New York: Teachers College Press, Columbia University.

Goodman, K. S. (1976). Reading: A psycholinguistic guessing game. In M. Singer & R. Ruddell (Eds.), *Theoretical models and processes of reading*. Newark, DE: International Reading Association.

Gronlund, N. E. (1985). *Measurement and evaluation in teaching*. New York: Macmillan.

Guszak, F. (1985). *Diagnostic reading instruction in the elementary schools*. New York: Harper and Row.

Hammill, D. D. (1985). *Detroit Tests of Learning Aptitude*. Austin, TX: PRO-ED.

Hammill, D. D., Brown, L., & Bryant, B. R. (in press). *A consumer's guide to tests in print*. Austin, TX: PRO-ED.

Hammill, D. D., & Bryant, B. R. (1986). *Detroit Tests of Learning Aptitude–Primary*. Austin, TX: PRO-ED.

Hammill, D. D., & McNutt, G. (1981). *Correlates of reading*. Austin, TX: PRO-ED.

Haring, N. G., & Schiefelbusch, R. L. (1967). *Methods in special education*. New York: McGraw-Hill.

Harris, A. (1970). *How to increase reading ability* (5th ed.). New York: David McKay.

Heilman, A. W. (1972). *Principles and practices of teaching reading* (3rd ed.). Columbus, OH: Charles E. Merrill.

Henry, S. (1948). Children's audiograms in relation to reading attainment. *Journal of Genetic Psychology, 71*, 3–63.

Hieronymus, A. N., Lindquist, E. F., & Hoover, H. (1982). *Iowa Tests of Basic Skills*. Chicago: Riverside.

Ingram, C. P. (1950). *Education of the slow-learning child* (3rd ed.). New York: Ronald Press.

Jastak, S. R., & Wilkinson, G. E. (1984). *Wide Range Achievement Test–Revised*. Wilmington, DE: Jastak Associates.

Johnson, M. S. (1957). Factors related to disability in reading. *Journal of Experimental Education, 26*, 1–26.

Kaluger, G., & Kolson, C. J. (1978). *Reading and learning disabilities*. Columbus, OH: Charles E. Merrill.

Karlsen, B., Madden, R., & Gardner, E. F. (1974). *Stanford Diagnostic Reading Test*. San Antonio, TX: The Psychological Corporation.

Kaufman, A. (1983). *Kaufman Assessment Battery for Children*. Circle Pines, MN: American Guidance Service.

Kennedy, E. C. (1977). *Classroom approaches to remedial reading*. Itasca, IL: Peacock.

Kephart, N. (1971). *The slow learner in the classroom* (2nd ed.). Columbus, OH: Charles E. Merrill.

Kirk, S. A. (1940). *Teaching reading to slow learning children*. Boston: Houghton Mifflin.

Kirk, S. A., Kliebhan, J. M., & Lerner, J. W. (1978). *Teaching reading to slow and disabled learners.* Boston: Houghton Mifflin.

Knox, G. E. (1953). *Classroom symptoms of visual difficulty. Clinical studies in reading: II* (Supplementary Educational Monographs No. 77). Chicago: University of Chicago Press.

Loban, W. (1963). *The language of elementary school children* (NCTE Research Report No. 1). Urbana, IL: National Council of Teachers of English.

MacGinitie, W. H. (1978). *Gates-MacGinitie Reading Tests* (2nd ed.). Boston: Houghton Mifflin.

Newcomer, P. L., & Bryant, B. R. (1986). *Diagnostic Achievement Test for Adolescents.* Austin, TX: PRO-ED

Newcomer, P. L., & Curtis, D. (1983). *Diagnostic Achievement Battery.* Austin, TX: PRO-ED.

Rabinovitch, R. D. (1968). Reading problems in children: Definitions and classifications. In A. H. Keeney & V. T. Keeney (Eds.), *Dyslexia: Diagnosis and treatment of reading disorders* (pp. 1–10). St. Louis, MO: C. V. Mosby

Reid, D. K., & Hresko, W. P. (1981). *A cognitive approach to learning disabilities.* New York: McGraw-Hill.

Reid, D. K., Hresko, W. P., & Hammill, D. D. (1981). *Test of Early Reading Ability.* Austin, TX: PRO-ED.

Richek, M. A., List, L. K., & Lerner, J. W. (1983). *Reading problems: Diagnosis and remediation.* Englewood Cliffs, NJ: Prentice-Hall.

Robinson, H. M. (1953). *Why pupils fail in reading.* Chicago: University of Chicago Press.

Slosson, R. (1983). *Slosson Oral Reading Test.* East Aurora, NY: Slosson.

Smith, E. B., Goodman, K. S., & Meredith, R. (1976). *Language and thinking in school* (2nd ed.). New York: Holt, Rinehart and Winston.

Spache, G. (1981). *Diagnosing and correcting reading disabilities.* Boston: Allyn & Bacon.

Spache, G. D., & Spache, E. B. (1977). *Reading in the elementary school* (4th ed.). Boston: Allyn & Bacon.

Strickland, R. (1969). *The language arts in the elementary school.* Lexington, MA: D. C. Heath.

Sullivan, E. T., Clark, W. W., & Tiegs, E. W. (1978). *Short Form Test of Academic Aptitude.* Monterey, CA: CTB/McGraw-Hill.

Sweetland, R. C., & Keyser, D. J. (Eds.). (1983). *Tests.* Kansas City, MO: Test Corporation of America.

Taylor, S. E., Frackenpohl, H., & White, C. E. (1979). *EDL core vocabularies in reading, mathematics, science and social studies.* New York: McGraw-Hill.

Vernon, M. D. (1957). *Backwardness in reading.* Cambridge, MA: Cambridge University Press.

Vogel, S. A. (1974). Syntactic abilities in normal and dyslexic children. *Journal of Learning Disabilities, 7*, 103–109.

Vogel, S. A. (1975). *Syntactic abilities in normal and dyslexic children.* Baltimore: University Park Press.

Wechsler, D. (1974). *Wechsler Intelligence Scale for Children–Revised.* San Antonio, TX: Psychological Corporation.

Wiederholt, J. L. (1985). *Formal Reading Inventory.* Austin, TX: PRO-ED

Wiederholt, J. L., & Bryant, B. R. (1986). *Gray Oral Reading Tests–Revised.* Austin, TX: PRO-ED

Wiig, E., & Semel, E. H. (1976). *Language disabilities in children and adolescents.* Columbus, OH: Charles E. Merrill.

Woodcock, R. W. (1973). *Woodcock Reading Mastery Test.* Circle Pines, MN: American Guidance Service.

Zintz, M. V. (1970). *The reading process: The teacher and the learner.* Dubuque, IA: William C. Brown.

8 / ASSESSMENT FOR INSTRUCTION

In previous chapters the nature of reading has been described, and some commonly used procedures for determining the presence and degree of a reading problem have been delineated. As critical as this information is, it does not indicate a student's specific instructional needs. Therefore, in this chapter five assessment procedures for determining instructional needs are presented. First, the assessment of environmental factors that may affect reading achievement are discussed. Second, the student's attitudes and feelings about reading are considered. Next, methods for analyzing the reading miscues made by students are described. Techniques for matching a student to print are then noted, and strategies for analyzing specific vocabulary and skill abilities of students are discussed.

ASSESSMENT OF THE READING ENVIRONMENT

Students are usually considered for an in-depth assessment in reading because they are experiencing difficulty in their reading program. In the past these students received the bulk of attention in the assessment efforts. However, the common practice of limiting assessment to the learner and his or her difficulties has been criticized repeatedly and soundly (e.g., Englemann, Granzin, & Senerson, 1979; Roser & Schallert, 1983; Wiederholt, Hammill, & V. Brown, 1983; Ysseldyke & Marston, 1982). These professionals advocate beginning assessment with the reading environment rather than the learner. The goal of such initial assessment efforts is to determine which aspects of the environment are inadequate, to find out precisely how they are inadequate, and to determine what must be done to correct their inadequacy.

Two major environments that influence reading achievement are the home and the school. A discussion of environmental assessment practices in each of these follows. We strongly recommend that assessment for instruction begin with these environments.

Home Environment

Most children enter school with a great deal of skill and knowledge that they have learned primarily in the home environment. These children have developed an extensive oral grammar and vocabulary; they have learned concepts that help them understand numerous events; they are able to communicate about many things with other people. This oral language proficiency provides much of the basis for learning to meaningfully interpret written language.

Prior to entering school, most children have also learned a great deal about written language. For example, they have learned that many stories follow a set of rules governing their structure; that is, stories generally consist of a setting, theme, plot, and resolution. They have also learned to match their own grammar with the somewhat different sentence construction of written language. They have learned how to ask and answer questions about stories and perhaps to recognize some letters and words. They have learned how to handle a book (e.g., open and hold the book properly, where to start reading, left to right progression, top of page and bottom of page, etc.). Some children have also learned to read simple stories.

Parents play an active role in the development of this written language ability. In a recent synthesis of research on learning to read by The National Academy of Education, The National Institute of Education, and the Center for the Study of Reading (Anderson, Hiebert, Scott, & Wilkinson, 1985), the role parents play in their child's reading achievement is stressed. The findings are that

> parents play roles of inestimable importance in laying the foundation for learning to read. A parent is a child's first guide through a vast and unfamiliar world. A parent is a child's first mentor on what words mean and how to mean things with words. A parent is a child's first tutor in unraveling the fascinating puzzle of written language. A parent is a child's one enduring source of faith that somehow, sooner or later, he or she will become a good reader. (p. 27–28)

The authors of this report by The Commission on Reading also note that once children are in school, their parent's expectations, home language, and the experiences parents provide their children continue to influence how much and how well children read.

How Parents Can Help.   Since parents are believed to play such a critical role, several researchers have attempted to isolate specific factors in the home that facilitate reading achievement (e.g., Anderson et al., 1985; Farr & Fay, 1982; Gates, 1961; Morrow, 1985; National Assessment of Educational Progress, 1981; Taylor, 1983, Teale, 1984). Some of the factors isolated are as follows:

- *Parent language:* Parents who talk to their children about their experiences, who ask thought provoking questions, and who encourage their children to think about events removed from the here and now are helping build an experiential base necessary for reading comprehension.

- *Parents who read to children:* Parents who often read aloud to their children and who also engage the child as an active participant through discussions, naming letters and words as well as talking about the meaning of words in context, are helping their children develop an understanding of written language.

- *Parents who model reading:* Parents who read not just newspapers and work related materials but who also model recreational reading of magazines and novels are demonstrating the pleasure that can be derived from written language.

- *Parents who provide experiences:* Parents who take their children to parks, zoos, museums, and so on, are helping their children develop the background knowledge necessary for mastering school material.

- *Parents who enforce television rules:* Parents who are selective about what their children watch on television and who set time limits (i.e., up to about ten hours a week) are providing their children opportunities both to learn from television and to spend some of their free time with written materials.

- *Parents who provide instructional materials:* Parents who ensure that their children are exposed to a wide variety of materials like pencils, chalkboards, magnetic boards, books, records, tapes, and such "toys" are laying the foundation for use of the instructional materials in the school.

- *Parents who assume responsibility for instruction:* Parents who believe that it is their responsibility to convey information about written language to their children are increasing the exposure the child has to instruction.

- *Parents who monitor progress:* Parents who maintain constant and consistent interactions with teachers and their own children about reading progress are helping their children stick with the sometimes lengthy and arduous task of learning to read.

Assessing Parental Involvement. Of course, many students who come from homes where these factors are not present still learn to read quite well. However, when assessing a student who is experiencing reading problems, it is always advisable to determine the amount and type of involvement of the parents. This can be done informally through interviewing the parents about their practices on the previously mentioned home factors.

The instructional implications of the results of the interview are quite apparent. For example, if parents do not read to their children, they should be encouraged to do so. If television watching is not monitored, then recommendations to do so would be appropriate. If parents do not provide experiences for their children in the community, then they could be told what experiences might be appropriate.

If parents are unable to (or simply will not) follow the recommendations, then teachers must provide the necessary environment in school within the limits of their ability. For example, if parents do not model recreational reading, then the teachers will need to do so; if parents have not provided an experiential background base about things that are learned in school, then teachers will need to do so; and so forth.

The important role that parents play in their child's academic achievement has been recognized for several decades. Consequently, governmental agencies have funded numerous projects that focus at least part of their attention on parental involvement (e.g., Head Start, Project Follow Through). As Madeleine Will (1986) from the U.S. Department of Education recently stated:

> The establishment of school-parent programs for developing an atmosphere in the home which is conducive to academic achievement has been found to increase supervised homework; encourage parent-child conversations about school and everyday events; encourage reading; reduce nonproductive television viewing; and have an outstanding record of success in promoting achievement. (p. 414)

School Environment

The school environment is where students receive most of their formal reading instruction. As in the case of the home environment, research has isolated factors that appear to affect reading achievement in school. The primary factors studied are (a) time on task, (b) programs used, (c) methods employed, and (d) teacher behaviors.

Time. With the schools' emphasis placed on the importance of learning to read, as well as the scheduled time allocated daily in most classrooms to this activity, research findings indicate that time spent actually reading is surprisingly quite small. By "actual reading" researchers mean contextual reading, not the use of worksheets, isolated phonics training, waiting for a turn to orally read, and so forth. Anderson et al. (1985) found that the amount of time students spend contextually reading was as follows: "An estimate of silent reading time in the typical primary school class is 7 or 8 minutes per day, or less than 10% of the total time devoted to reading. By the middle grades, silent reading time may average 15 minutes per school day" (p. 76). They also note that students spend up to 70% of the time allocated for reading in independent practice in workbooks or skill sheets.

Ysseldyke and Algozzine (1983) report similar results in their research (i.e., 10 minutes of actual contextual reading per day). This was found in spite of the fact that the average reading periods were 65 minutes long. They report that the majority of time was spent by the students waiting for instruction or listening to the teacher or another student, writing, discussing, or simply looking around. They conclude their report by stating that only when it can be shown that the student is actively engaged for sufficient time in actual reading should assessment be directed toward other causes of reading difficulty. We strongly concur with this statement.

As in the case of assessment of home environments, observations and interviews are the mode of assessment when analyzing time on task. The observations can be done simply by watching the student during several reading periods and noting how often he or she is engaged in actual reading. Or a structured system such as the *Code for Instructional Structure and Student Academic Response* (Greenwood, Delquadri, & Hall, 1978) can be used. In this system, 12 activity codes (e.g., academic subject areas, free time, class business), 8 task codes (e.g., workbooks, student readers, discussions), and 19 student response codes (e.g., writing, reading aloud, silent reading) are coded and analyzed.

Interviews, though probably less reliable than observations, can also be used in assessing time on task. Simply asking the teacher and/or student how much time is spent in actual contextual reading can yield a general estimate. However, when interviewing the teacher, it is important to remember that there are likely to be significant differences among individual students in a given classroom. These differences are described by Ysseldyke and Algozzine (1983) in the following manner.

Vast differences were observed in how individual students were engaged during class time. Time engaged in active academic responding varied from 30.7 to 62.8 minutes, time engaged in task management responding ranged from 56.2 to 154.7 minutes, and time engaged in inappropriate responding varied from 6.4 to 45.6 minutes. These ranges demonstrated that some students were engaged in learning behaviors more often than others were, some "wasted" more time than others did, and some displayed more inappropriate behaviors than others did. (p. 65)

Therefore, simply finding out how many minutes per day are specified for actual reading is likely to have little relevance for a specific student with a reading problem. It is important to focus upon the individual student and his or her actual day-to-day engaged time in contextual reading.

The instructional implications of the results of the observations and/or interviews are quite apparent. Where insufficient time is spent in contextual reading, efforts should be made to increase the time. This may require changing the classroom schedule to allow for time. Or, in the case of an individual student who has the time but will not read, a system such as contigency management may need to be employed.

Programs.   Reading is taught in the schools in a number of different ways. Those who assess reading achievement will be interested in the manner in which reading has and is being taught, particularly when the child is not making progress. Often, a change in the program will be made for a particular student. As a result, the various types of reading programs used in the schools are overviewed in this section as well as some factors that need to be assessed and considered before changing a program for a particular student.

Farr and Roser (1979) list seven types of reading programs commonly employed. These include basal programs, individualized reading, language experience, phonics, artificial alphabets, linguistics, and systems approaches. They also present a description of any special materials needed, the specific skills emphasized, the teaching procedures used, and the language controls of each approach. More recently, Bartel (1986) has listed six types of approaches to the teaching of reading: complete basals, synthetic phonics, linguistic phonemic, individualized reading, diagnostic prescriptive, and language experience approaches. Bartel also provides a listing of major programs within each approach and where they can be purchased, as well as the advantages and disadvantages of each approach.

Table 8.1 presents a combination of the Farr and Roser (1979) and the Bartel (1986) lists. An analysis of the table provides an overview of the unique characteristics of each approach. A student who is experiencing difficulty in one type of program may benefit from another type. However, before recommending a change of program, several factors will need to be assessed.

(a) *How appropriately the program is being used*—If a reading program has been carefully prepared to be delivered in a specific way and if these procedures are not followed conscientiously, then the student may not have had a fair chance to master the content of the program. For example, perhaps the preparatory language or vocabulary manual of the program being taught has been neglected. Any departure from the instructor's manual should be for the purpose of providing a better way to help an individual and should have a clearly expressed rationale.

(b) *How the supplementary activities and materials that accompany a particular program are used*—Programs often provide additional experiences designed to supplement the core material and to make it more meaningful. Sometimes, these enrichment experiences are ignored. Or, as noted previously, the workbooks become the focal point of instruction, and the core materials are ignored. In such cases, modifications will need to be made.

It can be seen that the assessment of the reading materials entails more than simply noting what programs are being used. One cannot automatically assume that the program should be changed simply because the student is not achieving. It could be that the program has not been delivered in an appropriate manner. Only after it has been determined that the materials have been used appropriately should recommendations for modifications or changes be made.

Methods. Methods are those procedures that teachers use to organize the reading instruction. Methods can also be referred to as the *management system* that may be superimposed over the classroom material. These management systems often specify the techniques for grouping students, for monitoring progress in the material, the order of presentation of the lessons, the manner in which lessons are to be taught, the reinforcement procedures used, the verbal and physical behaviors of the teacher during instruction, and so forth. For example, one popular method, the Direct Instruction model, is described by Jenkins and Heliotes (1981) in the following manner.

> The direct instruction approach focuses not only on the content of the material presented, the selection of skills and teaching examples, but also on the initial introduction and sequencing of those skills and examples, the frequency with which practice items are introduced and reviewed, and the development of specific instructional strategies. Certain teacher presentations are also characteristics of the direct instruction approach, such as simple, clear, and usually scripted teacher directions; error corrections; and use of both group and individual responses. (p. 27)

Some programs specify very clearly the methods to be used. Other programs, particularly those called language experience, stand independent of any commercial material. Still other programs loosely or incompletely define the methods or simply ignore them altogether in the teacher's manual.

TABLE 8.1. Summary of Six Types of Programs for Teaching Reading

Programs	Are special materials needed?	Are specified skills emphasized?	Are specific teaching procedures used?	Is the language of the reading materials controlled?	Advantages/disadvantages	Where available
Basals. These usually consist of reading texts, teacher's manual, and supplementary materials such as workbooks. They are often sequenced in a series from K to Grade 6 or 8. The instructional approach is one of introducing a controlled sight vocabulary coupled with an analytic phonics emphasis.	Yes. Special materials include student reader and teacher's manuals. Student workbooks, tests, and other supplementary materials are often available.	Yes. Basals usually try to include a wide range of reading skills. Although the sequence and number of emphasized skills vary, most basal programs build on a systematic introduction of skills in a prescribed order.	Yes. Basals usually encourage teachers to use a wide variety of teaching procedures. While specific teaching procedures are described in a teachers' manual, teachers are encouraged to supplement with other teaching procedures.	Yes. Basals usually are developed from "graded word lists" and other controls on the difficulty of the student materials.	1. Lend themselves well to the 3-reading-group arrangements, less well to individualizing. 2. Content usually designed for the "typical" child, often not appealing to inner-city children or rural children. 3. Generally well-sequenced and comprehensive, attend to most aspects of developmental reading. 4. Most have complete pupil packets of supplementary materials, saving teacher searching time. 5. Sufficiently detailed and integrated that successful use is possible for a teacher lacking in confidence or experience.	Holt Basic Reading Ginn 720 Series American Book Company Readers Scott, Foresman Reading Houghton Mifflin Reading Program Macmillan Series E Lippincott Basic Reading Pathfinder (Allyn & Bacon)

TABLE 8.1. continued

Individualized reading. Each child reads materials of own choice and at own rate. Word recognition and comprehension skills are taught as individual children need them. Monitoring of progress is done through individual teacher conferences. Careful record keeping is necessary.	No. In this approach, the teacher is encouraged to collect and use a wide variety of reading materials.	No. The emphasis is on teaching the skills that are needed when they are needed.	No. Yet the individual student conferences, record keeping concerning student progress, and flexible grouping are common factors in the organization of the program.	No. Because a wide variety of materials are used, this is not possible.	1. Children are interested in content. 2. Promotes good habits of selection of reading materials. 3. Need an extensive collection of books from which to choose. 4. Teacher needs comprehensive knowledge of reading skills to make sure all are covered. 5. Required record keeping can be cumbersome.	Trade books of many different types, topics, and levels
Language experience. Based on teacher recording of child's narrated experiences. These stories become basic for reading. May be based on level of group or individual child. Stories are collected and made into a "book."	No. In this approach the materials are often student developed stories based on shared or individual experience.	No. The emphasis is on comprehension, helping children to see the relationship between language and print.	Yes. The procedures for eliciting experience stories from children are fairly well specified. However, the procedures for teaching word-recognition skills are left unspecified.	No. The reading materials are based on the oral language patterns of the children being taught.	1. Relationship of child's experience is explicit. 2. Firmly establishes reading as a language/communicative act. 3. Provides no systematic skill development (left up to the teacher to improvise). 4. Can become reinforcing only at child's existing level, rather than pushing him or her on. 5. Highly adaptable to pupils with unique needs and backgrounds.	Teacher-made materials
Synthetic Phonics. Similar to above in some ways, but emphasis is on mastering component phonics skills, then putting together into words.	Yes. Phonics can be taught using any of a wide variety of materials. However, there are various special phonics programs that come with prepared materials.	Yes. The emphasis is on teaching word recognition skills emphasizing sound-symbol relationships.	No. Various teaching procedures can be used.	Yes. Instructional materials are usually carefully developed to introduce a sequence of sound-symbol relationships.	1–5. Same as Basals. 6. Evidence is that a synthetic approach to word attack is rarely used by good readers.	Open Court Reading Program, Lippincott's Basic Reader Series, Distar Reading I, II, III, Swirl Community Skills Program (SW Regional Laboratory)

TABLE 8.1. continued

Programs	Are special materials needed?	Are specified skills emphasized?	Are specific teaching procedures used?	Is the language of the reading materials controlled?	Advantages/ disadvantages	Where available
Linguistic phonemic. Vocabulary that is used is highly controlled and conforms to the sound patterns of English (e.g., Nan, Dan, man, fan, ran, etc.). Most programs contain children's texts, teacher's manual, and supplementary materials.	Yes. Linguistics usually means that children's language patterns and/or regular spelling patterns are employed.	Yes. The skills involved initially include attention to regular sound-symbol relationships, and move from simple to complex.	No. A wide variety of teaching procedures are used.	Yes. The emphasis is on language patterns used by children.	1. Content and usage in stories (especially early ones) sometimes contrived because of controlled vocabulary. 2. Same as for Basals.	Let's Read (Bloomfield), SRA Basic Reading Series, Merrill Linguistic Readers Programmed Reading (Webster, McGraw-Hill), SRA Lift-Off to Reading, Palo Alto Program (Harcourt Brace Jovanovich)
Diagnostic-prescriptive. These consist of entry testing and exit testing of skills related to specific areas. Students who pass entry test go on to other needed areas. Reading objectives fully stated.	Yes. These are special instructional packages, including tests, workbooks, A-V aids, and sometimes computer assisted instruction.	Yes. Usually work recognition skills are emphasized because they can be programmed more easily; however, a wide variety of skills are taught.	Yes. The instructional package usually specifically tells the teacher what to do.	Yes. The skills to be taught are arranged in carefully sequenced patterns.	1. Skills are usually well sequenced. 2. Pupils work at own pace. 3. Learning may be boring, repetitive, or mechanistic. 4. Provide for ongoing assessment and feedback. 5. De-emphasize the language basis of reading (interaction and communication with other people). 6. Only those skills that lend themselves to the format are taught.	Print: Wisconsin Design for Reading Skill (National Computer Systems), Fountain Valley Reading Support System (Richard Zweig), Ransom Program (Addison-Wesley). Non-Print: Computer Assisted Stanford University CAI Project, Harcourt Brace CAI Remedial Reading Program

Adapted from *Teaching a Child to Read* (pp. 448–489) by Roger Farr and Nancy Roser, copyright © 1979 by Harcourt Brace Jovanovich, Inc. Reprinted by permission of the publisher.

One program in which the methods of instruction are clearly outlined is the *DISTAR Reading Program* (Engelmann & Bruner, 1974, 1975). This method is very specific about the order of the lessons, the manner in which they are to be taught, the reinforcement procedures used, and the verbal and physical behavior of the teacher during instruction. Teachers are admonished not to improvise or augment the program.

Another method that stands independent of commercial material is the Multisensory/Language Experience approach of Grace Fernald (1943). Her method is one of the earlier language experience approaches. In general she recommends that the student tell a story which is written down by the teacher, that the teacher then write each word to be learned from the story on a card, that the student trace and pronounce each word aloud, and that the student write each word independently and check its correctness. The methodology for the multisensory/language experience approach to teaching reading is just as detailed as that recommended by the authors of DISTAR. However, it is a different methodology, as it is not tied to any specific materials.

Most methods used to teach reading in today's classrooms are not as specific as the two discussed previously. Therefore, it may be necessary to assess:

(a) *The methods used to teach reading*—The assessment of the method used will entail several parts. First, the recommended method, if any, in the teacher's manual will need to be analyzed. This may include recommended strategies to get the attention and involvement of the reader in the activity, strategies that are used to provide success experiences, methods for reinforcement for appropriate responses, techniques for reinforcing learning through drill or repetition, and the like. Second, the teacher's use of the recommended methods should be determined. In some instances, teachers may not follow the recommended methods. In such cases, students may have insufficient guidance to allow them to progress in the material. Third, where methods of instruction are not specified clearly in the teacher's manual, it will need to be determined what methods, if any, are being used.

(b) *The grouping practices used in the classroom*—Some reading experts believe that it is not so much ability that determines reading achievement as the reading group into which a student is placed. These specialists believe that students placed in low achievement groups receive less instruction, are treated differently from other students, are less engaged in their reading tasks than other groups, and come to view themselves as being poor readers (Anderson et al., 1985). Yet, despite these pervasive beliefs and research evidence, Roser and Schallert (1983) note that most reading teachers still continue to group their students into static thirds (i.e., high, middle, low). However, many alternative groupings are available, as depicted below.

	Heterogeneous	Homogeneous
Achievement	X	X
Social	X	X
Interest	X	X
Tutoring	X	X

The types of groups that can be formed are those related to students' achievement, social needs, interests, and being tutored by peers. These groups can be either heterogeneous or homogeneous, allowing a teacher eight alternative types of groups. Other alternatives include assigning fewer students to the low achievement group so that instructions can be more closely monitored and more whole class instruction.

(c) *The methods used to teach reading in content areas*—In many instances students are referred for in-depth assessment when they are required to read social studies and science texts. In such cases many students simply lack the background vocabulary and concepts necessary to deal with the content. Despite the fact that reading instruction and subject matter content should be integrated, there is little indication that this often occurs. It is therefore necessary that some assessment efforts be directed toward determining how teachers integrate the teaching of reading and content subjects. Where reading methods are not employed, recommendations for doing so should be made. Herber (1978) and Santeusanio (1983) offer a number of suggestions on how this can be done.

In sum, the assessment of reading methods includes an analysis of program recommendations, the teacher's adherence to such recommendations, any other methodologies employed, as well as grouping practices and the use of methods to teach reading in the content areas. As is true of parental involvement, time on task, and reading programs, the implications for instruction are usually quite clear. Where consistent methodology is not employed, it should be developed and used; where grouping is by achievement level, it should be extended to other types of groups; and when reading is not taught in content areas, it should be integrated into subject matter instruction.

Teacher Behaviors. It will come as no surprise that some teachers are better than others in fostering reading achievement. In point of fact, Rosenshine and Stevens (1984) have reviewed studies on the quality of instruction and conclude that about 15% of the variation among children in reading achievement is attributable to factors relating to the skill and effectiveness of the teachers. Some of these factors can be classified as general characteristics, while others are related to specific verbal behaviors of teachers.

Anderson et al. (1985) discuss some of the general characteristics of successful teachers:

> Teachers who are successful in creating *literate environments* have classrooms that are simultaneously stimulating and disciplined. The successful teacher creates varied opportunities for language use. The successful teacher asks questions that make children think and requires children to answer in ways that communicate ideas clearly. The successful teacher uses language in a manner that sparks children's interest in the meaning and origins of words. In the classrooms of successful teachers, the children are encouraged to ask questions and present information about class experiences, current world events, television programs, and so on. (pp. 85–86)

Skilled teachers were also found to have established routines for making transitions between activities, distributing supplies, getting help with assignments, and making clear the purpose of every activity. Effective teachers place a premium on subject matter learning and have high expectations for learning. They also are committed to the belief that all students can learn to read.

The pace of instruction is also related to year-to-year gains in reading (Barr & Dreeben, 1983). Allington (1984) reports data on the variation of the pace of instruction in 60 elementary school classrooms from different states, figures that ranged from 600 words read per week to 8,900 words per week. The rule of thumb is that pace is optimum when children accurately identify 95% or more of the words in a text or when they answer about 80% of the teacher's questions satisfactorily. The lessons are believed to be too fast paced if they fall below these figures.

In addition to these general types of characteristics, some very specific verbal behaviors of teachers have been identified as relating to reading achievement (Allington, 1980; Hoffman & Clements, 1983; Hoffman, O'Neal, Kastler, Clements, Segel, & Nash, 1984; Pflaum, Pascarella, Boskwick, & Aner, 1980). Basically, it has been found that teachers respond differently to students in high and low groups. Teachers were found to interrupt proportionately more often following miscues in lower groups than in higher achieving groups. They told the words more often to the lower groups and gave these students less time to work out words for themselves than they did with the higher groups. It is suggested that poorer readers may be poorer because teachers treat them differently.

Hoffman (1979) examined teachers' feedback to students' oral reading miscues and specified three dimensions. These include the teacher (a) selecting *which* miscue to respond to, (b) deciding *when* the miscues should be responded to, and (c) determining *how* the miscues should be responded to.

Hoffman and Baker (1981) provide a systematic procedure by which the characteristics and the effect of feedback can be assessed. This system is called FORMAS (Figure 8.1). Both expected and observed miscues are written at the far left of the figure. In Cluster I the type of miscue and its characteristics are noted; Cluster II provides space for recording the student's reaction to the miscue; and Cluster III provides space for recording the teacher's feedback. When coding group instruction, Cluster IV is used to record any other student's verbal feedback to the miscue. Finally, in Cluster V the observer can record what happens ultimately to the observed miscue.

In assessing their verbal feedback, teachers can tape record a sample of their oral reading instruction and analyze the recorded lesson at a later time. Or another person can assess the actual lesson on the FORMAS feedback sheet while oral reading is in progress—although considerable skill and efficiency would be required to do so.

The assessment of teacher behavior can be a thorny issue. Teachers often resent such a process, and teachers' unions are sometimes opposed. However, simply cueing teachers as to what has been found relative to reading achievement often helps focus their behaviors in different directions. Certainly, ignoring a teacher's behavior when it comes to assessing a student with a reading problem would result in an incomplete evaluation. If the teacher is inadequate, then assessment focusing only on the student with recommendations for program change is likely to be a futile effort.

Recommendations for instruction when it comes to teacher behavior is as straightforward as that relative to parents, time on task, programs, and methods. Teachers may need to improve their discipline procedures, ask thought provoking questions, encourage children to communicate their ideas better, establish efficient transition practices, develop higher expectations, and modify the pace of the instruction. In addition, in their feedback to student miscues, they may need to make changes in their behavior and observe the effect of these changes on the student's achievement. For example, as Hoffman and Baker (1981) note, they may want to extend the wait period between the occurrence of a miscue and the initiation of feedback. Later observation of this change would allow teachers to analyze their own success in extending the wait time as well as to examine changes in a student's behavior, such as an increase in the number of self-corrections.

This section on assessment for instruction has focused on environmental influences, which have been found to affect reading achievement. These influences include parental involvement and support for their child's reading progress, the amount of time that the student spends in contextual reading, the program and materials employed, and the teacher's skill and effectiveness. The strategies used to assess these environmental factors include observation (ranging from informal to structured) and interviews. Where environmental factors are found to be inadequate, some suggestions for correcting these inadequacies were given.

FIGURE 8.1. The FORMAS System of Assessing Feedback

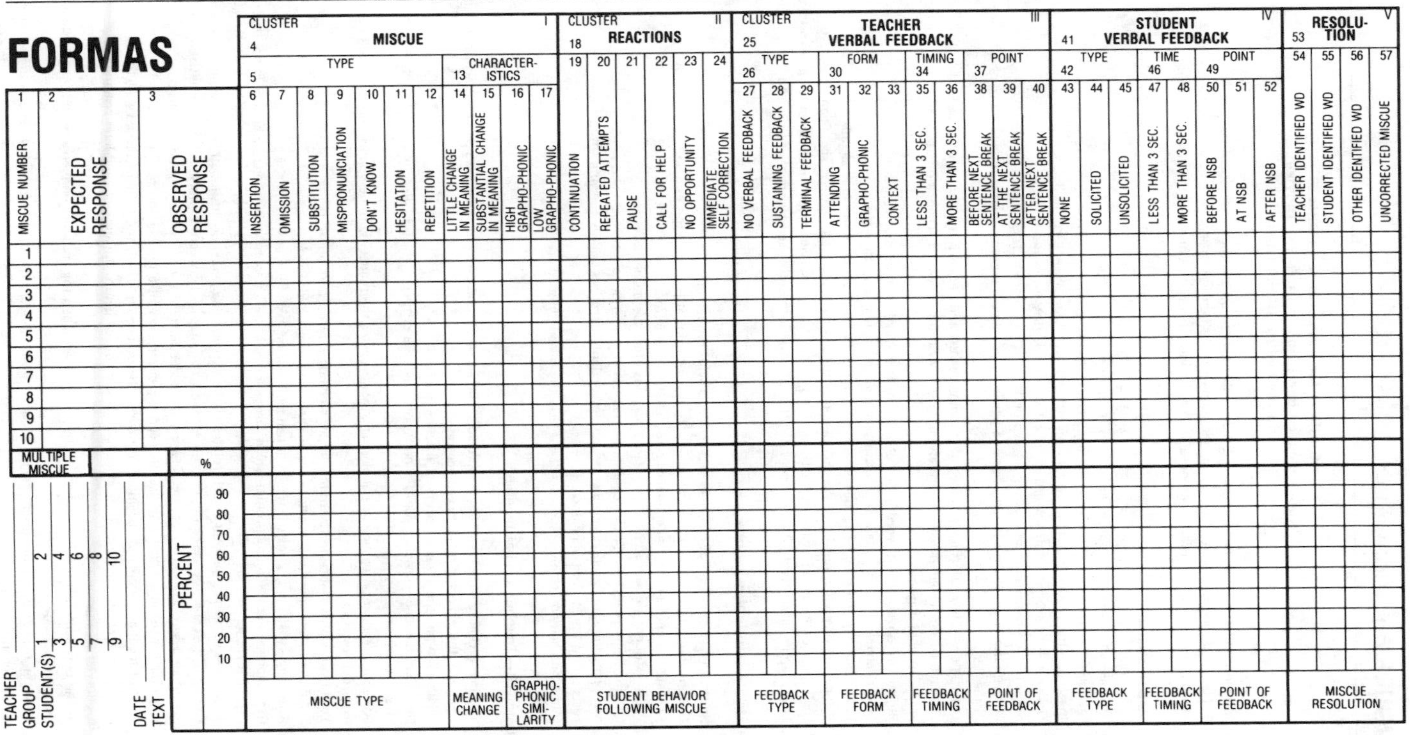
FORMAS

1 MISCUE NUMBER
2 EXPECTED RESPONSE
3 OBSERVED RESPONSE

CLUSTER 4 MISCUE I
5 TYPE
6 INSERTION
7 OMISSION
8 SUBSTITUTION
9 MISPRONUNCIATION
10 DON'T KNOW
11 HESITATION
12 REPETITION
13 CHARACTER-ISTICS
14 LITTLE CHANGE IN MEANING
15 SUBSTANTIAL CHANGE IN MEANING
16 HIGH GRAPHO-PHONIC
17 LOW GRAPHO-PHONIC

CLUSTER 18 REACTIONS II
19 CONTINUATION
20 REPEATED ATTEMPTS
21 PAUSE
22 CALL FOR HELP
23 NO OPPORTUNITY
24 IMMEDIATE SELF CORRECTION

CLUSTER 25 TEACHER VERBAL FEEDBACK III
26 TYPE
27 NO VERBAL FEEDBACK
28 SUSTAINING FEEDBACK
29 TERMINAL FEEDBACK
30 FORM
31 ATTENDING
32 GRAPHO-PHONIC
33 CONTEXT
34 TIMING
35 LESS THAN 3 SEC.
36 MORE THAN 3 SEC.
37 POINT
38 BEFORE NEXT SENTENCE BREAK
39 AT THE NEXT SENTENCE BREAK
40 AFTER NEXT SENTENCE BREAK

41 STUDENT VERBAL FEEDBACK IV
42 TYPE
43 NONE
44 SOLICITED
45 UNSOLICITED
46 TIME
47 LESS THAN 3 SEC.
48 MORE THAN 3 SEC.
49 POINT
50 BEFORE NSB
51 AT NSB
52 AFTER NSB

53 RESOLU-TION V
54 TEACHER IDENTIFIED WD
55 STUDENT IDENTIFIED WD
56 OTHER IDENTIFIED WD
57 UNCORRECTED MISCUE

1
2
3
4
5
6
7
8
9
10
MULTIPLE MISCUE
%

TEACHER
GROUP
STUDENT(S) 1 2 3 4 5 6 7 8 9 10
DATE
TEXT

PERCENT
90
80
70
60
50
40
30
20
10

MISCUE TYPE
MEANING CHANGE
GRAPHO-PHONIC SIMI-LARITY
STUDENT BEHAVIOR FOLLOWING MISCUE
FEEDBACK TYPE
FEEDBACK FORM
FEEDBACK TIMING
POINT OF FEEDBACK
FEEDBACK TYPE
FEEDBACK TIMING
POINT OF FEEDBACK
MISCUE RESOLUTION

FIGURE 8.1. continued

Definitions for categories on FORMAS
(Number coded and listed in the order they appear
on the coding sheet/chart)

1. Miscue number—the sequence for each miscue in relationship to other coded miscues.
2. Expected response—a text word and/or its numerical position in the sequence of text words.
3. Observed response—a student response and/or the identification number of the student reading.

Cluster I—Miscue

4. Miscue—an observed response that differs from an expected response.
5. Miscue type—classification scheme for observed miscues.
6. Insertion—the reader inserts a word or an affix which is not present in the text.
7. Omission—the reader omits a word or an affix which is present in the text.
8. Substitution—the reader substitutes a word or an affix for one which is present in the text.
9. Mispronunciation—the reader substitutes a partial or complete nonsense utterance for a word or affix which is present in the text.
10. Don't know—the reader stops before attempting a word and verbally requests teacher assistance.
11. Hesitation—the reader pauses before attempting a word for at least 3 seconds or the teacher intervenes before the 3 second period elapses.
12. Repetition—saying a text word or set of adjacent text words two or more times.
13. Miscue characteristics—qualitative features of each particular type of miscue.
14. Little change in meaning—the miscue alters the author's intended meaning only slightly.
15. Substantial change in meaning—the miscue alters the author's intended meaning significantly.
16. High graphophonic similarity—at least 2 of the 3 parts of the observed response conform to the expected response.
17. Low graphophonic similarity—less than 2 of the 3 parts of the observed response conform to the expected response.

Cluster II—Student reactions

18. Student reactions—how the reader initially deals with his/her miscue.
19. Continuation—student continues reading with no apparent attention to the miscue.
20. Repeated attempts—the reader makes repeated attempts at identifying the text word.
21. Pause—student stops reading for at least 2 seconds after the miscue occurs.
22. Call for help—reader explicitly requests teacher assistance after miscue has been made.
23. No opportunity for reaction—teacher or another student intervenes within 2 seconds of the miscue and before any other reaction by the student is evidenced.
24. Immediate self-correction—student self-corrects the miscue immediately.

Cluster III—Teacher verbal feedback

25. Teacher verbal feedback—initial verbal teacher behavior that follows a miscue and reader's reaction to the miscue and relates to the expected or observed response.
26. Feedback type—the general nature of teacher feedback.
27. No verbal feedback—teacher displays no verbal feedback strategy which is directly related to the identification of the target word.
28. Sustaining feedback—teacher verbal feedback that provides the reader with the opportunity to identify part or all of an expected response.
29. Terminal feedback—teacher identifies target word or calls on another student.
30. Feedback form—specific characteristics of sustaining teacher feedback.
31. Attending—sustaining feedback which is noncue focusing, e.g., "Try again."
32. Graphophonic—a sustaining prompt which relates to visual and/or sound-related characteristics of the miscue and/or the expected response.
33. Context—a sustaining prompt which relates to the surrounding semantic (meaning) or syntactic (structure) features.
34. Timing of teacher feedback—the time (in seconds) that elapses between the miscue and the initiation of feedback.
35. Less than 3 seconds—time elapsing between the occurrence of a miscue and teacher feedback.
36. More than 3 seconds—time elapsing between the occurrence of a miscue and teacher feedback.
37. Point of feedback—sentence position, relative to the miscue, at which the teacher provides feedback.
38. Before the next sentence break—teacher feedback is offered before the student completes reading the sentence containing the target miscue.
39. At the next sentence break—teacher feedback is offered when the student completes reading the sentence containing the target miscue.
40. After the next sentence break—teacher feedback is offered when the student has read beyond the sentence containing the target miscue.

FIGURE 8.1. continued

Cluster IV—Other student verbal feedback

41. Other student verbal feedback—verbal behavior of a student other than the reader relating to the expected or observed response.
42. Student feedback type—the general nature of other student verbal feedback.
43. None—no other student offers verbal feedback directly related to the miscue.
44. Solicited—a student's verbal feedback is requested by the teacher
45. Unsolicited—verbal feedback is volunteered by a student and not requested by a teacher.
46. Timing of student feedback—the time (in seconds) that elapses between the miscue and the initiation of a student's feedback.
47. Less than 3 seconds—time elapsing between the occurrence of a miscue and student feedback.
48. More than 3 seconds—time elapsing between the occurrence of a miscue and student feedback.
49. Point of feedback—sentence position, relative to the miscue, at which a student provides feedback.
50. Before the next sentence break—other student feedback is offered before the reader completes the sentence containing the target miscue.
51. At the next sentence break—other student feedback is offered when the reader completes the sentence containing the target miscue.
52. After the next sentence break—other student feedback is offered after the reader has progressed beyond the sentence containing the target miscue.

Cluster V—Miscue resolution

53. Miscue resolution—whether or not the miscue is corrected, and the individual correcting the miscue.
54. Teacher identifies word—teacher identifies word (or corrects a student's miscue).
55. Student identifies word—reader self-corrects the miscue.
56. Other identifies word—person other than the teacher or student reading identifies target word.
57. Uncorrected word—student continues reading with miscue left uncorrected.

Multiple miscue

58. Multiple miscue—a tally of student generated miscues that involve two or more consecutive text words which are not attended to individually either through self-correcting or teacher feedback.

From "Characterizing Teacher Feedback to Student Miscues During Oral Reading Instruction" by J. V. Hoffman and C. Baker, 1981, *The Reading Teacher, 34,* 907–913. Reprinted by permission of J. V. Hoffman and C. Baker and the International Reading Association.

Once the environment has been found to be supportive of reading achievement, and the student is still not making progress, then assessment effort directed toward the learner and his or her difficulties is necessitated. The procedures recommended in this effort are the focus of discussion in the next section.

ASSESSMENT OF THE STUDENT'S ATTITUDES

There is widespread agreement that students' attitudes toward themselves and the reading act are important parts of learning to read. Spache (1981) specifies some of the characteristics of students who have difficulty reading. He notes that in dealing with students with reading problems, educators

> must deal frequently with personality deviations and low self-concept. Among the feelings and behaviors that seem to be fairly common are aggressiveness or hostility toward both adults and peers, especially among boys; a tendency

to social conformity among girls; negative attitudes to adult suggestion; withdrawal from active social or personal relationships; anxiety and tension about reading; as well as poor social acceptance by classmates. (p. 106)

When encountering low achieving readers with these types of characteristics, examiners will need to assess them in the area of personality and behavior. Certainly, in cases where emotional problems are found, program plans should include treatment of *both* the reading problem and the personality and behavior problem. In addition to assessment of affective variables in seriously disturbed students, many students with reading problems can profit from specific assessment in the areas of (a) interest in reading and (b) passive failure about learning to read.

Interest in Reading

We have noted in previous sections that learning to read primarily comes with actual involvement in contextual reading. Yet Morrow (1985) states that "a substantial number of children do not choose to read either for pleasure or for information" (p. 1). She cites one study that found that fifth grade students used only 5.4% of their leisure time reading, and 22% of the students reported not reading at all. The Commission on Reading reports even bleaker figures for recreational reading. They found that the majority of children spend about 1% of their free time reading from books or magazines (Anderson et al., 1985).

Assessment of Attitudes. As a result, one of the major instructional goals for students with reading problems may be to get them involved in reading. Consequently, some assessment efforts should be directed toward discovering their interest in reading. The first step would be to determine their attitudes toward reading. This can be done by simply interviewing the students about their attitudes. Some examiners prefer using a checklist during this interview. Two checklists that typify this approach are presented here.

Estes, Estes, Richards, and Roettger (1981) have developed an attitude checklist that can be used to determine interest. The first scale (Figure 8.2) is for use with elementary aged children. Children respond on a 3-point Likert scale with the options of *Agree, Don't Know,* or *Disagree.* On the secondary scale (Figure 8.3), older students can respond on a 5-point Likert scale: 5 = strongly agree, 4 = agree, 3 = cannot decide, 2 = disagree, and 1 = strongly disagree. A perusal of each response will yield information on the student's attitude toward reading. We suggest that examiners probe the student on specific items to gather more in-depth information.

FIGURE 8.2. Attitude Checklist for Use with Elementary Aged Children

Reading Attitude Scale

	A	?	D
	Agree	Don't Know	Disagree
15. Reading is fun for me.	A	?	D
16. Books are boring.	A	?	D
17. Reading is a good way to spend spare time.	A	?	D
18. Reading turns me on.	A	?	D
19. Books do not make good presents.	A	?	D
20. Reading is rewarding to me.	A	?	D
21. Reading becomes boring after about a half hour.	A	?	D
22. Free reading teaches me something.	A	?	D
23. There should be time for free reading during the school day.	A	?	D
24. There are many books I hope to read.	A	?	D
25. Reading is something I can do without.	A	?	D
26. A certain amount of time during summer should be set aside for reading.	A	?	D
27. Books usually are good enough to finish.	A	?	D
28. Reading is not exciting.	A	?	D

$$\boxed{} + \boxed{} = \boxed{}$$

STEP 1   STEP 2   STEP 3

From *Estes Attitude Scales: Measures of Attitudes Toward School Subjects* by R. H. Estes, J. J. Estes, H. C. Richards, and D. Roettger, rev. 1981, Austin, TX: PRO-ED. Reprinted by permission.

FIGURE 8.3. Attitude Checklist for Use with Secondary Aged Children

Reading

	Strongly Agree 5	Agree 4	Cannot Decide 3	Disagree 2	Strongly Disagree 1
1. Reading is for learning but not for enjoyment.	☐	☐	☐	☐	☐
2. Spending allowance on books is a waste of good money.	☐	☐	☐	☐	☐
3. Reading is a good way to spend spare time.	☐	☐	☐	☐	☐
4. Books are a bore.	☐	☐	☐	☐	☐
5. Watching T.V. is better than reading.	☐	☐	☐	☐	☐
6. Reading is rewarding to me.	☐	☐	☐	☐	☐
7. Books aren't usually good enough to finish.	☐	☐	☐	☐	☐
8. Reading becomes boring after about an hour.	☐	☐	☐	☐	☐
9. Most books are too long and dull.	☐	☐	☐	☐	☐
10. There are many books which I hope to read.	☐	☐	☐	☐	☐
11. Books should only be read when they are assigned.	☐	☐	☐	☐	☐
12. Reading is something I can do without.	☐	☐	☐	☐	☐
13. Some part of summer vacation should be set aside for reading.	☐	☐	☐	☐	☐
14. Books make good presents.	☐	☐	☐	☐	☐
15. Reading is dull.	☐	☐	☐	☐	☐

From *Estes Attitude Scales: Measures of Attitudes Toward School Subjects* by T. H. Estes, J. J. Estes, H. C. Richards, and D. Roettger, rev. 1981, Austin, TX: PRO-ED. Reprinted by permission.

Huskins (1981) developed a sentence completion interview test for primary aged and older students (Figure 8.4). She recommends that in interpreting the responses there are no *correct* answers. Instead, a summary sheet for collating responses in six areas is used: teachers, reading lessons, peer relations, the act of reading, reading interests, and other areas. Spache (1981) comments about the use of this test.

> This approach will yield specifics as well as overall impressions of the reactions of children toward situations involving reading and reading instruction. They may or may not act out these feelings in their relations with teachers and peers, for there is often a real tendency for these children to be anxious about their feelings, to conceal them . . . the "good child facade" of passivity, depression, and apparent compliance with adult demands. Thus, when overt behavior and the impressions gained from this instruction are not consistent, the value in probing behind the behavioral facade is demonstrated. The behavioral manifestations of aggressiveness, hostility, or negativism are readily observed by the teacher; but when these are concealed, instruments of this type are particularly valuable in helping us understand some of the reasons for the child's reading failure. (p. 112)

Assessment of Interest. The second step in dealing with students in this area is to assess them on their specific reading interests. Summers (1979) suggests a forced choice method that provides a gross numerical index of the type of material the student would prefer to read (Figure 8.5). The student is asked whether he or she would prefer a mystery or a sports story, a mystery or a science story, a mystery or a history story. A plus sign is recorded in each cell if the student prefers the first named category (the vertical list, to the left of the matrix) and a zero sign if not. Summers' suggestions can be modified by adding different types of reading material depending upon the age of the student (e.g., fairy tales, romance, etc.).

Another way to assess interest in reading is to question the students about certain materials they might wish to read. There are many recreational materials aimed specifically at school aged children. Kline (1980) reports interesting consumer data about the reading material regarding its prominence in the United States in 1979. Of 12,000 magazines published, 13 aimed specifically at juveniles are among the top 1½% in circulation: *Mad Magazine, Boy's Life, Highlights for Children, Seventeen Magazine, Co-Ed, Sesame Street, American Girl, National Lampoon, Jack and Jill, Tiger Beat,* and *Teen Beat*. Each edition of the following four magazines tops one million copies: *Mad Magazine, Boy's Life, Seventeen Magazine,* and *Highlights for Children*. In terms of books, there are 40,000 children's book titles in print. One best selling author, Beverly Cleary, has more than a million copies of her books in print. Asking students if they read copies of these—or if they have access to them—will yield additional information on reading interest.

FIGURE 8.4. An Incomplete Sentence Test for Elementary Children

For Primary. This is a game called "Say the First Thing," I will say a word or a few words and then pause. When I stop, you tell me the very first thing that came to you. I will write down just what you say. Are you ready?

For Older Pupils. Finish each sentence with the first idea that comes to your mind. Let's try the first one together.

1. Reading is fun with _____
2. My teacher reads _____
3. Reading is _____
4. I cannot read when _____
5. Reading is not fun with _____
6. I find reading_____
7. Reading about _____
8. My classmates read _____
9. Reading is most fun when _____
10. My reading group_____
11. Reading in school is _____
12. The best reading group is _____
13. Reading with _____
14. I read _____
15. Reading games _____
16. When I read all by myself _____
17. Reading is best _____
18. When reading, new words _____
19. Reading before the class _____
20. I like reading when _____
21. Reading out loud _____
22. The best reader in my class is _____
23. I read best _____
24. Last year's reading teacher _____
25. Reading in the group _____
26. I don't like reading when _____
27. I always want to read about _____
28. I read better _____
29. I learn reading best when _____
30. I don't want to read about _____
31. I cry when I read about _____
32. I don't read when_____
33. The best thing about reading _____
34. I began reading_____
35. I laugh when I read about _____
36. When reading I feel _____
37. My class thinks I read _____
38. When I read at home _____

FIGURE 8.4. continued

39. At home I read _____
40. At home my mother reads _____
41. My teacher thinks I read_____
42. My teacher makes me mad when _____
43. I like reading when my teacher_____
44. I like it when my teacher _____
45. My reading teacher _____
46. My teacher makes me happy when _____
47. I like my teacher best when _____
48. I don't like my teacher best when_____
49. If I were the teacher _____
50. My teacher smiles_____
51. The teacher thinks the reading class_____
52. Last year my teacher did_____
53. The teacher talks loud when _____
54. This year my teacher does _____
55. The teacher thinks I_____
56. The teacher is angry when_____
57. The teacher is happy when _____
58. Next year I want my teacher to_____
59. The teacher thinks the class _____
60. The best book I know about _____
61. Books with pictures _____
62. My books _____
63. Books with no pictures _____
64. The book I like _____
65. The school's books _____

Summary Sheet

Write the student's response to each item listed in each problem area, if the response seems related to that area. If a response obviously reflects another problem area, or several, enter it there. Summarize your evaluation of the tone and specific indications in each problem area.

Teachers—2, 24, and 41 to 59

Reading Lessons—5, 8, 10, 11, 12, 13, 19, 21, 25, 26, 29, 43

Peer Relations—1, 4, 5, 8, 10, 12, 15, 16, 22, 25, 37

The Act of Reading—3, 4, 6, 7, 9, 17, 18, 19, 21, 26, 28, 32, 36

Reading Interests—3, 7, 9, 14, 16, 17, 20, 23, 27, 30, 31, 33, 35, 38, 60, 61, 62, 63, 64, 65

Other Areas—34, 38, 39, 40

From "Incomplete Sentence Test for Elementary Children" (pp. 447–449) by F. Huskins in *Diagnosing and Correcting Reading Disabilities* (2nd ed.), edited by G. D. Spache, Boston: Allyn & Bacon. Reprinted by permission.

FIGURE 8.5. Summers' Matrix Method for Determining Reading Choices

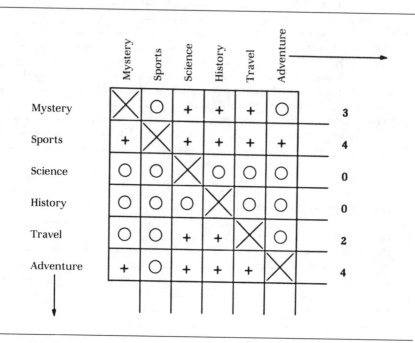

From *The Resource Teacher: A Guide to Effective Practices* (2nd ed., p. 155) by J. Lee Wiederholt, Donald D. Hammill, and Virginia L. Brown, 1983, Boston: Allyn & Bacon. Reprinted by permission.

The instructional implications for probing attitudes and interest in reading are straightforward, as in areas where the purpose is program development. If a student has a poor attitude toward reading, he or she will need to be provided with successful and pleasurable reading experience. To accomplish this, the student needs to be provided interesting material to read, as well as specified time for reading the material. Those students who cannot read words in context should be read to from material of their choice.

Passive Failure

Some students with reading problems show varying degrees of resignation to failure about learning to read. Goodman (1982) describes this type of reader in the following manner.

The use of the term *readers in trouble* will be used here by the author for all those who are not doing as well as they think (or someone else thinks) they should do in the development of reading proficiency. The common denominator among such readers is that they have become their own worst enemies. They have acquired a view that the world is populated by two kinds of people: those who can read and those who cannot. They believe that if they could just learn the phonics rules, just get enough word attacks, just master the skills, then they could do what good readers do easily and well. However, they know that they cannot because something is wrong with them; they just do not learn like "normal" people. (p. 87)

Johnston and Winograd (1985) refer to this type of attitude as a "passive failure" syndrome. They have pulled the following characteristics of this type of reader from relevant research in the area of metacognition, attribution theory, learned helplessness, and achievement motivation theory.

- history of continual failure
- inaccurate perceptions of the extent of their successes and failures
- difficulty in perceiving relationships between elements in reading tasks
- tendency to use task-inappropriate strategies spontaneously or effectively
- general unawareness of what strategies they do use in reading
- failure to monitor their own performance
- tendency to attribute their failure to their own low ability
- belief that ability is a fixed entity
- low expectation of success
- successful experiences are attributed to external factors beyond their control such as teacher help, luck, or task ease
- lack of persistence in the face of failure
- low self-esteem, resignation, apathy, and generally depressed affect
- making many negative affective statements and few positive ones while performing learning tasks.

Johnson (1985) notes that these affective and motivational factors are conspicuously absent in most reading assessment efforts. He further states:

We need to consider more seriously explanations which stress combinations of anxiety, attributions, maladaptive strategies, inaccurate or nonexisting concepts about aspects of reading, and a huge variety of motivational factors.

Although these aspects are more likely to exist in combination, I suspect that each alone is powerful enough to engender some degree of reading failure. (p. 174)

In assessing students who might be suffering from passive failure syndrome, several formal research instruments are available for use (e.g., Crandall, Katkovsky, & Crandall, 1965; Dweck, 1975; Fowler & Peterson, 1981; Nicholls, 1979). However, Johnston and Winograd (1985) note several problems with these instruments, including (a) the current uncertainty about the most salient causal dimensions of reading achievement; (b) the fact that these measures treat reading as a unitary construct rather than a construct with various dimensions that occur across a wide variety of situations; and (c) that the information they provide is incomplete. They, therefore, recommend that assessment of passive failure can best be done by observing students' responses during their actual reading. By attending to overt responses students make for outcomes, the length of time they persist at solving problems, how flexibly they use reading strategies, and the extent to which they persist in the face of failure, a picture of the specific components of passive failure can be observed.

The implications for educational intervention are based upon the isolation of behaviors that relate to passive failure. For example, if students appear unaware of the strategies they use in reading, a metacognitive approach to instruction may be appropriate. If they fail to monitor their own performance, then strategies for doing so, such as self-questioning, may be useful. Contingency management, praise, and the provision of successful experiences can also be helpful in dealing with students who demonstrate the passive failure syndrome.

ASSESSMENT OF THE STUDENT'S READING MISCUES

There is a long history of having students read orally and noting their deviations from print. The deviations (miscues) are then analyzed and interpreted as to their interference with reading achievement. However, as Spache (1981) notes, there is little agreement in the definition of miscues or even what should be noted as a miscue during oral reading. In this section two different approaches to miscue analysis are discussed. These include the graphic/phonemic linguistic and the semantic/syntactic linguistic approaches. However, prior to these discussions, some comments are made regarding the relationship between oral and silent reading, since only oral reading is used to assess miscues.

Oral and Silent Reading

Implicit in having a student read orally for the purposes of miscue analysis is the belief that oral reading reflects what the student would do when reading silently. However, as early as 1967, William S. Gray noted that the relationship between oral and silent reading was not great enough to accurately predict one from the other (Gray & Robinson, 1967). In apparent agreement, Goodman (1976) more recently noted:

> There are periods in the development of reading competence when oral reading becomes very awkward. Readers who have recently become rapid, relatively effective silent readers seem to be distracted and disrupted by the necessity of encoding oral output while they are decoding meaning. Ironically, then, "poor" oral reading performance may reflect a high degree of reading competence rather than a lack of such competence. (p. 489)

The research on the relationship of oral and silent reading has yielded contradictory results. In reviewing relevant studies, Juel and Holmes (1981) note that (a) some studies have found that comprehension is greater in silent reading than oral reading, (b) other studies have found that oral reading comprehension is superior, and (c) still other studies have found no consistent differences in comprehension between silent and oral reading.

However, the majority of authorities in reading appear to agree that the most appropriate reflection of an individual's competence is attained through the assessment of silent reading. This is because silent reading (a) is the more natural way fluent or more mature readers read; (b) emphasizes reading for comprehension while de-emphasizing accurate word calling; (c) allows the reader to adjust rate in relation to familiar or unfamiliar ideas; (d) may facilitate the use of context to help derive the meaning of new or difficult words; and (e) permits the reader to use a variety of methods of word analysis resulting in the deduction of word meanings—not necessarily their pronunciation.

Durkin (1983) notes that while silent reading is of paramount importance, oral reading can be used for some kinds of evaluation. She further observes that when oral reading is assessed, the student should be tested privately and on unfamiliar materials. She does not suggest, however, that oral reading is a perfect reflection of what would happen if the student read the same material silently.

In sum, when assessing oral reading miscues, examiners should keep in mind that the relationship between oral and silent reading is at the present time unknown. They should also be aware that the oral reading miscues may not be the same type of miscues a student would make during silent reading. Finally, they should recognize that silent reading comprehension is the best criterion for reading competence. With these points in mind, examiners have at their disposal the following two major approaches to miscue analysis.

Graphic/Phonemic Linguistic Approaches

In graphic/phonemic approaches, examiners are primarily interested in how a miscue looks (graphic) or sounds (phonemic) like the word in the text. This is basically a bottom-up approach (see Chapter 6) in that the focus is upon the exact correct reproduction of text. To illustrate how this is done, the following eight types of miscues are assessed on the 1967 version of the *Gray Oral Reading Tests* (Gray & Robinson, 1967).

1. *Aid.* When the pupil hesitates for *five seconds* without making an audible effort to pronounce the word, or *ten seconds* if he appears to be trying to pronounce it, the examiner pronounces the word. The error is marked by an underlined bracket.

> Example: [geologists].

2. *Gross mispronunciation of a word.* A gross mispronunciation is one in which the pupil's pronunciation bears so little resemblance to the proper pronunciation that the examiner must be looking at the word to recognize it. Such an error is marked by drawing a straight line under the entire word and writing the pupil's pronunciation phonetically above the word.

> fratific
> Example: traffic

3. *Partial mispronunciation.* When a word is partially mispronounced specific types of errors should be noted and recorded as follows:

> a. When the examiner pronounces a part of the word for the pupil, enclose that part in underlined parentheses.
>
>> Example: re(gard)   (1 error)
>
> b. Wrong sound of letters or groups of letters. Underline the part mispronounced and write the error or errors
>
>> above it. Examples: veins, that, dăzzling, himself.
>
> (1 error for each)
>
> c. Omission of one or more elements. Examples: house (s), st (r)aight, (al)most.   (1 error for each)
>
> d. Insertion of an element. Example: already for
>
>> al
>> ready marked, ∧ ready   (1 error)

e. Wrong syllabication. Examples: pier / ced, alm / ost (1 error)

f. Wrong accent. Example: re'cord instead of record' (1 error)

g. Inversion. Example: on for no, marked (n/o) (1 error)

4. *Omission of a word or group of words.* Circle the omitted word or group of words. Examples: I saw a (hungry) dog on the street. (1 error)

They fly passengers, (freight and mail) from one city to another. (1 error)

5. *Insertion of a word or group of words.* Place an insert mark and write the word(s) above the point at which they were added. Examples:

clear
The ∧ sky was bright blue.   (1 error)

pretty little
He called his   ∧   dog.   (1 error)

6. *Substitution of one meaningful word or several for others.* Examples:

many
The sun shone into <u>my</u> large window.   (1 error)

there was
Once <u>upon a time</u> a boy . . . .   (3 errors)

sat on
A boy <u>had</u> a wagon . . . .   (2 errors)

sat on
A boy <u>had</u> a wagon . . . .   (1 error)

The number of errors depends on the number of words replaced by the substitution.

7. *Repetition of one or more word(s).* (Except when due to stuttering.) Underline with a wavy line. Examples:

The boy ran <u>away</u>.   (1 error)

The boy ran <u>far into</u> the woods.   (1 error)

Repetition of the same word or group of words more than once counts as only one error. Example: They played <u>for a</u> long time. (2 repetitions of 2 words but only 1 error.)

In case the repetition is to correct an error, mark the repetition and cross out the corrected error. Example:

live
<u>His</u> pet bird sat on mother's hat.   (1 error)   (repetition only)

If there is no repetition in correcting mistakes, no errors of any kind are recorded.

8. *Inverting or changing word order.* Mark as in the example.

He ran ⟨rapidly there⟩.   (1 error)[1]

Monroe (1932) used a similar classification of miscues, including: faulty vowels, faulty consonants, reversals, additions of sounds, omission of sounds, substitutions of words, omission of words, and words aided. Other similar systems are those found on the *Durrell Analysis of Reading Difficulty* (Durrell & Catterson, 1955), the *Gates-McKillop Reading Diagnostic Tests* (Gates & McKillop, 1962), the *Gilmore Oral Reading Test* (Gilmore & Gilmore, 1965), and the *Diagnostic Reading Scales* (Spache, 1981).

Leu (1982) characterizes many of the miscues measured on the above tests as surface level in that intraword features of the graphic/phonemic relationship to the text word are analyzed. Recently, those interested in assessing oral reading have begun to focus upon semantic and syntactic features of miscues.

Semantic/Syntactic Linguistic Approaches

In semantic/syntactic approaches examiners are primarily interested in analyzing how a deviation from print relates to the text word in meaning (semantic) and in grammatic (syntactic) similarity. However, in most cases those who use these approaches also give attention to the graphic/phonemic similarities between the words. This is basically an interactive model but with primary emphasis on top-down strategies of reading comprehension (see Chapter 6).

To illustrate the semantic/syntactic approach, a story read by Jonathan is analyzed (Figure 8.6). This story was taken from the new *Gray Oral Reading Tests–Revised* (GORT–R) (Wiederholt & Bryant, 1986). The five types of reading miscues scored by the GORT–R are listed below.

1. *Meaning Similarity.* Allows the examiner to judge the extent of the student's use of comprehension strategies in reading. For example, in line 1 of the story in Figure 8.6, the following three miscues were noted in Jonathan's performance:

Text Word	Miscue	Meaning Similarity
perched	sitting	1
a	the	1
for	at the	0

---

[1]From *Gray Oral Reading Tests* (pp. 5–6) by W. S. Gray and A. M. Robinson, 1967, Austin, TX: PRO-ED. Reprinted by permission.

FIGURE 8.6. Example of Miscue Marking Procedure from GORT–R

A-5 Prompt: Say, "THIS STORY IS ABOUT ANIMALS HAVING A PROBLEM. READ THE STORY TO FIND OUT WHAT THE PROBLEM IS AND HOW IT WAS SOLVED."

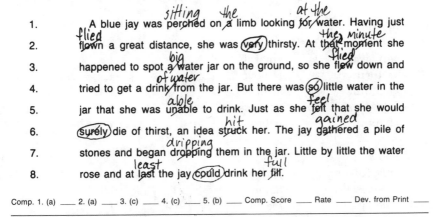

1. A blue jay was perched on a limb looking for water. Having just
2. flown a great distance, she was very thirsty. At that moment she
3. happened to spot a water jar on the ground, so she flew down and
4. tried to get a drink from the jar. But there was so little water in the
5. jar that she was unable to drink. Just as she felt that she would
6. surely die of thirst, an idea struck her. The jay gathered a pile of
7. stones and began dropping them in the jar. Little by little the water
8. rose and at last the jay could drink her fill.

Comp. 1. (a) ___ 2. (a) ___ 3. (c) ___ 4. (c) ___ 5. (b) ___ Comp. Score ___ Rate ___ Dev. from Print ___

From *Gray Oral Reading Tests–Revised* (p. 12) by J. L. Wiederholt and B. R. Bryant, 1986, Austin, TX: PRO-ED. Reprinted by permission.

In the first two cases (i.e., *sitting* for *perched, the* for *a*), the meaning of the passage is not significantly changed. The examiner would use a 1 to indicate meaning similarity for each case. In the third case (i.e., *at the* for *for*), meaning is significantly changed. The examiner would use a 0 to indicate that there is no meaning similarity.

2. *Function Similarity.* Allows the examiner to judge the extent to which the student uses appropriate grammar in reading. In line 1 of the example, Jonathan's miscues can be analyzed as follows:

Text Word	Miscue	Function Similarity
perched	sitting	1
a	the	1
for	at the	1

In all three miscues correct grammatical forms were used. Therefore, the student is given 3 points for function similarity. Examiners will want to note function similarity in the context of what is read orally. They may wish to read the sentence or phrase aloud when scoring to facilitate interpretation of function similarity.

3. *Graphic/Phonemic Similarity.* Allows the examiner to inventory the specific word attack strategies used in oral reading. Specifically, the examiner

decides whether the miscue has similar affixes, roots, vowel sounds, and/or consonant sounds. For example, the following miscues would all be given 1 point for graphic/phonemic similarity:

Text Word	Miscue	Graphic/ Phonemic Similarity
Affixes		
*un*mannerly	*un*motherly	1
*a*typical	*a*moral	1
re*turn*	re*move*	1
hand*ful*	arm*ful*	1
close*ness*	near*ness*	1
hat*s*	bat*s*	1
Roots		
*play*ful	*play*room	1
re*do*	*do*ing	1
*merr*y	*merr*ily	1
Vowel Sounds		
*i*f	*i*n	1
st*ay*	w*eigh*	1
*au*to	l*aw*	1
Consonant Sounds		
*c*at	*c*ome	1
*sh*out	*sh*ove	1
*st*one	*sh*one	1

In each instance where the miscue meets one or more of these criteria (i.e., affixes, roots, vowel sounds, and/or consonant sounds), the student is given 1 point.

In some instances a student will pronounce the text word so that it is not recognizable (e.g., *solitary* as *sōlitary*, *majestic* as *mājestic*). In these instances examiners should treat the word as a nonword and give a 0 for both meaning and function similarity. However, if any of the criteria for graphic/phonemic similarity are met, the student would receive 1 point under that category. The notation for an inappropriate emphasis on sounds can be a long mark over the miscue, as in the above mispronunciations of *solitary* and *majestic*.

Some of Jonathan's miscues would be classified as follows:

Text Word	Miscue	Graphic/ Phonemic Similarity
perched	sitting	0
moment	minute	1
gathered	gained	1
struck	hit	0

4. *Multiple Sources.* Allows the examiner to note those miscues that fit more than one classification. This is an optional category, but by counting miscues that fit more than one category, examiners can derive information about students' use of multiple reading strategies. Using line 1 in the example in Figure 8.6, *sitting* and *perched* can be noted as having both meaning similarity and function similarity by recording a 1 in the appropriate column:

Text Word	Miscue	Multiple Sources
perched	sitting	1

5. *Self-Correction.* Allows the examiner to judge the extent to which the student uses strategies to correct miscues. The notation for the miscue in line 2 of the example indicates that the student used self-correction.

Text Word	Miscue	Self-Correction
that	the↺	1

K. Goodman (1969) presents a detailed semantic/syntactic approach that includes the analysis of 28 different types of miscues. His system was designed for research purposes. Y. Goodman and Burke (1972) describe a simpler version of K. Goodman's system that includes the analysis of seven types of miscues. These are miscues that have graphic similarity, sound similarity, grammatical function, syntactic acceptability, semantic acceptability, meaning change, and correction and semantic acceptability to the text word.

There are also several methods for counting miscues. Some professionals separate graphic and phonemic miscues. In analyzing graphic miscues, some employ the complex formula proposed by Weber (1970). Others use Goodman's (1969) 10-point scale or Cohen's (1974–75) 5-point scale. Still others are not explicit about their criteria and simply note that there was "some" similarity to the text word. In counting miscues in meaning or grammatic similarity, some combine the two; others separate them. Finally, some investigators, like Leu (1982), note the study of quantitative differences among miscues according to the amount of information the reader brings to each deviation from print. The GORT–R provides percentages for each miscue category. For example, if 20 miscues are evidenced and 10 are classified as Meaning Similarity, then the score is reported as 50%. Such a system allows for comparisons across contexts (e.g., types of reading materials, different reading situations) and time.

Summary

The assessment of a student's reading strategies is based on oral reading behavior. Implicit in this practice is the belief that a relationship exists between oral and silent reading. Yet this belief is unsubstantiated. In analyzing oral reading miscues, examiners at the present time focus on graphic/phonemic, syntactic, and semantic miscues. The manner in which this is done varies from professional to professional.

Any oral reading miscue analysis should be interpreted with great caution, because miscue patterns are subject to considerable variation and are believed to be largely idiosyncratic due to complex interactions among several factors. Some of these factors include the methods by which students have been taught reading, their knowledge of the structure of the language of a particular text, the age of the students, their awareness of the content being expressed in the writing, the clarity of writing style in the passage, and the purpose for reading a text.

The instructional implications of the results of a miscue analysis are of course straightforward. Where students consistently make certain types of miscues, *and where their silent reading comprehension is below what would be expected for their age and ability*, they should be taught to use either graphic/phonemic cues, function cues, meaning cues, and/or self correction strategies. In addition, their progress in silent reading comprehension should be evaluated.

MATCHING STUDENTS TO TEXTS

Perhaps the most difficult and challenging assessments of reading are those that are directed toward matching students to texts. These texts may be particular basal reading series; content area books in social studies, science, and mathematics; or recreational reading materials such as novels, short stories, magazines, and trade books. This assessment task is challenging because not only must the difficulty level of the text be considered but also the student's background knowledge, interests, abilities, and reading strategies. In this section a discussion of the manner in which students are placed in texts is presented. These include the use of (a) readability formulas, (b) individual reading inventories, and (c) cloze procedures.

Readability Formulas

In the past, when professionals and textbook publishers spoke of text difficulty, they were primarily referring to such matters as the density of different words among the total number of words, the syllabic length of words, the number of words per sentence, and the complexity of sentence structure (i.e., simple vs. compound and complex sentences). In constructing the lower level of texts, attempts were usually made to minimize the density of different words, shorten syllabic and sentence length, and use simple sentences. At higher levels of texts, density and length increased, and sentence structure became more complex. Readability formulas that mathematically measured these factors were used to demonstrate the increased complexity of stories. The measurements were reported in terms of grade level difficulty (e.g., a text was given a third grade level score or a fifth grade level score), which meant it was appropriate for students in those classes.

Problems with Readability Formulas. Unfortunately, as Durkin (1981) states, "almost as old as the readability formulas are doubts about their ability to yield accurate information" (p. 32). For example, short sentences—a criterion for a low readability level—were at one time believed to be easier to read than long sentences. However, Irwin (1980) found that some short sentences are more difficult to read, because they require the reader to make inferences about previously stated or unstated information.

Another difficulty with readability formulas is that different formulas yield different reading levels. As a result, a textbook that claims to be at the fifth grade level may be considered an eighth grade level text if a different formula were used in analyzing it. Consider, for example, the story taken from the FRI (Wiederholt, 1985) in Figure 8.7. This story was subjected to a readability analysis on four computerized formulas: Flesch, Dale-Chall, Farr-Jenkins-Paterson, and Danielson-Bryan. Since each formula focuses somewhat differently on various text factors listed in the figure, they yielded grade level scores ranging from a low of fifth grade to a high of eighth grade.

Most importantly, readability formulas are suspect because several critical factors other than those measured by traditional techniques are related to readability. Some of these factors include the syntax of the sentences, the logical connections between sentences and clauses, and the coherence of topics. Meyer and Rice (1984) refer to this as text structure, which means

> . . . how the ideas in a text are interrelated to convey a message to a reader. Some of the ideas in the text are of central importance to the author's message, while others are of less importance. Thus, text structure specifies the logical connections among ideas as well as subordination of some ideas to others. (p. 319)

FIGURE 8.7. Readability Analysis of Passage

1   Once there was a turtle who chattered so much that she had no

2   friends. One day she met an eagle traveling to far-away lands

3   across the sea. The turtle had always wished for an adventure.

4   It would make a wonderful tale and win her many friends. So the

5   eagle agreed to take the turtle along. He flew with a strong

6   stick in his claws while the turtle held the stick fast in her

7   mouth. But when they were far out to sea, the turtle could no

8   longer keep silent. As soon as she opened her mouth, she fell

9   straight into the ocean below. Why did the turtle want to go

10 with the eagle? The turtle in this story is smart, careless.

11 The eagle in this story is helpful, interesting. Why do you

12 think the eagle agreed to take the turtle on the journey?

Total Words	143.00
Total Sentences	12.00
Average Sentence Length (Words)	11.90
Average Word Length (Syllables)	1.31
Average Word Length (Letters)	4.15
Percentage Difficult Words (not on Dale list)	16.00
Percentage Technical Terms	0
Percentage of Sentences with Passive Verbs	50.00

Readability Measure	Score	Graded Reading Level
Flesch (Reading Ease)	83.85	7
Dale-Chall	6.39	7
Farr-Jenkins-Paterson	70.26	8
Danielson-Bryan	75.69	5

The research on readability formulas resulted in a joint communique from the presidents of the International Reading Association and the Council of Teachers of English on November 7, 1984 suggesting that everyone involved with text selection stop rating reading level of difficulty primarily by word and sentence length (Cullinan & Fitzgerald, 1984). The key word in the above statement is "primarily." Readability formulas do have some utility. Klare (1984) analyzed the extensive research in this area and offers some suggestions for the use of these formulas. Specifically, he notes that they can be used as *surface* indicators of the readability of the text.

Most textbook publishers do provide an index of the readability of their books. Where an index may not available, professionals can choose from any of the previously mentioned formulas or those provided by Gray and Leary (1935), Lorge (1959), or Spache (1953). A very simple and easy formula is presented in Figure 8.8. This index is called the Fry Readability Scale (Fry, 1972). Directions for its use are found in the figure.

Analyzing Texts. The analysis of text structure, unlike readability scores, is somewhat more difficult to accomplish. Meyer and Rice (1984) describe techniques to analyze structure including the prose analysis systems (e.g., Frederiksen, 1975, 1977, 1979; Kintsch, 1974; Meyer, 1975) and story grammar approaches (e.g., Rice, 1980; Rumelhart, 1975). They also note that there is still much to be learned about analyzing texts.

> A number of different elements operate in the organization of prose. It is possible to describe a passage from the point of view of the content it presents, from a purely structural standpoint (as in story grammars), in terms of the cohesive relations which tie sentences together, or from the point of view of the emphasis patterns being used by the author to underscore his/her own interpretation of the relative importance of the ideas expressed. At present, no single system attempts to combine all of these possible organizations, and it is not clear that such a combination is desirable. The story grammar approach abstracts the structural features of a passage and does not deal with the others. Systems used for expository prose tend to combine content and structural elements. . . . Systems which represent cohesive relations and emphasis patterns are limited to very short passages. . . . It is possible that a representation system which integrated all of these elements would be too unwieldy. On the other hand, it is important to recognize that each of these elements may contribute significantly to the organization of a prose passage. (p. 342)

Recommendations. Since much remains to be investigated about how to analyze text structure, it is not recommended at this time that those charged with reading assessment employ any of the structured methods cited above. Instead, examiners should informally assess texts on such factors as clarity, coherence, organization, interest, and literary quality. In addition, demands should be put upon publishing companies to also attend to the above

FIGURE 8.8. The Fry Readability Scale

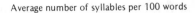

Average number of syllables per 100 words

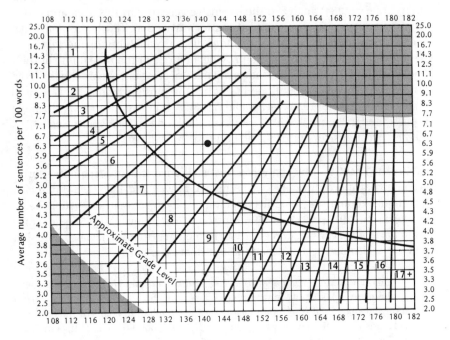

DIRECTIONS: Randomly select 3 one hundred word passages from a book or an article. Plot average number of syllables and average number of sentences per 100 words on graph to determine the grade level of the material. Choose more passages per book if great variability is observed, and conclude that the book has uneven readability. Few books will fall in gray area, but when they do, grade level scores are invalid.

Count proper nouns, numerals, and initializations as words. Count a syllable for each symbol. For example, "1945" is 1 word and 4 syllables and "IRA" is 1 word and 3 syllables.

EXAMPLE:	SYLLABLES	SENTENCES
1st Hundred Words	124	6.6
2nd Hundred Words	141	5.5
3rd Hundred Words	158	6.8
AVERAGE	141	6.3

READABILITY 7th GRADE (see dot plotted on graph)

From *Reading Instruction for Classroom and Clinic* (p. 232) by Edward Fry, 1972, New York: McGraw-Hill. Reprinted by permission.

factors. As the Commission on Reading stated, "Large publishing companies invest upward of $15,000,000 to bring out new basal reading programs. Within budgets of this size, surely it is possible to hire gifted writers who can create stories far superior to the standard fare" (Anderson et al., 1985, p. 48). This same statement could definitely be said about content area textbooks as well.

Until such time as the issues discussed in this section are solved, we also recommend that the emphasis placed on matching children to texts receive less attention, especially in recreational reading. We agree with C. Chomsky's (1972) recommendation that

> Our reading results indicate that exposure to the more complex language available from reading does seem to go hand in hand with increased knowledge of the language. This would imply that perhaps wider reading should find a place in the curriculum. The child could be read to, stimulated to read on his own, not restricted to material deemed "at his level" but permitted access to books well "above his level" to get out of them whatever he may. Perhaps he should be encouraged to skim when he reads, to skip uninteresting portions and get to the "good parts" instead of concentrating at length on controlled texts. In general it may be that the effort should be towards providing more and richer language exposure, rather than limiting the children with restrictive and carefully programmed materials. In this way the child would be permitted to derive what is accessible to him from a wide range of inputs, and put it to use in his own way. This approach would seem to be more closely in accord with the nature of language acquisition as we are coming to understand it. (p. 33)

In sum, when determining the readability level of texts, formulas can be used to derive surface level indicators of difficulty. Attention should also be directed toward informally analyzing texts according to their clarity, coherence, organization, interest, and literary quality. Finally, less attention should be given to prescribed reading levels and more attention given to having students read, in any way they choose, what they wish to read.

Individual Reading Inventories

One of the most common procedures for matching a student to print is the individual reading inventory. These inventories consist of a series of graded passages taken from the basal series or content area texts used in classrooms. Students read the passages orally and/or silently in sequence until they make so many errors that a frustration level is reached. Comprehension questions are usually asked at the conclusion of each passage read. The number of errors made is translated in terms of three reading proficiency levels: independent, instruction, and frustration. These levels are used to determine placement in classroom materials and to measure progress in reading. Some inventories are commercially available, while others are teacher-made.

Reading inventories vary on several dimensions (e.g., what they measure, how they measure it, what they count as errors, etc.). For this reason, a summary of an extensive inventory is found in Table 8.2. This summary inventory is taken from Durrell's (1955) analysis of reading difficulty and includes assumptions, nature, purposes, scope, content, equipment needed, time of administration, records made, and materials provided. Examiners who wish may develop their own inventory following some or all of the recommendations found in the table. However, prior to doing so they should consider some of the following problems with such inventories.

Problems with Reading Inventories. Research findings and theoretical speculations have been increasingly critical of individual reading inventories. For example, many of these inventories lack demonstrated reliability and validity (Jongsma & Jongsma, 1981; Newcomer, 1985; Pikulski, 1974; Wiederholt, 1985). Obviously, a test without some evidence of its consistency in results and its relationship to actual reading must be held suspect.

In regard to teacher-made inventories, research indicates that teachers have difficulty in selecting reading samples, as there is significant variation in the readability of passages within the same text (Bradley & Ames, 1978; Pikulski, 1974). Comprehension questions also pose problems. Professionals such as Allington, Chodos, Domaracki, and Truex (1977) found that many questions are passage independent. That is, the questions can often be answered correctly without reading the passage (e.g., "What color was the apple?" or "What did the sun do at nightfall?"). Where questions are passage dependent, Anderson (1972) found that readers can respond correctly to questions by simply matching similar text features such as the shapes or sounds of words in the question with those in the passage. For example, if the question was "What was the boy's name?" and Bill is the only name used in the sentence, a student could respond correctly by matching the two words.

Many published inventories also suffer from the same problems as the teacher-made inventories. In addition, where they do not accompany a particular series or textbook, the grade level passage cannot be expected to relate appropriately to classroom material. Consequently, these inventories cannot be used with assurance to match a student to print.

The use of independent, instruction, and frustration levels by both teacher and commercial inventories is also under attack. The rather stringent original criteria used to determine these levels is taken from Betts (1946). They are as follows.

TABLE 8.2. Summary of the Durrell Reading Analysis Inventory

ASSUMPTIONS	A. Nature of analysis: Observation and evaluation of weaknesses and faulty habits
	B. Assumes:
	  1. Lack of adequate background abilities to perform the task
	  2. Failure to master early elements of reading
	  3. Instruction not adjusted to level and rate of child's abilities
	  4. Faulty habits
	  5. Lack of transfer skills (i.e., discover "system" that generalizes for the child)
	  6. Continued failure and ineffective motivation
	C. Seeks those difficulties to be corrected by specific teaching
	D. Gives teacher an orderly plan
	E. Fixes responsibility on the school
	F. Assumes physical well-being of the child
	G. Assumes that emotional problems are usually the result of continued failure
	H. Requires teaching experience in the subject taught (i.e., reading)

NATURE	Series of tests, checklists, and situations. Provides record of difficulties; norms; one form.
PURPOSE(S)	To discover weaknesses and habits correctable in a remedial reading program.
SCOPE	Nonreader to 6th grade ability

CONTENT	A. *Oral Reading Tests*
	  1. 8 paragraphs with comprehension questions
	  2. Checklists for observation of phrase reading; word skills; voice; enunciation and expression; general reading habits
	  3. Norms
	B. *Silent Reading Tests*
	  1. 8 paragraphs of equal difficulty to oral paragraphs; with aided and unaided oral recall
	  2. Checklists for mechanics, recall characteristics, comparison with oral reading, imagery
	  3. Norms
	C. *Listening Comprehension Tests*
	  7 paragraphs, one at each level, with comprehension questions

TABLE 8.2. continued

CONTENT (cont.)	D. *Supplementary Paragraphs*
	8 paragraphs, equal in difficulty to oral and silent paragraphs; for supplementary use (e.g., retesting, writing)
	E. *Word Recognition and Analysis*
	Word cards and tachistoscope; Lists, grade 1, grades 2–6; Norms and checklists for word recognition and analysis; Phonics inventory for primary grades.
	F. *Visual Memory for Word Forms*
	Identification at Primary level; Writing from memory for Intermediate grades; Norms for both
	G. *Auditory Analysis of Word Forms*
	(Same as F)
	H. *Spelling and Handwriting*
	Two spelling lists: Primary and Intermediate. Checklists; Norms; Norms for speed of handwriting from copy; Checklists
	I. *Supplementary Determinations*
	  1. Suitability of textbook instruction
	  2. Evaluation of study abilities
	  3. Detailed analysis of word abilities and spelling
	  4. Reading interest and effort
	J. *Profile Chart*
	Record Book, p. 1
	K. *Check List of Instructional Needs*
	Record Book, p. 2
	L. *General History Form*
	Record Book, p. 3: School record; medical record; psychological factors and home history; remedial plans
	M. *Special Tests for the Nonreader*
	  1. Visual Memory of Word Forms, Primary Test
	  2. Auditory Analysis of Word Elements. If child knows letters, this constitutes the Primary Test. If not, Learning to Hear Sounds in Words Test is used.
	  3. Letter Recognition: naming; identifying letters named; matching letters; copying letters
	  4. Phonics: sounds of letters and blends
	  5. Learning rate: sight words remembered
	  6. Listening Comprehension

EQUIPMENT NEEDED	Stopwatch or second hand; pencil; forms

TABLE 8.2. continued

TIME FOR ADMINISTRATION	30–90 minutes per child

RECORDS MADE	A. Time required for each paragraph to be read
	B. Number of questions answered correctly
	C. Vertical lines between phrases the child reads
	D. Error Record:
	  1. Circle omitted words or word parts
	  2. Write child's pronunciation above each word mispronounced (phonetic spelling)
	  3. Put an *R* above all words repeated; if groups, then put a line above group repeated, with an *R* above that line
	  4. Write a *P* above all words pronounced for the child after a 5-second hesitation
	  5. Insertion of words or syllables is noted by a with child's insertion written above
	  6. If errors are too rapid, line through words mispronounced
	  7. *X* through all periods and commas ignored
	  8. Put a ✔ above words on which child hesitates
	  9. Checklist of difficulties should be filled in
	  10. Eye-voice span should be checked and noted according to directions given
	  11. Correct questions are noted by a (+) sign
	  12. Incorrectly answered questions are noted by a (−) sign
	  13. Two or more unanswered questions indicates poor comprehension or low attention: note

MATERIALS PROVIDED	A. Manual of Directions B. Reading Paragraphs on Card Book C. Tachistoscope and Lists D. Record Booklets for Each Child E. Group Summary Sheet

LEVEL OF DIFFICULTY DETERMINATION OF PARAGRAPHS	Not stated

Levels	Word Recognition (%)	Comprehension (%)
Independent	99	90
Instruction	95	75
Frustration	90	50

Spache (1981) notes that these terms—instruction, independent, and frustration—are purely arbitrary and without any basis in research. To illustrate this point, Powell and Dunkild (1971) questioned to what extent a word recognition problem must be present before comprehension is seriously affected. More specifically, Ekwall, Solis, and Solis (1973) used physiological means to measure frustration during reading and concluded that the frustration level in reading series varies from person to person depending upon such variables as general reading ability, measured intelligence, and personality.

Finally, what is counted as a miscue in oral reading often includes only the graphic/phonemic miscues and ignores semantic/syntactic orientations to miscue interpretation. For example, many inventories count miscues such as insertions, omissions, or reversals as errors. In regard to insertions and omissions, D'Angelo and Mahlios (1983) found that:

> The insertions and omissions (of) miscues made by either good or poor readers at instructional or frustration levels cause very little syntactic and semantic distortions. Consequently, time spent coding and interpreting insertion and omission miscues is probably of little use in classroom practices and could be eliminated. (p. 781)

Reversals are errors or miscues that are often present in beginning readers. Some authorities have attributed their presence to brain dysfunction, perceptual deficits, and other problems. However, long ago, Payne (1930) noted that reversals tend to disappear as reading skill matures.

Individual reading inventories can be useful in matching students to print if these criticisms are considered in the development and use of such a measure. Two examples of inventories that consider some of these criticisms are given in this section. One inventory is teacher-made; the other inventory is commercially available.

A Teacher-Made Inventory. Swaby (1984) specifies guidelines for developing an informal reading inventory that is consistent with current thinking about the noting of oral reading miscues. Her guidelines are as follows.

Preparing an Informal Reading Inventory

To prepare an IRI, you need a series of graded texts. Try to obtain texts two grade levels above and below your current grade assignment because you will most likely have a wide range of readers in your classroom.

Step 1. Choose a reading selection of between fifty (for grade 1) and two hundred (for grade 6) words from the middle of each text. The passage should make sense in isolation. You will need one copy of each selection for each student and as many copies for yourself as there are students so you can record each child's reading.

Step 2. Count and record the number of words in each sample.

Step 3. Prepare between six and ten comprehension questions for each selection. Include a variety of questions to assess different levels of comprehension (factual, inferential, vocabulary, cause and effect, evaluative).

Administering the Informal Reading Inventory

The Informal Reading Inventory is administered to each child individually. To administer the IRI, start the child reading in a passage approximately two years below his or her estimated reading level. This ensures success at the start of the test. Then take the following steps.

Step 1. Briefly provide a context for reading the selection. For example, you might say to the child, "The passage you are about to read is about a young boy with a problem. Read to find out what his problem is."

Step 2. Have each child read the selection orally.

Step 3. As the child reads, accurately record the errors on your copy. If the child encounters an unknown word, encourage him or her to try it out. Wait a few seconds and then provide the word. It is helpful to have a clear and consistent marking system to record oral reading errors. A suggested recording system is as follows.

Substitutions: Write the substituted word above the correct word.

The man lifted his *can*. cane.

Omissions: Circle the omitted word.

The man lifted (his) cane.

Additions: Insert a caret and write the word.

The man lifted his ^*long* cane.

Hesitations: Place a slash mark before the word in question.

The man lifted his / cane.

Unknown word: Place a *P* above the word you had to pronounce for the child.

The man lifted his *P* cane.

Repetitions: Underline the repeated word or phrase.

The man lifted <u>his cane</u>.

Self-corrections: Mark original error then place Ⓒ above the error.

The man lifted his ⓒ
The man lifted his <u>cane</u>.

Mispronunciations of names of people and places or pronunciations that reflect the child's dialect are not usually counted as errors.

Step 4. After the child has read the passage and you have recorded the errors, ask comprehension questions and record the child's responses.

Analyzing Oral Reading

The IRI places a child at one of three reading levels:

1. The independent reading level, at which the child scores
   98% or above on vocabulary
   90% or above on comprehension
2. The instructional reading level, at which the child scores
   90% to 97% on vocabulary
   70% to 89% on comprehension
3. The frustration reading level, at which the child scores
   89% and below on vocabulary
   50% and below on comprehension

The passage on which the child scores at the instructional level indicates the appropriate level for placement within the series.

In analyzing miscues, there are four important questions teachers should ask.

1. How well does the child use phonic information during reading? If the child said /rid/ for *ride* and /fum/ for *fume*, he or she knows initial and final consonants and uses them appropriately. But he or she does not use the final *e* construction.
2. How well does the child use syntactic information during reading? The text says, "The boy looked sadly to the right." The child reads, "The boy looked *slowly* to the right." In this case, the miscue is syntactically acceptable because it is syntactically similar to the text (both words are adverbs). If the child reads "The boy looked *sound* to the right," not only does the sentence lose meaning but the miscue is syntactically unacceptable because it is grammatically different from the text.
3. How well does the child use semantic information during reading? The text reads, "The day was very cold." The child reads, "The day was *quite* cold." In this instance, the miscue has not significantly changed the meaning of the text. On the other hand, if the child reads, "The day *wasn't* very cold," the meaning of the text has been dramatically changed.
4. How well does the child monitor reading and correct miscues without being prompted? If a child corrects his or her errors, the child is attending to meaning.

Analysis of miscues helps teachers determine the type of instructional and remedial work each child needs. The child who uses some phonic information but little syntactic and semantic information could benefit from extensive work in using context clues in conjunction with phonic information. The child who uses syntactic and semantic information well but ignores phonic information may need phonic instruction in whole language settings. The child who fails to correct errors needs to be continually asked the question, "Does that make sense?" and needs to be encouraged to use context and phonics to make sense of print.

Analyzing Comprehension
As the child answers the questions at the end of each passage, the teacher should analyze the type of questions answered correctly and incorrectly. Does the child tend to fail on vocabulary, factual, inferential, predictive, evaluative, or cause-and-effect questions? Does the child establish a success or failure pattern in comprehension? This information can be used to guide specific instruction in the strategies the child lacks.

Strange (1980) proposed one useful scheme for understanding possible causes for children's miscomprehension. He identifies seven major classes of errors:

1. *No existing schemata.* Children lack appropriate schemata (concepts) for understanding content.

2. *Naive schemata.* Children have underdeveloped or insufficient schemata for understanding.

3. *No new information.* The text provided no new information, and consequently the child is bored and inattentive.

4. *Poor story or passage.* The passage was poorly written and thus failed to activate children's existing schemata.

5. *Many schemata appropriate.* The material may be ambiguous or open to several interpretations.

6. *Schemata intrusion.* Children's existing schemata block comprehension, resulting in responses that have little or no relation to the text.

7. *Textual intrusion.* Children focus on irrelevant, incidental, or unimportant segments of the text and fail to attend to critical elements.

When teachers have identified the sources of miscomprehension, they can assist children in acquiring the schemata necessary for understanding.[2]

Swaby's inventory is especially relevant in that it includes a miscue analysis that focuses on semantic and syntactic characteristics. She also includes procedures for analyzing comprehension responses as recommended by Strange (1980). We find this addition to inventories especially valuable in that it focuses on the student's background knowledge, the literary quality of the passage, and the student's metacognitive skills. Finally, Swaby's procedures can be used to develop inventories specific to basal reading series as well as content area textbooks.

---

[2]From *Teaching and Learning Reading: A Pragmatic Approach* (pp. 221–225) by B. E. R. Swaby, 1984, Boston: Little, Brown. Reprinted by permission.

A Commercially Available Inventory.

Newcomer (1986) developed an inventory that overcomes many of the problems plaguing other commercially available devices. Her test, called the *Standardized Reading Inventory* (SRI), is based on the vocabulary used in five popular basal reading series: *Scott, Foresman Basics in Readings,* Scott, Foresman and Co., Glenview, IL, 1978; *Houghton Mifflin Reading Series,* Houghton Mifflin Co., Boston, 1979; *HBJ Bookmark Reading Program,* Harcourt Brace Jovanovich, New York, 1979; *Macmillan Reading Series,* Macmillan Co., New York, 1980; and *Ginn Reading Series,* Ginn and Co., Lexington, MA, 1982.

There are two equivalent forms of the SRI from reading level pre-primer to eighth grade, along with a graded word list to assess word recognition and to facilitate easy placement of the student into paragraph reading. Standardized procedures for administration and scoring are provided along with reliability and validity data. Passage dependent comprehension questions of a factual, inferential, and lexical nature are used. An example story from the SRI is as follows.

Form B, Level 3

Motivation: Have you ever seen the lovely birds at the seashore? Read this story to learn about a trip that some of these birds made.

Paul was a hungry gull who lived on a pier in Mexico with many squawking neighbors. One day he and seven gulls in his family left their poor village. They flew over an ocean and a mountain. After many days, they perched in a tower near a harbor at the California shore. Paul was thin, and he had lost some of his chest feathers. But as he looked to the east, he saw the rich country. He knew the dangerous trip through the darkness and chilly weather was a good idea. California was a state of gold and honey. As his doubt disappeared, he felt new courage. His war against hunger was over.

Comprehension Questions

(F) 1. What was Paul?

(F) 2. When the story began, where did Paul live?

(I) 3. Who were Paul's squawking neighbors?

(I) 4. Why did Paul leave his village?

(F) 5. After their flight, where did Paul and his family land?

(I) 6. Did Paul have an easy time reaching California?
How do you know?

(F) 7. What did Paul look like when he landed?

(V) 8. Paul's trip was dangerous. What does dangerous mean?

(F) 9. After Paul landed in California, what did he see when he looked to the east?

(V) 10. Paul felt new courage in California. What does courage mean?

Comprehension Responses

1. *A gull, a bird.*
2. *In Mexico.* If the child says, "On a pier or in a village," say "Yes, but in what country?" The child must provide Mexico to receive credit.
3. *Other gulls.*
4. *There was no food, they were poor.*
5. *California.* If the child says, "In a tower or harbor," say, "Yes, but where was the tower (harbor)"?
6. *No. He flew far, flew over an ocean and mountain, he got thin, he lost feathers, the trip was dangerous.*
7. *Thin, lost feathers.* If the child says, "He looked awful," say "Yes, but exactly how did he look?" No credit unless child is specific.
8. *Risky, could harm him, something bad could happen to him.* If the child says, "He shouldn't do it," say, "Yes, but tell me more about dangerous." To receive credit the child must get the idea of risk or harm.
9. *The rich country, the gold and honey of California, the wealth of California.*
10. *Bravery, not being afraid.* Give no credit for a response that conveys the notion of determination or resolve.

Technical Information

113 words
10 sentences
11.3 words per sentence
82 novel words
12 words used in 3 or more reading series
22 words used in 2 reading series

Scoring Guide

Word Recognition Errors	
Independent	0–2
Instructional	3–11
Frustration	12+

Comprehension Errors	
Independent	0–1
Instructional	2–3
Frustration	4–5[3]

Newcomer's (1986) test is unique in that reliability and validity data are provided. In addition, the test is related to five of the most popular reading series used in the schools today. Consequently, it is possible to use it with some assurance in matching the student with any of these basal programs.

Individual reading inventories do suffer from some inherent difficulties. However, when used with these weaknesses in mind, they can be helpful in matching students to print as well as measuring progress over time.

Cloze Procedures

The cloze procedure, originally referred to in 1897 as the Ebbinghaus Completion Method, has been used frequently as a measure of reading com-

---

[3]From *Standardized Reading Inventory* (pp. 57–59) by P. L. Newcomer, 1986, Austin, TX: PRO-ED. Reprinted by permission.

prehension as well as a measure of intelligence, imagination, and language abilities. Basically a cloze measurement is developed by selecting a passage and having a student fill in every Nth word that has been deleted. Obviously, if the student consistently fills in the blanks correctly, he or she is comprehending the material.

Problems with Cloze Tests. Professional opinion as well as research findings have been generally favorable toward the use of cloze in measuring reading comprehension and matching students to print (see, for example, reviews in the *Eighth Mental Measurement Yearbook*, 1978). However, some criticisms have been leveled toward this procedure such as the belief that standard cloze tests do not measure ability to synthesize information beyond the sentence level (Shanahan, Kamil, & Tobin, 1982). Other criticisms are that (a) a cloze procedure measures only one passage in a text, and passages are not equal throughout most texts, (b) cloze procedures often measure the redundancy of text, and (c) cloze procedures do not measure skills such as making inferences from the text.

While there may be some problems with the cloze test, it can still provide a quick, efficient, and general measure of a student's ability to comprehend a given text. Because of its ease of administration and development, we recommend it over the development of an individual reading inventory when the purpose is to match a student to print.

Development of a Cloze Test. In developing a cloze test, examiners should follow these procedures.

1. Select a reading passage from any textbook that is intended to be used. The passage should consist of 250 to 275 words.

2. Leave the first sentence intact and select at random any one of the first five words of the second sentence. That word is dropped from the running text, as is every fifth word thereafter.

3. Type the passage. For every fifth word type fifteen underlined spaces until 50 underlined blanks have been noted.

In scoring a cloze test it is recommended that only exact replacements be counted as correct. The total number of exact word replacements is then multiplied by two, and the following guidelines used to interpret scores.

Score	Interpretation
0–38%	Frustration Level
40–56%	Instructional Level
58%+	Independent Level

An Example. McCombs and Rosa (1978) illustrate the cloze test procedure with a passage taken from an ecology textbook. This example is as follows.

Example 1 Sample Cloze Test for Science

Along the coastal plains of the Atlantic and Gulf coasts to the south, scrub-pine forests are common. However, where these _____ are not disturbed by _____ or by fires, they _____ be replaced over a _____ of years by hardwoods _____ as hickory, oak, and _____.

Of course, each of _____ kinds of forest could _____ further sub-divided. The divisions _____ them are not abrupt. _____ are regions where mixtures _____ two kinds of forest _____. Yet it is clear _____ it would be possible _____ divide the forest into _____ based upon the major _____ of trees present.

Would _____ divisions be useful? Are _____ different forests different from _____ other in significant ways?

_____ you wandered through these _____, you would indeed notice _____ differences between them. In _____ coniferous forests of the _____, the pines or other _____ trees form a thick _____ overhead throughout the year. _____ of the light and _____ is intercepted by the _____ needles of the trees. _____ small trees or shrubs _____ in this forest. The _____ is covered with a _____ of fallen needles and _____ debris from the trees. _____ and mosses and a _____ flowering plants are scattered _____ over the ground.

The _____ inside the forest is _____ warmer than in the _____. Wind is almost entirely _____ by the coniferous forest. _____ may hear a gale _____ the tops of the _____, but scarcely more than _____ breeze can be felt _____ the forest floor.

The _____, or deciduous, forests are _____ different. Here a much _____ amount of light and _____ reaches the forest floor, particularly in the winter, when the leaves have fallen from the trees. Although the trees block the wind to a great extent, the wind within a hardwood forest is much stronger than the wind in the coniferous forests of the north.

Answers to Sample Cloze Test

1. forests	13. that	25. evergreen
2. logging	14. to	26. layer
3. may	15. regions	27. Most
4. period	16. kinds	28. rainfall
5. such	17. such	29. crowded
6. magnolia	18. these	30. Few
7. these	19. each	31. grow
8. be	20. As	32. ground
9. between	21. forests	33. layer
10. There	22. great	34. other
11. of	23. the	35. Ferns
12. exist	24. north	36. few

37. sparsely	42. You	47. hardwood
38. temperature	43. grow	48. quite
39. noticeably	44. trees	49. greater
40. clearings	45. a	50. rainfall[4]
41. blocked	46. on	

Uses of Cloze Tests. Santeusanio (1983) suggests that additional diagnostic information can be gleaned by examining the student's responses on the cloze test. These suggestions are as follows:

- The student's ability to use context clues. The lack of this skill is particularly evident when the inserted word is grammatically correct, but the word makes little sense.

- The student's skill in spelling. This skill can be determined by examining the spelling of both correct and incorrect insertions and analyzing the student's spelling on both technical and nontechnical words.

- The student's ability to perceive grammatical structure. This skill can be determined by examining blanks that require noun-verb agreement and those requiring articles, prepositions, adjectives, and adverbs.

Cloze procedures can be efficiently developed and administered, thereby making their use more desirable than developing an individual reading inventory. Like the inventories, however, they are not without their weaknesses. Examiners should bear this in mind and carefully monitor students' progress when they have begun to contextually read the text to which they are assigned.

Conclusion

As can be seen, matching a student to text is indeed difficult, and no foolproof method exists to do so. However, readability formulas, text structure analysis, informal reading inventories, and cloze procedures, although lacking in precision, do provide some ways to get into the general ballpark. Other techniques, such as having a student silently and/or orally read a passage and retell what he or she has comprehended, should not be overlooked. However, the most effective way to match a student to text is to observe his or her reading a text over a period of time and to make judgments based upon daily performance.

---

[4]From *What is Ecology?* (pp. 14–16) by L. McCombs and N. Rosa, 1978, Reading, MA: Addison-Wesley. Reprinted by permission.

SKILL ASSESSMENT

Up to this point we have focused on assessing students' performance in reading connected texts. This is because when one is involved in connected text, one is actually "reading." However, some examiners may be interested in the student's use of skills in word recognition and identification. Others will be interested in developing behavioral objectives to be used to teach reading. These two aspects are discussed in this section.

Word Recognition and Identification

While some professionals may use the terms *word recognition* and *word identification* interchangeably, there are important distinctions between the two that must be considered in assessment for instruction. Smith (1971) succinctly describes this distinction.

> "Identification" involves a decision that an object now confronted should be treated in the same way as a different object met before; that the two should be put into the same category. There is no implication that the object being identified should itself have been met before. "Recognition," on the other hand, literally means that the object now confronted has been seen before although it does not require identification. We *recognize* a person when we know we have seen him before, whether or not we can put a name to him. We *identify* a person when we put a name to him, whether or not we have met him before. (p. 106)

In word recognition assessment, examiners are usually concerned with what words a student already knows. For example, it is generally assumed that very young children need to be able to recognize words automatically that occur with high frequency before becoming proficient in reading connected text. There are many such high frequency word lists, for example, the Dolch Sight Vocabulary (Dolch, 1936), Durr list (1973), Harris-Jacobson list (1972), Johnson list (1971), Moe list (1973) and Otto-Chester list (1972). More extensive lists of words found in both basic readers and content area subjects are those developed by Carroll, Davies, and Richman (1971), which contain 86,741 different words found in 5,088,721 words of running text taken from 1,045 published texts in grades 2 through 9; and the *EDL Core Vocabularies in Reading, Science and Social Studies* (Taylor, Frackenpohl, & White, 1979).

Finally, most basal series usually specify the vocabulary that is introduced. Content area texts also often list new words that are employed.

One word list, Johnson's (Johnson & Pearson, 1978) basic vocabulary for beginning reading, is found in tables 8.3 and 8.4. Table 8.3 is first grade words; Table 8.4 is second grade words. These lists were developed based

TABLE 8.3. Johnson's First Grade Words

a	day	I	off	table
above	days	if	old	than
across	did	I'm	one	that
after	didn't	in	open	the
again	do	into	or	then
air	don't	is	out	there
all	door	it	over	these
am	down	its		they
American		it's	past	think
and	end		play	this
are	feet	just	point	those
art	find		put	three
as	first	keep		time
ask	five	kind	really	to
at	for	let	red	today
	four	like	right	too
back		little	room	took
be	gave	look	run	top
before	get	love		two
behind	girl		said	
big	give	make	saw	under
black	go	making	school	up
book	God	man	see	
boy	going	may	seen	very
but	gone	me	she	
	good	men	short	want
came	got	miss	six	wanted
can		money	so	was
car	had	more	some	way
children	hand	most	something	we
come	hard	mother	soon	well
could	has	Mr.	still	went
	have	must		what
	he	my		when
	help			where
	her	name		which
	here	never		who
	high	new		why
	him	night		will
	his	no		with
	home	not		work
	house	now		
	how			year
				years
				yet
				you
				your

From *Teaching Reading Vocabulary* by Dale D. Johnson and P. David Pearson. Copyright © 1978 by Holt, Rinehart and Winston. Reprinted by permission of CBS College Publishing.

TABLE 8.4. Johnson's Second Grade Words

able	different	last	real	water
about	does	leave	road	were
almost	done	left		west
alone		light	same	while
already	each	long	say	whole
always	early		says	whose
America	enough	made	set	wife
an	even	many	should	women
another	ever	mean	show	world
any	every	might	small	would
around	eyes	morning	sometimes	
away		Mrs.	sound	
	face	much	started	
because	far	music	street	
been	feel		sure	
believe	found	need		
best	from	next	take	
better	front	nothing	tell	
between	full	number	their	
board			them	
both	great	of	thing	
brought	group	office	things	
by		on	thought	
	hands	only	through	
	having	other	together	
called	head	our	told	
change	heard	outside	town	
church		own	turn	
city	idea			
close		part	until	
company	knew	party	us	
cut	know	people	use	
		place	used	
		plan		
		present		

From *Teaching Reading Vocabulary* by Dale D. Johnson and P. David Pearson. Copyright © 1978 by Holt, Rinehart and Winston. Reprinted by permission of CBS College Publishing.

on high frequency of a given word in children's spoken language and high frequency in appearance in general printed English.

The usual procedure for assessing a student's recognition of words is through having him or her say the words aloud. When a student pronounces a word correctly, the student is believed to be able to also recognize the word when it appears in connected passages. Conversely, when a student does not recognize the word, it is often believed that direct instruction is necessary.

Problems with Word Lists.   There are basic problems with most sight word lists. Johnson and Pearson (1978) note two of the problems: (a) The student may or may not know the meaning of the word and/or (b) the student may not know the syntactic function of the word in connected texts. In addition, words often have multiple meanings. For example, Balch (1976) found that 26% of the words on the Dolch Basic Sight Vocabulary, 40% of the words on the Harris-Jacobson list, and 42% of the words on the Otto-Chester list had multimeanings. Santeusanio (1983) demonstrates how words change their meaning when they appear in the context of different content areas by the following example.

> English: foot, meter, object, case, mood, notice, perfect
> Social Studies: period, ticket, cabinet, bill, trust, left, race
> Mathematics: sign, base, point, root, power, mean (p. 26)

What this implies is that meaning is very often derived from context. Therefore, in addition to having the student recognize the word, assessment should also include (a) defining the word *where appropriate* (e.g., asking a child to define *is* or *the* is obviously ludicrous), (b) having the student use the word in a sentence, or (c) having the student use the same word in different sentences that affect its meaning.

Two Techniques for Assessing Word Recognition.   Anders and Bos (1984) suggest two additional techniques that have been useful for assessing word recognition in content area texts. These include the Pre-Reading Plan (PReP) and semantic mapping. In PReP the examiner first reads the text and selects a word, phrase, or picture that exemplifies the key concepts presented. The student is then asked to free associate about the stimulus. The free associations are written on the board, and students discuss what triggered the associations. The analysis of the students' free associations indicates whether they have the necessary knowledge and conceptual vocabulary to comprehend the text. In making interpretations, Anders and Bos suggest that students whose free associations reflect superordinate concepts, definitions, analogies, or a linking of the key concept to another concept demonstrate *much* integration of the key concept with concepts already in the accessible memory store. Comprehension for these students should be adequate. Students whose free associations are primarily examples, attributes, or defining characteristics have *some* knowledge concerning the concept being taught. Comprehension should be adequate, but some instructional activities that assist the students in making the critical links between existing and new knowledge will probably be necessary. Students whose free associations reflect morphemes (prefixes, suffixes, root words), rhyming words, or firsthand experiences demonstrate *little* knowledge of the concept. These students need direct concept instruction before reading commences, with the reported firsthand experiences as a reference point for starting instruction. (p. 57)

The second assessment technique that has been useful is called semantic mapping. Again, free associations are used that the examiner relates to key concepts using a networking procedure of words that relate to class, example, and property. Figure 8.9 presents a semantic map of a student's concept of *desert*. As can be noted in that figure, the student did not give any super-ordinate class relations such as type of geographical region. Also, the property and example relations were limited and lacked technical vocabulary. Instruction would therefore be needed in word recognition regarding the vocabulary related to deserts.

Word Identification. As noted previously, word identification is different from word recognition. In word identification, examiners are interested in the student's ability to say a new word using cues he or she learned before with other words. In many cases, students will have previously learned skills such as how to identify the sounds of consonants and vowels, how to phonetically syllabicate, and how to do structural and contextual analyses. As a result, they can identify the new word.

Smith and Johnson (1976) developed a word identification test for teachers. Their test is found in Figure 8.10. By administering this or a similar test, examiners will be able to determine how the student attacks unknown words.

In approaching assessment of word recognition and word identification, examiners may wish to use *The Reading Teacher's Book of Lists* (Fry, Polk, & Fountoukidis, 1984). As the authors note about the book, "it basically has very little prose and consists primarily of lists of words, phonetic elements, meanings, symbols, and miscellaneous ideas" (p. vii). Sections include words that look alike; words that sound alike; words that are used in different school subjects in the primary, intermediate, and secondary levels; words that express feelings; ways to test vocabulary; and much more.

The skills of word recognition and identification may need to be developed by students who are experiencing contextual reading difficulty.

FIGURE 8.9. Semantic Map of Learning Disabled Student's Concept of Deserts

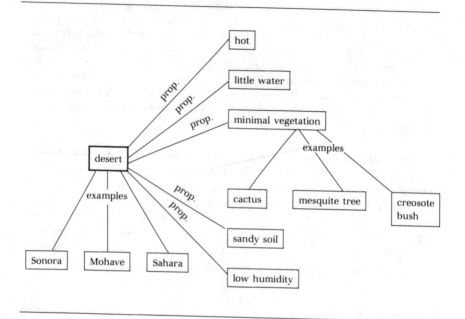

From "In the Beginning: Vocabulary Instruction in Content Classrooms" by P. L. Anders and C. S. Bos, 1984, *Topics in Learning and Learning Disabilities, 3*(4), 53–65. Reprinted by permission.

However, these skills should be developed only as part of a reading program. To repeat, students should be read to from interesting stories as well as encouraged to "read" whatever they wish to read, getting out of it whatever they can.

Behavioral Objectives

Many examiners, particularly those who are required by federal laws in special education, are interested in assessments that lend themselves directly to writing behavioral objectives. Specifically, when students demonstrate that they do not use a particular skill such as word identification, then this skill is usually written as a behavioral objective and taught. For example, two behavioral objectives are as follows.

• Brenda will divide ten randomly selected synthetic words into phonic syllabication with 90% accuracy.

- Linda will be able to recognize the following initial consonants with 90% accuracy when presented auditorily: m, b, h, j, g, r, s, d, c(k), c(s).

Unfortunately, this approach has led in many cases to the teaching of "splinter" skills that can be precisely measured but that may have little to do with learning to read. It is not unusual in schools today to see students spending their "reading" period doing skill worksheets or reading orally with an emphasis almost completely on the exact pronunciation of words and with minimum attention devoted to the syntax, semantic, or enjoyable aspects of reading. The use of behavioral objectives does not necessitate ignoring actual reading. For example, a more legitimate behavioral objective for both Brenda and Linda would be:

- Brenda will self-select reading material and increase the amount of time she spends on continuous silent reading from 5 to 20 minutes by the end of a four-week period.

- Linda will read cloze passages in the content area of social studies and use with 90% accuracy words that are syntactically and semantically correct.

Because of the prevalence of this approach and because it is so often misused to teach "splinter" skills, we present two approaches to developing behavioral objectives. These approaches were selected because they are consistent with current beliefs about reading and learning to read. The first is the reading subtest from the *Basic School Skills Inventory–Diagnostic* (BSSI–D) (Hammill & Leigh, 1983); the second is Guszak's (1985) economical set of reading objectives.

The BSSI–D. As the authors of BSSI–D note, their test (a) is composed of items identified by teachers as essential for reading success, (b) is devised with a format that permits direct translation into behavioral objectives, (c) contains national norms on students age 4–0 to 7–5 for comparing a student's performance to age mates, (d) has established reliability and validity, and (e) is easy to administer and score.

The BSSI–D has six subtests: Daily Living Skills, Spoken Language, Reading, Writing, Mathematics, and Classroom Behavior. The reading subtest consists of 20 items. These items are as follows.

1. *Has the child acquired beginning book-handling skills?*
   Before children develop proficiency in reading, they must first learn basic information pertaining to the physical characteristics of print in books. Give a book to the child and say, "SHOW ME HOW YOU WOULD READ THIS BOOK." The child should open the book and hold it in a proper orientation for reading. Then ask the child to show you where she would start reading.

FIGURE 8.10. Smith and Johnson's Word Identification Test for Teachers

---

GENERAL DIRECTIONS

The Word Identification Test for Teachers is divided into five parts: consonant correspondences, vowel correspondences, phonic syllabication, structural analysis and contextual analysis. Totally there are 50 questions. Score two points for each correct answer to determine percentage correct. On the first 39 questions you are asked to write a brief statement indicating the generalization or reason for your response. These written statements will not be scored but should be discussed.

Part I Consonant Correspondences

Read each synthetic word on the left. Note the underlined letter(s). Circle the word on the right whose underlined letter(s) represents the same sound. Write the generalization which applies below each item.

1.	ceft	sugar	kiss	sell
2.	cupe	king	sew	sure
3.	galp	measure	gym	pig
4.	genn	gone	agile	raquet
5.	tuce	wash	sand	Ken
6.	bition	hat	battle	dish
7.	quan	choir	ark	wag
8.	rebbing	ledge	bend	dent
9.	fax	zebra	sticks	eggs
10.	gliph	hophead	cuff	cup
11.	knilp	now	kite	acne
12.	cump	ship	sin	kin
13.	gome	log	garage	lock

FIGURE 8.10. continued

Part II *Vowel Correspondences*

Read each synthetic word on the left. Note the underlined letter(s). Circle the word on the right whose underlined letter(s) represents the same sound. Write the generalization which applies below each item.

1. peff	bed	came	she
2. laup	fuse	baby	gone
3. gite	bird	mild	pin
4. toib	book	bone	boy
5. dunt	tube	put	much
6. moad	open	coin	out
7. frage	sand	want	bake
8. wot	bond	of	off
9. wapple	game	call	black
10. de	her	team	tend
11. chy	lip	tree	pine
12. frotion	away	mild	lion

Part III *Phonic Syllabication*

Read each synthetic word and draw a line dividing it into syllables. Write the generalization below the word.

1. mapen	4. flotten
2. dochone	5. boncle
3. finter	

Part IV *Structural Analysis*

Draw a line dividing each synthetic word according to "meaningful" parts (which may or may not be pronounceable parts). Below each word explain why you divided where you did.

1. unwok	5. moltn't
2. rothing	6. glennest
3. lidenalk	7. palps
4. narthless	

FIGURE 8.10. continued

Part V *Contextual Analysis*

Read each sentence and note the underlined word. Circle the word it replaces from the choices below.

1. Mary bought an old flabber (a wood burning range) at the auction.

   icebox   stove   fireplace

2. The swarm of moopies destroyed the farm.

   locusts   trout   singers

3. Being much heavier than Ruth, Anna brizzled her in the match.

   overwhelmed   tied   defeated

4. His cheeriness was rantwilious on this heart-rending occasion.

   needed   out of place   typical

5. On the grey, cloudy February evening I felt very seroptick.

   cold   hopeful   lonely

Read the short paragraph and write a word that fits in each blank space.

Answer Key

Part I	Part II	Part III	Part IV	Part V
1. sell	1. bed	1. ma/pen	1. un/wok	1. stove
2. king	2. gone	2. do/chone	2. roth/ing	2. locusts
3. pig	3. mild	3. fin/ter	3. lide/nalk	3. overwhelmed
4. agile	4. boy	4. flo/tten	4. narth/less	4. out of place
5. sand	5. much	5. bon/cle	5. molt/n't	5. lonely
6. dish	6. open		6. glenn/est	6. skills
7. choir	7. bake		7. palp/s	7. teaching
8. bend	8. bond			8. do
9. sticks	9. black			9. basic
10. cuff	10. team			10. a
11. now	11. pine			11. that
12. kin	12. away			
13. log				

From *Teaching Children to Read* (pp. 119–123) by R. J. Smith and D. D. Johnson, 1976, Boston: Addison-Wesley. Reprinted by permission.

1. To receive credit for the item, the child must indicate a page at or near the beginning of the book and demonstrate an awareness of the orientation of print and other cues by holding the book in a proper upright position.

2. *Does the child know what letters are?*
   Children generally must have a concept of "letters" before acquiring many specific letter names and sounds. Show the picture coded RD2 to the child and ask, "WHAT ARE THESE?" The child receives credit either by saying "letters" or by providing the correct names of the letters. However, the child does not have to name the letter individually to receive credit. If the child responds by giving incorrect letter names, say, "YOU DON'T HAVE TO NAME EACH OF THEM, BUT CAN YOU TELL ME WHAT THEY ARE?"

3. *Can the child identify and name lower-case vowel letters?*
   The child's knowledge of lower-case vowel letters can be checked, if necessary, by showing the picture coded RD3 to the child. Point to each of the letters and ask, "WHAT LETTER IS THIS?" The child should correctly identify at least three of the five letters to receive credit for the item.

4. *Can the child name twelve or more capital letters of the alphabet when they are presented to him out of sequence?*
   The child must realize that each of the graphic symbols of the alphabet has its own name. To determine whether she has this knowledge, the individual capital letters of the alphabet are presented in random order, using alphabet flash cards. The child should correctly identify a minimum of twelve letters to receive credit for this item.

5. *Can the child recognize letters when the letter names are provided?*
   In early reading activities, teachers will often refer to individual letters by name. The child must develop the ability to recognize the letters upon hearing their names. Show the picture coded RD5 to the child and say, "POINT TO THE *K*." Repeat the instructions for the *C* and *S*. The child must correctly identify all three letters to receive credit.

6. *When shown a word, can the child find the same word in a group of three other words?*
   This is a word matching task. The child does not have to know the meanings of the words involved in order to complete the item successfully. Since you may use a variety of matching activities in your classroom, you probably already will know the children who can and cannot do these activities. A four-word series of word discriminations, coded RD6, is provided if you want to verify your judgments concerning the word-matching abilities of a particular pupil.

7. *Does the child attempt to read words in the proper left-right sequence?*
   To pass this item, the child must exhibit knowledge of the order in which words are read in a passage. Point to the first word on a page in a first grade reader and say, "IF I START READING HERE, SHOW ME WHICH WORD I WILL READ NEXT." Ask the child to continue to point to each word that

would be read until the end of the line is reached. The child must then indicate the first word in the second line of print in order to receive credit.

8. *Can the child identify and name letters when he hears their sounds?*
This is a sound-symbol association task. Show the card with three letters, coded RD8, to the child. Ask, "WHICH LETTER MAKES THE SOUND /t/?" Repeat the question, substituting the sounds /b/ and /m/. The child must both point to and name all three correctly to receive credit. The sounds /t/, /b/, and /m/ were selected because most children have mastered their articulation in speech by age four. To do this task the child should have the sounds in her speech, know the alphabet, know the names of the letters, and know at least the three letters that made the three particular sounds.

9. *Can the child identify the beginning consonant sound in a word after seeing and hearing the word?*
A beginning awareness of sound-symbol relationships is indicated when a child is able to identify initial consonant sounds of words. Show the picture coded RD9 to the child and pointing to the first word, say "THIS WORD IS *BOY*. WHAT SOUND DOES THE WORD *BOY* START WITH?" Repeat the task for the word *man*. If the child responds by giving the letter name, say, "WHAT SOUND DOES THAT LETTER MAKE IN THE WORD *BOY (MAN)?*" The words should be spoken naturally without placing emphasis on the beginning sounds. To pass the item, the child must identify both sounds correctly.

10. *Does the child have a basic sight vocabulary of at least five words?*
Most children are anxious to read and as a result have acquired a small number of sight words. These can be words that have been picked up by the children on their own or words that have been systematically taught to them by preschool teachers or by parents. Since children will differ in initial sight words acquired, you will have to score this item on the basis of past or current observation of the child. In any event, first grade teachers point out that those pupils who already know some words seem to be the ones who do well in beginning reading.

11. *Can the child identify a sentence that corresponds to a picture he has seen?*
Many beginning reading books provide pictures which accompany the reading passages. To use such visual cues effectively, children must learn that a correspondence exists between the pictures and words that appear on the page. Show the picture of the chick in the egg and the three sentences, coded RD11, to the child. Ask, "WHICH ONE OF THESE THREE SENTENCES GOES WITH THE PICTURE?" The child may not even be able to read all of the words in each sentence, but still receives credit for associating the correct sentence with the picture.

12. *Can the child predict missing words from a passage based upon context?*
All children occasionally encounter an unknown word when reading. At such times, the ability to predict an appropriate word based upon the context in which it occurs is highly useful. Have the child read the story coded RD12. To pass the item, the child must provide words that would appropriately fit into the two blanks. Any words the child provides which "make sense"

in the story are acceptable. For example, the child may fill in the second blank with words such as "water," "lake," or "swimming pool."

13. *Can the child answer questions pertaining to characters or events in a story she has read?*
This item requires the child to provide specific information from a simple story which she has just read. After the child has read the story, coded RD13, ask these two questions: (1) "HOW MANY COOKIES DID JACK HAVE?" (2) "WHO DID JACK GIVE A COOKIE TO?" Do not allow the child to read the story again to find the information. The child must answer both questions correctly to pass the item.

14. *Can the child group words read according to different concepts or categories?*
To perform well on this task, children must not only be able to recognize basic sight words, but also must detect relationships that exist between words based upon categories of meaning represented by the words. Show the child the six words, coded RD14. Say to the child, "THREE OF THESE WORDS BELONG TOGETHER BECAUSE THEY ARE EXAMPLES OF THE SAME THING. THE OTHER THREE WORDS ALSO BELONG TOGETHER BECAUSE THEY REFER TO SOMETHING DIFFERENT. SHOW ME THE WORDS WHICH BELONG TOGETHER." To receive credit, the child must point to or say *red, green, blue,* and then *cat, horse, dog.* The child does not have to label or describe the concepts represented by each group.

15. *Is the child able to describe the main events in a simple story she has read?*
Many reading skills, such as knowledge of sound-symbol relationships, are of little value unless a child is able to understand and remember what has been read. Ask the child to read the story coded RD15. After the child has finished, remove the card and say, "NOW TELL ME THE STORY YOU READ." If the child omits part of the story, prompt the child one time by saying, "DID ANYTHING ELSE HAPPEN IN THE STORY?" To receive credit, the child must mention at least *three* of the four events from the story (girl walking to school, girl seeing flower, girl telling teacher about flower, and flower missing after school).

16. *Can the child predict the ending of a story she has read?*
Prediction of the conclusion of a story requires children to understand both content and sequence within the story. Ask the child to read the story coded RD16. When the child finishes, say, "WHAT DO YOU THINK HAPPENED NEXT?" The child receives credit for providing any ending that logically relates to the events in the story (such as "The bird flew up to the sky," "The bird fell down to the ground," or "The bird flapped his wings but couldn't fly").

17. *Can the child place words in alphabetical order?*
An understanding of alphabetical order must be acquired before children learning to read can locate words in a dictionary, glossary, or index. Show the five words, coded RD17, to the child. Say to the child, "POINT TO THESE WORDS IN ALPHABETICAL ORDER." Other general instructions may be provided if necessary (like "POINT TO THE WORDS IN ORDER ACCORDING TO THE WAY THEY ARE SPELLED," or 'POINT TO THE WORDS IN THE SAME

ORDER THEY WOULD BE IN THE DICTIONARY.") However, it is not permissible to tell the child explicitly how to perform the task or to demonstrate the meaning of "alphabetical order." The child must point to all five words in the correct sequence to pass the item.

18. *Can the child follow printed instructions?*
Pupils are frequently expected to perform behaviors indicated in written directions. Point to each command written in RD18, and say, "DO WHAT THE SENTENCE SAYS TO DO." The purpose of the item is to determine whether the child has developed sufficient beginning reading skills to enable him to interpret and carry out printed instructions independently. Accordingly, the child must read both of the sentences and perform the tasks without assistance from the teacher to pass the item.

19. *Can the child identify sentences she read that are incorrect grammatically?*
Good readers are able to derive meaning from grammatical cues or markers that are present in any passage of print. Show the child each of the three pairs of sentences coded RD19. Point to each pair in turn and say, "ONE OF THESE SENTENCES HAS SOMETHING WRONG WITH IT. SHOW ME THE SENTENCE THAT IS NOT RIGHT." The child may or may not possess the verbal ability to explain why a particular sentence is incorrect. Credit is given if the child identifies the incorrect sentences from all three pairs, since such responses indicate that the child is sensitive to grammatical aspects of print.

20. *When shown four words out of order, can the child use them to form a meaningful sentence?*
This item involves the child's ability to sequence meaningful symbols. The four words, coded RD20, are shown to the child. Say, "USE THESE WORDS TO MAKE A SENTENCE." The pupil should say aloud: a cow eats grass. Children who succeed on this task demonstrate not only word decoding skills but also knowledge of syntactic information, which is critical to reading.[5]

The assessment of these skills is readily translated into behavioral objectives. For example, item 11, if failed, could be written as follows:

- Don will correctly identify with 90% accuracy, 20 sentences that correspond with specific pictures taken from the basal readers.

- Jim will correctly group 30 words with 90% accuracy taken from the categories of animals, jobs, colors.

Guszak's Reading Objectives. Guszak (1985) developed what he terms an "economical testing of reading objectives." His positions, like Hammill and Leigh's (1983), are consistent with current thinking about reading. Therefore, we have reproduced in totality his discussion on behavioral reading objectives taken from his book *Diagnostic Reading Instruction in the Elementary Schools.*

---

[5]From *Basic School Skills Inventory–Diagnostic* (pp. 30–35) by D. D. Hammill and J. E. Leigh, 1983, Austin, TX: PRO-ED. Reprinted by permission.

Having experienced the extremes of general, nebulous objectives as well as highly detailed lists of behavioral objectives, my colleagues and I felt the need to have a more economical set of reading behaviors that we could use to manage daily instruction. To do that, the objectives needed to be organized into some type of system that would permit us to communicate among ourselves, communicate the objectives to pupils, and communicate the objectives to concerned parties like principals, parents, supervisors, and visitors.

In setting up the system, we established the readiness set first. It was followed by the word recognition set, the connected reading set, and the comprehension set. The ordering was not intended to suggest that a teacher would proceed, in order, from A to B to C; it was simply to gather related skills into a meaningful set.

Whereas we spent a lot of time with beginning readers in the readiness set in the early years, we subsequently saw the greatest value for all readers coming from the connected reading and comprehension sets, which became the focal points of our instruction.

After seeing and reading about the components of each set, you will recognize the priorities given to each.

Figure 10.1 shows the reading objectives.

FIGURE 10.1   An economical listing of reading objectives.

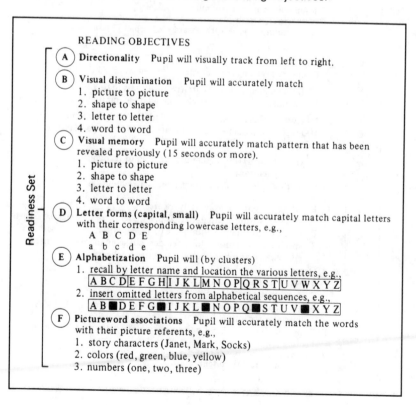

FIGURE 10.1 continued.

Word Recognition Set

(G) **Auditory discrimination** Pupil will accurately repeat sound pairs from reading checklist or phonetic element to be taught.

(H) **Sound to symbol relationships** Pupil will correctly assign symbols to consonant and vowel sounds:
1. initial consonant f, m, c, d, j, s, g, l, h, n, r, b, t, p, w, k
2. final consonant t, d, m, n, b, p, f, c, g, r, s
3. media vowel (CVC) bat bet bit bot but

(I) **Substitution** Pupil will correctly pronounce patterns with substituted letters.

(J) **Contextual application** Pupil will demonstrate substitution skills by reading controlled pattern stories (e.g., A Pig Can Jig, A Hen in a Fox's Den) at a rate of 60 wpm or better:
1. initial consonants: e.g., Dan can fan Nan.
2. initial and final consonants: e.g., Dan had a bag.
3. initial, final, media: e.g., A fat pig fed the hot duck.

(K) **Closure** Pupil will accurately predict covered words in connected reading materials (readers, etc.).

(L) **Word card composition** using previously learned words, pupil will
1. construct correct sentence from scrambled words
2. construct a set of correct sentences from scrambled words
3. construct responses to appropriate questions

(M) **Phrase card composition** using previously learned words in patterns, pupil will construct communications, e.g.,
Noun + verb
Noun phrase + verb phrase + adverbial phrase

Comprehension Set (PLORE) **Connected Reading Set**

(N) **Connected reading (oral or silent)** Pupil will read the following:

N^1 (independent) or N^N (narrative) with less than 3 miscues per 100 words, a good rate (see chart), and high comprehension

N^2 (instructional) or N^C (content) with less than 9 miscues per 100 words, acceptable minimum rate (see chart), and majority comprehension

N^3 (recreational) (no requirements for word recognition, rate, or comprehension)

(PR) **Predicting** Pupil will accurately predict elements and events.

(LO) **Locating** Pupil will accurately locate
1. specifics within written materials, e.g., sentences, paragraphs, parts
2. specific information with book parts, e.g., titles, contents, index
3. specific information with reference aids, e.g., maps, dictionaries, encyclopedias, phone books, classifieds, schedules

(OR) **Organizing** Pupil will
1. retell sentences, paragraphs, stories, sections
2. outline sequences
3. reorganize communication into another form, e.g., summary, illustration, caption

(RE) **Remembering** Pupil will remember various amounts in accordance with reading purpose.

(EV) **Evaluating** Pupil will render value judgments about validity, consistency, reality, intent, etc.

The Readiness Set

In Chapter 7, the primary discussions dealt with reading readiness as a complex of skills that enabled a person to respond effectively to selective reading tasks. It was further suggested that the most fruitful beginning reading tasks were reading aloud to children, the shared-book experience, the language-experience approach, and the teach-a-sentence approach. It is through these activities that pupils respond to the print-match task we call reading. Through these activities, such outcomes as directionality, visual discrimination, visual memory, letter forms, alphabetization, and picture-word associations occur naturally. For some children, the readiness set objectives can have value if used carefully.

A. Directionality *Directionality* normally involves worksheets on which the pupils would have the car going into the garage, the horse galloping into the barn, and the dog heading for the doghouse (Figure 10.2). To me, these tasks are a waste of paper and pupil time. Directionality does not appear to be developed through such experiences but rather through the process of following the left-to-right progression of a reader's finger through numerous reading experiences. For this reason, we have discarded the visuals and put more emphasis on the modeling of the moving finger in repetitive reading materials (the ones the pupils learn to put in their memory banks early).

FIGURE 10.2 Example of a directionality worksheet.

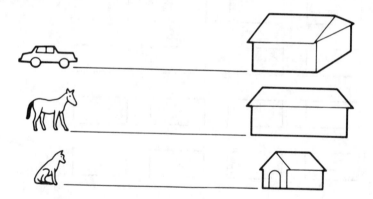

B. Visual discrimination *Visual discrimination* refers to pupils' abilities to differentiate various letter stimuli. Typically, workbook tasks would produce pictures, shapes, letters, and words for increasingly difficult discrimination tasks such as the following:

Directions read to pupils: Circle the pattern that is just like the first one.

j		k	l	t	j
m		n	m	w	x
is		si	zi	iz	is

While such tasks may have some values for helping pupils differentiate shape, size, orientation, and the like, they really present a very small portion of the reading act that requires meaning. We stopped using such tasks a long time ago.

C. Visual memory   *Visual memory* represents a far more formidable task than visual discrimination because it requires the pupil not only to discriminate unique features but to hold that configuration in mind. This skill seems to have a solid research basis (Barrett, 1965), so we continue to use concentration games that require pupils to organize what they are viewing. Starting with five or six pairs of matching items, the pupil turns over the first card, views it, returns it to the face-down position, turns up another card, and attempts to recall if the two cards match. (Figure 10.3) If they do, the matched pair remain face up and the game continues. The game can be played with more than a single player. In addition to being motivating, the game seems to help pupils systematize their viewing of letter and word stimuli.

D. Letter forms   *Letter-form* knowledge is important because beginners frequently have trouble when they see the same word with very different letters, such as *ride, Ride; and, AND*. We have internalized the criteria, but they have not. Basically, this task is probably more important for production (writing). Still, opportunities to match capital and lowercase letters with answer keys for reference seems to be a useful activity.

FIGURE 10.3   Visual memory cards used to play the concentration game.

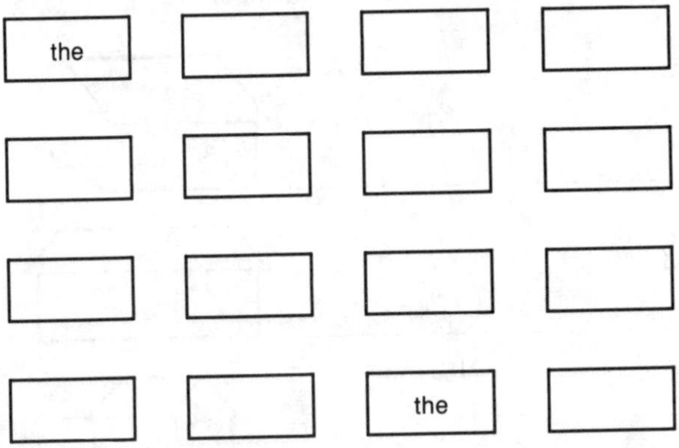

E. Alphabetization   *Alphabetization* is primarily a locational device. As such it will come into use when pupils need to locate things by alphabetical listing. For this reason, the skill seems useful from kindergarten on so that pupils can locate names on lists, words in dictionaries, articles in encyclopedias, telephone numbers, and so on.

F. Picture-word associations   *Picture-word associations* are the natural products of children's interacting with their environments. It doesn't seem to hurt if that environment is made more word-plentiful by pupil-brought logos, words on common objects, and the like. Children like to see the words for the various things around them.

The Word Recognition Set

The Chapter 5 word recognition skills of context, sight words, and word mediation are included, but in a different order, in the word recognition set. Within
this set, the first breakdown deals with word mediation: auditory discrimination (G), sound-to-symbol relationships (H), substitution (I), and contextual application of phonics skill (J). The context set is made up of closure (K), while the
sight word set is composed of word card composing (L) and phrase card composing (M).

G. Auditory discrimination *Auditory discrimination,* in the word mediation subset, simply states that pupils will accurately repeat sound pairs pronounced by another speaker. Before pupils can accurately pronounce the
different phonemes, they must discriminate them auditorially. This skill is
included because we sometimes find teachers attempting to teach sound-to-
symbol associations to pupils who cannot articulate the sounds involved. These
pupils simply don't discriminate the sounds auditorially. It is important that
teachers test pupils in advance of teaching any sound elements to determine
if the pupils can hear the elements. The easiest way to test is to pronounce word
pairs and ask the pupil to pronounce them after you (e.g., *pin* and *pan*). If they
can do it, proceed. If not, they need help in discriminating differences. The same
applies to trying to teach pupils to sound out or spell involved words in which
they do not hear the segmented sounds as evidenced by partial reproductions
(e.g., the teacher says *in-vig-or-at-ing* and the pupil repeats *in-vig-at-ing*).

H. Sound-to-symbol relationships *Sound-to-symbol relationships* is the
concept that symbols have associated sounds. Such associations are developed
naturally by most beginning readers, but some children need special assistance
in learning how some of the more stable patterns work. I use the word *stable*
because some letters are notorious for the multiple sounds that are associated
with them. Because stability is greater with certain consonants in the initial position and certain vowels in the medial position, we start as indicated in Chapter 5.

I. Substitution *Substitution* refers to the skill of using letter-sound relationships to attack new words. The term *blending* may also be used to represent
the process whereby pupils use the letter-sound relationships to formulate an
estimate of a word. The estimate is instantly checked against its likelihood for
carrying meaning in the passage.

J. Contextual application *Contextual application,* the final item in the word
mediation subset, refers to the pupil's ability to apply blending skills in a reading
context as opposed to a word list. Pupils need situations in which they can apply
their emerging skills to real stories. Controlled-pattern books such as the S.R.A.
Linguistic Series, the Merrill Linguistic Series, and the Palo Alto Linguistic Series
provide such materials at a modest cost. Ultimately, the final test of contextual
application must be the pupil's application of the skill in challenge-level reading.

K. Closure *Closure,* the context subset of the word recognition set, refers
to the reader's ability to effect closure across text. This entails figuring out words
and word meanings through the use of the surrounding information. Closure

is a part of the prediction skill of the comprehension category. As such, it is one of the most critical reading-thinking skills.

L. Word card composition   *Word card composition* is a sight word task in which the pupils construct sentences from word cards. The practice helps pupils to learn the words as a result of practice and syntactic reinforcement. Tasks can be arranged using words of certain types so that pupils can gain additional insights into the word order of sentences:

Names or things	Helping words	Action words
Tom	can	play
The cat	will	run

M. Phrase card composition   *Phrase card composition* is an extension of word card composition that allows the pupils to work with basic phrases in an effort to speed up the rapidity of their phrasing:

Noun phrases	Verb phrases	Prepositional phrases
The little boy	ran wildly	down the hill
A swift black bird	swooped gracefully	over the tree
Two thin chickens	climbed quietly	onto the big limb

O'Shea and Sindelar's (1983) application of this strategy to pupils' reading materials in the form of segmented discourse improved the fluency and reading accuracy as measured by miscues of first through third grade readers.

The Connected Reading Set

By now, you must suspect that this is the "biggie" insofar as I'm concerned. For years, the notations N^1 and N^2 have become (for independent reading and instructional reading) synonymous for easy and challenge reading for a good number of teachers, children, and parents. Not only are they easier to read and write, but they also save countless time in oral communications as we discuss pupils' reading progress with those concerned (which includes not only teachers, pupils, and parents, but administrators, specialists, and aides as well).

What people choose to call connected reading practice is really unimportant. Whereas terms like SQUIRT, USSR, SSR, R^1 and R^2 have been developed, the important consideration is that there is a means for communication.

Easy or independent reading is referred to by N^1. The behavioral objectives reiterate that such reading means less than 3 errors per 100 words with a good rate and high comprehension. Independent reading (N^1) time seems to be the all-time favorite reading activity because the children enjoy reading materials that are comfortable. Cooper's (1952) findings that pupils prosper greatest when reading at such a level of ease further strengthen its value.

Challenge or instructional reading (N^2) seeks to stretch pupils by challenging them with the materials. This challenge theory has worked well for us when the challenge has not been too great. When it is too great, we have frustration. Caution is advised in applying the criterion that allows as many as 9 errors per 100 words. This is too many for some pupils. Only an alert teacher can make the judgment of difficulty.

Recreational reading (N^3) is any reading a child chooses to pursue. Recall that a pupil's choices are limited by criteria of performance in the preceding categories, but in recreational reading (N^3) the child can read anything he or she wishes to read. This sometimes means that pupils bite off more than they can chew, but we still wish to allow them to do so. Sometimes special interests compensate for missing skills and allow a lot to happen. At other times pupils realize their limits and make different choices at recreational reading times.

When students become relatively accomplished readers at the third and fourth reading levels, there seems to be less need for continuing the idea of easy and challenge reading of basically narrative materials. The reading diet should be expanded in the direction of narrative reading (N^n) and content reading (N^c).

Narrative reading (N^n) means that pupils continue to read easy narrative materials on a daily basis. This allows them the pleasures of such reading but does not limit them to a total diet of narrative reading (which some might well like). Also, it means that they don't have to do detailed comprehension or PLORE tasks over this narrative material because we have had the opportunity to verify that they can perform the various tasks successfully.

Content reading (N^c) recognizes the need for reading in content materials such as content texts, news magazines, newspapers, and the like. In association with such tasks, pupils have the opportunities to learn to organize reports, outline materials, summarize, and learn content reading techniques such as SQRRR (Survey, Question, Read, Recite, Review).

The Comprehension Set Predicting, Locating, Organizing, Remembering, and Evaluating (PLORE)

As discussed in Chapter 6, this set includes the skills related to predicting, locating, organizing, remembering, and evaluating. Obviously, its last-place position doesn't indicate its relative importance.

PRIORITIZING THE OBJECTIVES

For the day-to-day teaching of reading, I suggest the following prioritization of the behavioral objectives:

First Priority: The Connected Reading Set
Independent or narrative reading (N^1 or N^n)
Instructional or content reading (N^2 or N^c)
Recreational reading (N^3)

In keeping with the principles of diagnostic reading instruction stated at the outset of the book, I believe that pupils learn to read by reading extensively. If time permits nothing else, connected reading must be the reading activity of the day.

Second Priority: The Comprehension Set (PLORE)

Predicting (PR)
Locating (LO)
Organizing (OR)
Remembering (RE)
Evaluating (EV)

After pupils have read their instructional-level materials (narrative or content), they need to demonstrate understanding by constructing written responses to a variety of comprehension tasks. As can be seen in Chapter 12, these tasks vary from simple manipulative answers to remembering questions to the array of PLORE questions.

Third Priority: The Word Recognition Set

Word mediation subset

Auditory discrimination (G)
Sound-to-symbol relationships (H)
Substitution (I)
Contextual application (J)

Context subset

Closure (K)

Sight word subset

Word card composition (L)
Phrase card composition (M)

Pupils needing assistance in mediating words could be taught and rehearsed in the necessary word mediation skills.

Fourth Priority: The Reading Readiness Set

Directionality (A)
Visual discrimination (B)
Visual memory (C)
Letter forms (D)
Alphabetization (E)
Picture-word associations (F)

The earliest reading efforts of preschoolers reveal a startling awareness of most of these elements. Consequently, it seems ill advised to spend large amounts of time on these tasks in situations isolated from the whole of reading.

SUMMARY

Objectives may be expressive or behavioral. Expressive objectives concern things that cannot or should not be measured, such as appreciation. Behavioral objectives, on the other hand, involve things that can be specified and measured.

Behavioral objectives that contain the given conditions, the behavioral statements, and the criteria of acceptable performance can be overly prescriptive or useful, depending on their kinds and amounts. An economical set of reading objectives is provided as a useful guide to planning and implementing instruction. The listing contains four sets: the readiness set, the word recognition set, the connected reading set, and the comprehension set. The connected reading and comprehension sets are the highest-priority sets for reading programs from kindergarten through the higher grades.[6]

As can be seen, Guszak (1985) places priority in learning to read on connected (contextual) reading (i.e., independent or narrative reading, instructional or content reading, and recreational reading). The lowest priority is what he calls the "the reading readiness set" (i.e., directionality, visual discrimination, and picture-word associations). We wholeheartedly endorse his statement that it is ill advised to spend large amounts of time on these latter readiness tasks in situations that are isolated from the whole of reading.

CONCLUSION

We have certainly not exhausted the number of various assessment strategies that are useful when assessing for instruction. However, we have delineated the numerous aspects of the reading act that need to be considered when teaching a student with reading problems. Specifically, these include the analysis of (a) the home and school environment, (b) the student's attitudes and interest in reading, (c) the student's reading strategies, (d) appropriate texts to use with specific students, and (e) skills believed to be important in learning to read.

REFERENCES

Allington, R. L. (1980). Teacher interruption behaviors during primary-grade oral reading. *Journal of Educational Psychology, 12,* 371–377.

Allington, R. L. (1984). So what is the problem? Whose problem is it? *Topics in Learning and Learning Disabilities, 3*(4), 91–99.

Allington, R. L., Chodos, L., Domaracki, G., & Truex, P. (1977). Passage dependency: Four diagnostic oral reading tests. *The Reading Teacher, 30,* 369–375.

---

[6]From *Diagnostic Reading Instruction in the Elementary Schools* (pp. 190–199) by F. Guszak, 1985, New York: Harper and Row. Reprinted by permission.

Anders, P. L., & Bos, C. S. (1984). In the beginning: Vocabulary instruction in content classrooms. *Topics in Learning and Learning Disabilities, 3*(4), 53–65.

Anderson, R. C. (1972). How to construct achievement tests to access comprehension. *Review of Educational Research, 42,* 145–170.

Anderson, R. C., Hiebert, E. H., Scott, J. A., & Wilkinson, I. A. G. (1985). *Becoming a nation of readers.* Washington, DC: The National Institute of Education.

Balch, M. C. (1976). *A problem with sight vocabulary lists: Multi-meaning words.* Unpublished master's thesis, The University of Wisconsin, Madison.

Barr, R., & Dreeben, R. (1983). *How schools work.* Chicago: University of Chicago Press.

Bartel, N. R. (1986). Teaching students who have reading problems. In D. D. Hammill & N. R. Bartel (Eds.), *Teaching students with learning and behavior problems* (pp. 23–89). Austin, TX: PRO-ED.

Betts, E. (1946). *Foundations of reading instruction.* New York: American Books.

Bradley, J. M., & Ames, W. S. (1978). You can't judge a basal by the number on the cover. *Reading World, 17,* 175–183.

Buros, O. K. (1978). *Eighth mental measurement yearbook.* Highland Park, NJ: Gryphon Press.

Carroll, J. B., Davies, P., & Richman, B. (1971). *Word frequency book.* Boston: Houghton Mifflin.

Chomsky, C. (1972). Stages in language development and reading exposure. *Harvard Educational Review, 42,* 1–33.

Cohen, A. S. (1974–75). Oral reading errors of first grade children taught by a code emphasis approach. *Reading Research Quarterly, 10,* 615–650.

Crandall, V. C., Katkovsky, W., & Crandall, J. V. (1965). Children's beliefs in their own control of reinforcement in intellectual academic achievement situations. *Child Development, 36,* 91–109.

Cullinan, B., & Fitzgerald, S. (1984). *Background information bulletin on the use of readability formulas.* Urbana, IL: National Council of Teachers of English.

D'Angelo, K., & Mahlios, M. (1983). Insertion and omission miscues of good and poor readers. *The Reading Teacher, 36,* 778–782.

Dolch, E. W. (1936). A basic sight vocabulary. *Elementary School Journal, 36,* 456–460.

Durkin, D. (1981). What is the value of the new interest in reading comprehension? *Language Arts, 58,* 23–43.

Durkin, D. (1983). *Teaching them to read* (4th ed.). Boston: Allyn & Bacon.

Durr, W. K. (1973). Computer study of high frequency words in popular trade journals. *The Reading Teacher, 27,* 37–42.

Durrell, D. D., & Catterson, J. H. (1955). *Durrell Analysis of Reading Difficulty.* San Antonio, TX: The Psychological Corporation.

Dweck, C. S. (1975). *Durrell Analysis of Reading Difficulty.* New York: Harcourt Brace Jovanovich.

Ekwall, E. E., Solis, J., & Solis, E. (1973). Investigating informal reading inventory scoring criteria. *Elementary English, 50,* 271–274.

Engelmann, S., & Bruner, E. C. (1974). *DISTAR Reading II.* Chicago: Science Research Associates.

Engelmann, S., & Bruner, E. C. (1975). *DISTAR Reading III.* Chicago: Science Research Associates.

Engelmann, S., Granzin, A., & Senerson, H. (1979). Diagnosing instruction. *Journal of Special Education, 13,* 355–363.

Estes, T. H., Estes, J. J., Richards, H. C., & Roettger, D. (1981). *Estes Attitude Scales.* Austin, TX: PRO-ED.

Farr, R., & Fay, L. (1982). Reading trend data in the United States: A mandate for caveats and caution. In G. R. Rustin & H. Garber (Eds.), *The rise and fall of national test scores* (pp. 83–141). New York: Academic Press.

Farr, R., & Roser, N. (1979). *Teaching a child to read.* New York: Harcourt Brace Jovanovich.

Fernald, G. M. (1943). *Remedial techniques in basic school subjects* (1st ed.). New York: McGraw-Hill.

Fowler, J. W., & Peterson, P. A. (1981). Increasing reading persistence and altering attributional style of learned helpless children. *Journal of Educational Psychology, 73,* 251-260.

Frederiksen, C. H. (1975). Acquisition of semantic information from discourse: Effects of repeated exposures. *Journal of Verbal Learning and Verbal Behavior, 14,* 158–169.

Frederiksen, C. H. (1977). Semantic processing units in understanding text. In R. O. Freedle (Ed.), *Discourse production and comprehension* (pp. 57–87). Norwood, NJ: Ablex.

Frederiksen, C. H. (1979). Discourse comprehension and early reading. In L. B. Resnik & P. A. Weaver (Eds.), *Theory and practice of early reading* (Vol. 1, pp. 155–186). Hillsdale, NJ: Lawrence Erlbaum.

Fry, E. (1972). *Reading instruction for classroom and clinic.* New York: McGraw-Hill.

Fry, E. B., Polk, J. K., & Fountoukidis, D. (1984). *The reading teacher's book of lists.* Englewood Cliffs, NJ: Prentice-Hall.

Gates, A. I. (1961). Results of teaching a system of phonics. *The Reading Teacher, 14,* 248–252.

Gates, A. I., & McKillop, A. S. (1962). *Gates-McKillop Reading Diagnostic Tests.* New York: Teachers College Press.

Gilmore, J. V., & Gilmore, E. C., (1965). *Gilmore Oral Reading Test.* New York: Harcourt Brace Jovanovich.

Ginn Reading Series. (1982). Lexington, MA: Ginn.

Goodman, K. S. (1969). Analysis of oral reading miscues: Applied psycholinguistics. *Reading Research Quarterly, 5,* 9–30.

Goodman, K. S. (1976). Behind the eye: What happens in reading. In H. Singer & R. B. Ruddell (Eds.), *Theoretical models and processes in reading* (pp. 470–496). Newark, DE: International Reading Association.

Goodman, K. S. (1982). *Language and literacy: The selected writings of Kenneth S. Goodman.* Boston: Routledge and Kegan Paul.

Goodman, Y. M., & Burke, C. L. (1972). *Reading miscue inventory: Manual and procedures for diagnosis and evaluation.* New York: Macmillan.

Gray, W. S., Leary, B. E. (1935). *What makes a book readable, with special reference to adults of limited readability: An initial study.* Chicago: University of Chicago Press.

Gray, W. S., & Robinson, H. M. (1967). *Gray Oral Reading Tests.* Austin, TX: PRO-ED.

Greenwood, C. R., Delquadri, J., & Hall, R. V. (1978). *Code for instructional structure and student academic response: CISSAR.* Kansas City, KS: Juniper Gardens Children's Project, Bureau of Child Research, University of Kansas.

Guszak, F. (1985). *Diagnostic Reading Instruction in the Elementary Schools.* New York: Harper and Row.

Hammill, D. D., & Leigh, J. E. (1983). *Basic School Skills Inventory–Diagnostic.* Austin, TX: PRO-ED.

Harris, A. J., & Jacobson, M. D. (1972). *Basic elementary reading vocabularies.* New York: Macmillan.

HBJ Bookmark Reading Program. (1979). New York: Harcourt Brace Jovanovich.

Herber, H. L. (1978). *Teaching reading in content areas* (2nd ed.). Englewood Cliffs, NJ: Prentice-Hall.

Hoffman, J. V. (1979). On providing feedback to reading miscues. *Reading World, 18,* 342–350.

Hoffman, J. V., & Baker, C. (1981). Characterizing teacher feedback to student miscues during oral reading instruction. *The Reading Teacher, 34,* 907–913.

Hoffman, J. V., & Clements, R. (1983). Reading miscues and teacher verbal feedback. *Elementary School Journal, 4,* 423–439.

Hoffman, J. V., O'Neal, S. F., Kastler, L. A., Clements, R. O., Segel, K. W., & Nash, M. F. (1984). Guided oral reading and miscue focused verbal feedback in second-grade classrooms. *Reading Research Quarterly, 19,* 367–384.

Houghton Mifflin Reading Series. (1979). Boston: Houghton Mifflin.

Huskins, F. (1981). Incomplete sentence test for elementary children. In G. D. Spache (Ed.), *Diagnosing and correcting reading disabilities* (2nd ed., pp. 447–449). Boston: Allyn & Bacon.

Irwin, J. (1980). The effects of explicitness and clause order on the comprehension of reversible causal relationships. *Reading Research Quarterly, 15,* 477–488.

Jenkins, J. R., & Heliotes, J. G. (1981). Reading comprehension instruction: Findings from behavioral and cognitive psychology. *Topics in Language Disorders, 1*(2), 25–41.

Johnson, D. D. (1971). A basic vocabulary for beginning reading. *Elementary School Journal, 72,* 29–34.

Johnson, D. D., & Pearson, P. D. (1978). *Teaching reading vocabulary.* New York: Holt, Rinehart and Winston.

Johnson, P. (1985). Understanding reading failure: A case study approach. *Harvard Educational Review, 55,* 153–177.

Johnston, P. H., & Winograd, P. N. (1985). Passive failure in reading. *Journal of Reading Behavior, 4,* 279-300.

Jongsma, K. S., & Jongsma, E. A. (1981). Test review: Commercial informal reading inventories. *The Reading Teacher, 34,* 697–705.

Juel, C., & Holmes, B. (1981). Oral and silent reading of sentences. *Reading Research Quarterly, 40,* 545–568.

Kintsch, W. (1974). *The representation of meaning in memory.* New York: Lawrence Erlbaum.

Klare, G. R. (1984). Readability. In P. D. Pearson (Ed.), *Handbook of reading research* (pp. 681–744). New York: Longman.

Kline, L. W. (1980). Market research: What young people read. *Journal of Reading,* *24,* 284–286.

Leu, D. J. (1982). Oral reading error analysis: A critical review of research and application. *Reading Research Quarterly, 3,* 420–437.

Lorge, I. (1959). *The Lorge formula for estimating difficulty of reading materials.* New York: Bureau of Publication, Teachers College, Columbia University.

Macmillan Reading Series. (1980): New York: Macmillan.

McCombs, L., & Rosa, N. (1978). *What is ecology?* Reading, MA: Addison-Wesley.

Meyer, B. J. F. (1975). *The organization of prose and its effect on memory.* Amsterdam: North-Holland.

Meyer, B. J. F., & Rice, G. E. (1984). The structure of text. In P. D. Pearson (Ed.), *Handbook of reading research.* New York: Longman.

Moe, A. J. (1973). Word lists for beginning readers. *Reading Improvement, 10*(2), 11–15.

Monroe, M. (1932). *Monroe Diagnostic Reading Test.* Bradenton, FL: C. H. Nevins.

Morrow, L. M. (1985). Developing young voluntary readers: The home—the child— the school. *Reading Research and Instruction, 25,* 1–8.

National Assessment of Educational Progress. (1981). *Reading, writing, and thinking.* 1979–1980 Report. Washington, DC: U.S. Printing Office.

Newcomer, P. L. (1985). A comparison of two published reading inventories. *Remedial and Special Education, 6,* 31–36.

Newcomer, P. L. (1986). *Standardized Reading Inventory.* Austin, TX: PRO-ED.

Nicholls, J. (1979). Development of perception of our attainment and causal attributions for success and failure in reading. *Journal of Educational Psychology, 71,* 94–99.

Otto, W., & Chester, R. (1972). Sight words for beginning readers. *The Journal of Educational Research, 65,* 435–443.

Payne, C. (1930). The classification of errors in oral reading. *Elementary School Journal, 31,* 142–146.

Pflaum, S. W., Pascarella, E. T., Boskwick, W., & Aner, C. (1980). The influence of pupil behaviors and pupil status factors on teacher behaviors during oral reading lessons. *Journal of Educational Research, 74,* 99–105.

Pikulski, J. (1974). A critical review: Informal reading inventories. *The Reading Teacher, 28,* 141–151.

Powell, W., & Dunkild, C. (1971). Validity of the IRI reading levels. *Elementary English, 10,* 637–642.

Rice, G. E. (1980). On cultural schemata. *American Ethnologist, 1,* 152–171.

Rosenshine, B. V., & Stevens, R. (1984). Classroom instruction in reading. In P. D. Pearson (Ed.), *Handbook of reading research* (pp. 745–798). New York: Longman.

Roser, N., & Schallert, D. L. (1983). Reading research: What it says to the school psychologist. In T. R. Kratochwill (Ed.), *Advances in school psychology* (pp. 237–268). Hillside, NJ: Lawrence Erlbaum.

Rumelhart, C. E. (1975). Notes on a schema for stories. In D. G. Bobrow & A. M. Collins (Eds.), *Representation and understanding* (pp. 211–236). New York: Academic Press.

Santeusanio, R. P. (1983). *A practical approach to content area reading.* Reading, MA: Addison-Wesley.

Scott, Foresman Basics in Reading. (1978). Glenview, IL: Scott, Foresman.

Shanahan, T., Kamil, M. L., & Tobin, A. W. (1982). Cloze as a measure of intersentential comprehension. *Reading Research Quarterly, 17,* 229–253.

Smith, F. (1971). *Understanding reading: A pscholinguistic analysis of reading and learning to read.* New York: Holt, Rinehart, and Winston.

Smith, R. J., & Johnson, D. D. (1976). *Teaching children to read.* Boston: Addison-Wesley.

Spache, G. (1953). A new readability formula for primary grade reading materials. *Elementary School Journal, 53,* 410–413.

Spache, G. (1981). *Diagnosing and correcting reading disabilities.* Boston: Allyn & Bacon.

Stein, N. L., & Glenn, C. G. (1979). An analysis of story comprehension in elementary school children. In R. O. Freedle (Ed.), *New directions in discourse processing.* Norwood, NJ: Ablex.

Strange, M. (1980). Instructional implications of a conceptual theory of reading comprehension. *The Reading Teacher, 33,* 391–397.

Summers, E. G. (1979). *Literature preferences of elementary age children.* Vancouver, Canada: University of British Columbia.

Swaby, B. E. R. (1984). *Teaching and learning reading: A pragmatic approach.* Boston: Little, Brown.

Taylor, D. (1983). *Family literacy: Young children learning to read and write.* London: Heineman.

Taylor, S. E., Frackenpohl, H., & White, C. E. (1979). *EDL core vocabularies in reading, mathematics, science and social studies.* New York: McGraw-Hill.

Teale, W. (1984). Reading to young children: Its significance for literacy development. In H. Goelman, O. Berg, & F. Smith (Eds.), *Awaking to literacy.* London: Heineman.

Weber, R. M. (1970). A linguistic analysis of first-grade reading errors. *Reading Research Quarterly, 5,* 427–451.

Wiederholt, J. L. (1985). *Formal Reading Inventory.* Austin, TX: PRO-ED.

Wiederholt, J. L., & Bryant, B. R. (1986). *Gray Oral Reading Tests–Revised.* Austin, TX: PRO-ED.

Wiederholt, J. L., Hammill, D. D., & Brown, V. L. (1983). *The resource teacher.* Austin, TX: PRO-ED.

Will, M. C. (1986). Educating children with learning problems: A shared responsibility. *Exceptional Children, 52,* 411–415.

Ysseldyke, J. E., & Algozzine, B. (1983). Where to begin in diagnosing reading problems. *Topics in Learning and Learning Disabilities, 2*(4), 60–69.

Ysseldyke, J. E., & Marston, D. (1982). Gathering decision making information through the use of non-test–based methods. *Measurement and Evaluation in Guidance, 15,* 58–69.

9 / DIAGNOSTIC CLASSIFICATIONS OF READING PROBLEMS

In the previous chapters, we described the nature of reading and identified techniques and instruments that are used to measure the reading abilities of students. A discussion of reading assessment would be incomplete, however, without some mention of the classification of students with reading problems into various diagnostic categories. Two major categories are used to describe those who experience reading difficulties. Dyslexic readers are those whose disability is the result of damage to the central nervous system. Corrective readers are those whose reading problem is not organically based. In addition to dyslexic and corrective readers, some individuals' reading abilities are affected by a particular handicapping condition (e.g., mental retardation, learning disabilities, visual impairments). While handicapped readers may exhibit characteristics of dyslexic or corrective readers, their uniqueness lies in the existence of their handicapping conditions. This chapter provides descriptions of the three major types of disabled readers: dyslexic readers, corrective readers, and handicapped readers. Prior to these descriptions, a brief overview of the historical aspects of reading disabilities is presented to show how these diagnostic categories were developed.

HISTORICAL OVERVIEW

One would suspect that for as long as man has used written symbols to communicate, there have been individuals who have been unable to associate meaning with the symbolic system. Benton (1964) and Albert (1979) report that the loss of reading ability due to brain damage had been documented as early as A.D. 30, when Valerius Maximus described a man's loss of memory for letters after he was hit on the head with an axe. In the sixteenth century, St. Teresa of Jesus recorded that, at times, words and letters were incomprehensible to her (Critchley, 1970). Albert (1979) notes that at about the same time, Murcuriable in 1588 discovered, "a truly astonishing thing; this man [following a seizure] would write but could not read what he had written" (p. 60). In the seventeenth century, Johon Schmidt, a physician, described instances of reading loss, and in the mid 1800s, Professor Lordat of Montpelier described a reading loss following his recovery from a speech disorder. In 1853, Wilde noted that children without known brain damage were exhibiting language behaviors similar to those encountered in brain damaged adults.

Thomson (1984) reports that, in the mid 1800s, autopsies were performed on patients who had acquired reading disorders following head injury. One of the most noteworthy developments of this period occurred in 1871, when Dejeune wrote of his post-mortem operations, "There always existed a lesion far back in the posterior temporal region in the left hemisphere where the parietal and occipital lobes come into contiguity" (Thomson, 1984, p. 4). Dejeune's autopsy research was paralleled at that time by Broadbent, whose efforts are described by Critchley (1970).

> [He] described the case of a man who had been knocked down in the street and had been taken to the Casualty department of St. Mary's hospital, London. The injured man could not express himself very well and pointing to some printed words on the wall, said "I can see them, but cannot understand." He had had a slight stroke a year before, since when, although able to write, he could not make sense of printed or written words with the exception of his own surname. Though able to converse pretty well he could never recall the names of objects put before him. Shortly afterwards he died from another vascular accident. Autopsy revealed two lesions, the older one, regarded by Broadbent as being responsible for the unusual type of aphasia, being in the region of the left angular and supramarginal gyri. (pp. 1–2)

As a result of Dejeune's and Broadbent's autopsies, researchers concluded that a loss in reading ability could be attributed to physiological causes (e.g., a loss of reading comprehension being a result of a left unilateral lesion). These hypotheses would lay the foundation for subsequent research and discussion.

In 1877, Kussmaul used the term *word blindness* to describe speech disorders resultant of brain damage to the left hemisphere of the brain, the area of the brain that is responsible for language. This term dominates the early literature in the field of reading disabilities. In 1872, Berlin first used the term *dyslexia* as an alternative term describing reading disorders (Thomson, 1984).

An important development occurred in 1895, when Hinshelwood published the first of several studies describing the loss of reading ability of brain damaged individuals. Critchley (1970) reports that the paper was read by Pringle Morgan, who wrote Hinshelwood a letter stating, "It was your paper—may I call it your classical paper?—on word blindness and visual memory published in the *Lancet* on 21st December, 1895, which first drew my attention to this subject, and my reason for publishing this case was that there was no reference anywhere, so far as I knew, to the possibility of this condition being congenital" (p. 6).

The case Morgan refers to was that of a 14-year-old boy who attended school in the town where Morgan practiced medicine. Excerpts from Morgan's (1896) report are presented here as evidence of the anecdotal nature of early writings.

> He has always been a bright and intelligent boy, quick at games, and in no way inferior to others of his age.
>
> His great difficulty has been—and is now—his inability to learn to read. This inability is so remarkable, and so pronounced, that I have no doubt it is due to some congenital defect.
>
> He has been at school or under tutors since he was 7 years old, and the greatest efforts have been made to teach him to read, but, in spite of this laborious and persistent training, he can only with difficulty spell out words of one syllable. The following is the result of an examination I made a short time since. He knows all his letters, and can write them and read them. In writing from dictation he comes to grief over any but the simplest words. . . . In writing his own name he made a mistake, putting "Precy" for "Percy," and he did not notice the mistake until his attention was called to it more than once. . . .
>
> I then asked him to read me a sentence out of an easy child's book without spelling the words. The result was curious. He did not read a single word correctly, with the exception of "and," "the," "of," "that," etc., the other words seemed to be quite unknown to him, and he could not even make an attempt to pronounce them. Words written or printed seem to convey no impression to his mind, and it is only after laboriously spelling them that he is able, by the sounds of the letters, to discover their import. . . .
>
> He seems to have no power of preserving and storing up the visual impression produced by words—hence the words, though seen, have no significance for him. His visual memory for words is defective or absent; which is equivalent to saying that he is what Kussmaul (1877) has termed "word blind." . . .
>
> I may add that the boy is bright and of average intelligence in conversation. His eyes are normal, there is no hemianopsia, and his eyesight is good. The school master who has taught him for some years says that he would be the smartest lad in the school if the instruction were entirely oral.[1]

---

[1]From "A Case of Congenital Word-Blindness" by W. P. Morgan, 1896, in *British Medical Journal*, 2, 1378. Reprinted by permission.

Morgan's work, and that of James Kerr in 1895, typified the descriptive work that was done in the 1800s. Most of the research of the early 1900s focused on the notion that the disorder was the result of either damage to, or a delay in, the left hemisphere of the brain—more precisely, in the supramarginal hemisphere believed to be crucial to visual-memory images of words (Hynd & Cohen, 1983). Several reports of this nature were written at the time, including those of Brunner (1905), Variot and Lecomte (1906), and Stephenson (1907). In 1917, Hinshelwood wrote a monograph titled "Congenital-Word Blindness." Here, *congenital word blindness* was described as "occurring in children with otherwise normal undamaged brains, characterized by a disability in learning to read so great that it is manifestly due to a pathological condition and where the attempt to teach the child by ordinary methods has completely failed" (p. 40).

In his classic text, *Reading, Writing, and Speech Problems in Children*, Orton (1937) hypothesized that factors such as eyedness, handedness, and footedness affected reading performance. In his discussion of the effects of brain injury to language loss, Orton discounted the then prevalent theory of faulty development of particular areas of the brain. Instead, he made the following proposition.

The existence of demonstrable mixtures between right and left motor preferences with a strong familial background implies that comparable intergrading may exist between the critical areas for the various functions of the language faculty in the two hemispheres of the brain, thus giving rise to a series of developmental disorders in language. (p. 67)

To describe this condition, Orton (1937) adopted the term *strephosymbolia*, which means

a delay or difficulty in learning to read which is out of harmony with a child's intellectual ability. At the outset it is characterized by confusion between similarly formed but oppositely oriented letters, and a tendency to a changing order of direction in reading. (p. 214)

Up to this point in history, most of the research in the field of reading disabilities had been conducted by physicians. The physicians were joined in the mid 1900s by psychologists in their effort to determine the cause of reading disabilities. The interest shifted from localizing brain functioning to clinically organizing the behaviors of reading disability cases into symptom complexes or syndromes that were hypothesized to be due to brain injury, heredity deficiencies, late maturational patterns, or to metabolic diseases. A description is provided below concerning the syndromes that have been offered to account for disorders in reading. Specifically, these disorders relate to dyslexic readers, corrective readers, and handicapped readers.

DYSLEXIC READERS

Some individuals experience reading impairment as a result of frank or hypothesized damage to the central nervous system. These individuals are called dyslexic readers, and they are generally divided into two major categories. Acquired dyslexia occurs when brain damage results in a loss of previously learned reading skills. Developmental dyslexia is a condition exhibited by behaviors similar to those seen in acquired dyslexics, yet no known brain damage has occurred or the damage has occurred prior to the attainment of reading skills. Each condition is described here.

Acquired Dyslexia

Simply put, acquired dyslexia refers to the loss of previously learned reading skills as a result of damage to the central nervous system. Most often, this condition occurs as a result of brain injury following an accident or stroke. Brain injury to a young child who had not yet developed reading skills would not result in acquired dyslexia; nor would disorders occurring in the pre-, peri-, or postnatal periods, since the child obviously would not have developed any reading skills. In describing this form of dyslexia, Young and Tyre (1983) note:

> In all cases of acquired dyslexia, the specialists can point to hard signs or to soft signs to support the view that the difficulties are in some ways caused by brain damage. *Hard* signs are, for instance, the physical injury or wound to the brain itself, the evidence revealed by an operation or autopsy or other evidence which may show that there have been cerebral lesions or haemorrhage as in a stroke. *Soft* signs are provided by unusual EEG (electroencephalogram) patterns, abnormal reflexes or difficulties. (p. 8)

Rabinovitch (1968) describes acquired dyslexia as "reading retardation secondary to brain injury." He describes the disorder as follows.

> Capacity to learn to read is impaired by frank brain damage manifested by clear-cut neurological deficits. The picture is similar to . . . adult dyslexic syndromes. Other definite aphasic difficulties are generally present. History usually reveals

the cause of the brain injury, common agents being prenatal toxicity, birth trauma or anoxia, encephalitis, and head injury. (p. 5)

Several attempts have been made to categorize the reading disabilities that occur within the general category of acquired dyslexia, sometimes referred to as *alexia*. Doehring, Trites, Patel, and Fiedorowicz (1981) provide a description of six such types of central nervous system related problems associated with dyslexia.

Alexia without agraphia (i.e., reading disability without writing disability) is a relatively rare disorder that results in the impairment of word reading and color naming.

Alexia with agraphia (i.e., reading disability with an accompanying writing disorder) involves "a reading-writing-spelling problem that extends to letters as well as to words and is accompanied by mild language impairment of the type classified as Wernicke's or fluent aphasia, as well as certain nonlanguage disorders" (p. 10).

Wernicke's aphasia with alexia and agraphia (i.e., reading and writing disability resulting from damage to Wernicke's area of the brain) is similar to alexia with agraphia but involves a predominant language deficiency characterized by severe difficulty with comprehending and repeating spoken language and naming.

Broca's aphasia with alexia and agraphia (i.e., reading and writing disability resulting from damage to Broca's area of the brain) results in letter reading deficits that are more severe than word reading deficits. This problem with letters results in poor writing and spelling.

Transcortical aphasia is a rare disorder affecting listening comprehension and speech but not affecting spoken language repetition. With this disorder, reading and writing are extremely impaired.

Visual agnosia (i.e., the inability to recognize visual stimuli) is characterized by lesions in the right hemisphere of the brain. These lesions affect visual perception and visual-motor construction that may deter the recognition of letter shapes.

Varney and Damasio (1982) choose to categorize the types of alexias within the subtypes verbal alexia and literal alexia. They state:

> In verbal alexia, understanding of the written word is impaired whereas letter "recognition reading" is intact: There is "word blindness" without "letter blindness." In literal alexia, both letter reading and word reading are defective: There is both letter blindness and word blindness. (p. 305)

Ellis (1984) provides a summary of the research in alexia (Table 9.1). This review is offered as a succinct overview of the subtypes associated within this disorder.

TABLE 9.1. Varieties of Acquired Dyslexia

1. Attentional dyslexia (alias literal dyslexia).
   Patient makes frequent visual segmentation errors when shown groups of words. Difficulty naming letters in strings but not letters in isolation.

   Main reference: Shallice and Warrington (1977).

2. Letter-by-letter reading (alias word-form dyslexia).
   Patient appears to name each letter of a word either aloud or subvocally before identifying the word, therefore reading time increases with the number of letters in the word. According to Warrington and Shallice (1980) reading is mediated via the patient's intact *spelling* system.

   Main references: Warrington and Shallice (1980); Patterson and Kay (1983).

3. Visual dyslexia.
   Patient makes frequent visually based errors in word recognition despite sometimes being able to name all the component letters of the target word. Deficit possibly due to "slippage" within the visual word recognition system.

   Main references: Marshall and Newcombe (1973); Newcombe and Marshall (1982).

4. Phonological dyslexia.
   Patient is able to read many familiar words aloud with understanding, though may have some problems with function words and inflected words. No effects of regularity, imageability, or length. Virtually unable to read unfamiliar words or nonwords aloud suggesting impairment of grapheme-phoneme conversion and/or phonemic assembly.

   Main references: Beauvois and Derousne (1979); Shallice and Warrington (1980); Patterson (1982).

5. Non-semantic reading (alias direct dyslexia).
   Occurs in some patients having "presenile dementia." Intact word naming (and apparently nonword naming) despite a lack of any indication that the patient understands the words being read. Arguably reading aloud is sustained by intact connections between visual word recognition units and phonemic word productions units despite disintegration of the semantic system.

   Main references: Schwartz, Marin, and Saffran (1979); Schwartz, Saffran, and Marin (1980); Shallice, Warrington, and McCarthy (1983).

6. Surface dyslexia (alias semantic dyslexia).
   Patient appears to read by phonic mediation. Some whole-word reading retained, but patient may misinterpret homophones showing that final access to the semantic system is via the auditory word recognition system. For many words the patient attempts to assemble a pronunciation with a consequent liability to "phonic" errors; other errors appear to be visual approximation similar to the errors of visual dyslexics. Regular words are read more successfully than irregular words. Principal deficits appear to be disconnectiton of visual word recognition system from the semantic system together with unavailability either of some visual word recognition units or some connections between those units and the corresponding phonemic word production units.

   Main references: Marshall and Newcombe (1973); Marcel (1980); Shallice and Warrington (1980); Henderson (1982).

7. Deep dyslexia (alias phonemic dyslexia).
   A complex syndrome whose central, defining symptom is the occurrence of semantic errors in single-word reading. Other symptoms include visual, visual-then-semantic and derivational errors, difficulty reading abstract words and function words, and an almost total inability to read nonwords. Several components of the reading system have been lost (e.g., Morton and Patterson, 1980), and Coltheart has argued that the remaining reading capacities are largely those of the right hemisphere.

   Main references: Marshall and Newcombe (1973); Coltheart, Patterson, and Marshall (1980).

From *Reading, Writing, and Dyslexia: A Cognitive Analysis* (pp. 134–135) by A. W. Ellis, 1984, London: Lawrence Erlbaum. Reprinted by permission.

Developmental Dyslexia

In the previous section, we described acquired dyslexia as a reading loss that occurs as a result of frank damage to the central nervous system. It has been well documented that behaviors associated with this condition have been seen in children with no history of brain injury (see the historical review at the beginning of this chapter). Readers who exhibit characteristics of acquired dyslexics but whose disability occurs not as a direct result of brain injury, or whose brain damage occurred before reading skills were acquired, are usually called developmental dyslexics.

Numerous definitions have been given for developmental dyslexia, including one by the Research Group on Developmental Dyslexia of the World Federation of Neurology. This definition is provided by Critchley (1970) as follows.

> A disorder manifested by difficulty in learning to read despite conventional instruction, adequate intelligence, and socio-cultural opportunity. It is dependent upon fundamental cognitive disabilities which are frequently of constitutional origin. (p. 11)

This definition has come under attack by several authors who question the value of such an ambiguous description. Rutter (1978), for example, points out that the definition "suggests that if all the known causes of reading disability can be ruled out, the unknown (in the form of dyslexia) should be involved. A council of despair, indeed" (p. 12). Similarly, Eisenberg (1978) questions "how a distinguished group of neurologists come to agree on a non-definition of a non-entity" (p. 31).

Such criticisms aside, the definition was an attempt to assure that dyslexia would not be confused with reading problems that are not associated directly to such conditions as mental retardation or cultural deprivation. Thomson (1984) describes a definition proposed by Wheeler and Watkins (1979) that adds inclusionary criteria to accompany the exclusionary criteria provided in the previous definition.

> Dyslexia is experienced by children of adequate intelligence, as a general language deficit which is a specific manifestation of a wider limitation in processing all forms of informtaion in short-term memory, be they visually, or auditorily presented. This wider limitation exhibits itself in tasks requiring the heaviest use and access to short term memory, such as reading, but particularly spelling. This limitation can have a multiplicity of causes (e.g., genetic, or birth trauma) and observable effects (e.g., clumsiness, reversals, and bizarre spelling). It may make sense in a number of circumstances to talk about sub-categories of dyslexia, e.g., genetic dyslexia, traumatic dyslexia, visual or auditory dyslexia if it helps in the diagnosis, prognosis and, most importantly, remediation of the symptoms of this general limitation. The choice of these subcategories does not detract

from the use of the term dyslexia to describe this general language deficit, as dyslexia is a generic concept. (p. 15)

Rabinovitch (1968) describes developmental dyslexia as "primary reading retardations." He defines this disorder as follows.

Capacity to learn to read is impaired without definite brain damage suggested in the history or on neurologic examination. The defect is in the ability to deal with letters and words as symbols, with resultant diminished ability to reflect a basic disturbed pattern of neurologic organization. . . . This etiology is biologic or endogenous. (p. 5)

There have been several attempts to describe subtypes of developmental dyslexia. Among these are efforts by Johnson and Myklebust (1967) (visual and auditory dyslexia) and Boder (1970) (dysphonic, dyseidetic, and dysphonic and dyseidetic forms of dyslexia). A description of the classification systems offered by these authors is presented to provide the reader with examples of the work that has been accomplished to classify subtypes of dyslexia.

Johnson and Myklebust System. Johnson and Myklebust (1967) identify two primary subtypes of dyslexia: visual dyslexia and auditory dyslexia. According to those researchers, visual dyslexia occurs as a result of central nervous system dysfunction and affects "children who can see but who cannot differentiate, interpret, or remember words" (p. 152). The severity of the disability varies, with some children failing to learn to read at all, while others simply experience trouble developing a sight vocabulary or learning the rules of syllabication.

Several features are identified by these professionals that are believed to accompany visual dyslexia. These include (a) visual discrimination difficulties that may result in the confusion of similar letters and words (e.g., *beg* for *bog*, *snip* for *ship*); (b) slow rate of perception (i.e., slow scrutiny of words even though discrimination is accurate); (c) reversal tendencies (e.g., *dig* for *big*); (d) inversion tendencies (e.g., spelling *pan* as *pna*, *apn* for *nap*); (e) visual memory deficits (i.e., a difficulty to revisualize characteristics of form); (f) inferior drawings that omit relevant details from even simple objects common to the child; (g) visual analysis and synthesis difficulties, demonstrating part-whole inadequacies; (h) relative strengths in auditory skills (i.e., visual performance below auditory performance in readiness and reading diagnostic tests); (i) auditory activity preferences that sometimes hide visual deficiencies; and (j) troublesome types of games or sports that children cannot grasp visually (e.g., model building).

When children have difficulty performing intrasensory auditory functions (e.g., distinguishing similarities and differences in sounds, perceiving a sound within a word, synthesizing sounds into words, and dividing words into syllables), they will have difficulty learning to read (Johnson & Myklebust, 1967). Unlike the child with visual disabilities, the auditory dyslexic "sees the similarities in word parts but does not relate them to their auditory counterparts so he does not make the generalizations required in learning to read" (p. 173). The authors provide five characteristics of auditory dyslexics.

1. They have numerous auditory discrimination and perceptual disorders which impede use of phonetic analysis. One of the most common is the inability to "hear" the similarities in initial or final sounds of words. . . . Discrimination of short vowel sounds is one of the greatest problems of the auditory dyslexic. Although he understands words such as *pin*, *pan*, and *pen* in context, he is unable to perceive differences among them when they are heard in isolation. . . . Because of one or more of these auditory disturbances, rarely is the dyslexic able to make generalizations about new words that he encounters.

2. These dyslexics have difficulty with auditory analysis and synthesis. Although their spoken language generally is good, those with a disturbance of analysis cannot break a word into syllables or into individual sounds. . . . It interferes with the development of syllabication skills for reading and because of an inability to break a word into its various components, entire syllables may be omitted when writing. Those with problems of synthesis cannot combine parts of words to form a whole. . . . We have observed children with this disability who know all of their letter sounds but, because of an inability to blend, were unable to learn to read by a phonic or elemental approach.

3. Many in this group cannot reauditorize sounds or words. When they look at a letter they cannot remember its sound, or when they look at a word they are unable to say it even though they know its meaning. The auditory dyslexic, therefore, may be able to read silently better than orally. . . . Because of these various types of disturbances, it is critical that more than one measure of reading be used. . . .

4. Some have a disturbance in auditory sequentialization. If auditory verbal symbolic functions are affected, they may distort the pronunciation of multisyllable words (*emeny* for *enemy*), or when writing, they may transpose letters because they cannot retain a sequence of sounds.

5. Behaviorally, auditory dyslexics tend to prefer visual activities. . . . They are inferior on tasks which involve auditory memory, sequence, and discrimination.[2]

Such descriptions provide guidelines within which Johnson and Myklebust (1967) determine whether disabled readers are visual or auditory dyslexics. Boder (1970) provides an alternative classification system.

---

[2]From *Learning Disabilities* (pp. 174–175) by D. J. Johnson and H. R. Myklebust, 1967, New York: Grune & Stratton. Reprinted by permission.

Boder System. In 1970, Boder reported the results of a study that examined the reading-spelling patterns of children with developmental dyslexia. The patterns were found to cluster in three groups, forming the basis for reporting three subtypes of dyslexia. She claims that "one or another of these three reading-spelling patterns have been found in all severely retarded readers who fulfill standard diagnostic criteria for developmental dyslexia. None of these patterns has been found among normal readers and spellers" (p. 219).

The pattern of the first group of children, the *dysphonic group*, reflects "a primary deficit in letter sound integration and in the ability to develop phonetic skills" (p. 289). Fundamental to this condition is the lack of rudimentary phonic skills, resulting in the inability to read words that are not in the child's sight vocabulary. Spelling errors demonstrate a general lack of any awareness of sound-symbol relationships. For example, such nonphonetic spellings as *rsty* for *guess*, *iklie* for *like*, and *aleg* for *laugh* were made by children in the dysphonic group. Boder claims that most nonreaders fall into this category.

The second group is called the *dyseidetic group* and includes children who demonstrate an inability to perceive words in their totality or, as Boder (1970) describes, an inability to perceive words as gestalts. Reading-spelling patterns observed in this group represent the opposite patterns found in children in the dysphonic group; that is, the dyseidetic group demonstrates an overapplication of phonetic principles. Boder reports that these children read phonetically, sounding out almost all of the words they encounter, whether familiar or unfamiliar. Spelling errors (e.g., *posishin* for *position*, *biznis* for *business*, and *dowt* for *doubt*) are consistent with this pattern.

The third pattern resulted in the identification of children as being in the *dysphonic and dyseidetic group*. That is, the children exhibit deficiencies common to both the first and second groups. Boder (1970) declares that, without remediation, children in this group are likely to remain nonreaders. Examples of this group's spelling errors include *u* for *work*, *mo* for *mother*, and *ntk* for *next*.

Importance of Classification. The instructional relevance of identifying subtypes of dyslexia has been the subject of debate for years. At the very least, the efforts of Johnson and Myklebust (1967), Boder (1970), and others provide professionals with information to consider when examining the behaviors of students with reading problems.

In the mid 1900s, professionals drawing from some of the work of neurologists and psychoneurologists became primarily interested in organizing reading disability cases into functional reading disorder subtypes. Causation, while not discounted, became secondary in importance to placing students with certain types of behaviors into diagnostic categories. These diagnostic categories were usually tied to funding sources. Once a student was found to be eligible for a specific category, he or she was placed in a special program and provided remediation or treatment. Major categories were found in both regular and special education. In the next section, the principle category of slow readers in regular education programming (i.e., corrective readers) is discussed. Following this, a description of special education categories is presented.

CORRECTIVE READERS

The majority of students with reading problems in today's schools would be classified as corrective readers. Students in this category are reading below what might be expected based on their aptitude, but their deficiency is not due to any damage to the central nervous system. There may be any number of reasons for the reading failure, including poor teaching, failure of the system to account for cultural diversity, bilingualism, and the like. Regardless, the corrective reader is one who is reading below an appropriate level and whose disability is not caused by brain damage.

Kress (1971) provides the following description of a corrective reader.

> For this child, the principal deterring factor, which inhibits progress in reading, is the inability of his classroom teacher to place instruction on a level which is within the child's present range of word-recognition and comprehension skills. . . . The child's problem may involve inadequacies in experience background, concept development, word recognition, and/or word comprehension, but there is no basic neurological or psychological learning difficulty present. No special learning techniques need to be employed to effect satisfactory progress, except for adjustment of instructional practices to the level where the child's present skills for dealing with languages can be applied and the new skills developed. (p. 146)

Rabinovitch (1968) describes a type of reading disability that occurs not as a result of frank or suspected neurological impairment. He describes "reading retardations secondary to exogenous factors" as follows.

> Capacity to learn to read is intact but is utilized insufficiently for the child to achieve a reading level appropriate for his mental age. The causative factor is exogenous, the child having a normal reading potential that has been impaired by negativism, anxiety, depression, emotional blocking, psychosis, limited schooling opportunity, or other external influence. (p. 6)

Goldberg and Schiffman (1972) note that corrective readers can usually be brought to grade level with the proper remedial methods. Dechant (1971) separates corrective readers into two groups, those with general retardation and those with specific retardation (Table 9.2). As is evident upon exam-

---

TABLE 9.2. Characteristics of the Corrective Reader

Case of General Retardation	Case of Specific Retardation
The reading level is substantially lower than the mental age, but no other specific problem exists. He is a case of partial disability. ↓	There is a definite weakness in a given area. This is usually a skill weakness. ↓
He is a pupil who learns only after undue and laborious effort; he is like the underweight child whose eating habits are not conducive to gaining weight but who, if he follows the proper diet, will gain. He learns after inhibiting factors have been removed. ↓	This is a case of reading retardation not complicated by neurological difficulties. ↓
The pupil may not have been ready for initial reading experiences, and thus fell farther and farther behind as his schooling continued. ↓	Learning capacity is adequate, but deficiencies in regard to certain specifics in word analysis or comprehension indicate that he has not profited from regular class work as well as he might. He has missed or has not profited from basic instruction in a given area. ↓
Instruction and reading materials generally have been above the pupil's level of ability and above his level of achievement in word-recognition and comprehension skills. ↓	Although each pupil presents a distinct pattern of acquisition and remediation, there will usually be others in the class with similar problems. ↓
He perhaps was absent from school at critical periods. ↓	His overall reading performance may be high in relation to his ability, but diagnostic testing will reveal a low subscore on a test. ↓
He perhaps was not stimulated to learn because instruction was below his ability level. ↓	There is usually a need for training in the area of weakness rather than a need for total remediation in the basic skills. ↓
The reading profile of the generally retarded pupil is relatively uniform. ↓	The pupil should be kept in the regular classroom in which reading is taught to subgroups of three to five.
He needs more experience in reading, including systematic instruction at his level of ability. Usually a visual-auditory technique or method is adequate. He does not need a VAKT method of teaching such as the Fernald or Gillingham method. There is a need for major adjustment in materials and instruction and for a reading program that motivates the pupil to learn. ↓	
On the secondary level, the pupil may be referred to the remedial teacher. ↓	
The pupil should be kept in the regular classroom.	

---

ining the characteristics, most if not all of the problems may be taken care of in a remedial program, probably in the confines of the regular classroom.

Categories Unrelated to Cause

Attempts have been made to describe the reading behaviors of students without regard to causation. In 1957, Bond and Tinker grouped disabled readers into four types: simple retardation cases, specific retardation cases, limiting disability cases, and complex disability cases. Bond, Tinker, Wasson, and Wasson (1984) modified these terms somewhat, preferring to call them general reading immaturity, specific reading immaturity, limiting reading disability, and complex reading disability. These categories relate not only to the severity of the problem but to the nature of the programming adjustments needed to educate them.

A child exhibiting *general reading immaturity* is one "who is significantly behind in reading when compared with other children of his general reading expectancy, but who has no unusual or limiting characteristic about his reading pattern" (p. 45). Children of this type usually do not require a re-education in reading, simply an adjustment in materials or instruction. *Specific reading immaturity* denotes a specific limitation in reading. While fundamentally able readers, these students have failed to adapt general basic reading skills and abilities to all of their reading purposes. Students who exhibit *limiting reading disabilities* are those "who have serious deficiencies in their basic skills and abilities which limit their entire reading growth" (p. 46). Re-education is required to unlearn some of what they have learned and to learn new approaches and strategies. *Complex reading disability*, a subtype of limiting reading disability, occurs with students whose reading deficiencies are "complicated by unfortunate attitudes toward reading and by undesirable adjustments to their failure to progress in reading" (p. 47). By identifying students as fitting into one of the diagnostic categories, it is hypothesized that remedial strategies can be formulated to meet their instructional needs.

In the classic text, *Remedial Techniques in Basic School Subjects*, Fernald (1943) divides cases of reading disability into two groups: those with total or extreme disability and those with partial disability. Children are classified according to the degree of the disability; that is, virtual nonreaders are placed in the total or extreme disability group, while those with "the same general characteristics as the cases of extreme disability but in less marked form" (p. 57) are assigned to the partial reading disability group.

Simply put, those with a total or extreme disability would fit Kussmaul's (1877) description of "word blindness." Thus, nonreaders of this type would probably be classified as developmental dyslexics. Those with partial disability would more likely be termed corrective readers.

Partial Disability

Fernald (1943) identifies three types of difficulties that are associated with partial disabiilty. The first is called "poor reading due to inability to recognize certain words" (p. 57) and occurs when readers fail to recognize common words, thus markedly reducing their ability to comprehend. As Fernald states, "the tendency of unfamiliar words to attract the attention blocks the individual as he is reading and throws him into a panic if he has to cover a certain amount of material in a limited time or if he is reading aloud" (p. 58).

According to Fernald (1943), the second type of difficulty occurs with "slow reading and poor comprehension due to [the] fact that [the] individual reads word by word" (p. 58). The meanings of most words are pondered before the next word is read, and while the various words that are encountered may be known, or perhaps even word groups are recognized, the student "has to go over the content several times to get the meaning of the thing as a whole" (p. 58).

The final type of partial disability is referred to by Fernald (1943) as "poor reading due to failure to comprehend [the] content read" (p. 58). This occurs with individuals who appear to have little difficulty reading with adequate rate and word recognition but who are unable to answer even basic literal questions about what has been read. The breakdown occurs when the reader has to use what was read.

Fernald's (1943) Visual-Auditory-Kinesthetic-Tactile (VAKT) approach to remediating reading disabilities is still used with effectiveness today. Where the student enters the remedial program is based upon whether he or she has a total disability or only a partial disability. Either way, the program remains the same. Thus, it is the degree of the disability more than the cause that forms the basis for remedial strategies. This being the case, one could argue that knowing the cause of a reading disability makes little practical difference, an argument that is often heard among professionals involved in reading assessment and instruction.

If for no other reason, knowing the cause of the reading problem is of value to the diagnostician or other professional when recommending placement in either a remedial or a special education program. If the student is a corrective reader, programs within regular education will be used to remediate the reading deficit. If the cause of the disability relates to a specific handicapping condition, then the student qualifies for special education services. Having already described corrective readers, the remainder of this chapter will address handicapped readers. That is, a discussion will focus on those reading problems encountered among the learning disabled, mentally retarded, and so on.

HANDICAPPED READERS

Within any school population there is a group of individuals who are handicapped. These special students have learning characteristics that often differ markedly from the norm. While it is recognized that each handicapping condition consists of a heterogeneous group of students, particular problems associated with reading have been identified for each group. These problems are presented in the remainder of this chapter, specifically as they relate to students with hearing impairments, learning disabilities, mental retardation, and visual impairments.

Hearing Impairment

In defining hearing impairment, Green (1985) provides the description selected by the Ad Hoc Committee to Define Deaf and Hard of Hearing. In 1975, this group provided the following definition.

> Hearing Impairment—A generic term indicating a hearing disability that may range in severity from mild to profound. It consists of two groups, the deaf and the hard of hearing:
>
> A deaf person is one whose hearing disability precludes successful processing of linguistic information through audition, with or without a hearing aid.
>
> A hard-of-hearing person is one who, generally with the use of a hearing aid, has residual hearing sufficient to enable successful processing of linguistic information through audition. (pp. 192–193)

As with most exceptional learners, hearing impaired students present difficulties in school achievement. Many of the difficulties involve language deficiencies. As Blake (1981) notes, the language deficits associated with hearing impairment inhibit attainment of functional literacy. This idea is echoed by Quigly and Kretschmer (1982), particularly with regard to deaf children. They state that "the average deaf child does not have a basic knowledge of the language he or she is learning to read. . . . Thus, the task of learning to read often becomes a language-learning process at the same time" (p. 66).

As early as 1917, Pinter and Patterson reported that deaf children aged 14 to 16 years had median reading scores equal to those of 7-year-old hearing children (Quigley & Kretschmer, 1982). Myklebust (1964) reports that the reading vocabulary of deaf high school seniors was that of 9-year-old normals. Wrightstone, Aranow, and Moskowitz (1963) examined the reading abilities of hearing impaired students and reported that, for the group ages 10.5 through 16.5, average reading was at the third grade level. Quigley, Wilbur, Power, Montanelli, and Steinkamp (1976) found that the average

18-year-old deaf student could not use or understand the basic syntactic structures of a 10 year old. Moores (1967) reports significant deficits in vocabulary and syntax for deaf students when their performance was compared to that of hearing students who were matched on reading achievement levels. Quigley and Kretschmer (1982) summarize the research by pointing out that "studies of various aspects of the reading task—word analysis, vocabulary, syntax, and inferencing ability, indicate that all of these present difficulties for the deaf child learning to read" (pp. 76–77).

The prognosis for reading success depends heavily upon the age at onset of the hearing loss. Lenneberg (1967) notes that exposure to language even for a short period of time is usually "sufficient to give a child some foundation on which later language may be based" (p. 239). Blake (1981) concurs, stating that a child who is born deaf is likely to grow up without acquiring adequate speech and language skills. However, those who have a mild to moderate hearing loss can usually learn to speak and use language effectively with proper intervention. Certainly, the prognosis for learning to read is much more favorable for these individuals than for those with complete hearing loss. This belief is reinforced by Williams and Vernon (1970), who examined the reading levels of 93% of the deaf students in the U.S. who were over 16 years old. They noted that 60% of these students were reading below grade level, while 30% were functionally illiterate.

Furth (1973) summarizes the problem of educating hearing impaired students.

> Here in a nutshell is the problem of education of deaf children. The one educational objective to which all energies are tuned is language. The colossal reading failure reflects a deficiency in the knowledge of language and not, as would be the case with hearing children, a reading disability. . . . A person who has been profoundly deaf from birth and who can read at grade 5 or better is invariably an exception. (pp. 92–93)

Furth's (1973) comments are relevant not only for the education of deaf students but for the assessment of their reading abilities as well. Any evaluation of a deaf student's reading skills must include an appraisal of the student's overall language abilities. Thus, comprehension performance and miscues noted in oral reading can be examined within the context of the student's global language competence.

Learning Disabilities

It is important to recognize the limited reading skills of learning disabled readers, especially considering the findings of Kirk and Elkins (1975), who note that reading was the primary disability in over two-thirds of the 3,000 learning disabled students receiving services in the 24 federally funded Child Service Demonstration Centers. Before describing the characteristics of learning disabled readers, it is first important to identify the population that we are discussing.

Of the numerous definitions provided for learning disabilities, the most appropriate is the one recommended by the National Joint Committee for Learning Disabilities. This group is composed of representatives from the American Speech-Language-Hearing Association (ASHA), The Council for Learning Disabilities (CLD), The Association for Children and Adults with Learning Disabilities (ACLD), the Division for Children with Communication Disorders (DCCD), the International Reading Association (IRA), the Orton Dyslexia Society, and the Division for Learning Disabilities (DLD). The definition states,

> Learning disabilities is a generic term that refers to a heterogeneous group of disorders manifested by significant difficulties in the acquisition and use of listening, speaking, reading, writing, reasoning or mathematical abilities. These disorders are intrinsic to the individual and presumed to be due to central nervous system dysfunction. Even though a learning disability may occur concomitantly with other handicapping conditions (e.g., sensory impairment, mental retardation, social and emotional disturbance) or environmental influences (e.g., cultural differences, insufficient-inappropriate instruction, psychogenic factors), it is not the direct result of those conditions or influences. (Hammill, Leigh, McNutt, & Larsen, 1981, p. 336)

To a large extent, this definition is similar to the definition of dyslexia described by Critchley (1970). The reason for this is quite obvious. For all practical purposes, dyslexic individuals are learning disabled. Both definitions presume that the deficit is the result of central nervous system dysfunction, and both provide exclusionary criteria. Therefore, all of the characteristics that have been described as pertaining to developmental dyslexic readers can be applied to learning disabled readers. These include reading aloud in a slow, choppy, word-by-word manner, reversing words and/or letters, transposing letters within words, confusing similar words (e.g., *write* and *white*), and repeating words and phrases (Sanders, 1962, cited by Reid & Hresko, 1981). Reid and Hresko (1981) note that oral reading errors often occur concurrently with speech defects, including "articulation defects, stammering and stuttering, and concept reversals, such as confusion of *over* and *under* and *yesterday* and *tomorrow*" (p. 233).

It was noted earlier that identifying the cause of a reading problem can be important in identifying students as handicapped. This is particularly true in the case of learning disabilities. If the student is identified as a dyslexic student, then he or she is eligible for special education services as a learning disabled individual.

Mental Retardation

Grossman (1977) provides the definition of mental retardation that is presented by the American Association on Mental Deficiency (AAMD).

> Mental retardation refers to significantly subaverage general intellectual functioning existing concurrently with deficits in adaptive behavior, and manifested during the developmental period. (p. 11)

As noted in Chapter 7, general intelligence is viewed by some as a factor that may impact the development of reading abilities. Certainly, those severely impaired in mental maturity are likely to suffer severe delays in their development of reading skills. Gillespie and Johnson (1974) describe studies that examine the characteristics of retarded readers. In 1954, Dunn reported that retarded boys were deficient in vowel understandings, context clues, sound omission, and both silent and oral reading when their performance was compared to that of normals at a similar mental age. Gates (1930) noted that in order to learn words appearing in basal readers, retardates needed more repetitions than their normal counterparts. Bliesmer (1954) studied the comprehension skills of retarded readers and noted deficiencies in locating or recognizing factual details, recognizing main ideas, drawing inferences and conclusions, listening comprehension, and total comprehension. Shotik (1960) found deficiencies for retardates in the use of context clues and figurative language, and Cawley, Goodstein, and Burrows (1972) note that retarded readers are inferior in the use of word attack skills.

Many of the difficulties retarded readers have may involve spoken language deficiencies. It is generally acknowledged that while they develop language skills in a similar way as normals, retarded readers do so at a slower rate (Blake, 1981; Ryan, 1975). Delays in sentence length and complexity and speech sound discrimination are noted by Spreen (1965), and Bowerman (1976) hypothesizes that the language delays of retardates may be the result of "delayed development in the prerequisite cognitive structures required for meaningful communication" (Berdine, 1985, p. 372).

As with other handicapping conditions, mentally retarded individuals are a heterogeneous group. Their abilities and disabilities differ markedly from one individual to another. In reading assessment, it is important to consider the individual's strengths and weaknesses in a number of areas that are related to reading, especially language proficiency.

Visual Impairment

Caton (1985) states that definitions describing children in terms of their educational goals are more practical than those describing vision problems in terms of acuity alone. In this vein, she offers:

This kind of [educational] definition, first proposed in 1957. . . , is now widely accepted by educators of visually impaired children. Educationally defined, the blind child is one whose visual loss indicates that he or she should be educated chiefly through the use of braille and other tactile and auditory materials. The partially seeing child is defined as one who has some remaining useful vision and can use print and other visual materials as part of the educational program. (p. 248)

Since this book deals solely with print reading, we will not describe braille reading or that done with instruments such as the Optacon. For readers interested in this information, we suggest the works of Barraga (1983) and Caton (1985).

It has been reported that partially sighted children can learn to read print if certain conditions are met. Such conditions include providing proper lighting, reducing glare, selecting appropriate print size, providing adequate spacing, and using low vision aids. The low vision aids include (a) magnifiers that are attached to the frames of eyeglasses, or perhaps to the lenses themselves, (b) stand magnifiers that are mounted to maintain a specific distance from the printed page, (c) magnifiers that are held by the reader, (d) telescopic aids that are similar to a pair of binoculars, and (e) television viewers that are used to enlarge the print on the page and project the print to a screen (Caton, 1985). Perhaps one of the most common tools used with the partially sighted reader is large print. Figure 9.1 shows an example of different print sizes that are used in books for the visually impaired.

Barraga (1983) reports that for years the notion was that large print materials would make reading easier for partially sighted readers. However, in her review she notes the following:

> Two ophthalmologists, Faye (1970) and Fonda (1966), have said that many children may have been encouraged or even forced to read large-print books and materials when, in fact, they could more easily have read material in regular print size, either with or without magnification. Sykes (1971, 1972) found that high school students, when provided with magnifying devices from which to choose and special lamps and/or lighting arrangements, were just as efficient with regular-sized print materials as they were with large-print materials, in fact, some lower degrees of measured vision were even more efficient with regular-sized type. Reading standard print was found to be no more tiring than reading large print, implying that the concern should not be with the size of the type but with the quality of the print and illumination. (pp. 113–114)

Caton (1985) describes conditions of lighting and print quality that are conducive to reading for partially sighted readers. With regard to lighting, she notes that evenly distributed fluorescent light bulbs in the room are the most conducive. Buff colored paper also helps reduce the glare from lights, and this paper is often used in combination with dark print to provide sharp contrast, an important feature.

FIGURE 9.1. Samples of Three Type Sizes

---

12 Point   When darkness fell, the women began
preparing a great heap of wood for the
circle of ceremonial fires. Then Chanuka
slipped into the river and swam silently

18 Point   When darkness fell, the
preparing a great heap of
circle of ceremonial fires.
slipped into the river and

24 Point   When darkness fe
preparing a great he
circle of ceremonial
slipped into the rive

Blake (1981) notes that visually impaired students have language restrictions that can cause difficulty in academic achievement. Particularly, words and concepts that signify some concrete stimuli and concepts experienced through vision provide difficulties. Such deficiencies may inhibit the reader from getting the information that the writer is trying to convey, and any time this occurs, comprehension suffers.

Given the information presented above, it is obvious that the assessment of visually impaired individuals must focus on physical surroundings, along with the student's ability to deal with spoken and written language. Chapter 7 addresses the student's language competence, and Chapter 8 deals with the analysis of the learning environment. These sections may hold particular relevance for the assessment of the visually impaired student.

SUMMARY

This chapter has presented information about the various diagnostic categories that exist for reading disabilities. It was noted that a student whose reading disability relates to frank or presumed damage to the central nervous system would be classified as a dyslexic reader. A student whose reading disability is not organically based would be called a corrective reader. It was also explained that there exists a third group of students, those that have handicapping conditions. While handicapped readers may exhibit symptoms associated with dyslexic or corrective readers, their uniqueness lies in the fact that they are handicapped.

Previous chapters dealt with the nature of reading and the means that are used to measure the reading abilities of students. Together, the chapters provide the reader with a comprehensive examination of the reading abilities and instructional needs of students.

REFERENCES

Albert, M. L. (1979). Alexia. In K. M. Heilman &. E. Valenstein (Eds.), *Clinical neuropsychology* (pp. 59–91). New York: Oxford University Press.

Barraga, N. (1983). *Visual handicaps and learning.* Austin, TX: Exceptional Resources.

Benton, A. L. (1964). Developmental aphasia and brain damage. *Cortex, 1,* 40–52.

Berdine, W. H. (1985). Mental retardation. In W. H. Berdine &. A. E. Blackhurst (Eds.), *An introduction to special education* (2nd ed., pp. 345–389). Boston: Little, Brown.

Blake, K. A. (1981). *Educating exceptional pupils: An introduction to contemporary practices.* Reading, MA: Addison-Wesley.

Bliesmer, E. P. (1954). Reading abilities of bright and dull children of comparable mental ages. *Journal of Educational Psychology, 45,* 321–331.

Boder, E. (1970). Developmental dyslexia: A new diagnostic approach based on the identification of three subtypes. *Journal of School Health, 40,* 289–290.

Bond, G. L., & Tinker, M. A. (1957). *Reading difficulties: Their diagnosis and correction.* New York: Appleton-Century-Crofts.

Bond, G. L., Tinker, M. A., Wasson, B. B., & Wasson, J. B. (1984). *Reading difficulties: Their diagnosis and correction* (5th ed.). Englewood Cliffs, NJ: Prentice-Hall.

Bowerman, M. C. (1976). Semantic factors in the acquisition of rules for word use and sentence construction. In D. Morehead &. A. Morehead (Eds.), *Normal and deficient child language* (pp. 99–179). Baltimore: University Park Press.

Brunner, W. E. (1905). Congenital word-blindness. *Ophthalmology, 1,* 189–195.

Caton, H. (1985). Visual impairments. In W. H. Berdine &. A. E. Blackhurst (Eds.), *An introduction to special education* (2nd ed.). Boston: Little, Brown.

Cawley, J. F., Goodstein, H. A., & Burrows, W. H. (1972). *The slow learner and the reading problem.* Springfield, IL: Charles C Thomas.

Chapey, R. (1986). *Language intervention strategies in adult aphasia* (2nd ed.). Baltimore: Williams &. Wilkins.

Critchley, M. (1970). *The dyslexic child* (2nd ed.). Springfield, IL: Charles C Thomas.

Dechant, E. V. (1971). *Detection and correction of reading difficulties.* New York: Meredith.

Doehring, D. G., Trites, R. L., Patel, P. G., & Fiedorowicz, C. A. M. (1981). *Reading disabilities: The interaction of reading, language, and neuropsychological deficits.* New York: Academic Press.

Dunn, L. M. (1954). A comparison of reading processes of mentally retarded boys of the same M. A. In L. M. Dunn & R. J. Capobianco (Eds.), *Studies of reading and arithmetic in mentally retarded boys.* Monograph of the Society for Research in Child Development, *19*, 7–99.

Eisenberg, L. (1978). Definition of dyslexia: Their consequences for research and policy. In A. L. Benton & D. Pearl (Eds.), *Dyslexia: An appraisal of current knowledge* (pp. 29–42). New York: Oxford University Press.

Ellis, A. W. (1984). *Reading, writing and dyslexia: A cognitive analysis.* London: Lawrence Erlbaum.

Fernald, G. M. (1943). *Remedial techniques in basic school subjects.* New York: McGraw-Hill.

Furth, H. C. (1973). *Deafness and learning: A psychosocial approach.* Belmont, CA: Wadsworth.

Gates, A. I. (1930). *Interest and ability in reading.* New York: Macmillan.

Gillespie, P. H., & Johnson, L. (1974). *Teaching reading to the mildly retarded child.* Columbus, OH: Charles E. Merrill

Goldberg, H. K., & Schiffman, G. B. (1972). *Dyslexia: Problems of reading disabilities.* New York: Grune & Stratton.

Green, W. W. (1985). Hearing disorders. In W. H. Berdine & A. E. Blackhurst (Eds.), *An introduction to special education* (2nd ed.). Boston: Little, Brown.

Grossman, H. J. (1977). *Manual on terminology and classification in mental retardation.* Washington, DC: American Association on Mental Deficiency.

Hammill, D. D., Leigh, J., McNutt, G., & Larsen, S. C. (1981). A new definition of learning disabilities. *Learning Disability Quarterly, 4.*

Hinshelwood, J. (1917). *Congenital word-blindness.* London: H. K. Lewis.

Hynd, G., & Cohen, M. (1983). *Dyslexia: Neuropsychological theory, research, and clinical differentiation.* New York: Grune & Stratton.

Johnson, D. J., & Myklebust, H. R. (1967). *Learning disabilities.* New York: Grune & Stratton.

Kennedy, E. C. (1977). *Classroom approaches to remedial reading.* Itasca, IL: Peacock.

Kirk, S. A., & Elkins, J. (1975). Characteristics of children enrolled in child service demonstration centers. *Journal of Learning Disabilities, 8,* 630–637.

Kress, R. A. (1971). When is remedial reading remedial? In E. Dechant (Ed.), *Detection and correction of reading difficulties* (pp. 145–149). New York: Meredith.

Kussmaul, A. (1877). Disturbance of speech. *Cyclopedia of Practical Medicine, 14,* 581–875.

Lenneberg, E. H. (1967). *Biological foundations of language.* New York: John Wiley & Sons.

Moores, D. (1967). *Applications of "cloze" procedures to the assessment of psycholinguistic abilities of the deaf.* Unpublished doctoral dissertation, University of Illinois, Urbana.

Morgan, W. P. (1896). A case of congenital word-blindness. *British Medical Journal, 2*, 1378.

Myklebust, H. R. (1964). *The psychology of deafness* (2nd ed.). New York: Grune & Stratton.

Orton, S. T. (1937). *Reading, writing, and speech problems in children.* New York: Norton.

Quigley, S. P., & Kretschmer, R. E. (1982). *The education of deaf children.* Austin, TX: PRO-ED.

Quigley, S. P., Wilbur, R., Power, D., Montanelli, D., & Steinkamp, P. M. (1976). *Syntactic structures in the language of deaf children.* Urbana, IL: Institute for Child Behavior and Development.

Rabinovitch, R. D. (1968). Reading problems in children: Definitions and classifications. In A. H. Keeney & V. T. Keeney (Eds.), *Dyslexia: Diagnosis and treatment of reading disorders* (pp. 1–10). St. Louis, MO: C. V. Mosby.

Reid, D. K., & Hresko, W. P. (1981). *A cognitive approach to learning disabilities.* New York: McGraw-Hill.

Rutter, M. (1978). Prevalence and types of dyslexia. In A. L. Benton & D. Pearl (Eds.), *Dyslexia: An appraisal of current knowledge* (pp. 3–28). New York: Oxford University Press.

Ryan, J. (1975). Mental subnormality and language development. In E. Lenneberg & E. Lenneberg (Eds.), *Foundations of language development* (Vol. 2, pp. 269–277). New York: Academic Press.

Shotik, A. L. (1960). *A comparative investigation of the performance of mentally retarded and intellectually normal boys on selected reading comprehension and performance tasks.* Unpublished doctoral dissertation, Syracuse University.

Spreen, O. (1965). Language functions in mental retardation: A review. *American Journal of Mental Deficiency, 69*, 482–494.

Stephenson, S. (1907). Six cases of congenital word-blindness affecting three generations of one family. *Ophthalmoscope, 5*, 482–484.

Thomson, M. E. (1984). *Developmental dyslexia: Its nature, assessment and remediation.* London: Edward Arnold.

Variot, G., & Lecomte, A. (1906). Un cas de typholexia congenitale (Cecite congenitale verbale). *Bulletins et Memoirs de la Societe-Medicale des Hopitaux de Paris, 23*, 995–1001.

Varney, N. R., & Damasio, A. R. (1982). Acquired alexia. In R. N. Malatesha & P. G. Aaron (Eds.), *Reading disorders: Varieties and treatments* (pp. 305–313). New York: Academic Press.

Wheeler, T., & Watkins, E. J. (1979). A review of symptomology. *Dyslexia Review, 2*, 12–16.

Williams, B. R., & Vernon, M. (1970). Vocational guidance for the deaf. In H. Davis & S. R. Silverman (Eds.), *Hearing and deafness* (3rd ed., pp. 457–479). New York: Holt, Rinehart, and Winston.

Wrightstone, J. W., Aranow, M. S., & Moskowitz, S. (1963). Developing reading test norms for deaf children. *American Annals of the Deaf, 108*, 311–316.

Young, P., & Tyre, C. (1983). *Dyslexia or illiteracy?* Milton Keynes, England: The Open University Press.

PART IV

ASSESSING
WRITING

Stephen C. Larsen

The ability to write effectively is becoming increasingly important in today's complex society. To express oneself by writing is not only a requirement for many types of employment but is often essential for the expression of personal feelings and ideas in social discourse. It is not surprising, therefore, that writing is an integral part of most school curriculums. It is also to be expected that many students fail to acquire functional competence in this area, because writing is a highly complex method of communication that requires the integration of eye-hand, linguistic, and conceptual abilities.

The purpose of this section is to provide the psychologist, teacher, or other interested person with a frame of reference for the assessment of writing problems. The rationale used in preparing this text is that assessment personnel first must be knowledgeable regarding the nature of writing, because it is only from this knowledge that viable assessment data will be forthcoming. The reader will be introduced to what actually constitutes the act of writing and then will be exposed to the procedures for conducting an in-depth assessment of writing problems.

Chapter 10 is devoted to discussing some of the elements that make up the writing process. Included in this chapter is a definition of writing and the stages through which one goes when actually composing a written piece. Additionally, the components of writing (i.e., mechanics, production, conventions, linguistics, and cognition) are described. Finally, a generalized scope and sequence of specific writing skills is presented to acquaint the reader with facets of the writing curriculum taught in the schools.

Chapter 11 discusses how to determine the presence and extent of writing problems. In particular, standardized and nonstandardized procedures are recommended for this purpose. The characteristics of these types of assessment techniques are described, as are specific devices that may be used to ascertain whether a student does, indeed, have a problem and the extent of the problem.

Finally, Chapter 12 introduces the reader to assessment strategies useful for assessing writing for instructional purposes. This important chapter contains suggestions that extend beyond merely analyzing a student's written products. Techniques for evaluating the instructional environment as well as student characteristics that may affect writing performance are discussed. The reader is encouraged to take a broad perspective of the student and his or her environment prior to planning and implementing an instructional program.

10 / THE NATURE OF WRITING

Writing is a highly complex form of human communication. To write effectively, a person must generate ideas to write about, select words that adequately express the thoughts, and use acceptable grammar. Additionally, the writer must transcribe the message through handwriting or typewriting, using punctuation, capitalization, and spelling rules to make it as readable as possible. To fully understand the nature of writing, the reader should be knowledgeable in several important areas: (a) what writing is; (b) the stages of writing; (c) the mechanical, productive, conventional, linguistic, and cognitive components of writing; and (d) the scope and sequence of writing skills that are usually taught in the public schools.

WHAT IS WRITING?

Writing may be defined in many ways. When treated as a noun, the term means the art, practice, style, or form of literary composition. When used as a verb, however, Smith (1982) feels the term *writing* has two quite different meanings. One meaning relates to the act of composing, the other to the act of transcribing the piece into a readable form. A description of writing from the perspective of both composing and transcription is provided below:

> Two people might in fact claim to be writing the same words at the same time, although each is doing different things. An author dictating to a secretary or

into a tape recorder could claim to be writing a book without actually putting a mark on paper. The secretary or person doing the transcribing could also claim to be writing the same words, by performing a conventional act with a pen, pencil, or typewriter. (p. 19)

During writing, composition and transcription are inseparable. For convenience, however, these two aspects of writing are dealt with individually in the discussion that follows.

Composition

Composition refers to how an author arranges the ideas that will make up the content of a piece and uses vocabulary and grammar to render it comprehensible to a particular audience. Obviously, composing a written message involves high level cognitive abilities and requires much thinking and rethinking of a topic to ensure that the message is organized and stated in a readable form. Composing has been described by Cooper and Odell (1977) as involving

> . . . exploring and mulling over a subject; planning the particular piece (with or without notes or outline); getting started; making discoveries about feelings, values, or ideas, even while in the process of writing a draft; making continuous decisions about dictation, syntax, and rhetoric in relation to intended meaning and to the meaning taking shape; reviewing what has been accumulated, and anticipating and rehearsing what comes next; tinkering and reformulating; stopping, contemplating the finished piece and perhaps, finally, revising. (p. xi)

In the view of Petty and Jensen (1980), writing consists of a number of elements reflecting the writer's thinking. Regardless of the form taken in the written message (e.g., book report, personal letter, original story), all of the compositional elements must be discernible if genuine communication is to be effected. The specific elements offered by Petty and Jensen are given below:

1. A clear cut, controlling purpose;

2. Content details relevant to this controlling purpose;

3. Systematic arrangement of content (e.g., order of importance, spatial relationships, cause and effect, time sequence, general to specific or concrete to abstract);

4. Use of comparison and contrast, valid evidence and generalization, and formal and informal language style as appropriate to content and audience;

5. Clear sentence construction;

6. Varied sentence structure. (p. 363)

Types of Composition. When discussing composition, one should keep in mind the usual forms that a written piece may take and that are taught in most school curriculums. In most instances, the basic goal of instruction in written composition is to foster expository ability. Simple exposition (i.e., factual, functional, and utilitarian writing) involves using clear, concise, specific language forms in a logical order and writing clear definitives. The formats in which expository writing are addressed, especially in the schools, are varied. For example, writing reports entails summarizing, paraphrasing, and interpreting reference materials. Report writing also requires documenting sources, handling accepted forms in footnoting and bibliography, and learning the difference between honest borrowing and plagiarizing. Descriptive writing demands the use of concrete words, selection of details to support a single impression, and accurate use of words and phrases. Argument and opinion, higher forms of composition, rely upon the accumulation of evidence, logical thinking, and writing to support the argument or opinion expressed by the author. Critical writing and analysis, particularly relating to advertising, newspaper editorials, commonly used abstractions (e.g., success, honesty, school spirit), and various forms of literature, require high level compositional skills. These skills include analysis of literary and mass-media sources to develop awareness of logical fallacies, semantic traps, propaganda techniques, and stylistic features of literature.

Creativity in Composition. Learning to write in a fashion that permits the expression of individual creativity rather than the simple reporting of facts is another important facet of composition. Developing the ability to write in humorous, literary, or fantasy styles requires exposure to a variety of pieces written in these styles. Additionally, the writer who wants to write creatively must become sensitive to the subtleties of a specific style of interest and practice writing in that style diligently.

When composing, individuals must rely upon their past experiences, emotions, familiarity with the writing of others, and attitudes toward writing itself. Smith (1982) suggests that no matter how proficient one becomes in writing, effective composition does not stem from the mere practice of writing. Rather, the acquisition of compositional skills requires that the student read and is read to. Through the exposure to written language of others, youngsters can see and hear how words and sentences are used to express ideas. When first learning to write, the child and adult typically share writing experiences.

Transcription

As stated in the preceding section, composition and transcription are highly interrelated in writing and are difficult or impossible to clearly delimit in actual practice. When transcription is considered independently, however, the activities associated with it include the physical act of writing (penmanship or typewriting), spelling, capitalization, and punctuation. It is not unusual to find that the major emphasis of writing instruction in some schools focuses upon the skills involved in transcription. This is done, apparently, with the mistaken belief that how a written piece looks is more important than the ideas that are being expressed.

Regrettably, a person who has learned to be more concerned with conventions such as punctuation, capitalization, and spelling than with the quality and organization of the concepts to be expressed will often find writing a tedious affair and will not be very good at it. Consequently, when writing an original piece, initial attention should be directed at generating and refining the ideas and vocabulary that comprise the content of the message. Once these have been put on paper in a form and organization acceptable to the writer, the transcription can be edited or otherwise cleaned up to render the piece as readable as possible. In other words, efforts directed toward polishing the transcription of a written piece should come after the compositional features have been thoroughly addressed.

The transcriptional aspects of writing are important because inappropriate or sloppy use of transcription skills can make a composition unattractive and at times unreadable. For example, a piece that contains good ideas and vocabulary is of little value if it is illegible. Additionally, the presence or absence of a comma may, in some instances, alter the meaning of a sentence. To illustrate, the meaning of the sentence, "When listening, vocabulary plays a major role in understanding what is said," is affected when the comma is omitted. Without the comma between listening and vocabulary, the sentence has little rational meaning, and the reader is tempted to "miscue." Misspelled words and improper use of capitalization can confuse readers and encourage them to put the written material aside because it is too difficult to decipher. As a writer masters the skills of transcription, he or she will use them automatically. Smith (1982) states that when competency of transcriptional skills is acquired, their spontaneous use may actually aid efforts at composition.

THE WRITING STAGES

In producing a written composition, individuals typically pass through several stages. These stages have been termed (a) *prewriting*, (b) *writing*, and (c) *postwriting* by Graves (1975) and Blake and Spennato (1980). This section discusses the stages of writing from the perspective of how the activities associated with each contribute to the completion of a written product.

Prewriting

During the prewriting stage, the writer selects a topic for the written piece, obtains information about the topic, and outlines information that will be discussed. The author also carefully considers the audience for which the writing is intended. Ong (1975) contends that writers must engage in the mental exercise of imagining how another person will read and react to his or her piece as one step toward fully understanding how the message should be constructed.

Several activities help an individual in the prewriting stage. Blake and Spennato (1980) suggest that once a topic is selected, relevant questions may be developed. For example, if a male student wishes to write about a football team, he might ask before he writes: (a) Who are the team's best players? (b) How many games have they won or lost? (c) What have been the most exciting episodes of the season? (d) Are there any players with unusual habits or interesting "quirks"? and (e) Do they have a chance to win a championship? Having developed a list of questions, the writer can determine those having the greatest interest to the proposed audience and those that will be included in the written product. Sequencing of the topics in a logical manner also greatly aids the readability of the written piece. Such activities are the heart of the prewriting phase and serve to facilitate the writing and postwriting phases.

Writing

During the writing stage, an author should be concerned primarily with meaning. In all likelihood, this stage will have many pauses—periods of rereading what has been written, interactions with others (verbal discussion of what is being written), consultations with additional resources such as encyclopedias, talking with oneself regarding the viability of what has been written and what is to be written, and reformulations of the ideas and organization of the topic under consideration.

As writers write, they begin to fully understand what must be written. During this phase, teachers must be willing to tolerate (and, in fact, encourage) crossed out words and sentences, incorrect spelling, punctuation, and capitalization, sentence fragments, and less than perfect handwriting. These characteristics of writing in progress are to be encouraged, since they demonstrate that the student is actively reconceptualizing certain portions of the content and is willing to experiment with its form. Once the ideas have been adequately stated, supported, and organized in a manner that enhances the understanding of the target audience, those activities that polish the piece and make it conform to literary standards may be focused on.

Postwriting

Postwriting entails editing and revising a written product. During this stage, the completed passage is read by the writer, and the gaps within the presentation are identified. Where additional facts, details, or examples are needed, they are added while maintaining the basic sequence of items discussed. The main ideas of the composition, as well as those of individual passages, are clarified and relationships among them strengthened, if necessary. Transitional phrases between paragraphs and sentences are considered to aid readability. The writer should delete irrelevant material and correct errors in capitalization, punctuation, grammar, and spelling. This facet of the postwriting phase is termed *copyediting*. Copyediting also involves rewriting awkward sentences and watching for inconsistencies.

Murray (1968) suggests that writers solicit corrective feedback from others. In most cases, the individual providing the feedback will be a teacher, a parent, or an older student. Sometimes the feedback will be mild and involve few suggested corrections, while in other cases a complete rewriting of the piece will be recommended. The author should be helped to consider criticism objectively without feeling unduly shamed or frustrated. Simple criticism, however, is not always adequate (especially with young writers) and should be expressed carefully. Suggestions for improvement should be incorporated into the feedback whenever possible.

Next, care is given to the handwriting or typewriting to effect a polished copy. At the conclusion of the postwriting stage, the written piece is given to the intended reader.

THE COMPONENTS OF WRITING

Hammill and Larsen (1983) suggest that:

> To write meaningfully, one must master at least five basic abilities. These include the ability (1) to form letters, words, numerals, and sentences in a legible manner, (2) to generate enough meaningful sentences to express one's thoughts, feelings, and opinions adequately, (3) to write in compliance with accepted standards of style, especially those governing punctuation, capitalization, and spelling, (4) to use acceptable English syntactic, morphological, and semantic elements, and (5) to express ideas, opinion and thoughts in a creative and mature way. (p. 2)

These abilities can be classified in terms of five components: mechanics, production, conventions, linguistics, and cognition. There are two good reasons for using these components to represent writing. The first, and most important, is that each of these has been considered essential to writing as theorized by Smith (1982), Nodine (1983), and Martin (1983). Second, they are used as the framework for analyzing written products that will be presented later. The five components are discussed next.

Mechanics

The mechanical component refers to an individual's ability to use a pen or pencil for forming letters, words, numerals, and sentences. To write requires eye-hand coordination, knowledge of left-right designation, established hand preference, small muscle coordination, and visual discrimination of letters and words. Handwriting is a visual-motor task that, depending upon the quality of its execution, can make reading a student's written product easy or difficult. Skill in handwriting develops gradually as a result of practice and as the student's neuromuscular mechanism matures and will tend to plateau from third grade on (Herrick & Okada, 1963). When mastery is established, penmanship is fluid, rapid (perhaps up to 60 words per minute), and sometimes beautiful. At the least, it should be serviceable. When problems occur, handwriting is characterized by illegibility, slowness, tension, and fatigue. Hammill and Larsen (1983) discuss the importance of penmanship.

> Poorly formed letters and words, uneven spacing, improper alignment, and general sloppiness make the reader's task unnecessarily difficult. In some instances, handwriting is so poor that regardless of the linguistic and conceptual competency of the person composing the message, the written product is totally illegible. For this reason, the quality of a student's handwriting must be considered . . . (p. 3)

Penmanship is not synonymous with written language but is merely a means by which it is expressed. When letters and words are ill-formed, however, the content of a written piece may be lost to the reader.

Handwriting and Comprehension. To illustrate how handwriting may adversely affect readability, the reader is asked to read the two passages in Figure 10.1. The reader probably could not read the first passage and possibly had difficulty reading the second. The samples were written by two fourth grade boys who evidenced no motor difficulties but who are referred to by their teachers as having handwriting problems severe enough to warrant remedial attention. Both students were asked to write the following passage: "The little boy went to the store. He was going after a candy bar and a box of crackers. His name was Frank. He ran all the way home to his mother." The penmanship difficulties exhibited by both students seriously impair the readability of their written products. Both students could benefit from an error analysis to find out which errors contribute to the relative illegibility. In some cases, teaching students to type might be the only way to enable them to produce messages that someone can read.

FIGURE 10.1. Samples of Poor Handwriting

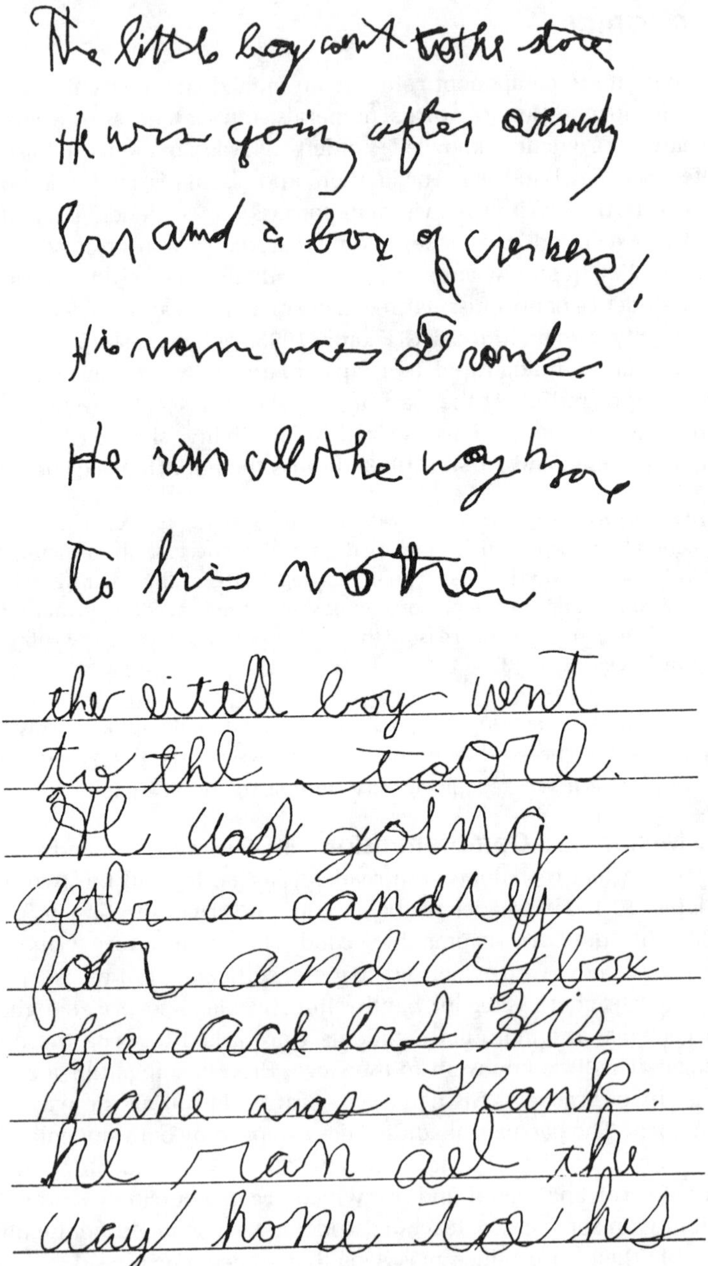

Development of Handwriting. Handwriting develops gradually from the scribbling done by preschool children. Scribbling, in addition to being a precursor of handwriting, is also preliminary to drawing. Scribbling becomes significant when it is deliberately produced on a horizontal plane. Children may even insert gaps in their horizontally oriented scribbles in an attempt to mimic spaces between words. Smith (1982) suggests that such visual-motor activities of young children are possible only when they see and become sensitive to some conventions of print. A scribble with the above mentioned characteristics is intended to represent language, "a remarkably sophisticated achievement similar to the blocking out of lines by a graphic designer to indicate the place of printed words in the layout of an advertisement or a page of text" (p. 180).

When a child scribbles to represent language, the result is even more significant when done within a certain context. For example, when four-year-old Sally takes a pencil and paper, sits down at a table, indicates that she is "going to write a letter to grandma," and produces scribbles that obviously represent an attempt to communicate with her grandma, the process of writing is apparently understood. As children begin to receive instruction in handwriting, some progress faster than others. Factors that discriminate between youngsters who are ready to learn to write and those who are not include the following: (a) Proper sitting and writing position is maintained; (b) when presented with a printed word, the child can copy the word correctly; (c) printing is within the lines; (d) the child is able to print first and last names; and (e) the direction of printing is from left to right. As a minimum requirement for learning to write, a kindergarten age student should be able to easily discriminate among different letters of the alphabet. If a student is unable to do this, he or she will have serious deficits in handwriting.

Diagnosis and Remediation. As stated previously, poor handwriting can adversely affect a reader's ability to understand a written message, regardless of the ideas expressed. In these cases, the specific causes of the handwriting problems must be identified through specific diagnostic efforts. Chapter 11 contains a discussion of common errors associated with the mechanical component of written language and offers numerous techniques useful in determining appropriate remedial efforts.

Production

If a written piece is to express the thoughts and feelings of its author, a sufficient number of words, sentences, and paragraphs must be generated. Students who, for various reasons, do not produce an adequate number of meaningful units of writing will likely be viewed as ineffective writers. Their written passages will tend to be composed of short, simple sentences and disjointed phrases unsupported by corresponding thoughts and will be limited in factual content. Pieces written in this fashion will inadequately express an author's intended message, and it will be difficult to judge whether the student is unable to produce sufficient written material or is simply prone to writing with such brevity that essential meaning is lost.

An example of how the quantity of words and sentences in a written message can affect its overall quality is demonstrated by the following passages written by an eight-year-old boy who is progressing adequately in all other phases of school performance.

> My mother sent me to the stor. Ther are many things in the stor. We spent alot of money in the stor.

> I have 3 friends. They are all good guys. We like to play with a football. We run a lot.

Note the short sentences and the complete absence of connectors that would necessitate punctuation marks. These two passages were written as a part of a school assignment. The topics were assigned by the teacher: (a) what you did after school yesterday and (b) what you and your friends do for fun. The teacher felt that these and other written pieces, all of similar length and pattern, were indicative of a potential writing problem.

The student was interviewed in both school and home situations. The mother of this student showed some written products that the youngster had composed while at home. An example is given below:

My trip to the moon.

> One day a spac ship landed in my back yard. A man and a woman got out of it and told me not to be scard. Thay asked me if I wanted to go to the moon and see a firworks sho. Some of there frends were having a picnik and wanted someone for there chilren to play with. We blasted off and got there in abot 12 minits. There frends were green but there 2 chilren were very nic. We plaed and wached the firworks Thay took me home and told my mother whar we went. My mother sent me to bed. First she gave me some cookes.

THE END!!

Comparison of the products generated at school and at home is interesting. It shows that production may be affected by the environment in which the writing takes place.

A student may demonstrate a low production in written expression for many reasons. While diagnoses of these cases are presented later, some of the more commonly occurring reasons are reviewed at this time. Wiederholt, Hammill, and Brown (1983) list seven factors that may account for a lack of meaningful units incorporated in a child's written product. These factors include:

1. Few or restricted opportunities for learning and practicing written expression.
2. Student knows the content, but does not know how to organize and express ideas.
3. Student lacks the essential content required to meet requirements of written expression
4. Student hesitates to write because judgmental standards are too high.
5. Student knows how to write; does not choose to do so.
6. Problems with subskills such as spelling, handwriting, and grammar.
7. Student is a slow worker. (pp. 230–231)

Conventions

Conventions are the rules for capitalization, punctuation, and spelling. Peculiarities in English make learning these rules a difficult task for many students (Barenbaum, 1983). The sometimes arbitrary rules governing punctuation, capitalization, and spelling imply a "contract" between the writer and the reader—a contract that becomes increasingly important as youngsters mature in writing abilities and write for unknown audiences. Hammill and Larsen (1983) discuss these conventions:

> Many of the rules governing the use of punctuation and capitalization (together called "style") are arbitrary in nature, based in tradition, and do not necessarily facilitate meaning. The place of the period in relation to the quotation marks in the following sentence is an example of this point: Mary said, "I saw the boy." Whether the period is placed inside or outside of the quotation marks does not affect the meaning of the sentence. Other rules, however, are essential to understanding the sense of sentences and passages. For example, the meaning of the sentence, "When reading, comprehension will be impaired greatly by poor vocabulary development," is altered considerably if the comma is omitted. Without the comma between reading and comprehension, the sentence has no rational meaning. The situation is much the same with spelling generalizations. Whether the child writes bear or bar does not usually affect the meaning of the sentence greatly, for the meaning is generally evident from the context of the sentence; for example: "The big grizzly bar chased the boy up the tree." On other occasions, misspelled words can confuse the reader considerably. (p. 3)

Spelling. When considering spelling as a potential "trouble spot," several factors should be noted. In learning to spell any word, a student has to (a) discover how to spell a word (e.g., by looking it up in the dictionary or by asking someone who knows the correct spelling) and (b) remember the word. In early writing, spelling is often inventive due to the fact that new writers don't know how to spell many words, and correct spellings of words are preceded by misspellings.

Researchers have shown that strategies for learning to spell develop in roughly the same sequence for most children. Graves (1979) determined that spelling begins with word inventions, followed sequentially by "words in transition" (inconsistent spellings), stable inventions (consistent but not conventional spellings), and then sight words (words that have been memorized and are spelled correctly). Deviations in spelling are usually considered indications of the stages mentioned above, ranging from approximations of correct spellings to the random ordering of letters. Gentry and Henderson (1978) believe that deviant spelling at the intermediate and secondary levels tends to be illogical, consisting of random letter choices.

Capitalization and Punctuation. The skills necessary to learn the rules of capitalization and punctuation appear to be different from those necessary to learn spelling rules. Smith (1982) indicates that mastering capitalization and punctuation rules requires more than mere memorization. Simply observing how sentences are punctuated and capitalized will not teach a writer the rules of capitalization and punctuation; the purposes of those rules must be deduced. Understanding the rules of capitalization and punctuation is gained by understanding the intent of what is actually written.

Linguistics

The linguistic ability required for successful writing includes the knowledge and use of English syntactic and semantic structures. The grammatical forms and vocabulary items used will significantly affect a reader's impression of the overall quality of the composition. This is particularly true for the writing of older students and adults, who are expected to be competent writers. For example, a letter, book report, or formal paper that contains errors in the use of verbs (e.g., *come* for *came*, *throwed* for *threw*) or pronouns (e.g., *them* for *those*, *theirselves* for *themselves*) or that contains double negatives (e.g., *haven't no* for *have no*) may adequately convey the intended meaning but will usually be judged as inferior to those products that are grammatically correct. The creative use of words to describe events and to explain concepts also influences how written passages are viewed by their readers.

Like punctuation, capitalization, and spelling rules, the linguistic standards required for acceptable writing are also often arbitrary. One major difference between the conventional and linguistic aspects of writing, however, should be noted: Whereas capitalization, punctuation, and spelling must be learned primarily through reading or direct instruction, the rudiments of grammar and vocabulary are learned incidentally through oral language (Smith, 1982). The conventions of written expression must be seen in print and cannot be inferred from listening to people talk; the grammar and vocabulary of written language can be heard. Logan, Logan, and Paterson (1972) report that many young children are aware of the grammatical features of written language. When asked to "tell it again so it can be written down," children will commonly use the vocabulary and grammar associated with text rather than repeat verbatim what they have just said. This sensitivity to the stylistic features of writing should be encouraged by teachers as the child is introduced to writing instruction.

Some youngsters, of course, do not have access to books, were not read to at an early age, or have not been exposed to individuals who speak in a grammatically correct fashion. These children will tend to use grammatical and vocabulary forms that Otto and Smith (1980) refer to as "illiterate or homely." In other words, they will write the way they and others around them talk. The illiterate style is associated with uneducated persons who use forms such as "he don't have none" or "them girls gone away." Whether used orally or in writing, these forms are clearly unacceptable in most school settings and are a source of concern to most educators. The homely style is more tolerated but contains some irregularities such as "me and Bob went" and "I have ate a cake." These patterns are common in the speech and writing of many students and will require instruction to gradually bring them into line with acceptable standards. While adequate grammatical usage and varied vocabulary are basic to what might be termed *effective writing*, the reader should note that exercises in the finer points of each will make sense only to students who are already writing.

Cognition

To write a piece that is logical, sequenced, and to some extent abstract requires a high level of cognitive ability. Regardless of whether a field trip report, an original story, a letter to a friend, or a book report, the piece must be organized and structured in such a way as to be readily understandable to a reader. Hammill and Larsen (1983) observe:

> The maturity of a product is usually evident if the writer employs titles, paragraphs, definite endings, character development, dialogue, and humor, or expresses some philosophical or moral theme. The cognitive component is not as easily defined as are other components, but a product that is immature in its development of expression is frequently viewed as "sloppy" in the presentation of ideas, disjointed in thought sequence, lacking in theme, or simply difficult to understand. (p. 4)

Hall (1981) states that cognitive abilities evolve from an inherent language base that is typically expressed first in a youngster's speech. Most children, even at a very early age, tell stories of some length and complexity. Their stories usually have a beginning, middle, and end, as well as containing adequate elaboration so that major and minor themes are clear to the listener. Children are likely to receive corrective feedback from others in their environment as to how they can make their stories more interesting, varied, and clear to the listeners. Bereiter and Scardamalia (1983) indicate that the difficulties youngsters have in telling stories have little to do with content. Rather, children seem to have global ideas of what a story should relate but are unsure where to begin and how particular ideas should be linked. Put another way, children sometimes exhibit difficulties in organizing and sequencing the events in a narrative, a problem evidenced in the writings of many adults as well.

As the student gains confidence, pleasure, and maturity in the organizing and sequencing of ideas, he or she will move on to increasingly more difficult types of expository and creative writing. For example, advanced narration skills will be evidenced by different ways of ordering ideas, increasingly complex detail added to develop one central theme, and increasingly accurate use of language, interpreting, and paraphrasing skills. In addition, students will deal with their own and others' ideas from a critical and analytical viewpoint and will be able to review another author's purpose and theme by examining dominant tone, mood, and symbolism. Gaining proficiency in these skills will increase the arenas in which students are able to function when writing, indicating growth in the cognitive component of writing.

While the five components of writing have been discussed as separate entities, one must remember that they are heavily interrelated. Deficits in one component interfere with performance in the others. Similarly, proficiency in one area will not necessarily mean proficiency in all. To illustrate, a student with adequate (possibly even beautiful) penmanship may be unable to compose even two or three sentences that follow in a logical fashion. Conversely, an individual may be quite sloppy in his or her handwriting but be able to organize and sequence ideas in a way that is readily understandable to any reader. Which of the two students would be considered a good writer? Obviously, skill in the cognitive and linguistic components of writing are the most valued and should be acquired before the mechanical and conventional components are heavily stressed in the instructional sequence. In essence, a writer must develop and integrate the skills of all five components in order to be effective and independent. Students who are judged to be deficient in writing ability must be assessed in the major aspects of these areas to ascertain the nature and extent of the problem. To do otherwise is to encourage superficial and possibly incorrect diagnosis of an individual's difficulties in written expression.

SCOPE AND SEQUENCE OF WRITING SKILLS

A useful tool available to those who would understand and evaluate writing is a scope and sequence of skills that comprise a typical writing curriculum. Table 10.1 is an example of a comprehensive scope and sequence of skills that incorporates most of the content included in writing instruction in the schools. The major components of this table are capitalization, punctuation, vocabulary, word usage, grammar, sentence construction, and paragraph construction. The grades for which various writing skills are listed are one through eight.

Assessment personnel need to be aware of scope and sequence of skills employed by the referring teacher to, initially, ascertain whether or not the skill for which the student has been referred has, in fact, been taught. Take, for example, a third grade student who is referred because he or she has difficulty linking verbs and predicate nominatives, fails to recognize transitive and intransitive verbs, and has no apparent knowledge of contractions. Perusal of the scope and sequence chart provided in Table 10.1 indicates that these particular skills in word usage and vocabulary are not generally taught until the fifth grade. Perhaps the teacher making the referral is new to the system and is not aware of when certain skills are introduced within the curriculum or has set unrealistic expectations for the students in her class. In this case, remedial efforts will probably best be directed toward acquainting the teacher with realistic standards for the writing of third grade students and not toward students who are inappropriately referred.

Another use of scope and sequence charts is in developing criterion referenced tests. Hills (1981) suggests that scope and sequence charts can be the best source of content for generating various nonstandardized scales to be used in the assessment of writing. This is particularly true when the scope and sequence used is based on the curriculum of that particular school. In this way, the examiner can be relatively assured that items used in various assessment devices correspond to what the student is being taught (a form of content validity). In any case, knowledge of the particular skills presented to a student in a given school, as well as when they are introduced, will improve the examiner's effectiveness in assessment of writing.

TABLE 10.1. Scope and Sequence of Composition Skills

	Grade 1	Grade 2	Grade 3	Grade 4	Grade 5	Grades 6, 7, and 8
Capitalization	The first word of a sentence The child's first and last names The name of the teacher, school, town, street The word *I*	The date First and important words of titles of books the children read Proper names used in children's writings Titles of compositions Names of titles: Mr., Mrs., Miss	Proper names: month, day, common holidays First word in a line of verse First and important words in titles of books, stories, poems First word of salutation of informal note, such as Dear First word of closing of informal note, such as Yours	Names of cities and states in general Names of organizations to which children belong, such as Boy Scouts, Grade Four, etc. Mother, Father, when used in place of the name Local geographical names	Names of streets Names of all places and persons, countries, oceans, etc. Capitalization used in outlining Titles when used with names, such as President Lincoln Commercial trade names	Names of the Deity and the Bible First word of a quoted sentence Proper adjectives showing race, nationality, etc. Abbreviations of proper nouns and titles
Punctuation	Period at the end of a sentence that tells something Period after numbers in any kind of list	Question mark at the close of a question Comma after salutation of a friendly note or letter Comma after closing of a friendly note or letter Comma between the day of the month and the year Comma between the name of the city and the name of the state	Period after abbreviations Period after an initial Use of an apostrophe in a common contraction such as isn't, aren't Commas in a list	Apostrophe to show possession Hyphen separating parts of a word divided at end of a line Period following a command Exclamation point at the end of a word or group of words that make an exclamation Comma setting off an appositive Colon after the salutation of a business letter Quotation marks before and after a direct quotation Comma between explanatory words and a quotation	Colon in writing time Quotation marks around the title of a booklet, pamphlet, the chapter of a book, and the title of a poem or story Underlining the title of a book Period after outline Roman numeral	Comma to set off nouns in direct address Hyphen to compound numbers Colon to set off a list Comma in sentences to aid in making meaning clear Comma after introductory clauses

TABLE 10.1. continued

Vocabulary

New words learned during experience	Words with similar meanings; with opposite meanings	Extending discussion of words for precise meanings	Dividing words into syllables	Using antonyms	Extending meanings: writing with care in choice of words and phrases
Choosing words that describe accurately	Alphabetical order	Using synonyms	Using the accent mark	Prefixes and suffixes; compound words	In writing and speaking, selecting words for accuracy
Choosing words that make you see, hear, feel		Distinguishing meanings and spellings of homonyms	Using exact words that appeal to the senses	Exactness in choice of words	Selecting words for effectiveness and appropriateness
		Using the prefix un and the suffix less	Using exact words in explanation	Dictionary work: definitions; syllables: pronunciation; macron; breve	Selecting words for courtesy
			Keeping individual lists of new words and meanings	Contractions	Editing a paragraph to improve choice of words
				Rhyme and rhythm: words with sensory images	
				Classification of words by parts of speech	
				Roots and words related to them	
				Adjectives, nouns, verbs—contrasting general and specific vocabulary	

Word Usage

Generally in oral expression	*Generally in oral expression*	Using *there is* and *there are*; *any* and *no*	Agreement of subject and verb	Avoiding unnecessary pronouns (the boy he)	Homonyms: *its, it's; their, there, they're; there's, theirs; whose, who's*
Naming yourself last	Avoiding double negatives	Using *let* and *leave; don't* and *doesn't; would have,* not *would of*	Using *she, he, I, we,* and *they* as subjects	Linking verbs and predicate nominatives	Using parallel structure for parallel ideas, as in outlines
Eliminating unnecessary words (my father he)	Using *a* and *an; may* and *can; teach* and *learn*	Verb forms in sentences:	Using *bring* and *take*	Conjugation of verbs, to note changes in tense, person, number	Verb forms in sentences:
Using *well* and *good*	Eliminating unnecessary words (this here)	throw, thew, thrown	Verb forms in sentences:	Transitive and intransitive verbs	beat, beat, beaten
Verb forms in sentences:	Verb forms in sentences:	drive, drove, driven	blow, blew, blown	Verb forms in sentences:	learn, learned, learned
is, are	rode, ridden	wrote, written	drink, drank, drunk	as, was, been	leave, left, left
did, done	took, taken	tore, torn	lie, lay, lain	say, said, said	light, lit, lit
was, were	grow, grew, grown	chose, chosen	take, took, taken	fall, fell, fallen	forgot, forgotten
see, saw, seen	know, knew, known	climbed	rise, rose, risen	dive, dived, dived	swing, swung, swung
ate, eaten	bring, brought	broke, broken	teach, taught, taught	burst, burst, burst	spring, sprang, sprung
went, gone	drew, drawn	wore, worn	raise, raised, raised	buy, bought, bought	shrink, shrank, shrunk
came, come	began, begun	spoke, spoken	lay, laid, laid	Additional verb forms:	slide, slid, slid
gave, given	ran, run	sang, sung	fly, flew, flown	climb, like, play, read, sail, vote, work	
		rang, rung	set, set, set		
		catch, caught	swim, swam, swum		
			freeze, froze, frozen		
			steal, stole, stolen		

TABLE 10.1. continued

Grammar	Not applicable	Not applicable	Nouns: recognition of singular, plural, and possessive Verbs: recognition	Noun: common and proper; in complete subject Verb: in complete predicate Adjective: recognition Adverb: recognition (telling how, when, where); modifying verbs, adjectives, other adverbs Pronoun: recognition of singular and plural	Noun: possessive, object of preposition; predicate noun Verb: tense; agreement with subject; verbs of action and state of being Adjective: comparison; predicate adjective; proper adjective Adverb: comparison; words telling how, when, where, how much; modifying verbs, adjectives, adverbs Pronoun: possessive; object of preposition Preposition: recognition; prepositional phrases Conjunction: recognition Interjection: recognition	Noun: clauses, common and proper; indirect object Verb: conjugating to note changes in person, number, tense; linking verbs with predicate nominatives Adjective: chart of uses; clauses; demonstrative; descriptive; numerals; phrases Adverb: chart of uses; clauses; comparison; descriptive: *ly* ending; modification of adverbs; phrases Pronoun: antecedents; declension chart—person, gender; case; demonstrative; indefinite; interrogative; personal; relative Preposition: phrases Conjunction: in compound subjects and predicates; in subordinate and coordinate clauses Interjection: placement of in quotations
Sentences	Writing simple sentences	Recognizing sentences; kinds; statement and question Composing correct and interesting original sentences Avoiding running sentences together with *and*	Exclamatory sentences Using a variety of sentences Combining short, choppy sentences into longer ones Using interesting beginning and ending sentences Avoiding run-on sentences (no punctuation) Learning to proofread one's own and others' sentences	Using command sentences Complete and simple subject; complete and simple predicate Recognizing adjectives and adverbs; pronouns introduced Avoiding fragments of sentences (incomplete) and the comma fault (a comma in place of a period) Improving sentences in a paragraph	Using a variety of interesting sentences: declarative, interrogative, exclamatory, and imperative (you the subject) Agreement of subject and verb; changes in pronoun forms Compound subjects and compound predicates Composing paragraphs with clearly stated ideas	Developing concise statements (avoiding wordiness or unnecessary repetition) Indirect object and predicate nominative Complex sentences Clear thinking and expression (avoiding vagueness and omissions)

TABLE 10.1. continued

	Not applicable	Not applicable	Keeping to one idea Keeping sentences in order; sequence of ideas Finding and deleting sentences that do not belong Indenting	Selecting main topic Choosing title to express main idea Making simple outline with main idea Developing an interesting paragraph	Improving skill in writing a paragraph of several sentences Selecting subheads as well as main topic for an outline Courtesy and appropriateness in all communications Recognizing topic sentences Keeping to the topic as expressed in title and topic sentence Using more than one paragraph Developing a four-point outline Writing paragraphs from outline Using new paragraphs for new speakers in written conversation Keeping a list of books (authors and titles) used for reference	Analyzing a paragraph to note method of development Developing a paragraph in different ways: e.g., with details, reasons, examples, or comparisons Checking for accurate statements Using a fresh or original approach in expressing ideas Using transition words to connect ideas Using topic sentences to develop paragraphs Improving skill in complete composition—introduction, development, conclusion Checking for good reasoning Using bibliography in report based on several sources
Paragraphs						

Adapted from "Problems in Written Composition" by Donald D. Hammill in *Teaching Students with Learning and Behavior Problems*, 4th ed. (pp. 96–99) by Donald D. Hammill and Nettie R. Bartel, 1986, Newton, MA: Allyn & Bacon. Reprinted by permission.

REFERENCES

Barenbaum, E. (1983). Writing in the special class. *Topics in Learning and Learning Disabilities, 3,* 12–20.

Bereiter, C., & Scardamalia, M. C. (1983). From conversation to composition: The role of instruction in developmental process. In R. Glasser (Ed.), *Advances in instructional psychology,* Vol. 2 (pp. 163–188). Hillsdale, NJ: Erlbaum.

Blake, H., & Spennato, N. A. (1980). The directed writing activity: A process with structure. *Language Arts, 57,* 317–318.

Cooper, C. R., & Odell, L. (1977). Evaluating writing. National Council of Teachers of English.

Gentry, J. R., & Henderson, E. (1978). Three steps to teaching beginning readers to spell. *The Reading Teacher, 31,* 632–637.

Graves, D. C. (1979). What children show us by revision. *Language Arts, 56,* 312–319.

Graves, D. H. (1975). An examination of the writing process of seven year old children. *Research in the Teaching of English, 9,* 231–236.

Hall, J. K. (1981). *Evaluating and improving written expression.* Boston: Allyn & Bacon.

Hammill, D. D., & Larsen, S. C. (1983). *Test of Written Language.* Austin, TX: PRO-ED.

Herrick, V. E., & Okada, N. (1963). The present scene: Practices in the teaching of handwriting in the United States. In V. E. Herrick (Ed.), *New horizons for research in handwriting.* Madison: University of Wisconsin Press.

Hills, J. R. (1981). *Measurement and evaluation in the classroom.* Columbus, OH: Charles E. Merrill.

Lavine, L. O. (1977). Differentiation of letterlike forms in prereading children. *Developmental Psychology, 13,* 89–94.

Logan, L. M., Logan, V. G., & Paterson, L. (1972). *Creative communication.* New York: McGraw-Hill.

Martin, N. (1983). Genuine communication. *Topics in Learning and Learning Disabilities, 3,* 1–11.

Murray, D. M. (1968). *A writer teaches writing: A practical method of teaching composition.* Boston: Houghton Mifflin.

Nodine, B. F. (1983). Forward: Process not product. *Topics in Learning and Learning Disabilities, 3,* ix–xii.

Ong, W. J. (1975). The writer's audience is always a fiction. *PMLA, 90,* 9–21.

Otto, W., & Smith, R. J. (1980). *Corrective and remedial teaching.* Boston: Houghton Mifflin.

Petty, W. T., & Jensen, J. M. (1980). *Developing children's language.* Boston: Allyn & Bacon.

Smith, F. (1982). *Writing and the writer.* New York: Holt, Rinehart and Winston.

Wiederholt, J. L., Hammill, D. D., & Brown, V. (1983). *The resource teacher: A guide to effective practices.* Austin, TX: PRO-ED.

11 / DETERMINING THE PRESENCE AND EXTENT OF WRITING PROBLEMS

The presence and extent of writing problems is determined by the administration of standardized or nonstandardized assessment procedures. The purposes of administering these types of assessment procedures are to (a) identify students who are evidencing educationally significant writing problems; (b) determine the degree to which a problem is evidenced; and (c) isolate the various subareas of writing that may be particularly troublesome (e.g., spelling, grammar, punctuation). This chapter is intended to acquaint the reader with the characteristics of standardized and nonstandardized assessment and to discuss specific tests and techniques that are particularly recommended for use.

STANDARDIZED ASSESSMENT OF WRITING

Standardized assessment of academic achievement has an extensive history in the schools. In the case of writing, standardized assessment procedures have been used since the 1920s to determine which students have problems as well as the extent of such problems. The diverse testing formats used to measure various writing abilities range from analyzing a spontaneously written story according to a rating scale to selecting a misspelled word from three or four words that are spelled correctly. This section presents the characteristics of standardized assessment and discusses commonly used standardized tests that measure writing abilities.

Characteristics of Standardized Assessment

While much has been written about standardized assessment, few writers have defined the term precisely. In an effort to resolve confusion regarding this topic, Hammill and Bartel (1986) stipulate that three elements must be present in a standardized procedure: (a) a set of administration instructions, (b) objective scoring criteria, and (c) a specified preferred frame of reference. Authors of standardized assessment techniques must also show evidence of statistically derived reliability and validity as a proof of technical adequacy. Without satisfactory proof of technical adequacy, no assessment procedure can be considered standardized.

Set administration procedures are a hallmark of standardized assessment. Administration procedures in most standardized devices are rigorous and frequently indicate exact instructions that are to be given to a student. Additionally, the materials that are to be used by individuals during the course of the evaluation are usually provided. For students of different ages, directions are given as to where to begin and where to stop. Some standardized techniques that require the examiner to enunciate certain test items, such as dictated spelling tests, provide pronunciation guides to be used when administering the test.

A second criterion of standardized assessment is the provision of some system for objectively scoring the responses or behaviors of students being evaluated. This ensures that the tester will know what constitutes a correct or incorrect response. In addition, depending upon the type of assessment format being used, instructions may need to be given as to how a particular type of student-teacher interaction will be coded or how a response to an interview question will be judged.

A third criterion of standardized assessment is the presence of some specified frame of reference that guides how the obtained results will be interpreted. While several different frames of reference may be employed, the one most commonly used in the assessment of writing has been termed *norm referenced*. Norm referenced interpretation involves taking the results of an individual student's evaluation and applying them to normative or average performance standards. Such an application of a student's score results in statements like "Leon is at the 32nd percentile in spelling" or "Ruth has obtained a standard score of 10 on written vocabulary." The result of a norm referenced interpretation is knowledge of where a student falls in relation to youngsters of similar age, geographic location, sex, and so forth.

The elements of standardized assessment mentioned above are to be followed precisely. There are important reasons for such rigor in administering, scoring, and interpreting standardized measures. As Hammill stated earlier in this volume:

> Adherence to the stated procedures is so important that any divergence is considered to invalidate the results to some extent. As a consequence of using these

guidelines, there is a higher degree of consistency in results among examiners. This is a basic assumption underlying standardized assessment—namely, that different examiners will obtain more or less the same results when using the same procedure. Following the provided procedures minimizes error and increases the probability that what an examiner sees or hears will truly reflect the student's abilities, knowledge, or behavior.

As a definitive proof that an assessment procedure is indeed standardized, an evaluator must also consider its stated reliability and validity. Reliability refers to the consistency with which a person performs on a given procedure. Validity refers to whether an evaluation procedure measures what it is said to measure. Reliability and validity are essential to any standardized assessment procedure and must be demonstrated, typically through logical or experimental means. A discussion of the types of reliability and validity and how they are computed is beyond the scope of this book. Readers are encouraged to consult Anastasi (1982) and Salvia and Ysseldyke (1985) for a detailed discussion of these topics.

Standardized Tests of Writing

Virtually all standardized measures of writing ability are in the form of tests. According to the American Psychological Association (1974) manual, *Standards for Educational and Psychological Tests*, a test is defined as

> a set of tasks or questions intended to elicit particular types of behavior when presented under standardized conditions and to yield scores that will have desirable psychometric properties such as high reliability and validity. (p. 2)

Table 11.1 lists the most commonly used standardized tests of writing, including their mode of administration, testing format, and writing components assessed. Regardless of whether the test is group or individually administered, most of the devices employ a contrived format. The contrived format is particularly useful in the evaluation of punctuation, capitalization, spelling, and grammar.

The reason contrived testing formats are a part of all standardized writing tests will become obvious. If a student is required to produce a spontaneously written passage, he or she would probably not use enough of the rules of punctuation, capitalization, and grammar or an adequate number of correctly spelled words to accurately estimate competency in these areas. For

TABLE 11.1. Standardized Tests of Writing

Test	Administration		Format		Components Measured					
	Group	Individual	Contrived	Spontaneous	Handwriting	Punctuation and Capitalization	Spelling	Grammar	Vocabulary	Ideas and Organization
Iowa Test of Basic Skills	X		X			X	X	X		
California Achievement Test	X		X			X	X	X		
Metropolitan Achievement Test	X		X			X	X	X		
SRA Achievement Series	X		X			X	X			
Comprehensive Test of Basic Skills	X		X			X	X	X		
Stanford Achievement Test	X		X			X	X			
Peabody Individual Achievement Test		X	X				X			
Wide Range Achievement Test		X	X				X			
Woodcock-Johnson Psychoeducational Battery		X	X			X	X			
Diagnostic Achievement Battery		X	X	X		X	X		X	
Test of Written Language		X	X	X	X	X	X	X	X	X
Test of Adolescent Language		X	X				X	X	X	
Test of Written Spelling		X	X				X			

example, a story written by a student may fail to demonstrate that the student knows that proper names are capitalized, quotation marks set off direct dialogue, and that "child" is the correct singular form of "children," simply because the story did not require the use of those conventions. Consequently, tests that assess these component areas will use various formats to try to determine a youngster's competency.

One commonly used contrived testing format for punctuation, capitalization, spelling, and grammar is multiple choice. For example, the *Comprehensive Test of Basic Skills* (CTB/McGraw-Hill, 1982) asks 6th to 8th grade students to identify the misspelled words among the following stimulus items: (a) constantly, (b) interpret, (c) benefit, (d) explanation, and (e) none misspelled. On the same instrument, grades 4 through 6 youngsters are asked to indicate the item that contains a capitalization error:

A. This selection comes

B. from the "silent world,"

C. a book about exciting

D. deep sea adventures.

In other types of contrived testing formats, the *Test of Written Spelling* (Larsen & Hammill, 1986) and the *Wide Range Achievement Test* (Jastak & Wilkinson, 1985) measure spelling ability by asking a student to write a word after hearing that word used in a sentence. The *Test of Written Language* (Hammill & Larsen, 1983) measures grammar by requiring a student to "fill in the blank" by selecting an appropriate grammatical form determined by the context of a sentence (e.g., "We built the bridge all by _____.")

Evaluators interested in standardized assessment of writing will likely be concerned with vocabulary and ideas and organization as well as punctuation, capitalization, spelling, and grammar. Assessment of these areas requires the use of either a student's spontaneously written story or relatively unique contrived formats. Table 11.1 indicates that only three tests measure linguistic (i.e., vocabulary) and cognitive (i.e., ideas and organization) aspects of written expression. These are the *Test of Written Language*, the *Diagnostic Achievement Battery*, and the *Test of Adolescent Language*. Each of these tests is discussed in some detail, because they are the only instruments that provide data pertaining to these important components of writing and because they are examples of technically well-constructed tests of writing.

Test of Written Language. The *Test of Written Language* (TOWL) (Hammill & Larsen, 1983) is one of the most commonly used test of writing abilities. This instrument may be used to identify students who perform significantly poorer or better than their peers in written expression and to delineate a student's particular strengths and weaknesses in various writing abilities. Additionally, this instrument is appropriate for documenting progress in writing programs and for conducting research in writing. The TOWL is standardized on 3,418 students who reside in 14 states. Normative statistics are presented and may be used with students from 7-0 years to 18-11 years of age. Two kinds of normative data are provided for the user: percentiles and standard scores.

The TOWL can be administered in approximately 40 minutes to either a group of students or to an individual student. In total six subtests comprise the TOWL, three of which are obtained from analyzing written products produced by the student (i.e., Handwriting, Vocabulary, and Thematic Maturity). In order to obtain the written product, the student is asked to write a story based upon three stimulus pictures that depict a space migration theme. The remaining three subtests (Spelling, Style, and Word Usage) are measured using a contrived format that asks the student to respond to actual test items. Descriptions of each of these six subjects to the TOWL are presented below:

1. *Thematic Maturity*—measures the ability to write in a fashion that conveys meaning. A sample of the student's spontaneous writing is evaluated according to 20 specific criteria relating to the quality of the story written. Examples of the 20 scoring criteria: (a) writes in paragraphs, (b) gives personal names to main characters, (c) writes a story that has a definite ending, and (d) expresses some philosophic or moral theme.

2. *Vocabulary*—measures the ability to use "mature" words. In a story containing 50 or more words, the student receives one point for each word written that contains seven or more letters.

3. *Spelling*—is composed of 25 words, some of which are phonetically regular and others that can be considered "demons." The student writes words from dictation.

4. *Word Usage*—measures the pupil's ability to form tenses and plurals, use objective and nominative case, and so forth. In this subtest, students are to fill in the blanks in sentences in a traditional Cloze format.

5. *Style*—requires pupils to read sentences written without any punctuation or capitalization and rewrite them using correct stylistic forms.

6. *Handwriting*—estimates the quality of a pupil's penmanship by rating samples of his or her spontaneous writing.

Interpreting the TOWL is facilitated by plotting the individual subtests on a profile sheet and comparing the Written Language Quotient to other test scores representing various cognitive abilities. The individual subtests are plotted on a standard score scale with a mean of 10 and a standard deviation of 3. A guide for interpreting standard scores associated with the subtests is as follows:

Superior	18–20
Above average	14–17
Average	7–13
Below average	3–6
Poor	0–2

The Written Language Quotient is also a standard score providing a broad index of writing competence. The Written Language Quotient has a mean of 100 and a standard deviation of 15. A convenient guide for the interpretation of the Written Language Quotient is:

Superior	131–145
Above average	116–130
Average	85–115
Below Average	70–84
Poor	55–69

A TOWL face sheet is presented in Figure 11.1. Perusal of this face sheet indicates that the student is below average in the areas of Spelling, Word Usage, Style, and Handwriting. Her Written Language Quotient is below average with a standard score of 76. Generally, it can be said that this student is experiencing difficulty in the area of writing as indicated by her Written Language Quotient and is most notably deficient in Spelling, Word Usage, Style, and Handwriting. Significantly, she is on grade level in the cognitive and linguistic areas of Thematic Maturity and Vocabulary. Recommendations for this student would be referral for an in-depth assessment in her classroom setting as well as an error analysis of those writing components in which she is most deficient. Obviously, a well-designed and constructed test of writing can be helpful to an evaluator who desires to conduct an assessment of writing abilities.

Test of Adolescent Language. The *Test of Adolescent Language* (TOAL–2) (Hammill, Brown, Larsen, & Wiederholt, 1987) is a comprehensive test of language designed for pupils aged 12–0 to 18–5. In addition to writing, the test also assesses listening, speaking, and reading. The purposes of the TOAL–2 are essentially the same as for the *Test of Written Language.*

The two subtests that specifically measure written expression are (a) Writing/Vocabulary, in which a student reads a word and is required to write a meaningful sentence that includes the word, and (b) Writing/Grammar, which entails reading two to six sentences and then combining them into

FIGURE 11.1. TOWL Summary Sheet

TOWL

Test of Written Language

SUMMARY AND PROFILE SHEET

Donald D. Hammill
Stephen C. Larsen

Name _____ *Laurel L.*
Male _____ Female ✓

	Year	Month	Day
Date Tested	*78*	*12*	*6*
Date of Birth	*68*	*2*	*1*
Age	*10*	*10*	*5*

School *Harris Elem.* Grade *5th*
Examiner's Name *M. Bagley*
Examiner's Title *School Psychologist*

SECTION I RECORD OF SCORES

SUBTESTS	Raw Scores	%iles	Std. Scores
I Vocabulary	*9*	*50*	*10*
II Thematic Maturity	*2*	*25*	*8*
III Spelling	*2*	*5*	*5*
IV Word Usage	*8*	*9*	*6*
V Style	*1*	*2*	*4*
VI Handwriting	*3*	*9*	*6*
Sum of Standard Scores =			*39*
Written Language Quotient (WLQ) =			*76*

SECTION II OTHER TEST SCORES

NAME	DATE	STD. SCORE	TOWL EQUIV.
WISC VS	*10-78*	*95*	*95*
WISC PS	*10-78*	*100*	*100*
WISC FS	*10-78*	*96*	*96*
Reading CTBS	*5-77*	*4 (stanine)*	*93½*
Math CTBS	*5-77*	*4 (stanine)*	*93½*
Lang. CTBS	*5-77*	*3 (stanine)*	*85*
TOLD-I	*9-78*	*93*	*93*

SECTION III PROFILE OF SCORES*

Std. Scores	VOCABULARY	THEMATIC MATURITY	SPELLING	WORD USAGE	STYLE	HANDWRITING	Std. Scores	Std. Scores	TOWL WLQ	IQ GENERAL	IQ VERBAL	IQ NONVERBAL	READING	SPOKEN LANGUAGE	MATH	OTHER	Std. Scores
20							20	150									150
19							19	145									145
18							18	140									140
17							17	135									135
16							16	130									130
15							15	125									125
14							14	120									120
13							13	115									115
12							12	110									110
11							11	105									105
10	X						10	100			X						100
9							9	95	X								95
8		X					8	90		X		X	X	X			90
7							7	85								X	85
6				X		X	6	80									80
5			X				5	75	X								75
4					X		4	70									70
3							3	65									65
2							2	60									60
1							1	55									55

*In the sixth printing of the TOWL (1983) manual, the criteria for interpreting scores were changed. The guidelines restrict the average range to 8–12 for standard scores and 90–110 for quotients. Specific descriptions of the guidelines are printed in Section IV of this sheet.

From *Test of Written Language* (p. 30) by D. D. Hammill and S. C. Larsen, 1983, Austin, TX: PRO-ED. Reprinted by permission.

one sentence that retains the meanings of the original sentences. For example, a student is presented with the following three sentences:

Samantha had a picnic.
It was last Friday.
It was after school.

A permissible response to this item would be "Samantha had a picnic last Friday after school" or "Last Friday after school, Samantha had a picnic." The standard scores for the two written language subtests can be analyzed separately or combined into an overall quotient. The scores may be plotted on the cover sheet to depict strengths and weaknesses in writing ability.

The TOAL–2 was standardized on a sample of 2,628 students residing in 20 different states and three Canadian provinces. The TOAL–2 is a reliable test with adequate to above estimates of criterion related and construct validity. Since the TOAL–2 is one of the few standardized norm referenced tests that address adolescent language, it is particularly valuable in educational diagnosis and research with this age group.

Diagnostic Achievement Battery. The *Diagnostic Achievement Battery* (DAB) (Newcomer & Curtis, 1984) measures the constructs of spoken and written language and mathematics and is appropriate for use with children aged 6–0 to 14–11. The four writing subtests included in the DAB are Capitalization, Punctuation, Vocabulary, and Spelling.

The Spelling subtest is composed of 20 words that are written by the student after he or she hears them spoken in sentences. Capitalization and punctuation skills are measured in a somewhat different way than on other standardized tests. A paragraph containing a variety of errors in capitalization and punctuation is provided to the student. The student is then required to insert the correct capitals and punctuation marks. The first sentence of one paragraph is written as follows:

the handsome young man ben jones decided to apply for a job with a newspaper the daily chronicle.

The corrected version of the sentence would read

T   B J
the handsome young man, ben jones, decided to apply for a job with a
      T D C
newspaper, the daily chronicle.

Written vocabulary is assessed, similarly to the TOWL, by asking a student to write a story in response to three stimulus pictures. The three pictures represent a modified version of "The Tortoise and the Hare." Once the student has written the story, the vocabulary maturity is evaluated by counting the number of seven or more letter words written.

The four writing subtests of the DAB may be analyzed separately or can be combined to form a composite score for writing. The DAB's normative tables were based upon testing of 1,756 students located throughout the United States. The scores that are used for interpretation of the results include percentiles and standard scores. The DAB presents high levels of reliability and validity to support its claim that the instrument is highly standardized. Because this test employs innovative contrived formats for assessing punctuation and capitalization and uses a spontaneously written story as the basis for assessing vocabulary usage, it provides an excellent indicator of student performance in these writing abilities.

The Value of Standardized Testing. In summary, the use of standardized assessment procedures is an effective way to identify students who exhibit writing problems, to determine the degree to which the problem is present, and to isolate the writing components that are particularly deficient. Standardized tests permit the relatively precise measurement of various writing skills because they conform to certain criteria: set procedures for administration, objective scoring criteria, and use of a normative frame of reference for interpretation. Additionally, these tests provide, to some extent, statistics that demonstrate their reliability and validity.

Evaluators are responsible for becoming thoroughly familiar with the technical features of standardized instruments used in their environment. For example, a thorough knowledge of the type of formats used to measure different writing abilities is helpful in judging whether a particular instrument will adequately reflect the student's competency in a given writing component. It is also good practice, when attempting an in-depth standardized assessment of writing, to use instruments that measure a wide variety of writing skills, including vocabulary, ideas, and organization. Of the tests reviewed in Table 11.1, the test that best meets this criterion is the *Test of Written Language* (Hammill & Larsen, 1983). The *Test of Adolescent Language* (Hammill, Brown, Larsen, & Wiederholt, 1987) and the *Diagnostic Achievement Battery* (Newcomer & Curtis, 1984) are also recommended, since they tap writing abilities in ways that are not found in other standardized achievement tests.

NONSTANDARDIZED ASSESSMENT OF WRITING

Nonstandardized assessment of writing may also be used to determine the presence and extent of a writing problem. Specifically, these procedures may be employed to (a) identify students who are notably deficient in writing;

(b) estimate the severity of the problem; and (c) indicate the components of writing that may present particular difficulties for the student. Nonstandardized assessment relies upon the examiner's expertise and judgment as a primary means of deciding whether an individual's writing is in need of remediation. To become proficient in the use of nonstandardized assessment, evaluators should become familiar with the characteristics of this type of assessment and the steps necessary to conduct a nonstandardized writing evaluation. These points are considered in this section.

Characteristics of Nonstandardized Assessment

The presence and extent of a writing problem may be determined through the use of standardized and/or nonstandardized assessment procedures. Standardized techniques have many advantages, not the least of which is that they yield reliable and valid results. However, it should be noted that standardized procedures require regimentation in their administration and interpretation. Consequently, the flexibility permitted the examiner to use his or her judgment to select the content to be evaluated, as well as to improvise during the assessment process, is virtually nonexistent with standardized procedures.

There are numerous occasions during phases of writing evaluation when evaluators will need information that is impossible to acquire through the use of standardized procedures. Nonstandardized assessment is chosen when the information desired can be derived only from the use of relatively unstructured procedures that permit the examiner freedom to probe and change directions as needed during the evaluation. The freedom afforded the examiner through nonstandardized assessment is particularly valuable when working with special populations and in cases where intuitive judgment of the examiner is more desirable than a standard score.

Nonstandardized assessment of writing when identifying students with problems and the areas in which problems are particularly notable has several characteristics. Most important, the determination of whether or not a problem exists and in what areas it is most pronounced is accomplished through the subjective judgment of the evaluator. There is no attempt to tabulate errors or to edit a composition written by a student. Instead, the examiner attempts to generally estimate the student's proficiency in whatever aspect of writing is of interest.

Another characteristic of nonstandardized assessment is that evaluators strive to limit the subjectivity of judgment so that results obtained can be considered reasonably reliable. This can be accomplished by becoming familiar with writing associated with students at different age levels. Having an internal "data base" upon which judgments are made increases the confidence one can place in the results of nonstandardized assessment.

In summary, nonstandardized procedures are useful in the evaluation of writing ability. Use of this type of assessment permits the examiner flexibility as to how an evaluation will be conducted, as well as what aspect of writing will be assessed. Subjectivity of judgments made by evaluators is a necessary ingredient in nonstandardized assessment but must be continually monitored so that it does not unduly affect the reliability of results. Specific nonstandardized procedures appropriate for use in the evaluation of writing are discussed in the following section.

Conducting a Nonstandardized Assessment

Nonstandardized assessment, when used to determine the presence and extent of a writing problem, is dependent upon the judgment of the evaluator. In view of the general lack of "items" and specified performance criteria necessary for standardized measurement, nonstandardized assessment is necessarily subjective in nature. Obviously, it is necessary for the examiners to develop a set of "internalized norms" to guide their judgments. Hammill and Bartel (1986) suggest that when evaluating written compositions, it is wise for evaluators to take precautions to minimize undue subjectivity as well as to increase the reliability of the process.

Hammill and Bartel (1986) suggest that the first step in calibrating judgments is to standardize the topics of written pieces that are to be assessed. For example, if the writing to be evaluated is of students in grades five through eight, the examiner should select three topics (e.g., "What I Did Last Summer," "What I Would Like To Do When I Finish School," "My Most Memorable Person") and have twenty or so representative students at each grade level write a brief composition on each topic. Reading approximately 60 essays on the same subject written by students of similar grade levels is very helpful. This activity will likely provide the evaluator with a better-than-intuitive idea of what constitutes good, average, and poor writing with regard to particular topics. This set of internalized norms can then be used to estimate whether a student's writing presents a significant problem and to what degree the writing is below average relative to students at similar age and grade levels.

Nonstandardized Procedures. Once the evaluator has calibrated his or her perceptions of good and poor writing at various grade intervals, there are several ways in which nonstandardized assessment may be initiated. One method would entail the evaluator reading short essays written on a similar topic by each student in a class in which a reported problem writer is located. By using his or her set of internalized norms, the evaluator could sort the papers into three or more categories reflecting general quality. Particular attention can be directed to the writing of students reported to be deficient in this area to be sure that their compositions are categorized appropriately. Following this method of nonstandardized assessment will determine the presence and extent of a writing problem with a high degree of accuracy. In some cases, it will be impossible to secure writing samples from the classmates of suspected problem writers. When this occurs, the evaluator will read only the compositions of students who are thought to be in need of remedial assistance. Employing their knowledge of the writing of students at the same age and grade, the evaluator makes a judgment that writing quality is generally good or bad, above or below average, in need of further assessment, and so forth. As stated previously, the reliable use of such nonstandardized procedures depends upon the accuracy of an evaluator's perception of quality writing at varying grade levels. Competent evaluators will continually attempt to refine their judgments of writing ability to ensure the accurate identification of students with serious writing problems.

Nonstandardized assessment procedures may also be used to isolate the various components of writing that present particular difficulty. Components include (a) penmanship, (b) conventions (punctuation, capitalization, and spelling), (c) linguistics (vocabulary and grammar), and (d) cognition (ideas and organization). When judging a student's proficiency in the various writing abilities, the evaluator should not attempt to make corrections or revisions. To do so would distort the purpose of assessment, which is simply to determine the presence and extent of a writing problem. Instead, the evaluator should strive to make relatively quick judgments about a student's mastery of the various components of writing.

Rating Scales and Checklists. It is usually helpful for the evaluator to employ a rating scale or checklist when evaluating the adequacy of the various writing abilities. For example, a rating scale represented by the descriptions "good," "average," and "poor" would appear as follows.

	Good	Average	Poor
Handwriting			
Punctuation			
Capitalization			
Spelling			
Vocabulary			
Grammar			
Ideas			
Organization			

A checklist, when used to evaluate these same areas, requires the examiner to simply indicate whether or not a problem exists. An example of a checklist is provided below.

	Yes	No
Handwriting		
Punctuation		
Capitalization		
Spelling		
Vocabulary		
Grammar		
Ideas		
Organization		

The standardized and/or nonstandardized assessment of writing to determine the presence and extent of a problem is a necessary and valuable first step in the overall evaluation effort. Not only will this phase of assessment clearly delineate who does and does not possess a significant writing problem, but it can also direct attention to those writing components that require more in-depth analysis. The isolation of error patterns associated with each writing component is essential for instructional programming and is considered in the next chapter.

REFERENCES

American Psychological Association. (1974). *Standards for educational and psychological tests*. Washington, DC: Author.

Anastasi, A. (1982). *Psychological testing* (5th ed.). New York: Macmillan.

CTB/McGraw-Hill. (1982). *Comprehensive Tests of Basic Skills*. Monterey, CA: Author.

Hammill, D. D., & Bartel, N. R. (Eds.). (1986). *Teaching students with learning and behavior problems* (4th ed.). Austin, TX: PRO-ED.

Hammill, D. D., Brown, V., Larsen, S. C., & Wiederholt, J. L. (1987). *Test of Adolescent Language*. Austin, TX: PRO-ED.

Hammill, D. D., & Larsen, S. C. (1983). *Test of Written Language*. Austin, TX: PRO-ED.

Jastak, J., & Wilkinson, G. S. (1985). *Wide Range Achievement Test*. Wilmington, DE: Guidance Associates.

Larsen, S. C., & Hammill, D. D. (1986). *Test of Written Spelling*. Austin, TX: PRO-ED.

Newcomer, P. L., & Curtis, D. (1984). *Diagnostic Achievement Battery*. Austin, TX: PRO-ED.

Salvia, J., & Ysseldyke, J. E. (1985). *Assessment in special and remedial education* (3rd ed.). Boston: Houghton Mifflin.

12 / ASSESSING WRITING FOR INSTRUCTIONAL PURPOSES

Once the presence and extent of a writing problem has been ascertained, the evaluator may wish to further clarify the parameters of the problem. The first step in this regard often entails probing aspects of (a) the classroom environment and (b) characteristics of the student to gain insight into why the problem has occurred. This type of information is diagnostic in nature and suggests what changes need to be made to mitigate the problem. In addition, the evaluator will frequently conduct an error analysis of the student's writing to isolate the components of writing that are particularly problematic. This chapter discusses the diagnostic assessment of the instructional environment and student characteristics, as well as procedures appropriate for error analysis of writing problems.

ANALYSIS OF THE INSTRUCTIONAL ENVIRONMENT

Consideration of the instructional environment will always prove helpful, even if undertaken on only a few occasions. While the focus of the assessment conducted in the classroom will vary markedly from setting to setting, the evaluator should usually note (a) opportunities provided students to write, (b) type and quality of instruction afforded, and (c) the teacher's attitude toward and knowledge of writing. Techniques that will be used by assessment personnel when collecting information regarding instructional environment include interviews with teachers and students and observations of teacher-student interactions. Regardless of how information is obtained, insights into the workings of the classroom that pertain to writing will be valuable to the total evaluation effort.

Opportunities Provided for Writing Practice

An obvious but frequently overlooked fact is that individuals learn to write by writing. Since the complexities involved in producing viable written products cannot be mastered in any other way, all teachers should devote classroom time to writing. This is as true for first graders as it is for students in twelfth grade. If time is not provided for youngsters to practice writing in various contexts, their writing performance as measured by standardized or nonstandardized assessment procedures will probably be notably low. Ideally, writing will be an indispensable ingredient of all content areas taught within the classroom.

Teachers can integrate writing with other content areas in various ways. Wiederholt, Hammill, and Brown (1983) suggest that writing may be incorporated into science and mathematics instruction by requiring the students to write down their structured observations and explaining their calculations. In the area of social studies, students may write reports, answer questions, and participate in the creative writing of letters and stories. Field trips provide rich and varied experiences that may be used to elicit writing products. As a result of a field trip, the teacher could provide starter sentences such as "I saw at the zoo . . ." or "The fireman I spoke to told me . . ." to help initiate student's writing. Of course, the teacher will need to provide encouraging corrective feedback to writers of all ages in order to foster continued efforts in this area.

Not only must students be provided rich and varied experiences upon which to base their writing, but they must also be offered assistance before, during, and after the writing experience. For example, some classrooms provide wall charts that are of use to students in terms of handwriting and formats appropriate for structuring personal and business letters, book reports, and so forth. Teachers should also endeavor to have ample writing supplies and supplementary materials available to students. Observers will be able to quickly determine whether tangibles such as crayons, card and picture files, envelopes, extra "writing" paper, and graph paper are available for students' writing projects. Students in intermediate grades—junior and senior high school—should have ready access to dictionaries, thesauruses, books of quotations, and similar reference material to facilitate written composition. The examiner should also note whether youngsters are encouraged to work in groups for the purpose of generating ideas when producing creative works. These and other classroom characteristics will provide the evaluator with valuable knowledge regarding the opportunities provided students for writing practice.

Writing Instruction

A student's writing problem may be due, at least in part, to the type and quality of writing instruction afforded. To illustrate this point, in many classrooms the writing program's focus is on drilling students in the mechanics of spelling, memorization of vocabulary, and the rules of punctuation and capitalization. Obviously, these aspects of writing are important; but drilling is not the only way that these skills can be taught. Other methods are equally effective and certainly more fun for the students. Ideally, teachers will give equal attention to teaching ideation, organization, and other cognitive aspects of written expression.

In any event, the expectations held by teachers should be made known to students in an organized and systematic way. Wiederholt, Hammill, and Brown (1983) provide a seven-point guide for use in ascertaining the writing standards held by teachers under observation. Evaluators may use these points as a guide for observing teaching styles and/or teacher-child interactional patterns.

1. Instruction should precede or accompany evaluation.

2. Such instruction is developed slowly and carefully with the students.

3. The student is not expected to know usage and mechanics of written expression simply because they were in last year's curriculum guide.

4. Instructional opportunities in mechanics and usage arise from naturally occurring occasions and from occasions that the teacher deliberately creates within the classroom, and not from a textbook or curriculum timetable.

5. Standards are reasonable; for example, adults often disagree about the correct punctuation of a sentence or paragraph.

6. Constructive assistance is provided to help the student with rewriting before a final, evaluatable draft is handed in.

7. Content is considered separately from other factors and is also evaluated differently from those factors. (pp. 220–221)

Teacher's Attitude and Knowledge Regarding Writing

Another area needing to be assessed is the teacher's attitudes toward writing and his or her degree of knowledge in this particular area. Determination of a teacher's attitude and knowledge must be deduced rather than directly observed. A knowledgeable teacher with a positive attitude toward writing will be more successful in instilling writing proficiency in students than an instructor who is noncommittal toward writing and whose writing skills are poor. Perhaps the most valid indicator of teacher attitude is the manner in which the teacher fosters writing in the classroom and the extent of such encouragement. If writing is a common occurrence in the instructional setting and the teacher appears to enjoy interacting with students regarding their written products, the teacher's attitude toward writing is probably positive. In all likelihood, this teacher is also knowledgeable about the various components of writing and is capable of providing adequate corrective feedback.

A teacher's knowledge base is somewhat more difficult to determine than attitude. While there are many reasons that a teacher may not encourage writing in the classroom, it seems reasonable to conclude that a teacher who gives a Friday spelling test as the only writing activity during the week may not have grasped the importance of writing. Or the teacher may lack the confidence and skill to institute an active writing program. In any event, the successful teaching of written expression does require a positive attitude on the part of the teacher that underlies sincere encouragement of writing and a knowledge base that is conducive to providing expert and meaningful editorial advice.

In summary, many important factors should be considered when evaluating the adequacy of the instructional environment. Obtaining some notion as to whether writing is viewed as an important activity in the classroom is the first step to understanding why children are experiencing certain problems in writing. The teacher and his or her expectations, attitudes, and instructional style are instrumental in promoting writing proficiency and should be viewed as potential causative factors before subjecting the student's written production to detailed analysis. During the period that the classroom environment is under scrutiny, the evaluator may also wish to view and interact with the individual student in question to better understand various learner characteristics that may be impeding writing performance.

ANALYSIS OF LEARNER CHARACTERISTICS

Knowledge of the instructional environment will provide the evaluator with some specific ideas of the extent and nature of the writing programs employed within an individual classroom. An additional diagnostic focus that will likely prove beneficial is the characteristics of the student in question. While many factors may impact student performance in writing, assessment personnel should consider the following points: (a) educational history, (b) physical and intellectual ability, and (c) motivation. Each of these is discussed below.

Educational History

Important facts about a student's educational history can be obtained through a student's cumulative records, through interviews with teachers who have known the student in previous grades, and through structured conversations with the student. Cumulative records are useful to the evaluator, because they provide a year by year account of the student's grades as well as the results of standardized measures of achievement. Also, cumulative records frequently contain anecdotal reports by teachers who instructed the student in earlier years. Long periods of school absences that may have affected academic performance in general can be noted also.

Interviewing the student's previous teachers is an important source of information. During these interviews, questions should be asked about the type of writing instruction used by that teacher and his or her perceptions of how the student responded. Particular motivational devices used by these teachers to stimulate a student's interest can also be ascertained. Interviews with the child's previous teachers can also clarify anecdotal comments that have been included in the cumulative files.

Particular attention should be devoted to finding out how often the student changed schools. Students who are members of transient families may have attended as many as ten different schools by the time they are in the fifth grade. In these cases, academic performance can be affected negatively. Careful attention to these and other aspects of a student's educational history will be useful to the examiner who is attempting to determine why a student is experiencing writing problems.

Physical and Intellectual Ability

Intelligence and physical ability are two important characteristics that will influence a student's writing performance. Since writing is a highly complex skill, intelligence is of great importance when considering a child's performance. Estimates of the student's intelligence can be obtained with standardized intelligence tests. Because many factors may influence how a child scores on an intelligence test, IQ scores should always be substantiated by direct interaction with the student. In most cases, it is not difficult to determine whether a student has adequate intellectual abilities to write proficiently if the student engages in activities that connote normal intellectual development. Asking the child questions regarding hobbies, sports, or other areas of interest will provide the examiner with insights into the student's abilities to deal with complex topics. When interviewing the student for this purpose, the examiner will need to employ intuitive judgment as to whether a student has the intellectual ability to write at levels expected of his or her age and grade level.

Physical characteristics can also impact a student's writing performance (e.g., hearing and vision problems, eye-hand abilities). Obviously, if students are deficient in their ability to hear or see, proficiency in all academic areas, including writing, will be negatively affected. For example, *dysgraphia* is a neurological disorder manifested in spontaneous writing, although the ability to copy remains intact. Dysgraphia is characterized by bizarre writing patterns, including highly irregular use of vocabulary or grammar or extremely unusual ways of expressing ideas. These patterns typically are so unusual that they may readily be distinguished from writing that is poor due to lack of practice or motivation. In cases where a student is suspected of being dysgraphic, the examiner should consult a language specialist whose expertise may be required for in-depth assessment and planning a remedial system.

Motivation to Write

Many students are considered problem writers by their teachers simply because they have no motivation to write. There are many possible reasons for this lack of motivation to write. In some instances, the student may have been exposed to a teacher who conveyed to students the idea that writing is an arduous and tedious undertaking. Consequently, a student exposed to this type of instruction, particularly in the early school years, will show a disinterest in writing and will avoid writing tasks.

An unfortunate but common situation in schools today is that scholastic success is not highly prized by the student or the parents. In these instances, students may have received adequate instruction in writing, but because writing is not prized or modeled in their homes, they will show little interest in it. Evaluators who suspect that a writing problem may be due to lack of encouragement in the home can quickly confirm their suspicions through interviews with the students and parents. For example, questioning the students regarding the amount of writing done in the home and meeting with parents to determine the frequency with which students are encouraged to write in this environment will be beneficial. Interactions with parents and students will yield valuable diagnostic insight into motivation.

Obviously, many variables influence the student's writing. Some of these variables are characteristics of the student and require careful observation and interviewing strategies to pinpoint those that are of particular concern in an individual situation. Once the evaluator has obtained a reasonably complete concept of the peculiarities of the instructional environment and the characteristics of the learner, analysis of the actual written products of the student can be undertaken. This analysis will provide the evaluator with the information necessary for planning remedial strategies.

ANALYSIS OF WRITTEN PRODUCTS

The analysis of written products is undertaken to identify error patterns useful for instructional planning. This type of assessment typically focuses on specific facets of writing such as capitalization, punctuation, spelling, and vocabulary. This section discusses procedures useful for analyzing writing errors in the following areas: (a) penmanship, (b), capitalization and punctuation, (c) spelling, (d) vocabulary and grammar, and (e) ideas and organization. These components of the written product that are discussed here have been addressed in Chapter 10 under the broad headings of mechanics, conventions, linguistics, production, and cognition, respectively. The reader is encouraged to reread these discussions, if necessary, to facilitate understanding of what skills are associated with each area. Additionally, the evaluator should keep in mind that the procedures presented in this section will often require adaptation to accommodate the idiosyncrasies of particular writing samples.

Penmanship

The mechanical component of written expression refers to handwriting (i.e., penmanship). Penmanship is a crucial element in communicating thoughts through writing. If a reader cannot decipher the handwriting of an individual, regardless of how well the passage is composed, its meaning is lost (see Chapter 10).

Considerable research has been conducted on penmanship assessment. Knowledge of this research is helpful to the examiner, especially as a means of identifying common errors. Particularly noteworthy research efforts include those of Newland (1932), Pressy and Pressy (1972), and Horton (1970). These researchers recorded the quantity and quality of errors associated with the handwriting of elementary age students. By and large, their results indicate that a relatively small number of letter malformations contribute to the illegibility of students' handwriting. Newland, for example, determined that almost one-half of the illegibilities associated with handwriting of 2,381 individuals involved the letters a, e, r, and t. If teachers are familiar with the most common errors exhibited by students, they can recognize them in a student's written work. The ten most common handwriting errors, according to Newland, are:

1. Failure to close letters (e.g., a, b, f, etc.).

2. Top loops closed (i like t, e like i).

3. Looping nonlooped strokes (i like e).

4. Using straight up-strokes rather than rounded strokes (n like u, c like i).

5. End-stroke difficulty (not brought up, not brought down, not left horizontal).

6. Top short (b, d, h, k).

7. Difficulty crossing t.

8. Letters too small.

9. Closing c, h, u, w.

10. Part of letter omitted.

In addition to letter malformations, other variables require consideration when assessing penmanship. Greene and Petty (1967) mention seven common handwriting deficits that should be noted by professionals: too much slant, spacing too wide, and writing too straight, heavy, light, angular, and irregular.

When evaluating handwriting, the first task of the teacher is to secure a representative sample of the student's penmanship. The sample must not be collected when the student is fatigued and under undue pressure and should contain an adequate number of words and sentences to provide the basis for meaningful assessment. Gueron and Maier's (1983) checklist, presented in Table 12.1, directs an educator's attention to such aspects of handwriting as letter size, proportion, figures, and fluency. Directions are provided for administering the checklist and for making specific judgments about the appropriateness of responses. While this checklist yields valuable information, it does not provide specific data about particular handwriting deficits. More detailed analyses will be necessary to gather this type of information.

Professionals need to consider six areas when attempting to isolate specific deficits in penmanship: (a) letter formation, (b) spacing, (c) slant, (d) line quality, (e) letter size and alignment, and (f) fluency or rate (Zaner-Bloser, 1968; Burns, 1980).

Letter Formation.   One method for assessing letter formation is suggested by Hammill (1986). This procedure entails evaluating the way a pupil forms letters according to the criteria listed in Figure 12.1. If a student writes the letters differently than indicated in the column marked "right," the degree of perceived illegibility will increase. Hammill states, "the handwriting examples under the 'wrong' column indicate the most common errors made in the formation of the eight letters. These particular errors are often referred to in the language arts literature as the fifteen handwriting demons

FIGURE 12.1. Letter Formation

	Wrong	Right
1. a like o	*o*	*a*
2. a like u	*u*	*a*
3. a like ci	*ci*	*a*
4. b like li	*li*	*b*
5. d like cl	*cl*	*d*
6. e closed	*e*	*e*
7. h like li	*li*	*h*
8. i like e with no dot	*e*	*i*
9. m like w	*w*	*m*
10. n like u	*u*	*n*
11. o like a	*a*	*o*
12. r like i	*i*	*r*
13. r like n	*n*	*r*
14. t like l	*l*	*t*
15. t with cross above	*t*	*t*

From "Correcting Handwriting Deficiencies" by Donald D. Hammill in *Teaching Students with Learning and Behavior Problems*, 4th ed. (p. 165) by Donald D. Hammill and Nettie R. Bartel, 1986, Newton, MA: Allyn & Bacon. Reprinted by permission.

TABLE 12.1. Analysis of Handwriting Errors

Directions: Analysis of handwriting should be made on a sample of the student's written work, not from a carefully produced sample. Evaluate each task and mark in the appropriate column. Score each task "satisfactory" (1) or "unsatisfactory" (2).

I. Letter formation
   A. Capitals (score each letter 1 or 2)

A _____	G _____	M _____	S _____	Y _____
B _____	H _____	N _____	T _____	Z _____
C _____	I _____	O _____	U _____	
D _____	J _____	P _____	V _____	
E _____	K _____	Q _____	W _____	
F _____	L _____	R _____	X _____	

Total _____

Score
(1 or 2)

   B. Lowercase (score by groups)
      1. Round letters
         a. Counterclockwise
            a, c, d, g, o, q   _____
         b. Clockwise
            k, p   _____
      2. Looped letters
         a. Above line
            b, d, e, f, h, k, l   _____
         b. Below line
            f, g, j, p, q, y   _____
      3. Retraced letters
         i, u, t, u, w, y   _____
      4. Humped letters
         h, m, n, v, x, z   _____
      5. Others
         r, s, b   _____

TABLE 12.1. continued

C. Numerals (score each number 1 or 2)

1 _____	4 _____	7 _____	10–20 _____
2 _____	5 _____	8 _____	21–99 _____
3 _____	6 _____	9 _____	100–1,000 _____
			Total _____

II. Spatial relationships

Score
(1 or 2)

A. Alignment (letters on line)   _____

B. Uniform slant   _____

C. Size of letters
1. To each other   _____

2. To available space   _____

D. Space between letters   _____

E. Space between words   _____

F. Anticipation of end of line (hyphenates, moves to next line)   _____

Total _____

III. Rate of writing (letters per minute)

Score
(1 or 2)

Grade 1: 20
2: 30
3: 35
4: 45
5: 55
6: 65
7 and above: 75   _____

Scoring

	Satisfactory	Questionable	Poor
I. *Letter formation*			
A. Capitals	26	39	40+
B. Lowercase	7	10	11+
C. Numerals	12	18	19+
II. *Spatial relationships*	7	10	11+
III. *Rate of writing*	1	2	6

From *Informal Assessment in Education* by G. R. Gueron and A. S. Maier, 1983, Palo Alto, CA: Mayfield. Reprinted by permission.

and are purported to cause or contribute to most of the illegibilities in children's cursive writing" (pp. 165–166).

Another effective method of assessing individual letter formation is to use a "letter finder" (see Figure 12.2). A letter finder is simple to make by merely cutting a hole a little larger than a written letter in a piece of cardboard. Place the hole of the letter finder over each letter or numeral in a passage and place a small check next to those that are illegible. Having the student practice those letters that are consistently malformed should increase the overall readability of written sentences and paragraphs.

FIGURE 12.2. Letter Finder

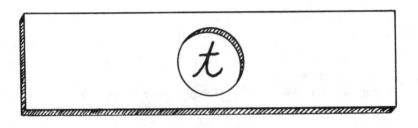

Spacing. Spacing refers to the way letters are distributed within words and how words are spaced within sentences. The criteria for effective spacing within words are subjective; however, it is apparent that uniformity should be observed and extremes avoided. The space between words in a sentence should be little more than the width of one lower case letter. An illustration of spacing errors and recommended marking is provided below.

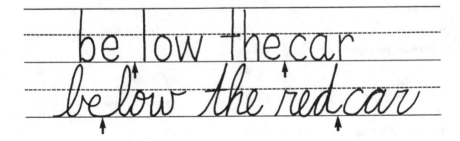

Slant. The slant of handwriting, whether printed or cursive, should be relatively uniform. The most straightforward technique for evaluating slant is to draw straight lines through individual letters. This procedure will quickly indicate those letters that markedly deviate from others or are "off slant." An example of this technique is shown below.

Line Quality. Inconsistencies in thickness or thinness of lines within a letter can have an enormous effect on legibility. The appropriateness of line quality can be ascertained quickly by using the letter finder shown in Figure 12.2. Place the hole over individual letters and mark those that are hard to read due to the quality of line. If all letters are readable, but it is apparent that inconsistent line quality is detracting from legibility, mark those letters that are too thick or too fine. Simply bringing these inconsistencies to the attention of the student may be enough to mitigate the deficit.

Letter Size and Alignment. Size and alignment can be effectively assessed by using a ruler to draw a baseline that touches the bottoms of as many letters as possible. It is important to note that the lower case letters i, u, and e should be one-fourth of a space high; d, t, and p should be one-half of a space high; and capitals and l, h, k, d, and b should be three-fourths of a space high. Lower loop letters ideally go a half space below the line.

Fluency. The fluency of handwriting becomes more important as increased writing demands are placed upon students in the school setting. A certain minimum level of speed is mandatory if a student is to accomplish a normal amount of work in class. The conventional procedure for ascertaining handwriting speed is to simply count the number of letters produced per minute. The actual rate of handwriting speed is calculated by dividing this figure by the number of minutes allowed for the writing. According to Zaner-Bloser (1968) handwriting scales, students should be writing at or above the following rates:

Grade	1	2	3	4	5	6	7
Words per Minute	25	30	38	45	50	67	74

When a professional is determining fluency of penmanship, the stimulus sentences should be given to the students, and they should be allowed to practice writing them. Typically, students are asked to write for two minutes when handwriting speed is being determined.

Capitalization and Punctuation

Educators desiring to analyze the conventional components of written language will be concerned primarily with capitalization and punctuation. These two skill areas are among those listed by Smith (1982) as critical elements of "transcription" of a written message. They are the conventions used by most literate persons when putting a message on paper which often but not always contribute to its ultimate readability. Most people who write are aware that many of the rules associated with punctuation and capitalization are arbitrary and may not enhance meaning. For example, meaning is usually not affected by whether the comma is placed inside or outside quotation marks, by whether a word is or is not capitalized, or by whether most words are spelled correctly. For this reason, some writing programs have not stressed these skills; consequently, many children do not have a firm grasp of the rules of capitalization and punctuation and, therefore, do not use them appropriately in their writing. This situation is indeed regrettable, since inappropriate capitalization and punctuation will sometimes detract from the intended meaning of the written product. Also, such errors often mark the writer as poorly educated. Therefore, when a student is experiencing problems in writing, educators should be prepared to evaluate mastery of the writing conventions.

Sequence of Capitalization and Punctuation Skills. Capitalization and punctuation need to be analyzed relatively frequently, so it is essential that the evaluator be thoroughly knowledgeable in these areas. If necessary, the examiner should study a listing of the rules of capitalization and punctuation and the approximate grade levels in which they are acquired. The sequences in which these skills are taught will vary slightly from school to school; however, the basic information presented will be consistent across basal programs. Petty and Jensen (1980) list the capitalization and punctuation skills that a student should have acquired upon completion of elementary school. This list includes skills necessary for minimal competency in these areas.

Capitalization

Grade One
1. The first word of a sentence
2. The child's first and last name
3. The name of the teacher, school, town, street
4. The word I

Grade Two
1. Items listed for the previous grade
2. The date
3. First and important words of titles of books read
4. Proper names used in children's writings
5. Titles of composition
6. Names of titles: Mr., Mrs., Ms., Miss

Grade Three
1. Items listed for previous grades
2. Proper names: month, day, common holiday
3. First and important words in titles of books, stories, poems
4. First word of salutation of informal note, as Dear
5. First word of closing of informal note, as Yours and Your friend

Grade Four
1. Items listed for previous grades
2. Names of cities and states
3. Names of organizations to which children belong, as Boy Scouts, Grade Four, and so on
4. Mother and Father, when used in place of the name
5. Local geographical names

Grade Five
1. Items listed for previous grades
2. Names of streets
3. Names of all places and persons, countries, oceans, and so on
4. Capitalization used in outlining
5. Titles when used with names, such as President Lincoln
6. Commercial trade names

Grade Six
1. Items listed for the previous grades
2. Names of the Deity and the Bible
3. First word of a quoted sentence
4. Proper adjectives showing race, nationality, and so on
5. Abbreviations of proper names and titles

Punctuation

Grade One
1. Period at the end of a sentence which tells something
2. Period after numbers in any kind of list

Grade Two
1. Items listed for the previous grade
2. Question mark at the close of a question
3. Comma after salutation of a friendly note or letter
4. Comma after closing of a friendly note or letter
5. Comma between the day of the month and the year
6. Comma between the name of a city and a state

Grade Three
1. Items listed for the previous grades
2. Periods after abbreviations
3. Period after an initial
4. Use of an apostrophe in common contractions, such as isn't, aren't
5. Commas in a list

Grade Four
1. Items listed for the previous grades
2. Apostrophe to show possession
3. Hyphen separating parts of a word divided at end of a line
4. Period following a command
5. Exclamation point at the end of a word or group of words that makes an exclamation
6. Comma setting off an appositive

      7. Colon after the salutation of a business letter
      8. Quotation marks before and after a direct quotation
      9. Comma between explanatory words and a quotation
    10. Period after Roman numerals in an outline

Grade Five
      1. Items listed for the previous grades
      2. Colon in writing time
      3. Quotation marks around the title of an article, the chapter of a book, and the title of a poem or story
      4. Underlining the title of a book

Grade Six
      1. Items listed for the previous grades
      2. Comma to set off nouns in direct address
      3. Hyphen in compound numbers
      4. Colon to set off a list
      5. Commas to set off transitional/parenthetical words (e.g., yes, no, of course, however)[1]

When evaluating capitalization and punctuation, the examiner should watch carefully for those errors most likely to occur and note when rules are used appropriately. Ferris (1971) suggests that mastery of capitalization rules includes knowing when not to capitalize. Punctuation errors in a student's writing will most commonly fall into seven categories: (a) omission of periods at the ends of sentences, (b) omission of periods in other situations (e.g., in abbreviations), (c) failure to use colons, (d) omission of question marks after interrogative sentences, (e) failure to set off nonrestrictive clauses by commas, (f) failure to set off a series by commas, and (g) failure to use commas to set off appositives.

The writing samples on which the evaluation is based can be either a student's spontaneously written composition or a piece written in response to a teacher's prepared stimulus. When using a spontaneously produced sample, the evaluator simply asks the student to write a story, theme, or letter and notes errors that are made. In this way, the student's grasp of rules can be estimated from his or her natural writing sample. The weakness of this approach is that a limited number of capitalization and punctuation rules may be actually utilized, so the examiner will not be able to assess the full range of skills in these areas. To circumvent this shortcoming, Burns (1974) suggests that the evaluator prepare a series of short sentences and/or paragraphs in which specific punctuation and capitalization rules are used.

---

[1]From *Developing Children's Language* (pp. 421–424) by W. T. Petty and J. M. Jensen, 1980, Boston: Allyn & Bacon. Copyright © 1980 by W. T. Petty and J. M. Jensen. Reprinted by permission.

The evaluator dictates the passages, and students write them down following the correct rules. The educator then evaluates the written products. In most instances, performance on the dictated sentences should closely approximate performance on the spontaneously written pieces. Frequent assessment and comparison of the student's spontaneous writing and dictated passages will indicate whether progress is being made in the correct use of capitalization and punctuation.

Table 12.2 provides samples of charts that can be used with an entire class or an individual student for the analysis and recording of punctuation and capitalization errors. Charts similar to these can help the examiner document the progress of students as well as simply providing a list of specific errors.

Spelling

Analysis of spelling errors is important in the in-depth assessment of writing ability. Prior to initiating a spelling assessment, the examiner should be cognizant of some general facts regarding spelling performance. One useful study was made by Edgington (1967), who analyzed the writing of children and youth and compiled a list of the most frequent spelling errors found in their writing. Evaluators attempting an error analysis of spelling should be especially sensitive to the following types of mistakes:

1. Addition of unneeded letters (e.g., sleevess)

2. Omissions of necessary letters (e.g., now for know)

3. Reflection of dialectical speech patterns (e.g., Imapala for Impala)

4. Reflection of mispronunciations (e.g., wabbit for rabbit)

5. Reversals of letters in an entire word (e.g., was for saw)

6. Reversal of consonant order (e.g., lcock for clock)

7. Reversal of consonant or vowel placement (e.g., peice for piece)

8. Reversal of syllables (e.g,. phonetele for telephone)

9. Phonetic spelling of nonphonetic words or parts thereof (e.g., pepl for people)

10. "Neographisms" for letter placed in a word and bears no discernible relationship with the other letters in the word (e.g., candlet for candle)

11. Varying degrees and combinations of these or other possible deficit spelling patterns. (p. 59)

Once evaluators are aware of the most common spelling errors, they may use a number of techniques to isolate specific errors. Once such tech-

TABLE 12.2. Charts Useful for the Analysis of Punctuation and Capitalization Errors

Capitalization

Pupils' Names	First word of sentence	The word "I"	Proper names	Titles	Proper adjectives	First word of quotation	Words for the deity	Appropriate abbreviations	Salutation and closing of letter	Words such as mother, father when used as a name	Trade names

Punctuation

Pupils' Names	Period	Comma	Semicolon	Colon	Quotation mark	Apostrophe	Question mark	Hyphen	Underlining

From *Diagnostic Teaching of the Language Arts* (p. 90) by C. Burns, Itasca, IL: F. E. Peacock Publishers, Inc., 1974. Reprinted by permission.

nique is analytic teaching. Generally, this approach involves: (a) observing students' efforts to spell; (b) noting particular strengths and weaknesses; (c) demonstrating alternative ways of spelling words; and (d) documenting progress as a result of the teaching efforts. Anderson and Groff (1968) outline several specific tasks that will help the teacher gain a clear perspective of a student's ability to deal with various aspects of spelling. These tasks may be viewed as variations of the more traditional spelling tests. Anderson and Groff's suggestions include asking the student to:

1. Circle or underline vowels in certain words

2. Mark long or short vowels in certain words

3. Select the words of more than one syllable

4. Mark word accent and divide into syllables

5. Write abbreviations of words

6. Alphabetize words

7. Change all single words to plurals

8. Show contraction or possession

9. Demonstrate ability to generalize from practiced to new words (p. 40)

The judicious use of these procedures will yield useful information regarding a student's particular spelling problems. As with all assessment activities, the ultimate objective is to provide appropriate data that are directly applicable to teaching. There is little doubt that specialized assessment strategies are of significant assistance to the teacher who chooses to use them.

Grammar

Perhaps the single most frequently mentioned complaint regarding students' writing is that of poor grammar. Consequently, evaluators will need to analyze errors in grammar made by students who have been referred for writing problems. The first step in the analysis is to have a systematic format for coding grammar deficits. Burns (1974) has developed a grammatical analysis system that addresses the linguistic forms of verbs, pronouns, adjectives/adverbs, and words. The chart used in this analysis and an example of errors associated with each form are presented in Table 12.3. This chart is to be used to record particular errors and/or frequency with which the error is made. Consultation of the list of common errors corresponding to the individual linguistic forms should make analysis a relatively straightforward matter. Examiners should modify the chart to reflect the needs of particular assessment situations.

Another important area to be addressed when analyzing a student's writing is the variety of syntactical forms used. Syntax refers to the order of words within a sentence and the various types of sentences used in the expression of ideas. Assessment in this area may begin by determining the type and variety of syntax employed by students in spontaneous writing. Hall (1981) suggests questions such as whether the student uses:

1. Simple sentences exclusively?

2. When and/or where phrases in simple sentences?

3. Descriptive phrases?

4. Any compound or complex sentences?

5. A variety of sentence types and lengths?

6. Correct word order in all sentences? (p. 37)

Syntactical Units. Once the educator has observed the student's writing in regard to syntax, more in-depth analysis may be warranted. Perhaps the most common technique used to estimate syntactical complexity involves analysis of Terminal-Units (Hunt, 1977). Hunt defines Terminal-Units (i.e., T-Units) as the shortest syntactically complete sentences that a passage can be divided into without creating fragments. Analyzing the types of units produced helps establish the student's competence in the linguistic component of writing. The T-unit concept has been studied extensively and has proved useful in describing some of the changes in the syntax of sentences produced by students as they grow older (Deno, Martson, & Mirkin, 1982; Siegelman, 1982; Failey, 1977; Veal, 1974).

Hunt (1977) provides an example of how to score T-Units. The following example, totally without punctuation, was written by a fourth grader:

I like the movie we saw about Moby Dick the white whale
the captain said if you can kill the white whale Moby
Dick I will give this gold to the one who can do it and
it is worth sixteen dollars they tried and tried but
while they were trying they killed a whale and used the
oil for the lamps they almost caught the white whale. (pp. 75–76)

An educator reading this passage may be confused as to where to begin scoring to determine the actual syntax. The following is a breakdown of the T-Units:

1. I like the movie we saw about Moby Dick the white whale

2. The captain said if you can kill the white whale Moby Dick I will give this gold to the one who can do it

TABLE 12.3. A Grammatical Analysis System

Analysis Chart of Grammar

Pupils' Names	Verbs				Pronouns				Adjectives/ Adverbs		Words				
	Tense form	Tense shift	Agreement	Auxiliary missing	Subject or object position	Pronoun/adjective	Antecedents	Form	Confusion	Article Comparision	Addition	Omission	Substitution	Plural	Substandard

**Sample Items and Errors
of the Analysis Chart**

Items	Example of Errors
Verbs	
1. Tense form	He seen it.
	I have come home.
	Bill come home.
2. Tense shift	Inappropriate shift between sentences.
3. Agreement	They was here.
4. Auxiliary missing	He standing there.

TABLE 12.3. continued

Pronouns	
1. Subject or preposition object	Him did it.
	With Sam and I he went.
2. Demonstrative adjective	Them books are mine.
3. Unclear antecedents	Mary and Jane were there and she saw him do it.
4. Form	Our'n, her'n
Adjectives/Adverbs	
1. Confusion (*good* for *well*)	Everything went good
2. Article (*a* for *an*)	She and I go to an store.
3. Double comparison	He is more bigger than I am.
Words	
1. Additions	This here dog is pretty.
2. Omissions	She went the movie.
3. Substitutions	Sally sat on the there.
4. Plurals	The two boy played.
5. Substandard	I ain't going there.

From *Diagnostic Teaching of the Language Arts* by P. C. Burns, Itasca, IL: F. E. Peacock Publishers, Inc., 1974. Reprinted by permission.

3. and it is worth sixteen dollars

4. they tried and tried

5. but while they were trying they killed a whale and used the oil for the lamps

6. they almost caught the white whale

It is obvious that the passage does indeed contain a number of complete sentences that could be easily overlooked if the T-Unit or some similar technique is not employed to discover them.

The adequacy of the T-Units can be judged by comparing the results of the analysis with those of children of the same age and grade level. In general, students will spontaneously increase the number of words per T-Unit as they become older. In addition, students tend to consolidate into their T-Units a larger number of embedded clauses as they mature in writing ability. Undoubtedly, use of the T-Unit concept will aid educators in determining the number and quality of syntactical structures employed in a student's writing.

Immature Connectors. There are other indicators that distinguish adequate from inadequate syntax usage. The extensive use of "immature" connectors such as *and, but,* and *so* tend to create run-on sentences. Hunt (1970; 1977) determined that fourth graders wrote sentences equal in length to those written by twelfth graders. This is because the younger children used immature connectors to join main clauses (many main clauses, in some instances). Hunt describes the run-on sentences as a stylistic rather than syntactic offense. However, these types of sentences are indicative of less mature writers and should be considered in assessment efforts. Veal (1974) discovered that the relative absence of simple connectors distinguishes good from poor writers. Supporting this point, Potter (1967) determined that the connectors *and* and *but* accounted for 91% of inadequate writers' multiple T-Unit sentences. Thus, the teacher should note the overuse of immature connectors in a student's writing and direct remedial attention toward this problem.

Sentence Combining. Another technique that can be used to evaluate a student's ability to generate syntactically mature sentences has been termed the *sentence combining* technique. Phelps-Gunn and Phelps-Terasaki (1982) state that sentence combining involves a linguistic approach to written language and entails "reforming simple expressions into more complex ones" (p. 144). This procedure does not make use of the student's spontaneous writing but, rather, is presented in a contrived format. This procedure requires the evaluator to present a student with a series of two or more sentences. The student is asked to rewrite the sentences into one sentence without losing or changing the meaning of the stimulus sentences. For example, these two sentences:

> The lions were angry.
> They began to growl.

could be written as:

> The angry lions began to growl.
> The lions began to growl because they were angry.

Either of these sentences is an acceptable combination of the two stimulus sentences.

Immature writers tend to form compound sentences using *and* or *but.* Older students and mature writers will use any number of grammatical strategies to combine sentences. Burns, Broman, and Wantling (1971) give several examples of how sentences can be combined.

1. Possessives:
   Bill has a dog.
   The dog is gentle.   Bill's dog is gentle.

2. Comparisons:
   John is strong.
   Tom is stronger.   Tom is stronger than John.

3. Relatives (such as that, which, who, whom):
   The girl played the piano.   The girl who played the
   The girl is my sister.   piano was my sister.

4. Appositives:
   Clara is my youngest sister.   Clara, my youngest sister,
   She went to California.   went to California.

5. Coordination:
   The phone rang.   The phone rang, but no
   No one answered it.   one answered it.

6. Subordination:
   The man was strong.
   He was tall.   The man was strong, tall,
   He was handsome.   and handsome.

   The wind was strong.   The leaves fell to the ground
   The leaves fell to the ground.   because (as, since, when) the
                                         wind was strong.

7. Sentence connection:
   I am not going to the movie.   I am not going to the movie;
   I am going to the dance.   however I am going to the
                                         dance.

Several sources are available to help professionals interested in using the sentence combining procedure. The activities and discussions presented in Strong (1973), Clark and Clark (1977), and Phelps-Gunn and Phelps-Terasaki (1982) provide particularly helpful insights into how sentence combining can be used as an effective assessment tool.

Semantics. An obvious linguistic feature that frequently requires analysis is semantics. Semantics refers to the intentions expressed in a written product. Most commonly, the term *semantics* is used to describe the appropriate and meaningful use of vocabulary. Obviously, individuals with well-developed vocabularies will evidence greater ease in expressing themselves than those whose vocabularies are deficient. To this point, Loban (1961) states:

. . . it seems logical that children with large and readily accessible vocabularies would find expression easier than those with limited vocabularies. Certainly vocabulary ought to be included in any examination of fluency. (p. 35)

Vocabulary

As with the assessment of syntax, the evaluation of vocabulary should begin with a perusal of the student's writing sample. Noting whether the student uses a wide variety of words, different classes of words, words of his or her own invention, literary devices (e.g., onomatopoeia), and so forth will provide some insight into the level of vocabulary usage. Obviously, the assessment of vocabulary is a necessarily subjective task, because the main bases for determining adequacy in this area are comparison with peers and general readability of the written passage. Burns (1980) recommends a simple rating system based on the educator's subjective judgment of a student's written vocabulary. In essence, this scale involves a ranking of 3 if a student's composition contains a variety of clear, precise, descriptive, vivid words that (a) appeal to the senses, (b) develop shades of meaning, (c) define action, (d) enhance word pictures, and (e) reflect effective similes and/or metaphors. A ranking of 2 is given if the words in the composition are adequately descriptive, if there is some use of similes and/or metaphors, and if there is sporadic use of vivid words or phrases. A ranking of 1 is awarded if there is little variety of word choice, very few descriptive or picture words, and common or overworked similes and metaphors. A ranking of 0 is appropriate if only trite, ineffective, dull, and monotonous words are employed.

While the assessment procedures described above will provide general estimates of vocabulary usage, evaluators will frequently wish to make a more detailed analysis of how students use words.

Serapiglia (1980) has devised a checklist for assessing oral vocabulary that can be easily used to evaluate written vocabulary as well. The assumption underlying the use of this checklist is that students must have an inherent understanding of words before the words can be produced in either oral or written language. Consequently, the checklist provides for the assessment of both understanding and production. The educator can effectively use the checklist by first finding out whether the student has a good command of certain vocabulary elements and whether the student used them in certain specified contexts. The results of this analysis should greatly enhance the professional's knowledge of the student's vocabulary development. Table 12.4 presents Serapiglia's checklist.

Ideas and Organization

The cognitive aspect of writing deals with the ability to incorporate ideas in a logical, coherent, and well-organized fashion. This aspect of written

TABLE 12.4. Checklist for Vocabulary Development

Basic Vocabulary/ Semantics	Identifies				Produces			
	Identifies persons, things, or events labeled	Comprehends words in sentences in familiar contexts	Comprehends words in sentences in unfamiliar contexts		Labels persons, things, or events	Uses words in sentences in familiar contexts	Uses words in sentences in unfamiliar contexts	
1. Body Parts								
2. Clothing								
3. Classroom Objects								
4. Action Verbs								
5. Verb Tasks								
6. Animals and Insects								
7. Outdoor Words								
8. Family Members								
9. Home Objects								
10. Meals								
11. Food and Drink								
12. Colors								
13. Adverbs								
14. Occupations								
15. Community								
16. Grooming Objects								
17. Vehicles								
18. Money								
19. Gender								
20. School								
21. Playthings								
22. Containers								
23. Days of the Week								
24. Months								
25. Emotions								
26. Numbers								
27. Celebrations and Holidays								
28. Spatial Concepts								
29. Quantitative Concepts								
30. Temporal Concepts								
31. Shapes								
32. Greetings and Polite Terms								
33. Opposites								
34. Materials								
35. Music								
36. Tools								
37. Categories								
38. Verbs of the Senses								

From "Language" by T. Serapiglia. In *Diagnosing Basic Skills* (p. 203) by K. W. Howell and J. S. Kaplan, 1980, Columbus, OH: Charles E. Merrill. Copyright 1980 by J. S. Kaplan. Reprinted by permission.

language is the most difficult for students to master, since a high level of abstraction is required. This abstraction is manifested in the ability to plan, organize, and write a passage that conveys the intended meaning of the author. Often students will need special evaluative and instructional assistance to become proficient in these skills. Regardless of how well a student can mechanically form letters, spell, write individual sentences, or use a wide variety of words, the ideas and organization must be adequate if meaning is to be conveyed. When educators are confronted with a student who has difficulty composing and organizing a written passage, they must be prepared to assess the extent of the deficiency in order to plan effective intervention strategies.

Content. Of all aspects involved in assessing writing, evaluating the content of what is written presents the most difficulties. The ideas and levels of abstraction contained in a passage are so dependent upon the language experiences, cultural background, interests, and intelligence of the student that assessment of this area requires special care and attention. Students who are having problems with the content of writing exhibit several characteristics that are all too familiar to experienced teachers. Most frequently, these students tend to be "stimulus bound," that is, the idea upon which a passage is based will be supported by only a simple listing of obvious details, use of simple declarative sentences, and/or inclusion of irrelevant details. The story will typically be quite short and contained within one paragraph, will display little evidence of originality of thought, and will tend to focus only upon the immediate personal experiences of the student. Hall (1981) summarizes the characteristics of a student experiencing problems in the content of writing:

> The limited writer lacks planning skill, which includes the ability to make relevant generalizations and to select the appropriate supporting details which would help develop the personal narrative or story. Ideas are handled in expected patterns and little, if any, originality or personal style is evident. Once the story is written, the writer feels that it is complete and does no further work on it. (p. 14)

An example of the work of a "limited" writer who is in the fifth grade is provided below. The student was asked to write a story about a camping trip.

> My dad took me camping. I took a spoon, knife, fork. I saw nice trees, bushes, leefs, and senry. I slept in a tent. I got cold. The car brok down. My dad got mad. I caught two fishes. Girls shouldn't go camping. They would get to scared. I had to go to bed early.

Reading this story indicates several features important in the assessment of the content of a written passage. The story consists of a mere listing of events experienced on the trip. No elaboration of ideas is evident. Irrelevancies appear in the mention of the car breaking down, the father becoming angry, and the idea that girls shouldn't go camping. The writing is obviously egocentric, and few descriptive details of the trip are present. No emotion is exhibited, and the story possesses little action. The sequence of activities is uneven and makes reading the passage difficult.

The weaknesses of this story become even more evident when considering the following passage, also written by a fifth grader, on the same topic.

My Family's Camping Trip

My entire family went on a camping trip last summer. The weather was warm, but we were not too uncomfortable. We planned for the trip by making a list of all the things we would be needing. I was surprised that we didn't forget too many things.

We camped by a beautiful river. My father, brother, and sister caught many fish. Some were perch and some were catfish. We ate them all. My sister and I also went swimming. The water was cold, but felt good on the hot days. One day the whole family rented a boat and went for a ride. That was really fun, especially for my baby brother.

There was one thing that made me sad. The campgrounds were very dirty. There were old pop and beer cans everywhere. The people who were there before us did not even pick up their old food containers. It took my family two hours to clean up our grounds before we could feel comfortable. I wish people would stop poluting the environment! Everyone would like to stay in a clean place, wouldn't you?

All in all we all had a very good time. We cleaned up the grounds before we left. When we were leaving, we told the manager of the camp that we would see him next summer.

The End

This story is clearly superior to the previous one for several reasons. In this case, the writer provided a number of elaborations and descriptions regarding camping, including going fishing and boating, and indicated that these activities were enjoyed by his or her family. In general, the sequence of events was clearly shown in the use of paragraphs. Clear beginning, middle, and ending sentences were employed. A title directed the reader's attention to the topic under discussion. Information appears to have been deliberately selected for inclusion rather than just incorporated in a haphazard way. A definite philosophical theme was evident in the student's concern with pollution of the environment. An attempt was made to appeal to the emotion of the readers by asking if they would like to stay in a "clean place." The personal style of the writer is quite clear, cohesive, and consistent in terms of content and purpose.

Organization. An additional aspect of the cognitive component of writing is the manner in which students arrange their ideas (i.e., organization). A student's problem in organization usually can be traced to a lack of planning. Failure to plan what is to be written can result in a lack of topic sentences, ineffective paragraph development and sequencing, and few related summaries and/or conclusions. Unless a written product is appropriately organized, its meaning will be distorted and perhaps lost entirely.

The evaluation of organizational skills is somewhat subjective, because few hard and fast rules govern the organization of written material. Hall (1981) lists nine questions that can guide the educator in evaluating a student's organizational abilities. Hall's questions can be adapted as an error analysis checklist, as shown in Table 12.5.

TABLE 12.5. Error Analysis Checklist

Organization	Yes	No
1. Did student include a title		
2. Did student have a clear introduction to story (i.e., a statement of the problem or beginning of story line)?		
3. Did student add relevant supportive information?		
4. Did student avoid gaps in organization of story line?		
5. Did student write more than one paragraph?		
6. Did student indent at beginning of paragraphs?		
7. Did student sequence information appropriately?		
8. Did student attempt any other form of sequencing of ideas other than narrative (such as spatial or logical)?		
9. Did student include only relevant information (or did student include irrelevant information)?		

Adapted from *Evaluating and Improving Written Expression*, 4th ed. (p. 36) by J. K. Hall, 1981, Boston: Allyn & Bacon. Adapted by permission of publisher.

It is obvious from considering the organizational aspects of writing that the paragraph plays a major role. While the paragraph is a familiar concept to all literate persons, many individuals have difficulty actually defining the function of a paragraph. In essence, the primary function of a well-written paragraph is to categorize and classify ideas. The ideas expressed in sentences must be sequenced in a logical fashion. Dallman (1976) specifies the knowledge and skill necessary to write effective paragraphs:

1. Knowledge of what a paragraph is.

2. Knowledge of the characteristics of a good paragraph.

3. Knowledge of the importance of the use of good paragraphs.

4. Skill in the use of topic sentences.

5. Skill in making all sentences in a paragraph contribute to its central thought.

6. Skill in relating points in the correct order.

7. Skill in using good beginning sentences.

8. Skill in using good ending sentences.

9. Skill in making transitions from one paragraph to another. (p. 306)

Although a broad listing of requirements is useful in understanding what constitutes a good paragraph, such a list does little to help the teacher analyze a student's work for apparent weaknesses. At least six elements should be considered when a student's performance in writing paragraphs is charted. The teacher should ask the following questions to outline patterns of difficulty:

1. Does the paragraph deal with only one topic?

2. Are the major points of the paragraph presented in a correct sequence?

3. Does the paragraph have a beginning sentence that adequately introduces the idea to be discussed?

4. Does the paragraph have an end sentence that concludes the idea discussed?

5. Is each new paragraph started on a new line?

6. Is the first word of the paragraph indented?

7. Are there are any run-on or fragmented sentences?

Many activities can be used to assess a student's ability to sequence related sentences within a paragraph and also to provide practice in this important skill. Hall (1981) suggests choosing a paragraph and writing each sentence from the paragraph on a separate strip of paper. Include one sentence that is totally irrelevant. For example:

> It is necessary to take good care of your teeth.
> You should brush them two times a day.
> If you cannot brush, at least rinse your mouth.
> It is fun to play in the gym.
> Use dental floss frequently.
> Visit your dentist twice a year.
> Too many sweets can cause cavities.

Mix the sentences together; then ask the student to read all the sentences, identify the irrelevant sentence, remove the irrelevant sentence, and then sequence the sentences to reorganize the paragraph. This activity will show the evaluator whether the student is capable of constructing paragraphs.

An adaptation of this technique uses common jokes, rhymes, jingles, or short fables. Write each sentence in a specific passage on a separate strip of paper. Mix the sentences together (do not mix the sentences from the separate passages) and ask the student to arrange them in logical order. Once the student has finished the task, he or she can read the series of sentences that constitutes the paragraph to see whether the sequence makes sense. Educators should have little difficulty in generating similar activities to evaluate a student's skill in organizing the content of a written passage.

REFERENCES

Anderson, P. S., & Groff, P. J. (1968). *Resource materials for teaching of spelling* (2nd ed.). Minneapolis: Burgess.

Burns, P. C. (1974). *Diagnostic teaching of the language arts.* Itasca, IL: Peacock.

Burns, P. C. (1980). *Assessment and correction of language arts difficulties.* Columbus, OH: Merrill.

Burns, P. C., Broman, B. L., & Wantling, A. L. L. (1971). *The language arts in childhood education.* Chicago: Rand McNally.

Clark, H. C., & Clark, E. V. (1977). *Psychology and language: An introduction to psycholinguistics.* New York: Harcourt Brace Jovanovich.

Dallman, M. (1976). *Teaching the language arts in the elementary school* (3rd ed.). Dubuque, IA: William C. Brown.

Deno, S. L., Martson, D., & Mirkin, P. (1982). Valid measurement procedures for continuous evaluation of written expression. *Exceptional Children, 48,* 368–370.

Edgington, R. (1967). But he spelled them right this morning. *Academic Therapy Quarterly, 3* 58–59.

Failey, L. L. (1977). *Measuring growth in college writing.* Paper presented at the annual meeting of the Conference on College Composition and Communication. Kansas City, MO (ERIC Document Reproduction Service No. ED 143-028)

Ferris, R. D. (1971). Teaching children to write. In P. Lamb (Ed.), *Guiding children's language learning.* Dubuque, IA: William C. Brown.

Greene, H., & Petty, W. (1967). *Developing language skills in the elementary school.* Boston: Allyn & Bacon.

Gueron, G. R., & Maier, A. S. (1983). *Informal assessment in education.* Palo Alto, CA: Mayfield.

Hall, J. K. (1981). *Evaluating and improving written expression.* Boston: Allyn & Bacon.

Hammill, D. D. (1986). Correcting handwriting deficiencies. In D. D. Hammill & N. Bartel (Eds.), *Teaching students with learning and behavior problems* (4th ed., pp. 155–177). Austin, TX: PRO-ED.

Horton, L. (1970). Illegibilities in the cursive handwriting of sixth graders. *Elementary School Journal, 70,* 446–450.

Hunt, K. W. (1970). Syntactic maturity in school children and adults. *Monographs of the Society for Research in Child Development, 35.*

Hunt, K. W. (1977). Early blooming and late blooming syntactic structures. In C. R. Cooper & L. Odell (Eds.), *Evaluating writing: Describing, measuring, judging* (pp. 91–104). United States: NCTE.

Loban, W. (1961). *Language ability: Grades seven, eight, and nine* (Cooperative Research Monograph No. 18). Washington, DC: U.S. Department of Health, Education and Welfare, Office of Education.

Newland, T. E. (1932). An analytical study of the development of illegibilities in handwriting from the lower grades to adulthood. *Journal of Education Research, 26,* 249–258.

Petty, W. T., & Jensen, J. M. (1980). *Developing children's language.* Boston: Allyn & Bacon.

Phelps-Gunn, T., & Phelps-Terasaki, D. (1982). *Written language instruction.* Rockville, MD: Aspen.

Potter, R. R. (1967). Sentence structure and prose quality: An exploratory study. *Research in the Teaching of English, 1,* 17–28.

Pressy, S. L., & Pressy, L. C. (1972). Analysis of 300 illegibilities in the handwriting of children and adults. *Educational Research Bulletin, 6,* 270–273.

Serapiglia, T. (1980). Language. In K. W. Howell & J. S. Kaplan (Eds.), *Diagnosing basic skills* (pp. 183–242). Columbus, OH: Charles C. Merrill.

Siegelman, L. A. (1982). *The evaluation of written products in school aged subjects.* Unpublished doctoral dissertation, University of Texas at Austin.

Smith, F. (1982). *Writing and the writer.* New York: Holt, Rinehart and Winston.

Strong, W. (1973). *Sentence combining: A composing book.* New York: Random House.

Veal, L. R. (1974). Syntactic measures and related quality in the writing of young children. *Studies in Language Education* (Report No. 8). Department of Education, University of Georgia.

Wiederholt, J. L., Hammill, D. D., & Brown, V. (1983). *The resource teacher: A guide to effective practices.* Austin, TX: PRO-ED.

Zaner-Bloser Staff. (1968). *Evaluation scale.* Columbus, OH: Zaner-Bloser.

PART V

ASSESSING
ARITHMETIC

Herbert P. Ginsburg

Many students experience difficulty with elementary arithmetic. This difficulty makes them feel inadequate as learners and impedes their progress through the mathematics curriculum. In severe cases, the difficulty prevents them from functioning adequately in everyday life situations.

The aim of these chapters is to help you conduct instructional assessments of students' difficulties with elementary arithmetic. The focus is on arithmetic rather than other branches of mathematics, because arithmetic is basic for all students, regardless of age. Instructional assessment uses both standardized tests and flexible interviews to provide information on the individual's areas of strength and weakness and also the mental activities or strategies he or she uses to do arithmetic. The result is an analytic teaching approach which suggests specific remedial procedures that can be of practical educational value in correcting arithmetic difficulty.

Instructional assessment is useful to a wide variety of professionals concerned with assessing students' arithmetic abilities—the school psychologist, the diagnostician, the writer of the Individualized Education Program (IEP), the clinical psychologist, the classroom teacher, and all others charged with the task of assisting students to overcome their difficulties. While the emphasis is on students experiencing serious problems, the techniques described in the following chapters are also useful for correcting ordinary, everyday difficulties with school arithmetic.

This text focuses on both the content and methods of assessment. It describes key arithmetic concepts and calculations that are important to assess and explains how to assess them using several techniques, ranging from standardized tests to flexible interviewing. The assessments are appropriate for students of various ages who suffer from an inability to master elementary arithmetic: elementary school children, older special education students, or even adolescents.

The first chapter provides an introduction to instructional assessment of arithmetic. It describes the goal of instructional assessment and discusses the types of questions that are useful to ask. Chapter 14 presents background information concerning the development of arithmetic thinking. Chapter 15 describes various approaches to testing and offers instruction in a major assessment tool, the technique of flexible interviewing. This material sets the stage for the concluding chapters, which discuss the substance of assessment in arithmetic: how to assess students' basic arithmetic concepts and skills and how to assess number facts, calculation, and understanding.

13 / INTRODUCTION TO THE INSTRUCTIONAL ASSESSMENT OF ARITHMETIC

This chapter provides an introduction to the instructional assessment of arithmetic. First, the chapter describes the types of students you are likely to encounter and what assessment can do for them. Second, the chapter discusses questions that are important to ask to understand and help these students as effectively as possible.

YOUR STARTING POINT AND GOAL

You begin with students who are clearly experiencing difficulties in arithmetic. The most common cases are students at the elementary school level who exhibit persistent difficulty in arithmetic and perform poorly in other subjects as well. Their grades are low, their achievement test scores are below average, and in class they seem lost. These students are not usually seriously retarded or emotionally disturbed, although they are certainly distressed about performing poorly. Frequently, these students are poor and members of minority groups. They are often considered low achievers. Some have so much difficulty that you may think they are learning disabled. Often, the teacher feels a sense of helplessness with students like these, since nothing seems to improve their performance in arithmetic.

Here is an example of the kind of student you may encounter. Butch, a member of a working class family, is in the third grade. His teacher identi-

415

fied him as having severe problems in learning elementary school arithmetic. Both his grades and achievement test scores are low, in arithmetic as well as in other school subjects. Butch is a candidate for repeating third grade. He is not retarded nor has he been identified as emotionally disturbed. Outside of the classroom, on the playground, he is lively and boisterous. His everyday behavior seems to reveal at least average intelligence. Yet in the classroom he is quiet, appears depressed, and obviously neither performs well in school arithmetic nor understands it. When asked what he is doing in school, Butch says that he is working with fractions.

Interviewer: Fractions? Can you show me what you are doing with fractions?

Butch: [writes] $8\,\overline{)\,16}$

Interviewer: OK. So what does that say?

Butch: 8, 16.

Interviewer: What do you do with it?

Butch: You add it up and put the number up there.

Interviewer: OK. What is the number?

Butch: [writes] $8\,\overline{)\,16}$ with 23 above

Obviously, Butch is doing something unusual. He seems to be trying hard but confuses fractions with division and obtains an apparently arbitrary answer to the problem. He seems to lack an understanding of school arithmetic and engages in highly irregular procedures. You may encounter low achievers or learning disabled students who are similar to Butch: They perform poorly and seem to do odd things.

Another possibility is that you will have to deal with older students who are retarded, learning disabled, or seriously emotionally disturbed. Their grades are poor, and they cannot seem to master the most elementary subject matter in arithmetic. They do not seem able to add or subtract and may even write the numbers improperly. Their school performance is clearly very inadequate, and they require considerable help.

In these and other cases, difficulty with arithmetic leads to several undesirable outcomes. First, arithmetic failure makes the student feel inadequate as a learner; this in turn may lead to deleterious effects on the student's school learning in general. Second, arithmetic failure prevents the student from advancing in the mathematics curriculum; it is hard to learn algebra, for example, if the student cannot do basic computations in arithmetic. Third, poor knowledge of arithmetic may leave the student— particularly the retarded student—poorly equipped to deal with practical problems in everyday life; it is hard to engage in successful monetary transactions if the student lacks knowledge of simple arithmetic.

Your goal is to help low achieving, learning disabled, retarded, and severely disturbed students learn to the best of their abilities, whether these are genuinely limited or have been seriously underestimated. In most cases, students should be able to master elementary arithmetic; it contains nothing so difficult that the person of normal intelligence is prevented from learning it. By contrast, in cases of mental retardation, there are severe limits on what students can learn in arithmetic. Nevertheless, some amount of learning may be possible, and your job is to facilitate it. You can help do this by conducting an *instructional assessment*. This attempts to provide an understanding of students' behavior and thought and to suggest specific remedial procedures that are of practical value in correcting arithmetic difficulties. An instructional assessment tool involves several questions, which we now discuss.

THE QUESTIONS YOU NEED TO ASK

To help students learn, you first need to understand them. You need to understand their areas of strength and weakness and obtain insight into how they think about arithmetic. To achieve this kind of understanding, you need to ask several questions, including the following: (a) How severe is the student's problem? (b) In what areas does the student experience difficulties and strengths? (c) What kind of thinking is responsible for the student's difficulties and strengths? and (d) Can the student learn to overcome the difficulties? Consider each in turn.

How Severe Is the Student's Problem?

When we encounter a student who experiences difficulty in arithmetic, we want first to determine the severity of the problem. How badly is the student doing in his or her arithmetic work? Is the student extremely far behind or only moderately far behind? Questions like these involve an implicit comparison of the student with peers. The questions are *normative*, since they ask how the student's level of work compares with the norms established by his or her peers.

In the case of Butch, for example, we need to know whether the inability to do fractions and division is normal for his grade level or represents a real deficit in achievement. This involves comparing Butch with typical third graders. If typical third graders can do at least elementary forms of these operations, then Butch's achievement is slow; if they cannot, then perhaps Butch's behavior is typical.

What Are the Student's Areas of Difficulty and Strength?

A second type of question involves the student's areas of difficulty and strength: In what area does the student exhibit real weaknesses? Does the student give evidence of any areas of strength? We ask questions like these to identify the areas of instruction in which the student needs help. Does the student need extra instruction in basic counting skills or in fundamental concepts of arithmetic like equality?

In the case of Butch, the weaknesses are more apparent than the strengths. He seems confused about what fractions are and appears unable to calculate a simple division problem. Are there no strengths? Most students are strong in at least some area. Other portions of the interview showed that Butch was no exception. He could correctly write and solve simple addition problems like $15 + 7$ and simple multiplication problems like 5×7. A good instructional assessment provides a comprehensive picture of strengths and weaknesses like these.

What Kind of Thinking Does the Student Use?

Suppose we know that the student is generally doing poorly relative to his or her peers and that performance is characterized by a particular pattern of strengths and weaknesses. For example, we may find out that Butch is generally performing two years behind his peers, that he is extremely deficient in division, but that he has minimal strengths in addition and multiplication. The next set of questions deals with *why* the student does poorly in some areas and well in others. What kinds of thinking are responsible for the errors and for the successes? How does he go about solving the problems? Questions like these are sometimes called *cognitive*, since they attempt to identify the mental strategies underlying the student's strengths and weaknesses. The next excerpt from the interview with Butch gives insight into why he has trouble with division and why he has some strength in addition.

Recall that Butch had just written

$$\frac{23}{8 \overline{)\ 16}}$$

Interviewer: How did you do that?
Butch: I went, 16, 17, 18, 19, 20, 21, 22, 23. I added from 16.

The question "How did you do that?" revealed that Butch got the answer 23 just as he earlier said he did: "You add them up." He added by counting up from the larger number. In doing this, he made an execution error in counting and therefore ended up with the answer 23 instead of 24.

In this brief excerpt, the interviewer got preliminary information about Butch's thinking—his understanding of arithmetic and the strategies he uses to deal with it. On the negative side, Butch used the word *fractions* but wrote a division problem, and he attempted to solve the division problem by adding. This shows that he has particular problems in understanding the spoken and written symbolism of arithmetic. He does not know what the word *fractions* means, and he seems to believe that addition should be written as division. On the positive side, he can do a simple addition calculation, even though he makes a minor mistake in the counting procedure. The apparently bizarre answer 23 makes some sense if we understand how Butch conceived the "division" problem—for him, it was an addition problem. The excerpt thus provides intriguing—although obviously incomplete—insights into Butch's thinking.

Why is it useful to ask questions about how the student solves arithmetic problems? If you can get information about how the student solves problems and why he or she makes mistakes, you can recommend instructional procedures that will capitalize on existing strengths and remove sources of the difficulty. For example, with Butch, you might recommend instruction explicitly designed to remove confusion concerning symbolism, and you might also propose that instruction make use of his informal understanding of addition as counting. The more detailed information we have about the immediate reasons for students' failure, the more effectively can we help them.

Note that our focus is on students' *thinking* or *strategies* as the immediate cause of academic difficulty, not on other possible causes like emotional problems. This kind of focus is useful, because academic difficulties sometimes may cause emotional conflicts rather than the other way around. Thus, if you can help students improve their understanding and strategies, the emotional disturbance may take care of itself. In brief, we focus on thinking or mental strategies as the immediate cause of the student's difficulties, since this seems to be the most practical approach to the solution of educational problems. If the focus on thinking does not work, then you may find it useful to delve into the student's emotional problems or to seek further professional assistance for the student.

Can the Student Learn to Overcome Arithmetic Difficulties?

A final set of questions, and perhaps the most important, involves the student's ability to learn. It does you little good to understand why Butch makes errors in division and to discover his counting strategies for addition if you cannot help him get over the errors and use his existing strategies to learn something new. So you need to ask: What can the student learn? Can Butch learn to use the proper symbolism for addition? Can he learn the standard algorithm for adding? Can he learn new techniques for dealing with fractions?

You can begin your inquiry into learning with the assumption that almost all students can learn a significant amount of mathematics. There is no evidence that any group of biologically "normal" students—that is, students without clear neurological impairment—cannot learn a significant amount, regardless of such factors as social class or cultural background. Under the right conditions, almost all students can be taught simple arithmetic and even higher forms of mathematics. This proposition may be problematical only in the case of retarded students or some—but not all—students diagnosed as learning disabled. Yet while these students may not learn as much as or in the same way as other students, they seem capable of learning something. For almost all students, the question is not *whether* learning can take place but *how much* and *under what conditions*.

HOW TO ANSWER YOUR QUESTIONS

Our goal in instructional assessment is to improve the learning of students who experience difficulty in arithmetic. Achieving this goal first requires asking sound questions concerning severity of the student's problem, areas of weakness and strength, thinking, and potential for learning. Then it requires using penetrating assessment techniques to answer the questions. The following chapters are designed to help you do both of these things—to ask the right questions and then go about answering them.

To ask sound questions, you need to know what to look for. This means knowing something about the psychology of students' arithmetic, particularly the thought processes involved in doing arithmetic and how they develop. Chapter 14 provides background information on the psychology of arithmetic. It shows how, even before entering school, children spontaneously develop some key arithmetic concepts and skills, and it shows how students use this informal knowledge to assimilate the formal arithmetic taught in school. If you understand the psychology of arithmetic as described in Chapter 14, then you will have the background knowledge for asking sound questions about students' learning difficulties in school.

Of course, this background knowledge is not sufficient in itself. You also need to understand the major techniques used in the instructional assessment of arithmetic. Chapter 15 provides an overview of these assessment techniques, including tests and flexible interviewing. It shows you what each of these procedures is good for and places special emphasis on describing methods for flexible interviewing.

After you have acquired background knowledge concerning the psychology of arithmetic and techniques of assessment, you will be ready to learn to conduct focused instructional assessments. Chapter 16 gives detailed information concerning the assessing of early arithmetic concepts and skills. Finally, Chapter 17 deals with more advanced arithmetic abilities in the areas of number facts, calculation, and understanding.

14 / THE DEVELOPMENT OF ARITHMETIC THINKING

This chapter provides an overview of the development of arithmetic thinking from infancy through the elementary school years. (See Ginsburg, 1982, for a more complete account.) The chapter discusses key aspects of both *informal mathematical thinking*—what children learn about arithmetic outside of school—and *formal mathematical thinking*—what they understand of the arithmetic taught in school.

This background information is intended to accomplish three purposes. First, it will provide an appreciation of the normal development of mathematical thinking, so that you will have a standard by which to judge the students you encounter. Second, it will help you understand and conduct the intensive assessments of specific concepts and skills discussed in chapters 16 and 17. Third, it will help you formulate your own questions concerning students' arithmetic and develop your own tasks for assessing key concepts and skills.

INFORMAL MATHEMATICAL THINKING

Recent work in psychology has revealed some surprises about young children. One is that informal mathematical thinking begins as early as infancy and develops throughout the preschool years. Obviously, the infant or the preschooler does not understand mathematics in the same way that adults do. Understanding at early ages is very practical and intuitive; it is not formulated with any precision and involves virtually no written symbolism. This informal mathematical thinking is full of contradictions: Sometimes the young child is capable of intellectual activities that we adults think are impossible for the child to do; and sometimes the child may have difficulty with what we consider to be the most elementary of tasks. The unexpected strengths and weaknesses of the young child's mathematical mind seldom fail to surprise us. Consider first the remarkable fact that informal mathematical thinking begins in infancy. After that, we will review the development in preschoolers of key informal concepts.

Infancy

The world of infants is filled with quantity. Infants lie in cribs with a large number of bars. Some of their toys are bigger than others, some are identical, and others are equal in size. If they push a toy, it moves; and the harder they push, the harder it moves. Their parents go into the room and out of it over and over again. The stories read to them are often about number and size: *The Three Little Pigs* and *Goldilocks and the Three Bears* (about big, medium, and small). Infants thus have ample opportunity to learn about number, repetition, regularity, quantity, size, and the like.

While quantity surrounds infants, do they notice any of it? And if they do, to what aspects are they sensitive? Recent research (Starkey & Cooper, 1980) shows that young infants can tell the difference between 2 events and 3; they can discriminate among small numbers. Piaget (1952) reports that at 9 months his son, Laurent, ". . . imitates the sounds which he knows how to make spontaneously. I say *papa* to him, he replies *papa* or *baba*. When I say *papa-papa* he replies *apapa* or *ababa*. When I say *papa papa papapa* he replies *papapapa*" (p. 141). These apparently trivial imitations indicate a primitive appreciation of quantity. They show that Laurent was able to hear the differences among the different numbers of sounds his father made (otherwise, how could he have imitated them?). The infant also made strings of sounds that roughly corresponded in number to Piaget's. This seems a rather large accomplishment for a 9 month old! Furthermore, infants' concern with quantity is reflected in their earliest words. One of the first words for many babies is "more" or " 'nother." Babies find quantity so important that they must describe it in words.

The Preschool Years

From about 2 to 5 years of age, young children develop many informal mathematical concepts and skills (Fuson & Hall, 1983). These are called *informal*, since they need not be learned in the context of formal schooling.

Instead, children seem to acquire these concepts and skills in various informal ways: through imitation of adults; through watching programs like *Sesame Street*; through informal instruction by adults, siblings, and peers; and through spontaneous interaction with the environment. Some aspects of informal mathematics—for example, the infant's ability to discriminate among numbers of events, as described above—may even be innate. Also, informal mathematics is extremely widespread across social classes, racial groups, and cultures. In Western societies, black and white children—both lower and middle class—seem to possess important elements of informal mathematical thinking (Ginsburg & Russell, 1981). In traditional African societies, even illiterate children seem to possess key informal skills (Ginsburg, Posner, & Russell, 1981). It is indeed remarkable that almost all children and adults seem to have the rudiments of informal mathematics. These rudiments include the concepts of *more, conservation, counting, enumeration, addition,* and *subtraction.* Consider each in turn.

The Notion of More. Among the earliest informal concepts is the notion of *more.* If you present a young child with two randomly arranged collections of objects like pennies and ask which has more, the child will be accurate, even when as many as 12 or 13 objects are in each collection. To verify the child's sensitivity to more, let the child choose between two bowls of ice cream or two collections of M&Ms. Do you think the child will voluntarily choose the one with less? By 4 or 5 years, children know that the spoken word "seven" indicates a larger number than the word "three" (Ginsburg & Russell, 1981). As time goes on, children refine such elementary concepts of more into an intuitive number line (Resnick, 1983). Using this number line, children know for example that 2 and 8 are farther apart than 8 and 10. Children have a feel for which numbers are larger than others and which are close to one another. Of course, this knowledge is typically informal and intuitive; children cannot talk about the number line in formal, adult terms.

Conservation. Another informal concept is *conservation,* discovered by Jean Piaget, the well-known Swiss psychologist, whose major contribution was to show that children's minds often work differently from our own. (For an introduction to Piaget's theory, see Ginsburg and Opper, 1979.) In a conservation problem, the interviewer begins by asking an individual child to construct two collections of objects having the "same number" of items. Thus, the child may be told, "I'm going to put out this row of dolls. Now, what I'd like you to do is put out just as many hats as there are dolls—the same number of hats as dolls." The interviewer typically puts out 6 or 7 objects, and most children by the age of 4 or 5 construct a row identical in number and physical appearance. Then, as the child watches, the interviewer makes the line of dolls longer than the line of hats. That is, the interviewer rearranges one of the collections so that it looks different from the other but its number is unchanged. The question is whether the child recognizes that the equivalence between the two sets is *conserved* despite the irrelevant change in appearance. Surprisingly, the young child maintains that there is no longer the same number in both collections: The longer one has more. Moreover, even if the child counts each of the rows accurately, he or she still maintains that the longer row has more! Piaget concludes that, for young children, equivalence is based on mere physical appearance, not a deeper concept of number. The child's concept of equivalence is not the same as the adult's. The key point is not that children get wrong answers but that they sometimes approach the world in a manner which is different from ours. To teach them, we must learn to understand their distinctive perspectives.

Counting. Among the most important informal skills is *counting*. As early as 2 or 3 years of age, young children learn the counting words "one, two, three . . ." They hear these number words in stories and on popular television programs like *Sesame Street* and *Mr. Rogers*. Children try to learn the counting words themselves but experience considerable difficulty. One problem is that there seem to be an awful lot of words like these. If you learn to say "one, two, three," someone will always come along and say "four, five, six." The end is never in sight. Also, people are very fussy about the way you say the words. You have to say "four, five, six"; for some reason, it is not OK to say "four, six, five."

So young children are faced with two important problems with respect to the counting words: There are a lot of them to learn, and they must be learned in a certain order. After hearing the numbers over and over again, children gradually learn to see patterns in the apparent chaos of number words. They learn that the initial counting words follow one another in an arbitrary order, which must simply be memorized. There is no reason "three" comes after "two": It just does, and the child has to learn it. Parents try to make the task simpler by imposing on it some rhyme (if not reason): "One, two, buckle my shoe . . . ," but it takes children a long time to learn the first 12 or so number words.

After this, there are of course many more number words to learn, but, in a paradoxical way, learning the bigger number is easier than memorizing the smaller ones. This is because the larger numbers can be constructed by rule; they do not need to be memorized like the smaller ones. For example, children learn that you create the tens numbers (20, 30, etc.) by modifying the units. That children are in fact following a rule like this when creating numbers is indicated by amusing mistakes like "two-ty" for "twenty," "three-ty" for "thirty," and so forth. Children also learn that you generate big numbers by adding on the units to the tens numbers. Thus, after fifty (or "five-ty"), you simply add on the numbers from one to nine. Evidence for use of this rule is again provided by mistakes like "fifty-ten," "fifty-eleven," and so forth. This kind of rule learning extends into the school years. Children continue to memorize a few words ("thousand," "million," etc.) and learn rules to combine these with other numbers. All this is relatively easy: The hardest task has been accomplished by the 4 year old who discovered that patterns underlie number words, and rules can be used to generate them.

Enumeration. Next, children have to learn *enumeration*—how numbers are used to count things. In the natural environment, children sometimes see their parents pointing to things as they say the number words. They poke a finger at a block and say "one," at another block and say "two," and so forth. What's the secret to doing this? If you just say "one, two, three," to as high a number as you know, you are apt to be wrong. Perhaps the secret is poking the finger. How should that be done? Young children have to struggle with the problem of attaching the numbers they can already say to the objects they can see.

Initially, children's enumeration is inconsistent. The first time they count objects, they get one answer; the next time, another. They do not know which answer is right or may even think that both are! Why should enumeration cause so much trouble? The problem is not faulty knowledge of the number words: Often children can *say* the words perfectly well up to a reasonable limit but cannot *count* a set of objects whose number is well below that limit. They enumerate incorrectly, because they skip objects or count others twice. To get the right answer, children must learn to count each member of the collection once and only once; skipping and double counting are not allowed. They must also learn to make a one-to-one correspondence between each number word and each thing. The word "one" has to go with this object and "two" with that one. "One" cannot go with both. Each object must be assigned one and only one number word.

It takes many years for children to learn simple enumeration. One reason for their difficulty is that they lack a systematic plan for making sure that a particular object has been considered once and only once. Instead, when counting things, they proceed in a haphazard manner, touching one object and then another in a random fashion. Since there is so much to keep in mind at the same time, they frequently forget and, therefore, count some things twice and some not at all. As they grow older, children learn various tricks that make enumeration easier. One trick is simply to push an object aside after it is counted. This reduces the load on memory by eliminating the objects already counted. But this works only with small, moveable objects, so other tricks are useful, too. One is to count systematically from left to right or from top to bottom, so as to avoid skipping objects. Another is to count objects in convenient groups of 2 or 5 or 10; this reduces the sheer labor of counting. All these tricks are so obvious to you, but they are major discoveries for children. There is a lesson in this: You can't take anything for granted about children's thinking; they may lack basic knowledge that you assume is available to all.

Addition and Subtraction. Many ordinary experiences in the natural environment afford preschool children the opportunity to develop intuitions about addition and subtraction. The young child eats up the food on his or her plate, and the parents give her or him more; she has a toy, and a sister takes it away. Adding and subtracting are vital skills for young children. Obviously, they prefer addition to subtraction: They generally like to get things, not lose them. While this preference indicates that they see a difference between the two, how much do they understand of each? Some interesting research by Brush (1978) sheds light on this issue.

Suppose that a young child is shown two identical rows of eight coins each and judges that they have the same number. The interviewer places each collection in a separate box, so the child can no longer see the coins. Next, as the child watches, the interviewer takes a new coin and places it in one of the boxes. Which box has more coins, or do they both still have the same number? Notice what the problem is from the child's point of view. The child knows at the outset that both boxes contain the same number of coins, although they cannot be seen. The only visible event is the placing of a new coin in a box. The question, therefore, is whether the child realizes that the addition of an object to one of two equal sets makes that set have more than the other. Brush's research shows that almost all children at ages 4 and 5 have no difficulty with this problem or with an analogous subtraction problem (taking one coin from a box). These little experiments are easy to do. Try them out yourself.

Some elegant research by Gelman (1975, 1980), a pioneer in this area, shows that children as young as 2 or 3 years of age combine their concepts of addition and subtraction with their counting skills. The result is far more competence than we would ordinarily expect. Here is an example from Gelman's work: Vivian, a preschooler typical of her age, was shown one plate with 3 toy mice on it and another plate with 5. The plates were hidden from view, and the interviewer surreptitiously removed 2 mice from the 5 mouse plate, so each plate then had 3. The plates were again shown to Vivian. The question was: How would the child interpret the secret subtraction of 2 mice? She saw first that one plate had 3, then she looked at the other.

Vivian: Wait. There's 1, 2, 3. It has 3.
Interviewer: What happened?
Vivian: Must have disappeared.
Interviewer: What?
Vivian: The other mouses.
Interviewer: Where did they disappear from?

Vivian: One was here and one was here. There was one there, one there, one there, one there, one there. This one is three now, but before it was five.

Interviewer: What would you need to fix it?

Vivian: I'm not really sure because my brother is real big and he could tell.

Interviewer: What do you think he would need?

Vivian: Well, I don't know. Some things have to come back.
[The interviewer gave Vivian some objects including four mice. Vivian put all four mice on the plate.]

Vivian: There. Now there's 1, 2, 3, 4, 5, 6, 7. No, I'll take these two off and we'll see how many are left.

Vivian's approach to this apparently simple task was complex, illustrating several intellectual processes. She *remembered* that the plates she had seen contained 3 and 5 mice, respectively. She *saw* that there were fewer toys on one plate than there had been before—some mice had "disappeared." She *knew* how many had disappeared. She knew that the subtraction could be undone by an addition—that is, she *understood* something of the relationship between addition and subtraction. And finally, she *counted* to perform the necessary addition. So the preschooler does all this mental work to deal with subtraction in the real world!

During the years from 2 to 5 or 6, children develop counting methods for dealing with problems that we would solve by addition and subtraction. Their solutions involve at least these two steps. First, they have to interpret the problem: They have to decide whether the situation demands adding things together or taking some things away. Second, they have to implement what they have decided to do. If they think the problem requires adding 2 and 3, they have to figure out a way to get the result; after all, at this age they usually do not know the number facts.

By 5 years of age, most children interpret simple addition and subtraction problems correctly. They can deal with concrete situations like, "Here are 2 cookies, and here are 3 cookies. How many do I have altogether?" Or, "Here are 5 marbles; if I take away 2, how many will be left?" Moreover, children at this age usually solve problems of this type (involving small numbers) correctly. Their method is usually to count the objects one by one, starting with the first. After a period of time, they spontaneously learn to streamline their method: They count on from the larger number. Thus, given the addition problem above, the young child says: "Three cookies and 2 cookies is 3, 4, 5." Often, children use finger counting to solve addition and subtraction problems. This is almost a universal method, spontaneously invented by children all over the world.

Summary

In the years before schooling typically begins, children develop considerable knowledge of elementary arithmetic. They have notions of more and less, equivalence, and addition and subtraction. These concepts are sometimes like the adult's and sometimes take a distinctive form. Children learn rules for generating the counting numbers and strategies for enumeration. They develop techniques for calculation—for adding and subtracting real objects. One result is that children generally develop a body of mathematical knowledge that adults would usually not expect children to grasp. Another result is that virtually all children possess a foundation on which they can build a more formal and precise understanding of mathematics. They can assimilate what is taught in school into their informal knowledge.

FORMAL MATHEMATICAL THINKING

In school, students are instructed in formal, written mathematics with explicit rules, principles, and procedures. They study conventions, number facts, calculations, and concepts. Sometimes children learn this material as it is taught. But often, as they interpret what the school presents within the framework of what they already know, students develop distinctive forms of mathematical knowledge. They learn both informal tricks that result in successful calculation and systematic rules that result in incorrect calculation. This section discusses students' methods of doing school mathematics. It explains both how they succeed and how they fail in mastering (a) conventions, (b) number facts, (c) calculations, and (d) concepts.

Conventions

To understand formal mathematics, the student must be familiar with certain elementary conventions concerning the reading and writing of numbers. These include memorizing the digits, place value, and alignment.

Memorizing Digits. At first, students have to memorize the first ten digits, from 0 to 9. These are completely arbitrary and must be learned by rote. There is no reason that the written number *4* should stand for the spoken number "four" or why you should say the word "five" when you see the symbol *5*. This is all a matter of convention. We could just as well write "six" as *8* or *. So students have to learn through memorization that *1* represents "one," *2* represents "two," and so forth. In a few years, virtually all students accomplish this, although along the way they sometimes make reversal errors—like ⌐ for 7. These reversals are very common in the writing of young students around 5 or 6 years of age and may even persist after that time. There is generally no reason for concern: The reversals usually drop out without special instruction.

Place Value. Once students overcome the arbitrariness of the first ten digits, they encounter a more meaningful system, which must be learned in a different way. The written numbers above 9 are organized by place value. We write our numbers—like 2,345—so that a digit acquires its value by virtue of its left to right location. The 5 on the extreme right stands for five ones; the 4 for 4 tens; the 3 for 3 hundreds; the 2 for 2 thousands. We could say the number as "two thousand, three hundred, forty (four tens), and five (ones)." We write the number in shorter and more convenient form, because we can drop out explicit reference to thousands and hundreds and merely represent these by left-right position. Obviously, students cannot memorize all of the written numbers above 9. Just as students learn rules for saying larger numbers, they must learn rules for reading and writing them. Thus, to write "four thousand three hundred and eighty four," the student must know the necessary rules—the place value system—for constructing hundreds, thousands, and so on.

It takes several years for students to master the place value system. In the process, they often make the mistake of writing numbers the same way they say them. Thus, the student may write "twenty three" as *203*. Obviously, students have not been taught to write numbers like this. The errors are generated by a system of rules invented by the students themselves. These rules base writing on the spoken language, not the place value system. Since you say "twenty three," you write 203 as well. Children in the first grade often make errors of this sort (Ginsburg, 1982). Older students make the same type of error with larger numbers, as when they write "four hundred thirty three" as 400303.

Alignment. Children also have difficulty with conventions involving the alignment of numbers for written calculations. For example, given the problem, "Write down and solve: How much is 23 + 7?" students may make alignment errors like the following:

$$\begin{array}{r} 23 \\ +7 \\ \hline \end{array}$$

When addends with uneven numbers of digits are involved, students often line up all numbers to the left. Such errors may imply a lack of understanding of place value. The student may not realize that units have to be added to units. In any event, misalignment often leads to absurd answers—sums that are drastically incorrect.

Number Facts

Among the earliest acquisitions in the learning of school mathematics are the number facts. Children must know that 2 and 2 are 4 or that 5 times 3 are 15. Having the number facts under control is important for an obvious reason: It makes calculation easier. Knowing the number facts also facilitates the understanding of calculation. If students are not bogged down in details of figuring, they may have the opportunity to notice important general principles, like the fact that in addition the sum must be larger than either addend. Learning the number facts is a far more complex process than we usually realize. Three separate types of learning seem to be involved: counting, remembering, and reasoning (Baroody & Ginsburg, 1982).

Counting. Most likely, the earliest method the student uses for obtaining the number facts is some variant of counting. Thus, faced with a simple problem like 3 + 2, the student obtains the answer by counting, perhaps using objects if they are available, perhaps fingers, or perhaps counting in his or her head. Incorrect number facts may result from faulty use of the counting method. Students may count forward too far, take away too much, forget the amount to be counted on, or lose track of where they started.

Remembering. A second method for obtaining the number facts is simply to remember them in a rote fashion. Thus, the student knows, or remembers, that 6 × 6 is 36 or that 21 divided by 3 is 7, probably because of repeated drill. But memory may break down: Sometimes, the student may simply forget that 3 + 2 is 5 and falsely remember that the sum is 7. On other occasions, the student may confuse addition with multiplication and conclude that 3 + 2 is 6.

Reasoning. A third method for knowing the number facts is rather subtle. It involves reasoning. Suppose that through drill the student memorizes that 4 + 2 is 6. Suppose, too, that the student knows that the order of adding numbers makes no difference—that is, the principle of commutativity holds. When Laura encounters the new addition problem 2 + 4, she may simply deduce from knowledge of 4 + 2 and of the commutativity principle that 2 + 4 must also be 6. She does not count; she does not remember 2 + 4; she reasons that 2 + 4 is 6. This process of reasoning can go wrong, too. The student may not know the relevant principle and hence cannot apply it; or the student may know the principle, but not think of applying it. In either case, the student either gets the number fact problem wrong or has to resort to a less efficient procedure.

In brief, students obtain the number facts by counting, by remembering them in a rote fashion, or by reasoning about them. Any of these processes may break down. Students may have poor knowledge of elementary number facts because they make mistakes in counting, their memory for number facts is faulty, or they do not reason adequately about number facts.

Calculation

Knowledge of the elementary conventions of reading and writing numbers and of the basic number facts permits students to learn written calculation. Some students gradually develop successful methods for calculation; other students are less fortunate. Current research teaches us to focus not only on right and wrong answers but on the mental processes students use to obtain the answers. These processes or strategies may take unexpected forms, and knowledge of them can help to suggest and direct remedial efforts. Consider first the student's successful methods and then the unsuccessful ones.

Successful Methods. Successful methods take several forms. The two major types are algorithms and invented procedures.

Algorithms. Sometimes students use the standard school method, or algorithm, as it was taught. Thus, students usually learn to perform column addition by the carrying or regrouping method. Jane does 48 + 14 by saying to herself: "8 plus 4 is 12, put down the 2, carry the 1; 1 plus 4 is 5, 5 plus 1 is 6; put down the 6; so the answer is 62." The standard school algorithm involves carrying out a series of operations (combining the elementary number facts) in a specified sequence. Jane must (a) remember that 8 and 4 is 12; (b) write down the units digit, 2; (c) carry the tens digit, 1; (d) add all the tens digits; and (e) write down the result in the tens column. This sequence of activities is what we mean by executing the standard algorithm.

Invented procedures. Often students do not use the standard algorithm taught in school. Some students solve computational problems by means of invented procedures—that is, methods that are at least partially invented by the students themselves and that in some way draw on or modify what is taught in school (Ginsburg, 1982; Groen & Resnick, 1977). The simplest invented procedure is probably the inclusion of counting with the standard algorithm. Suppose Mickey is given Jane's problem (48 + 14) but, unlike her, does not remember that 8 + 4 is 12. He gets around this difficulty by counting on his fingers. He says to himself: "8 plus 4 is 8, 9, 10, 11, 12; put down the 2, carry the 1; then I go, 4, 5, 6; put down the 6." Mickey's procedure is not the standard algorithm as taught in class. Rather, using his past experience, he has developed a minor modification of the standard algorithm—an invented procedure.

Other invented procedures are more elaborate and sophisticated. For example, given the problem 42 + 33, Susie proceeds as follows: "I know that 40 plus 30 is 70, because 4 plus 3 is 7; and then 2 and 3 is 5; so the answer is 75." Susie recasts the written problem in a simpler form, which can be solved through the use of familiar facts. Note that implicit in the simplification method is the notion that numbers can be broken down into tens and units; this is an intuitive understanding of the base ten system. Simplification is, of course, not limited to children. Many adults use it when pencil and paper are not available, and particularly when quick estimates need to be made.

Some students rely heavily on mental calculation and prefer to avoid written work entirely. They sometimes manage an effective solution on a mental level. Thus, many students can solve addition problems, without paper and pencil, by counting on from the larger number ("23 plus 13 is 23, 24, 25, . . . 36"). Research has shown that students who normally perform poorly with paper and pencil are sometimes capable of impressive feats of mental calculation (Ginsburg, 1982). Indeed, cross-cultural research (Petitto & Ginsburg, 1982) reveals that in some African cultures even individuals who are completely unschooled (hence, illiterate) are capable of complex and accurate forms of mental calculation.

The research on invented procedures and mental calculation shows that students who calculate poorly may nevertheless possess informal skills that offer considerable potential for sound work in arithmetic. Even though such students may not be able to execute the standard algorithm accurately, they may be capable of various informal procedures, which can serve as the foundation for instruction in more orthodox methods of calculation. For example, the simplification method described above implicitly conceptualizes numbers in terms of tens and units. The base ten concept is contained within the informal method. Instruction can attempt to make this knowledge explicit. In a sense, the student using the invented strategy of simplification already knows about place value; formal instruction can build upon this foundation.

In brief, informal skill in mathematical calculation is widespread. Some students use invented procedures to solve written problems. Other students, who fail when presented with written mathematics, can succeed when allowed to solve problems mentally. Both kinds of informal skill provide the potential for formal mathematical learning. Indeed, according to the respected psychologists Vygotsky (1978) and Piaget (1970), one of the main approaches to effective education is tapping informal knowledge to promote formal instruction.

Unsuccessful Methods. The use of both standard algorithms and invented procedures may break down in several ways and result in errors of calculation. The major types of breakdowns are these: poor knowledge of number facts, "slips," and systematic error strategies or "bugs." Consider each in turn.

Number facts. Accurate knowledge of the elementary number facts (e.g., from 0 + 0 to 9 + 9 in addition) underlies efficient calculation. If students' knowledge of number facts is faulty, all calculations are likely to be wrong. Indeed, the most important single cause of difficulties in calculation is poor knowledge of number facts. According to VanLehn (1981), about 50% of students making computational errors know the algorithm quite well but use it poorly because of faulty number fact knowledge or various slips (to be defined below). Accurate knowledge of number facts provides a solid foundation for calculation. When students are comfortable and fluent in number facts, they can concentrate on calculation and even come to appreciate abstract mathematical principles.

Slips. These are minor deficiencies in the execution of a readily available procedure (VanLehn, 1981). Consider as an example slips in the subtraction algorithm. Lizbeth seems to exhibit adequate knowledge of the "borrowing" algorithm. She may even understand that borrowing involves taking a group of ten from the tens column to make up for a deficit in the ones column. Yet on some occasions, perhaps when hurrying or distracted, Lizbeth may fail to adjust the numeral in the tens column to reflect the result of borrowing, and hence obtains a wrong result. Such a slip is transitory and does not seem to reflect Lizbeth's true competence with respect to knowledge of subtraction. Sometimes slips may be the result of "memory overload." For example, suppose Jim is required to calculate a long column of numbers. He knows the number facts perfectly well and understands many principles of addition. Yet when many numbers are involved, Jim loses track of what has and has not been added, adds some numbers twice, and forgets to add others. Such slips do not seem to be result of faulty knowledge; given a larger memory capacity, Jim would have no difficulty with the problem. In brief, slips in the standard algorithm are relatively minor execution errors and do not seem to result from basic faults in understanding or serious defects in the calculational procedure.

The student may be especially susceptible to slips in invented procedures, since these place heavy demands on memory. One common invented procedure involves counting forward or backward. Thus, Andrea calculates 17 + 7 by starting with 17 and counting on 7. These invented procedures or tricks can easily break down when large numbers are involved or when much has to be remembered. If Andrea, starting with 46, tries to count on 23, she may lose track of the counting process, particularly if she uses her fingers! In brief, invented procedures are liable to result in slips because of various performance factors like limits on memory or attention.

Bugs. Some mistakes do not result from faulty number facts or from slips but rather are generated by a systematic error strategy or "bug." This is a procedure that is fundamentally defective and in certain situations leads to regular, predictable errors. The student applies the systematic error strategy quite conscientiously and accurately, but it is so fundamentally flawed that it must generate errors in certain problems. Some error strategies are frequent and well-known. For example, in subtraction, one common bug occurs when the student operates according to his own rule, "Always subtract the smaller from the larger." Applied to 23 − 16, this bug results in the answer 13, because the student subtracts the 3 from the 6 in the units column. Sometimes this bug may lead to a correct response, as in the case of 25 − 11, since borrowing is not an issue.

The notion of the systematic error strategy or "bug" asserts that wrong answers may not be random or meaningless. The student makes mistakes for a reason. Errors result from use of misguided but systematic procedures (Brown & Burton, 1978). Moreover, these procedures usually have sensible origins (Ginsburg, 1982) in the student's learning history. For example, the rule "Always subtract the smaller from the larger" may have originated from early subtraction lessons; the student's mistake was to generalize it beyond its proper domain. In brief, many calculational errors are not random; they derive from systematic error strategies which often have sensible origins.

Summary. Calculational errors may result from a variety of processes. One important factor is weak number fact knowledge, perhaps the most common reason for calculational difficulty. Another factor involves slips in the execution of an adequately known algorithm or informal strategy. Systematic errors or bugs are the final source of errors on our list: Calculational mistakes are usually not random but result from systematic strategies having sensible origins.

Concepts

Instruction in elementary mathematics should involve not only calculation but also should establish an understanding of fundamental concepts. The student must learn both to figure and to understand. Correct answers are essential, but it is also important for the student to know why the answers are correct and how the algorithms work to produce them. Common experience shows that many students calculate without understanding much about the underlying rationale. They say: "That's just the way you do it," or "You get the right answer that way, but I don't know why you do it." But some students come to understand calculation: They make a connection between the calculational routines taught in school and various aspects of their existing knowledge. In other words, students can gain insight or meaning by integrating what they are taught with what they already know. These interpretations may involve simpler procedures, everyday experiences, and formal mathematical theory. We consider each in this section.

Simpler Procedures. One way to understand a written calculation or algorithm is to interpret it in terms of a simpler, informal procedure. Children often assimilate the written procedure taught in school into their more elementary and comfortable counting schemes. A very simple example of this was given by Sonia, a first grader, who was asked why the written statement 6 + 3 = 9 is true. She replied: "6 plus 3 equals 9 'cause you can tell ... adding 3 more is 9 ... 6, 7, 8, 9." As she said these numbers, she counted on her fingers. This example shows that Sonia understood the number fact in terms of her own counting. She believed the written statement, because she could get the same result by counting on her fingers. In a sense, Sonia's counting understood her writing.

Everyday Experiences. Similarly, students may understand various principles of calculation by referring to everyday experiences. For example, Jennifer, a third grader, had difficulty in judging the relative magnitudes of written numbers. Thus, she believed that 8, 80, and 800 are all "the same," because "zero doesn't make any difference." In other words, her rule was that if zero is "nothing," then adding it to a number doesn't change anything. In the course of the interview, Jennifer was asked about the ages of various acquaintances. As it turned out, she had a friend 10 years of age. The interviewer asked "Which is larger, 1 or 10?" and wrote the numbers on paper. Jennifer answered: "They're both the same, because zero doesn't make any difference." But suddenly an expression of comprehension lit up her face. "Oh, that's *one* and that's *ten*!" Jennifer had assimilated the written numbers into her knowledge of ages. Now the written numbers were connected to something meaningful—a body of informal knowledge that Jennifer had been building up over the years—and the "zero makes no difference" rule could be abandoned.

Formal Mathematical Theory. While some students interpret calculation in terms of informal knowledge, others understand it in terms of formal mathematical theory. They assimilate algorithms into other aspects of their formal mathematical knowledge. For example, Jane, a third grader, began the interview by misaligning a subtraction problem. She wrote:

$$\begin{array}{r} 132 \\ -\ 14 \\ \hline \end{array}$$

Then she looked puzzled and said, "Maybe it's supposed to look like this":

$$
\begin{array}{r}
132 \\
-\ 14 \\
\hline
\end{array}
$$

At this point, she had a look of real insight and excitement. "That's the way it's suppose to go, because that's in the one's place, that's in the ten's place, and that's in the hundred's place." As she said this, she pointed to the appropriate numerals in both 132 and 14. She then proceeded to solve the problem.

Jane's example shows how understanding can improve performance. Jane saw how to correct her mistake only when she understood the algorithm by connecting it with her knowledge of place value. The connection allowed her to see exactly where she had gone wrong and to improve her calculations.

CONCLUSION

We have seen that arithmetic thinking begins with the informal concepts and counting activities of the preschooler. It is vital for you as educator to understand these basic concepts and skills, because they can and should form the foundation on which the student builds an understanding of the formal arithmetic taught in school. An instructional assessment must establish whether students experiencing difficulty with arithmetic nevertheless possess these essential concepts and skills. If so, you can devise effective remedial activities for students experiencing difficulty. It is also vital for you to understand the ways in which students assimilate the arithmetic taught in school into their own ways of understanding and doing. Students do not always do arithmetic as it is taught: They may invent their own procedures that can lead to surprising successes and to errors that on the surface appear to be chaotic. The more you understand the student's *personal* arithmetic, the more you can suggest effective educational interventions.

Now that we have an overview of mathematical thinking, both formal and informal, we can consider methods for assessing it. We turn next to this topic.

REFERENCES

Baroody, A. J., & Ginsburg, H. P. (1982). Generating number combinations; rote process or problem solving? *Problem Solving, 4,* 3–4.

Brown, J. S., & Burton, R. B. (1978). Diagnostic models for procedural bugs in basic mathematical skills. *Cognitive Science, 2,* 155–192.

Brush, L. R. (1978). Pre-school children's knowledge of addition and subtraction. *Journal for Research in Mathematics Education, 9,* 44–54.

Fuson, K. C., & Hall, J. W. (1983). The acquisition of early number word meanings: A conceptual analysis and review. In H. P. Ginsburg (Ed.), *The development of mathematical thinking*. New York: Academic Press.

Gelman, R. (1975). How young children reason about small numbers. Paper delivered at the University of Indiana.

Gelman, R. (1980). What young children know about numbers. *Educational Psychologist, 15,* 54–86.

Ginsburg, H. P. (1982). *Children's arithmetic: How they learn it and how you teach it.* Austin, TX: PRO-ED.

Ginsburg, H. P., & Opper, S. (1979). *Piaget's theory of intellectual development* (2nd ed.). Englewood Cliffs, NJ: Prentice-Hall.

Ginsburg, H. P., Posner, J. K., & Russell, R. L. (1981). The development of mental addition as a function of schooling and culture. *Journal of Cross-Cultural Psychology, 12,* 163–178.

Ginsburg, H. P., & Russell, R. L. (1981). Social class and racial influences on early mathematical thinking. *Monographs of the society for research in child development, 46,* serial no. 193.

Groen, G. J., & Resnick, L. B. (1977). Can preschool children invent addition algorithms? *Journal of Educational Psychology, 69,* 645–652.

Petitto, A. L., & Ginsburg, H. P. (1982). Mental arithmetic in Africa and America: Strategies, principles, and explanations. *International Journal of Psychology, 17,* 81–102.

Piaget, J. (1952). *The origins of intelligence in children.* NY: International Universities Press.

Piaget, J. (1970). *Science of education and the psychology of the child.* New York: Orion.

Resnick, L. B. (1983). A developmental theory of number understanding. In H. P. Ginsburg (Ed.), *The development of mathematical thinking*. New York: Academic Press.

Starkey, P., & Cooper, R. G. (1980). Perception of numbers by human infants. *Science, 210,* 1033–1035.

VanLehn, K. (1981). *Bugs are not enough.* Palo Alto, CA: Xerox.

Vygotsky, L. S. (1978). *Thought and language.* Cambridge, MA: MIT Press.

15 / ASSESSMENT TECHNIQUES: TESTS, INTERVIEWS, AND ANALYTIC TEACHING

As pointed out in Chapter 13, understanding the individual student requires that you ask several sorts of questions: (a) How severe is the student's problem? (b) In what areas does the student experience difficulties and strengths? (c) What kind of thinking is responsible for the student's difficulties and strengths? and (d) Can the student learn to overcome the difficulties? To answer these questions, you may use three different techniques of assessment: tests, flexible interviewing, and analytic teaching. The aim of this chapter is to describe these techniques, particularly the logic and nature of flexible interviewing—a technique that is sometimes undervalued and poorly understood.

TESTS

Tests are particularly useful for determining the severity of the student's problem and for establishing areas of weakness and strength. Some efforts have also been made to use tests to investigate students' thinking.

Determining the Severity of the Problem

One effective use of tests is to determine the severity of a student's problem. This requires comparing the student with peers. Is the student far behind or only slightly below average? Is the student's difficulty serious or minor? Suppose that a third grade student has trouble with understanding place value. You first need to determine whether the difficulty is unusual or typical of third graders. Answering this question involves a statistical comparison. You need to compare the student's performance with the norms characterizing typical students at the same grade level.

Comparisons of this type are efficiently accomplished through standardized tests with empirically established norms. Such tests have three important features. First, test administration is standardized: The test items are presented in the same fashion to all students, to ensure comparability of the results. Second, the student's performance is scored objectively, so there can be no controversy about what score each student receives. Third, the test provides norms, based on an appropriate sample, so the individual student's score can be compared with those of peers.

Several standardized, normative tests of this type are available in the areas of arithmetic and elementary mathematics. Chief among them are the *KeyMath* (Connelly, Nachtman, & Pritchett, 1976), the *Test of Early Mathematics Ability* or TEMA (Ginsburg & Baroody, 1983), and the *Test of Mathematical Abilities* or TOMA (Brown & McEntire, 1984). For example, the *KeyMath* can be used to establish whether a child has an especially severe difficulty in the area of computational skill; the TEMA can be used to determine whether the child is deficient in informal arithmetic; and the TOMA can provide information on whether the child is below average in interpreting story problems. Further information concerning the use of these tests is provided in chapters 16 and 17.

Establishing Strengths and Weaknesses

A second effective use of standardized, normative tests is to assess the individual student's pattern of strengths and weaknesses. Tests like the *KeyMath*, TEMA, and TOMA contain several subscales that measure different aspects of children's mathematics. For example, the TOMA can be used with students from grades 3 to 10 to measure attitudes toward mathematics, vocabulary, computation, general information, and story problems. This allows the tester to determine the student's relative strengths and weaknesses in these areas. The tester can learn from the TOMA, for example, that the student has a poor attitude toward mathematics, is weak in the areas of story problems and vocabulary, but is skilled in calculation and general information.

Investigating Thinking

A third and less frequent use of tests has been to investigate the individual student's thinking or mental strategies. In this case, the test does not have a normative aim; it does not attempt to compare the student with peers. Instead, its aim is to describe how the student solves, understands, or otherwise deals with a particular arithmetic task. Thus, from a test designed to assess thinking you might learn that the student has trouble with column addition because he or she systematically misaligns the numerals or uses some other specific strategy that results in wrong answers. Such tests may vary in their degree of standardization. Typically, there are semistandardized in that the examiner begins by administering the problems in a fixed way but has some latitude in following up on the student's responses.

The first successful test of thinking was developed by Buswell and John (1926). It attempted to measure students' mental strategies for both successful and unsuccessful computation. Recently, Ginsburg and Mathews (1984) have developed the *Diagnostic Test of Arithmetic Strategies* or DTAS, which measures students' strategies for writing and aligning numbers, for computation in the four operations of arithmetic, and for mental calculation. Further information concerning the DTAS is provided in Chapter 17.

While useful in measuring clearly defined aspects of thinking, tests of this type suffer from a major limitation: If the student employs a strategy that the test is not designed to measure, little of value can be learned. The tester is restricted to the standard administration of the original problems, perhaps with some follow-up, but is not free to go beyond what has been planned. Thus, the tester is prevented from adequately exploring novel and unexpected responses. A more effective (but also more difficult) procedure for investigating thinking is flexible interviewing, to which we now turn.

FLEXIBLE INTERVIEWING

Flexible interviewing was originally developed by Piaget (1929), who called it the "clinical interview method" and used it with great success to investigate thinking. The method has become increasingly popular in developmental psychology and has great potential for instructional assessment. The aim of this section is to present the logic and major features of flexible interviewing. The section begins with an example of flexible interviewing and continues with a description of its logic and main components.

An Example of Flexible Interviewing

Flexible interviewing in the area of students' arithmetic has several important features. To illustrate them, consider the interview with Butch described in Chapter 13.

Interviewer: What are you doing now in school?
Butch: Fractions.
Interviewer: Fractions? Can you show me what you are doing with fractions?
Butch: [writes:] $8 \overline{)\ 16}$
Interviewer: OK. So what does that say?
Butch: 8, 16.
Interviewer: What do you do with it?
Butch: You add it up and put the number up there.
Interviewer: OK. What is the number?
Butch: [writes:] $8 \overline{)\ \overset{23}{16}}$
Interviewer: How did you do that?
Butch: I went, 16, 17, 18, 19, 20, 21, 22, 23. I added from 16.

Several features of the interview stand out. First, the interviewer gives Butch some freedom to determine the topic for discussion and does not impose on him a preconceived plan of interviewing. The interviewer's aim is to explore the issues that concern the student, to discover the topics that might cause him difficulty. Second, the interviewer tries to get Butch to explain in his own words what he is doing. The questions were designed to be open-ended, like "What do you do with it?" so Butch can answer them in a way that would reveal his thinking or mental strategies. Third, the interviewer's questions are not standardized. They are responsive to or contingent upon the student's answers. The interviewer's questions were not formulated beforehand but depend on what the student said. The aim is to follow up on interesting responses and to discover how the student thinks. In brief, the flexible interview gives the student some freedom to determine the content of the interview, employs open-ended questions that allow the student to reveal his or her thinking, and uses a contingent method in which the interviewer's questions are determined in part by the student's responses. These basic features of flexible interviewing distinguish it sharply from standardized testing.

Components of Flexible Interviewing

The flexible interview is a more complex technique than the standardized or semistandardized tests discussed earlier. It involves four components: (a) establishing rapport with the student; (b) discovering thinking processes or mental strategies; (c) describing how these thinking processes operate; and (d) determining levels of competence. Thus, after putting the student at ease, you may want to discover if he or she can do some kind of mental calculation; to describe exactly how he or she does it; and to determine whether current performance represents competence—the best the student can do.

Flexible interviewing can be used with varying degrees of intensity. You can interview a student for a full hour to obtain detailed information concerning mathematical knowledge. This may be desirable, but it is hard to do and in any event is usually impractical. More likely, you will have the time to engage in only a brief sequence of flexible interviewing designed to clarify the student's understanding of a particular topic, like column subtraction. But the briefer approach is valuable too: Even when used on a short-term basis with a limited focus, flexible interviewing can provide valuable information that is difficult or impossible to get from existing tests.

Whether the flexible interview is lengthy or brief, the general principles and techniques for conducting it are essentially the same. The next sections are designed to help you learn them. Consider next how to use flexible interviewing to establish rapport, discover thinking processes, describe how they operate, and determine levels of competence.

Establishing Rapport. Usually, students must be properly motivated—trying hard to exhibit their highest level of performance. Of course, it is possible for some students to exhibit their competence, or lack of it, while half asleep, especially if the task is so easy that virtually no effort is required to solve it ("How much is 1 plus 1?") or so hard that no amount of trying will suffice ("In your head, find the square root of 43"). Yet if the task is challenging, as much arithmetic is for young students, a high degree of motivation is required for students to perform to the best of their abilities. Hence, in flexible interviewing, you must try to establish a good relationship—good rapport—with the student so that the level of effort will be high. If the student works hard in the interview session, then you may be able to pin down the intellectual causes of the failure in mathematics—for example, a lack of understanding of place value or an inability to remember number facts. By contrast, if the student is not properly motivated, it will be hard for you to know what causes poor performance in the interview session. Perhaps the student fails because of lack of effort or because of intimidation by the interviewer, or perhaps the student fails because of a genuine lack of understanding of the material.

In standardized testing, the tester attempts to establish rapport by simple instructions, which often stress that the test is a game the student will enjoy playing. Sometimes such instructions are effective; but often they are not, especially in the case of students who are doing poorly in school or who are culturally different. These students do not always reveal their competence under standard testing conditions. Indeed, from a Piagetian point of view, the use of standardized directions to establish rapport is a contradiction in terms. If you wish to create proper motivation, you need to treat the student as an individual; you need to tailor the task to his or her personal needs. While this is prohibited by standardized testing, it is the essence of flexible interviewing. Consider next several important methods for establishing sound rapport with the student.

The interview should be conducted in a setting that is quiet and free from distractions. It is difficult for the student (and you!) to work when the school band is playing in the room next door, or other students are passing by and making funny faces, or adults interrupt to make phone calls, or you are testing in a supply closet. These are real examples; no doubt you can think of many more difficulties with which interviewers and students have to contend. In general, no other persons should be present beside you and the student; you should operate "one on one." This allows you to establish a good relationship with the student, to control the questioning, and to focus on the student's behavior. But there are exceptions to the rule (just as there are to most rules of flexible interviewing). If, despite your best efforts, the student refuses to talk, you might consider bringing in another student and having the pair work as a team. You could encourage them to help each other, to explain problems to each other, and generally to talk to each other as much as possible. Under these conditions, you might be able to elicit some verbal information from the student who is silent when tested one on one. Of course, the danger here is that the students might influence each other to the extent that you will not be able to determine who is responsible for what.

Perhaps the most important element of establishing sound rapport is the personal relationship between student and interviewer. Remember that the interview situation can be a threatening, frightening experience for the student. After all, the student would not be seeing you unless he or she were in some kind of difficulty. Typically, students are quite aware that they are not doing well in school work; and if they do not know, their peers will usually inform them in no uncertain terms. Under these circumstances, students may feel guilt about their failure or may feel anxiety at the prospect of revealing their ignorance to a strange adult. A student may even see the interview as punishment for his or her "bad" behavior. Or a student may simply be afraid of strange adults. So there are many reasons that the interview can be an unpleasant prospect for the student.

You can do several things to make the interview a positive experience that will motivate and interest the student. If at all possible, try to spend some time with the student before initiating the interview itself. It may be useful to drop by the class and introduce yourself to the student or to spend some time with the student in the playground. Simple contact like this may serve to reduce the student's anxieties: You are not so threatening a person after all!

When the student enters the testing room, don't begin the interview immediately but try first to set the student at ease. Sometimes you can do this with pleasant conversation about the student's interests or family. This can be superficial, but it may work. Sometimes, as Opper (1982) suggests, it may be useful to let the student—particularly a young child—engage for a while in activities like drawing: These may let the child demonstrate some competence and relax as well.

When it seems that the student is ready to begin, explain the purpose of the interview in an honest way that the student can understand. You may say that you are interested in how the student does arithmetic. Information about how he or she solves some problems or has trouble with others will help you determine how to teach effectively. For example: "I want to know how you do your math. If I find out how you're doing your work and why you're having trouble, I can help you learn better." Make clear that you are interested in how the student does the problems, not in how many he or she gets right or wrong.

Your tone should be warm and supportive. Your behavior should make it clear to the student that you are interested in what he or she does and says. You should encourage effort on the student's part and should never criticize wrong answers or inability to produce correct ones. The student who tries hard should realize that he or she is doing well and that you are not critical of failures. All this should help establish rapport and get the student off to a good start.

Discovering Thinking Processes. One basic task for assessment is to discover unanticipated thinking processes or mental strategies used by students in a variety of contexts. As an interviewer, you should not prejudge students by assuming that they think the way you think or the way current theories propose they think. You should always be alert to the possibility that the student may do something that is both unexpected and important to know about. Thus, we saw previously that Butch talked about fractions, wrote division, but solved the problem by counting on. These activities could not have been anticipated; the interviewer needed to discover them. And knowledge of these activities could be very important in helping a student like Butch. In Chapter 14 we saw that students sometimes use rare "bugs" or strategies that systematically produce wrong answers. It is impossible to design a test that in a brief amount of time can identify every rare bug. Hence, the tester needs to use flexible methods to discover bugs that could not have been anticipated.

In flexible interviewing, the student is the "teacher" and you are the "student." You must let the student teach you about the interesting kinds of mathematical thinking that are employed. You must let the student lead while you follow, so that you may learn about unsuspected strengths and weaknesses. When the aim is discovery, the student cannot give "wrong" answers. All answers are correct insofar as they allow you to discover something important about the student. Discovery in flexible interviewing is like the initial mapping of a new terrain. The goal is to identify the major landmarks, the important features that cannot be anticipated and that later must be explored and described in precise detail.

In brief, one aim of flexible interviewing is to discover aspects of the individual student's mathematical thinking—both strengths and weaknesses—that are new and unexpected and that, therefore, cannot be identified by predetermined diagnostic tests. As Piaget (1929) put it, the flexible interview is an open-ended procedure intended to give the student a chance to display his or her "natural inclination."

To accomplish the aims of discovery, several techniques are used: (a) The interviewer employs a task that is open-ended; (b) the interviewer asks questions that follow up on the student's answers to reveal interesting aspects of the student's thinking; and (c) the interviewer elicits a good deal of reflection (or introspection) on the part of the student to obtain further evidence concerning the methods of thinking employed. Consider how you should use each of these techniques.

Tasks to be used. Even when the aim is exploration, you should begin the flexible interview with several prepared tasks. A *task*, as the term is used here, is a problem, sometimes involving concrete objects, sometimes paper and pencil, and sometimes just questions stated orally. A task can involve presenting the student with two groups of marbles and asking her or him to determine how many there are altogether; asking the student to solve a column addition problem with paper and pencil; or asking "What is the commutative property?" Tasks are necessary to draw out the student's strengths and weaknesses; in most cases, the student will not spontaneously reveal them. The nature of the tasks presented will be determined by the extent of your knowledge of and interaction with the student. If you are not familiar with the student, you might begin an interview with general questions relating to work currently being undertaken in the classroom. Recall that Butch's interview began with, "What are you doing in arithmetic?" It is not necessary for you to be quite so general: You can ask somewhat more specific questions like, "What kinds of addition are you working on now?" or "What did your teacher show you today in math?" In general, it is better to have the student do something than just talk to you. The student may be apprehensive about a strange adult but is accustomed to working with paper and pencil and with concrete objects. Hence, you might say, "Show me what kinds of adding you are working on," or "Show me what your teacher did today in math."

If you know what material is being covered in the classroom—and it is a good idea to find this out before you start—you can direct the tasks at particular areas of mathematical content. For example, you can ask, "What did you work on today in borrowing?" or, better still, you can have the student work on a particular type of subtraction problem. It is strongly recommended that before beginning the first interview you observe the student's ordinary behavior in the classroom. Not only will you learn in detail what material is being covered, but you will have the chance to get an impression of the student's motivation, to see how he or she interacts with peers and the teacher, and to assess the quality of his or her work. All this information is important for directing your exploration as well as for assessing motivation and for other reasons to be discussed below. Indeed, if you are working with the student over a period of time, it will be useful for you to visit the classroom at regular intervals, partly to observe any changes that may be occurring.

Suppose you know Sally reasonably well and feel that she is capable of insight into her own behavior. Then you might try asking what problems she is having and what she thinks is responsible for them. Often students know the areas of work with which they are having difficulty; sometimes they can even tell you the reasons for the difficulty, like "I don't know how to carry" or "I make mistakes in counting." A self-diagnosis like this may be useful for at least two reasons. One is that it may be accurate and save you some work. Another is that it involves the student in the process of self-help. It communicates to the student that you are taking her or him seriously and that the student's efforts can contribute to solving her or his own problems. Any time you can involve students as active participants in their own learning, you have already won a significant victory.

Open-ended tasks. The task should be open-ended. It should be designed to discover how the student operates and to determine how the student structures and interprets the task. Effective questions allow students to reveal their own thought processes; you must try not to let your preconceptions influence their responses. Thus, suppose you want to know how a student does column addition. You might present a written addition problem and ask, "What do you do with this problem?" This would be preferable to asking, "Can you add these numbers for me?" since you should not assume that the student knows the problem involves adding at all; perhaps the student thinks that such problems are solved by multiplication. Remember how Butch thought that a problem he wrote as division should be added. Even if the student does know the problem involves adding, she or he may add in a way you did not expect, for example, by a mental simplification method rather than by carrying. Try to ask questions that let the student present you with surprises. Avoid preconceptions about what the student will do. The only "correct" answers are the ones that shed light on how the student operates. Whether the student gets the right answer is of less concern than your discovery of how the answer was obtained in the first place.

Opper (1982) recommends several techniques that you may find useful in creating open-ended questions. One is simply to request more information without biasing the student's response. Thus: "Can you tell me more about this?" or "What do you have in mind?" Another is simply to nod, smile, pause, or say "uhmmm" in a manner indicating that more information is sought. A third is to repeat the student's last statement in a questioning manner—"So when you add zero to something it makes zero?"—in the hope that the student will elaborate on it. In brief, the essence of flexible interviewing is that you are guided by what the student says, not by a plan predetermined in detail. When you want to discover the student's methods and meanings, you need to employ open-ended questions.

Following up on answers. The essence of flexible interviewing is varying the task to follow up on the individual student's response; the essence of standardized testing is presenting tasks in the same way to all students regardless of their responses. In flexible interviewing, the interviewer is sensitive to the student; in standardized testing, the student reacts to the test. Consequently, in flexible interviewing, you must always attempt to ask questions that pursue leads suggested by the student's answers to previous questions. Often your follow-up will attempt to discover how the student went about doing a particular problem. For example, when Butch indicated that he would write fractions as division, the interviewer did not tell him he was wrong but pursued Butch's response by asking him how he would do it. When Butch got the answer 23 to what appeared to be the problem 16 divided by 8, the interviewer did not go on to some predetermined question but instead followed up on the answer to see how Butch got it. Thus, you must always attempt to be sensitive to the student's answer and pursue it where it leads. Remember that the student is the teacher and you the student; the student is the leader and you the follower.

In following up on the student's response, you should keep in mind a key danger of flexible interviewing: Avoid putting words in the student's mouth by suggesting answers. This results only in the illusion of discovery: You will find only what you expected to find, not what is really there. Suggestions may infiltrate the interview in rather subtle ways. As Opper (1977) points out, the very wording of a question may suggest an answer. For example, if you present the student with two statements like 2 + 2 = 4 and 2 + 2 = 5 and say, "Which of these answers is wrong?" you are perhaps unintentionally conveying the message that one of the answers must be wrong, that it is not possible to get different answers to the same problem. But the student may not believe this at all. From the student's perspective, both answers may be right. The question suggests an answer and prevents the student from expressing a contrary belief. Sometimes, too, the interviewer can convey suggestions in a subtle manner just by tone of voice or by reactions to various aspects of the student's behavior. For example, the interviewer may say, "What do you mean by that?" in such an incredulous way that the student realizes that he or she has done something seriously wrong and then tries to hide it. Or the interviewer may look so pleased when the student does something that the student decides to do more of it when he or she otherwise would have gone on to something else. Children are extraordinarily sensitive to adult reactions; many believe that their survival in school often depends on "psyching out" what the teacher is thinking and anticipating the teacher's next question. So it is all too easy for you to engage in practices that unintentionally suggest answers; try to pose follow-up questions in as open-ended and neutral a fashion as possible.

Reflection. In flexible interviewing, you need to request reflection—self-analysis—on the part of the student to obtain further information concerning his or her methods of solution. The interviewer asks the student to verbalize his or her thoughts, to give reasons for his or her actions, and generally to reflect on what he or she has done. The interviewer asks such questions as: "How did you get that answer?" or "Why did you do it that way?" The focus is on the students' methods of solution and on their explanation of their actions, not on the right and wrong answers. At the same time, the interviewer is careful not to believe everything that the student says nor to take statements at face value. Instead, the interviewer listens "with the third ear," aiming to determine what lies *behind* the student's response. Since students' use of language may be different from that of adults, the concern must be with what the student *meant*, not necessarily with what was said. For example, asked whether two sets of 7 elements each have the same number, a young student said, "They both have the mostest." Taken literally, this statement is gibberish, but the actions and other statements of the 4 year old indicated that the statement meant "They both have the same." So you may have to look beneath the surface of the student's language to see what is really meant. Listen not just to what is said, but look at what is done and try to assume the student's perspective to make sense out of what might appear to be nonsense.

Describing Thinking.

Once interesting aspects of students' mathematics have been discovered, the thinking processes or mental strategies must be described in detail. You need to learn as much as possible about the student's methods of solution. If, for example, we find from exploratory work that a student adds by counting, we next need to describe the strategy in detail. Flexible interview techniques can help us to do this, too. When description is the aim, the interviewer employs many of the techniques discussed above (like asking follow-up questions and requesting reflection) and in addition stresses channeling responses into areas of interest and testing hypotheses.

Channeling responses. Now you are less interested in exploring the student's strategies than in describing them with some precision. Hence, if you are about to begin an interview, you should prepare a fairly extensive plan concerning how to proceed. If you are in the middle of an interview, you need to improvise as you go along. This aspect of flexible interviewing is, of course, difficult, but it is also challenging and potentially rewarding.

Suppose you are interviewing Butch and have just observed that he gets the answer 23 to the problem 16 divided by 8. Furthermore, he says that he "added from 16." All this was unexpected; you have stumbled on an interesting discovery concerning Butch. Apparently, he solves written addition problems by counting on from the larger number, even though he is very confused about what calculations are called and how to write them. You want to find out more about Butch's addition method. But the one bit of evidence you have so far is not enough; you need to investigate a number of matters in greater detail. For example, does Butch always count on from the larger number, or will he sometimes proceed from the smaller? Does he use mental addition when the numbers are very large? To answer questions like these, you need to plan a sequence of tasks designed to provide specific information concerning Butch's methods.

Two general principles may help guide your efforts at designing such interviews. One principle is that the sequence of tasks should proceed from general to specific. At the outset, you will often find it useful to ask non-directive questions like "What would you do with these numbers?" or "How would you add these numbers?" Questions like these do not bias the student's response and may allow you to get preliminary information concerning his or her strategy. But then you need to focus the interview more narrowly and ask such questions as: "Which number did you start to count with?" or "Did you use your fingers when you were counting?" You should ask specific questions like these only when you have enough information to know that they will not bias the student's methods. Thus, if you already know that the student is counting on the fingers, it may be useful to ask what he or she does after he gets to 10. But if you are not sure about how the student calculates, a specific question about finger counting may suggest that procedure when it otherwise may not have been used.

A second principle in designing flexible interviews is that the sequence of tasks should generally proceed from simpler to harder. The student is apt to feel comfortable with the simpler tasks, use familiar strategies, and achieve some success with them. After the student has had this positive experience, you can challenge him or her with more difficult tasks designed to stimulate the use of advanced strategies. Thus, if you have learned that the student counts on the fingers and want to find out how he or she does it, you might begin by asking the student to do 3 + 2, a problem that is simple partly because it can be done on one hand. Will the student count on the fingers or will he or she just remember the number facts? After you have identified the student's methods on such simple problems, you can proceed to harder ones like 4 + 5 (requiring two hands) and eventually to problems like 8 + 6, which are harder still since they involve sums larger than the available number of fingers.

The simpler to harder sequence may also be illustrated by an example concerning Butch. You might begin by presenting him with a series of mental addition problems containing no written material and designed to determine the limits of the counting on strategy. The sequence could start with simple problems like: "I want you to add some numbers in your head. Tell me how you do it each time. Let's start with 14 plus 5." Butch might well use counting on for relatively small problems like these. Then you could introduce harder problems for which counting on is an inefficient strategy. For example, it is extremely tedious to count on in the case of 321 + 567. Under these circumstances, can Butch use a more powerful strategy like simplification? If he does, you might then introduce written addition problems of a simple type, perhaps with no carrying required. If Butch now does reasonably well on these, it might then prove useful to give him harder addition problems that involve carrying.

In brief, try to arrange the questioning so that it proceeds from general to specific, and the tasks from simple to difficult. These techniques will usually allow you to obtain progressively more detailed information concerning the student's strategies and the conditions influencing them.

Testing hypotheses. The flexible interview also employs a technique that is usually not recognized as characteristic of it—namely, hypothesis testing. This may sound awesome but is analogous to the kind of "detective work" we do in many everyday situations. For example, suppose the car doesn't start and we want to find out why this has happened. We may begin with two competing hypotheses. One is that the battery is dead and the other is that the gas tank is empty. How can we test out the hypotheses? If we turn the key and the engine doesn't turn over, the cause is likely to be a dead battery. But this first test is not conclusive. Perhaps the battery is good, but there is some problem in the connection between the battery and the engine. We can test out this hypothesis by trying to turn on the headlights. If they go on, then the battery is good. If they don't, then we have support for the idea that the battery is dead. Suppose we do all this and the engine turns over and the lights go on. We know that the battery is not the cause, and we would go on to explore other possibilities like the empty gas tank.

You are often faced with situations like these in everyday life. Something happens, you don't understand why, and you want to discover the cause. Why doesn't Edie want to go to school today? Maybe she is unprepared for an exam, or maybe she is really sick. You need to discover which is true or if there is another explanation entirely. You try out various "experiments" to discover the cause. For example, if she is not sick, she might not like the idea of staying in bed all day and missing her afternoon swimming lesson. So hypothesis testing simply involves coming up with ideas to explain something that has happened and then testing them out with experiments that can tell you whether one explanation is more likely than another.

Hypothesis testing in flexible interviewing may be illustrated by an interview with a third grader named Patty. It began with an addition problem on which Patty used a misalignment strategy. Given the problem 29 + 4, she wrote:

$$
\begin{array}{r}
29 \\
+\ 4 \\
\hline
69
\end{array}
$$

Asked to describe the problem in words, she said, "29 plus 4 is 69." The interviewer then decided to see whether Patty really believed this.

> **Interviewer:** Are you sure that 29 and 4 are 69?
> **Patty:** Altogether?
> **Interviewer:** Yes.
> **Patty:** No.
> **Interviewer:** How much are 29 and 4?
> [Patty then used tallies to calculate the correct result, 33.]
> **Interviewer:** How come this (the written problem) says 69?
> **Patty:** 'Cause you're not doing it like that [pointing to the tallies].

The interviewer then conceived of two hypotheses to explain the student's behavior. One is that Patty experienced difficulty with written addition problems, misaligning addends with different numbers of digits, and yet could solve essentially the same problems when they were presented in concrete form. This hypothesis seemed plausible, because many students who fail on written problems nevertheless exhibit skill in informal calculation. A second hypothesis, which seemed less likely, is that the source of Patty's difficulty involved the word "plus." When she or the interviewer used this word, Patty misaligned the addends. When the word "altogether" was used, she had no difficulty.

To decide between the two hypotheses, the interviewer proceeded as follows:

> **Interviewer:** Let's do this. Here are 10 chips, and here's one more. How many do you think altogether?
> **Patty:** Altogether, it would be 11.
> **Interviewer:** OK. What about 10 plus 1, not altogether but plus?
> **Patty:** Then you'd have to put 20.
> [She apparently said this because she would write:]

$$
\begin{array}{r}
10 \\
+\ 1 \\
\hline
20
\end{array}
$$

Interviewer: Now what if I write down on paper, here's 20, now I write down another 1, and you want to find out how much the 20 and the 1 are altogether?

Patty: It's 21.

Interviewer: Now what would 20 plus 1 be?

Patty: 20 plus 1?

[She wrote:]

$$
\begin{array}{r}
20 \\
+\ 1 \\
\hline
30
\end{array}
$$

Note that to decide between the alternative hypotheses, the interviewer deliberately varied certain features of the problem. She began by using two different words—altogether and plus—to ask about the addition of the same concrete objects. Patty solved the "altogether" problem correctly but not the "plus." This seemed to indicate that the language was the culprit. But is this always true? The possibility exists that the words are influential only when concrete objects are involved. Therefore, the interviewer introduced another variation: She now used written problems rather than concrete objects. The question was whether written problems cause further difficulties or whether language is the only source of Patty's misalignment. In brief, the interviewer thought that there were two possible explanations of Patty's behavior and played off one against the other. She tried to set up the situation so that if the first explanation were true, Patty would do one thing; and if the second were true, she would do another. This kind of clever detective work is at the heart of hypothesis testing in the flexible interview.

So when you are conducting a flexible interview, you may wish to ask yourself what could have been responsible for a particular answer: Was it strategy A or strategy B? If it was A, what would the student be expected to do, and how would that be different from what B would produce? Then try to set up problems that the student would solve in one way if strategy A were used and in another way if strategy B were used. For example, suppose you want to find out how William gets the answer to small subtraction problems. You cannot decide whether he is counting in his head or whether he remembers the answers, but you are pretty sure he uses one method or the other. You ask him and he doesn't tell you; you've got to find out some other way. You think of timing his response: How long does it take him to get the answer? When very small problems like 3 − 2 are involved, the results are ambiguous, since counting back can be done as quickly as remembering. When large problems like 17 − 8 are used, the results are also ambiguous, since William cannot use either counting or memory to get the answer. Therefore, to decide between the two alternatives, you need to design problems in just the right range—about the magnitude of 7 − 2. Given problems like these, William should take a fairly long time if he solves them by counting and a shorter time if he remembers.

In brief, hypothesis testing involves first coming up with alternative explanations of the student's behavior and then devising situations that will show whether the student uses one procedure or another. This is no different from what you do in everyday life when you try to figure out why people do what they do or why objects work (or fail to work) as they do.

Determining Competence. An important aim of the flexible interview is the assessment of competence. Your aim is to identify the best that the student can do—the highest level of performance. Typically, you have begun the interview with knowledge that the student has not been doing well in some area of mathematical work. For example, the teacher reports that Butch's performance has been inadequate in arithmetic. Now you want to find out how extensive his problems really are. Does his classroom performance represent the best he can do? What is his true competence in arithmetic? Perhaps in the classroom Butch does not work very hard but could do better if he were properly motivated. Perhaps in the classroom he does not understand what the teacher is trying to get him to do, but if he did understand he could do a lot better. Perhaps Butch seems to accept some incorrect mathematical principles but does not really believe that they are correct. So your aim is to establish Butch's true competence—the best he can do. And this aspect of flexible interviewing involves three components. You need to (a) foster a high level of motivation in the student; (b) determine whether the student understands the task in the way intended; and (c) discover whether the student's beliefs are deeply held. Each of these components requires different techniques.

Motivation. As pointed out in the section on rapport earlier in this chapter, usually the student must be properly motivated—trying hard—to exhibit his or her highest level of performance. Motivation is likely to fluctuate in the course of the interview, so you must always be alert for signs of disinterest, boredom, and the like. Often the onset of yawning and stretching is a good sign that things are getting too difficult or boring. You can encourage motivation in some of the same ways used to establish rapport in the first place. The general approach is to be warm and supportive throughout. Encourage effort and display interest in the student's responses. Do not criticize, interrupt, or use a harsh tone. Do not push too hard if the student is experiencing difficulty. Make it clear that your job is to learn something from the student so you can improve his or her classroom performance; it is your intent to evaluate the student by counting up successes and failures. If the student's motivation seems to be waning, it may be a good idea to take a break or to change tasks. Sometimes it is a good idea to leave a task for a while only to return to it later. And try to put some fun into the tasks; don't let the atmosphere get too dismal.

These are only general suggestions. Personal relationships do not operate according to standardized procedures, so you will have to adjust your behavior according to the needs of the individual student. In general, feel free to break the rules, to do almost anything—even criticize the student—if that's what it takes to get him or her motivated.

Understanding. Usually the student must understand the task demands—particularly the instructions—to exhibit his or her highest level of competence. The student has to understand what the task involves and what he or she is required to do. If the student does not understand and instead interprets the problem to involve something else, then you cannot come to any useful conclusions concerning competence.

This kind of misunderstanding is by no means uncommon. Recall that Butch talked about doing fractions, wrote something that appeared to be division, and then proceeded to do addition. Children will often interpret the problem in ways you find unusual and did not intend. For example, suppose you say to Andy, "Here are some numbers, 12 plus 34; add them up," and the student gets an answer of *10*. You are surprised by this result and ask him how he got it. The answer is: "I did what you said. I added them up: 1 + 2 + 3 + 4 is 10." In this example, the problem the student did was not the one you intended; therefore, you would be incorrect to conclude anything about his competence in addition. Before making any conclusions of this type, you would have to establish that the student indeed understood what your problem requires. In brief, the assessment of competence depends on the student's understanding of the problem in the way intended.

How to avoid misunderstandings? One approach is to attempt to employ language suited to students' level of understanding. You can try out instructions informally before using them in a diagnostic setting. For example, through informal experimentation you may discover that students react more comfortably to "take-away" than "subtraction," or understand "multiply these numbers for me" better than "give me the product of these numbers." Try to assume the student's perspective and use words that he or she can understand. Don't worry about whether you are using the "correct" or "official" terminology (unless, of course, your main interest is in determining whether the student understands it). While the textbook may talk about the "union of sets," you may be more effective in getting the student to understand if you ask him or her to "add this up." For the purposes of interviewing, the correct instruction is generally the one that allows the student to understand what the problem involves.

Unfortunately, the interviewer cannot always anticipate the student's difficulties in understanding; perfect instructions and questions are hard to develop. The only solution to this all too frequent situation is to vary the wording of your questions. While beginning with some predetermined questions for initiating the interview, you should feel free to modify them as necessary. One great advantage of flexible interviewing is that you are not obligated to give the same instructions to or ask the same questions of all students. If the student does not seem to understand one set of instructions ("multiply these numbers"), present them in another way ("times these numbers"). If the student does not seem to understand the wording of a question ("Why do we add from right to left?"), substitute a different phrasing ("Why do we add going this way?"). Even if the student indicates that he or she understands, it may be useful for you to check comprehension through further questioning: You may be surprised to find that the student still requires clarification concerning some points. In brief, try to ask questions appropriate to the student's level, but if that doesn't work, feel free to modify the wording until the student understands what the task involves.

Belief. In the course of flexible interviewing, you may find that you are unsure of how seriously the student holds certain beliefs. For example, if you ask Albert to tell you how much is 6 + 6 and he gives the answer *555*, you may wonder whether he is serious, distracted, or simply puttting you on. Or if you ask him to explain borrowing and he repeats the textbook definition word for word, you may wonder whether he really understands the concept or is merely parroting what he has read or heard.

To determine the strength and quality of belief, you can use two types of challenges, or "counter-suggestions," as described by Opper (1982). One challenge involves telling the student that other students disagree with his answer; they believe something quite different. For example, if the student seems uncertain about his belief in borrowing, you might point out that other students maintain that you should always subtract the smaller from the larger number. What does he or she think about that? Such challenges often force students to think through their responses and decide if they do indeed entertain the belief in question. Another type of challenge involves presenting the student with extreme cases. Does the student maintain his or her belief under these conditions? For example, Norma aligned numbers to the left and given 10 + 1 wrote:

She maintained that this was a sensible procedure. What would she do with the more extreme problem, 100 + 1? If she maintained that the answer obtained through misalignment (200) was correct, then we might conclude that her belief is firm. But the extreme case might stimulate her to rethink her belief. In brief, it is important to know how seriously the student holds certain beliefs; you may have to challenge the student to find out.

How to Use Flexible Interviewing

As you have seen in this chapter, flexible interviewing is an enormously powerful technique for identifying students' thinking and learning processes in arithmetic. Used properly, flexible interviewing is more sensitive than standardized tests and can provide you with invaluable information for instructional assessment. As you have also seen, flexible interviewing is a subtle activity, requiring skill and sensitivity: You must know both how to interview and what to interview about.

Is it practical for *you* to engage in flexible interviewing? The answer is yes, if you start slowly and on a small scale. The wisest plan is to begin by using flexible interviewing to extend existing tests. Suppose that you find some students' responses to items from the TEMA particularly intriguing and would like to know more about their thinking in that area. Use flexible interviewing to expand on the existing questions and go beyond them. By giving you a definite starting point and a rough destination, this procedure should make you feel comfortable with flexible interviewing and allow you to conduct it reasonably effectively. After practice of this type, you might try to proceed somewhat more independently by devising your own starting points instead of using those provided by existing tests. But don't be too ambitious: Investigate a relatively restricted area of thinking without extending yourself too far. Go slowly and give yourself plenty of time to build up your skills in flexible interviewing. But don't be afraid of trying it; the result is ultimately worth the effort. As you practice, you may find it useful to refer to Table 15.1, which summarizes key aspects of flexible interviewing.

ANALYTIC TEACHING

One important question for instructional assessment is whether the student can learn to overcome whatever difficulties have been encountered. Suppose you have established through flexible interviewing that Helen has severe difficulty with subtraction. She always "takes away the smaller from the larger," even when it is inappropriate to do so. Thus, she writes:

TABLE 15.1. Suggestions for Good Flexible Interviewing

To Establish Rapport:

• The setting should be quiet and free from distractions.
• You should be the only adult present.
• Spend time with the student before the interview.
• Before beginning the interview, put the student at ease with small talk or, if the student is young, by letting him or her engage in activities like drawing.
• If the student will not talk to you, bring in another student and have the pair work as a team.
• Explain the purpose of the interview in an honest way that the student can understand. "I want to know how you do your math. If I find out why you're having trouble, I can help you learn better."
• Be warm and supportive. Encourage effort. Do not criticize wrong answers.

To Discover Thinking Processes:

• Begin by observing the student's behavior in the classroom.
• Find out what material is being covered in the classroom.
• Ask the student to devise and solve some problems reflecting material being taught in class at the present time. "What kinds of addition are you working on now?" "What did your teacher show you today in math?"
• Ask the student to indicate the areas in which he or she is having difficulty. "What are you having trouble with now?" "Why do you think you are having trouble with that?"
• Make the tasks as open-ended as possible. "What do you do with this problem?"
• Request information concerning how the student solves the problems. "How did you do this one?" "How did you get that answer?" "Can you tell me more about it?"
• Nod, smile, pause, or say "uhmm" when you want the student to talk more.
• Repeat the student's last statement in the hope that he or she will elaborate on it.
• Follow up on the student's last response until you are sure of his or her strategy.
• Don't put words in the student's mouth.

To Describe How Thinking Operates:

• When you have an idea about how the student is solving problems, prepare some tasks that will test your hypothesis.
• Try to use tasks that the student will solve in one way if using one strategy and in another way if using a different strategy.
• The tasks should proceed from general ("What do you do with these numbers?") to specific ("Can you add these up with carrying?")
• The tasks should proceed from easy to hard.

To Assess Competence:

• Encourage effort and display interest in the student's work.
• Don't criticize or push too hard if the student is having a hard time. If the student seems tired, take a break or change tasks.
• Use language suitable to the student's level of understanding.
• If the student does not seem to understand the question, vary the wording. "Can you do subtraction? Can you do take-away?"
• If the student seems to be parroting the teacher or text, ask him or her to rephrase the answer. "Can you put that in your own words?"
• To determine the strength of belief, challenge student's answer. "How could that be true?" "Johnny doesn't do it that way."

General Advice:

• Start your flexible interviewing slowly and on a small scale.
• Get your initial questions by expanding on existing tests.
• Later, devise some of your own problems.
• Do short interviews concentrating on a limited amount of material.

$$\begin{array}{r} 23 \\ -19 \\ \hline 16 \end{array}$$

The important question that now arises is whether she can learn to eliminate this "bug" and employ instead the proper algorithm of subtraction with borrowing. You may wonder how rigid she is in the application of the bug and whether she can readily profit from instruction to correct her behavior. These questions concerning learning potential are key aspects of the instructional assessment. The student who learns very slowly and with great difficulty requires different instructional techniques than the student who learns quickly and easily.

The only way to determine learning potential is to conduct a miniature teaching experiment. This involves using what seem to be the best available means, materials, or stratagems in an effort to correct the student's difficulty and then examining the extent to which the student learns. The assessor uses whatever techniques seem most effective for promoting learning. Different techniques might be effective for different children. These might involve verbal instruction, like telling the student described above that "You don't always take away the smaller number from the larger; you have to borrow. . . ." Or it might involve presenting the student with materials, like an abacus, that provide a concrete representation of the concept in question. The aim, of course, is not to remedy all of the student's possible deficiencies and misunderstandings, but to discover whether and how the student learns.

This kind of teaching experiment is sometimes called *analytic teaching* (see Chapter 1) and has several features. First, it focuses on the student's learning. The main aim of analytic teaching is not to discover what the student knows and how he or she thinks, but to get information concerning the student's learning ability. Second, analytic teaching usually concentrates on the acquisition of academic knowledge, like arithmetic or reading. There are, however, some notable exceptions, for example, Feuerstein (1980), who assesses the learning of abstract, nonacademic material. Third, analytic teaching can be employed in conjunction with flexible interviewing. The assessor-teacher may begin with an interview to determine what the student knows and how the student thinks. Then teaching is used in the attempt to modify particular aspects of the student's knowledge of strategies. After this is done, the assessor-teacher may again interview the student to determine what, if anything, has been learned. The assessor-teacher uses flexible interviewing, as well as observation, to *analyze* the student's potential for learning.

In brief, analytic teaching is a key aspect of instructional assessment. It involves the use of potentially effective instructional techniques to conduct a direct investigation of students' ability to learn academic material. Chapters 16 and 17 suggest techniques useful for investigating various aspects of students' potential for learning arithmetic.

CONCLUSION

This chapter began with the assertion that understanding the student requires that you answer four questions: (a) How severe is the student's problem? (b) In what areas does the student experience difficulties and strengths? (c) What kind of thinking is responsible for the student's difficulties and strengths? and (d) Can the student learn to overcome the difficulties? We saw that several assessment techniques are useful for getting answers to these questions. Tests are valuable primarily for answering the first two questions regarding severity and strengths and weaknesses. Flexible interviewing is most valuable for answering the third question concerning thinking. And analytic teaching is essential for answering the fourth question concerning learning potential. We turn now to a discussion of how to use these assessment methods to investigate specific aspects of students' arithmetic.

REFERENCES

Brown, V. L., & McEntire, E. (1984). *Test of Mathematical Abilities*. Austin, TX: PRO-ED.

Buswell, G. T., & John, L. (1926). *Diagnostic studies in arithmetic* (Supplementary Educational Monograph No. 30). Chicago: The University of Chicago.

Connelly, A. J., Nachtman, W., & Pritchett, E. M. (1976). *KeyMath Diagnostic Arithmetic Test*. Circle Pines, MN: American Guidance Service.

Feuerstein, R. (1980). *Instrumental enrichment*. Baltimore: University Park Press.

Ginsburg, H. P., & Baroody, A. J. (1983). *Test of Early Mathematics Ability*. Austin, TX: PRO-ED.

Ginsburg, H. P., & Mathews, S. C. (1984). *Diagnostic Test of Arithmetic Strategies*. Austin, TX: PRO-ED.

Opper, S. (1977). Piaget's clinical method. *Journal of Children's Mathematical Behavior, 1*, 90–110.

Opper, S. (1982). *The clinical interview method*. Unpublished manuscript, University of Hong Kong.

Piaget, J. (1929). *The child's conception of the world*. New York: Harcourt, Brace, and World.

16 / HOW TO ASSESS BASIC ARITHMETIC CONCEPTS AND SKILLS

The need for assessment of basic concepts and skills typically arises in the classroom when you encounter a student who is performing poorly in the most fundamental areas of school arithmetic. The student has trouble with simple column addition or with writing elementary numerals. Often, the student is young—5, 6, or 7 years of age—and is in a regular classroom in one of the lower grades. Occasionally, the student may be older: Perhaps he or she is an 8 or 9 year old who has been kept back, or perhaps the student has made it to the third or fourth grade but does not seem to understand much about the arithmetic taught at that level. Sometimes, the student may be a member of a special education class; perhaps the student is retarded. In all these cases, you typically know that the student is having trouble, but you have several questions: How severe is the difficulty? What are the student's areas of strength and weakness? The first part of this chapter discusses how you can use tests to get answers to these questions. Next, you may ask: "What strategies does the student use to do arithmetic?" and "Can the student learn?" The second part of this chapter shows how you can use flexible interviewing and analytic teaching to get answers to these questions.

WHAT IS THE NATURE AND SEVERITY OF THE DIFFICULTY?

Two individually administered standardized tests—the *KeyMath* (Connelly, Nachtman, & Pritchett, 1976) and *Test of Early Mathematics Ability* or TEMA

(Ginsburg & Baroody, 1983)—provide a measure of students' overall level of mathematical functioning and a rough indication of their strengths and weaknesses in basic mathematical abilities. Consider each.

The KeyMath

The *KeyMath* is designed to be used with students from kindergarten through about grade 6. The test includes a large number of items, ranging from the counting of objects to fractions, and yields several types of scores. One is a grade equivalence score, based on total test performance, which gives a gross indication of a student's standing relative to peers. This score may tell us, for example, that the student is performing at the second grade level. Such information may be useful in establishing the general severity of the student's problem but can tell you little else. Other *KeyMath* scores are intended to provide more specific information. For example, the *area performance* score describes the student's performance in the three mathematics areas of content, operations, and applications, and the *subtest performance* score describes the student's relative standing in 14 areas like numeration, addition, and word problems. You should be cautious in interpreting these scores, however, since it is not always evident that they measure what they are intended to measure. For example, the Numeration subtest score is said to measure "basic mathematics knowledge," but it is not clear how this is accomplished by the items provided. Typical activities include reading numerals like 7 (which can be solved by a kind of rote memory) and determining the ratio of 4 to 20 in lowest terms (which can be solved by simple computational tricks).

The TEMA

The TEMA (Figure 16.1) is designed to be used with students from kindergarten through about grade 4. The test includes items ranging from elementary notions of *more* through written subtraction with borrowing and provides several types of scores. One type of score is the Math Quotient or MQ, which is an index of the student's overall mathematics ability relative to peers. The MQ ranges from 55 to 145 at each grade level, with the lowest scores indicating poor ability, scores from 85 to 115 average ability, and the highest scores superior ability. The authors of the TEMA caution that the MQ is intended to provide only a ranking, allowing you to get a rough notion of the student's level of functioning, and does not tell you why a student has performed well or poorly.

An important and perhaps unique feature of the TEMA is its focus on both informal and formal aspects of mathematical thinking. The test includes items that measure mental addition, the mental number line, and other aspects of informal mathematics, as well as items that measure the reading and writing of numbers, written calculation, and other aspects of the formal mathematics taught in school. Therefore, the test not only provides an indication of the student's relative performance in school work but also describes the student's relative standing with respect to informal knowledge— the concepts and skills not taught through direct formal instruction but acquired in other ways by the student. It is important for you to learn about this informal knowledge because, as we will see later in this chapter, it can serve as the foundation for remedial efforts.

WHAT STRATEGIES DOES THE STUDENT USE?

Suppose Sylvia has been shown by the *KeyMath* or TEMA to be performing far below grade level. You also know from administration of the TEMA that she performs poorly at simple aspects of formal arithmetic like writing single digit numerals or doing basic calculations. At the same time, the TEMA shows that Sylvia is not entirely lacking in informal arithmetic skills: She is relatively advanced in mental addition. Now you want to get more specific information to facilitate her school learning. You want to find out more about Sylvia's thinking and to determine what she is capable of learning. Unfortunately, there does not seem to be available an appropriate test that can help you answer these questions concerning basic concepts and skills. Hence, you will have to employ flexible interviewing and analytic teaching.

A useful strategy for conducting instructional assessments of students whose basic mathematical abilities are at issue is beginning with an exploration of the student's informal knowledge. This approach has two advantages: (a) it provides you with valuable information and (b) it gives the student an opportunity to demonstrate some real competence and thereby develop positive feelings about the testing session. You might find it useful to conduct the assessment as follows. First, investigate the student's informal addition strategies, related enumeration activities, and, if necessary, even counting words. If the student exhibits difficulty in these areas, explore even more basic concepts concerning addition and the concept of *more*. After you have established the student's informal competence, turn to formal areas that are likely to be giving the student trouble—the reading and writing of numerals and elementary calculation. Consider each of these areas in turn.

Assessing Informal Addition Calculation

Begin with simple addition problems involving concrete objects. You can invent some yourself or use some like those below (which are modeled after

FIGURE 16.1. The TEMA Scoring Sheet

TEMA
The Test of Early Mathematics Ability

Herbert P. Ginsburg
Arthur J. Baroody

Section III.

PERFORMANCE RECORD

Item#	Score	Item#	Score
4> 1.	⎫	26. (a)	___
2.	⎬	27.	___
3.	⎬ 5	8> 28. (b)	___
4. (a c)	⎭	29. (a)	___
5> 5. (a)	___	30. (a)	___
6.	/	31. (a)	___
7. (c)	/	32. (a)	___
8. (a)	/	33. (a)	___
9. (c)	/	34. (a)	___
6> 10. (a)	/	35.	___
11. (b)	0	36. (a)	___
12.	/	37. (a)	___
13.	/	38. (a)	___
14. (a)	0	39. (a)	___
15.	/	40. (b)	___
16. (a)	/	41. (b)	___
17. (a)	/	42.	___
18.	/	43.	___
19.	0	44. (a b)	___
7> 20. (a)	0	45.	___
21.	0	46.	___
22. (a)	0	47. (b)	___
23. (a)	0	48. (a)	___
24. (b)	___	49. (b)	___
25. (a)	___	50.	___

Total Raw Score _____

a Item using Picture Card(s)
b Item using the Student Worksheet inside this form
c Item requiring pennies or chips

Section I.

IDENTIFYING INFORMATION

Name: _Alison_

Female ☑ Male ☐

School: _Ridgecrest_

Teacher's Name: _Mrs. Clair_

Examiner's Name: _Mr. Syage_

Examiner's Title: _Sp. Ed. Teacher_

Referred by: _Mrs. Clair_

Section II. CHILD'S AGE

	Yr.	Mo.
Date Tested	81 82	14 7
Date of Birth	74	8
Age	7	6

Section IV. TEMA RESULTS

Total Raw Score ___16___

Math Quotient ___82___

Percentile Score ___12___

Math Age ___6-10___

Section V. OTHER TEST RESULTS

Test	Date	Standard Score Results
Binet	1/82	95
___	___	___
___	___	___

FIGURE 16.1. continued

Section VI. TESTING CONDITIONS (Check as appropriate)

	Interfering	Not Interfering
Child Motivation		✓
Distractions		✓
Lighting		✓
Noise Level		✓
Temperature		✓

Section VII. ITEM PROFILE

Age	Informal	Formal	Age
9-6 or greater	43, 45, 46, 50	42, 44, 47, 48, 49	9-6 or greater
9-0 to 9-5	—	39, 40, 41	9-0 to 9-5
8-6 to 8-11	36	33, 34, 35, 37, 38	8-6 to 8-11
8-0 to 8-5	—	29, 30, 31, 32	8-0 to 8-5
7-6 to 7-11	27	25, 26, 28	7-6 to 7-11
7-0 to 7-5	19, 21	20, 22, 23, 24	7-0 to 7-5
6-6 to 6-11	15, 16, 17, 18	14	6-6 to 6-11
6-0 to 6-5	12, 13	—	6-0 to 6-5
5-6 to 5-11	9	10, 11	5-6 to 5-11
5-0 to 5-5	6, 7, 8	—	5-0 to 5-5
4-6 to 4-11	3, 4, 5	—	4-6 to 4-11
4-0 to 4-5	1, 2	—	4-0 to 4-5

Section VIII. INTERPRETATIONS & RECOMMENDATIONS

Alison clearly has difficulty with formal aspects of math thinking. She cannot write even the simplest numerals. Her informal knowledge is relatively strong. Her counting is good, and she can perform simple mental addition. Formal instruction should be related informal strengths. Has good potential for learning math.

From *Test of Early Mathematics Ability* by H. P. Ginsburg and A. J. Baroody, Austin, TX: PRO-ED. Reprinted by permission.

TEMA item 4). Present the student with two small sets of objects like pennies or chips—anything that can be counted and easily moved around. The sets should be clearly separate, with one in an area to the student's left and another to his or her right. At the outset, place two objects in one set and one in the other. Make up a story in which the sets are brought together by some action. Here is an example: "Jill has two pennies. She is walking to the store and finds one more penny. How many does she have altogether?" (As you tell the story, point to the appropriate sets.) Of course, the content of the story can be changed for the sake of variety. "Jack has one flower. He is walking in the field and finds two more flowers. How many does he have altogether?" The important feature of the story is not the specific content but the active joining of two sets. The sets must be brought together by some kind of clear action. If the student is successful with these simple problems, you can gradually increase the size of the sets. It does not matter a great deal whether you place the objects in a straight line or arrange them randomly, because you eliminate the student's need to count by always announcing the number in each set.

You can use problems like these to learn how the student does informal addition and what he or she understands about the process. On informal addition problems, the student may achieve a correct solution by means of any one of several different strategies, including counting and number facts. We consider these strategies next. Then we turn to the student's ability to choose strategies appropriate for different problems and to the student's learning potential.

Counting. The earliest procedures for dealing with addition problems involve some way of *counting concrete objects*. In one form of such counting, the student counts all of the objects in both sets, pointing to each one in turn. Thus, if there are two objects in one set and three in the other, the student will say, while pointing to each object, "One, two [pause], three, four, five." Sometimes the student even pushes the two sets together before counting them. This strategy of "counting all" is the most primitive form of addition: It involves combining the two subsets into a larger set and then counting all of the elements. A second form of counting is more efficient, and most students eventually come to use it: Recognizing that there is no need to count all of the objects, the student "counts on" from the larger set. Thus, the student does the 3 + 2 problem by saying, as he or she points, "Three [pause], four, five." Occasionally, the young child may not point to the objects but instead uses fingers or even blocks to represent the elements of the set. Thus, the child applies the count all or count on strategy to his or her fingers instead of pennies or chips. It is usually very easy to observe use of these strategies in young children: They point in obvious ways and say the counting words out loud. Ordinarily, no interviewing is required.

What does use of the counting all or counting on strategies tell us about the student? Accurate counting signifies that the student can first *interpret* an elementary word problem and then can *calculate* it in the simplest way possible. To deal with the problem "How much does Jack have altogether?" the student must have at least an intuitive understanding of what "altogether" means and must also realize that such problems may be solved through counting. Of course, the student may not know any of this explicitly and may not be able to tell you about the concept of addition or about the calculational routines used. But the student's understanding, while intuitive and implicit, is real, because it allows the solution of addition problems. Furthermore, the student's understanding may be substantial, even if the answer is wrong in minor ways. Sometimes the student may miscount, concluding that 3 + 2 = 4. But the student's knowledge that combining and counting is an appropriate way to deal with an addition problem is more important than a minor error in counting. Don't forget that the student may know what to do, but may not do it perfectly. Don't be concerned only with the right answer; look at what the student is trying to do and at the strategy being used.

Another strategy for solving addition problems is *mental counting*. For example, after the problem is presented, Steve may quietly look at the objects, perhaps moving his lips a bit, and perhaps barely pointing his finger at the objects from a distance. These behaviors may indicate that the student is attempting to use the counting all or counting on strategies on a mental level. He is "counting to himself." In this case, the student not only knows intuitively how to interpret and calculate the problem but also is beginning to internalize his problem solving activities, to use them on a mental level. Fortunately for the examiner, the young student is not very subtle about all this. While trying to count mentally, the student retains some of the outward signs of counting out loud or pointing. If you are unsure of what the student is doing, ask: "How are you figuring that problem?" or "What are you saying to yourself?" If those questions do not work, try "How are you doing that problem?" Remember to concentrate on the strategy, not just on the answer. A wrong answer may result from a sensible strategy poorly executed. In this case, it will be important to find out why the student counts poorly—Is it sloppiness? inattentiveness?—but do not overlook the possibility that the student may understand the problem well even if he or she gets a wrong answer.

Number Facts. Another approach a student may use to deal with addition involves number facts. In this case, which is rarer than those discussed above, the student quickly responds with the correct answer, apparently without calculating. Asked how he or she got the answer, the student says, "I don't know" or "I just knew it." The use of number facts on addition problems is usually a rather advanced strategy, and students using it typically have a reasonable understanding of the concept of addition. A later section discusses how students arrive at the number facts and how you can find out whether these facts indicate understanding. For now, just note that use of number facts is one way of solving these simple addition problems and probably indicates an adequate concept of simple addition.

Adjusting to Different Problems. It is important to examine not only strategies used on individual problems but also the extent to which the student can adjust to the demands of different types of problems. For example, very simple problems like 2 + 1 can be solved easily, even by very young children, through the use of number facts. But it is hard to solve larger problems, like 6 + 5 (which is "large" for a 6 year old), through the use of number facts. Consequently, given the larger problem, the student should adjust by using some kind of counting strategy. Or suppose that the student solves a relatively small problem like 3 + 2 with a mental counting strategy. While working well for the small problems, mental counting may break down in the case of larger sums like 6 + 5. Hence, the adaptive course of action in dealing with larger problems may be to abandon the mental approach and instead be very careful to point to each element, saying the numbers out loud. So compare the student's performance on different problems to determine if he or she can adjust to changing circumstances by adapting strategies. Of course, if the student is functioning at the lowest level and possesses only a counting all strategy, there are no alternatives available, and the question of adaptation does not arise.

If the student shows some degree of success on problems involving the addition of concrete objects, you should next explore the addition of imaginary objects. One simple way of doing this is by using story problems similar to those discussed above. For example: "Joan is holding two teddy bears. She walks into her room and picks up three more. How many is she now holding altogether?" Many students will have no difficulty in responding to such problems expressed on a totally verbal level. If it seems necessary to simplify the problem, however, you can show the student concrete objects (like sets of teddy bears) at the outset then remove them from view so the student cannot arrive at a solution merely by counting objects. Thus, at the outset you can show the student two teddy bears then put them where the student cannot see them, repeat the process with the three teddy bears, and then have the student solve the problem. In this situation, the student has the chance to see what the problem involves but must solve the problem mentally in the absence of the objects.

When imaginary addition problems of this type are used, students generally use number facts or a counting strategy. Number facts are likely to be used particularly on smaller problems and can be identified mainly by the student's rapid response. Counting all or counting on are likely to be used on larger problems and may be executed entirely on a mental level. Or the student may carry out a counting strategy by representing the absent objects with fingers or whatever objects are available like blocks or chips.

Thus, given the problem 3 + 2, the student first holds out three fingers, then two, and then counts the lot. Of course, when the calculations are being carried out on a mental level, there is even more room for minor execution errors than on the concrete addition problems. So remember to concentrate on the student's strategy rather than on accuracy alone. And don't forget to see how the student adapts strategies to deal with problems involving numbers of different magnitudes.

Success on imaginary addition problems represents a more advanced level of functioning than does the solution of concrete problems. Now the student can solve problems mentally and does not require the presence of concrete objects. He or she feels increasingly comfortable in using abstract thought to deal with mathematical problems.

Learning Potential. Suppose the student does poorly at the concrete or imaginary addition problems. He or she does not just make minor execution errors; rather, the student seems to lack any sensible strategy for solving the problems. The next question is: Does the student have the *potential* to understand addition, or is he or she totally incapable of understanding the concept? A complete lack of understanding is rare, but it can occur in learning disabled students and particularly in retarded students. The only way to determine whether the potential for understanding exists is to see what happens when you teach the student addition. Perhaps with a bit of help the student will learn effective addition strategies.

The best way to provide this help is through simple games involving concrete objects. You might try something like the car race game (Figure 16.2), developed by Baroody and Gannon (1983) for the purpose of teaching retarded students. Or better still, develop your own games. The essence of the car race game is a competition between you and the student to see whose car can arrive first at the finish line of an imaginary race track. The number of spaces a player can move is determined by throwing two large dice (very large dice created from blocks of wood, so that it is easy to count the dots) and then figuring out the sum of their dots. The student and you take turns, although the student adds up your dots as well as his or hers. Children seem to enjoy the game and can play it for a very long time. It is easy to produce many variations of the game by using, for instance, horses instead of cars or by modifying popular games like *Sorry* to use dice instead of playing cards.

Analytic teaching in games like these should involve the most elementary form of counting—counting all. The student can be told, "Here's a way for you to find out how many spaces you can move. Just count each of the dots like this. Start with the dots on this side, count them one by one very carefully, and then go on to these over here." This may seem like a trivial task, but for some students it is not. These students require persistent help in remembering to count both dice and in learning to count all the dots once and only once. As you play the game with students, it will be interesting

FIGURE 16.2. The Car Race Game

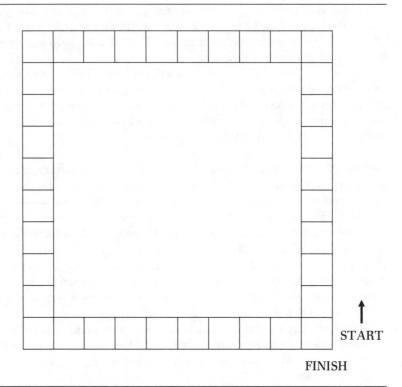

START

FINISH

Adapted from "The Use of Economical Mental Addition Strategies by Young Children" by A. J. Baroody and K. E. Gannon, 1983, paper presented at the annual meeting of the American Educational Research Association, Montreal. Printed by permission of the authors.

to observe not only whether they can learn the basic counting on strategy but also whether they can go beyond it. For example, does the student learn to see the numbers of certain configurations of dots without counting them (e.g., the dots that look like a triangle are three, the ones that look like a box are four)? Can the student short-cut the counting all strategy by using counting on (e.g., if he or she sees that one die has three because it has a triangle, the student can just count on from there to get the sum)? Does the student eventually remember that $2 + 2 = 4$ without having to calculate?

A simple task like the car race game can reveal a good deal concerning students' potential. You may find that given a bit of instruction, a student will "take off," surprising you with how much he or she can do. It's as if the student is saying, "Oh, is that what you mean by addition? That's easy;

watch what I can do!" When this happens, you have tapped a previously unrecognized potential, and the chances for educating the student successfully are greatly enhanced. Or, in a less happy case, you may find that the student simply cannot learn the game. He or she always forgets to count some of the dots or fails to consider both dice no matter how much help you provide. Here the potential for understanding is limited, hence, the educational prognosis is not favorable. In this case you may wish to pursue the assessment of enumeration, counting, and informal concepts as described below.

Assessing Informal Subtraction Calculation

To this point we have discussed only addition, since it is usually the first operation children learn. But you may also wish to explore subtraction, which is a somewhat harder operation but not out of the reach of young children. To investigate subtraction, use the same types of techniques as those described above. Just modify the stories to describe "take away." For example, "Alan has three flowers. He drops one on the floor. How many does he have left?" Children's strategies will be very similar to those used for addition. But instead of counting all or counting on, they will typically count backward or use some other form of counting to subtract.

Assessing Enumeration and Counting

If the student has performed well on the addition or subtraction tasks described above, his or her enumeration (i.e., the counting of *objects*) and counting skills (i.e., knowledge of the counting *words*) are likely to be basically sound, and there is no need to investigate them further. But if calculation was poor, then you need to investigate enumeration and counting more thoroughly. Through activities like the car race game, you will have the opportunity to observe how students enumerate objects. That is, you can see whether students carefully count each dot once and only once, or whether they make errors of various types. Some students approach the task in a haphazard way, without a plan, and apparently do not even try to count many of the dots. You may wonder whether these students know that it is necessary to count all the dots once and only once or whether they know it but execute enumeration very badly. To answer this question, you might first ask the student what he or she is trying to do. For example: "Are you supposed to count these dots too?" "To get the right answer, do you have to count all the dots?" If the student seems to misunderstand the goal of enumeration, you may wish to see whether he or she can learn it if taught. Is the concept of enumeration totally beyond the student, or can he or she grasp it with a bit of help?

By the age of 5 or 6, most students seem to understand what enumeration requires but do it so poorly that they often skip dots and sometimes count dots twice. You may wonder whether this is the result of sloppiness and inattention or whether it reflects deep-seated limitations of the student. One way to find out is simply to encourage the student to work carefully at enumeration, especially by slowing down if he or she is rushing. Tell the student to enumerate very carefully by counting all of the dots, not skipping any or counting any twice. Some students respond favorably to this kind of external "conscience." If so, then you know that careful enumeration is not beyond the limits of the student, even though he or she may require frequent reminders to keep counting accurately. Eventually, students must learn to administer these reminders themselves, and perhaps the teacher can help them to learn this form of self-control.

If the student persists in skipping or omitting dots, you may wonder whether the student even recognizes his or her own mistakes. One way to find out is to say: "Watch me closely. I'm going to count the dots now, and I want you to tell me if I make any mistakes." You can then occasionally skip a dot or count a dot twice to determine whether the student recognizes any of your mistakes. As we all know, it is sometimes easier to identify mistakes in others than to recognize (let alone correct them!) in ourselves.

Some students may enumerate badly because they cannot count well. The student may point to each dot and not omit any but incorrectly count: "One, two, three, five, eight." In this case, the student is obviously quite immature and requires extensive remedial work in counting.

Assessing Informal Concepts

Suppose that the student performs very badly on enumeration tasks, and attempts to help do not produce much of an improvement. At this point you may find it useful to explore the student's knowledge of certain informal concepts that are fundamental for the understanding of arithmetic. If, despite the other weaknesses, the student understands these concepts, he or she can learn at least some arithmetic. If these concepts are weak or lacking, then the prognosis for successful remediation is poor, and it may be appropriate to seek further diagnostic services.

The Notion of More. As pointed out in Chapter 14, the notion of *more* is among the earliest and most fundamental of informal concepts. It seems to provide the intuitive foundation for later and more sophisticated ideas concerning the inequality of numbers. Recognizing that 5 dots are more than 2 is the precursor to knowing that 5 is a larger number than 2. You can easily measure a student's grasp of this concept by presenting the student with pairs of randomly arranged sets of objects (e.g., 5 pennies vs. 9 pennies), as illustrated in Figure 16.3, and asking him or her to: "Tell me quickly which side has more. Don't count them; just show me quickly whether this side has more or whether this one does. Just show me the one that has more." Start with simple problems like 3 versus 1, 5 versus 2, and so forth to make the task clear for the student. If the student seems not to understand, then give him or her feedback after the first few simple problems: "No, this one has more, and that one has less." But once the student has caught on, there is no need to tell the student whether he or she is right or wrong. Proceed to somewhat larger problems like 8 versus 4 or 6 versus 9. Remember to randomize the position in which you place the larger set; don't put it only on the left or right.

Conservation. The conservation problem, pictured in Figure 16.4 and described earlier in Chapter 14, investigates the student's notion of equivalence. In particular, is the student's concept of equivalence distorted by mere physical appearance? You can begin the conservation problem by asking the student to construct two rows of objects with the same number of items. For example: "Here are some red blocks in a line. Now take some of these green blocks and make a row with exactly the same number—just the same number of green blocks as red ones." If you use about 5 or 6 blocks, the typical 5 or 6 year old will construct a row of the same number and same length as the model (your row). Next, as the student watches, take your red row and stretch it out so that it is longer than the other. "Now are there are as many red blocks as there are green ones, or are there more red or more green?" If the child does not seem to understand the question, feel free to modify the question, using the flexible interviewing techniques described in Chapter 15. You can ask: "Do they have the same number?" or "Do we both have the same?" You want to determine whether the young

FIGURE 16.3. The Concept of More: Randomly Arranged Pennies

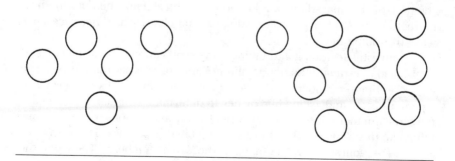

FIGURE 16.4. The Conservation Task

PHASE
1

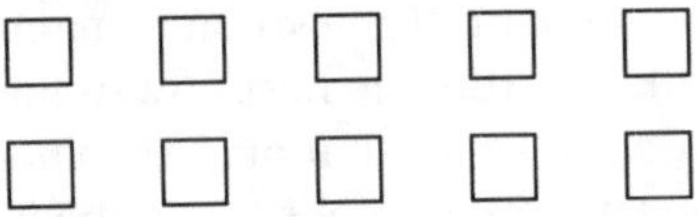

Transition: One row is spread out

PHASE
2

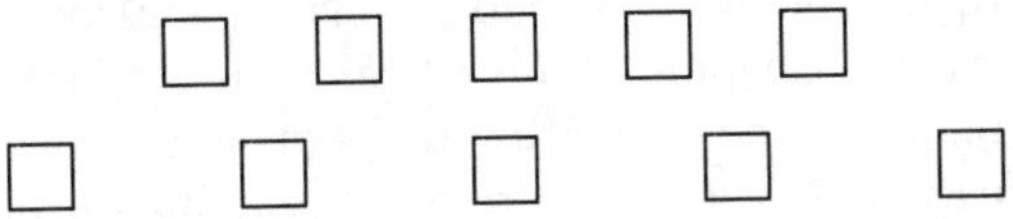

---

child recognizes that the equivalence between the two sets is conserved or maintained despite the irrelevant change in appearance, or whether the student believes that lengthening a set (or even shortening it) makes it more numerous than it was before. To be sure of your conclusion, give the student several conservation problems with different objects. Also, on at least one problem, ask him or her to count the objects in each set to see if this helps the student to conserve. On another problem, use small numbers of elements—perhaps 3 or 4 items in each set—to see if the size of sets affects the student's response.

Adding and Taking Away. Does the student understand that *adding* to a set makes it have more and that *taking away* makes it have less? This is essential for the later learning of elementary arithmetic. The techniques of written addition will make no sense unless the student knows that in a problem like 23 + 14 the addition of 14 to 23 results in a sum larger than 23. As pointed out in Chapter 14, most young students have an intuitive understanding of the operations of addition and subtraction. The question now is whether the student you are testing has such knowledge. Here are some ways of finding out.

To investigate adding and taking away, you can use the same coins or chips used to evaluate the notion of *more* and for conservation tests. Begin by presenting the student with two equal sets of objects, like two rows of 5 pennies each, and asking him or her to determine whether the sets have the same number of objects (Figure 16.5). Your instructions might be something like this: "Look at this. Here are two lines of pennies. This is my line and this is yours. Do we both have the same number?" Then put the

FIGURE 16.5. The Adding Experiment

PHASE
1

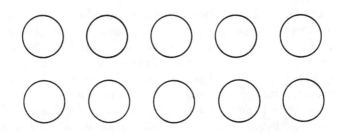

Transition: Pennies are placed in identical containers

PHASE
2

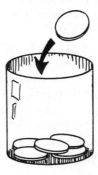

5 pennies are in each container, and a penny is added to one.

coins into two separate containers into which the student cannot see, one on his or her left and one on the right. Say, "See, I'm hiding this line of pennies in this box and this line of pennies in this box so you can't see them any more." At this point, you can check on the student's understanding of the situation by asking: "Can you remember whether both boxes have the same number of pennies, or does one have more?" If the student is uncertain or incorrect, you can demonstrate again that the two sets have the same amount. Don't go on until the student clearly understands that the two sets are equal in number. Next, take a new coin and dramatically drop it into one of the containers, so the student can see it falling through the air into the box. Say, "Watch carefully what I'm going to do next. I'm taking this penny, and I'm dropping it into this box." The question, of course, is whether the student realizes that adding to the collection in the box makes it have more than the other set. Say, "Do these two boxes have the same number of pennies, or does one have more?" If students do not spontaneously explain their answers, ask them to do so. Often students will express their understanding of the adding task quite clearly, as in: "You added more to that one, so it has more."

After this, you can do some interesting variations on the task. For example, you can take away the penny you added. Does the student recognize that this inverse action restores the original equality? Or, after you have hidden the two equal sets, you can add 3 pennies to one set and 1 to the other. Which set has more now? You can use similar problems to investigate subtraction. After hiding the two equal sets, you can do the following: (a) Take away one penny from a set, (b) return the penny you just removed, and (c) take away 3 pennies from one set and 2 from the other. Again, try to get the students to verbalize their reasoning: Do they demonstrate real understanding of the principles of addition and subtraction?

An especially interesting and difficult variation of the task is this. Begin with two clearly unequal sets—say, 8 in one and 3 in the other—and hide them as before. Then add one penny to the *smaller* set, so that now there are 8 in one and 4 in the other. Now what does the student say? He or she could maintain that the set with 8 still is larger. Or he or she could make the mistake, as many students do, of saying that the other set is larger "because you added something to it." This is true in a sense, since the set with 4 is larger than it was before. But does the student understand that a set can be added to (as in the observed 3 + 1 set) but still have less than another set (the set with 8)? This is a subtle notion—that something can get bigger but still be smaller than something else which did not get bigger— and the student may not understand it.

Implications for Teaching. Usually, by the time they enter elementary school, most students understand basic informal concepts like more, equivalence, and adding and taking away. These concepts are so solid that you can use them as the intuitive foundation on which to build an understanding of school arithmetic. But what if your informal assessment reveals that the student does not understand such notions as adding or grasps them only weakly? In that event you have no alternative but to undertake instruction on the most basic level and attempt to teach the student these basic informal concepts. This is a risky venture, since there is no body of evidence demonstrating that this can be done effectively. Nevertheless, you must try, and the procedure most likely to succeed is one that uses games derived from the assessment tasks. For example, you can create a contest in which students get points (perhaps for moving their cars around the track in the car race game) if they correctly determine which set has more in the adding task. But feel free to use any strategy that seems effective in teaching these concepts, since they are a necessary first step in the learning of arithmetic.

Formal Concepts

Suppose you find through informal assessment that the student experiencing difficulty in early school arithmetic has reasonable skill in informal addition and adequate knowledge of informal concepts like more and adding. Indeed, this is the most likely finding: Almost all students in elementary school have a solid foundation in informal mathematics. Now you need to explore the student's school work. You can begin with an examination of the student's ability to use some form of writing to represent number.

Representation of Number. The most fundamental aspect of written arithmetic is the ability to use written symbolism to signify the numbers in a set. This can be done by a device as simple as tallies or by conventional written numbers. The first question then is: Can the student use some form of writing to represent quantity? The test of this is very simple: Just show the student a collection of objects and ask him or her to describe in writing the number in the set. The following game-like situation is useful for this purpose. As a puppet, doll, or toy character is placed behind an imaginary wall, the student is told: "Puppet is going to hide behind this wall so he can't see. But he wants to know exactly how many pennies there are on the other side of the wall." At this point you can place some pennies in front of the student, but of course, where Puppet cannot see them. Encourage the student to count the objects carefully to get the right number. "Can you write down something on paper to tell Puppet exactly how many pennies are here?" After the student writes down the answer, he or she is asked to read it to Puppet. This gives you information on what the student intended to write. If the student produces either pictures or tallies, ask him or her to try another method: "Can you write the number another way so that Puppet will know exactly how many pennies there are?"

In this situation, students produce several kinds of responses (Figure 16.6). The most immature response is simply to draw the objects, often ignoring their number. Here the student can create a symbol—the picture—to represent the objects, but the symbol is not very abstract: It closely resembles the objects depicted and does not provide accurate information concerning quantity. A more advanced response is to use tallies. These are symbols that ignore the appearance of the objects but that attempt to specify number. However, tallies are cumbersome: To know the number represented by the tallies, you have to count the tallies. They preserve information about number but do not communicate it in a convenient way. The most mature response, of course, is to write down a numeral. This is an abstract symbol that conveys exact information about number.

Suppose the student uses pictures in this situation, even after you suggest that he or she use another method. This suggests that the student has limited ability to represent number in an abstract fashion and needs help

---

FIGURE 16.6. Student Representations of Number

What the student sees:

What the student draws:

A. Picture

B. Tallies

C. Numeral

---

to do it. Games revolving around communication might be useful. For example, you can ask the student to communicate in writing the number of a set of pennies to a hidden friend, who must then reproduce the collection's exact number. Say, "Write down for your friend exactly how many pennies there are here so that he can show me. If he gets it right, you'll both get a prize." The game can become even more interesting if the students take turns as writer and reader. Activities like these can help the student learn methods of representing number that are more efficient than the drawing of pictures. If the student uses tallies in the puppet game, he or she exhibits some skill in abstract representation but needs to receive training in the use of conventional numerals. The game involving communication between friends can be modified for this purpose. Say, "Write down for your friend a number that tells him (or her) exactly how many pennies there are." In the puppet game, most students will write numerals, not pictures or tallies, and it is to the writing of numerals that we turn next.

Writing Numerals. As pointed out in Chapter 14, students have to memorize the first ten digits, from 0 to 9, in order to write them. They have to learn that the numeral 6 is written when you want to convey "six." One of the most frequent mistakes the student makes in learning to write numerals is visually reversing them. If you administer the puppet task, or if you simply ask a student to write down some spoken numbers, he or she may write ⟨ for 7, ⊆ for 2, ℮ for 9, and so forth. It is natural that students do this, because previous experience has taught them that an object's left-right orientation generally makes no difference and should be ignored. For example, a car is the same whether it faces left or right. Why should numerals or letters be any different? But they are different, and the student has to learn that orientation is now relevant and cannot be overlooked. Fortunately, most students learn this on their own without extensive instruction, so there is generally no need for concern. The teacher should just point out to the student once in awhile that his or her numerals are reversed and encourage the student to straighten them out. It is only if the reversals persist over a long period of time—say, into the second grade—that you need to worry about the possibility of a perceptual problem or learning disorder.

Another major type of writing error occurs when the student writes relatively large numbers. Suppose you ask the student to write down "twenty-three" and "forty-five." He or she may very well write 203 and 405. As pointed out in Chapter 14, the errors are not random but result from the student writing the number as it sounds. This is a strategy; it can be considered the student's original attempt to write the numbers according to a systematic rule. Errors of this type usually drop out without extensive instruction, only to reappear again when the student encounters still bigger numbers. Now he or she may write 80023 for "eight hundred twenty-three." Again, do not be overly concerned with errors like these unless they persist for a long time.

REFERENCES

Baroody, A. J., & Gannon, K. E. (1983). *The use of economical mental addition strategies by young children.* Paper presented at the annual meeting of the American Educational Research Association, Montreal.

Connelly, A. J., Nachtman, W., & Pritchett, E. M. (1976). *KeyMath Diagnostic Arithmetic Test.* Circle Pines, MN: American Guidance Service.

Ginsburg, H. P., & Baroody, A. J. (1983). *Test of Early Mathematics Ability.* Austin, TX: PRO-ED.

17 / HOW TO ASSESS NUMBER FACTS, CALCULATION, AND UNDERSTANDING

The need for assessment of number facts, calculation, and understanding may arise in the classroom when a student performs poorly in addition, subtraction, multiplication, or division. Typically, the student is in a regular classroom, in grades 2, 3, 4, 5, or even 6. Occasionally, the student may be older, perhaps a junior high school student who still experiences difficulty with basic arithmetic. Sometimes the student may be a member of a special education class; perhaps the student is retarded. In all these cases, you want to determine the severity of the student's difficulty and the causes of it, and you want to offer suggestions for remedial work. This chapter helps you do this by discussing separately the assessment of number facts, calculation, and understanding of basic concepts.

NUMBER FACTS

What do we mean by knowing number facts? The facts involved are the relatively small number combinations of addition, subtraction, multiplication, and division. The definition of *small* is somewhat arbitrary, but typically the combinations are considered to range from $0 * 0$ (where $*$ can indicate any of the four arithmetic operations) to $10 * 10$ or perhaps even $12 * 12$. The student is considered to know the number facts when he or she has them at the tip of the tongue—that is, when they are easily accessible. Indeed, we are willing to say that the student knows the number facts *if and only* *if* he or she gets the answer very quickly. If the student comes up with a correct answer only after laborious calculation, we do not usually talk of number fact knowledge; instead we say that the student has figured the answer but did not "know" it. So knowing the number facts refers to getting a quick and correct answer to relatively small number combination problems.

There are good reasons for the student to know the number facts. First, having the number facts under control makes calculation easier. It is hard to do a complex multiplication problem like 456 × 321 if you have to struggle to find the product of 1 × 6. Second, knowing the number facts makes it easier to understand calculation. If you don't have to devote your attention to determining the sum of 1 + 2, you will have more time and energy to discover some general principles that can help you understand why you calculate as you do. Third, knowing the number facts allows you to do effective estimation. For example, suppose you want to estimate the sum of 5,234 + 8,765 by rounding. You say, "That's about 5,000 plus 9,000. I know that 5 + 9 = 14, so the sum should be about 14,000." Your estimation procedure could not have succeeded unless you knew the key number fact that 5 + 9 = 14.

What are the mental activities that allow the student to know the number facts? As pointed out in Chapter 14, knowing the number facts may involve at least three separate processes. The student might get the correct answer to the problem 2 + 5 (a) by *counting* quickly (in fact, so quickly that you might not realize he or she is doing it), (b) by remembering the answer in a rote fashion, or (c) by *reasoning* (as when the student concludes that 2 + 5 must be 7, because he or she already figured out that 5 + 2 = 7). Similarly, the student might get a wrong answer if he counts inaccurately, if his memory is poor, or if his reasoning is faulty.

Research and clinical experience show that students with learning difficulties in mathematics often suffer from poor number fact knowledge. Hence, it is important for you to find out as much as possible about reasons for students' poor performance in this area. Your assessment may lead to specific teaching recommendations.

You can assess number fact knowledge in at least two ways. The TEMA can be used to give a rough indication of the severity of the student's problem with number facts. The flexible interview can provide insight into the thought processes the student uses to get the number facts and into whether he or she can learn them. Each of these procedures is considered in the following section.

Severity of the Difficulty

The TEMA contains several items, each demanding quick response to two number fact problems. These items can be used to get a rough indication of the student's level of functioning in addition, subtraction, and multiplication. The norms show that students at about ages 7–0 to 8–5 or grades 2 and 3 should do reasonably well with items 20 (2 – 2, 6 – 6), 22 (3 + 4, 6 + 3), 25 (6 + 4, 7 + 3), 29 (8 – 4, 12 – 6), and 30 (8 + 8, 7 + 7). Similarly, students at about ages 8–0 to 9–6 or grades 3 and 4 should perform adequately with items 32 (3 × 1, 6 × 1), 34 (10 – 3, 10 – 6), 39 (8 + 5, 9 + 7), and 48 (3 × 2, 8 × 2). If the student at the second or third grade level experiences considerable difficulty—that is, getting almost all wrong—with the first set of items, or if the student in the third or fourth grade has serious trouble with the second set of items, the student's level of functioning is low relative to that of his or her peers, and you should probably undertake further assessment of the kind described below. Of course, individual schools vary in their timetables for introducing the four operations of arithmetic, so you may need to adjust the norms accordingly.

Thinking Processes and Learning

To conduct flexible interviews concerning the number facts, begin with a set of problems useful for distinguishing among students' thinking strategies and for determining learning potential. The common families of facts can be useful as a starting point for your assessment. Definitions of the main families and examples are given in Table 17.1. For example, some addition number facts are taken from the family of doubles, as in 1 + 1 or 5 + 5; others from the family of N + 0 facts, as in 4 + 0 and 7 + 0; others from the "small, easy" family, as in 3 + 2; and others from the "large, difficult" family, as in 8 + 6 or 9 + 7. (Remember, of course, that "easy" and "difficult" are relative to the student's level; for a particular student, 3 + 2 may be quite hard.) In subtraction, one important family is N – 0 (as in 5 – 0) facts; another is N – 1 (as in 5 – 1); and another is N – N (as in 6 – 6).

Using Table 17.1, you can easily construct a series of number fact problems in addition, subtraction, multiplication, or division. Devise many problems, since it may be necessary to test and retest the student in a certain area if the results are not clear. You can present the problems in either written or oral form. If you are sure that the student has no difficulty in reading simple numerals, flashcards may be useful to present the number fact problems. If the student has trouble reading, present the number facts orally so you don't confuse inability to read with poor knowledge of the number facts.

Instructions might take this form: "Now I'm going to show you some adding problems. Tell me *quickly* what you think the answer is. How much is six and four altogether? Just tell me what pops into your head when I say, 'How much is six and four altogether?'" These instructions are intended to get the student to respond spontaneously, without engaging in extensive

TABLE 17.1. Number Fact Families

Addition

N + 0: 1 + 0, 2 + 0, 3 + 0, etc.

N + 1: 1 + 1, 2 + 1, 3 + 1, etc.

N + 2: 1 + 2, 2 + 2, 3 + 2, etc.

N + N: 1 + 1, 2 + 2, 3 + 3, etc.

Small, easy: 1 + 1, 2 + 1, 2 + 2, 3 + 1, 3 + 2, 4 + 1, 4 + 2, 4 + 3, etc.

Large, difficult: 7 + 5, 7 + 6, 7 + 8, 7 + 9, 8 + 5, 8 + 6, 8 + 7, etc.

Subtraction

N − 0: 1 − 0, 2 − 0, 3 − 0, etc.

N − 1: 1 − 1, 2 − 1, 3 − 1, etc.

N − 2: 2 − 2, 3 − 2, 4 − 2, etc.

N − N: 1 − 1, 2 − 2, 3 − 3, etc.

Small, easy: 1 − 1, 2 − 1, 2 − 2, 3 − 1, 3 − 2, 3 − 3, 4 − 1, 4 − 2, etc.

Large, difficult: 7 − 2, 7 − 3, 7 − 4, 8 − 2, 8 − 3, 8 − 5, 9 − 2, etc.

Multiplication

N × 0: 1 × 0, 2 × 0, 3 × 0, etc.

N × 1: 1 × 1, 2 × 1, 3 × 1, etc.

N × 2: 1 × 2, 2 × 2, 3 × 2, etc.

N × N: 1 × 1, 2 × 2, 3 × 3, etc.

Small, easy: 1 × 1, 2 × 1, 2 × 2, 3 × 1, 3 × 2, 3 × 3, 4 × 2, 5 × 2, etc.

Large, difficult: 5 × 6, 5 × 7, 5 × 8, 5 × 9, 6 × 4, 6 × 5, 6 × 7, 6 × 8, etc.

Division

N ÷ 1: 1 ÷ 1, 2 ÷ 1, 3 ÷ 1, etc.

N ÷ 2: 2 ÷ 2, 4 ÷ 2, 6 ÷ 2, etc.

N ÷ N: 1 ÷ 1, 2 ÷ 2, 3 ÷ 3, etc.

Small, easy: 2 ÷ 1, 2 ÷ 2, 3 ÷ 1, 3 ÷ 3, 4 ÷ 1, 4 ÷ 2, 4 ÷ 4, 5 ÷ 1, 5 ÷ 5, 6 ÷ 1, 6 ÷ 6, etc.

Large, difficult: 8 ÷ 2, 10 ÷ 2, 12 ÷ 3, 15 ÷ 3, 18 ÷ 3, 21 ÷ 3, 20 ÷ 4, 24 ÷ 4, etc.

calculation. Moreover, the student is given only 3 seconds to respond; the examiner goes on to the next problem if he or she takes longer.

The order of administration of the problems will vary according to the student's level and your purposes. If the student seems to know few number facts, you obviously have to present only simple problems. If you suspect that the student has particular difficulty with reasoning, then you may focus on problems designed to deal with that strategy (these are discussed below). If you don't know too much about the student, then just plunge in with problems that seem appropriate for his or her age level.

After developing problems representing the various kinds of number facts, you can attempt to answer the following questions concerning students who are having difficulty with number facts. (a) What strategy is the student using? (b) Can the student generalize a counting or reasoning stategy to new problems? (c) Can the student check his or her answer? (d) If the student cannot remember a number fact, can he or she get it by counting? (e) Can the student learn new number facts by counting or memory? (f) How should the student be taught? Consider each question in turn.

What Strategy Is the Student Using? Children experiencing difficulty with the number facts often make errors for one of two reasons: (a) They count badly or (b) they remember poorly. To investigate counting, present the student with problems selected from relatively large or difficult families. Remember that for a 6 year old, "relatively large" may mean 3 + 2 or even 2 + 1; you always have to adjust the problems to the student's level. You will need to observe and record the question and the student's answer, the time it takes him or her to get it, and any signs of counting, obvious or subtle.

You may observe several different behavioral patterns. The simplest pattern is if the student counts in an obvious manner—whether out loud, on his or her fingers, or in whispers. If you observe this behavior, you have clear evidence of the student's strategy. But usually you won't be so lucky. Instead, you are likely to see either a slow response with a slightly wrong answer or a slow response with a very wrong answer. In the first case, suppose that the student responds slowly to a problem like 6 + 5 and gets the answer 10. A reasonable interpretation is that the student solved the problem by counting but made a minor error of execution. In the second case, suppose that the student responds slowly but gets the answer 19. You might conclude that he or she was guessing, since it is unlikely that counting could have gone so far wrong. You can try to engage in flexible interviewing to pin down the student's strategy. "How did you do that problem?" "What did you do to get that answer?"

To investigate memory for number facts, present the student with problems like 2 + 1, selected from relatively small and easy families, or with problems from the doubles family, like 2 + 2, which are also usually committed to memory. Again, there are several possible types of response. If the student answers slowly and comes up with an answer fairly close to the correct one, he or she probably counted. If, on the other hand, the student answers quickly but produces an answer that is dramatically wrong or even absurd, as in 3 + 6 = 2, he or she probably guessed or perhaps pulled out of memory something that should not have been stored in there in the first place. Again, you can try to determine the student's strategy through flexible interviewing.

To investigate reasoning, present the student with problems like 6 + 0, selected from families that illustrate a simple principle (in this case, that the addition of zero doesn't change anything or, more formally, the *identity axiom*). Be careful to include problems that could not be remembered but that must be solved through reasoning—in this case, problems like 185 + 0. Obviously, if the student gets problems like these correct, he or she is likely to have reasoned. If the answers are *systematically* wrong, the students also may have reasoned. For example, given the N × 0 multiplication family, the student may respond by saying that 6 × 0 = 6, 8 × 0 = 8, and so forth, because "zero doesn't make any difference." He or she has solved the problems by reasoning, but has used the wrong principle in doing so. (Probably the identity axiom from addition was misapplied.)

In brief, as a result of the flexible interview, you are likely to find that the student's failure at number facts results from inaccurate counting, from wild guesses, from faulty memory, from misguided reasoning, or perhaps from a combination of the four. Next you can ask more subtle questions.

Can the Student Generalize a Counting or Reasoning Strategy?
Suppose you find that the student counted to get number fact answers with reasonable accuracy. Does this mean that he or she can use counting on all relevant problems? Not necessarily. Sometimes students can use counting only on small problems but not larger ones. To determine whether the strategy is a general one, you need to present the student with new problems (particularly larger ones), examine speed and accuracy of response, and look for overt signs of counting. Similarly, suppose you find that the student used a principle like "Zero doesn't change anything" to get the number fact 6 + 0 = 6. This does not necessarily mean that the student can use the same principle on other problems. He or she may not realize, for example, that the same principle applies to numbers larger than 100. Again, the only way to determine whether the strategy is a general one is to challenge the student with new problems.

Can the Student Check Answers?
Suppose the student uses any strategy described above to deal with a number fact problem. How does he or she know whether the answer is right or wrong if there is no authoritative means (like a table in a book) to validate it? Does the student know that there are ways to check? To find out, you need to give the student almost any

number fact problem. After he or she solves the problem, ask, "Do you think that's the right or wrong answer?" When the student answers, you challenge him or her by saying, "How do you know?" or "How could you find out?" Generally, there are two ways of finding out. One way is to count. This may be tedious but always works if you do it right. A second way is to reason from what you already know. Thus, "4 + 5 = 9 because I know that 4 + 4 = 8 and the other is just one more, so it must be 9." Of course, if you insist on asking how the student knows that 4 + 4 = 8, he or she may have to count. In brief, it is important to determine whether the student has a means to check number facts; books and calculators are not always around (and sometimes books and calculators need checking, too!).

If the Student Cannot Remember a Number Fact, Can Counting be Used?
Suppose the student tries to remember the number facts but can't. The strategy is memory, but the student's memory is empty, at least with regard to the fact being sought. Can the student find the fact by another means? The most feasible alternative is likely to be counting. One way to find out if the student can use this alternative strategy is to ask, after he or she has failed to remember a fact, "Is there any other way you could do it besides remembering? Can you find the answer another way?" Often the response to a question like this is that the student didn't know that he or she was allowed to do it any other way, or that any other method is cheating. Once you relieve the concerns on this matter, the student will often show that he or she can easily get the answer by counting. Sometimes the student may genuinely lack skills like counting. If this seems to be the case, you are led to the next question.

Can the Student Learn to Use Counting or Memory?
Suppose you have found that the student does not seem capable of getting the facts by counting or memory. Can he or she be taught to use either strategy? These are the key issues for instruction: Can the student learn to get number facts by counting, and can he or she learn to remember number facts? In both cases, you need to do a teaching experiment. In the first case, you need to deliberately teach counting strategies and then determine whether the student can use them accurately and generalize them to new number fact problems. In the second case, you need to engage in repetitious drill to determine whether the student is capable of retention.

How Should the Student be Taught?
The answer to this question depends on what the student's problem is. Suppose that the student's number fact errors result mainly from faulty reasoning. Believing, for example, that "Multiplying by zero makes no difference," the student concludes that

6 × 0 = 6. In this case, your best strategy is to deal with the faulty reasoning directly. Disabuse the student of the faulty principles and teach the right ones. This kind of instruction is most effective when it makes extensive use of examples. Only after giving the student experience with patterns in the number fact tables should you verbalize the relevant principle. Thus, show the student the sequence 1 × 0 = 0, 2 × 0 = 0, 3 × 0 = 0, and so forth, let him or her practice it, and then teach the explicit rule by which the student can reason to get the facts.

Suppose that the student's problem is faulty counting. In this case, too, you need to attack the deficiency directly. Give the student instruction in careful counting. Practice in the counting of concrete objects may even be required. You may have to teach the student not to skip objects and not to count them more than once each. You may wish to use simple games, like the car race game described in Chapter 16, in which the number of moves is determined by getting the sum of dots on two dice. More likely, the student will need practice in the mental counting of verbally presented numbers, as well as reassurance that doing it is acceptable. Tell the student that it is all right to get the number facts by counting—at least at first—and help him or her do it efficiently. The student may need practice in how to count forward for addition and backward for subtraction. Multiplication is harder to do mentally but can be approached through "skip counting" on a number line. Thus, multiplying by 2s is just like counting by 2s: You start with 2 and then systematically skip one number on the number line ("jump over 3 and go to 4; then jump over 5, going to 6," etc.). Multiplying by 3s is just like jumping to every third number on the line, and so on. Division is very difficult to teach in this way; don't even try.

Suppose that the student cannot remember the number facts. If he or she can count to get them, encourage that instead. Perhaps after enough repetitious counting the student will begin to remember them. But what if memory is lacking, and the student does not have counting to fall back on? In this case, the first approach should be through drill. Flashcards are often effective and so is computer drill. Now you can choose from many computer programs—complete with rockets, space ships, and alien invaders—that do little more than present showy flashcards designed to provide individualized drill in as exciting a manner as possible. Children often enjoy these programs; they are worth trying. But suppose they don't work and nothing else does either to get the student to remember the number facts. What should be done? One approach at this point is to give up, concluding that it is not possible for the student to learn arithmetic. This would be a mistake; some students can do interesting arithmetic even if they don't know the number facts. Instead of giving up, by-pass the problem by giving the student an alternative to remembering, counting, or reasoning. Provide a calculator and let the student depend on it. Forget about teaching the number facts and go on to new topics in mathematics.

CALCULATION

This section considers calculation—the paper and pencil computation that students perform in the areas of addition, subtraction, multiplication, and division. When you encounter a student experiencing difficulty in column addition with carrying or long multiplication, you will need to determine how poorly the student is performing relative to peers, to identify the thinking processes underlying calculational mistakes, to discover whether the student can learn to eliminate the mistakes, and to implement effective instructional procedures. These are the topics considered next.

Level of Performance in Calculation

Several standard tests allow you to assess students' levels of performance with respect to ordinary calculation. Part II of the *KeyMath*, (Connelly, Nachtman, & Pritchett, 1976) contains straightforward problems involving the four operations of arithmetic and may be used to obtain normative information concerning students at any grade level in elementary school. The *Test of Mathematical Abilities* (TOMA) (Brown & McEntire, 1984), appropriate for students in grades 3 through 12, contains a computation subtest that deals with the four arithmetic operations, as well as more advanced topics like ratios and square roots. This test, too, can be used to obtain preliminary information concerning students' overall levels of functioning with respect to calculation.

Thinking Processes in Calculation

As pointed out in Chapter 14, students solve calculational problems in several different ways. Sometimes they succeed by using the standard method or algorithm (like column subtraction with borrowing) as it was taught in school. Sometimes they get the right answer by more creative means: They use procedures that are at least in part invented, often modifying the techniques taught in school, or they perform mental calculation to solve written problems. These potentially successful methods can fail in any of several ways. For example, the student may get wrong answers because of a systematic error strategy or bug—like "Always subtract the smaller from the larger" (which gives $21 - 19 = 18$). Consider first the use of tests to measure thought processes like these.

Tests. Some tests of calculation focus on the student's strategies of solution, not just on right and wrong answers. These tests attempt to identify both the methods that lead to correct answers (algorithms, invented strategies) and those that lead to failure (bugs and others to be discussed). The first test of this type, devised by Buswell and John (1926), focused on strategies systematically leading to error, which they called the "bad habits" of arithmetic and which we now call bugs. The Buswell-John test was brilliantly conceived and far ahead of its time. The only serious flaw in the test was that Buswell and John considered invented strategies—like mental calculation—to be bad habits. We know now that they are not. Indeed, invented strategies are good habits; they provide the informal foundation for a sound understanding of calculation. Despite this, the Buswell-John test is a model for later efforts.

Recently, Ginsburg and Mathews (1984) have continued in the tradition of Buswell and John by developing the *Diagnostic Test of Arithmetic Strategies* (DTAS), which attempts to identify strategies underlying success and failure in addition, subtraction, multiplication, and division. The DTAS contains three sections: setting up the problem, calculational processes, and informal skill.

Alignment. Section I of the DTAS deals with several basic ways in which the student may set up the written algorithm incorrectly. For example, given the problem "Write down and solve: How much is 23 + 7?" the student may write:

In this case, the student's error involves misalignment or faulty organization. When addends with uneven numbers of digits are involved, students often line up all numbers to the left and get seemingly absurd answers— sums that are drastically incorrect. Such errors may imply lack of understanding of place value. The student may not realize that units must be added only to units, tens only to tens, and so on. Similar mistakes occur in subtraction and multiplication.

A related error involves sloppy alignment. Even though knowing that alignment should begin on the right, first with units, then tens, and so on, the student may execute the alignment in a sloppy fashion so that it is not clear what goes with what. Thus, he or she may write:

$$\begin{array}{r} 2{\_}3 \\ +\ 7 \\ \hline \end{array}$$

Such sloppy alignment often, but not always, leads to calculational error. Sometimes students survive the sloppiness; they remember to add units to units, tens to tens, and so on, despite the fact that the alignment of the problem does not help them to do this.

In the case of division, the major error in setting up the problem is not vertical alignment, but incorrect organization of the numbers with respect to the division sign. For example, asked to do 32 divided by 12, one student wrote:

$$32\overline{)12}$$

This is a reversal of divisor and dividend, a serious error of organization that clearly leads to calculational mistakes. The DTAS is designed to identify errors of this type as well.

In brief, one important reason for students' errors of computation is incorrect alignment or organization strategy. Typically, it involves lining up numbers from left to right or reversing divisor and dividend. The DTAS investigates these faulty strategies by a simple method: The student is asked to write out calculational problems with uneven numbers of digits, for example 92 + 7, 147 − 32, 32 × 4, and 96 ÷ 3. While simple and apparently obvious, this method is seldom used. Most tests present the student with problems already written in the proper manner and require him or her to solve the problems, not to arrange them in the first place. Yet this is precisely where many students experience difficulty.

Once you have identified alignment or organization errors, it is relatively easy to deal with them on one level, and harder on another. The easy part is to get the student to change his or her behavior. Usually, if you just point out the faulty misalignment procedure and then show the student how to align properly, he or she will not have much trouble doing so. But does the student now understand why alignment takes the form it does? Not necessarily. And that is much harder to teach, as you will see in the last section of this chapter.

Bugs. Section II of the DTAS presents students with a collection of calculational problems (in any of the four operations), correctly aligned and organized (since this section is not concerned with setting up the problem) and carefully designed to identify several different sources of error. The chief source of error is bugs. As we saw in Chapter 14, a bug is an organized method—a systematic strategy—for solving problems that contains a fundamental flaw and hence can result in wrong answers even if carefully and conscientiously applied. For example, the student may use the bug "Write all sums below the line regardless of place value" (or "Never carry") to work this problem as follows:

$$\begin{array}{r} 28 \\ + 13 \\ \hline 311 \end{array}$$

Many wrong answers result from bugs; the student's errors are not random or capricious.

The DTAS is designed to identify the most frequent bugs (about five or six) in each of the four arithmetic operations. The test does this by presenting the student with carefully selected written calculational problems and asking him or her to think out loud. For example, suppose the student employs the bug just described, "Never carry." Identifying this bug requires presenting the student with problems in which something should be carried so the bug can have a chance to operate. Obviously, if no carrying is required, then it is impossible to determine whether the student uses the bug in question. The student's overt response to the problem (the numbers written) and his or her verbalizations (if any) both may be used to shed light on the method of solution. The DTAS manual carefully describes the major bugs in the four operations and shows you how to identify them. Once you get used to thinking about bugs, you will find that they are easy to spot.

In the unlikely event that you have trouble identifying bugs, you can turn to some clever materials devised by Ashlock (1982) and by Brown and Burton (1978) to help you. After presenting a clear description of common bugs, Ashlock offers exercises you can engage in to get practice in spotting and identifying bugs. Brown and Burton have developed a computer program, BUGGY, which also provides such practice. It works like this. The computer flashes on the screen a simple subtraction problem along with an answer that is clearly wrong. A bug is the culprit, and your job is to figure out which one. The computer then gives you some more examples of problems with answers produced by using the same bug. From all this, you try to figure out what the bug could be. Next, the computer flashes on the screen a new problem, and this time you have to predict the answer produced by use of the bug that has been identified. You type in what you think the answer would be. If you are right, the computer congratulates you profusely; if you are wrong, the computer tells you what the answer would be using the particular bug in question, and you have a chance to try again. It is actually a lot of fun to search for bugs and find them.

Number fact errors. The second section of the DTAS also measures slips and number fact errors in use of the standard algorithm. Slips are minor mistakes in the execution of a sound procedure, usually the standard algorithm. We usually consider slips to be stupid, trivial mistakes, and don't pay much attention to them. They do not seem to result from basic misunderstandings of arithmetic or serious defects in the calculational routine. Slips usually occur when the student is in a hurry, is distracted, or is trying to remember too much at once. When this happens, he or she may forget to add one of the relevant numbers or may write down the wrong number, and so forth. It is fairly easy to identify slips by observing the student's methods of calculation. If you can get students to talk aloud, which is usually not hard to do, they will probably reveal how they execute the standard algorithm, and you may be able to see them skipping a relevant number or adding another twice, or making some other slip. In such cases, the answer itself tells you little about the soundness of the student's method. A very small slip—especially in the hundreds column—can result in a very large error! Hence, concentrate on the methods, which can be essentially sound even though the answers are seriously wrong.

One of the most frequent errors in calculation occurs when students make number fact errors as they execute the standard algorithms in an otherwise correct manner. The student's knowledge of the algorithm is fine; he or she knows all the steps, including carrying and borrowing, and does them in the right order. The student would always get the right answer if only he or she could get the number facts right. And, of course, minor number fact errors can result in answers that are seriously incorrect. Again, to identify errors of this type you need to look at the student's method of solution. As the student talks aloud—"I start with 3 plus 2. That's 6."—you should be able to identify most number fact errors.

Informal calculational processes.   Section III of the DTAS accentuates the positive. This final portion of the test determines whether students spontaneously use invented methods to solve calculational problems and, if not, whether they are capable of using informal procedures when asked to do so. The student is first asked to solve some arithmetic problems "in your head" and to talk out loud about the process. If the student persists in using the standard written methods, say, "Do it a different way in your head without written numbers." The intention is to discover the intellectual resources of a student who may have a great deal of difficulty with standard calculational algorithms.

Flexible Interviewing.   While the DTAS provides useful information about methods leading to both right and wrong answers, flexible interviewing may also be necessary if the student calculates in ways the test was not designed to measure. Children are very different from one another and sometimes come up with unique calculational methods that are hard to anticipate. For example, in the case of subtraction, several hundred distinct bugs have been identified to date. The DTAS measures only five or six bugs and cannot encompass more in the short time available for testing. Consequently, identifying students' distinctive methods of calculation requires individualized attention and flexible interviewing.

You can use the DTAS as a starting point for flexible interviewing. If the student does not seem to be using one of the bugs described in Section II, ask him or her to talk aloud about some of the problems and question him or her about methods of solution. Often this will allow you to develop ideas about what method the student is in fact using.

For example, suppose that the student solves subtraction problem #15 on the DTAS as follows:

$$\begin{array}{r} 4\,0\,3 \\ -\,2\,4\,7 \\ \hline 1\,4\,6 \end{array}$$

Clearly, the student is not borrowing in the standard way and has some kind of problem with the zero. Yet, the answer is not the result of using any of the bugs described by the DTAS. Flexible interviewing reveals the following:

> **Interviewer:** How did you do that problem?
> **Child:** I borrowed.
> **Interviewer:** How?
> **Child:** I went: 3 minus 7 you can't do. So I took a 1 from the 4 and made it 13. 13 minus 7 equals 6. Then 0 minus 4 is 4, because you always take away zero from a larger number. Then 3 minus 2 equals 1.

Flexible interviewing revealed that this student used a new bug, "borrow across zero," along with one already described, "always subtract the zero from the larger number." It was not hard to identify the bug once the student talked aloud.

The Student's Learning Potential

Finally, assessment can make a major contribution by focusing on learning potential. If you have discovered through the DTAS or by flexible interviewing that the student's calculation is characterized by slips, number fact errors, or bugs, you next need to determine whether the student can learn new procedures. You need to perform a miniature teaching experiment in which you attempt to help the student get accurate number facts, to avoid slips, and to abandon bugs in favor of effective procedures, usually algorithms. If students can learn in this situation, then they are likely to profit from more intensive instruction over the long term.

Helping the Student Learn Calculation

Once you know about the student's methods of calculation and his or her potential for learning, how can you improve instruction? You will probably find from the DTAS and from your flexible interviewing that most students performing poorly in school arithmetic fail because of specific difficulties in mathematical thinking—for example, bugs or slips. Moreover, you are likely to find that these students possess some informal understanding of elementary arithmetic—for example, an effective mental strategy—and that they are capable of learning new procedures. Recent research (Russell & Ginsburg, 1984), as well as clinical experience, suggests that most students doing poorly in school do *not* suffer from psychological disturbances, learning disabilities, intellectual deficits, and the like.

Given this point of view, your approach to instruction should focus on specific problems with academic content and should encourage existing strengths. Thus, if the student calculates incorrectly because of a particular bug, then the bug needs to be replaced by an accurate calculational procedure. To do this you don't need to try to raise the student's IQ or to teach general problem-solving skills; instead, you need to correct a specific problem in arithmetic. There are several effective strategies for doing this, including the exploitation of knowledge that the student already possesses, the encouragement of active learning, and the use of available materials. Specific suggestions for implementing these strategies are given in the DTAS manual.

UNDERSTANDING BASIC CONCEPTS

Arithmetic is more than number facts and calculation. The student must learn not only to get correct answers but to develop an understanding of key concepts. The student cannot always operate in a mechanical fashion. Dealing with new and unforseen problems often requires understanding. If your car breaks down, you have a better chance of fixing it if you understand something about how the engine works. Similarly, if the student encounters an unexpected problem (like adding 3 digit numbers having previously added only 2 digit numbers), he or she is more likely to deal with the problem effectively if the concept is understood.

You can help promote this understanding by providing a sound assessment of it. Unfortunately, it is no easy job to answer the question, What does the student understand about arithmetic? Understanding is as hard to assess as it is to teach. You cannot assume that students understand just because they get right answers. There is a big difference between behavior and thought, between employing some procedure in a mechanical fashion to get a result and understanding why the procedure works as it does. Just as you can drive a car without understanding anything about engines, so you can calculate without understanding arithmetic. Yet, despite its difficulty, the assessment of understanding must be done, so understanding is the topic of this section. In particular, the section deals with the understanding of written calculation and of story problems.

Written Calculation

What does the student need to understand about written calculation? He or she should know why numbers are written as they are and why the calculational algorithms operate as they do. Consider each type of understanding in turn.

What Written Numbers Mean. In the first few grades, students usually succeed at reading and writing individual numbers of reasonable size, like 345. But do they understand why numbers are written as they are? Why can't you write "three hundred and forty five" as 543? The answer, of course, refers to the place value system: We conceive of numbers in terms of units, tens, hundreds, and so forth, and in writing we represent these numbers in a particular order (units on the right, tens immediately to the left, etc.).

The assessment of place value understanding must involve flexible interviewing, since appropriate tests are unavailable in this area. You can start out by trying to determine whether the student has any rationale for the written form of numbers. First ask the student to write a two digit number like 24. Then use flexible interviewing to ask a series of questions designed to uncover the student's rationale, if any. The following is a real interview illustrating some useful questions and typical answers.

> **Interviewer:** Now I'm going to ask you something about 24. Why did you write twenty-four with a 2 and then a 4?
> **Robert:** 'Cause that's how I write 24.
> **Interviewer:** I see that when you write 24 you have a 2 on the left and a 4 on the right. What does that 4 stand for?
> **Robert:** 'Cause it's 24.
> **Interviewer:** What does the 2 stand for?
> **Robert:** That's how you write 24.
> **Interviewer:** Why don't you write it like this? [42]
> **Robert:** That's 42.

In this case, although the student can write two digit numbers accurately, he seems to have no understanding of the place value system for written numbers. He knows when numbers are written incorrectly (you can't write "twenty-four" as 42), but he does not know why numbers are written as they are.

Other students seem to have a reasonable understanding of place value, although they express it only with difficulty. For example, here is how one girl explained why "thirteen" is written as 13: " 'Cause there's one 10, right? So you just put 1. 13 is like 10 and 3, but the way we write it, it would be 103, so they just put 1 for one 10 and 3 for the extra 3 that it adds on to the 10." In interviewing young students, do not expect them to express ideas in a formal way, as they are presented in the textbook. The explanation of 13 given above is sloppy, inelegant, and hard to follow; but it is especially convincing precisely because it is stated in the student's imperfect language. Indeed, if students do repeat what is in the textbook, you should be alert to the possibility that they are just parroting something they do not understand.

How Algorithms Work. While students can often use an algorithm like addition with carrying, do they know what it means? Why are the numbers aligned on the right side, why does addition proceed down the columns, and why do we carry? Again, your investigation of these issues will employ flexible interviewing.

You can focus on several basic questions. One is whether the student understands the fundamental purpose of a written algorithm—that it is an efficient method for accomplishing what the student already knows how to do by informal means. Does the student realize that written addition and informal counting methods both accomplish the same purposes and should be expected to give the same results? Or does the student think that written addition is an arbitrary procedure, bearing no relation to his or her own informal methods? This is not an unlikely possibility; many students do not connect what they learn in school with what they already know. They think it quite reasonable that adding 12 and 13 on your fingers and on paper should give you entirely different answers. As a result, they have no way of checking their written calculations and accept bizarre answers as eminently reasonable.

You can investigate such misconceptions by confronting the student with discrepancies between written and informal calculations. Suppose the student makes an error in calculation, as when he or she uses the "zero makes zero" bug in the problem 23 – 20. The student explains: "3 take away 0 is 0 because 0 makes nothing. 2 take away 2 is 0. So the answer is 0." At this point, you should take away the pencil and paper and ask the student to think a bit. "Suppose you have 23 pennies and you give me 20. Would there be any left over?" Few students lack the informal knowledge necessary to answer that question correctly. Next: "Now figure out how many will be left. Use your fingers if you want to." At this point, the student will probably determine the correct answer. If so, you can ask him to compare the written and informal methods and the result obtained by each. "Do you remember when you wrote 23 minus 20 over here and got the answer 0? Is that anything like the problem you just did on your fingers when you took away 20 from 23?" Some students will deny any similarity between the two problems. They will maintain that the problems are different because one involves pennies and the other numbers, or because one was done on paper and the other on the fingers. They are, therefore, not surprised by getting two different answers, nor are they upset by it.

By contrast, suppose that the student is immediately upset by the discrepancy in results. This seems to indicate that he or she knows that the two methods are equivalent. At first, the student may try to eliminate the discrepancy by checking earlier calculations. When this does not work, he or she may become suspicious of the written result. "There's no way 23 minus 20 could be 0!" This indicates that the student places primary reliance on informal knowledge. This student may not know exactly how the algorithm is related to counting, but he or she does know in a general way that one calculation ought to do the same thing as the other, and that is the first step in understanding the written algorithm.

The next step is understanding the workings of the algorithm. You can focus on two basic ideas. One, already discussed, is the base ten system. The standard algorithm cannot be properly understood unless the student realizes that the numbers must be conceptualized in terms of units, tens, hundreds, and the like. You can pursue the line of questioning described earlier to examine understanding of base ten. The other basic idea is that calculation must be done on like groups whose value is specified by their spatial position: You can subtract only units from units (and you know they are units because they are on the right), tens from tens, and so forth. Related to that is the notion that if you run out of members of a given group, you have to take some from another (borrowing); and if you have too many members, you have to give some away (carrying).

While it is hard to question the student on carrying and borrowing and related notions in multiplication and division, it is worth a try. One useful technique is to have the student explain the concept in question to another student, hypothetical or real, who does not understand it.

Also, prompt the student with questions like: Why do you start adding on that side? How are the numbers in that column [units] different from the ones over there [tens]? Why do you carry that number? What is the number you are carrying? Also, it may be useful to challenge the student's explanations with countersuggestions. "You said that the number you're borrowing is really a 30. But why? It sure looks like a 3 to me." In evaluating the student's response, beware of parroting from the textbook. An explanation that sounds too good to be true probably is. Also, be tolerant of imprecise and informal explanations; it's very hard for most people to express these ideas with ease or lucidity, especially in the case of division.

Story Problems

One common form of school arithmetic involves story problems in which the student is presented with a situation like this: "Johnny has 5 apples and gives 2 to Sue. How many does he have left?" Subtest J of the *KeyMath* and items 1 through 10 of the Story Section of the TOMA involve standard story problems like the one just described. Hence, you can get a rough idea of the student's ability to deal with such problems by comparing performance on these items with the available norms.

How does the student solve such word problems? There seem to be basically two steps in the solution process. One is interpreting the problem, and the other is applying a calculational procedure. The first thing that the student needs to do is figure out what the problem is all about. Is it a story in which something is being taken away or something is added? This is often not so easy to determine, since the stories are often stated in rather round about, even devious terms. For example, suppose the problem is: "Jim has 8 apples. He has 3 apples more than Joe. How many apples does Joe have?" This problem contains a potential trap in the word *more*. If the student looks only at the surface, he or she might interpret the story like this: "We start with 8 apples and we get 3 more, so there are 11 altogether. Joe has 11." Once the story has been interpreted as requiring addition or some other operation, it is usually fairly easy for the student to carry out the relevant computations. The main point of giving the stories is to determine whether the student can interpret them properly.

To investigate the student's interpretation, a key step is the careful selection and analysis of story problems. You've got to pick useful problems and be aware of their potential traps. The easiest problems seem to involve simple combining and changing (Riley, Greeno, & Heller, 1983). An example of simple combining is: "Joe has 3 apples. Harry has 2 apples. How many do they have altogether?" A simple change problem is: "Jill had 5 apples; she gave 2 to Mary. How many does Jill have now?" Both types can be made more complex. Thus, a change problem with an unknown starting point is: "Ken had some apples. Tom gave him 4 more apples. Now Ken has 7 apples. How many apples did Ken have at the beginning?" A problem like this is tricky, because while the story is about adding ("Tom gave him 4 more"), the solution involves subtracting. The hardest kind of problem involves a comparison like this: "Ann has 5 apples. She has 3 apples less than Betty. How many apples does Betty have?" This problem is hard because the solution requires reversing the "less than" statement. It can easily be solved when it is interpreted as: "Ann needs 3 more to have the same as Betty. How many will both have then?" Figure 17.1 presents major types of word problems for addition and subtraction.

Your flexible interviewing should focus on the student's interpretation of different types of problems. What does the student think the problem requires? And what leads him or her to this interpretation? A useful way of proceeding is to ask the student to "think out loud" while working through the problem and to give reasons for his or her interpretation. For example, in the Ann and Betty apple problem, the student might say: "Ann has 5 apples. She has 3 less than Betty so Betty has 2." "How did you get 2?" "Because I took away 3 from 5." "Why?" "Because it says 3 less." In a case like this, the

FIGURE 17.1. Word Problems for Addition and Subtraction

Action	Static

CHANGE

Result unknown

1. Joe had 3 marbles.
   Then Tom gave him 5 more marbles.
   How many marbles does Joe have now?

2. Joe had 8 marbles.
   Then he gave 5 marbles to Tom.
   How many marbles does Joe have now?

Change unknown

3. Joe had 3 marbles.
   Then Tom gave him some more marbles.
   Now Joe has 8 marbles.
   How many marbles did Tom give him?

4. Joe had 8 marbles.
   Then he gave some marbles to Tom.
   Now Joe has 3 marbles.
   How many marbles did he give to Tom?

Start unknown

5. Joe had some marbles.
   Then Tom gave him 5 more marbles.
   Now Joe has 8 marbles.
   How many marbles did Joe have in the beginning?

6. Joe had some marbles.
   Then he gave 5 marbles to Tom.
   Now Joe has 3 marbles.
   How many marbles did Joe have in the beginning?

EQUALIZING

1. Joe has 3 marbles.
   Tom has 8 marbles.
   What could Joe do to have as many marbles as Tom?
   (How many marbles does Joe need to have as many as Tom?)

2. Joe has 8 marbles.
   Tom has 3 marbles.
   What could Joe do to have as many marbles as Tom?

COMBINE

Combine value unknown

1. Joe has 3 marbles.
   Tom has 5 marbles.
   How many marbles do they have altogether?

Subset unknown

2. Joe and Tom have 8 marbles altogether.
   Joe has 3 marbles.
   How many marbles does Tom have?

COMPARE

Difference unknown

1. Joe has 8 marbles.
   Tom has 5 marbles.
   How many marbles does Joe have more than Tom?

2. Joe has 8 marbles.
   Tom has 5 marbles.
   How many marbles does Tom have less than Joe?

Compared quality unknown

3. Joe has 3 marbles.
   Tom has 5 more marbles than Joe.
   How many marbles does Tom have?

4. Joe has 8 marbles.
   Tom has 5 marbles less than Joe.
   How many marbles does Tom have?

Referent unknown

5. Joe has 8 marbles.
   He has 5 more marbles than Tom.
   How many marbles does Tom have?

6. Joe has 3 marbles.
   He has 5 marbles less than Tom.
   How many marbles does Tom have?

From "Development of Children's Problem-Solving Ability in Arithmetic" by M. S. Riley, J. G. Greeno, and J. I. Heller in *The Development of Mathematical Thinking* (p. 160) edited by H. P. Ginsburg, New York: Academic Press. Reprinted by permission.

student is clearly focusing on one part of the problem, the word *less,* and misinterprets the word to indicate simple subtraction. Through interviewing of this sort, you should not have great difficulty in identifying the student's interpretations. Knowledge of these interpretations can be extremely useful in helping students cope with the pitfalls of word problems.

REFERENCES

Ashlock, R. B. (1982). *Error patterns in computation* (3rd ed.). Columbus, OH: Charles E. Merrill.

Brown, J. S., & Burton, R. B. (1978). Diagnostic models for procedural bugs in basic mathematical skills. *Cognitive Science, 2,* 155–192.

Brown, V. L., & McEntire, E. (1984). *Test of Mathematical Abilities.* Austin, TX: PRO-ED.

Buswell, G. T., & John, L. (1926). *Diagnostic studies in arithmetic* (Supplementary Educational Monograph No. 30). Chicago: The University of Chicago.

Connelly, A. J., Nachtman, W., & Pritchett, E. M. (1976). *KeyMath Diagnostic Arithmetic Test.* Circle Pines, MN: American Guidance Service.

Ginsburg, H. P., & Mathews, S. C. (1984). *Diagnostic Test of Arithmetic Strategies.* Austin, TX: PRO-ED.

Riley, M. S., Greeno, J. G., & Heller, J. I. (1983). Development of children's problem-solving ability in arithmetic. In H. P. Ginsburg (Ed.), *The development of mathematical thinking.* New York: Academic Press.

Russell, R. L., & Ginsburg, H. P. (1984). Cognitive analysis of children's mathematics difficulties. *Cognition and Instruction. 1,* 217–244.

PART VI

ASSESSING SOCIOEMOTIONAL DEVELOPMENT

Linda Brown

The evaluation of students' socio-emotional status is a major component of school appraisal programs. The term *socioemotional* is used here to encompass affect (feelings, moods, temperaments), emotion (strong, subjective feelings), and behavior (observable, goal directed responses) in both internal and interactive contexts. Because behavior is by nature overt, it is a good index of emotional or affective well-being and overall adjustment.

The purpose of this section is to describe the assessment of students' socioemotional problems. The chapters serve as a guide to understanding the reasons for undertaking such an assessment, to identifying the actions and feelings that tend to be most relevant in an educational setting, and to describing the assessment techniques that are most appropriate. All of this is done within an ecological frame of reference.

Chapter 18 addresses the nature of socioemotional assessment in the schools. The purposes for undertaking socioemotional assessment are explored: identification of students who need special or remedial education, documentation of the existence of a problem, generation of instructionally relevant information, and evaluation of child change and program effectiveness.

Chapter 19 describes the techniques used in socioemotional assessment in the schools. The chapter begins with a discussion of the general characteristics of assessment techniques, followed by detailed descriptions of specific procedures that are useful in socioemotional evaluations. The final section deals with the frames of reference that can be applied to interpret the results of assessment.

Chapter 20 delves into the issue of diagnosis. Diagnostic terminology is defined, and the legal requirements for diagnosing serious emotional disturbance in the schools are outlined.

In Chapter 21 examples are given of ways to apply the assessment techniques described in Chapter 19 to each of the socioemotional constructs identified in Chapter 18. Although some of the techniques are limited to use by personnel who hold specific licenses or who have undergone specialized training, most can be used by classroom teachers and counselors as well as by appraisal personnel such as psychological associates, psychometrists, and educational diagnosticians.

Finally, Chapter 22 introduces the reader to an ecological perspective of socioemotional assessment. The assumptions of ecological assessment are delineated, and ecological models are discriminated from more traditional approaches to assessment in the schools.

18 / THE NATURE OF SOCIOEMOTIONAL ASSESSMENT IN THE SCHOOLS

Socioemotional assessment, as used in the following chapters, refers to the evaluation of how students feel and act. *Socioemotional* is a blanket term that encompasses students' emotions, affect, and behavior. Although each of these words has a precise meaning of its own, school vernacular often permits them to be used interchangeably. Therefore, brief definitions are in order.

Emotions are complex feelings that generally are recognized to have physiologic manifestations and that can be placed along a continuum between pleasant and unpleasant. Psychologists have classified six different kinds of emotions. Primary emotions are such things as fear, joy, anger, or grief, while sensory/stimulative emotions include pain and disgust. Some emotions arise out of self-appraisal (e.g., shame and pride), while others grow out of inter-relationships (e.g., love and hate). Wonderment and humor are examples of appreciative emotions. Moods, such as anxiety or elation, constitute a sixth type of emotion.

Affect involves more prolonged, pervasive feelings. For this reason affect does not evidence the immediate physiologic changes associated with emotions. Affect can include longstanding emotions or moods as well as temperaments and other relatively stable, possibly innate, conditions. Affect is generally thought of as a nonintellectual or noncognitive state; thus, one often hears of affective-cognitive dichotomies.

Behavior constitutes the observable and recordable responses that an individual makes. Behavior is goal directed. It generally is overt, although covert behaviors (e.g., galvanic skin response or electrical responses in the brain) can be observed and measured when sophisticated equipment is available. Behavior is often evaluated for the purpose of judging the nature and degree of a person's affective status or emotional well-being.

All three of these concepts are subsumed in the term *socioemotional.* The affix *socio-* is included to indicate that many of the feelings or behaviors of particular concern in the school setting are elicited or controlled by social as well as internal variables; students' feelings and behaviors can be altered (or maintained) by the feelings and behaviors of others.

This chapter explores the nature of socioemotional assessment in the schools by defining the purposes for which it is undertaken, the specific constructs that are measured, and the contexts within which assessment occurs.

WHY ARE SOCIOEMOTIONAL PROBLEMS MEASURED IN THE SCHOOLS?

There are three principal reasons to undertake socioemotional assessment in the schools: (a) to identify students who need special or remedial education, (b) to generate information that can be used to plan interventions, and (c) to serve as a yardstick for evaluating the impact and effectiveness of interventions.

Identification of Students Who Need Special or Remedial Education

Identification of handicapped students is one of the primary goals of school-based assessment, and rigorous rules and regulations govern this process. Professionals involved in the identification process should be thoroughly familiar with the guidelines promulgated by federal, state, and local education agencies.

Four broad parameters for evaluation of this type are mandated in P.L. 94-142. First, testing must be nondiscriminatory: The assessment procedures should not be culturally or racially biased, and the student should be evaluated in the native language normally used at home. Second, parents have a right to be involved in the decision making process that is an outgrowth of evaluation. Third, multiple evaluation criteria must be employed and must be considered by a multidisciplinary team or committee. Fourth, the tests used in the evaluation must be valid for the purposes for which they are employed.

Evaluation for identification typically includes two phases: screening and diagnosis. Screening is the process of identifying students who are suspected of having socioemotional problems and/or who are at risk for developing these problems. More intensive appraisal follows screening to diagnose those children who actually have socioemotional problems. Screening in the affective domain usually is accomplished by soliciting referrals from teachers or parents. Unlike academic or intellectual screening, tests are rarely used for initial screening in the affective domain.

Diagnosis is a sophisticated means of hypothesis testing that attempts to find explanations for the feelings and behaviors observed. The concept of diagnosis has been borrowed from medicine; in an analogy the socioemotional patterns are symptoms, and the label that subsequently is applied (e.g., emotionally disturbed, psychotic, obsessive, socialized delinquent) is the diagnosis that explains the symptoms. An entire chapter is devoted to the diagnosis of socioemotional problems (see Chapter 20). While diagnosis is important in obtaining special education for handicapped students, it is not particularly important in planning that special education program.

Generation of Educationally Relevant Information

Data gathered through a well-planned socioemotional assessment will help the professional (a) to identify the goals or targets of an intervention plan, (b) to order these goals in a logical sequence, and (c) to determine when the goals have been mastered. Viable assessment data also may help professionals decide among several potential interventions: Would Casey respond better to a behavioral self-control program than to an externally monitored behavior modification program? Is Ms. Simpson better able to deal with acting out students than Mr. Morley? Is the self-contained ED class a more appropriate placement for Michael than the resource room?

As in the academic domain, intervention goals for the socioemotional domain usually are established within the student's weak areas, those areas where the student is unable to meet the expectations of the classroom. In addition to the goal of changing the student's feelings, behavior, or emotional processes, intervention goals also may include: changing the expectations of the environment, changing the teacher's behavior, or changing the environment itself. This process is discussed more fully in Chapter 22.

The differences between the academic and socioemotional domains become more apparent when one attempts to order the intervention goals into a logical sequence. Even though there are affective and social skills curricula on the market, the scope and sequence charts that accompany them are not nearly so comprehensive or valuable as those that accompany academic curricula, such as reading, spelling, or mathematics. Table 18.1 depicts a typical scope and sequence chart that has been taken from the

TABLE 18.1. Scope and Sequence Chart from Magic Circle

Level	Grade	Age	Groupings	Strategies	Objectives
Pre-School		4	Single Circle 5–10	Encouragement to talk, listen, succeed.	Improve self-control and ability to listen and express; develop self-confidence and understanding of interpersonal interaction. Tolerance for individual differences. Understanding of universalization principle—emphasis on common human traits.
Kinder-garten		5	Single Circle 8–12	As above. Deal with negative as well as positive topics.	Increase self-acceptance and listening skills. Begin coping with mixed feelings.
I	First	6	First one circle 8–14; then add self-controlled children to outer ring until whole class is in two concentric rings. Teacher and child leaders alternate.	As above. Discuss: 1) ambivalence in feelings, thoughts, behaving; 2) effective and ineffective behavior; 3) reality and fantasy. Discuss variables of inclusion, warmth, coldness, making of decisions. Begin leadership experiences.	As above. Effective self-control, ability to comfortably experience ambivalence, improve reality testing, self-confidence, effective meeting of needs, increase responsibility, tolerance, empathy, skill in making helpful suggestions. Sharing in decision making and recognition of leadership abilities.
II	Second	7	As above.	As above. Continued presentation of methods of awareness, coping, social interaction. Character development is fostered by challenge, commitment, and direct interpersonal communication with peers. Continued decision making and child leadership.	As above. Articulation of wide range of experiences in positive and negative feelings, thoughts, and behavior. Self-confidence and positive self-concept. Ability to distinguish between reality and fantasy. Motivation to be responsible, productive, kind. Share in decision making. Leadership as service, not exploitation. Ability to make helpful suggestions to guide leaders to better functioning.

TABLE 18.1. continued

Third	III	8	As above.	As above. Further challenge to self-sufficiency, integration, honesty. Emphasize responsibility to social interaction, keeping commitments.	As above. Self-control as a matter of personal pride. Verbal facility, skillful and tolerant listening. Ability to tolerate ambivalent feelings in self and others. Skill in observing differences between verbalization and performance. Wise decision making and responsible, constructive leadership. Courage in taking the initiative to build good social relationships.
Fourth	IV	9	As above.	As above. Challenge to recognize psychological similarities and differences between the sexes. Role playing. Micro Lab. Experiences with authenticity and duplicity and problem solving. Exploring dreams and practice at problem solving.	As above. Accepting and reflective listening. Deeper self-awareness and understanding of social relationships. Fuller acceptance of responsibility for own behavior.
Fifth	V	10	Three general plans for articulation presented.	As above. Focus on importance of flexible outlook and behavior. Units no longer assigned to a certain number of days of the week. Supplemental affective activities presented in a variety of subject areas.	As above. Increased understanding of how trusting relationships are developed. Awareness of the complexities in social situations. Development of a sense of identity. Dealing with Role Expectations, such as sex role demands. Increasing awareness of one's own capabilities and likeable qualities.
Sixth	VI	11	As above.	As above. Focus on responsibility for one's own behavior. Increased supplemental affective activities presented in a variety of subject areas.	As above. Increased self-confidence through validation of self and others. Increased sense of self-identity and group identification. Increased practice at problem solving and decision making. Exploring the complexities in conflict resolution.

From *Magic Circle: An Overview of the Human Development Program* (p. 12), edited by G. Ball, 1974, La Mesa, CA: Human Development Training Institute.

Human Development Program's Magic Circle curriculum (Palomares & Ball, 1974).

Three questions should be considered when the purpose of the assessment is to plan an intervention strategy. First, what aspects of the environment can be changed easily to have a salient effect on the socioemotional problems? Assessment will include an evaluation of the impact of such things as seating arrangements, class assignments, and other systemic or environmental variables. Second, what problems are most disturbing? The most disturbing behaviors often make good goals for initial intervention because their change may make the student more palatable to teachers, classmates, and family members. Third, what problems is the student committed to changing or improving? The importance of this commitment cannot be overemphasized when intervention is undertaken.

Zionts and Wood's (1983) *Pupil Assessment System Survey* (PAS) provides a way to organize assessment data so that they will be pertinent in the school setting. The PAS record form is reproduced in Figure 18.1. It takes into account four variables or elements: the disturber element, the problem behavior element, the setting element, and the disturbed element. The disturber element is concerned with who or what is perceived to be the focus of the problem. The problem behavior element is concerned with determining the specific problematic behaviors exhibited by the student. The setting element is concerned with where the problems are observed and what expectations are operating in that particular setting. Finally, the disturbed element is concerned with who is disturbed by the student's problems.

Evaluation of Child Change and Program Effectiveness

Assessment data provide a useful and essential yardstick for monitoring student progress and evaluating the success (or failure) of a particular intervention. Periodic evaluations tell where a student started, where the student is functioning currently, if there has been any change, and whether change is in the desired direction. Rate of progress also may be evaluated so that projections and future plans can be made.

Professionals should know if the teaching methods or other interventions they are using with a student have been successful. If no progress is indicated, one must examine the appropriateness of the goal and/or the appropriateness of the intervention. Certainly, something is amiss and it is a waste of valuable time and effort to continue along nonproductive lines. Similarly, it is improvident to continue teaching students material that they already know or to employ a slower instructional pace than is necessary. Periodic reevaluation, which is prescribed in federal law and included in most state and local regulations, mitigates these problems.

FIGURE 18.1. The PAS Record Form

The Disturber Element: Who or what is perceived to be the focus of the problem?

1. List pertinent demographic and historic events:

   Name:

   Age:

   Sex:

   Parent or Guardian:

   Previous Educational Placement:

   Significant Historic Events:

2. Is the child's intellectual functioning a problem?
   Does the child have an unusual variation among subtests?
   List the intelligence test documentation here:

FIGURE 18.1. continued

3. What personality characteristics does the child exhibit?
   List brief personality test summaries (projective tests, peer evaluations self-ratings, and teacher ratings):

4. Does the child have perceptual-motor or other specific psychoeducational strengths or weaknesses? List:

5. How is the student functioning academically? List evidence:

6. What patterns of behavior does the child exhibit? (Describe intensity, frequency, and duration if available).
   Rating scale or checklist information:

   Observational information:

   The Problem Behavior Element: What specific behaviors does the child exhibit (or not exhibit) that create a problem?

List the student's behavioral characteristics (you may use information from Disturber Element no. 6) and have rater/observer define them as they relate to student.

FIGURE 18.1. continued

The Setting Element: In what setting(s) does the problem behavior occur? (There may be multiple settings if student is disturbed rather than disturbing.)

1. List the specific educational settings (math, English, social studies, special education, gym)

2. List the nonacademic school settings (playground, recess, lunchroom, bus)

3. List the social settings (home, community, agency clubs)

4. How does student's behavior compare to that of other students in that setting?

The Disturbed Element: Who regards the behavior as a problem?

1. Diagnostician

2. Previous teacher(s)

3. Present teacher(s)

4. Parent(s)

5. Peer(s)

6. Others

From *The Pupil Assessment Summary* by P. Zionts and P. Wood, 1983, Mt. Pleasant, MI: RETCO. Reprinted by permission.

A related use of assessment data is to determine when a student has met the exit criteria of a particular program or instructional arrangement. Special education is based upon the premise that a continuum of services is available to students and that, whenever possible, students will be moved into increasingly less restrictive instructional environments. Schools tend to have very specific regulations governing the entry of a student into a special education program; unfortunately, they tend to be less thorough and diligent when delineating the exit skills that a student must exhibit to leave special education and re-enter the regular classroom or to enter a less restrictive special education placement. This is particularly true for students with socioemotional problems; changes in students' abilities to cope with their problems or to control their own behavior should be accompanied by appropriate changes in instructional placement.

WHAT SOCIOEMOTIONAL CONSTRUCTS ARE MEASURED IN THE SCHOOLS?

Six specific socioemotional constructs related to success and performance in school are described in this section. These include attitudes, interests, locus of control, self-concept, social skills, and other personality traits. Each definition is followed by a brief discussion of the importance of that particular construct to school performance. The reader will note that behavior is not included in this list, even though behavior itself is the most frequent target of socioemotional assessment in the schools. This is because behaviors will be evaluated as part of each of the constructs identified below.

Attitudes

Definition. Attitudes are the feelings that people learn to associate with particular individuals, ideas, activities, or objects. Expression of attitudes usually takes the form of actions or words reflecting the favor (or disfavor) in which an object is held. Attitudes tend to be enduring aspects of one's socioemotional development, "a dispositional readiness to respond to certain situations, persons, or objects in a consistent manner which has been learned and has become one's typical mode of response" (Freeman, 1962, p. 596). Anderson (1981) thinks it is important to remember that attitudes are learned. He says that "the feelings themselves may or may not be learned. What is learned, however, is the attachment of feelings to particular targets. For example, favorableness may or may not be a learned feeling. However, individuals learn to attach feelings of favorableness (or unfavorableness) to a wide variety of targets such as automobiles, churches, or teaching as a profession" (pp. 32–33). Whether they are expressed or not, attitudes tend to influence a person's thinking or behavior in fairly predictable ways. When attitudes direct behavior, both conceptual/cognitive and emotional or motivational factors are involved.

Importance in School. At school, we may be concerned with the pupil's attitude toward school in general, toward teachers or a specific teacher, toward the curriculum, toward classmates, or toward other aspects of education and instruction. We also may be concerned with measuring the attitudes of teachers and other school personnel—their attitudes toward teaching, toward handicapped students, and so on. Staff attitudes permeate a school and must be considered when planning any school based interventions.

Interests and Preferences

Definition. Interests also are learned. According to Anderson (1981) they are "high intensity affective characteristics. They impel people to seek out things. . . . Since interests tend to be action oriented, [their] targets tend to be actions and skills more frequently than objects or understandings" (p. 33). We usually think of interests as being present or absent and of people as being interested or disinterested. Emmerich (1968) says that attitudes toward tasks or actions, acquired experientially, provide the base from which interests develop.

Preferences are related to interests, except that they involve two or more targets. Preference involves making a choice between or among alternatives and is reflected in the use of qualitative adjectives (e.g., more-less). Preferences also tend to be more stable than interests. A student who prefers to play computer games rather than to read during free time may, in fact, elect to read sometimes. However, it is likely that computer games will be selected (because they are preferred) more often than reading.

Importance in School. Students' interests and preferences can be used effectively to motivate and reinforce learning and to provide relevance for school tasks whenever possible. The manner in which interests are manifested is important in school, too; especially in children, interests can be fleeting, and they are subject to change without notice.

Locus of Control

Definition. Locus of control is the place where an individual assigns responsibility for his or her behavior. The literature refers to internal locus of control (meaning responsibility is assigned to oneself) and to external locus of control (meaning responsibility is assigned to other people or to events).

Anderson (1981) relates locus of control to "preferences for accepting or denying responsibility for one's behavior, its consequences, or both . . . [which are] most likely learned from careful observation of events that precede and follow various behaviors" (p. 36).

Importance in School. This is an extremely important concept when working with emotionally or behaviorally disordered students. Redl (1959) notes colorfully that ED children are victims of evaporation of the self-link in the causal chain: They are unable to see the part they play in the chain of events linking a behavior to its consequences. Therefore, they tend to repeat behaviors that seem to an observer to have consequences sufficiently aversive to stop or reduce the frequency of the behavior. These children often also develop superstitious behaviors, attributing events to circumstances, fate, or luck. Altering the locus of control and establishing a realistic cause-effect relationship in the student's mind is a major—and difficult—goal of educational programs for the emotionally disturbed. Most of the milieu therapies (e.g., Hobbs, 1966; Redl, 1959) and rational approaches such as reality therapy (Glasser, 1965) or rational-emotive therapy (Ellis, 1973) have locus of control as a central theme.

Self-Concept

Definition. Self-concept is simply the way that one sees or perceives oneself. As used here, it is synonymous with self-esteem. In Coopersmith's (1967) study of self-esteem, he concludes that one's self-concept is learned inferentially, principally from the comments and actions of other people—particularly people who are important to us—and from life experiences in general. The adjectives usually associated with this construct are high-low (as in high or low self-esteem) or positive-negative (as in positive or negative self-concept).

Importance in School. If self-concept is a learned feeling or trait, then it is important to remember that school experiences play a major role in developing students' feelings about themselves, their skills, and their place in the scheme of life. Although we tend to think of self-concept as a powerful characteristic capable of generating or eliciting strong emotional responses, Anderson (1981) makes an interesting observation concerning academic self-esteem: "Consider a student who has negative academic self-evaluations (lousy, dumb, slow) but who believes that school and success in school are unimportant. It seems likely in this instance that the intensity of this student's academic self-esteem might be quite low" (p. 36).

Social Skills

Definition. Social skills, sometimes referred to as social competence, include those traits, abilities, and behaviors that permit a person to function successfully and appropriately in society. According to D. Walker (1973), social skills include such diverse things as leadership, popularity, personal relationships with peers and authority figures, conformity, cooperation, and social status. H. Walker and his colleagues (Walker, McConnell, Holmes, Todis, Walker, & Golden, 1983) define social skills within the classroom context: "These are social responses and skills that: (1) Allow one to initiate and maintain positive relationships with others, (2) Contribute to peer acceptance and to a successful classroom adjustment, and (3) Allow one to cope effectively and adaptively with the social environment" (p. 1). They go on to classify social skills into two major categories: critical classroom behaviors (e.g., paying attention, following directions) and peer-to-peer social skills (e.g., carrying on a conversation, meeting new people).

Importance in School. Inadequate social skills have been linked to a variety of emotional and school problems and to juvenile delinquency (Cowen, Pederson, Babigan, Izzo, & Trost, 1973; Roff, Sells, & Golden, 1972). In addition, social skills often prove to be a stumbling block for handicapped children and adults seeking to enter the mainstream (Bryan & Bryan, 1978; Gresham, 1981).

Other Personality Traits

Definition. This category includes a broad array of personality traits such as anxiety, dependence, autonomy, perseverance, aggression, sexuality, depression, and social introversion. Rather than define each of these terms here, since they will be used so seldom at school, we encourage readers to seek definitions and behavioral descriptions that are appropriate for their particular needs.

Importance in School. In general, these concepts will be important only for the most severely disturbed students, and their appraisal will be within the purview of professionals other than the teacher. Their educational relevance is debatable and must be viewed in terms of the specific behaviors in which personality traits manifest themselves.

IN WHAT CONTEXTS ARE SOCIOEMOTIONAL PROBLEMS MEASURED?

Since socioemotional problems do not occur in a vacuum, one must consider the environments and interactions in which they occur and are observed or measured. These contexts include students' interactions with themselves, with peers, with family members, with authority figures, and with aspects of the school environment itself. In each instance, the context is defined and a description of its importance in school based evaluations is offered.

Student/Self Context

Definition. This term refers primarily to a student's self-evaluations, self-concept, and self-esteem. In-school evaluations are particularly concerned with students' self-concepts with regard to school and academic tasks as well as their overall self-evaluations.

Importance in School. Student/self interactions merit attention at school because they have been shown to be related to the amount and kind of attention students give to school work, to the anticipatory set students bring to school, and to the way in which students perceive reality. Students' ideas, experiences, and perceptions are filtered through and colored by the self-concepts they have acquired or learned. As Newcomer (1980) points out, ". . . behavior cannot be understood from the examination of simple, observable events. An interaction as uncomplicated as a teacher praising a child may produce varied results depending on the child's perceptions of the event. One child may find praise gratifying . . . whereas another may view praise as insincere and be threatened or upset by it. . . . As the child's perceptions are intrinsically related to its self-concept, it is the dimension of self that is the critical determinant of behavior" (pp. 44–45).

Student/Peer Context

Definition. These are child-to-child relationships and for the purposes of school evaluations will usually involve classmates. Appraisal usually focuses on students' attitudes toward peers (and vice versa), on the locus of control that is evidenced in peer interactions, and on social control.

Importance in School. Student/peer interactions are a major indicator of students' abilities to function in social situations, to assume responsibility for their own behavior, to form lasting relationships with other people, and to take into account perceptions other than their own. These interactions are a principal aspect of overall classroom adjustment.

Student/Family Context

Definition. These are interactions with family members, including parents, siblings, and other members of the family unit. In some instances they will include extended family members such as grandparents or aunts and uncles who may be living in the home. They also may include relationships with surrogate caregivers in institutional settings, foster homes, or similar placements.

Importance in School. The importance of student/family interactions in school based evaluations will vary considerably from one situation to another. The impact of the home on a student's feelings and behavior is undeniable; however, school personnel can do little to alter the home environment. Therefore, student/family interactions become important to the understanding of a student's behaviors and to interventions that teach the student to cope with the environment but are not usually so important to direct treatments or interventions. In cases where the student is in a 24-hour care setting or where the family is involved in therapeutic or educational programs, the importance of assessing student/family interactions for programmatic purposes increases.

Student/Authority Context

Definition. This category of student interactions refers to relationships with authority figures. In most instances, relationships with school authorities such as teachers, principals, and other staff will be of most interest to the evaluator. The evaluator also may be interested in the student's relationships and interactions with authority figures at home (parents, older siblings, houseparents, foster parents) and in the community (police, scout leaders, gang leaders, employers).

Importance in School. As with student/peer interactions, student/authority interactions are important indicators of social responsibility and cooperation. Individuals who are unable to accept and work with people in positions of authority are unlikely to experience success and satisfaction at school, on the job, or in many leisure time activities requiring conformity and rules compliance. The attitudes of authority figures, particularly school personnel, toward students in general or toward a particular student are extremely important, too, but they often are overlooked in assessment.

Student/School Context

Definition. This category involves students' interactions with the school itself (school rules, classroom arrangements, availability of reinforcement), with the physical environment of the classroom (temperature, lighting), and with the curriculum (actual skill requirements, expectations, teacher competence).

Importance in School. Student/school interactions cut across many of the affective characteristics that are important in socioemotional evaluations (e.g., attitudes, interests, locus of control, self-concept). In addition, the teacher may have great control over these interactions. It is easier, for instance, to change a student's location in the classroom, to alter the reinforcement schedule or menu, or to change instructional arrangements than it is to alter a student's self-concept or to have an impact on the home environment.

SUMMARY

Socioemotional problems are as important in school as academic problems. Socioemotional problems are evaluated to identify students for special education programs, to generate information that will be helpful in planning instruction, and to document program effectiveness and pupil change. Typical focuses of socioemotional evaluations at school include attitudes, interests and preferences, locus of control, self-concept, social skills, and other personality traits. These socioemotional constructs are measured within the contexts of student/self, student/peer, student/family, student/authority figure, and student/school interactions.

REFERENCES

Anderson, L. W. (1981). *Assessing affective characteristics in the schools.* Boston: Allyn & Bacon.

Bryan, T. H., & Bryan, J. H. (1978). Social interactions of learning disabled children. *Learning Disability Quarterly, 1,* 33–38.

Coopersmith, R. (1967). *The antecedents of self-esteem.* San Francisco: W. H. Freeman.

Cowen, E. L., Pederson, A., Babigan, H., Izzo, L. D., & Trost, M. A. (1973). Long term follow-up of early detected vulnerable children. *Journal of Consulting and Clinical Psychology, 41,* 438–446.

Ellis, A. (1973). *Humanistic psychotherapy: The rational-emotive approach.* New York: Julian.

Emmerich, W. (1968). Personality development and concepts of structure. *Child Development, 39,* 71–96.

Freeman, F. S. (1962). *Theory and practice of psychological testing* (3rd ed.). New York: Holt, Rinehart & Winston.

Glasser, W. (1965). *Reality therapy.* New York: Harper & Row.

Gresham, F. M. (1981). Social skills training with handicapped children: A review. *Review of Educational Research, 51,* 139–176.

Hobbs, N. (1966). Helping disturbed children: Psychological and ecological strategies. *American Psychologist, 21,* 1106–1115.

Newcomer, P. L. (1980). *Understanding and teaching emotionally disturbed children.* Boston: Allyn & Bacon.

Palomares, V. H., & Ball, G. (1974). *Human development program.* La Mesa, CA: Human Development Training Institute.

Redl, F. (1959). The concept of a therapeutic milieu. *American Journal of Orthopsychiatry, 9,* 721–734.

Roff, M., Sells, B., & Golden, M. (1972). *Social adjustment and personality development in children.* Minneapolis: University of Minnesota Press.

Walker, D. K. (1973). *Socioemotional measures for preschool and kindergarten children.* San Francisco: Jossey-Bass.

Walker, H. M., McConnell, S., Holmes, D., Todis, B., Walker, J., & Golden, N. (1983). *The Walker social skills curriculum: The ACCEPTS program.* Austin, TX: PRO-ED.

Zionts, P., & Woods, P. (1983). *The Pupil Assessment System Survey.* Mt. Pleasant, MI: RETCO.

19 / USEFUL TECHNIQUES FOR ASSESSING SOCIOEMOTIONAL PROBLEMS

This chapter is a guide to the many assessment tools that are commonly used to evaluate socioemotional problems in the schools. Although some of these assessment techniques will be limited to use by professionals who hold specific certificates and licenses or who have undergone a specified course of study, the majority can be used easily and productively by most school professionals. Teachers, counselors, educational diagnosticians, psychological associates, and school psychologists will be able to utilize most of these tools.

To be sure, this is not a comprehensive listing of available procedures. However, those measures discussed here are drawn from a wide range of theoretical and philosophical preferences, and their adequacy rests on a large body of empirical evidence reported in the literature.

In addition to their versatility in professional use, most of these tools can be adapted to appraise any of the socioemotional constructs described in the previous chapter. Very few of the techniques are limited to measurement of a specific construct or to use within a single context. Professionals can select those tools that best meet their particular needs.

In the first section of this chapter, the general characteristics of assessment techniques are delineated. Six specific tools are described in detail in the second section.

GENERAL CHARACTERISTICS OF ASSESSMENT TECHNIQUES

Three characteristics are described here: the degree of standardization that is ascribed to a technique, the proofs of that standardization, and the frame of reference that is used to interpret the obtained results.

Standardization

In most testing and appraisal texts, standardization is defined as the process of establishing norms for tests by compiling reliable and valid test results from large, representative groups of test subjects. Unfortunately, this definition limits the concept of standardization to a single type of appraisal technique (testing) and limits the interpretation of the obtained results to a single frame of reference (normative interpretation). This text adheres to a much broader definition: A standardized assessment procedure is one that has a specified (or standard) system for administration, for scoring, and for interpretation and that has empirical proof that the results of the procedures are reliable and valid. Using this definition, it is apparent that most of the appraisal techniques discussed in this chapter can be standardized to varying degrees.

By specifying criteria for administration, scoring, and interpretation, the examiner or developer of the procedure ensures a degree of objectivity, because the technique will not vary considerably from one testing situation to another, from one student to another, or from one examiner to another. The instructions and materials will not vary, the time allotted to the procedure will be the same, and consistent scoring criteria will be imposed each time the technique is applied (e.g., a particular response always will be incorrect-correct, appropriate-inappropriate, normal-abnormal). The frame of reference for interpretation (to be discussed in the next section) also will be uniform (e.g., normative tables will be provided for norm referenced interpretation, criteria for mastery will be specified for criterion referenced interpretation). This consistency in administration, scoring, and interpretation can be practiced as rigorously for so-called informal appraisal tools, such as direct observation or a teacher-made rating scale, as it is for commercially published norm referenced and criterion referenced test batteries.

Proofs of Standardization

The difference between formal and informal tools often lies not with methodical administration, scoring, and interpretation, but with the empirical evidence of a technique's reliability and validity. These two concepts are referred to here as "proofs" of standardization. The proofs of reliability and validity are a necessary component of standardization and provide a touchstone of reality to verify the quality of an appraisal tool and the results that the tool yields. Without belaboring points that can be found in Hammill's introductory chapter (Part I) and in most good assessment texts (e.g., Anastasi, 1982; Gronlund, 1985; Salvia &. Ysseldyke, 1985), the concepts of reliability and validity will be discussed briefly.

Reliability. Reliability is the dependability or consistency of a test or other measurement technique. Reliability accounts for several kinds of error that are inevitable in most assessment procedures.

Content sampling error refers to error that can be attributed to the items on a test, the questions in an interview, the objects of direct observation, and so on. Content sampling error, or internal consistency reliability, usually is measured or estimated by the application of such statistical formulas as the split-half procedure, the various Kuder-Richardson equations, or coefficient Alpha.

Time sampling error refers to the error that results when a period of time elapses between testing sessions or between the use of other appraisal tools. Correlating results or testing mean differences between results obtained at different times (called test-retest reliability) accounts for this type of error.

Interobserver sampling error refers to error that can be attributed to discrepancies between two (or more) different testers or observers. This is measured by determining the percent of agreement between examiners or observers, by correlating their results, or by testing the mean differences between their scores or quantified observations. Interobserver or interscorer reliability is particularly important for techniques that rely on the skill and judgment of the examiner, such as direct observation or projective personality testing; it is less important in instances where scoring is highly objective, such as a multiple choice test.

Validity. Validity is evidence that an appraisal technique measures what it purports to measure. There are three commonly recognized forms of validity: content, criterion related, and construct.

Content validity assures that the items or components of a technique are representative of the construct being evaluated. This kind of validity can be established logically, through nonstatistical means, by showing that items have been extracted directly from curricula in the area, by submitting items to a panel of experts, by demonstrating that items are consistent with current theory in the area, and so on. All of these logical deductions can be confirmed statistically through item analytic procedures. Statistical verification is preferred for procedures or techniques that will be marketed commercially or that will be used as principal evidence in the diagnosis of a student.

Criterion related validity is an empirical demonstration that the results of a technique are related as hypothesized to other measures of the same construct. This is accomplished most often by correlating results obtained from one technique with the results of other, similar measures; by comparing results to professional or parental judgments; or by predicting future performance.

Construct validity is concerned with the theoretical underpinnings of a particular measure. It is established by hypothesizing the elements that account for performance on a particular appraisal tool and then verifying the hypotheses. Such variables as age, sex, or intelligence might be hypothesized to have strong (or weak) relationships with the socioemotional construct being measured; relationships among various socioemotional constructs also might be hypothesized (e.g., the relationship of self-concept to locus of control). If these hypothesized relationships can be confirmed empirically, then evidence of the construct validity of the measure begins to accrue.

For purposes of defining or classifying the techniques described in this chapter relative to their standardization characteristics, the following rules of thumb can be applied. Techniques that do not exhibit all three of the standardization characteristics (i.e., consistent administration, scoring, and interpretation) are *nonstandardized*. Tools that incorporate all three characteristics but that do not provide the necessary proofs of standardization (i.e., appropriate empirical evidence of both reliability and validity) also are referred to as *nonstandardized*. Only those tools that meet the standardization criteria and also provide proof of reliability and validity may be considered *standardized* or, in the face of an unusually large body of supportive data, *highly standardized*.

It is possible, then, for a teacher-made behavior rating scale to be standardized if the teacher takes care in constructing it and provides the requisite proofs. It is more likely, however, that teachers will not establish the reliability and validity of the appraisal tools that they construct, so their techniques must be classified as nonstandardized. On the other hand, the fact that an assessment procedure, particularly a test, is marketed commercially does not ensure that it is standardized. Professionals who purchase and use such materials should be careful to determine the degree of standardization attributed to the technique and, therefore, the amount of confidence that can be placed in the results obtained by using the technique.

Frame of Reference

There are three frames of reference that a professional can use to interpret assessment data: norm referencing, criterion referencing, and nonreferencing. These are described briefly here. For more in-depth analyses, readers are referred to Hammill's appraisal component (Chapter 1) and to major assessment texts.

Norm Referencing. Norm referencing is most often associated with testing, but it can be applied to other appraisal techniques, too, such as developmental observations, teacher judgments, and so on. In norm referencing, the reference group is specified. For instance, it may be the national population as a whole, students in grades one through 12, algebra students in a particular class or school district, or blind students who have completed orientation and mobility training. The important considerations are that the reference group is specified, that the normative sample is demonstrated to be representative of the reference group, and that the reference group is an appropriate comparative population for the students being evaluated.

Norm referenced interpretations compare one student's performance to the performance of the individuals who make up the normative sample. Through this kind of interpretation, the examiner determines that the student's performance is the same as the average of the normative sample, better than average, or below average. Although most norms are derived statistically, norms that are based on professional judgment and experience are equally viable when they represent "conscientious, capable, and objective" evaluations (Salvia & Ysseldyke, 1985). Norm referenced interpretations are particularly helpful in screening and diagnosis, but they cannot be used effectively to plan instruction or to implement interventions.

Criterion Referencing. Criterion referencing differs from norm referencing in that the examiner is not concerned with how a student's performance stacks up against the performance of classmates, but with how a student's performance relates to such criteria as teacher expectations, curricular objectives, and skill mastery. The reference group here is not a group of individuals, but a group of tasks or skills. This type of interpretation is particularly useful when the goal of assessment is to place a student in a curriculum, to plan an instructional sequence, or to document progress or program effectiveness.

Nonreferencing. This is a new term that was coined for this particular series of books. Nonreferencing is concerned with the strategies and approaches that students use to obtain an answer or to solve a problem. In academic evaluations this is often referred to as *error analysis*. In the evaluation of socioemotional problems, it refers more often to the reasoning process by which a student selects a particular behavior or emotional reaction in a situation. The examiner employing nonreferenced evaluations is not concerned with why a student acts or behaves as he or she does, but with how a student decided to act or behave in that manner. Nonreferencing will be most helpful in planning instructional strategies and interventions.

SIX SPECIFIC ASSESSMENT TECHNIQUES

This section describes six categories of assessment techniques that can be used to evaluate socioemotional problems in the schools. These include reviews of students' records, tests, direct observation, applied behavior analysis, interviews, and other assessment techniques. The latter category incorporates Q-sorts, sociometrics, and analyses of classroom interaction.

Review of Records

Student records are one of the "most important [and] most overlooked sources of information" during appraisal (Wiederholt, Hammill, & Brown, 1983, p. 23). A thorough review of records will yield a gold mine of information and may prevent the proverbial re-invention of the wheel by duplicating assessment or treatment programs. Legal and regulatory dictates have resulted in burgeoning paperwork, so school records are often copious. Unfortunately, they may not be well-organized, and their disarray hampers the search for relevant information. Organization, therefore, is often the first order of business for the professional who wants to review school records.

Records usually are arranged in chronological order, with the most recent information appearing in the front portion of the file. While this organizational system is helpful in discriminating old and new information, it is not so helpful in determining the times, places, and other situational variables that may surround the behavioral problems documented in a student's records. In response to similar filing and retrieval difficulties in the medical profession, Weed (1971) developed a Problem Oriented Record Form for use in hospitals and medical settings where the same patient may be treated by several different professionals and have records maintained in several different clinics or departments. The advent of high technology and computerized versions of the problem oriented record system have made it possible, for instance, to identify potential child abuse victims who are treated at multiple hospitals and clinics in a community or region. Problem oriented record systems have subsequently been adopted by some social service agencies, schools, and other institutions characterized by shared professional responsibility for clients and students. An added advantage for schools that use this system to organize records of students with emotional and behavioral problems is that it permits assimilation of records from medical, social, and legal agencies outside the school, too.

Weed's system allows records to be organized in one of two ways: (a) according to the specific problem that is observed or (b) according to the setting in which the problem is observed. The current generation of computer software permits a user to customize the retrieval system by defining the important variables and establishing the coding system that will be used. For instance, school records may be organized according to specific problems such as truancy, defiance, failure to respond to verbal controls, aggressive responses to frustration, and so on. In this way, previously undetected behavioral patterns surrounding these responses may emerge. Records also may be organized according to situational expectations or requirements. Examples might be:

Setting: The behavior occurs at school and home, but not on the job.

Time of day: The behavior occurs in the afternoon only.

Specific classes: The behavior occurs only during language arts instruction.

Instructional style: The behavior occurs when student cooperation and group activities are required, but not during independent work or one-to-one instruction.

Task requirements: The behavior occurs in situations requiring conformity to rules and regulations.

The salient characteristics will vary from one class to another and from one student or teacher to another. Once the data are organized it will be necessary to (a) discard old information; (b) discard information that is suspect; and (c) identify the informational gaps that the appraisal plan is intended to fill.

By using some variation of this approach to organize existing student records, the teacher may be able to identify specific problems, situations that tend to elicit or aggravate the problems, aspects of the environment that may be reinforcing (or punishing), and the efficacy of various treatments and interventions that already have been used. Added to this, a chronological review of the records will provide an indication of the enduring or situational nature of the problem, its chronicity, and its apparent onset. This is valuable diagnostic information and may guide the formulation of hypotheses concerning further evaluation or intervention efforts.

Tests

Tests probably constitute one of the most widely used appraisal techniques in the public schools. The introduction to this book defined tests as having three properties: (a) Tests comprise tasks or questions (referred to as *items*), (b) they require a specific behavior in response to the items, and (c) they yield scores that can be acted on statistically. Obviously, many techniques meet these criteria and would have to be considered tests. This section describes common test formats, offers guidelines for constructing tests, and discusses specific tests that are used frequently in socioemotional evaluations.

Test Formats. Tests used to assess socioemotional problems usually are dichotomized by their formats into *nonprojective* and *projective* tests. Projective measures are reserved almost exclusively for the responses of the target students themselves, while the nonprojective formats incorporate responses from students as well as from their peers and classmates, teachers, family members, or impartial observers.

Projective tests assume that subjects will reveal their feelings, thoughts, motivations, or other "inner" emotions by projecting them onto a neutral or ambiguous stimulus (such as a picture or geometric design) or onto some creative activity (such as play or art). On a projective test, the student may be asked to

- look at a picture or design and describe it;
- complete sentence stems, such as, "I am afraid when . . ." or, "Other children think I . . .";
- draw pictures of themselves, their houses, or other people;
- copy geometric designs;
- play with puppets, dolls, or other symbolic toys.

Guidelines for interpreting the elicited responses are stated with varying degrees of specificity (standardization) by the developers of projective tests. It is not within the scope of this book to go into these scoring systems in detail. However, a summary of the indicators of emotional disturbance that Koppitz (1968) found in the human figure drawings of students with personality disorders is provided in Table 19.1 as an example. Koppitz' caution concerning the analysis of human figure drawings, and presumably other projective tests, bears reapeating.

> It is not possible to make a meaningful diagnosis or evaluation of a child's behavior or difficulties on the basis of any single sign on a [human figure drawing]. The *total* drawing and the combination of various signs and indicators should always be considered and should then be analyzed on the basis of the child's age, maturation, emotional status, social and cultural background and should then be evaluated together with other available test data. (p. 55)

Nonprojective tests are more direct measures and usually take the form of inventories, checklists, or rating scales. Inventories and checklists use variations on simple yes-no or true-false response formats and are helpful in verifying the existence of problems and identifying possible targets of inter-

TABLE 19.1. Indicators of Emotional Disturbance in Human Figure Drawings

Emotional Indicators	Emot. Probl.	Shy	Aggres-sive	Psycho-somatic	Stealing	Brain Injury	Poor Sch.Ach.	Special Class
Integration	X		O			X	X	X
Shading face	O							
Shading body	X	O			O			
Shading hands	X				O			
Asymmetry	X		X			X		X
Slanting figure	X				O	X	X	X
Tiny figure	X	X				X		X
Big figure	X		O		O			
Transparency	X		O		O	X		
Tiny head	O				O			
Crossed eyes								
Teeth	O		X					
Short arms	X	O		X				X
Long arms	O		X					
Clinging arms	O							
Big hands	X		X		X			X
Hands cut off	X	X				X		X
Legs together	O			O				
Genitals	O		X					
Monster	O						O	X
Three figures	O						X	O
Clouds	O			X				
No eyes	O							
No nose	O	X		X				X
No mouth	O	X		O			O	O
No body	O				O	X	X	X
No arms	O		O		O		X	X
No legs								
No feet	O	O						
No neck	X				X	X		

X: Item occurs significantly more often on HFDs of group indicated.
O: Item occurs more often on HFDs of group indicated.

From *Psychological Evaluation of Children's Human Figure Drawings* (p. 56) by E. M. Koppitz, 1968, New York: Grune & Stratton. Reprinted by permission.

ventions. Inventories and checklists use sentences, phrases, adjectives, and pictures to elicit responses (e.g., "Happy: like me—not like me," "Are you often ill: yes—no," "Other children like me: true—false").

Rating scales not only verify the existence of problems, but also provide guidelines for determining the seriousness, frequency, or severity of particular behaviors. Rating scales utilize a response continuum so that respondents can indicate the degree to which a behavior or emotion is observed rather than simply noting its presence or absence. Rating scales would include items such as: "Susan makes 'put down' remarks: frequently—sometimes—seldom—never," "Jo swears in class: 5 or more times daily—3–4 times daily—1–2 times daily—0 times daily," "Throwing temper tantrums is: very much like—somewhat like—somewhat unlike—very much unlike my child," "I find that lying is: very disturbing—disturbing—mildly disturbing—not disturbing at all."

Guidelines for Constructing Tests. There are unique theoretical demands for building and interpreting projective tests. For this reason, we do not recommend that most school personnel undertake such a task. Instead, on those rare occasions when projective evaluation seems to be in order, examiners should choose from among the commercially available projective tests described in the next section.

Nonprojective measures are more easily built by teachers and other school personnel. Personalized checklists, inventories, and rating scales will often be more specific to a particular student, classroom, or cluster of behaviors than commercially available tests and, therefore, will be more relevant to stated evaluation goals.

Bower and Lambert (1971) suggest that items for inventories, checklists, and rating scales should encompass three kinds of behaviors/feelings: (a) personal behaviors/feelings associated with the target student, (b) interpersonal behaviors/feelings observed between the target student and classmates, and (c) interactive behaviors/feelings observed between the target student and the teacher (or other authority figure of interest). To prevent the instrument from becoming so unwieldy as to be useless, Wiederholt, Hammill, and Brown (1983) suggest that these instruments be limited to approximately 30 items.

In building tests, it is important to keep in mind the standardization characteristics discussed earlier (i.e., stated criteria for administration, scoring, and interpretation). School personnel who build their own tests should write out specific and detailed instructions for giving the test and for scoring the results; guidelines for interpreting the results should be provided, too. This ensures that every member of the school staff who uses the instrument will use it in the same manner. Whenever possible, the test builder also should provide proofs of standardization by determining an instrument's reliability and validity. The statistical calculations associated with these concepts is beyond the scope of this book; however, many other texts, most notably Gronlund's (1985), provide step-by-step guidance for calculating reliability and validity data. At the very least, we suggest that test builders adhere to the spirit of these concepts. It is fairly easy, for instance, to ask a colleague to review test items for appropriateness and clarity, to "eyeball" simultaneous ratings of the same student as an estimate of interscorer reliability, or to ensure the content validity of an instrument by adhering to Sattler's (1982) guidelines:

> In evaluating content validity, consider the appropriateness of the type of items, the completeness of the item sample, and the way in which the items assess the content of the domain involved. Questions relevant to these considerations include the following: (1) Are the questions appropriate test questions and does the test measure the domain of interest? (2) Does the test contain enough information to cover appropriately what it is supposed to measure? (3) What is the level of mastery at which the content is being assessed? If these three questions can be answered satisfactorily, the test is thought to have good content validity. (p. 23)

In addition to reliability and validity, Anderson (1981) suggests that test builders should consider the communication value, objectivity, and interpretability of their instruments in attempting to standardize them. Questions that will help readers determine if a test they have built or intend to use exhibits these important characteristics are listed in Table 19.2.

There are three major formats that teachers and others may want to employ in building their own inventories, checklists, and rating scales. These are adjective checklists, Likert scales, and semantic differential scales. Each is described briefly here. Interested readers are referred to Anderson's (1981) excellent and detailed discussion of affective scaling techniques. His directions for building these three types of tests are presented in Table 19.3.

Adjective checklists.   Adjective checklists consist, quite simply, of a list of adjectives or adjective phrases which respondents check if they associate that item with a specified target. The target may be the respondents themselves, another person (e.g., the classroom teacher or a classmate), a place (e.g., school), or an object or thing (e.g., a toy, an activity, or a school assignment). The adjectives can describe behaviors, personality traits, and attitudes. These are easy instruments to develop and administer, and the format is appropriate for a wide variety of respondents, including target students themselves; teachers, aides, and other professionals; and parents. Adjective checklists lend themselves to oral as well as written formats, and the creative examiner may even be able to build a pictorial checklist. The range of possibilities is so great that Anderson (1981) warns his readers against information overload by obtaining so many responses to so many adjectives that the results are overwhelming and difficult to comprehend and interpret. Adhering to the 30-item limit suggested earlier will help alleviate this problem. Examiners must remember that adding up the various checks on an adjective checklist to obtain a total score is *not* an appropriate heuristic technique. Without empirical evidence to justify the clustering of scores, each adjective must stand on its own merit.

TABLE 19.2. Questions for Evaluating the Standardization of Tests of Socioemotional Constructs

Communication value
1. Do the directions clearly specify the nature of the task? That is, will the respondent know what to do and how to do it after reading the directions?
2. Do the directions clearly specify the general purpose for which the scale is being administered?
3. Do the directions clearly indicate that there are no "right" or "wrong" answers?
4. Do the directions contain a definition of the affective target? That is, do the directions try to ensure that all respondents will be reacting to the same meaning of the target?
5. What is the estimated readability of the scale?
6. How does the estimated readability of the scale compare with the reading level of the audience to whom you wish to administer the scale? Is the language as written too hard, too easy, or just right?

Objectivity
1. Are the scoring rules clearly specified?
2. Are the qualifications that the scorer must possess described?
3. Approximately how much error in scoring typically results when the scoring rules are used?

Validity
1. Are the steps used in constructing the items clearly stated? Do the steps appear to be logically related to one another and to the definition(s) on which the scale is based?
2. Are several scales included on the same instrument? Are these scales (called subscales) clearly pointed out? Are reasons given for suspecting subscales? To what extent do the results of appropriate statistical procedures support the hypothesized set of subscales?
3. With what other measures are scores on the affective scale related? Does the author of the scale provide a rationale for suspecting that the relationships exist?
4. Do the scores on the affective scale differentiate among groups of people who are known or suspected to be different in terms of the affective characteristic? Does the author of the scale give a reason for suspecting that the differences will exist?

Reliability
1. Does the author describe the sample that was used to estimate the reliability of the scale? Is the sample comparable to the group to whom you intend to administer the scale?
2. To what extent does the scale possess a satisfactory degree of internal consistency? What formula was used to estimate internal consistency?
3. To what extent does the scale possess a satisfactory degree of equivalence? What scales were used to estimate equivalence?
4. To what extent does the scale possess a satisfactory degree of stability? How long was the time period between administrations?

From *Assessing Affective Characteristics in the Schools* (p. 111) by L. W. Anderson, 1981, Boston: Allyn & Bacon. Reprinted by permission.

TABLE 19.3. Directions for Building Adjective Checklists, Likert Scales, and Semantic Differential Scales

Procedure for Adjective Checkists

Step 1: Select an appropriate number of adjectives. A good source of possible adjectives is Allport and Odbert's (1936) list of 17,953 trait words.

Step 2: Place adjectives on a sheet of paper.

Step 3: Write or select directions for responding to the adjectives. Usually the directions ask the respondent to place a check mark in front of the adjectives is Allport and Odbert's (1936) list of 17,953 trait words.

Step 4: Administer the checklist to a sample of the audience for whom the instrument is intended.

The Likert Technique

Step 1: Write or select statements that are clearly either favorable or unfavorable with respect to the underlying affective characteristic.

Step 2: Have several judges react to the statements. These judges should examine each statement and classify it as positive, negative, or neutral.

Step 3: Eliminate those statements that are not unanimously classified as positive or negative (since neutral statements are not acceptable for inclusion on a Likert Scale).

Step 4: Decide on the number of alternative choices to be offered for each statement. (*Note:* The original Likert scale had five alternatives: SD, D, NS, A, SA.)

Step 5: Prepare the self-report instrument. Include directions. The directions should indicate that the respondents should indicate how they feel about each statement by marking SA if they strongly agree, A if they agree, NS if they are not sure, D if they disagree, and SD if they strongly disagree.

Step 6: Administer the scale to a sample of the audience for whom the instrument is intended. (*Note:* You should have at least five times as many persons as statements.)

Step 7: Compute the correlation between each statement response and the total scale score.

Step 8: Eliminate those statements whose correlation with the total scale is not statistically significant (Likert's Criterion of Internal Consistency).

The Semantic Differential Technique

Step 1: Choose appropriate pairs of bipolar adjectives. The pairs you choose should contain adjectives that are clearly evaluative in nature with respect to the concept (target) under consideration. (Examples of such adjectives would include good-bad, tasty-distasteful, kind-cruel, brave-cowardly, clear-hazy, honest-dishonest, beautiful-ugly, calm-agitated, valuable-worthless, pleasant-unpleasant, happy-sad, relaxed-tense, nice-awful, fair-unfair, and healthy-sick.)

Step 2: Construct a response sheet. For example:

My Teacher

Fair_____ : _____ : _____ : _____ : _____ : _____ : _____Unfair

Step 3: Administer the scale to sample of the audience for whom the instrument is intended. (*Note:* You should have at least five times as many persons as statements.)

Step 4: Compute the correlation between each pair of bipolar adjectives and the total scale score.

Step 5: Eliminate those adjective pairs that do not correlate significantly with the total scale score.

From *Assessing Affective Characteristics in the Schools* (pp. 248, 257, 259) by L. W. Anderson, 1981, Boston: Allyn & Bacon. Reprinted by permission.

Likert scales. Probably the most popular format for informal instruments is the Likert scale. These scales usually contain an equal number of negative and positive statements which the respondent rates on a continuum between such evaluative phrases as Strongly Agree-Strongly Disagree, Never-Often, Highly Desirable-Highly Undesirable, and so on. A weight is attached to each point along the continuum. For instance, a weight of 3 might be assigned to Never, a weight of 2 assigned to Almost Never, a weight of 1 to Sometimes, and a weight of 0 to Always. The total score is calculated by summing these weighted scores. As Wallace and Larsen (1978) point out, Likert scales give the teacher "great flexibility in attending to the content of a given scale" (p. 114), which can be modified to measure a variety of behaviors, attitudes, interests, personality traits, or situations. These scales also can be used with several different groups of respondents, although readability of the items should be carefully considered because Likert scales do not lend themselves well to oral or nonverbal formats.

Semantic differential scales. Semantic differential scales present a concept or construct such as "doing math calculations" or "going to school." Pairs of adjectives that might describe the concepts are presented, and respondents select the one word in the pair that better describes their feelings. Possible adjective pairs might be valuable-worthless, difficult-easy, fun-boring, and so on. Semantic differential scales tend to be nonthreatening for the respondents, especially for students. They can become boring, though, and Anderson (1981) suggests that they be built to include no more than 10 adjective pairs for each concept being evaluated. The scales are easy to build and score, but the directions can be quite confusing. Once again, readability is an important consideration, and the examiner must ensure that the adjectives are in the respondent's reading or speaking vocabulary. In general, semantic differential scales are used to assess attitudes and interests more often than behaviors.

Specific Tests. This section includes two tables of tests that are commercially available and commonly used in socioemotional assessment. Table 19.4 describes tests of each of the six socioemotional constructs defined in Chapter 18. Table 19.5 describes tests that are more behavioral in their orientation; their results could be interpreted within the confines of several constructs. On both tables, the standardization of the tests' administration, scoring, and interpretation is indicated; the presence of reliability and validity data is noted; and the formats are described.

Direct Observation

Direct observation is one of the most efficient and informative technique used to evaluate behavior in the classroom. Two things must be considered when planning to use direct observation. First, this is a more time consuming technique than using, say, an adjective checklist or a behavior rating scale. It often is necessary to use an observer—such as a student teacher, an aide, or a classroom volunteer—to assist with the observation or to train students to monitor and assess their own behaviors. Obviously, this increases the time commitment. A second consideration is the overwhelming urge to interpret the behaviors that are observed, attributing particular motivations and meanings to them. Teachers and other appraisal personnel should remember that these attributions are their own projections and may not accurately reflect the child's feelings.

Most sources discuss three types of direct observation: automatic recording, analysis of permanent products, and observational recording. *Automatic recording* involves a highly sophisticated and mechanical technology such as that used in biofeedback training or in laboratory animal research. School personnel seldom have access to or a need for such equipment. *Analysis of permanent products* refers to the evaluation of tangible products of behaviors. Examples would be spelling tests, written or oral language samples, and so on. Since permanent products of affective characteristics are rare, this form of direct observation also will be used infrequently, if ever, in the observation of socioemotional problems. *Observational recording* is the principal direct observation technique used to measure classroom behavior and affective characteristics.

Data obtained from direct observation should be recorded in a systematic way that can be interpreted quickly and easily. Anecdotal records are usually presented in a narrative form. Data from the other techniques are usually presented in graphs such as those depicted in Figure 19.1, which can be used to note behavioral trends or to observe when the rate or duration of a behavior begins to increase or decrease.

Classroom observation can be accomplished by target students themselves. Indeed, self-observation is an integral part of a technique known as behavioral self-control. Interested readers are referred to Workman (1982) for a complete description of the process. In short, the self-assessment phase involves (a) identifying a target behavior, (b) devising a rating system for the student to use, (c) determining the time interval for the student to do the rating, and (d) establishing a reinforcement system. Self-observation has the advantage of freeing the teacher from a time-consuming task, of encouraging students to monitor and evaluate their own behavior, and of moving students to less tangible, more intrinsic forms of reinforcement, since the charting itself may be all the reinforcement that is needed.

Observational recording in the classroom involves one of six techniques: (a) maintaining anecdotal records, (b) event recording, (c) duration recording, (d) interval recording, (e) time sampling, or (f) planned activity check, each of which is described in the next sections.

TABLE 19.4. Tests of Six Socioemotional Constructs

Construct Measured	Test	Standardization			Proofs		Format
		Admin	Scoring	Interp	Rel	Val	
Attitudes	Estes Attitude Scales (Estes, Estes, Richards, & Roettger, 1981)	X	X	X	X	X	S responds to 75 statements about school subjects using a 5-pt Likert scale
	Family Relations Test (Bene & Anthony, 1957)	X	X		X	limited	S assigns pictures of emotions, attitudes, & feelings to figures of family members, nobody
	TOMA Subtest I: Attitudes toward Math (Brown & McEntire, 1983)	X	X	X	X	X	S responds to statements about math
Interests & Preferences	Manifold Interest Schedule (Heil, Sheviakov, & Stone, 1960)	X				limited	S responds to 420 items on 3-pt scale
	OASIS Interest Schedule (Parker, 1983)	X	X	X	X	X	S responds to 120 occupations on 3-pt scale
Locus of Control	ETS Locus of Control Scale (Shipman, 1970)	X	X	X		limited	S looks at 22 cartoons, explains success/failure by picking 1 of 2 choices
	Intellectual Achievement Responsibility Questionnaire (Crandall, Katkovsky, & Crandall, 1965)	X	X	X		limited	S reads 34 acad. ach. statements & picks 1 of 2 explanations for success/failure
Self-Concept	Animal Crackers (Adkins & Ballif, 1973)	X	X	X		limited	S picks 1 of 2 described that behaves like S
	Piers-Harris Children's Self-Concept Scale (Piers & Harris, 1984)	X	X	X		limited	S rates 80 items yes-no

TABLE 19.4. continued

Self-Concept (cont.)	*Self-Perception Inventory—Student Form* (Soares & Soares, 1974)	X	X	X	S rates bipolar items on 4-pt scale
	Tennessee Self-Concept Scale (Fitts, 1970)	X	X	X	S rates 100 items on 5-pt scale
Social Skills	ACCEPTS Placement Test & Checklist (Walker, McConnell, Holmes, Todis, Walker, & Golden, 1983)	X	X	limited	Teacher rates 28 S behaviors on 5-pt scale
	Cain-Levine Social Competency Scale (Cain, Levine, & Elzey, 1969)	X	X	limited	E interviews respondent who is familiar w/S
	Kohn Social Competence Scale (Kohn & Rosman, 1972)	X	X	limited	E rates S on 73 items using 7-pt scale
Other Personality Traits	*Bender-Gestalt Test for Young Children* (Koppitz, 1964)	X	X	limited	S copies 9 geometric patterns
	Blacky Pictures (Blum, 1967)	X	X	limited	S looks at Blacky cartoons, tells stories, answers questions, notes preferences for cartoons
	Children's Apperception Test (Bellak & Bellak, 1965)	X	X	limited	S tells stories about 10 animal pictures
	Draw-A-Person Test (Urban, 1963)	X	X		S draws a person
	House-Tree-Person Test (Buck & Jolles, 1966)	X	X	X	S draws house, tree, person, & describes pix orally
	IPAT Children's Personality Questionnaire (Porter & Cattell, 1975)	X	X	X	S selects 1 of 70 pairs of statements that best describes S
	Junior Eysenck Personality Inventory (Eysenck, 1965)	X	X	limited	S answers 60 questions yes-no

TABLE 19.5. Tests of Behavior

Test	Standardization			Proofs		Respondent
	Admin	Scoring	Interp	Rel	Val	
AAMD Adaptive Behavior Scales, Public School Version Part 2 (Nihira, Foster, Shellhaas, & Leland, 1975)	X	X	X		limited	Teacher
Barclay Classroom Climate Inventory (Barclay, 1971)	X	X	X		limited	Teacher & student
Basic School Skills Inventory–Diagnostic, Classroom Behavior (Hammill & Leigh, 1983)	X	X	X	X	X	Teacher
Behavior Evaluation Scale (McCarney, Leigh, & Cornbleet, 1983)	X	X	X	X	X	Teacher
Behavior Problem Checklist (Quay & Peterson, 1967)	X	X		X	X	Teacher
Behavior Rating Profile (Brown & Hammill, 1983)	X	X	X	X	X	Teacher, student, parents, peers
Devereux Adolescent Behavior Rating Scale (Spivak, Spotts, & Haimes, 1967)	X	X	X	X	X	Teacher
Devereux Elementary School Behavior Rating Scale (Spivak & Swift, 1967)	X	X	X	X	X	Teacher
Learning Environment Inventory (Anderson, 1973)	X	X	X	X	limited	Student
Pupil Behavior Rating Scale (Lambert, Hartsbough, & Bower, 1979)	X	X		X		Teacher, student, & peers
Test of Early Socioemotional Development (Hresko & Brown, 1984)	X	X	X	X	X	Teacher, students, parents, peers
Walker Problem Behavior Identification Checklist (Walker, 1970)	X	X	X	X	X	Teacher

FIGURE 19.1. Methods of Graphing Data

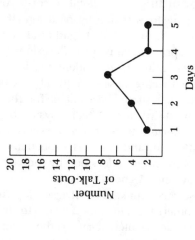

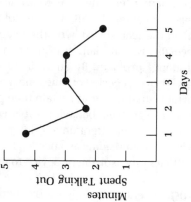

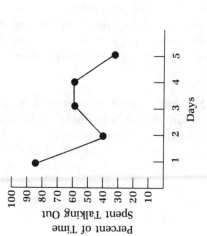

Anecdotal Recording. Anecdotal records provide an account of everything that is done to, with, for, by, or around the target child. Obviously, no one individual can take the time to gather all the anecdotal data that are required for a comprehensive record. Occasionally, other personnel such as trained volunteers, aides, or student teachers can be assigned some responsibility for gathering these data. Ideally, a videotape recording of the child's entire school day should be available for analysis, but, of course, this is not practical in most situations. A coding system or some form of shorthand may be devised to permit the observer to record as much data as possible in a short amount of time and space. The shorthand is transcribed later into narrative form that can be understood by individuals who are unfamiliar with the coding system. A coded entry in an anecdotal record might look like this: "1025—sci ctr—X pokes SL—SL cries, X pokes more—M, SR, PR also in ctr—M calls Δ, others tell X to quit—Δ comes to ctr." Translated, this means that at 10:25 in the science interest center, the target child (X) poked at Susan Lily (SL) until she cried, after which he continued poking her. The other children in the science center (M, SR, and PR) told the target child to quit poking and M called the teacher (Δ), who then came to the science center.

Anecdotal records are especially useful when one cannot identify the pattern of the student's problem. By analyzing a continuous recording of the student's behavior over a period of time, one may learn that the behavior occurs only in certain situations or at certain time periods in the day or that every occurrence of the problem behavior is followed by a positive reward, perhaps by increased teacher attention and interest. While it is possible to identify these variables from reading an anecdotal record, continuous recording is not a time-efficient measurement device to employ in most instances.

Event Recording. Event recording is a frequently used technique. It is, simply, a record of the number of times a defined behavior occurs. It is a behavioral frequency count. Using this technique, a teacher learns that Frances had 2 talk-outs during the 30-minute algebra class on Monday, 4 on Tuesday, 8 on Wednesday, 2 on Thursday, and 2 on Friday. These data are recorded in the form of a conventional graph in the third section of Figure 19.1.

Duration Recording. Duration recording is used when one is more concerned with how long a behavior lasts than with the frequency of occurrence. Knowledge of the duration of a child's temper tantrum, for instance, may occasionally be more important than a recording of the number of outbursts occurring during a given time period. Another example is provided by Linda, who has difficulty attending to the task at hand. It could be that she exhibits only one instance of off-task behavior during the independent work period; regrettably, that one instance lasts for twenty minutes.

Interval Recording. Interval recording combines the two previously described techniques, giving a measure of both the frequency and the duration of a behavior. An observation period is divided into equal, usually short, time periods. For instance, the 5 minutes after recess may be divided into thirty 10-second intervals. The observer watches continuously during the 5-minute session and notes whether or not the defined behavior occurs during each of the shorter intervals. For instance, if Pat talked without permission during twenty-five of the thirty 10-second intervals, the results would be reported as 83% of the time spent talking out. The form on which the observer recorded Pat's talking (T) would probably look something like the following:

T 1	T 2	T 3	T 4	T 5	T 6
T 7	T 8	T 9	T 10	11	12
T 13	T 14	T 15	T 16	T 17	T 18
T 19	T 20	T 21	T 22	T 23	T 24
T 25	T 26	T 27	T 28	29	30

Time Sampling. Time sampling is very similar to interval recording, but it is more useful because it does not require continuous observation. The observation period again is divided into equal, usually longer, time periods. For instance, Mr. Nixon, the world history teacher, may divide his 50-minute class period into five 10-minute intervals. He then conducts a time sampling of Henry's behavior while Henry is supposed to be answering his questions at the end of Chapter 14 in the world history textbook. After (not throughout) each 10-minute interval, Mr. Nixon observes to see if Henry is answering the questions. If Henry was working (W) four of the five times that Mr. Nixon observed him, he would be recorded as working 80% of the time. An example of Mr. Nixon's time sampling record follows.

W	W	W	W	

Planned Activity Check. Planned activity check, sometimes called *placheck*, is used to measure the behaviors of groups of children. Those who use this technique would be interested in the percentage of students engaged in a defined behavior. Perhaps a teacher would want to do a placheck of the children working on an assignment in an interest center. The teacher first would count the number of students working and then would count the number of students actually in the interest center. If ten students were in the center and only four were engaged in the assignment, the placheck record would be 40% on task. Placheck records often are taken on a time sampling basis. For example, Mr. Nixon, the world history teacher, may do placheck every ten minutes during his 50-minute class period. If 25 students are in the class and if 24 are working at the first check, 20 at the second check, 25 at the third and fourth checks, and 5 at the final check, the placheck records would be 96, 80, 100, 100, and 20%, respectively. Mr. Nixon might conclude that studying behavior dropped off during the final 10 minutes of his class, particularly if this pattern continued over a period of time. He might adjust his planning to make better use of that final 10 minutes.

Applied Behavioral Analysis

Applied behavioral analysis (ABA) is a generic term that refers to a variety of behavioral systems used to teach academic content or to control classroom behavior. Strictly speaking, ABA is not an assessment technique. It is an instructional system that uses direct observation techniques to determine the severity of reported problems and to document the efficacy of programs implemented to eliminate or ameliorate the problems. Still, ABA is included in this book for two reasons. First, it provides an example of the uses of direct observation. Second, it provides an excellent example of the ways in which validity can be established.

Each of the four major steps in implementing ABA is discussed here: (a) identifying target behaviors or activities; (b) observing and recording target behaviors; (c) formulating intervention goals; and (d) implementing and verifying the results of the intervention. For more detailed discussions than are possible here, interested readers are referred to Sulzer-Azaroff and Mayer's (1977) comprehensive and detailed book; to Craighead, Kazdin, and Mahoney's (1976) description of ABA techniques applied to cognitive, affective, and other nonobservable processes; and to the work of Lovitt and his colleagues (e.g., Haring, Lovitt, Eaton, & Hansen, 1978; Lovitt, 1975).

Identifying a Target Behavior. Identifying a target behavior involves describing behaviors that are both observable and measurable. If an observer can't see a behavior happening and can't quantify its occurrence, the behavior isn't an appropriate target. For instance, "improved self-concept" is not a suitable target behavior, but it can be defined operationally in terms of such observable and measurable behaviors as "making positive remarks about oneself." The definition should be sufficiently precise that observers agree when they have or have not seen an instance of the target behavior occur.

Observing and Recording Behaviors. Observing and recording behaviors involves the direct observation techniques described in the previous section. Data obtained through direct observation usually are presented in graphs. The days, class sessions, and other time intervals are plotted along the horizontal axis of the graph. The vertical axis is used to record the frequency, duration, or ratio of the target behavior. Both axes should be plainly labeled. Data from the different experimental phases or treatment conditions are divided on the graph by vertical lines; data points between conditions are not joined. The various experimental conditions are labeled as descriptively as possible. For instance, if three interventions were used (ignoring competing behaviors, reinforcing with tokens, and awarding free time) to increase Linda's attending behaviors, the resulting graph might resemble the one in Figure 19.2. Hall and Van Houten's (1983) *Managing Behavior: The Measurement of Behavior* is a good handbook of techniques for observing and recording behaviors.

Setting Goals for Intervention. Step 3 in ABA, setting goals for intervention, involves defining the desired outcome or terminal behavior as well as the intervening enroute objectives. Terminal objectives usually are written in the elicitor-behavior-reinforcer format suggested by Peter (1972); enroute objectives specify the intermediate steps that the student must accomplish in achieving the desired behavior. Magee and Newcomer (1980) outline this progression with the following example.

> Given the fifth-grade social studies book, Steve will read the assignment and correctly answer on paper the questions at the end of the chapter while receiving only regular teacher attention.

This terminal objective would fit into the model in this manner:

Elicitor	*Behavior*	*Reinforcer*
Fifth grade social studies book.	Read the assignment and correctly answer on paper the questions at the end of the chapter.	Regular teacher attention.

The third phase involves *writing enroute objectives*. Enroute objectives are a series of steps or skills that the student must learn or accomplish to move from his or her entering behaviors to the terminal objectives. Usually, the teaching procedures and curricular materials are specified in the enroute objectives. Enroute objectives are also written according to the elicitor-behavior-reinforcement model. Enroute objectives for Steve might include the following:

FIGURE 19.2. Graph of Three Interventions to Increase Attending Behavior

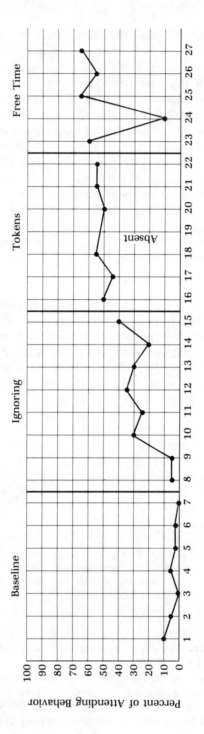

Elicitor	Behavior	Reinforcement
1. Fifth grade social studies book	Read one paragraph and answer correctly on paper two questions about the paragraph.	Five minutes free time to listen to the radio.
2. Fifth-grade social studies book	Read three paragraphs and answer correctly on paper three questions about the paragraphs.	Four minutes free time to listen to the radio and teacher praise.
3. Fifth-grade social studies book	Read one page and answer correctly on paper five questions about the content.	Good progress note to take home and teacher praise.

This list of enroute objectives should continue until the desired terminal objective is reached.[1]

A review of Mager's (1962) classic handbook *Preparing Instructional Objectives* will help in the formulation of appropriate ABA goals that specify the desired behavior, the situation in which the behavior will be taught (or observed), and the objective criteria for determining when the goal has been achieved.

Implementing an Intervention. The final step in ABA is implementing a treatment plan or intervention. The scope of this book does not include therapies or interventions. However, one of the principles of ABA is that the results of the treatment be verified scientifically. This is done through the use of one of four experimental research designs. The most common of the ABA designs is the *reversal design.* In this design, baseline data are recorded before the intervention program is initiated. Following baseline, treatment begins. To verify that observed changes in behavior are, indeed, the result of the treatment and not the result of some unaccounted or unknown variables, the treatment condition is terminated as soon as results begin to be apparent. This is the so-called reversal or return to baseline from which the design derives its name. Treatment then is reinitiated after a few days or sessions on the second baseline period. If the behavior approximates its original baseline level during the reversal phase and returns to its treatment level when intervention is started again, one can conclude that the behavioral change is the result of the treatment (i.e., the results are verified). Figure 19.3 is a graph of a reversal design.

---

[1]From "Educational Therapy" by P. Magee and P. L. Newcomer. In *Understanding and Teaching Emotionally Disturbed Children* (p. 240) edited by P. L. Newcomer, 1980, Boston: Allyn & Bacon. Reprinted by permission.

FIGURE 19.3. Graph of a Reversal Design

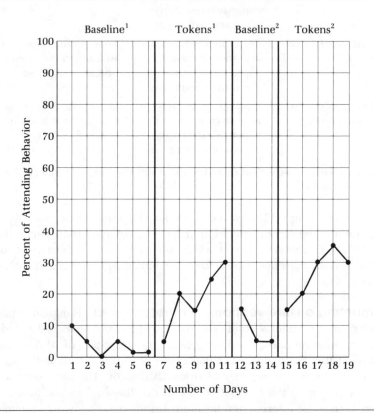

The *multiple baseline design* is another widely used ABA design. In this design, the teacher or therapist will be working with two or more behaviors at the same time. This may mean multiple behaviors observed in the same individual (e.g., talking without permission, being out of seat, and failure to complete assignments observed in Steve) or the same behavior observed in multiple individuals (e.g., talking without permission observed in Steve, Lee, and Don). Baseline data are gathered before treatment begins. Then, the intervention is applied to the first behavior (or the first student) while the other behaviors (or students) remain on baseline. Treatment is gradually introduced for each of the behaviors (or students) involved. If improvement is seen in each behavior when treatment is initiated, this provides verification that the results can be attributed to the treatment. A sample multiple baseline graph is presented in Figure 19.4.

FIGURE 19.4. Graph of a Multiple Baseline Design

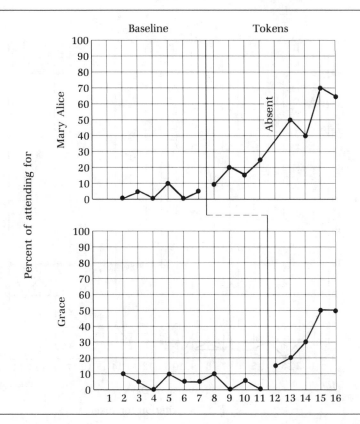

The *changing criterion design* is actually a form of behavioral shaping and no doubt is used unwittingly by many teachers. Baseline data are gathered. Treatment begins with a specified criterion that must be achieved to receive reinforcement (e.g., 2 problems must be completed to receive reinforcement). Later, the criterion is changed (e.g., 3, then 4, then 5 problems be completed to receive reinforcement). Scientific verification is inferred when the behavior continues to meet the successive approximations specified by the changing criterion. Cigarette smokers who reinforce themselves for gradually reducing the number of cigarettes smoked each day are using a changing criterion design, as are teachers who require students to work for increasing periods of time to earn free time privileges. A changing criterion design to improve Joye's attending behavior is depicted in Figure 19.5.

The final ABA design, *multi-element*, is something of a trial-and-error approach. Several potential interventions are planned, and a different one

FIGURE 19.5. Graph of a Changing Criterion Design

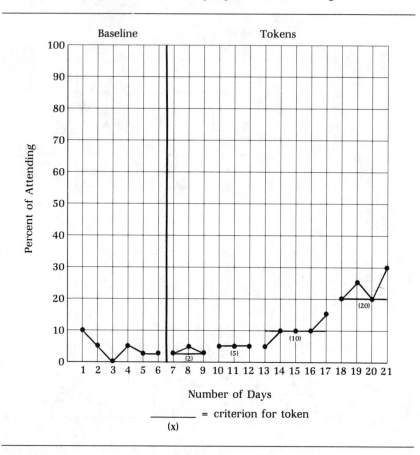

is picked at random to be implemented each day (or session). For instance, the awarding of tokens or free time for appropriate behaviors and the ignoring of inappropriate behaviors may be used to increase on-task responses; one of these consequences will be chosen at random each day and the results recorded. The direct relationship between the treatment and the observed behavioral change provides the necessary scientific verification. Figure 19.6 shows a multi-element design.

Interviews

Interviewing is a broad based assessment technique that can be used to gather information from parents, teachers, other professionals, and from students

FIGURE 19.6. Graph of a Multi-Element Design

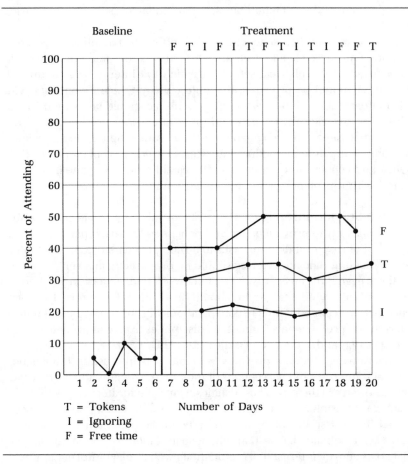

T = Tokens   Number of Days
I = Ignoring
F = Free time

themselves. Interviews can be used to convey information as well as to gather it and can be an effective tool for building rapport and establishing an atmosphere that will be conducive to the ongoing exchange of information. Interviews can be highly structured or loosely organized. Regardless of their formality, interviews should be planned and purposeful, and the interviewer should have specific goals in mind. Three kinds of interviews are discussed here: initial interviews, problem solving interviews, and diagnostic interviews.

Initial Interviews. At a first interview, interviewers should introduce themselves and briefly describe their roles in the school. They may want to gather background information at this time, such as family, medical, educational, and developmental histories. There is no need to repeat this line of questioning, though, if the information is readily and reliably available from a student's existing records. If additional records exist at another school or agency, an initial interview is the appropriate time to request permission to obtain them. Table 19.6 outlines some potential areas of interest during an initial interview.

Keeping in mind that school interviews often elicit a defensive reaction from other professionals as well as from parents, the interviewer should be cognizant of the physical setting in which the interview is conducted. The setting should be private and should convey the confidentiality with which information will be treated. The furniture should be as comfortable as possible—no child sized chairs!—and coffee or similar refreshments offered whenever possible. The adage about a-stitch-in-time applies to interviews: It is helpful to plan and conduct interviews *before* a problem arises. Confidence and cooperation are more easily established when one is not confronted with a problem that demands an immediate solution.

Problem Solving Interviews. At problem solving interviews, the interviewer will want to provide paper and pencils so that each participant can make a list of responsibilities or tasks to be completed before the next interview or meeting. The interviewer should be prepared to answer any direct questions, even if the answer is, "I don't know. I'll find out and let you know." It goes without saying that jargon should be avoided. Remember that even terms that are common in daily conversations at school may be unfamiliar to parents or professionals from other disciplines (e.g., comprehensive test battery, scope and sequence of skills, IEP, ARD, CSC).

Interviewing students provides valuable and interesting information about their interests and perceptions of their own strengths and weaknesses. Students often are their own best diagnosticians, if educators could only take advantage of the information! Through interviews, student ideas can be incorporated into classroom planning, and student commitment to behavioral change can be obtained. Questions about special interests, hobbies, and personal goals convey interest in the student as well as elicit information to be used in planning instructional programs or behavioral interventions.

Interviewing professionals who work with a particular student can generate new information and perhaps offer a different perspective on the problem. Interviews can help identify the expectations that other teachers (or parents) have for the student, the attitudes and values that are operating in other classrooms or agencies (or at home), and the extent of cooperation that can be anticipated. Skills and interests that the student demonstrates in other environments can be identified, as well as interventions that were particularly successful (or dismal).

The interviewer will have to use probe questions (see Table 19.7) to elicit in-depth information, to obtain specific behavioral descriptions, or to clarify responses. Remarks such as, "That's a good idea. How do you think we can

TABLE 19.6. Initial Interview Guide

A. Present Status

  1. Age
  2. Sex
  3. Grade—class—last year's teacher's name

B. Physical appearance and history

  1. General impression made by child
  2. Obvious physical strengths and limitations
  3. General mannerisms, appearance, etc.

C. Educational Status

  1. Present school achievement—kind of work—any samples of work
  2. Promotions—accelerations, retardations—causes
  3. Relations with individual teachers, present and past
  4. Books and other materials used in last educational setting
  5. Tests, individual or group, types of measures used

D. Personal Traits

  1. Personality (general statement)
  2. Attitudes toward home, friends, self, family, other students, school
  3. Hobbies, play life, leisure time activities
  4. Educational and vocational goals
  5. Marked likes and dislikes—foods, toys, TV programs, etc.

E. Home and Family

  1. Individuals in the home
  2. Socioeconomic level
  3. Relation with family members—favorite brothers/sisters, parent/other relative
  4. Regular chores, pets, etc.
  5. Home cooperation
  6. Record at social agencies

F. Work Experience

  1. Part-time jobs (summer, after school)
  2. Attitude toward work, etc.

G. Additional information needed

  1. Sending school
  2. Outside agencies
  3. Private sources, doctor, mental health center, etc. (need release forms)
  4. Health information

TABLE 19.7. Possible Probe Questions for a Problem Solving Interview

"Just how do you mean that?"

"Would you tell us a little more about what you have in mind?"

"Will you give me an example of what you mean?"

"What makes you think . . .?"

"Why?"

"In what way . . .?"

"You feel that . . .?"

"Tell me more."

"Isn't that interesting?"

"Uh huh," as in "Yes, go on. . . ."

implement it?" will elicit support from the interviewee and convey a cooperative attitude.

The interview should close on a positive note and should end before the respondent is tired, bored, or confused. Both parties to the interview should leave with new information. Commitments for tasks to be accomplished before a future meeting should be reviewed and an appointment made if necessary. The following checklist should be helpful.

1. Have a goal for the interview (obtaining specific information, getting to know one another, eliciting cooperation, etc.).

2. If necessary, write down or outline the questions to be asked and the information to be conveyed.

3. Take a moment to appraise the physical surroundings of the interview through the other person's eyes.

4. Use probe or guide questions to move the interview into appropriate areas or into new areas when a topic is dead or unfruitful.

5. Be alert to sensitive or touchy topics.

6. Monitor yourself for defensive behaviors or responses.

7. Indicate a willingness to cooperate and a desire to work together.

8. Encourage the interviewee to participate actively in the interview and to contribute information.

9. Complete the interview on an upbeat tone that will put future interactions on a positive footing.

10. If you didn't take notes during the interview, make a few notes as soon after the interview as possible.

11. If possible, videotape yourself in interviews and then evaluate your performance or ask others to do so. Role playing interviews or specific situations that you find difficult during interviews may be helpful, too.

Diagnostic Interviews. Interviews are frequently used in socioemotional assessment to evaluate the dynamics that influence the present (and future) behavior or personality development of an individual. These interviews are called clinical, psychodynamic, or diagnostic interviews. Kessler (1966) outlines a diagnostic guide for interviewing parents and children that will be helpful to school professionals (Table 19.8).

Interviewing is a deceptively easy task. Good interviewing requires planning and practice. Losen and Daiment (1978), McCallon and McCray (1975), and Stewart and Cash (1985) are useful resources. In addition, Turnbull, Strickland, and Brantley (1978) and Wiederholt, Hammill, and Brown (1983) offer excellent guidance for interviewing students.

Other Assessment Techniques

The remaining assessment tools to be discussed in this chapter are all interactive techniques: Q-sorts, sociometrics, and analyses of classroom interaction.

Q-Sorts. Q-sorts are used to compare two different interpretations of the same set of behaviors. Q-sort items may include descriptions of academic behaviors (e.g., reads a lot, enjoys reading, reads at home), social attributes (e.g., dates frequently, dances well, has friends of both sexes), personal responsibility (e.g., does assigned chores, gets ready for school on time, has a messy room), and a host of other characteristics that may be of interest.

TABLE 19.8. Kessler's Diagnostic Interview Guide

I. *From the Parents*

(In interviewing parents, one is concerned with obtaining factual information about the child, but also with assessing, if possible, the parents' attitudes and feelings. The best method is to start with general inquiries and follow up with specific questions.)

A. *General inquiry*

1. "What is the problem which concerns you?" The parents may be specific and well-informed about this, or vague and perplexed, or even so indifferent that they are there only because they were told to come.

2. "When did you first learn of the difficulties? What were you told? Have you done anything about this before?" The parents may seem astonished that a problem exists, and insist that they were never informed of it. If their account of what has been said to them is inaccurate, the distortions they introduce will be helpful in understanding them.

3. "Have you any ideas what the possible causes of the school problem might be?" The parent may blame the school, themselves, or some physical defect, or they may intuitively sense a psychological cause.

4. "Were there any problems before he started school? Did you anticipate his having difficulties?"

5. "What has been said to the child about his school failures? How does he feel about them?" One hopes to get an indication of the parents' closeness to the child and of their ability to communicate with him.

B. *Specific inquiry*

1. *Current behavior*

a. Other symptoms: Enuresis, thumb sucking, lip licking, sleep problems, feeding difficulties, fighting, dawdling, and so on.

b. Peer relationships: Choice of playmates, role usually taken by the child, interest in seeking companionship, close friendships, teasing, being teased, and so on.

c. Physical activity: Degree of interest and form it takes . . . reaction to instruction in sports involving physical contact with other players.

d. Family relationships: Acceptance of parental authority, of criticism, restrictions, requests, and punishment. Responsibility for self-care and for helping in home. Relationship to siblings, patterns of dominance, bickering, jealousy, and so on.

e. Expressed feelings about going to school: History of reluctance to attend, differences in mood during school and vacation periods, comments about work, successes and failures.

TABLE 19.8. continued

2. *Pre-school history*
   a. Birth and early development: Abnormalities . . . worries during the first years. Age of walking, development of speaking.
   b. Feeding: Usual appetite, food preferences, history of force feeding, present attitudes, age of weaning from bottle.
   c. Toilet training: Time if recalled, parents' recollection of relative easiness, history of constipation, history of force, participation by the parents.
   d. Early discipline: Easy or difficult to control, means used, manner of handling early aggression (e.g., biting and kicking), manner of handling verbal aggression.
   e. Mental development: Verbal development, intellectual curiosity (i.e., questions asked), expression of curiosity about sex differences, birth of babies, death, God, and so on. Nursery school.
   f. Medical history: Previous illnesses, operations, accidents, present defects (e.g., allergies, visual defects).
3. *Family history*
   a. Family illness or crisis: When, how explained to the child, his reactions.
   b. Chronic tensions in home: Financial, marital difficulties, in-laws, crowding, and so on.
   c. Separations from parents: When, how long, reasons, how explained, child's reaction.
   d. Parents' educational experiences: Schooling. Was it easy, enjoyable, difficult, or what? Their current occupations and attitudes toward them.
   e. Parental handling of current school problem: Degree of interest, what has been said and done, degree of accord between parents about handling of the problem, evidences of interplay between parents or parent and child.
   f. Indications of identifications: Father-son, mother-daughter, father-daughter.

II. *From the Child*
   No attempt is made here to describe the diagnostic usefulness of psychological procedures or to recommend any special battery of tests; this would require extensive presentation and a critique of the voluminous literature available. None is foolproof, and even those tests which differentiate diagnostic groups (e.g., organic versus functional) overlap to an embarrassing extent. In studying an individual child, one must evaluate the tests in the light of his history and behavior.
   A. *Attitudes*
      1. Child's awareness of the problem: Evaluation of his expressed feelings about the difficulty, particularly in terms of anxiety and involvement.

TABLE 19.8. continued

2. His self-concept: How does he see himself—as a top student, a bad child, or a foreordained failure?
3. Reactions to success and failure: Level of aspiration, realistic understanding of his limitations, pleasure in success, reactions to difficult questions, admission of lack of knowledge, and so on.

B. *General behavior*
1. Patterns of withholding and blocking: Kinds of situations which arouse these reactions.
2. Response to examiner: Degree of openness, readiness to establish a relationship, eagerness to confide, ability to verbalize reactions and experiences, tolerance for work involved in taking tests.
3. Special preoccupations: Aggression, violent ideas, intimations of catastrophe or danger, self-devaluation, intrusion of fantasy into tests.
4. Activity or passivity: Extent to which he is governed by a wish to be liked, to avoid trouble, and so on. What awakens spontaneity? Frequency with which he asks questions. Degree to which he resents being told what to do.

Jane W. Kessler, *Psychopathology of Childhood*, © 1966, pp. 221–223. Reprinted by permission of Prentice-Hall, Inc., Englewood Cliffs, NJ.

The first step in using the Q-sort technique is to obtain or devise the descriptor statements. There should be a different set of items for each area of interest. Although most Q-sorts have 25 or 36 items, any number of statements may be included as long as the items can be sorted into a perfect pyramid form, such as the one in Figure 19.7. (There is a variation on the Q-sort, called the F-sort, that is nonparametric and does not require an approximation of the normal curve. However, it is more difficult to construct and interpret.) Sample descriptor items are given in Figure 19.7 and in Table 19.9. Professionals who do not want to build their own items will find Kroth's (1973) article on the diagnostic Q-sort helpful. Other commercially available Q-sorts include Schachter, Cooper, and Gordet's (1968) *Child Development Center Q-Sort*, Baumrind's (1971) *Preschool Behavior Q-sort*, and Riley's (1971) *Animal Pictorial Q-sort* that is based on 36 Animal Lotto cards.

The descriptor statements are numbered and written on small cards, one item per card. The individual who is completing the sort reads each item and then places it onto the form board in the appropriate category (e.g., "most like me," "very much like me," etc.). All the squares on the pyramid must be used: None may be left blank, and none may be used more than once. Sorters may rearrange items until they are satisfied that their responses are representative. Students complete this process twice. On the first sort

FIGURE 19.7. Q-Sort Formboard

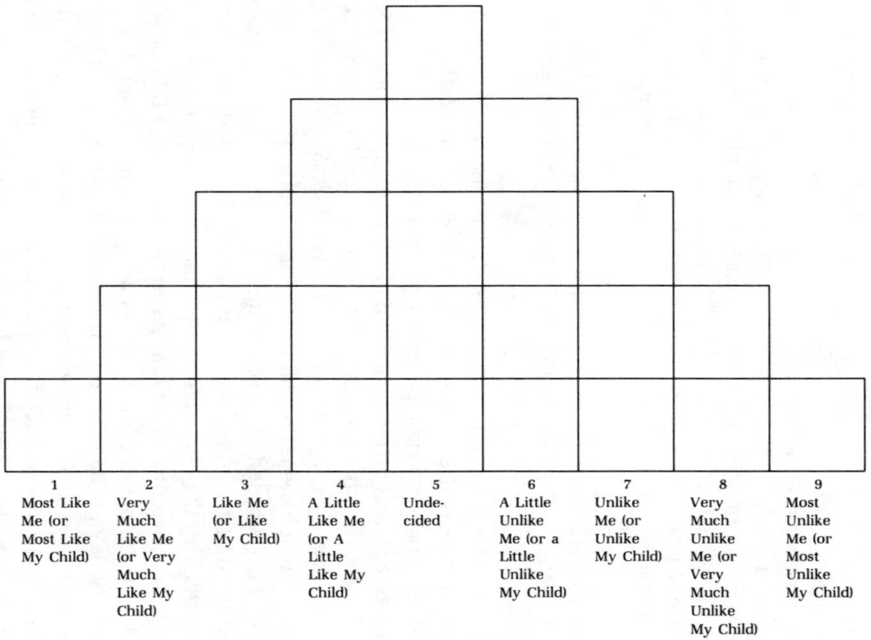

1
Most Like
Me (or
Most Like
My Child)

2
Very
Much
Like Me
(or Very
Much
Like My
Child)

3
Like Me
(or Like
My Child)

4
A Little
Like Me
(or A
Little
Like My
Child)

5
Unde-
cided

6
A Little
Unlike
Me (or a
Little
Unlike
My Child)

7
Unlike
Me (or
Unlike
My Child)

8
Very
Much
Unlike
Me (or
Very
Much
Unlike
My Child)

9
Most
Unlike
Me (or
Most
Unlike
My Child)

From "The Behavioral Q-Sort as a Diagnostic Tool" by R. Kroth, 1973, *Academic Therapy*, 8, p. 320, San Rafael, CA: Academic Therapy Publications. Reprinted by permission.

TABLE 19.9. Parent Q-Sort Items

1. Does assigned chores.	13. Eats between meals.
2. Does homework on time.	14. Is overweight.
3. Goes to bed without problems.	15. Is destructive of property.
4. Comes home when he should.	16. Gets ready for school on time.
5. Argues with parents.	17. Makes own decisions.
6. Has friends.	18. Chooses own clothes.
7. Likes school.	19. Is unhealthy.
8. Cries or sulks when he doesn't get his own way.	20. Fights with brothers and sisters.
	21. Has a messy room.
9. Throws temper tantrums.	22. Responds to rewards.
10. Likes to watch TV.	23. Does acceptable schoolwork.
11. Likes to read.	24. Is a restless sleeper.
12. Plays alone.	25. Stretches the truth.

From "The Behavioral Q-sort as a Diagnostic Tool" by R. Kroth, 1973, *Academic Therapy, 8,* p. 320, San Rafael, CA: Academic Therapy Publications. Reprinted by permission.

they arrange the items into categories that reflect their true perceptions; this is called the *real sort*. On the second sort (the *ideal sort*), items are arranged to represent subjects' ideal perceptions.

Responses are recorded on a form like the one in Figure 19.8. For example, if a student sorted Item 1 as "a little like me" on the real sort and "unlike me" on the ideal sort, a 4 would be recorded beside item 1 in the *S-1* column, and a 7 would be recorded in the *S-2* column. The difference between the sorts (3) is recorded in the *D* column, and the difference squared (9) is recorded in the *D²* column. This last column is added, and the sum (ΣD^2) is substituted into the correlation formula printed on the record form. This correlation coefficient will be neither greater than $+1.00$ nor smaller than -1.00. The farther the correlation is away from $r = .00$, the greater the agreement between the real and ideal sorts. A perfect correlation of $+1.00$ indicates that the items were sorted exactly the same way on the real and ideal sorts. A -1.00 coefficient is an indication that the sorts were exactly inverse (e.g., the item rated "most like me" on the real sort was rated "least like me" on the ideal sort).

In most socioemotional evaluations at school, the correlation coefficient will be of less interest than the items that have large discrepancies between them. Items with large differences probably constitute good target behaviors or goals for intervention. If the student rates an item such as, "likes to read," as "like me" on the ideal sort but "unlike me" on the real sort, the examiner may have identified an area in which the student is committed to change and will begin to work for improvement of the behavior or skill.

FIGURE 19.8. Q-Sort Record Form

Name of Subject _____ Sex _____ Date Tested _____

Address_____Phone_____Date of Birth_____

School_____ Teacher_____ Grade_____ Age_____

Name of Examinee_____ Relationship to Child_____

Card No.	Column S-1	Column S-2	D	D²	
1					$n = 1 - \dfrac{\Sigma D^2}{200}$
2					
3					
4					
5					
6					
7					
8					
9					
10					
11					
12					
13					
14					
15					
16					
17					
18					
19					
20					
21					
22					
23					
24					
25					
			$\Sigma =$		

From "The Behavioral Q-Sort as a Diagnostic Tool" by R. Kroth, 1973, *Academic Therapy, 8*, p. 323, San Rafael, CA: Academic Therapy Publications. Reprinted by permission.

Kroth's (1973) article on diagnostic uses of the Q-sort is excellent. He reminds readers of the versatility of the technique and suggests that Q-sorting be used with students' parents and teachers, too. The real sort would represent the way they believed their child/student actually behaved, while the ideal sort would represent the way they wished the child/student would behave. With a little creativity, many Q-sort comparisons are possible: the child's ideal sort compared with the parents' ideal sort, the regular class teacher's real sort compared with the special class teacher's real sort, the student's real sort compared with the teacher's real sort, and so on. Once again, particular discrepancies may be more valuable than the actual correlation coefficient that is obtained. For instance, if the regular class teacher rates "is a good reader" as "unlike my student" while the special education teacher rates the item as "like my student," an area that is worthy of further evaluation has been identified. Does the student actually read better in one class than the other, and if so, why? Or do the two teachers have different criteria for determining a good reader? Or does one of the teachers have a skewed perception of the student's reading ability that is not related to actual skill in reading? All are possible hypotheses that the examiner may draw.

Q-sort items can be read to nonreaders, although this has not been particularly successful. Subjects who cannot read the cards themselves tend to have difficulty manipulating the cards, especially when only a few slots remain on the form board, and some switching is necessary. Pictorial Q-sorts may be appropriate for these students. Subjects who are easily frustrated also have difficulty with the Q-sort technique, because they are forced to limit their responses to the existing categories. Most students, however, enjoy the activity and can complete it independently, even recording their own responses, after brief instructions have been given.

Sociometrics. Sociometric or peer nominating techniques are popular in educational measurement, particularly in the identification of emotionally disturbed, behaviorally disordered, and learning disabled students. Sociometrics generally are used in one of two ways (Moreno, 1953). They may be used to create a sociological map, analyzing the structure of groups and the relationships reported by the respondents. They also can be used to evaluate individuals within a group, identifying students who are popular, rejected, or isolated within their classes or peer groups.

Sociometric nominations can be obtained in several ways. The most common is to ask students to name classmates whom they would most (or least) like to do something with, for example, "Whom would you most (least) like to play with at recess?" Responses of this type can be mapped (see Figure 19.9), or they can be analyzed in the norm referenced manner described later for the *Behavior Rating Profile* (Brown & Hammill, 1983).

The *Birthday Test* (Northway, Weld, & Davis, 1971) is a sociometric technique that asks children to name three peers and three adults who they want to invite to their birthday parties. Several party situations are subsequently described, and children then select three of these original six people to be

FIGURE 19.9. Sociogram

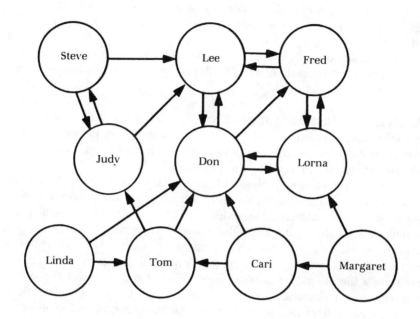

companions in each situation. This helps to highlight issues of independence and dependence as well as sociometric relationships. McCandless and Marshall (1957) and Moore and Updegraff (1965) both use photographs rather than names to complete their sociograms. Bower and Lambert (1971) use three different sociometric techniques for screening. Class Pictures consists of 10 pictures of children engaging in maladjusted behaviors and 10 of children engaging in neutral behaviors; students are asked to name a classmate who might be the subject of each picture. Class Play includes 20 hypothetical roles, and students are asked to nominate a classmate to play each role, to select roles for themselves, and to identify roles they think other students would select for them. Student Survey, the third Bower and Lambert technique, presents 10 terms descriptive of emotionally disturbed behaviors and 10 terms descriptive of positive or neutral behaviors. Children are asked to nominate classmates who typify each term and to identify those terms they believe are characteristic of their own behavior.

Some authorities (e.g., Gronlund, 1985) believe that responses to one set of sociometric questions should not be generalized to another pair of questions. For instance, responses to questions relating to cooperative school work should not be generalized to questions regarding social relationships. However, Brown (1980, April) found that popular, rejected, and ignored students in elementary grades tended to maintain their relative status across several stimulus questions, although children with middle status ranks seemed to be differentially chosen. They also found that the reliability of sociometric responses seems to be low moderate (correlations in the .15 to .30 range) and related to age and sex (older children and males are more stable in responding).

Analyses of Classroom Interaction. Tools have been devised to assist in the evaluation of other kinds of classroom interaction, principally interactions of the student with the teacher and interactions of the student with the general classroom climate and environment.

Flanders' Interaction Analysis Categories (FIAC) (Flanders, 1970) are the most prominent of several measures of teacher-pupil interaction. Flanders' system codes and analyzes 10 behaviors that are observed in the verbal interaction of a teacher with an entire class of students. These behavioral categories, defined in Table 19.10, include 7 teacher talk behaviors (3 responses and 4 initiations), 2 pupil talk behaviors (1 response and 1 initiation), and a silence or confusion category. Observations of these 10 behaviors are recorded in 4-second segments for several short, daily periods of time. No particular pattern of teacher-pupil interaction is considered to be inherently better than any other; however, it is important to know which patterns are favored by a particular teacher and which patterns are used sparsely or not at all.

Hough's (1967) Observation System for Instructional Analysis (OSIA) grew out of FIAC and was revised so that there would be an equal number of teacher and student talk categories. Thus, OSIA has 16, rather than 10, behaviors to code for a teacher and a class of students. By increasing the number of student talk categories, the examiner can begin to identify the kinds of student initiations and responses that are reinforced by a particular teacher. Another advantage of OSIA is that subsequent editions of the system have been tailored to measure specific kinds of verbal interaction that are unique to a particular academic content such as reading, mathematics, and physical education (Gauthier, 1980).

When examiners are more interested in the interaction of the teacher with a single student than with the entire class, they will find Brophy and Good's (1969) Dyadic Interaction Analysis to be more helpful. This system analyzes five sets of behaviors: (a) the pupil's response to the teacher's question (response opportunities); (b) oral presentation by the student (recitation); (c) general classroom management (procedural contacts); (d) interaction

TABLE 19.10. Flanders' Interaction Analysis Categories

TEACHER TALK	*Response*	1. *Accepts feeling.* Accepts and clarifies an attitude or the feeling tone of a pupil in a nonthreatening manner. Feelings may be positive or negative. Predicting and recalling feelings are included. 2. *Praises or encourages.* Praises or encourages pupil action or behavior. Jokes that release tension, but not at the expense of another individual; nodding head, or saying "Um hm?" or "go on" are included. 3. *Accepts or uses ideas of pupils.* Clarifying, building, or developing ideas suggested by a pupil. Teacher extensions of pupil ideas are included but as the teacher brings more of his own ideas into play, shift to category five.
		4. *Asks questions.* Asking a question about content or procedure, based on teacher ideas, with the intent that a pupil will answer.
	Initiation	5. *Lecturing.* Giving facts or opinions about content or procedures; expressing his own ideas, giving his own explanation, or citing an authority other than a pupil. 6. *Giving directions.* Directions, commands, or orders to which a pupil is expected to comply. 7. *Criticizing or justifying authority.* Statements intended to change pupil behavior from nonacceptable to acceptable pattern; bawling someone out; stating why the teacher is doing what he is doing; extreme self-reliance.
PUPIL TALK	*Response*	8. *Pupil-talk—response.* Talk by pupils in response to teacher. Teacher initiates the contact or solicits pupil statement or structures the situation. Freedom to express own ideas is limited.
	Initiation	9. *Pupil-talk—initiation.* Talk by pupils which they initiate. Expressing own ideas; initiating a new topic; freedom to develop opinions and a line of thought, like asking thoughtful questions; going beyond the existing structure.
SILENCE		10. *Silence or confusion.* Pauses, short periods of silence and periods of confusion in which communication cannot be understood by the observer.

From *Analyzing Teacher Behavior* (p. 186) by N. Flanders, 1970, Menlo Park, CA: Addison-Wesley. Reprinted by permission.

regarding the student's written work (work-related contacts); and (e) discipline or individual remarks about the student's behavior (behavioral contacts).

The Florida Climate and Control System (Soar, Soar, & Ragosta, 1971) uses similar but more elaborate observation categories to describe the interaction of the pupil with the physical environment of the class, the size and type of class, the nature of classroom activities, student and teacher tasks, classroom organization and structure, seating arrangements, the use of classroom displays, and so on. More than 50 environmental and interactive variables are coded in the Florida system, and potential users must complete at least 20 hours of training. Another, less structured, means for analyzing the overall climate of a classroom is offered by Medley, Schmuck, and Ames (1968) in their excellent little book.

All of these systems are useful because they describe objectively the interactive patterns that are characteristic of a particular class or teacher-pupil dyad. These tools can help teachers become aware of the ways they manage their classes and can further help teachers sharpen their observational skills. However, each of these systems is complicated, and each requires a great deal of supervised, formal training to master. Each also requires a great deal of teacher or observer time to implement. Therefore, we do not recommend their use routinely. We certainly do not recommend their use for purposes of teacher promotion and evaluation, a questionable and unfortunate practice in some school organizations.

SUMMARY

Socioemotional problems are evaluated with a wide variety of assessment techniques. Among the most frequently used tools are reviewing records, testing, observing, using ABA, interviewing, and analyzing interactions through Q-sorts, sociometrics, and classroom analysis techniques. All of these techniques can be informal or standardized. To be considered standardized, a tool must have specified criteria for administration, scoring, and interpretation, and also must have proof of its standardization in the form of empirical evidence of reliability and validity. Data obtained from these techniques can be interpreted through norm referenced, criterion referenced, and nonreferenced comparisons.

REFERENCES

Anastasi, A. (1982). *Psychological testing* (5th ed.). New York: Macmillan.

Anderson, G. J. (1973). *The assessment of learning environments: A manual for the Learning Environment Inventory and the My Class Inventory.* Halifax, NS, Canada: Atlantic Institute of Education.

Anderson, L. W. (1981). *Assessing affective characteristics in the schools.* Boston: Allyn & Bacon.

Barclay, J. R. (1971). *Barclay Classroom Climate Inventory.* Lexington, KY: Educational Skills Development.

Baumrind, D. (1971). *Preschool Behavior Q-sort.* Berkeley: University of California Press.

Bellak, L., & Bellak, S. S. (1965). *Children's Apperception Test.* Monterey, CA: Consulting Psychologists Press.

Bene, E., & Anthony, J. (1957). *Family Relations Test.* Windsor, England: NFER.

Blum, G. (1967). *The Blacky pictures: Manual of instructions.* New York: Psychological Corporation.

Bower, E. M., & Lambert, N. M. (1971). In-school screening of children with emotional handicaps. In N. J. Long, W. C. Morse, & R. G. Newman (Eds.), *Conflict in the classroom* (2nd ed.). Belmont, CA: Wadsworth.

Brophy, J., & Good, T. (1969). *Teacher-child dyadic interaction: A manual for coding behavior.* Austin, TX: The University of Texas Research and Development Center.

Brown, L. (1980, April). *The reliability of sociometric measures with elementary, junior high, and senior high school students.* Paper presented at the meeting of the International Council for Exceptional Children, Philadelphia.

Brown, L., & Hammill, D. D. (1983). *Behavior Rating Profile: An Ecological Approach to Behavioral Assessment.* Austin, TX: PRO-ED.

Brown, L., & Sherbenou, R. J. (1981). A comparison of teacher perceptions of student reading ability, reading performance, and classroom behavior. *Reading Teacher, 34,* 557–560.

Brown, V. L., & McEntire, E. (1984) *Test of Mathematical Abilities.* Austin, TX: PRO-ED.

Buck, N. J., & Jolles, I., (1966). *House-Tree-Person Test.* Los Angeles: Western Psychological Corporation.

Cain, L., Levine, S., & Elzey, F. F. (1969). *Cain-Levine Social Competency Scale.* Palo Alto, CA: Consulting Psychologists Press.

Craighead, W., Kazdin, A., & Mahoney, M. (1976). *Behavior modification.* Boston: Houghton Mifflin.

Crandall, V. C., Katkovsky, W., & Crandall, V. J. (1965). Children's belief in their own control of reinforcement in intellectual-academic situtions. *Child Development, 36,* 91–109.

Estes, T. H., Estes, J. J., Richards, H. C., & Roettger, D. (1981). *Estes Attitude Scales: Measures of Attitudes Toward School Subjects.* Austin, TX: PRO-ED.

Eysenck, S. B. G. (1965). *Junior Eysenck Personality Inventory.* San Diego: Educational & Industrial Testing Service.

Fitts, W. (1970). *Tennessee Self-Concept Scale.* Nashville, TN: Counselor Recordings & Tests.

Flanders, N. E. (1970). *Analyzing teacher behavior.* Menlo Park, CA: Addison-Wesley.

Gauthier, R. A. (1980). *A descriptive-analytic study of teacher-student interaction in mainstreamed physical education classes.* Unpublished doctoral dissertation, Purdue University, West Lafayette, IN.

Gronlund, N. (1985). *Measurement and evaluation in teaching* (5th ed.). New York: Macmillan.

Hall, R. V., & Van Houten, R. (1983). *Managing behavior series, vol. 1: The measurement of behavior* (2nd ed.). Austin, TX: PRO-ED.

Hammill, D. D., & Leigh, J. (1983). *Basic School Skills Inventory–Diagnostic*. Austin, TX: PRO-ED.

Haring, N. G., Lovitt, T. C., Eaton, M. D., & Hansen, C. L. (1978). *The fourth R: Research in the classroom*. Columbus, OH: Merrill.

Heil, L. M., Sheviakov, G. V., & Stone, S. (1960). Manifest interest schedule. In L. M. Heil, M. Powell, & I. Feifer, *Characteristics of teacher behavior and competency related to the achievement of different kinds of children in several elementary grades*. Washington, DC: U.S. Office of Education.

Hough, J. B. (1967). An observation system for the analysis of classroom instruction. In E. J. Amidon & J. B. Hough (Eds.), *Interaction analysis: Theory, research, and application*. Reading, MA: Addison-Wesley.

Hresko, W. P., & Brown, L. (1984). *Test of Early Socioemotional Development*. Austin, TX: PRO-ED.

Kessler, J. W. (1966). *Psychopathology of childhood*. Englewood Cliffs, NJ: Prentice-Hall.

Kohn, M., & Rosman, B. (1972). Kohn social competence scale. In J. Kohn, B. Parnes, & B. Rosman, *A rating and scoring manual for the Kohn Problem Checklist and Kohn Social Competence Scale*. New York: White Institute of Psychiatry, Psychoanalysis, and Psychology.

Koppitz, E. M. (1964). *Bender-Gestalt Test for Young Children*. New York: Grune & Stratton.

Koppitz, E. M. (1968). *Psychological evaluation of children's human figure drawing*. New York: Grune & Stratton.

Kroth, R. (1973). The behavioral Q-sort as a diagnostic tool. *Academic Therapy, 8,* 317–330.

Lambert, N. M., Hartsbough, C. S., & Bower, E. M. (1979). *Pupil Behavior Rating Scale*. Monterey, CA: CTB/McGraw Hill.

Losen, S. M., & Daiment, B. (1978). *Parent conferences in the schools*. Boston: Allyn & Bacon.

Lovitt, T. C. (1975). Applied behavioral analysis and learning disabilities: Characteristics of ABA, general recommendations, and methodological limitations. *Journal of Learning Disabilities, 8,* 432–443.

Magee, P., & Newcomer, P. L. (1980). Educational therapy. In P. L. Newcomer (Ed.), *Understanding and teaching emotionally disturbed children*. Boston: Allyn & Bacon.

Mager, R. (1962). *Preparing instructional objectives*. Palo Alto, CA: Fearon.

McCallon, E., & McCray, E. (1975). *Planning and conducting interviews*. Austin, TX: Learning Concepts.

McCandless, B. R., & Marshall, H. R. (1957). *McCandless-Marshall Sociometric Status Test*. Atlanta, GA: Emory University, Department of Psychology.

McCarney, S. B., Leigh, J. E., & Cornbleet, J. A. (1983). *Behavior Evaluation Scale*. Columbia, MO: Educational Services.

Medley, D., Schmuck, C., & Ames, N. (1968). *Assessing the learning environment in the classroom*. Princeton, NJ: ETS.

Moore, S., & Updegraff, R. (1965). *Minnesota Sociometric Status Test*. Minneapolis: University of Minnesota Institute of Child Development.

Moreno, J. L. (1953). *Who shall survive? Foundations of sociometry, group psychotherapy, and sociodrama* (2nd ed.). New York: Beacon House.

Nihira, K., Foster, R., Shellhaas, M., & Leland, H. (1975). *AAMD Adaptive Behavior Scales, Public School Version*. Washington, DC: American Association on Mental Deficiency.

Northway, M. L., Weld, L., & Davis, M. (1971). *Birthday Test: Junior Form*. Toronto: University of Toronto Institute of Child Studies.

Parker, R. M. (1983). *OASIS Interest Schedule*. Austin, TX: PRO-ED.

Peter, L. (1972). *Individual instruction*. New York: McGraw-Hill.

Piers, E. V., & Harris, D. B. (1984). *The Piers-Harris Children's Self-Concept Scale*, Revised Manual 1984. Nashville, TN: Counselor Recordings & Tests.

Porter, R. B., & Cattell, R. B. (1975). *The IPAT Children's Personality Questionnaire*. Champaign, IL: Institute for Personality & Ability Testing.

Quay, H. C., & Peterson, D. R. (1967). *Behavior Problem Checklist*. Champaign, IL: Children's Research Center.

Riley, J. E. (1971). *Animal Picture Q-sort*. Denton: Texas Woman's University.

Salvia, J., & Ysseldyke, J. E. (1985). *Assessment in special and remedial education* (3rd ed.). Boston: Houghton Mifflin.

Sattler, J. M. (1982). *Assessment of children's intelligence and special abilities* (2nd ed.). Boston: Allyn & Bacon.

Schacter, F., Cooper, A. & Gordet, R. (1968). *Child Development Center Q-Sort*. Chicago: Stoelting.

Shipman, V. C. (1970). *ETS Locus of Control Scale*. Princeton, NJ: ETS.

Soares, A. T., & Soares, L. M. (1974). *Self-Perception Inventory*. Princeton, NJ: ETS.

Soar, R., Soar, R., & Ragosta, M. (1971). *Florida climate and control system*. Gainesville: University of Florida Institute for the Development of Human Resources.

Spivak, G., Spotts, S., & Haimes, P. E. (1967). *Devereux Adolescent Behavior Rating Scale*. Devon, PA: Devereux Foundation.

Spivak, G., & Swift, M. (1967). *Devereux Elementary School Behavior Rating Scale*. Devon, PA: Devereux Foundation.

Stewart, C. J., & Cash, W. B. (1985). *Interviewing: Principles and practice* (4th ed.). Dubuque, IA: Brown.

Sulzer-Azaroff, B., & Mayer, G., (1977). *Applying behavior-analytical procedures with children and youth*. New York: Holt, Rinehart & Winston.

Turnbull, A. P., Strickland, B. B., & Brantley, J. C. (1978). *Developing and implementing individualized education programs*. Columbus, OH: Merrill.

Urban, W. H. (1963). *Draw-A-Person Test*. Los Angeles: Western Psychological Corporation.

Walker, H. M. (1970). *Walker Problem Behavior Identification Checklist*. Los Angeles: Western Psychological Corporation.

Walker, H. M., McConnell, S., Holmes, D., Todis, B., Walker, J., & Golden, N. (1983). *The Walker social skills curriculum: The ACCEPTS program*. Austin, TX: PRO-ED.

Wallace, G., & Larsen, S. C. (1978). *Educational assessment of learning problems: Testing for teaching*. Boston: Allyn & Bacon.

Weed, L. L. (1971). *Medical records, medical evaluation, and patient care: The problem-oriented record as a basic tool*. Cleveland, OH: Case Western Reserve University Press.

Wiederholt, J. L., Hammill, D. D., & Brown, V. L. (1983). *The resource teacher: A guide to effective practices* (2nd ed.). Austin, TX: PRO-ED.

Workman, E. A. (1982). *Teaching behavioral self-control to students*. Austin, TX: PRO-ED.

20 / DIAGNOSING SOCIOEMOTIONAL PROBLEMS IN THE SCHOOLS

Socioemotional problems run the full continuum of severity in classrooms. At the mild end they comprise such things as minor rule violations, transient problems that last only a few days or for a maturational phase, or slightly developmentally delayed social skills. These mild problems usually occur singly and infrequently; they are short lived and easily managed, with little effect on others. It is likely that these problems never reach proportions that are sufficiently grand for the teacher to make a referral outside the classroom; some may not even require special interventions on the part of the teacher and will be handled by the normal behavior management systems already operating in the class. In the middle of the continuum are problems generally referred to as behavior disorders. These problems usually are not severe enough to warrant a special education placement in programs for the emotionally disturbed but probably will require some specific intervention on the part of the teacher and at times may result in a referral for further evaluation. These moderate problems are stressful and occasionally disruptive. They are exhibited by students who often are unable to relate to others but who usually are aware of their own behavior and can sometimes control their behavior. The severe end of the continuum includes problems that are associated with serious emotional disturbance and warrant special education placement. These severe, referable problems are many and varied. They are extremely disruptive and are severe in both frequency and duration. Students in this category have little control over their own behavior, are unable to relate to others, have considerable confusion about reality, and rarely act appropriately.

Although these delineations seem clear, diagnosis of socioemotional problems is fraught with difficulty and hazards, particularly in the public schools. As Eli Bower (1982) once observed with tongue in cheek, "Along with the hazards of street crime, drunk driving, and Christmas shopping is that of defining what is meant by 'emotional disturbance'!" (p. 55). To help the reader through this diagnostic minefield, the discussion in this chapter is divided into three sections: the terminology associated with socioemotional problems in the schools, the legal requirements for diagnosing emotional disturbance in the schools, and applications of the DSM III criteria to school based diagnosis.

TERMINOLOGY ASSOCIATED WITH SOCIOEMOTIONAL PROBLEMS

The reader will not be surprised to learn that each discipline that concerns itself with socioemotional problems in the schools has its own vocabulary. Sometimes those of us in one profession understand the idiom of another profession, and sometimes we are not exactly sure what the words mean. This section does not purport to unravel that particular Gordian knot, merely to give readers a nodding acquaintance with the most prevalent terms.

From the outset, the reader should note that the diagnostic term used in the public schools is *serious emotional disturbance* and that a precise legal definition accompanies that term. The next section of this chapter is devoted to legal requirements for diagnosis in the public schools, and the relevant terminology is discussed.

In psychiatric parlance, the preferred terminology is taken from the third edition of the *Diagnostic and Statistical Manual of Mental Disorders* (American Psychiatric Association, 1980), commonly referred to as DSM III. Again, this is a diagnostic system, and there are specific criteria and characteristics associated with each DSM III classification. That classification system also is discussed in detail later in this chapter. What remains for discussion is the less scientific and less precise terminology that is bandied around teachers' lounges, multidisciplinary team meetings, and parent conferences.

Terms such as *emotionally disturbed* or *behavior disordered* purport to describe students themselves and refer to children whose behavior, personality characteristics, and/or social skills set them apart from their classmates. Emotionally disturbed students are considered to be more seriously involved than behavior disordered students, but both kinds of students are readily identifiable in the classroom. Sometimes these two terms are used interchangeably, so the professional who encounters them in reports or discussions should consider the context in which the words are employed. Educators tend to use *behavior disordered*, because they believe that the term carries less stigma and that behavior, not emotions, falls within their domain of concern. Psychologists, on the other hand, tend to use *emotionally disturbed*, because this term suggests a causative agent, (e.g., disordered emotions) instead of simply focusing on the more observable symptoms (e.g., disordered behavior).

Many professionals, particularly those in the schools, have a tendency to avoid describing the student as emotionally disturbed *or* behavior disordered, concentrating instead on describing the behavior itself as disturbed or disturbing. This is somehow believed to be less stigmatizing to the student who exhibits disturbed or disturbing behavior. Regardless of the stigma argument, which is questionable, the dichotomy raises an important distinction—namely, whether the behavior in question is characteristic of emotional disturbance or whether it is disturbing within the environment. Not all disturbing behaviors are disturbed.

Disturbing behaviors are defined largely by the tolerance ranges and flexibility of the classroom, the teacher, and the other students and, therefore, will vary from one situation to another. A behavior is disturbing when it upsets the equilibrium of the ecosystem. No more precise definition is possible.

Disordered behavior is chronic, frequent, and severe; it also is more universally recognized and defined. Quay, Morse, and Cutler (1966) found that teachers observed three distinct types of disordered behavior. *Conduct disorders* are hostile, acting out, overtly aggressive, and oppositional behaviors. Conduct disordered students usually do not have good relationships with their peers or with adult authority figures. *Personality problems* are more introverted and withdrawn behaviors. Students with personality problems are characterized by unhappiness, fear, anxiety, and general stress often accompanied by physical ailments. *Problems of inadequacy or immaturity* are chronologically or developmentally inappropriate behaviors and encompass such broad areas as passive or disinterested responses, laziness, and the lack of awareness of one's surroundings that is associated with autism. In later research, Quay (1975) added a fourth type of disordered behavior that he termed *socialized delinquency,* referring to the rule breaking behavior and other activities that are only condoned within a specific subgroup such as a gang.

LEGAL REQUIREMENTS FOR DIAGNOSIS

Seriously emotionally disturbed is the diagnostic term of choice in the public schools. This term is dictated by the provisions of P.L. 94-142 and the Federal regulations that implement the law (34 C.F.R. Part 300).

Seriously emotionally disturbed is defined as follows:

(i) The term means a condition exhibiting one or more of the following characteristics over a long period of time and to a marked degree, which adversely affects educational performance:

    A. An inability to learn which cannot be explained by intellectual, sensory, or other health factors;

    B. An inability to build or maintain satisfactory interpersonal relationships with peers and teachers;

    C. Inappropriate types of behaviors or feelings under normal circumstances;

    D. A general pervasive mood of unhappiness or depression;

    E. A tendency to develop physical symptoms or fears associated with personal or school problems;

(ii) The term includes children who are Schizophrenic. The term does not include children who are socially maladjusted, unless it is determined that they are seriously emotionally disturbed. (34 C.F.R. 300.5(b)(8))

Readers who are familiar with the emotional disturbance literature will recognize this as Bower's (1969) definition. Its major advantage, according to Rich (1982) and others, is that the definition is an amalgam of diverse theoretical and philosophical positions: "References to 'feelings,' 'mood,' and 'depression' are of a psychodynamic origin; the phrases 'inability to learn' and 'inappropriate types of behavior' are associated with behavior theory; and 'interpersonal relationships' suggests a sociological influence" (p. 54).

Unfortunately, the eclectic nature of the definition makes it difficult to operationalize in an objective manner. The next two sections are devoted to discussions of the characteristics that constitute serious emotional disturbance and the conditions under which those characteristics must be observed.

Characteristics

To understand better the conditions that satisfy each of the five conditions of the federal definition of seriously emotionally disturbed, we will paraphrase both Bower's (1969) original descriptions and Slenkovich's (1983) more recent and more succinct discussion.

1. *An inability to learn.* A child who is not learning will come immediately to the attention of the classroom teacher. Actual classroom achievement will be poor and progress practically negligible, facts that no doubt will be confirmed by tests of achievement. Bower says that one must first rule out the major causative factors of nonlearning (e.g., mental retardation, physical or sensory impairment) before considering socioemotional explanations. Slenkovich points out that getting failing grades or being behind in schoolwork is not sufficient. To satisfy this provision of the definition, one

must demonstrate "that the student actually be unable to learn. He must be so emotionally disturbed that he cannot learn" (p. 7).

2. *An inability to build or maintain satisfactory interpersonal relationships.* Says Bower, "It isn't getting along with others that is significant here. Satisfactory interpersonal relations refers to the ability to demonstrate sympathy and warmth toward others, the ability to stand alone when necessary, the ability to have close friends, the ability to be aggressively constructive, and the ability to enjoy working and playing with others as well as enjoying working and playing by oneself" (p. 22). Students with these problems are most recognizable to peers and to observant teachers.

3. *Inappropriate behavior or feelings.* According to Slenkovich this condition "appears to mean psychotic or bizarre behavior, not merely neurotic, hyperactive, compulsive, or immoral behavior, or insecure or uncertain feelings" (p. 7). Bower, long an advocate of a strong teacher role in the diagnosis of emotional disturbance in the schools, says that "appropriate or inappropriate is best judged by the teacher using her professional training, her daily and long term observation of the child, and her experience working and interacting with the appropriate behavior of large numbers of normal children" (p. 23).

4. *A general pervasive mood of unhappiness.* Slenkovich insists that this provision refers to "a heavy mood of depression, so heavy that it cannot be missed by anyone" (p. 7). Bower notes that children "may demonstrate such feelings in expressive play, art work, written composition, or in discussion" and that "in the middle or upper grades a self-inventory is usually helpful in confirming suspicions about such feelings" (p. 23).

5. *A tendency to develop physical symptoms.* Many children become nauseous before or after a test is administered, develop headaches or speech difficulties when called on in class, or develop repetitive illnesses to avoid even going to school. Bower points out that peers are often aware of fellow students who develop physical symptoms or illnesses in response to school pressure, as are parents, school nurses, and other noneducators. Slenkovich describes this condition as less severe than the other four and reiterates that "this characteristic (as well as the other P.L. 94-142 characteristics) must be the outgrowth of an established emotional disturbance" (p. 9).

The latter point is well taken. The characteristics, by themselves, do not constitute serious emotional disturbance; rather, they must stem from an emotional condition. The reader will remember that a diagnosis is not a listing of symptoms or observed behaviors, but is an explanation of (or a theory that attempts to explain) the presence of the symptoms. Each diagnosis is associated with its own cluster of symptomatic behaviors. P.L. 94-142 says that the diagnosis *serious emotional disturbance* is characterized by one or more of the five behaviors outlined above.

Conditions

In addition to the five characteristics described above, other conditions are specified in the law and must be met before a diagnosis of serious emotional disturbance can be made. The symptoms must have been observed "over a long period of time," must be present "to a marked degree," and must "adversely affect educational performance." The regulations give very little guidance to interpret these conditions. However, the literature does provide some information to assist professionals who are attempting to diagnose under this definition.

1. *Over a long period of time.* This condition implies that the characteristics must be chronic and must have been observed over a considerable period of time. So-called transient situational disorders that are typical of certain developmental life periods or that are adjustment reactions to crisis situations obviously do not meet this condition. But how long is long enough? Many of the DSM III definitions include a minimum time of 6 months duration for diagnosis, and all require a period of at least 3 months. Rich (1982) suggests that "at the very least, the basis for establishing the existence of chronic behaviors should include the last year, and preferably two, of a student's educational and general life experience" (p. 71).

Slenkovich (1983) says the legal test "appears to be this: If one of the more serious characteristics is involved, or if the disorder itself is one of the more serious disorders, the minimum length of time that the characteristic must have been established appears to be six months; if the characteristic or the disorder is one of the less serious (or one more susceptible to the student's control, such as 'school phobia'), the minimum length of time that the characteristic must have been established appears to be at least a year, and more likely two years" (p. 10). Clearly, then, serious emotional disturbance does not occur overnight, over the weekend, over a semester, or perhaps even over the course of a single school year.

2. *To a marked degree.* This condition refers to the frequency and severity of a behavior. Coleman (1986) contends that these concepts are inversely interrelated in diagnosis: The more severe the behavior, the less frequently it has to occur to be indicative of serious emotional disturbance. She offers the example of a student's anger and hostility that are expressed in two ways: by one student through the creative use of profanity and by another student through the creative use of explosives. Profanity must occur many, many times before it is treated with more than disciplinary action. Use of a bomb, or even a bomb threat, need occur only once to be considered marked. Rich (1982) suggests that the degree of intervention required is an indicator of the markedness of a particular behavior. If simple interventions within the realm of the classroom teacher will suffice (e.g., altering assignments or changing classes), then the characteristic isn't present to a marked degree. Slenkovich (1983) is more blunt: If it requires unusual insight,

special training, or unique assessment devices to detect a characteristic, then the characteristic isn't present to a marked degree.

3. *Adversely affect educational performance.* This is probably one of the more controversial aspects of the Federal definition of emotional disturbance. Regardless of the psychiatric severity of a child's presumed disturbance, if that child's academic performance is appropriate for the child's age and ability, the child cannot, by definition, be diagnosed as seriously emotionally disturbed under the provisions of P.L. 94-142. It is at this point that one becomes aware of the distinction between diagnosing a child as emotionally disturbed in general and diagnosing a student as seriously emotionally disturbed in the public schools. The distinction is an important one. It is valid for the educational purposes of the law; it is not valid for true mental health purposes.

Two other conditions, one inclusionary and one exclusionary, are mentioned in the law. *Schizophrenic students* (i.e., those suffering from withdrawal, reduced affect, and a general breaking away from reality without apparent intellectual or emotional deterioration) are specifically included within the diagnostic category of seriously emotionally disturbed *so long as* the three conditions outlined above are met. By contrast, *socially maladjusted students* (e.g., those with conduct or oppositional disorders, those who are antisocial, those who are classified as juvenile delinquent) do not qualify as seriously emotionally disturbed unless it can be demonstrated that they suffer from disturbance *in addition to* social maladjustment. The latter is another large bone of contention among educators and mental health professionals (Bower, 1982).

The law is very specific about the kinds of students who can be diagnosed seriously emotionally disturbed in a public school classroom.

1. Such students must have an emotional condition.

2. The emotional condition must result in one or more of five specified characteristics (e.g., inability to learn, inability to have satisfactory interpersonal relationships, inappropriate behavior, depression, or physical symptoms).

3. The characteristic(s) must have been observed to a marked degree and over a long period of time.

4. The characteristic(s) must adversely affect the student's academic performance.

5. The definition includes schizophrenic students whose conditions meet the other criteria and excludes socially maladjusted students.

USE OF DSM III IN THE SCHOOLS

DSM III is the third revision of the *Diagnostic and Statistical Manual of Mental Disorders* (American Psychiatric Association, 1980). This volume, and its predecessors, were written to standardize the terminology used to describe and define mental disorders. With publication of DSM III, the APA introduced an entire section entitled, "Disorders Usually Evident in Infancy, Childhood, or Adolescence." These disorders include:

I. *Intellectual*
   Mental retardation

II. *Behavioral*
   Attention deficit disorders
   Conduct disorders

III. *Emotional*
   Anxiety disorders
   Other disorders

IV. *Physical*
   Eating disorders
   Stereotyped movement disorders

V. *Developmental*
   Pervasive developmental disorders
   Specific developmental disorders

Each of these disorder groups is accompanied by specific diagnostic criteria. For instance, there are diagnostic criteria to distinguish among four specific areas within the category of conduct disorders: undersocialized, aggressive; undersocialized, nonaggressive; socialized, aggressive; and socialized, nonaggressive. The relevant criteria include physical violence, failure to establish longstanding friendships and interpersonal relationships, chronic rules violations, lying, stealing, and so on. The categories are not mutually exclusive, so a diagnosis can be labeled principal, probable, or provisional.

Although DSM III does not address the etiology or causes of the various disorders that it describes, a severity continuum is presumed, ranging from obvious organic conditions to apparently "normal" conditions. This makes it possible for a diagnostician to use one of the many so-called decision trees for differential diagnosis that are provided in the manual. For instance, a major problem in the public schools diagnosis of emotionally disturbed students is determining whether reported academic difficulties are the result of disordered emotions or of some other condition or constellation of conditions. One of the DSM III decision trees was designed to diagnose a problem differentially as a major academic or learning problem or as a predominant emotional disturbance. In the course of making the diagnostic decision, an examiner would consider the appropriateness of such alternate diagnostic categories as neurological disorders, mental retardation, specific developmental disorders, attention deficit disorders, conduct disorders, or oppositional disorders. Multiple diagnoses, of course, are possible outcomes of this process, too.

DSM III has been criticized on several grounds, in particular, failure to address potential causes for disorders and failure to indicate the treatment of choice or even the direction of treatment. In addition, the categories were derived deductively from assumptions about mental disorders; critics would prefer that they had been developed inductively through the observation of behaviors and interactive situations. The interobserver reliability of the diagnostic categories used in DSM II has been found to be in the mid .30s for adults and even lower for children (Stuart, 1970). This level is well below accepted reliability estimates of .80 or .90 for similar kinds of assessment. In addition, large numbers of patients (Rosen, Bahn, & Kramer, 1964) and students (Redick, 1973) are undiagnosed. Specific data relative to DSM III have not yet been published, but there is no reason to believe that the changes involved in the revision would affect reliability or overall diagnostic utility.

Slenkovich (1983) is an attorney who has analyzed the DSM III diagnostic categories as they relate to the requirements of P.L. 94-142. An example of her analysis of one of the conduct disorders is reproduced in Table 20.1. Educational diagnosticians and school psychologists may find her explications helpful if they decide to employ DSM III rather than behavioral diagnostic criteria.

TABLE 20.1. A Legal Analysis of a DSM III Diagnostic Category

312.00   Conduct Disorder, Undersocialized, Aggressive

DESCRIPTION OF DIAGNOSTIC LABEL: Conduct Disorder, Undersocialized, Aggressive is usually characterized by aggressive antisocial conduct (violence, thefts) and lack of social attachment or social conscience.

> *Note:* The above description is included so that the reader can have a general idea of what the term means; the description is not comprehensive and is not stated in the language of DSM III; it is expressly not intended to be used for diagnosis.

THE DISTURBANCE MUST BE a condition exhibiting one or more of the following characteristics:

TABLE 20.1. continued

1. **An inability to learn which cannot be explained by intellectual, sensory, or other health factors:** DSM III does not list this as a criterion, nor does it appear from the DSM III description that it is an aspect of this diagnosis. While academic achievement may be below the expected level, there is no indication that this is due to an actual *inability to learn which cannot be explained by intellectual, sensory, or other health factors.* Therefore, Conduct Disorder, Undersocialized, Aggressive does not appear to fit within this P.L. 94-142 characteristic.

2. **An inability to build or maintain satisfactory interpersonal relationships with peers and teachers:** DSM III does list this as a criterion. Therefore, Conduct Disorder, Undersocialized, Aggressive appears to fit within this P.L. 94-142 characteristic.

3. **Inappropriate types of behavior or feelings under normal circumstances:** DSM III does not list this as a criterion; however, DSM III does list behavior which is aggressive and in violation of the basic rights of others. To the extent that this constitutes *inappropriate types of behavior or feelings under normal circumstances,* Conduct Disorder, Undersocialized, Aggressive will fit within this P.L. 94-142 characteristic.

4. **A general pervasive mood of unhappiness or depression:** DSM III does not list this as a criterion, nor does it appear from the DSM III description that it is an aspect of this diagnosis. Therefore, Conduct Disorder, Undersocialized, Aggressive does not appear to fit within this P.L. 94-142 characteristic.

5. **A tendency to develop physical symptoms or fears associated with personal or school problems:** DSM III does not list this as a criterion, nor does it appear from the DSM III description that it is an aspect of this diagnosis. Therefore, Conduct Disorder, Undersocialized, Aggressive does not appear to fit within this P.L. 94-142 characteristic.

6. **Schizophrenia:** DSM III does not define nor describe this diagnosis as being Schizophrenia.

THE DISTURBANCE MUST NOT BE social maladjustment: By the DSM III definition of Conduct Disorder, Undersocialized, Aggressive, the essence of the diagnosis is *social maladjustment.* Since social maladjustment is expressly excluded from the P.L. 94-142 definition of seriously emotionally disturbed, Conduct Disorder, Undersocialized, Aggressive does not qualify as a P.L. 94-142 serious emotional disturbance.

DISCUSSION: Even though *an inability to build or maintain satisfactory interpersonal relationships with peers and teachers* and *inappropriate types of behavior or feelings under normal circumstances* may be characteristics of this diagnosis, since the diagnosis constitutes *social maladjustment* which is expressly excluded from the P.L. 94-142 definition of seriously emotionally disturbed, it does not qualify as a P.L. 94-142 serious

TABLE 20.1. continued

emotional disturbance. (If the student has another DSM III diagnosis, that diagnosis should be analyzed to determine whether or not it qualifies as a P.L. 94-142 serious emotional disturbance.)

In addition, the required characteristics do not appear to be of sufficient severity to meet the P.L. 94-142 requirement that they exist *to a marked degree.*

With respect to the *inappropriate behavior,* DSM III does not describe it as *inappropriate behavior under normal circumstances* which is *marked.* In other words, DSM III does not apply those descriptors to the behavior which would make it sound serious enough to meet the P.L. 94-142 requirement *to a marked degree.* While many types of behavior can be said to be *inappropriate,* in order to qualify under P.L. 94-142 the behavior must be *markedly* inappropriate under *normal circumstances. Markedly inappropriate behavior under normal circumstances* appears to mean *bizarre* or *psychotic* behavior, not merely neurotic, uncontrolled, deliberate, or immoral behavior. For this reason, this book takes the position that since the behavior involved in this diagnosis does *not constitute bizarre nor psychotic behavior*, it does not meet this P.L. 94-142 requirement.

With respect to the *inability to build or maintain relationships,* it is unclear whether or not it is severe enough to constitute a *marked* inability to build or *maintain satisfactory interpersonal relationships with peers and teachers.* If the student exhibits an actual *marked inability* to build or maintain satisfactory *interpersonal relationships with peers and teachers,* he will meet this P.L. 94-142 requirement; if he does not (for example, he has one or two friends), he will not meet this P.L. 94-142 requirement.

Therefore, even if this diagnosis were not exempted as social maladjustment, most of the required characteristics are not of sufficient severity to meet the P.L. 94-142 requirement that they exist *to a marked degree.*

From *P.L. 94-142 as Applied to DSM III Diagnoses* (pp. 30–31) by J. Slenkovich, 1983, Cupertino, CA: Kinghorn Press. Reprinted by permission.

SUMMARY

The diagnosis of socioemotional problems is plagued by sometimes arbitrary use of terminology. By adhering closely to the legal definition of serious emotional disturbance outlined in P.L. 94-142 and by employing a diagnostic system that defines terms explicitly, school personnel can avoid many of these problems.

REFERENCES

American Psychiatric Association. (1980). *Diagnostic and statistical manual of mental disorders* (3rd ed.). Washington, DC: Author.

Bower, E. M. (1969). *Early identification of emotionally handicapped children in school* (2nd ed.). Springfield, IL: Thomas.

Bower, E. M. (1982). Defining emotional disturbances: Public policy and research. *Psychology in the Schools, 19,* 55–60.

Coleman, M. C. (1986). *Behavior disorders: Theory and practice.* Englewood Cliffs, NJ: Prentice-Hall.

Quay, H. C. (1975). Classification in the treatment of delinquency and antisocial behavior. In N. Hobbs (Ed.), *Issues in the classification of children* (Vol. I). San Francisco: Jossey-Bass.

Quay, H. C., Morse, W. C., & Cutler, R. L. (1966). Personality patterns of pupils in classrooms for the emotionally disturbed. *Exceptional Children, 32,* 297–301.

Redick, R. (1973). *Utilization of psychiatric facilities by persons under 18 years of age* (Statistical Note 90). Washington, DC: Department of Health, Education, & Welfare.

Rich, H. L. (1982). *Disturbed students: Characteristics and educational strategies.* Austin, TX: PRO-ED.

Rosen, B. M., Bahn, A. K., & Kramer, M. (1964). Demographic and diagnostic characteristics of psychiatric clinic outpatients in the USA, 1961. *American Journal of Orthopsychiatry, 34,* 455–468.

Slenkovich, J. E. (1983). *P.L. 94-142 as applied to DSM III diagnoses.* Cupertino, CA: Kinghorn Press.

Stuart, R. (1970). *Trick or treatment: How and when psychotherapy fails.* Urbana, IL: Research Press.

21 / PROBING SPECIFIC SOCIOEMOTIONAL AREAS

One of the more memorable lines from the movie "Oh, God!" was George Burns' statement, "I'll paint the big picture; you fill in the details!" The first four chapters of this book are big picture chapters. The next two chapters offer guidance for filling in the details.

This chapter explores means of probing specific socioemotional problems. First, general guidelines are discussed. Then, assessment techniques that are appropriate for evaluating each of the six socioemotional constructs are described. The final section of this chapter is devoted to the evaluation of specific behavioral manifestations of problems within these constructs.

GENERAL GUIDELINES

Principles of assessment have been addressed with broad strokes throughout this book. The philosophical, theoretical, and technical issues can be distilled into seven rules of thumb to guide this phase of the socioemotional assessment process.

1. *Review the records that already are available.* There is not time to re-invent the wheel. Records provide valuable information about what is already known concerning the student's problems; about others' perceptions of the problems; about steps that already have been taken; about recommendations that have been ruled out. Records, quite literally, provide a historical perspective; to ignore them is to view each student as a *tabula rasa*.

2. *Early in the evaluation process, determine that a referred problem really is a problem.* The concept of deviance, or perhaps the concept of normalcy, is inherent in this guideline. In one sense, normalcy is a statistical artifact: Most people do this; most people do not do that. The rate (or frequency) of this behavior is within the average range; the rate of that behavior is higher (or lower) than average. These statements reflect a norm referenced interpretation. The examiner may (a) consult the normative tables that accompany a behavioral checklist or rating scale; (b) identify developmentally appropriate behavioral expectations; or (c) rely on extensive personal experience to distinguish between normal and deviant behavior. In this interpretation, students' behaviors are not normal when the behaviors deviate statistically from those of their classmates (i.e., too many or too few behaviors are observed) or when the behaviors deviate developmentally from age appropriate expectations.

This guideline is a utilitarian one. It helps to ensure that (a) teachers don't spend time trying to change behaviors that will improve or go away of their own accord as the student matures and (b) students don't become scapegoats for examiners' own preferences, biases, and tolerance ranges (more about this in Rule #7).

3. *Assess socioemotional problems in as natural and realistic a situation as possible.* Let us begin by recognizing two caveats. First, of necessity, much of the testing that is incorporated into a socioemotional appraisal is accomplished in the splendid isolation of a diagnostician's office. This arrangement permits the examiner to adhere scrupulously to the standardized administration directions associated with most tests. Second, school, in and of itself, is not a particularly natural setting. Redl (1959) has referred to school as a "harem society," replete with its own unique social and interactive situations. Still, school is usually the environment of interest in this type of evaluation, and it is helpful if the appraisal techniques (direct observation, applied behavioral analysis, sociometrics, etc.) are applied in a realistic environment.

This guideline serves two purposes. First, it ensures as nearly as possible that typical, representative information is obtained. Second, it does not isolate seemingly peripheral elements that may have a bearing on a student's socioemotional problems (e.g., the physical environment of the school and the classroom; the attitudes, interests, preferences, personalities, expectations, values, and skills of the teacher and other school staff; the curricular and nonacademic requirements and expectations placed on the student; the social structure and group processes operating in the class; the rules and regulations that are part of the school routine).

4. *Don't evaluate just the problem of concern; evaluate the situations in which the problem occurs, too.* In some ways, this is a corollary of the previous guideline. Behaviors don't occur in a vacuum, and feelings don't spring out of nowhere. It is important to examine the environmental parameters of a socioemotional problem: What conditions (people, settings,

tasks) seem to elicit, aggravate, or meliorate the problem? Are there camouflaged reinforcers in the environment that unwittingly maintain or encourage the problem? What are the consequences of the problem, and are they natural or artificial?

5. *Assess continuously.* The dichotomy between assessment and intervention is an artificial one. Appraisal is an ongoing process that is an integral part of effective instruction. The test-teach-test sequence is a familiar one. The ultimate goal of assessment in the schools (once a problem has been documented) is to help professionals decide what to do and how to do it (i.e., to set goals and to plan interventions). If the intervention is successful, then ensuing goals will be established and interventions planned to meet them. If the initial plan doesn't work, then school personnel will want to re-evaluate the appropriateness of the goals, to try another plan, or to do both. This approach to instruction is often referred to as diagnostic or clinical teaching, and it is predicated on the assumption that testing and teaching are contemporaneous activities, neither of which can be implemented fully without the other.

6. *Use broad definitions of "success" when evaluating child change and program effectiveness.* More than 25 years ago, Fritz Redl (1961) speculated on the concept of improvement and how school personnel can know that improvement is real. This discussion paraphrases his astute observations of six alternate explanations of apparently real improvement in the behavior or affect of disturbed children.

(a) Can the improvement be attributed to the student's defense against treatment or change? For instance, students in new placements often "clean up their act" until they feel comfortable or at ease in the new environment. Or some manipulative students may improve their own behavior while working behind the scene to goad classmates into oppositional or inappropriate behaviors.

(b) Is the improvement stable enough to transfer to other situations? For instance, if a student begins to make one friend (or to open up to one adult), will the student be able to make other friends (or open up to other adults)? If a student demonstrates an interest in a particular school project and can work on it for long periods of time, will that student be able to demonstrate a similar attention span for other school projects?

(c) Is the improvement "re-traumatization proof," meaning, "just how much of the old bad stuff could the youngster take without a relapse?" (p. 456). This is particularly important for school based appraisal because there are a good eighteen hours every day of a child's life over which educators have no control whatsoever. In fact, there are substantial parts of the school day itself over which individual educators have no control!

(d) Does the improvement rest on true change from within, or is it maintained only by unusual and rigid aspects of the classroom environment? For instance, students who are afraid of being abandoned may well improve their surface behavior under the impact of separation panic, but the real problem has not improved.

(e) Is the improvement worth the price the student must pay? For instance, does a student learn to control aggressive behaviors to the point of being labeled a sissy? Do the student's improvements estrange her or him unnecessarily from an important peer group?

(f) Is the improvement due simply to a temporary run of luck? "Sometimes, it just so happens we hit . . . one of those situations where a 'positive mood' simply is in the air from the first waking hour on, or where a lucky surprise, and unusual event, sets the tone so well that even disturbed children, with that much supportive luck, can really *live above their means for a while*" (p. 456). Redl goes on to remind his readers that improvement, even real improvement, does not mean a cessation of problems or even of problem behaviors.

7. *School personnel must take care to be aware of and wary of their own values, biases, and preferences in conducting socioemotional evaluations.* Students are not necessarily emotionally disturbed just because their behavior or feelings violate our own personal standards or disgust our moral taste. Algozzine (1977; Algozzine & Curran, 1979) notes that students whose behavior exceeds their teachers' ability to tolerate that behavior are likely to be referred, even though such students probably are merely disturbing and not truly disturbed. Rich (1982) cautions that one of the more difficult problems for professionals evaluating socioemotional problems in a learning environment is evaluating their *own* behaviors and emotions.

EVALUATING THE SOCIOEMOTIONAL CONSTRUCTS

The examiner who conducts a socioemotional evaluation will probe most, if not all, of the constructs defined in Chapter 18. Behavioral problems observed in the classroom probably stem from difficulties in one or more of the socioemotional constructs. Appraisal personnel will probe these constructs to confirm their suspicions or to rule out areas that do not seem to be problematic. These constructs are not behaviors nor does each construct necessarily have a characteristic set of behaviors associated with it (e.g., the behavioral description of a student with an attitude problem may well resemble the behavioral description of a student who is disinterested or who has a poor self-concept). Each construct is considered individually.

Attitudes

People's attitudes toward objects, tasks, situations, or other people are learned and cause them to associate feelings of favorableness/nonfavorableness with these targets in a fairly predictable and stable manner. Anderson (1981) suggests that students who have unfavorable attitudes about school learned them as a result of negative school experiences or as a corollary of the values in their culture. However, unfavorable attitudes are unlikely "causes of learning difficulties, largely because of their relatively low correlations with measures of learning" (p. 184).

Because attitudes are not always expressed overtly, the more behaviorally oriented evaluation techniques (e.g., direct observation or applied behavioral analysis) usually are not employed to measure this construct. Analyses of historical or documentary material, interviews, and projective tests are sometimes used in clinical settings to evaluate attitudes but are rarely used in schools.

Attitudes are most often evaluated through some sort of subjective paper-and-pencil task, such as an attitude scale, that yields quantitative information about the direction of an attitude (i.e., where it is placed on the favorableness continuum and the intensity with which it is held). The items of an attitude scale usually concentrate on one issue or a group of related issues (e.g., social conformity, doing math), and respondents rate items using a Likert scale or some similar scaling procedure.

In schools, the targets of attitudes usually are people (teachers, staff, peers, parents, family members), tasks (doing math), objects (some aspect of the classroom environment, a particular text, or curricular material), or situations (working in a group, being placed in a special class, talking to the counselor). Professionals can build their own scales (using techniques described earlier) to evaluate student attitudes toward these targets. It also may be important to measure the attitudes of school staff (e.g., attitudes toward teaching in general, toward teaching handicapped students, toward particular behaviors) or of a student's parents (e.g., toward child rearing, toward education).

Two measures of student attitudes toward curricular content areas that are available commercially are the *Estes Attitude Scales* (EAS) (Estes, Estes, Richards, & Roettger, 1981) and the Attitudes toward Math subtest of the *Test of Mathematical Abilities* (TOMA) (Brown & McEntire, 1984). EAS is a standardized, norm referenced measure of students' attitudes toward mathematics, reading, and science (for elementary school students) or mathematics, reading, English, science, and social studies (for junior and senior high school students). The TOMA subtest—also highly standardized and norm referenced—similarly addresses curricular attitudes of students in grades 3 through 12, but because this subtest is co-normed with other subtests measuring math aptitude and vocabulary, it permits the examiner to compare the relationship of attitudes to the actual performance of these skills.

Interests and Preferences

The measurement of interests and preferences accounts for an individual's likes and dislikes relative to various kinds of activities. Interests, if sufficiently strong, can compel an individual to attain specified goals or to acquire certain objects. Preferences involve a choice among two or more targets. Interests and preferences are learned and can range along a continuum of intensity. It may be important to evaluate the interests and preferences of staff as well as students.

A number of evaluation techniques lend themselves to the assessment of interests and preferences. Observation and personal interviews are excellent ways of acquiring this information. Tests—particularly checklists, forced choice instruments, and sentence completion measures—can be built by teachers or appraisal personnel. Test content can be verbal (words and phrases) or pictorial. Items can be grouped into specific areas (e.g., academic content, play activities); can be differentiated by social interactions (e.g., doing an activity by myself, with a friend, with a large group); or can contrast the type of activity (e.g., listening to a story about airplanes, making a paper or model airplane, or finding out how airplanes fly).

Relatively few general interest measures are available commercially. Most of the tests on the market relate to occupational interests. The *OASIS Interest Schedule* (Parker, 1983) is a recent, well-built and highly standardized measure of high school students' interests in 12 occupational areas: artistic, scientific, nature, protective, mechanical, industrial, business detail, selling, accommodating, humanitarian, leading-influencing, and physical performing.

Locus of Control

Locus of control measures attempt to determine where individuals place responsibility for their behavior and for what happens to them: Is responsibility attributed to their own actions or to luck, fate, the actions of others, and so on? Locus of control can be assessed through structured interviews; through projective measures such as art, storytelling, or free play; through structured problem solving interviews; and through tests.

Tests of locus of control usually ask the respondent to pick between two possible explanations for an event. Both positive and negative events are included among the test items. For instance, a positive event might be: "When you get a good grade on a final exam, is it because: (1) you studied hard all semester or (2) the teacher was in a good mood when he scored the tests?" An item concerning a negative event could be worded this way: "When you can't afford to buy a record album that you want, do you: (1) try to get a part-time job to earn spending money or (2) hope that your grandmother will send you a check for your next birthday?"

Most ready-made locus of control tests have been developed for research purposes. Although they usually aren't available for purchase, they can be located in the professional literature. The Intellectual Achievement Responsibility Questionnaire (Crandall, Katkovsky, & Crandall, 1965) was built for students in grades 3 and up. The 34 test items all describe things that happen at school. The Locus of Control Scale for Children (Nowicki & Strickland, 1973) has a much broader scope. Its 40 items address home, community, and social settings as well as school events.

Self-Concept

Self-concept is the perception and awareness of oneself. These self-perceptions can be subjective ("I am a good student") or objective ("I have a 3.5 GPA"). Self-concept usually is described as positive or negative; self-esteem, a related term that is used synonymously in this book, is usually described as high or low. Self-concept is learned as a result of day-to-day life experiences and comments made by people who are important to us.

Subjective self-concept is most often measured through direct observation, interviews, and projective measures. Objective self-concept is tapped through self-report tests—particularly checklists, rating scales, and Q-sorts—in addition to observations, interviews, and projectives. Stimulus items can require simple yes-no or true-false responses (e.g., I am smart, Other kids make fun of me, I am pretty, My parents treat me like a baby); or they can require a Likert-type response (e.g., Compared with other students in your grade, how hard is your school work? Very hard—hard—about average—easy—very easy).

Examples of commercial tests of self-concept include the *Piers-Harris Children's Self-Concept Scale* (Piers & Harris, 1984), the *Tennessee Self-Concept Scale* (Fitts, 1970), and *Animal Crackers* (Adkins & Ballif, 1973). The latter is unique because of its pictorial format, which makes it particularly suitable for very young children.

Social Skills

Social skills are the behaviors that allow an individual to interact with and cope successfully in the environment. The social skills required for success at school may be different from those required for success in the community or within particular peer groups. These differences should be taken into account when social skills are evaluated. Social skills are best evaluated through direct observation or testing procedures. Sociometric and peer nominating techniques can be used to evaluate the impact of a student's social skills.

Observation systems or checklist and rating scale items might be developed out of social skills curricula such as *Social Skills and Me* (Crane & Reynolds, 1983). Crane and Reynolds developed their curriculum for students with severe socioemotional problems, so the behaviors addressed are realistic and go beyond polite behaviors. Since the curriculum's 100 lessons are structured and highly sequential, the materials are well-suited to evaluative purposes. In fact, self-evaluation is a major skill that the curriculum teaches.

Walker and his colleagues have built two tests of social skills. *Assessment for Integration into Mainstream Settings* (AIMS) (Walker & Rankin, 1980) helps identify the social skills required in the mainstream classroom, the social skills that the mainstream teacher thinks are unacceptable, and the assistance that the mainstream teacher will need to integrate handicapped students successfully into the mainstream. The ACCEPTS Checklist and Placement Test (Walker et al., 1983) accompanies the ACCEPTS social skills curriculum to identify deficient social skills and to place students at the appropriate level in the curriculum. Both of these instruments were built for less severe socioemotional problems than those of Crane and Reynolds' curriculum.

Other Personality Traits

Personality traits is used in this text as a catholic term that encompasses an individual's behavioral, temperamental, emotional, and mental characteristics. Personality traits cannot be evaluated directly. Instead, such characteristics as anxiety, introversion, aggression, and perseverance are inferred from direct observation, from interviews, and from test results. Self-report rating scales and projective measures are used most frequently.

The issue of personality assessment has become troublesome in recent years. For one thing, according to Salvia and Ysseldyke (1985) "there are no reliable and valid measures of specific personality traits or disorders." They suggest that "school personnel refrain from using personality measures, especially projective tests, in schools. . . . [Psychologists] have had considerable difficulty defending the practice of personality assessment, both in terms of the psychometric adequacy of the devices and the educational relevance of the information provided by those devices" (p. 291).

Whether self-report tests, checklists, projectives, observations, or interviews are used to evaluate personality traits, the behaviors and responses that are recorded usually are not interpreted at face value. Instead, they are "interpreted" according to so-called deeper aspects of personality. Therefore, the skill and clinical expertise of the individual conducting the evaluations are as important, if not more important, than the manner in which the original data were gathered.

EVALUATING BEHAVIORAL MANIFESTATIONS

In most school based evaluations, the staff will concentrate on evaluating the behaviors that are observed rather than the socioemotional constructs that are presumed to underlie the problems. This usually is accomplished by looking at the developmental appropriateness and frequency of the behavior.

"A developmental approach to defining disturbance seems to be the most appropriate compromise. . . . Thus, disturbance can be defined by behaviors that reflect lower level functioning compared with chronological counterparts within the normal population" (Rich, 1982, p. 60). For instance, Havighurst (1966) notes that a certain amount of oppositional, testing behavior is normal in the adolescent years; therefore, such things as petty theft and vandalism might be considered borderline normal rather than deviant or disturbed.

In a similar study of child development, Senn and Solnit (1968) trichotomized behaviors into acceptable behavioral characteristics, minimal psychopathology, and extreme psychopathology. The acceptable characteristics include general good health and physical integration; acceptance of sexual roles; adequate impulse control; competitive peer interaction; general regard for social rules and fair play; and curiosity about nature and the child's surrounding environment. Behaviors that are characteristic of minimal problems at this same age range include anxiety and over sensitivity; acting out and temper tantrums; regressive behaviors such as soiling and wetting; tics and other ritualistic or compulsive behaviors; somatic illness and general fear of illness or bodily injury; moodiness and withdrawal; and few personal relationships. At the more severe end of the continuum are such behaviors as extreme withdrawal and apathy; self-destructive tendencies; chronic lying and stealing; intentional cruelty to animals; obsessive-compulsive behaviors such as phobias and fantasies; sexual exhibitionism; extreme somatic illnesses such as anorexia, obesity, or even failure to thrive; and a complete absence or deterioration of personal relationships.

Salvia and Ysseldyke (1985) suggest a more statistical, but related, approach. "If school personnel document the frequency and duration of occurrence of behaviors, and if they also have data on extent of occurrence of those behaviors in students' agemates or grademates, then decisions about who should be served can be based on normative peer comparisons" (p. 291).

Tables 21.1 and 21.2 will be helpful to professionals who are not engaging in the formal act of diagnosis but who still want to classify problem behaviors observed in the classroom, to determine the degree of disturbance associated with a particular behavior or set of behaviors, or to ascertain the need for referral. By comparing an observed behavior to the criteria outlined in Table 21.1, one can determine if that behavior is normal, if it constitutes a problem,

TABLE 21.1. Classification of Problem Behavior

Descriptor	Criteria		
	Normal	Problem	Referable
Intensity	Nondisruptive	Disruptive	Extremely disruptive
Appropriateness	Reasonable	Inappropriate	Excessive
Duration	Short lived	Moderately long	Long lasting
Frequency	Infrequent	Frequent	Habitual
Specificity	Occurs in specific situations	Occurs in several situations	Occurs in many situations
Manageability	Easily managed	Difficult to manage	Cannot be managed
Assessability of circumstances	Easily assessed	Difficult to assess	Cannot be assessed
Maturity	At class level	Below class level	Considerably below class level
Number	Rarely more than one	Usually more than one	Usually many and varied
Peer acceptance	Accepted	Difficulty getting along	Unaccepted
Recovery time	Rapid	Slow	Delayed
Contagion	Little effect on others	Considerable effect	Excessive effect
Reality contact	No confusion	Some confusion	Considerable confusion
Response to learning opportunities	Positive	Slow, weak	No response

From "Training Teachers to Recognize and Manage Social and Emotional Problems in the Classroom" by G. Gropper, G. Kress, R. Highes, & J. Pekich, 1968, *Journal of Teacher Education, 19,* 477–485. Reprinted by permission.

TABLE 21.2. Determining the Degree of Disturbance

Criteria	Degree		
	Mild	**Moderate**	**Severe**
Precipitating Events	Highly stressful	Moderately stressful	Not stressful
Destructiveness	Not destructive	Occasionally destructive	Usually destructive
Maturational appropriateness	Behavior typical for age	Some behavior atypical for age	Behavior too young/old
Personal functioning	Cares for own needs	Usually cares for own needs	Unable to care for own needs
Reality index	Usually sees events as they are	Occasionally sees events as they are	Little contact with reality
Social functioning	Usually able to relate to others	Usually unable to relate to others	Unable to relate to others
Insight index	Aware of behavior	Usually aware of behavior	Usually unaware of behavior
Conscious control	Usually can control behavior	Occasionally can control behavior	Little control over behavior
Social responsiveness	Usually acts appropriately	Occasionally acts appropriately	Rarely acts appropriately

From *Understanding and Teaching Emotionally Disturbed Children* (p. 111) by P. L. Newcomer, 1980, Boston: Allyn & Bacon. Reprinted by permission.

or if it is severe enough to warrant a referral for evaluation and possible diagnosis. Similarly, Table 21.2 helps determine if an observed behavior is mildly, moderately, or severely disturbed. Application of these terms is *not* diagnostic and in no way qualifies a student for placement in a special education program. Clarifying and specifying terminology will be helpful, though, for professionals who are determining if referral is necessary or who are working with a mild or moderate socioemotional problem in the classroom.

REFERENCES

Adkins, D. C., & Ballif, B. L. (1973). *Animal Crackers: A Test of Motivation to Achieve.* Monterey, CA: CTB/McGraw-Hill.

Algozzine, B. (1977). The emotionally disturbed child: Disturbed or disturbing? *Journal of Abnormal Child Psychology, 5,* 205–211.

Algozzine, B., & Curran, T. J. (1979). Teachers' predictions of children's school success as a function of their behavioral tolerances. *Journal of Educational Research, 7,* 344–347.

Anderson, L. W. (1981). *Assessing affective characteristics in the schools.* Boston: Allyn & Bacon.

Brown, V. L., & McEntire, E. (1984). *Test of Mathematical Abilities.* Austin, TX: PRO-ED.

Crandall, V. C., Katkovsky, W., & Crandall, V. J. (1965). Children's beliefs in their own control of reinforcement in intellectual-academic situations. *Child Development, 36,* 91–109.

Crane, C., & Reynolds, J. (1983). *Social skills and me.* Houston: Crane & Reynolds.

Estes, T. H., Estes, J. J., Richards, H. C., & Roettger, D. (1981). *Estes Attitude Scales: Measures of Attitudes Toward School Subjects.* Austin, TX: PRO-ED.

Fitts, W. (1970). *Tennessee Self-Concept Scale.* Nashville, TN: Counselor Recordings & Tests.

Havighurst, R. J. (1966). *Human development and education.* New York: Longmans, Green.

Nowicki, S., & Strickland, B. (1973). A locus of control scale for children. *Journal of Consulting and Clinical Psychology, 40,* 148–154.

Parker, R. M. (1983). *OASIS Interest Schedule.* Austin, TX: PRO-ED.

Piers, E. V., & Harris, D. B. (1984). *Piers-Harris Children's Self-Concept Scale, Revised Manual 1984.* Nashville, TN: Counselor Recordings & Tests.

Redl, F. (1959). The concept of a therapeutic milieu. *American Journal of Orthopsychiatry, 9,* 721–734.

Redl, F. (1961). Clinical speculations on the concept of improvement. In N. J. Long, W. C. Morse, & R. G. Newman (Eds.), *Conflict in the classroom* (pp. 453–465). Belmont, CA: Wadsworth.

Rich, H. L. (1982). *Disturbed students: Characteristics and educational strategies.* Austin, TX: PRO-ED.

Salvia, J., & Ysseldyke, J. E. (1985). *Assessment in special and remedial education* (3rd ed.). Boston: Houghton Mifflin.

Senn, M., & Solnit, A. (1968). *Problems in child development.* Philadelphia: Lea & Febinger.

Walker, H. M., McConnell, S., Holmes, D., Todis, B., Walker, J., & Golden, N. (1983). *The Walker social skills curriculum: The ACCEPTS program.* Austin, TX: PRO-ED.

Walker, H. M., & Rankin, R. (1980). *Assessment for Integration into Mainstream Settings.* Eugene: University of Oregon Center on Human Development.

22 / AN ECOLOGICAL PERSPECTIVE

A great deal of data, perceptions, and other information will be gathered concerning students who are suspected of having emotional or behavioral problems. Placement, diagnostic, and educational decisions all are predicated on the assumption that the presence and severity of the problem have been documented and that priorities for behavioral change have been established. We think it is important for situational variables surrounding the problem to be thoroughly investigated, too. This is best done through ecological means.

While traditional evaluation systems assume that the student being evaluated "owns" the problem, ecological assessment recognizes that behaviors do not occur in a vacuum but are highly related to situational, or ecological, variables. Ecological assessment views the classroom as an ecosystem that has an effect on and is affected by the student. In this chapter we address the basic assumptions of ecological models of assessment, describe two tests built on an ecological framework, and offer guidelines for the formulation of hypotheses for ecological assessment.

ASSUMPTIONS OF ECOLOGICAL ASSESSMENT

Ecological assessment assumes that learning and behavior are interactive. If this is true, it is important for the evaluative process to tap all of the relevant interactions in the classroom: teacher-student, student-peer, student-curriculum, student-self, and so on. In addition, it is not sufficient to evaluate students only in the environments where they are experiencing difficulty;

evaluation also must be conducted in the environments where success is being experienced. Unfortunately, many student evaluations yield information about only the negative aspects of a student's behavior without identifying or focusing on any of the positive aspects.

Each ecology has its own unique expectations and requirements, and a different set of skills is needed to be successful in each ecology. Some school environments, such as reading groups or speech therapy, require verbal skills, while others, such as art, have only minimal verbal requirements. Some environments, such as English composition, will require creativity and "deviance," while others, such as chemistry, demand conformity to rules. Obviously, these different requirements and expectations will affect student success and interest. Obviously, too, students must be able to make a smooth transition among several environments during the course of a typical school day.

In addition, each ecology may have a different physical environment. For instance, the lunchroom, the playground, the library, and the classroom are all quite different physically. Different kinds of motivation and reinforcement may be available, too. One teacher may be viewed as warm and reinforcing, while another is viewed with apprehension; using the computer learning center may be self-reinforcing for one student but a task that requires external reinforcement for another student; one classroom may be highly structured, while the other encourages independence and self-starting skills.

Ecologies also can be differentiated by the eyes through which they are viewed. A playground fight, for instance, will be perceived in one way by the aggressor and in another way by the victim. Different perceptions also will be forthcoming from other students observing from the sidelines, from the teacher or playground supervisor, or from a passerby. It is easy to see that more than one set of perceptions are important in determining what actually happened and in dealing with the students' subjective realities.

Ecological assessment, then, involves identifying the relevant ecologies, gathering performance and expectation data from each of the ecologies, and establishing goals for change that involve changing aspects of the environment as well as changing the behavior of the student in question (Laten & Katz, 1975). Attempting to change a student's behavior certainly is not the only intervention, and it may not be the best possible intervention. Other potential objects for change—the teacher, the classroom, the curriculum, the setting, the reinforcement system or ratio—should be considered, too.

TWO ECOLOGICAL TEST BATTERIES

Two test batteries that adhere to ecological principles have been built. These are the *Behavior Rating Profile* (Brown & Hammill, 1983) and the *Test of Early*

Socioemotional Development (Hresko & Brown, 1984). These instruments will be described in detail because of their unique formats and because the guidelines for interpretation and for further evaluation that are discussed by the authors will be helpful to school personnel constructing their own appraisal programs.

Behavior Rating Profile (BRP)

The BRP (Hammill & Brown, 1983) is a battery of five rating scales and a sociogram, all of which are norm referenced. The Teacher Rating Scale, Parent Rating Scale, Student Rating Scales (Home, School, and Peer), and Sociogram form the BRP. Because they are normed individually, each of the six components can be used individually as a rating scale, or the components can be administered as a battery to produce the ecological profile depicted in Table 22.1.

The BRP was normed on a large and unselected sample of 1,966 students from 6 through 18 years of age, 955 of their teachers, and 1,232 of their parents. The samples are representative of the United States population as a whole (based on the 1980 census) in terms of sex, race, ethnicity, and parental education and occupation. Internal consistency is established through the calculation of coefficients Alpha at five age levels. All of the coefficients exceed .70, and 84% of them exceed .80. Alpha coefficients of similar magnitude are reported for groups of learning disabled and emotionally disturbed subjects. Two week test-retest reliabilities are in the .80s. Validity was established by correlating the BRP scales with the *Behavior Problem Checklist*, the *Walker Problem Behavior Identification Checklist*, and the *Vineland Social Maturity Scale*; by intercorrelating BRP scales within ecologies; and by demonstrating the test's ability to discriminate matched groups of normal, learning disabled, and emotionally disturbed children. The components each generate standard scores and percentile ranks.

The BRP Teacher Rating Scale includes 30 descriptive sentence stems, which the teacher rates as "Very Much Like the Student," "Like the Student," "Not Much Like the Student," and "Not At All Like the Student." Examples of Teacher Rating Scale items are:

4. Tattles on classmates

17. Is an academic underachiever

30. Doesn't follow class rules

The Teacher Rating Scale takes less than 20 minutes to complete. The authors suggest that it may be helpful to obtain Teacher Rating Scale scores from all of the teachers who have the target student in class.

TABLE 22.1. Ecological Framework of the BRP

BRP Component	Respondent				Ecology		
	Student	Teacher(s)	Parent(s)	Peers	Home	School	Interpersonal
Student Rating Scale: Home	X				X		
Student Rating Scale: School	X					X	
Student Rating Scale: Peer	X						X
Teacher Rating Scale		X				X	
Parent Rating Scale			X		X		
Sociogram				X			X

From *Behavior Rating Profile* (p. 3) by L. Brown & D. D. Hammill, 1983, Austin, TX: PRO-ED. Reprinted by permission.

The Parent Rating Scale is similar in format to the Teacher Rating Scale. It also contains 30 sentence stems, which the parent rates from "Very Much Like" to "Not At All Like My Child." Sample items from the Parent Rating Scale are:

1. Is verbally aggressive to parents

10. Is shy, clings to parents

27. Won't share belongings willingly

This scale also is appropriate for use with parent surrogates such as close relatives, guardians, foster parents, or house parents.

The three Student Rating Scales are embedded within a single instrument. Each scale contains 20 items, which the student classifies as True-False. Examples of items from the Student Rating Scale: Home are:

1. My parents "bug" me a lot.

33. I have lots of nightmares and bad dreams.

47. I often break rules set by my parents.

Examples of Student Rating Scale: School items are:

14. I sometimes stammer or stutter when the teacher calls on me.

29. My teachers give me work that I cannot do.

59. The things I learn in school are not as important or helpful as the things I learn outside of school.

Examples of items from the Student Rating Scale: Peer are:

6. Some of my friends think it is fun to cheat, skip school, etc.

10. Other kids don't seem to like me very much.

31. I seem to get into a lot of fights.

The Student Rating Scales take about 30 minutes to administer, and it is appropriate for the examiner to read items aloud if students cannot read items for themselves.

The Sociogram is a peer nominating technique that was normed on the performance of individual classes of students. Students nominate three classmates in response to each of a pair of questions. Examples of the Sociogram questions are:

1. Which of the students in your class would you most (least) like to have as your friend?

2. Which of the students in your class would you most (least) like to work with on a project in school?

3. Which of the students in your class would you most (least) like to invite to your home after school?

Questions are offered to help BRP administrators interpret the results of the profile. They are reproduced here because teachers may be able to apply similar questions to the results of other rating scales that are standardized or teacher-made.

Does the student only score low (or high) on measures related to school? . . . or home? . . . or interpersonal relationships? If so, areas in need of further investigation or intervention have been identified. Successful as well as failure prone areas for the student also may be identified.

Is there discrepancy among raters? Do two of three teachers rate the student's behavior in the normal range while the third's evaluations are quite low? This may be an indication that the third teacher's perceptions are skewed or that the expectations in that class are very different from the expectations in the two other classes or that the student does, in fact, display deviant behavior in only one class. Remember that teacher expectations and actual requirements for success vary from class to class and teacher to teacher. Most students make this transition from one environment to another smoothly. Learning and behaviorally disordered students typically do not and it is likely that this difficulty would be apparent on the BRP profile. Deviance between mothers' and fathers' ratings also should be explored. When we developed the original norms for the BRP, we calculated mother and father responses separately. However, their scores were not statistically different and so we combined them into a single set of norms. Therefore, a profile which shows evidence that parents have vastly different views of the same child should be examined closely.

Is there some question about the reality of the perceptions expressed on the BRP components? In this case, it may be advisable to administer the relevant scales more broadly. In the classroom, for instance, several of the target student's classmates may be asked to complete the *Student Rating Scale: School* to determine if they, too, view that classroom in an unusually negative way. If the third teacher, who we discussed earlier, were asked to rate several students in the class, one might find that the teacher viewed most of the students as behaviorally deviant or exemplary, or that some individuation was apparent in the ratings. Similarly, at home the examiner may want to ask the parents to complete the *Parent Rating Scale* on all of their children, or the brothers and sisters of the target student may be asked to complete the *Student Rating Scale: Home*. This additional testing should help the examiner to pinpoint possible areas of difficulty that may be attributable to situations or people other than the target student him or herself, and may be helpful when the time comes to develop an intervention plan.

Does the student's self-evaluation seem to be in keeping with the evaluations of other raters? Does the student express negative self-ratings despite being successful in school, being well liked by peers, and having good relationships with parents and teachers? Perhaps the profile reflects another discrepancy: the student believes that his or her behavior is perfectly normal and acceptable but all other raters express negative perceptions. It is unlikely in this case that the self-ratings represent actual behavioral problems; more likely they are evidence of self-concept difficulties.

Is there some relationship between the student's academic and behavioral competence? This is a question that the BRP alone cannot answer, but it is an important area to consider. There is ample evidence that teachers' subjective evaluations of students' behaviors are affected by the students' academic competence and vice versa (Brown & Sherbenou, 1981); below average students seem to be allowed much less behavioral latitude than their more academically competent classmates. The inverse also may be true: a child who is out of kilter behaviorally may be perceived as being below average in academic tasks even when the facts belie this. This interweaving of perceptions should be taken into consideration.[1]

Test of Early Socioemotional Development (TOESD)

The TOESD (Hresko & Brown, 1984) is a downward extension of the BRP. It has four components—Student Rating Scale, Teacher Rating Scale, Parent Rating Scale, and Sociogram—which can be administered individually or as a battery, retaining the BRP's ecological frame of reference. The TOESD is suitable for use with target children from 3 through 7 years of age. It was standardized on the ratings of 1,006 children, 1,773 parents, and 1,006 teachers. Subjects lived in 15 states and exhibited the same demographic proportions of sex, race, ethnicity, and parental education and occupation that are reported in the 1983 census projections. Coefficients Alpha are reported at every one year age interval; all of the coefficients exceed .70, and more than half of them exceed .90. Two week test-retest coefficients are mostly in the .90s. Validity is established by correlating TOESD with the *Basic School Skills Inventory–Diagnostic*, the *Behavior Evaluation Scale*, and the *Behavior Rating Profile*; by intercorrelating the components; and by demonstrating the test's utility in discriminating among normal, mentally retarded, learning disabled, and emotionally disturbed students. The TOESD's scales yield both standard scores and percentile ranks.

The TOESD scales are similar in content and format to the BRP scales, except that oral administration is used on the TOESD Student Rating Scale.

---

[1]From *Behavior Rating Profile* (pp. 33–34) by L. Brown and D. D. Hammill, 1983, Austin, TX: PRO-ED. Reprinted by permission.

The items of each scale were built to ascertain perceptions of students' personal behavior, their behavior in interpersonal relationships, and their behavior with authority figures. The TOESD Sociogram questions elicit positive nominations but do not ask for negative nominations.

The BRP and TOESD results will be extremely helpful to classroom teachers and other school appraisal personnel, because they are rich with possibilities for interpretation. For instance, administering the school-related instruments to classmates of the target student and to several teachers may provide a broader picture of the problem behavior. Let's take the example of James, a student whose behavior is viewed as deviant by his fifth grade teachers. Do his other teachers—the art teacher, the physical education instructor, the band director, the special education teacher—view him similarly or do their responses on a behavioral checklist reveal markedly different perceptions? If so, is this because his behavior is different in each of these settings (something that could be determined through direct observation) or is it because the teacher's requirements and expectations are different (something that could be determined through an interview)? Likewise, if James views his class as a negative experience, is this perception shared by his classmates? Do they also find the class to be negative or is James's perception unique?

Similarly, the examiner may find it helpful to ask the student's parents to complete behavioral checklists on all of their children rather than just on the target child. Do the parents view their children similarly? Do mother and father express similar feelings or does each parent express different perceptions? The same axiom may be applied to inventories completed by the target student: Do brothers and sisters concur with that child's perceptions of the home ecology?

We emphasize that even though investigations of this scope are consistent with the principles of ecological assessment, they should be undertaken only when the need is warranted. The process can be quite time consuming, and there is no reason to lengthen it unnecessarily. We suggest these variations as a means of stimulating the formation of alternative hypotheses regarding problem behaviors. Brown and Hammill (1983) warn that "a low score [on a behavioral measure] . . . should not be interpreted flatly as a sign of deviance on the part of the child" (p. 32). It is the profile or pattern of scores that is important.

FORMULATION OF HYPOTHESES

Hypotheses are assumptions that are used as the basis for action. They are subject to verification or proof. In education, these assumptions usually concern how students can be helped to learn or behave better, and they are verified by evidence of change.

Based on initial impressions or referral data, the professional conducting socioemotional assessment will formulate hypotheses to explain the behavior that is observed and/or to propose interventions that have a high probability for success. These hypotheses guide the appraisal process and are subject to revision or clarification as additional information is obtained. This section suggests some questions to guide the formulation of hypotheses based upon an ecological frame of reference.

1. *What history does the referred student present?* Is there information in the student's records that sheds light on the current problem? A student with no history of behavioral difficulties probably isn't seriously emotionally disturbed but may be facing new problems that are situational (e.g., difficulties at home, a personality conflict with teachers or classmates) or developmental (e.g., being a teenager).

2. *How does school or school district policy affect the student's problems?* Has the student violated specific rules? Is the teacher or principal bound by policy to treat the observed problems in a specific manner? These are extremely important considerations, and ones which may not be negotiable. The teacher or examiner must be familiar with district policy concerning discipline, with the continuum of services available to students with behavioral and emotional problems, and with specific entry and exit criteria for these programs.

3. *Are behavioral problems observed in only one ecology or in several ecologies?* Problems that are observed in only one setting probably are not indicative of emotional disturbance. Even though they may be highly problematic and very disturbing, these behaviors are more likely to be situationally related than to be characteristic of true disturbance. Conversely, when behavioral or emotional problems are apparent in virtually every environment in which a student functions—at school, at home, in the community— the possibility of emotional disturbance must be considered. Similar reasoning would apply if the student's problems are reported by only one teacher or only in specific classroom situations.

4. *Are problems observed only in particular classes or with particular teachers?* The first focus of appraisal here would be to determine teacher expectations and skill requirements and then to discriminate those expectations that require skills that are within the student's behavioral repertoire from those that require new skills. If all of the teachers/situations seem to require similar skills, the examiner will want to determine (a) if the student has learned to generalize the skills to different settings, (b) if the student has difficulty making the transition from one setting to another, or (c) if the student simply chooses to behave differently in the various settings.

5. *What aspects of the environment seem to be related to the problem and which (if any) can be altered?* Some parts of the classroom environment are more amenable to change than others. Seating arrangements, for instance, can be altered fairly easily to account for personality clashes and to orient

students physically to the independent or group nature of the task at hand. Lighting and temperature, on the other hand, are difficult to adjust in most classrooms. In elementary schools, the time of day when instruction takes place can be manipulated more easily than in secondary schools. The curriculum obviously lends itself to changes within the parameters of the teacher's skill and flexibility (e.g., limiting the length of assignments, clarifying or highlighting directions, using study guides or other advance organizers, adjusting the readability of materials, making multimedia supplements available, providing alternative testing formats). Such things as classroom organization, classroom rules, and general classroom climate should be considered.

6. *What kinds of reinforcement is the child most responsive to, and are they available in the ecologies of interest?* Of interest here are such reinforcer variables as tangible-secondary (e.g., food vs. tokens or grades), extrinsic-intrinsic (e.g., external reinforcement vs. the reinforcement of a job well done), and immediate-delayed reinforcement (e.g., reinforcement delivered after the completion of each individual problem or when papers are returned the following day). It is important to determine if the consequences of both appropriate and inappropriate behavior are clearly delineated for students. Many children with academic and behavioral problems do not intuitively know the "rules of the game" and do not respond well to the sparse and often abstract kinds of reinforcement usually available in schools—a good grade, a star or Smilin' Sam, the teacher's smile, peer approval, or learning itself. It is important to know what the student likes to do that is available (or can be made available) in the classroom.

7. *Does the teacher have a highly structured or a flexible style of classroom management?* Neither of these styles is inherently better than the other, but it helps to match learning and teaching styles whenever possible. Many ED students, for instance, need a high degree of structure and predictability to feel secure and to experience success. Other children need avenues for divergence and creativity that are better provided in open or discovery classes. Some students respond best to group instruction; others require one-to-one instruction; still others function well in independent learning situations. Some students can work well independently, but only for short periods of time.

Other questions that are specific to a particular situation or to a particular student should be added to this list. By using these questions as a guide, it will be possible to implement a truly ecological affective assessment that will help identify potential interventions as well as the problems themselves.

REFERENCES

Brown, L., & Hammill, D. D. (1983). *Behavior Rating Profile*. Austin, TX: PRO-ED.

Hammill, D. D., & Leigh, J. (1983). *Basic School Skills Inventory–Diagnostic*. Austin, TX: PRO-ED.

Hresko, W. P., & Brown, L. (1984). *Test of Early Socioemotional Development*. Austin, TX: PRO-ED.

Laten, S., & Katz, G. (1975). *A theoretical model for assessment of adolescents: The ecological/behavioral approach*. Madison, WI: Madison Metropolitan Schools.

Walker, H. M. (1970). *Walker Problem Behavior Identification Checklist*. Los Angeles: Western Psychological Corporation.

AUTHOR INDEX

SUBJECT INDEX

ABA. *See* Applied behavioral analysis
ACCEPTS Checklist and Placement Test
  (Walker et al.), 541, 592
Achievement, 12-13
Addition and subtraction
  assessment of informal learning, 465, 468,
    473, 476-478
  informal learning of, 428-429
  word problems, 500-503
Adjective checklists, 353, 357. *See also*
  Checklists
Affect. *See also* Socioemotional assessment
  definition, 13, 507
  rating scales, 207
  relation to reading ability, 204, 206-207
AIMS. *See Assessment for Integration into
  Mainstream Settings*
Alexia, 322. *See also* Dyslexia
Algorithms, 499-500
Allomorphs, 56
Analytic teaching
  advantages, 22
  arithmetic assessment, 459, 461-462
  definition, 21
  example of, 21-22
  features of, 461
Animal Crackers (Adkins and Ballif), 540,
  591
Animal Pictorial Q-sort (Riley), 560
Aphasia, 322

Applied behavioral analysis. *See also*
  Behavior
  changing criterion design, 551-552
  identifying target behavior, 546
  implementing an intervention, 549-552
  multi-element design, 551-552
  multiple baseline design, 550-551
  observing and recording behavior,
    547-549
  reversal design, 549-550
  setting intervention goals, 547, 549
Aptitude, 12
Arithmetic assessment
  addition and subtraction, 465, 468, 473,
    476-478
  adjusting to different problems, 470-471
  algorithms, 499-500
  analytic teaching, 459, 461-462
  basic arithmetic concepts, 497
  calculation, 465, 468, 491-497
  checking the answer, 488-489
  conservation task, 475-476
  counting, 468-469, 473-474
  determining competence, 456-459
  enumeration, 473-474
  flexible interviewing, 443-459
  goal of, 415-417
  implications for teaching, 478
  interviewing, 495-496
  learning potential, 471-473
  meaning of written numbers, 498-499